Readings in Industrial and Organizational Psychology

Readings in Industrial and Organizational Psychology

Edited by
Frank J. Landy

The Dorsey Press

Chicago, Illinois 60604

Cover photo: Carol Lee

ISBN 0-256-03165-7
Library of Congress Catalog Card No. 85-73804

Printed in the United States of America

2 3 4 5 6 7 8 9 0 K 3 2 1 0 9 8 7 6

CONTENTS

INTRODUCTION

In the past 20 years, industrial and organizational psychology has become very complex. This increased complexity is due, in part, to the rapidly expanding technology of business and government. The introduction of computers and robots to the workplace, the laws that govern fair employment practices, and expansion of service jobs represent challenges to industrial and organizational psychology that did not exist 20 years ago. The expansion of the field is also due to the fact that theories have been developed where, before, there were none. In the late 1940s, applied psychology was characterized as "dust-bowl empiricism." This was meant to imply that there was little concern for *why* relationships between variables were observed. The concern seemed to be for predictability rather than understanding. That narrow concern for predictability has also changed. Theories of information processing, work motivation, leadership, and performance evaluation have appeared to fill the conspicuous substantive gaps that existed 20 years ago.

The most obvious symbol of this expansion in industrial and organizational psychology is the breadth and depth of research literature. The size of the body of knowledge supporting the field has grown geometrically. There are seven or eight major journals that serve the industrial-organizational student and researcher. Collectively, these journals represent about 5,000 *new* pages of reading material each year. In addition to these major journals, there are dozens of supporting journals that include articles of direct interest to the industrial and organizational psychologist. Add to the journal pages the information contributed by new *books* in the field and you begin to appreciate the meaning of the term *information explosion*.

This information explosion represents something of a dilemma. On one hand, there is simply too much for any one person to read. On the other hand, the *science* of industrial and organizational psychology demands an awareness of recent developments in theory and research findings. For the student, the dilemma is often addressed by finding a comprehensive textbook that covers most of the important material in the field. Necessarily, the student is reading predigested theory and research that has been already "processed" by the author of the textbook. This leaves something to be desired. As any author will tell you, there is no good substitute for reading original sources, i.e. the actual articles themselves rather than results or theory abstracted and modified to suit the purposes of the textbook author.

It is this dual concern for the integrity of original sources and the need to be selective in reading that provides the logical foundation for readings books. These books attempt to present to the reader a balanced selection of articles that are well written and comprehensive. If the readings are up to date and the selection representative of the field, the readings book can make an enormous contribution to the student's understanding of the field. This is what I hope to accomplish with this current book of readings. I have included articles in all of the major areas of industrial and organizational psychology—most of them published within the last five years. Others, though published earlier, remain central to an understanding of the nature of work behavior and thus deserve exposure.

In selecting the readings, several forces have influenced me. I mentioned two of those forces above—currency and comprehensiveness. In most sections, I have included a review piece that serves two purposes. First, it pulls together the major points of interest in a particular area for the student to consider simultaneously. Second, it presents the student with a comprehensive list of articles covering research and theory in that area. For the student who would like to pursue additional reading or research in that area, the most difficult part of the literature review is already completed.

Another influence in the selection of readings for each chapter has been application. In most sections, one or more real world problems is represented by a reading. This provides a link between the principles of behavior as manifest in industrial settings and the application of those principles. An additional influence was the desire to expose the student to the scientific method as it is practiced by industrial and organizational psychologists. As a result, each section has one or more research studies included to show how important questions are posed using the powerful language and analytic strategies that represent the scientific method. Finally, in each section, I have included nonempirical readings that are intended to stimulate original thinking and give the reader a break from the demanding characteristics of scientific reading. Most often, these nonempirical readings are in the form of an essay. They are intended to balance the comprehensiveness of the reviews and the technical detail of the empirical research with a broader and more thoughtful consideration of topics within an area. In other words, each section is heterogeneous in composition, with each reading directed toward a somewhat different end.

Although there are 14 major sections in the book, these sections can be reduced to four overarching categories: (*a*) personnel psychology, (*b*) industrial-social psychology, (*c*) human factors psychology, and (*d*) the field of industrial and organizational psychology in perspective. The first two areas receive a great deal more attention than the last two. Each section will be introduced by a brief description of what is to be covered in that section as well as a statement indicating how and why that section is important to the student of work behavior. In addition, each reading within the sections will be introduced by a paragraph explaining its unique contribution and thrust.

Approximately 25 percent of the readings have been condensed. More often than not this was accomplished by eliminating some of the statistical and technical detail. Occasionally, particularly in the case of review articles, summaries were substituted for detailed descriptions of reviewed literature. These reductions were necessary in order to maintain a book of reasonable length that was, nevertheless, comprehensive. Two other modifications were made to conserve space. All of the references from a reading appear in the general reference section at the end of the book. Article abstracts, reference notes, and some nonessential footnotes have also been eliminated from the readings. By making these minor concessions, I have been able to include additional pages of text material to better serve the student.

This readings book has been designed in a way that makes it compatible with any general text in industrial and organizational psychology. The sections and topics covered by the readings are representative of topics covered by most of the general texts in the industrial and organizational area. There is no doubt that I have included articles that other authors might not have included. Similarly, others might have included articles that I have ignored. Nevertheless, in my opinion, the readings that comprise this book represent an excellent cross section of theory, research, application, and speculation in the field of industrial and organizational psychology as it currently exists. I hope that those who use the book will agree.

In putting this book together, I had the assistance of a trio of reviewers who gave willingly of their time and expertise to guide me in the selection and editing of the readings. Jeff Burroughs, Kevin Murphy, and Bob Vance read all of my initial selections carefully and helped me decide what readings to keep, and they also helped identify others that I had not originally planned on including. Wendy Becker was also helpful in identifying articles for possible inclusion. I am grateful to them and, in some measure, any success that this book enjoys will be due to them.

Job Analysis and Job Evaluation

Personnel psychology is based on the proposition that a work task, a collection of tasks, or a job can be completely and accurately described in behavioral terms. Typically, this description is a list of duties and responsibilities—often called a job description. The process used to produce this description is called job analysis and this analysis can be carried out in several ways. One method of job analysis involves watching the worker perform the tasks under examination and making notes about those tasks. A second method is for the job analyst to actually perform the tasks or the job to get an appreciation for the duties and responsibilities. A third, and increasingly common, method of completing a job analysis is to ask people who hold the job to complete a questionnaire that tells the analyst about the relative importance of individual tasks and the frequency with which those tasks are performed.

Once the tasks are clearly and completely described, it is possible to identify the knowledges, skills, abilities, and other personal characteristics that an individual should possess in order to successfully complete those tasks. This second stage is often called an abilities analysis, and it accompanies and supports the job analysis. Once you know what knowledge, skills, and abilities the job requires, you can choose or develop the measures of those knowledges, skills, and abilities—the actual predictors of performance.

After the job and abilities analyses are completed, there are many possible applications of the resulting information. For example, it is then possible to develop tests to identify potentially successful employees and develop training programs for preparing individuals to meet the demands of a particular job. In addition, it is possible to use duties and requisite abilities to determine how much money to pay people who hold the job title under consideration. This last process is called job evaluation.

In this section, readings will be presented that address these three issues: job analysis, abilities analysis, and job evaluation.

The leading figure in abilities analysis in applied settings is Ed Fleishman. Over 30 years ago, he began to develop methods for identifying the unique abilities that workers use to carry out various tasks. He has conducted both field and laboratory research involving both military and civilian occupations. As a result of this research, he has developed a taxonomy or list of abilities that could be used to accomplish any task. In this reading, Fleishman describes the value of this taxonomy in applied psychology, some of the history of its development, and the relationship between abilities analysis and task analysis. A more recent review of research on this topic may be found in Fleishman, E.A., and Quaintance, M.K., Taxonomy of Human Performance: The Description of Human Tasks *(Orlando Fla.: Academic Press,).*

■ READING 1 ■

Toward a Taxonomy of Human Performance

Edwin A. Fleishman
University of California, Irvine

Much research in the behavioral sciences is concerned with the study of factors affecting human task performance. Thus, we may study the effects on task performance of different training methods, different environments and conditions of work, attitudinal and group factors, and individual differences in abilities. It is surprising, therefore, that more attempts have not been made to conceptualize a set of variables common to these areas, namely those associated with the kinds of *tasks* that people perform.

For some years, a number of us have been concerned with the need to develop a set of concepts that might help us make more dependable generalizations of research results to new tasks. The essential problem is the need to generalize the effect of some training, environmental, or procedural condition, from knowledge of its effect on one task, to its probable effect on some other task. What has been lacking is a system for classifying such tasks that would lead to improved generalizations and

predictions about how such factors affect human performance (cf. Fleishman, 1967b; Gagné, 1964). In particular, what is needed is a learning and performance theory that ascribes a central role to task dimensions.

Not too long ago a favorite distinction in psychology textbooks was between "mental" and "motor" tasks or between "cognitive" and "non-cognitive" tasks. Such broad distinctions are clearly too all-inclusive for generalizing results obtained on the effect of some learning or other condition to some new task. Job analysts, on the other hand, have developed highly detailed task analysis systems, but these are often too specific to particular jobs to help us arrive at general task dimensions applicable across many different tasks and jobs. Other psychologists (such as Alluisi, 1967; Gagné, 1964; Miller, 1966) have proposed categories of tasks in terms of broad human functions required to perform them. For example, such categories as *identification, discrimination, sequence learning, motor skill, scanning,* and *problem solving* are terms that have been used in the literature. However, everything we know from actual correlations among human performances indicates a considerable diversity of functions

Source: *American Psychologist*, December 1975, pp. 1127–1133; 1140–1142. Copyright 1975 by the American Psychological Association. Adapted by permission of the publisher and author.

within each of these broad areas. The recent work by McCormick and his associates (e.g., McCormick, Jeanneret, & Mecham, 1972) explicitly recognizes this.

The need for a better conceptualization of task dimensions relates to some other pressing problems of our field. The recent challenges to our selection methodology intensify the need to search for better methods of job analysis conceptually linked to more analytical criterion measures of job performance. A taxonomic system of task dimensions should assist in this.

It has been my feeling over the years that some kind of taxonomy of human performance is required which provides an integrative framework and common language applicable to a variety of basic and applied areas. Such a taxonomy should have certain characteristics. It should identify important correlates of learning, criterion performance levels, and individual differences *and* should be applicable to laboratory tasks and to tasks encountered in on-the-job situations.

Although the need has been recognized (e.g., Fitts, 1962; Melton & Briggs, 1960; Miller, 1962), it is only recently that concerted attempts have been made to explore more intensively some of the issues and alternatives in taxonomic development in psychology and to proceed on an *empirical* basis in the evaluation of these alternatives. I would like to review a program of research that has made at least some beginnings in this area.

Specifically, this article discusses briefly some general problems in the development of taxonomic systems applicable to descriptions of human performance and tasks. Some alternative approaches and provisional classification schemes developed are described. Then, some attempts to *evaluate* the utility and validity of these systems are reviewed.

SOME TAXONOMIC ISSUES[1]

Early in our research program we reviewed the literature bearing on taxonomic approaches

and concepts in the behavioral sciences as well as related developments in other sciences (Chambers, 1973; Farina, 1973; Theologus, 1973; Wheaton, 1973). We cannot provide the details of this review here, but we can indicate some issues that stood out.

Purpose of Classification

We need to be clear on why we are interested in task classification. The question is important because individuals who attempt such classification usually do not view the development of such a system as an end, in and of itself. Rather, they view the system of classification as a tool to increase their ability to interpret or predict some facet of human performance (Cotterman, Note 1). This goal is to be achieved by seeking relationships between that which is classified (e.g., tasks, processes mediating performance) and selected variables of interest to a particular investigator (e.g., distribution of practice, training regimens, environmental stressors).

We can elect to develop a system of classification having utility for a limited area (e.g., the classification of tasks with respect to which certain training methods are found most effective in promoting high levels of task performance), or we may look for a system from which a *variety* of applications may stem. For example, we might first classify tasks and *only then* relate stressors, learning principles, training regimens, etc., to each class of tasks in this system. In this case, classification is designed from inception to be general and to serve a variety of users by aiding in the interpretation, prediction, or control of a broad range of human performance phenomena.

With respect to systems having rather specific applied objectives, classifications dealing with training are most numerous. A number of investigators (Annett & Duncan, 1967; Gagné, 1962; Miller, 1966; Cotterman, Note 1; Eckstrand, Note 2; Folley, Note 3; Stolurow, Note 4) have called for systems intended to permit the classification of tasks into sets of categories that are relatively homogeneous with respect to principles of learning, training

[1]The author is indebted to George W. Wheaton for his contributions to the conceptual phase of this research.

techniques, etc. Bloom (1956) has attempted to develop a similar taxonomic system for the educational community. However, few empirical evaluations of such systems have been attempted.

Where broad task classification systems are developed as autonomous structures, which are only some time later to be applied to other variables, the classification exercise is an integral step in the development of theory. The resultant system provides a consistent conceptual framework, the elements of which eventually are to be used in the interpretation or prediction of human performance. One is not precluded from seeking specific applications for such classifications. The point is that a specific application does not dictate the composition and structure of the system.

Learning theorists have engaged in these pursuits (see Melton, 1964), but as yet there is no comprehensive system that effectively compares, contrasts, and interrelates the various human learning "categories."[2] Consequently, we have been unable to formulate a general theory of learning which allows dependable generalizations of learning principles to particular classes of tasks. Gagné (1964) has been the most systematic in the specification of general "learning categories" and their potential implications for ordering principles of learning.

The ability theorists also have attempted to isolate basic dimensions of behavior on which a general theory of human performance might be based. Guilford (1967) and I (Fleishman, 1964) have been perhaps the most explicit in attempting to integrate the ability dimensions identified within the general framework of experimental psychology. Thus, my associates and I have conducted research relating ability dimensions identified in research on individual differences to stages of learning (Fleishman & Hempel, 1954, 1955), stimulus-response relations (Fleishman, 1957), skill retention (Fleishman & Parker, 1962), part-whole task relations (Fleishman, 1965), effects of drugs (Elkin, Freedle, Van Cott, & Fleishman, Note

5), etc. This variety of studies was possible because we first attempted to develop a standard and consistent classificatory structure of human abilities and then attempted to test the feasibility of this framework across different areas of human performance. This approach is examined later in this article.

Conceptual Bases of Classification

After the consideration of the purposes of task classification, one needs to examine the descriptive bases of taxonomy. A concern here is with the definition and meaning of the concept *task*.

Definition of the Task. Task definitions vary greatly with respect to their breadth of coverage. At one end of this dimension are definitions that view the task as the totality of the situation imposed on the subject. For example, this definition would consider ambient stimuli an integral part of the task. The other end of this dimension is represented by definitions that treat a task as a specific *performance*. In this case, for example, one task could be to "depress the button whenever the light comes on." Suffice it to say that very different concepts may underlie definitions falling at either end of this dimension.

This diversity of opinion is also reflected in the extent to which tasks are defined as being external to or an intrinsic part of the subject. Some definitions take into account the propensity of subjects to redefine an imposed task in terms of their own needs, values, experiences, etc. In the grossest sense, these definitions treat a task as whatever it is the subject *perceives* the task to be. Other investigators (e.g., Hackman, 1970) define the task in terms of stimulus materials and instruction to the subject. The instructions indicate the activities to be performed with respect to the stimuli and the goals to be achieved. Merely giving a person a broken radio would not be assigning him a task.

Most investigators treat tasks as consisting of interrelated processes and activities. For example, Miller (1966) stated that "A task is any

---

[2] For a recent attempt in the area of instrumental conditioning, see Wood (1974).

set of activities, occurring at about the same time, sharing some common purpose that is recognized by the task performer" (p. 11).

Our conclusion was that we should not debate about *the* definition of a "task" as if only one were possible. Rather, we must adopt or develop a definition that will permit the derivation of terms that reliably describe tasks and distinguish among them. These derived terms can provide the conceptual basis for classification, as we shall see later.

There appear to be four major conceptual bases underlying current task description and classification.

Behavior Description Approach. In this conceptual approach to task classification, categories of tasks are formulated based on observations and descriptions of what operators actually do while performing a task. Most often, overt behaviors such as dial setting, meter reading, and soldering are employed. In spite of the large number of terms available for this approach to task description, relatively few descriptive systems have been developed that are based exclusively on operator behaviors or activities. McCormick (Note 6) has employed this descriptive approach in his studies of worker-oriented job variables (e.g., handling objects, personal contact with customers), and Fine (Note 7) has used this approach as a basis for describing worker functions in terms of handling (things), analyzing (data), and negotiating (with people).

Behavior Requirements Approach. A second approach to "task" description emphasizes the cataloging of behaviors that are assumed to be *required* in order to achieve criterion levels of performance. The human operator is assumed to possess a large repertoire of processes that will serve to *intervene* between stimulus events and responses. There has been a great deal of interest in codifying the required intervening processes (functions, behaviors, etc.), cataloging tasks in terms of the types of processes required for successful performance, and then relating to particular training methodologies the types of tasks that emerge (see Annett & Duncan, 1967; Gagné &

Bolles, 1963; Miller, 1966; and Eckstrand, Note 2). Typical of the functions used to differentiate among tasks are scanning function, short-term memory, long-term memory, decision making, and problem solving.

Ability Requirements Approach. The third conceptual basis for the description and classification of tasks, which we call the ability requirements approach (e.g., see Fleishman, 1972), is in many respects similar to the behavioral requirements concept. Tasks are to be described, contrasted, and compared in terms of the abilities that a given task requires of the operator. These abilities are relatively enduring attributes of the individual performing the task. The assumption is made that specific tasks will require certain abilities if performance is to be maximized. Tasks requiring similar abilities would be placed within the same category or would be said to be similar.

The abilities approach differs from the behavior requirements approach primarily in terms of concept derivation and level of description. The ability concepts are empirically derived through factor-analytic studies and are treated as more basic units than the behavior functions.

Task Characteristics Approach. A fourth approach differs from the preceding approaches in terms of the type of task description that is attempted. This approach (see Farina & Wheaton, 1973; Hackman, 1970) is predicated on a definition that treats the task as a set of conditions that elicit performance. These conditions are imposed on the individual and have an objective existence quite apart from the activities they may trigger, the processes they may call into play, or the abilities they may require. Having adopted this point of view, appropriate descriptive terms are those that focus on the task per se. The assumption is made that tasks can be described and differentiated in terms of intrinsic, objective properties they may possess. These properties or characteristics may pertain to the goal toward which the operator works, relevant task stimuli, instructions, procedures, or even to characteristics of the response(s) or the task content. The obvious problem is the selection of those task components that are to be described, as well as the particular terms or parameters by means of which description is to be accomplished.

We have seen that tasks can be defined in several ways, particularly in regard to the scope of definition; the extent to which tasks may be treated as objective entities, clearly apart from the operators who perform them; and the extent to which tasks are viewed as processes or structures.

SOME METHODOLOGICAL ISSUES

Within the scope of this article I cannot dwell on the more general problems of "how" to proceed with classification. I shall discuss instead a number of criteria for evaluating such systems.

The requirement for operational definition of terms becomes increasingly critical if the system is to be used by a broad range of specialists. The descriptive terms may be completely unfamiliar to many of these individuals, or even too familiar as in the case of the popular terms *decision making* and *problem solving*. Although homage is paid to the need for operational definitions, few investigators have actually generated such definitions. Also, as a minimum requirement, the descriptors employed in the differentiation and classification of tasks must permit *nominal scaling*. That is, a judge must at least be able to ascertain whether each descriptor applies or does not apply to the particular task being examined.

Also, descriptors must be defined and treated within a system of measurement so that they can be reliably evaluated. Another criterion requires that classes within the system be mutually exclusive and exhaustive.

A major criterion is that classes are desired that have specific behavioral implications, as with the interest of Annett and Duncan (1967) in classifying "tasks" so that each category or class of tasks has specific training requirements

associated with it. Ultimately, of course, any behavioral classification scheme must make the "match" between specific categories and behavioral effects. The degree to which the "match" can be made will determine the predictive power of the system. At one level, a statement might concern *whether or not* a particular environmental variable would affect performance. At another and more sophisticated level it might be possible to predict the *direction* and *magnitude* of the effect.

A final set of criteria includes efficiency and utility. The taxonomy should promote communication among its users, be they researchers in different areas or specialists who must use research findings in applied settings.

In our own program we found it useful to lay out these general issues, which we have elaborated elsewhere. In no sense can we say that our subsequent efforts met the rigorous standards called for. However, they at least provide indications of where we fell short and allow for successive iterations toward meeting these criteria.

In the remainder of this article, I illustrate some developments with two provisional systems, one based on the *ability requirements approach* and another on the *task characteristics approach*. I conclude with some attempts to link these two approaches.

THE ABILITIES APPROACH

Much of what is known today about the categorization of human skills, at least that which is based on empirical research, comes from correlational and factor analysis studies. Such correlational studies are typically carried out in the psychometric tradition, and until recently, little attempt has been made to integrate the ability concepts developed there into the more general body of psychological theory. Here the fact of individual differences is exploited to gain insights about common processes required to perform different groups of tasks. Abilities are defined by empirically determined relations among observed separate performances.

FIGURE 1   Examples of Tests Found Valid for Pilot Selection

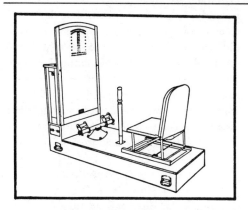

a. COMPLEX COORDINATION   b. ROTARY PURSUIT

It has been my feeling, over many years, that research using combinations of experimental and correlational methods, properly conducted, can lead to the development of a taxonomy of human performance which is applicable to a variety of basic and applied problems and that ability concepts may provide an integrative framework.

Elsewhere (e.g., Fleishman, 1962) I have elaborated on the concepts of *ability* and *skill*. Briefly, ability refers to a more general capacity of the individual, related to performance in a variety of human tasks. For example, the fact that spatial visualization has been found related to performance on such diverse tasks as aerial navigation, blueprint reading, and dentistry makes this ability somehow more basic.

My interest in this area began when I was responsible for developing psychomotor tests to select pilots for the Air Force. Figure 1a shows a test found valid for pilot selection. The test requires simultaneous manipulations of stick and rudder pedals and has a great deal of face validity. However, Figure 1b shows another test found equally valid. This test, the familiar pursuit rotor, has little face validity. The subject is required to keep a stylus tip in contact with a moving target. My feeling was that we needed basic research on the dimensions of perceptual-motor ability to identify what factors in these tests were common to the criterion performance in more complex tasks such as piloting.

An extensive series of interlocking experimental-factor-analytic studies, which we have conducted over many years, has attempted to isolate and identify the ability factors common to a wide range of perceptual-motor performances. Essentially, this is laboratory research in which tasks are specifically designed or selected to test certain hypotheses about the organization of abilities in a certain range of tasks. The experimental battery of tasks is administered to several hundred subjects, and the correlation patterns are examined through factor analysis methods. Subsequent studies tend to introduce task variations aimed at sharpening or limiting our ability factor definitions.

Through our investigation of a wide range of several hundred different tasks, we have been able to account for performance in terms of a relatively small number of abilities. The following display gives the labels of 11 perceptual-motor factors that consistently appear to account for the common variance in such tasks. In subsequent studies, definitions of these abilities and their distinctions from one another have become more clearly delineated. I will not define all of these here, but extensive definitions of each ability exist with illustrations of the tasks that best measure them (Fleishman, 1964).

PERCEPTUAL-MOTOR ABILITIES

Control precision
Multilimb coordination
Response orientation
Reaction time
Speed of arm movement
Rate control (timing)
Manual dexterity
Finger dexterity
Arm-hand steadiness
Wrist-finger speed
Aiming

Similar studies have been carried out in the physical proficiency area, and nine factors have been identified that account for performance in several hundred physical performance tasks:

PHYSICAL PROFICIENCY ABILITIES

Extent flexibility
Dynamic flexibility
Static strength
Dynamic strength
Explosive strength
Trunk strength
Gross body coordination
Equilibrium
Stamina

Perhaps it might be useful to provide some examples of how one examines the generality of an ability category and how one defines its limits. The specification of an ability category is an arduous task. The definition of the rate control factor may provide an illustration.

In early studies it was found that this factor was common to compensatory tracking, for example, keep a horizontal line in the center of the dial, by compensatory movements of a control, as well as to following pursuit tasks, for

example, keep a gun sight in line with a moving target (see Figure 2a). To test the generality of this factor, further tasks were developed to emphasize responses to stimuli moving at different rates, where the tasks were not conventional tracking tasks. For example, Figure 2b shows a task in which the subject had to *time* his movements in relation to different stimulus rates, but he did not have to follow a target or to compensate for the target's movement. The factor was found to extend to such tasks.

Later studies attempted to discover if emphasis on this ability is in judging the rate of the stimulus as distinguished from ability to

---

FIGURE 2 Examples of Tasks Used to Evaluate the Generality and Limitations of Rate Control Ability

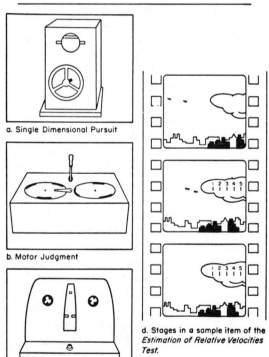

a. Single Dimensional Pursuit

b. Motor Judgment

c. Visual Coincidence

d. Stages in a sample item of the *Estimation of Relative Velocities Test.*

Source: From "On the Relation Between Abilities, Learning, and Human Performance" by Edwin A. Fleishman, *American Psychologist,* 1972, *27,* 1017–1032. Copyright 1972 by the American Psychological Association. Reprinted by permission.

respond at the appropriate rate. Thus, Figure 2c shows a task developed where the only response was the timing of button pressing in response to judgments about the location of stimuli moving at different rates. Performance on this task did not correlate with other rate control tasks. Finally, several motion picture tasks, such as the one in Figure 2d, were adapted in which the subject was required to extrapolate the course of an airplane moving across a screen. The only response required was on an IBM answer sheet. (At what point did the planes meet? Points 1, 2, 3, 4, or 5?) These moving picture tests involving only judgments about stimulus rate did *not* correlate with the group of tasks previously found

FIGURE 3   Percentage of Variance Represented by Loadings on Each Factor at Different Stages of Practice on the Discrimination Reaction Time Task

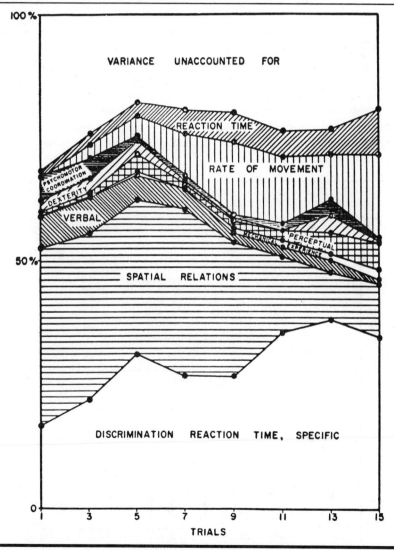

Note: Percentage of variance is represented by the size of the shaded areas for each factor.

Source: From "The Relation Between Abilities and Improvement with Practice in a Visual Discrimination Reaction Task" by Edwin A. Fleishman and Walter E. Hempel, Jr., *Journal of Experimental Psychology,* 1955, *49,* 301–312. Copyright 1955 by the American Psychological Association. Reprinted by permission.

to measure "rate control." Thus, our definition of this rate control ability was expanded to include measures beyond tracking and pursuit tasks, but was restricted to tasks requiring the timing of an actual adjustive movement to the changing stimulus.

A similar history can be sketched for each ability variable identified, and a great number of principles relating task characteristics and abilities measured can now be described. For example we know that multilimb coordination is common to tasks involving simultaneous control actions of two hands, two feet, or hands and feet, but some feedback indicator of coordination is required. Furthermore, this factor does not extend to tasks involving the body in motion, such as in athletic tasks. And we know that fast reaction times are general to auditory and visual stimuli, but as soon as more than one stimulus or response is involved in such tasks, the ability required shifts to re-

sponse orientation. And it is useful to know that there are four primary strength factors, not confined to muscle groups but dependent on specific task requirements (see Fleishman, 1964).

TASK CHARACTERISTICS APPROACH

In a second general approach to taxonomic development, our project staff (Farina & Wheaton, 1973) has worked with what has been termed the *task characteristics approach*. As mentioned earlier, this approach attempts to provide for the description of tasks in terms of a variety of task-intrinsic properties including goals, stimuli, procedures, etc. Knowledge of how performance varies, as a result of manipulating the characteristics of tasks, might provide a basis for estimating performance on

FIGURE 4   Conceptual Scheme of Task Characteristics: Relationship among the Terms *Task, Components,* and *Characteristic*

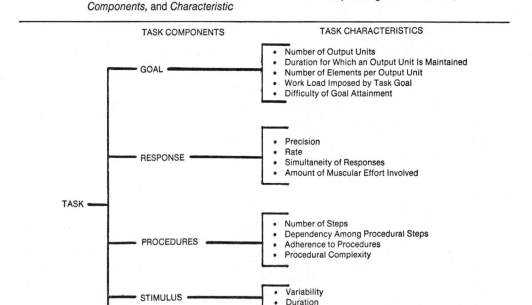

Source: From *Development of a Taxonomy of Human Performance: The Task Characteristics Approach to Performance Prediction* (AIR Tech. Rep. 726–7) by Alfred J. Farina, Jr., and George R. Wheaton.

other tasks whose characteristics could be described.

The development of task characteristics received initial guidance from a definition of the term *task*. A task was conceived of as having several components: an explicit goal, proce-dures, input stimuli, responses, and stimulus-response relationships. In order to differentiate among tasks, the components of a task were treated as categories within which to devise task characteristics or descriptors.

Figure 4 clarifies the relationship among the

FIGURE 5   Example of a Task Characteristic Scale

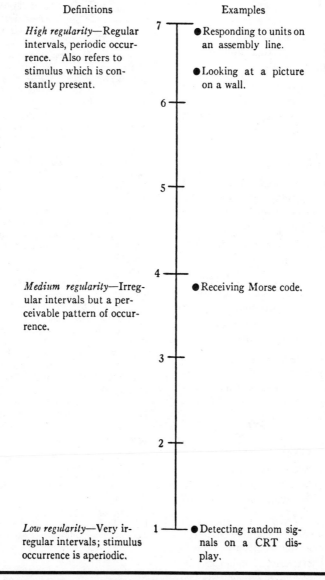

Rate the present task on this dimension.

Definitions

High regularity—Regular intervals, periodic occur-rence.   Also refers to stimulus which is con-stantly present.

Medium regularity—Irreg-ular intervals but a per-ceivable pattern of occur-rence.

Low regularity—Very ir-regular intervals; stimulus occurrence is aperiodic.

Examples

● Responding to units on an assembly line.

● Looking at a picture on a wall.

● Receiving Morse code.

● Detecting random sig-nals on a CRT dis-play.

Source: From *Development of a Taxonomy of Human Performance: The Task Characteristics Approach to Performance Prediction* (AIR Tech. Rep. 726–7) by Alfred J. Farina, Jr., and George R. Wheaton.

terms *task, task components*, and *characteristics.* Each characteristic was cast into a rating scale format that presented a definition of the characteristic and provided a seven-point scale with defined anchor points and midpoints along with examples for each point (Smith & Kendall, 1963). A sample rating scale is shown in Figure 5.

Many different reliability studies have been conducted. Relations between values obtained from three-judge groups and larger groups were high, and a human factors background by raters was found helpful. Of primary interest here are studies in which ratings of task characteristics have predicted actual task performance. In an illustrative study (Farina & Wheaton, 1973), judges rated 37 tasks on 19 scales. The criterion performance score reported for each task was converted to obtain the average number of units produced per unit time.

The six most reliable scales were chosen for analysis. For each of these scales, the ratings provided by three judges were averaged to obtain a single value on each scale for each of the tasks. The specific task descriptive scales employed in the study were (*a*) stimulus duration, (*b*) number of output units, (*c*) duration for which an output unit is maintained, (*d*) simultaneity of responses, (*e*) number of procedural steps, and (*f*) variability of stimulus location.

The results showed that four predictors accounted for approximately 70 percent of the variance in the criterion measure (after correction for small sample bias). It was possible to specify those task characteristics that contributed most to performance. Several replications of such studies have been completed, the most recent of which have employed more complex training devices used by the Navy (Mirabella & Wheaton, Note 11) where it was possible to predict *learning time* through a knowledge of the ratings of the tasks on critical task dimensions.

Overall these efforts have tentatively demonstrated that it is possible to describe tasks in terms of a task-characteristics language and that these task characteristics may represent important correlates of performance.

[1]Cotterman, T. E. *Task Classification: An Approach to Partially Ordering Information on Human Learning* (WADC TN 58-374). Wright-Patterson Air Force Base, Ohio: Wright-Patterson Air Development Center, 1959.

[2]Eckstrand, G. A. *Current Status of the Technology of Training* (AMRL-TR-64-86). Wright-Patterson Air Force Base, Ohio: Aerospace Medical Division, September 1964.

[3]Folley, J. D., Jr. *Development of an Improved Method of Task Analysis and Beginnings of a Theory of Training* (NAVTRADEVCEN 1218-1). Port Washington, N.Y.: U.S. Naval Training Devices Center, June 1964.

[4]Stolurow, L. *A Taxonomy of Learning Task Characteristics* (AMRL-TD 12-64-2). Wright-Patterson Air Force Base, Ohio: Aerospace Medical Research Laboratories, January 1964.

[5]Elkin, E. H., Freedle, R. O., Van Cott, H. P., & Fleishman, E. A. *Effects of Drugs on Human Performance: The Effects of Scopolamine on Representative Human Performance Tests* (AIR Tech. Rep. E-25). Washington, D.C.: American Institutes for Research, August 1965.

[6]McCormick, E. J. *The Development, Analysis, and Experimental Application of Worker-Oriented Job Variables* (Final report; ONR Nonr-1100 [19]). Lafayette, Ind.: Purdue University, 1964.

[7]Fine, S. A. *A Functional Approach to a Broad Scale Map of Work Behaviors* (HSR-RM-63/2). McLean, Va.: Human Sciences Research, September 1963.

[8]Baker, W. J., Geist, A. M., and Fleishman, E. A. *Effects of Cylert (Magnesium-Pemoline) on Physiological, Physical Proficiency, and Psychomotor Performance Measures* (AIR Tech. Rep. F-31). Washington, D.C.: American Institutes for Research, August 1967.

[9]Romashko, T., Brumback, G. B., and Fleishman, E. A. *The Development of a Procedure to Validate Physical Tests: Physical Requirements of the Fireman's Job* (AIR Tech. Rep. 375-1). Washington, D.C.: American Institutes for Research, June 1974.

[10]Romashko, T., Brumback, G. B., and Fleishman, E. A. *The Development of a Procedure to Validate Physical Tests: Physical Requirements of the Sanitation Man's Job* (AIR Tech. Rep. 375-2). Washington, D.C.: American Institutes for Research, October 1973.

[11]Mirabella, A., and Wheaton, G. R. *Effects of Task Index Variations on Transfer of Training Criteria* (NAVTRAEQUIPCEN 72-C-0126-1; American Institutes for Research Contract N61339-72-C-0126). Orlando, Fla.: U.S. Navy Training Equipment Center, September 1973.

[12]Wheaton, G. R., Shaffer, E. J., Mirabella, A., and Fleishman, E. A. *Methods for Predicting Job-Ability Requirements: I. Ability Requirements as a Function of Changes in the Characteristics of an Auditory Signal Identification Task* (AIR Tech. Rep. 73-5). Washington, D.C.: American Institutes for Research, September 1973.

[13]Rose. A. M., Fingerman, P. W., Wheaton, G. R., Eisner, E., and Kramer, G. *Methods for Predicting Job-Ability Requirements: II. Ability Requirements as a Function of Changes in the Characteristics of an Electronic Fault-finding Task* (AIR Tech. Rep. 74-6). Washington, D.C.: American Institutes for Research, August 1974.

The best known and documented research in the area of job analysis has been done by Ernest McCormick. He has developed a standardized questionnaire called the Position Analysis Questionnaire (PAQ) that can be used to analyze jobs. The PAQ provides data about information input activities, information processing or mediation activities, and information and response output activities. This reading describes some of the logic and background for the PAQ. In addition, McCormick describes how the PAQ (and job analysis data generally) can be used to determine the dollar value of different jobs.

■ READING 2 ■

A Study of Job Characteristics and Job Dimensions as Based on the Position Analysis Questionnaire (PAQ)

Ernest J. McCormick, Paul R. Jeanneret, and Robert C. Mecham
Purdue University

Most facets of industrial psychology and the associated functions of personnel administration and vocational counseling have (or at least should have) roots in job-related information. The implications of such information are quite obvious in the case of the practical processes of personnel selection, classification, placement, training, personnel appraisal, job evaluation, job design, etc. Further, basic research relating to many aspects of the relationship between human beings and their work and work situation hinge in part on an understanding of the composition of human work.

Knowledge about human work, either for use in ongoing activities or in a research context, usually is gained by conventional job-analysis procedures, which unfortunately often tend to be more "qualitative" than "quantitative" in form. Qualitative job information is

characterized by typically narrative, essay descriptions in the case of some types of job information (especially job content) or qualitative statements about other aspects of jobs (such as working conditions, context, personnel requirements, etc.). On the other hand, what we might think of as quantitative job information is characterized more by the use of "units" of job information such as job tasks, worker behaviors, and quantitative ratings of job characteristics. In general terms, the field of job and occupational analysis has not benefited substantially from the scientific, systematic approach that has characterized other domains. There have indeed been some exceptions, however, to this general pattern. These include the early work of Viteles (1922, 1932), that of Primoff (1957, 1959), and research performed by or for the United States Training and Employment Service (Jaspen, 1949; Lewis, 1969; McCormick, Finn, & Scheips, 1957; Trattner, Fine, & Kubis, 1955). In addition, special mention should be

Source: *Journal of Applied Psychology Monograph*, 56, no. 4 (August 1972), pp. 347–349; 363–361. Copyright 1972 by the American Psychological Association. Adapted by permission of the publisher and author.

made of the research of the United States Training and Employment Service (UST&ES) that is incorporated in the Dictionary of Occupational Titles (United States Employment Service, 1965), and the innovative research sponsored by the Personnel Division of the Air Force Human Resources Laboratory in the development and use of job inventories (Morsh, 1964; Morsh & Christal, 1966).

BACKGROUND OF PRESENT STUDY

The study consisted of two phases. The first involved the development of a structured job-analysis instrument that provided for characterizing jobs in terms of certain types of human behaviors, and the subsequent analysis of the dimensional or factorial structure of jobs based on such behaviors. The second phase was directed toward the potential use of quantitative data derived with this instrument in the prediction of aptitude requirements of jobs and of rates of pay.

With respect to the objective of the first phase, McCormick and his associates (Cunningham & McCormick, 1964; Gordon & McCormick, 1963; McCormick, Cunningham, & Gordon, 1967) have hypothesized that there is some underlying behavioral "structure" or order to the domain of human work. If there is some such underlying behavioral structure, such structure presumably would have to be characterized in terms of the manner in which more specific "units" of job-related variables tend to be organized across jobs. Thus, the "building blocks" or common denominators of any dimensional structure must consist of relatively unitary, discrete job variables of some class that can be identified and quantified as they relate to individual jobs. In turn, these building blocks need to be reflected by language, and, in most instances, the identification (by analysts) of such building blocks in individual positions or jobs depends on the interpretations of their descriptions as they relate to the positions or jobs in question.

The adequacy of any set of job dimensions that might characterize the structure of human work would depend on having a reasonably complete set of the specific building-block variables of some given class to use in characterizing individual jobs, and would depend further on the validity of the underlying assumption that one can in fact reconstitute jobs in their entirety from the specific building blocks used in the analysis of the jobs.

If meaningful job dimensions can be identified, they would be of considerable importance to both the theoretical and practical developments of the study of the world of work. The theoretical implications concern the development of a taxonomy of work behaviors which in turn could provide structure and continuity to many research findings in much the same manner that the taxonomic work of Fleishman and his associates has contributed understanding to both the conceptual and practical aspects of task performance (Fleishman, 1967; Fleishman, Kinkade, & Chambers, 1968; Fleishman & Stephenson, 1970; Fleishman, Teichner, & Stephenson, 1970).

The quantification of job characteristics, including the possible identification of job dimensions, would offer potential utility over a range of several practical applications. Such applications would be predicted on the hypothesis that communality across jobs based on similar human behaviors should have implications in terms of common aptitude requirements, corresponding rates of pay, and possibly other job-related variables. The second phase dealt with an experimental test of this hypothesis, in particular to predict—from strictly job-analysis data—the aptitude requirements of jobs and the rates of pay of jobs.

Jobs, of course, can be described in terms of different types or classes of variables. One class, for example, deals with worker traits as characterized by Fine and Heinz (1957); these are the human qualities or attributes that presumably are required for satisfactory performance on specific types of jobs. Other classes of job variables deal more with job content —in particular, the work activities. In this connection, Fine (1955) made the distinction between worker functions and work fields. In the formulation of the worker function concept Fine makes the point that all jobs involve some relation to things, data, and people, and that the involvement with each of these can be expressed as a hierarchy. In turn, the work fields concept is a reflection of what gets done, such as riveting, packing, appraising, and drafting. Another class of job variables deals with the work environment and working conditions. Other classes could also be mentioned. In the case of whatever type one is dealing with, the quantification thereof requires the initial identification of "units" or building blocks of the type of variable in question, and the measurement or judging of each such unit as it relates to individual jobs. Any set of job dimensions derived from variables or some given class would, of course, take on the coloration of the class of variables that serves as the basic units of analysis.

The present research is primarily concerned with job activities and related working conditions. In this connection McCormick (1959) makes the distinction between job-oriented and worker-oriented job elements. Job-oriented elements are descriptions of job content that have a dominant association with, and typically characterize, the "technological" aspects of jobs and commonly reflect what is achieved by the worker. On the other hand, worker-oriented elements are those that tend more to characterize the generalized human behaviors involved; if not directly, then by strong inference. Although the job-oriented and worker-oriented job-element concepts have certain parallels, respectively, to the work fields and worker functions set forth by Fine (1955), there is also a difference in these two frames of reference. The job-oriented concept typically would be reflected by the use of specific task statements such as those embodied in job inventories (Morsh, 1964; Morsh & Christal, 1966). In turn, the worker-oriented concept typically would be reflected by the use of descriptions of reasonably definitive human behaviors of many kinds, as contrasted (in the worker function approach) with an indication of the "level" of involvement in the hierarchies of things, data, or people.

In the context of our present discussion, the kinds of common denominators one would seek are those of a worker-oriented nature, since they offer some possibility of serving as bridges or common denominators between and among jobs of very different technologies. One cannot possibly relate butchering, baking, and candlestick-making to each other strictly in these "technological" terms; their communalities (if any) might well be revealed if they were analyzed in terms of the more generalized human behaviors involved, that is in terms of worker-oriented elements. A worker-oriented element can, in effect, be viewed collectively within the framework of the stimulus-organism-response paradigm or, in more operational terms, information input, mediation processes, and output. In addition to these types of behaviors, the concept can also embrace the behavioral "adjustment" required of individuals to the features of the work context.

POSITION ANALYSIS QUESTIONNAIRE (*PAQ*)

The basic job-analysis instrument used in the study was the Position Analysis Questionnaire (PAQ), a structured job-analysis instrument that consisted of 189 job elements of a "worker-oriented" nature. The PAQ was essentially a successor to an earlier instrument called the Worker Activity Profile (Gordon & McCormick, 1963; McCormick, Cunningham, & Gordon, 1967; McCormick, Cunningham, & Thornton, 1967).

The primary frame of reference underlying the development and organization of the PAQ followed the information-input, mediation, and work-output model mentioned above, there being individual job elements relating to each of these. Additionally, there were job elements relating to the interpersonal activities associated with jobs, to the nature of the work situation or job context, and to certain miscellaneous aspects of work. The following is a listing of the major divisions and subdivisions of the PAQ with the number of job elements in each; following each subdivision is the title of an illustrative job element (without its more detailed description).

Information Input (35)

Sources of job information (20): Use of
written materials

Discrimination and perceptual activities
(15): Estimating speed of moving
objects

Mediation Processes (14)

Decision making and reasoning (2): Reasoning in problem solving

Information processing (6): Encoding/de-
coding

Use of stored information (6): Using
mathematics

Work Output (50)

Use of physical devices (29): Use of keyboard devices

Integrative manual activities (8):
Handling objects/materials

General body activities (7): Climbing

Manipulation/coordination activities
(6): Hand-arm manipulation

Interpersonal Activities (36)

Communications (10): Instructing

Interpersonal relationships (3):
Serving/catering

Personal contact (15): Personal contact
with public customers

Supervision and coordination (8):
Level of supervision received

Work Situation and Job Context (18)

Physical working conditions (12):
Low temperature

Psychological and sociological aspects
(6): Civic obligations

Miscellaneous Aspects (36)

Work schedule, method of pay, and
apparel (21): Irregular hours

Job demands (12): Specified (controlled)
work pace

Responsibility (3): Responsibility for
safety of others

For most of the job elements there was an
appropriate scale such as "importance," "extent
of use," "time," etc., or a special scale applicable to the specific element; the analyst
rated each such element as it related to a given

position or job using in most instances a six-
point scale from "0" (does not apply) to "5"
(the highest scale value). Several elements were
of a dichotomous nature; in such instances the
analyst marked the element as "0" (does not
apply) or "1" (does apply).

Terminology

Because of the way in which certain terms
are used in this report, including certain ones
already mentioned and others to be discussed,
these terms will be briefly described here.

Job Element. The term job element refers
to a generalized class of behaviorally related
job activities, including the behavioral adjustment required to features of the work context;
illustrations are given above, these being presented for the various divisions of the Position
Analysis Questionnaire (PAQ). They are not
job tasks in the sense of characterizing specific
technologically related work activities, but
rather relate to generalized human behaviors
involved in work.

Attribute. The term attribute as referred to
below applies to constructs of various types of
human qualities most closely associated with
the common concept of human traits. As further mentioned below, some of these are of an
"aptitude" nature; others are of a "situational"
nature in the sense of imposing a requirement
on the individual to adapt to the situation in
question.

Job Dimension. The term *job dimension*
applies to statistically derived factors (technically principal components) of job-related data
based on the job elements of the PAQ. Two
types of job dimensions will be discussed;
namely (*a*) those based on job-analysis data resulting from the analysis of jobs with the
PAQ, and (*b*) those based on attribute profiles
of the job elements as described below.

Job dimension scores. Job dimension scores
are statistically derived factor scores (principal
components scores) of the various job dimensions as computed for individual jobs on the

basis of the PAQ job-element ratings for the jobs in question.

Uses of PAQ Data in Job Evaluation[1]

If behaviorally similar job characteristics exist in different jobs, it would seem that, as far as those corresponding characteristics are concerned, the jobs would be roughly equivalent in the demands made on the incumbents, and therefore should be roughly equivalent in their wage or salary rates. By extrapolation one might speculate about the possibility that total job values might somehow be based on the composite of the behaviorally characterized components of the jobs. Since the PAQ, with its worker-oriented job elements, seemed to offer a reasonably satisfactory base for quantifying such job characteristics, it was very logical to explore its potential use in the job-evaluation context. This phase of the study was then designed to determine the possible relationships that exist between the behavioral aspects of jobs as based on PAQ data, and rates of monetary compensation in the labor market. In a sense, then, the method was a "policy capturing" one, specifically aimed at finding those behavioral aspects of jobs that have a predictable and stable relationship with compensation rates for many types of jobs in the world of work.

Job Sample

The sample used in this phase consisted of 340 of the 536 jobs for which PAQs had been obtained in connection with the previous phases. These 340 jobs were from 45 different organizations, these being jobs for which optional (and confidential) wage or salary data had been reported. The sample contained jobs in each occupational category given in the *Dictionary of Occupational Titles* except for category four (farming, fishing, forestry, and related occupations).

[1]This phase of the study is reported in greater detail in Mecham (1970) and Mecham and McCormick (1969b).

Conversion of Wage and Salary Data to a Common Metric

Wage and salary rates were supplied with reference to various time periods (i.e., hourly wage, weekly salary, monthly salary, etc.) by different organizations, and therefore it was necessary, for statistical purposes, to convert all such rates to a common time base. The average monthly compensation rate was selected as this common time base.[2]

Analysis Procedures

As a first step in analyzing the data, the job sample was randomly divided into two subsamples (sample A with 165 jobs and sample B with 175 jobs). Secondly, the data in samples A, B, and the combined sample were independently evaluated to identify the PAQ-based variables that might be predictive of wage and salary rates; this was done using a correlational and regression analysis approach. Three types of PAQ predictor variables were used for each job: (*a*) ratings on individual job elements of the PAQ; (*b*) job dimension scores based on overall dimensions; and (*c*) job dimension scores for the 27 job-data dimensions based on the divisions of the PAQ.

As a third step, the predictors and their respective weights (derived using a stepwise-regression analysis procedure) for sample A were used to predict compensation rates in sample B and vice versa. This step constituted a double cross-validation procedure in which cross-validation coefficients were derived by correlating predicted rates with actual rates; sample B actual rates were correlated with rates predicted from sample A predictors and weights, and vice versa. The basic procedure is shown graphically in Figure 1.

After the cross-validation coefficients had

[2]This rate was computed as follows: Average monthly compensation = 173 × hourly wage rate; or 4.333 × weekly salary; or 1.00 × monthly salary; or 1/12 × yearly salary.

The computations were based on the rationale that employees typically work 40 hours per week and receive pay during vacations.

FIGURE 1   Illustration of Cross-Validation Procedure Used in the Job-Evaluation Phase of the Research

Sample A (165 jobs)	Sample B (175 jobs)
Identification and weighting of predictors in sample A	Identification and weighting of predictors in sample B
Sample B predictors and weights used to predict salary rates in sample A	Sample A predictors and weights used to predict salary rates in sample B

been derived using the above procedure, samples A and B were combined, and the best combinations of predictors and their respective weights were determined. It would be expected that the combined sample would yield the optimum combination of predictors and weights for any of the three types of predictors (i.e., job elements, overall job dimensions, and division job dimensions).

As a fourth and final step, the residuals (actual rate − predicted rate = residual) obtained with the optimum prediction equations (for each of the three types of predictors) were compared by "50-dollar" predicted compensation classes. This procedure was designed to determine if prediction was better in some sections of the compensation range than in others. Additionally, the standard deviation of residuals in each "50-dollar" class was computed as a way of determining the range of misprediction for each class. Finally, the generalized expected standard deviation of observed compensation rates around predicted compensation rates was computed and plotted.

Selection of Predictors. To select a set of tentative predictors from the PAQ job elements, ratings on each PAQ job element for the jobs in each sample were correlated with actual wage and salary rates for those same jobs. The 15 job elements having ratings with the highest positive correlations and the 10 having the most negative correlations in each sample were selected as tentative predictors. These 25 job elements for each sample comprised the job-element set used later in the stepwise-regression procedure. The overall job dimensions and division job dimensions were

used without any such selection procedure since it was not necessary to reduce the number of predictors in these analyses.

The next step consisted of subjecting all tentative predictors in each set for each sample to a "build-up" stepwise-regression analysis. This procedure produced sets of final predictors and corresponding regression weights for each sample on each type of predictor. Because the 25 job elements used as tentative predictors and the 27 division job dimensions did not produce important increases in predictive power beyond the ninth step, only these nine are reported as final predictors. With the remaining predictor set, overall job dimension scores, all five dimensions were used.

Results: Job Evaluation

The multiple correlation coefficients computed as part of the regression analysis for each set of predictors within each sample are given in Table 1. These coefficients ranged from .83 to .90 for the various job samples (A, B, and combined). As noted above, the shrinkage in cross validation was fairly nominal.

An examination of the pattern of relationships between job evaluation points and monthly compensation rates was made by dividing the entire range (from about $375 to $1,525 per month) into 25 classes. Although there were variations by class intervals, the basic relationship appeared to be linear except for the lower end of the scale, which tended to veer up a bit. However, there were very few jobs in the lower class intervals, so the pattern for these categories must be viewed cautiously. The standard deviations of the compensation

TABLE 1 Multiple Correlation and Cross-Validation Co-Efficients of Regression Equations Based on Job Data of the PAQ Used to Predict Compensation Rates

Nature of Data	Initial Sample		Cross-Validated Sample*		Combined Sample
	A	B	B	A	
Overall dimensions (5)	.83	.87	.87	.83	.85
Dimensions from PAQ divisions (9)	.87	.90	.85	.83	.87
Individual job elements (9)	.87	.89	.86	.86	.87

*The regression equation developed from the initial sample A (or B) was then cross validated by applying it to sample B (or A).

rates of jobs within each class interval can be viewed as an indication of misprediction. In general, it was found that the range of misprediction was narrower for lower level jobs than for higher level jobs; further, the range increased progressively as the predicted compensation rate increased, the increase in range being virtually a constant ratio of the compensation rates.

DISCUSSION AND CONCLUSIONS

Human work can be viewed from various frames of reference, and thus can be characterized in terms of different "classes" of job-related variables. This report is based on a probing effort relating to worker behaviors, or what are herein referred to as the worker-oriented aspects of jobs. It would seem that such behaviorally related variables could serve as possible common denominators on which to compare or contrast jobs of different technological areas. Further, it would seem that jobs that involve the same general "kind" of human behavior(s), even though in different technological settings, would have common implications—insofar as those particular features of the jobs are concerned—in terms of their apti-

tude requirements and possibly their appropriate rates of compensation.

Assuming that one could analyze jobs in terms of reasonably discrete, separate job elements of a worker-oriented nature, one would hope that these could in turn serve as the basis for building up statistically related groupings of such elements in order to describe the dominant dimensions of jobs. Job-dimension scores for individual jobs could then reflect variations among jobs along each such dimension, thus providing the basis for job profiles described in terms of such dimensions, and for a "reconstitution" of any given job from the analyzed elements.

A rigorous test of the adequacy of any such reconstitution of jobs is probably hard to come by, but some considerations that would be relevant in such an assessment might include the intrinsic integrity of each job dimension in terms of its statistical stability, the meaningfulness of the job dimensions, the extent to which the dimensions collectively encompass the totality of the class of variables being dealt with, and the practical utility of job data based on such dimensions in serving some useful purpose (in the present instance those in the synthetic validity and job evaluation contexts).

A boiled-down recapitulation of the premises implied in this research might be something like this: that there are common denominators of jobs of a behavioral nature that exist in jobs of different types, in most instances such common denominators existing in different jobs in varying degree; that these common denominators can be expressed in language that lends itself to the reliable and valid analysis of individual jobs; that the rather specific common denominators form reasonably stable, meaningful job dimensions; and that these dimensions collectively can serve as an adequate basis for characterizing jobs in their totality in terms of the type of behavioral variables in question.

The research was based on data derived from the Position Analysis Questionnaire (PAQ), a structured job analysis questionnaire developed with this frame of reference in mind. The various phases of the research lead to certain general conclusions, including those below:

1. The results lend further support to the thesis that it is possible to analyze human work in terms of meaningful "units" or job elements of a worker-oriented nature, and that this analysis can be carried out with acceptable reliability.

2. Further, there is evidence that such job elements tend to form reasonably stable job dimensions that characterize the "structure" of human work.

3. In addition, ratings of the "requirements" of such job elements in terms of various human attributes can be made by psychologists with substantial reliability, when pooling the ratings of several raters.

4. The resulting attribute "profiles" of job elements (expressed as medians of the several ratings of individual attributes) also tend to form reasonably stable job dimensions.

5. The data resulting from the use of the PAQ (by itself or in combination with the related attribute profiles of job elements) offer considerable promise of serving certain practical purposes such as job evaluation and the establishment of synthetically derived aptitude requirements of individual jobs.

The indications about the potential applications of the PAQ in the areas of synthetic validity and job evaluation still need to be viewed with some reservations. At the same time they are distinctly encouraging. If supported further, and worked into operational systems, the results might go a long way in aiding and abetting the development of aptitude requirements and the evaluation of jobs in industry. It does, in fact, appear to be within the realm of possibility to establish test-score standards of jobs strictly on the basis of job data from the Position Analysis Questionnaire (PAQ), thus minimizing the need for situational validation of tests (and the perhaps more common practice of selecting tests by "judgment"). Similarly, one might contemplate the derivation of job values, also on the basis of strictly job analysis data, thus eliminating the conventional job evaluation processes.

Perhaps more generally, however, the results may be viewed as a step in the direction of identifying and quantifying the "structure" of human work, toward the end of dealing more quantitatively with this relatively boggy domain, both for its theoretical and practical implications.

In this reading, Arvey and Begalla illustrate the type of information that comes out of the PAQ. They analyze the job of a homemaker and discover some things that are not surprising and other things that are unexpected. As an example, although you may not be surprised to learn that a homemaker's job is similar to that of a home economist, are you aware that the homemaker's job is even more similar to that of a police officer? The detailed analysis shows that a homemaker needs to know environmental conditions (e.g., beds to be made, floors to be scrubbed, and meals to be prepared). On the other hand, working on a regular schedule and discussing things with a "supervisor" or "subordinate" are less important parts of the job. Since most of us are aware of the job of a homemaker, this reading provides a nice illustration of the application of the PAQ to job analysis.

■ READING 3 ■

Analyzing the Homemaker Job Using the Position Analysis Questionnaire (PAQ)

Richard D. Arvey and Martha E. Begalla
University of Tennessee, Knoxville

The job of a housewife or homemaker is not immune to scientific analysis and study. Indeed, there are a number of reasons why it is becoming increasingly important to learn more about the tasks, duties, and functions performed by homemakers. First, it is important to understand the various tasks and responsibilities in *any* job to be able to train or change behavior to perform these tasks more efficiently.

Second, there is a growing concern that the work performed by women (or men) in homemaking jobs should be directly compensated or that at least some monetary value should be calculated that would have been paid if the services had been performed under contract. Perhaps an assumption behind this concern is that people who perform tasks and duties that are not compensated for are sometimes perceived

not to do work or hold a job. As one person put it, "because the homemaker works without pay we have difficulty in recognizing her labors as being of value or even as real work" (Briggs, Note 1, p. 1).

Third, we have begun, with some pushing from the feminist movement, to fully examine the homemaker job as a work role not unlike other jobs (Walker, 1973; Galbraith, 1973). For example, it may be that a homemaker's job requires certain skills and capabilities that are common to other jobs. If so, homemakers could perhaps move into these other occupational areas without excessive or long periods of training.

To these ends, an attempt was made to analyze the job of the homemaker using a particular job analytic instrument—the Position Analysis Questionnaire (PAQ)—utilized previously within industrial settings. Several objectives were involved in the present research: (*a*) to determine if the job was amenable to analysis using the PAQ and to describe the be-

Source: *Journal of Applied Psychology*, 60, no.4 (1975), pp. 513–17. Copyright 1975 by the American Psychological Association. Reprinted by permission of the publisher and author.

haviors and psychological processes involved in the job; (b) to attempt to associate a wage or salary figure with the job as described; (c) to learn which kinds of jobs were closely related to the homemaker job to make preliminary inferences concerning possible job transfer and training decisions; and (d) to examine possible correlates, such as age and education, of the PAQ descriptions provided by the homemakers.

METHOD

Instruments

The Position Analysis Questionnaire (PAQ), developed by McCormick and his associates (McCormick, Jeanneret, & Mecham, 1972), provides for the analysis of jobs in terms of 194 job elements. These elements either reflect directly or infer the basic human behaviors in jobs, regardless of the specific technological area or level of the job. In analyzing a job with the PAQ, the analyst judges the relevance of each job element (e.g., the use of mechanical devices) to the job using an appropriate rating scale such as importance or frequency.

On the basis of ratings on the 194 job elements, 32 basic "job dimensions" have been statistically derived using factor analytic techniques. Each dimension is characterized and defined by a group of job elements that tend to occur in combination in jobs (McCormick et al., 1972). The last 5 of the 32 dimensions are considered as "overall" dimensions because they reflect a larger number of job elements and tend to be more general in nature. Once a job has been analyzed with the PAQ, a computer data service processes the data so that scores on these 32 job dimensions are derived for a particular job. These scores are in the form of Z scores so that comparisons can by made between jobs on a normative basis.

The PAQ computer service also provides a profile similarity option and an estimated income value which can be used in the establishment of compensation rates for jobs (Mecham & McCormick, Note 2). The predicted income level is based on a procedure in which the job dimensions are weighted using a general non-linear regression equation previously derived from a sample of 531 jobs from approximately 50 different organizations (McCormick, Mecham, & Jeanneret, Note 3).

A two-page personal inventory sheet asking for age, income, education, and other information was also used.

Sample

An attempt was made to interview 60 homemakers. Phone calls were made on a random basis to Knoxville households listed in various economic-level areas in the city directory. The nature of the project was explained, and if the individuals considered themselves full-time homemakers with no other job they were asked to participate in the study. Those who agreed to participate were told that an interviewer would contact them later and set up an interview date and time.

About 65 individuals agreed to participate (out of about 100 contacted) and were scheduled to be interviewed. Actual interviews were conducted with 55 individuals, seven of whom were eliminated because of missing data or some acquaintance with the researchers/interviewers. The total sample thus consisted of 48 individuals who considered themselves full-time homemakers.

All 48 subjects were female, and their average age was 37.6 years ($SD = 11.02$). Twenty-seven subjects had children at home, the average number of children being 2.4 ($SD = 1.25$). Forty-four subjects were married, and 42 had had a previous full-time job outside the home sometime during their lifetime. The median income level for the total sample was approximately $14,500, reflecting a wealthier sample than the average Knoxville household (the median household income for this area was $9,270. Individuals reporting an income level less than $10,000 ($n = 11$) were classified as a relatively low socioeconomic group, those between $10,000 and $20,000 ($n = 20$) were considered a middle socioeconomic group, and those greater than $20,000 ($n = 17$) were classified as a relatively high socioeconomic group.

Procedure

Five interviewers were trained to analyze the job of the homemaker. These interviewers, after contacting the subjects and setting up appointments, spent about one and one-half to two hours interviewing each subject. The interviewers were instructed to let the subjects define their jobs broadly to obtain some general limits on what they felt their jobs contained. Subsequently, the interviewers administered the PAQ by asking the various questions verbally and providing the subjects with the appropriate response format. A small gift was presented to each person who participated. Informal feedback from the interviewers indicated that the subjects did not feel pressured or "guided" by the interviewers to respond in any particular manner.

The individual PAQ data sheets were scored along the 32 job dimensions using the various computer packages associated with the instrument. The 48 profiles were averaged to obtain a composite picture of the homemaker job along these dimensions. A predicted monthly salary figure was generated based on the composite profile. A profile similarity analysis was conducted by computing a distance score (D^2) between the homemaker job profile and approximately 1,000 jobs in the normative data bank.

One-way analysis of variance procedures were performed on each of the 32 job dimension scores using the socioeconomic groups as the independent variable to detect whether dimension scores were dependent upon socioeconomic differences.

Also, education and age were correlated with the dimension scores to determine if these variables were related to the descriptions based on the PAQ.

RESULTS

Subject Agreement

The intraclass correlation coefficient (Winer, 1962) for the 48 subjects was .98, indicating that the subjects were very similar in their descriptions across the 32 dimensions.

The coefficients for the high-, middle-, and low-socioeconomic groups were .86, .97, and .92, respectively.

Dimension Profile

The 32 job dimension Z scores and their standard deviations are shown in Table 1. Generally speaking, a high Z score signifies that the particular psychological or behavioral process is fairly important for the job being discussed on the job dimension compared to other jobs. (However, there are three bipolar dimensions that do not reflect a unidimensional continuum, in which case there is some question as to which end is high.) There are several things to note in this table. First, the scores seem to reflect a relatively "high" or demanding profile; almost all the scores except for four of the dimensions are greater than zero. The average Z score across the 32 dimensions for the sample was .90. It must be noted that these high scores could reflect a tendency on the part of the subjects to overinflate the nature of their jobs, instead of reflecting real job differences.

The four highest dimensional scores for the sample were on Dimensions 7 (being aware of body movement and balance), 30 (being physically active/related environmental conditions), 6 (being aware of environmental conditions), and 23 (engaging in personally demanding situations). All of these Z scores were greater than 2.00, suggesting that the behaviors involved in these dimensions far exceed those found in most other jobs. The negative score of Dimension 27 (-1.48) indicates that the subjects were on a highly variable schedule involving irregular hours compared to most jobs.

Job Similarities

Table 2 presents the 20 occupations that were the most similar to the homemaker profile using the data from the present study and from over 1,000 other jobs. Also shown are the D^2 values indicating the degree of profile similarity of the homemaker and other jobs.

TABLE 1   Position Analysis Questionnaire Job Dimension Z Scores and Standard Deviations

Dimension	Average Z Score	SD
1. Watching devices/materials for information	.16	.72
2. Interpreting what is heard or seen	.51	.78
3. Using data originating with people	.34	1.06
4. Watching things from a distance	.36	.86
5. Evaluating information from things	1.79	1.03
6. Being aware of environmental conditions	2.30	1.75
7. Being aware of body movement and balance	3.08	1.74
8. Making decisions	.13	.61
9. Processing information	.34	.90
10. Controlling machines/processes	− .08	.47
11. Using hands and arms to control/modify	1.36	.83
12. Using feet/hands to operate equipment/vehicles	1.96	1.28
13. Performing activities requiring general body movement	1.89	.91
14. Using hands and arms to move/position things	.41	.67
15. Using fingers versus general body movement	− .56	.71
16. Performing skilled/technical activities	.96	.89
17. Communicating judgments, decisions, information	.44	.68
18. Exchanging job-related information	1.69	1.27
19. Performing staff/related activities	1.28	.86
20. Contacting supervisor or subordinates	− .38	.94
21. Dealing with the public	1.43	1.63
22. Being in a hazardous/unpleasant environment	1.37	1.08
23. Engaging in personally demanding situations	2.05	.90
24. Engaging in businesslike work situations	.03	.47
25. Being alert to detail/changing conditions	.87	1.11
26. Performing unstructured versus structured work	− .32	.63
27. Working on a variable versus regular schedule	−1.48	.89
28. Having decision-making, community, and social responsibility	1.19	.74
29. Performing skilled activities	.49	.63
30. Being physically active/related environmental conditions	2.72	1.01
31. Operating equipment/vehicles	1.5	.99
32. Processing information	1.11	.96

Note. Based on 48 descriptions of homemaker job.

DISCUSSION

The results of this study indicate that the job of homemaker is amenable to analysis using the PAQ. The intraclass correlation data show that the subjects agreed quite reasonably in their descriptions of their jobs regardless of their socioeconomic levels. Further, the data depict a particular profile of job behavior that suggests that the job is personally demanding, requiring considerable attention to both the "work" environment and to oneself in relationship to this environment and a highly variable schedule. This profile must be viewed as providing only preliminary guidelines, however, as it is based on data gathered from a relatively small sample from one community.

Based on these data, the predicted wage for the homemaker using 1968–69 wage rates was $740 a month. This wage rate seems to be over-inflated compared to our general notions of the job compared to other jobs. It is possible that the scores on the job dimensions might be over-inflated due to tendencies on the part of the subjects to depict aspects of their jobs as being perhaps more important than they might in fact be. Another factor possibly contributing to the relatively high wage was that the sample, as a whole, was well above the median household income level for the particular geographical area. Thus, the high predicted wage may be due to the sample of higher income-bracket individuals. In any case, a wage rate was predicted that could serve as a starting point for further research and investigation. Other job analysis procedures and techniques should be applied along with other

TABLE 2 Jobs Most Similar to Homemaker Job Based on Profile Similarity (D^2) Scores

Job	D^2
1. Patrolman	6.69
2. Home economist	7.95
3. Airport maintenance chief	9.96
4. Kitchen helper	9.99
5. Fire fighter	10.21
6. Trouble man	10.23
7. Instrument-maker helper	10.67
8. Electrician, foreman	10.91
9. Maintenance foreman, gas plant	11.12
10. Hydroelectric-machinery mechanic	11.17
11. Transmission mechanic	11.55
12. Lineman, repair	12.25
13. Electric-meter repairman	12.36
14. Instructor, vocational training	12.43
15. Gas serviceman	12.75
16. Inspector, motors and generators	12.93
17. Lifeguard	12.84
18. Fire captain	13.05
19. Repairman, switch gear	13.22
20. Home economist, consumer service	13.47

Note. D^2 = generalized distance score (Nunnally, 1967). The smaller the D^2 values, the more similar are the profiles.

job evaluation processes to further establish a wage point. The authors do *not* wish this wage rate to be quoted out of context without careful attention to possible biases and artifacts involved in this research.

Learning about the kinds of jobs that are closely related to the homemaker job was another objective of this study. Perusal of the 20 most similar occupations suggests that several jobs are closely related to the homemaker job by name, for example, kitchen helper. More interesting, perhaps, is that a major theme which seemed to run through many of the other occupations was a troubleshooting, emergency-handling orientation. This theme would probably not go undisputed by many homemakers. Also to be noticed is the close similarity of the homemaker job to several supervisory jobs (electrician foreman, gas plant maintenance foreman, and fire captain).

While the profile similarity analysis yielded a number of jobs closely related to that of the homemaker, it would nevertheless still be difficult to state unequivocally that these jobs are the most amenable to entry by homemakers. There is a considerable amount of training required for many of the jobs and various necessary technological skills. However, it is interesting to note that the most similar job— patrolman—is an occupational role into which many women are presently moving and which, with mounting affirmative action pressures, represents a job area which seems ripe for entry by women. Certainly, it is interesting to consider the possibilities of organizations establishing training programs in order for people in homemaking jobs to gain entry into these particular job areas. A question that might be raised here is whether homemakers could be more easily trained and prepared for entry into these occupations in contrast to other less-related job areas.

Finally, several variables were associated with the PAQ descriptions given by the 48 subjects. Specifically, low-socioeconomic subjects described their jobs as being less important on eight dimensions than did middle- and high-socioeconomic subjects. Age and education were two other variables that exhibited considerable relationships with the job dimensions; the older and less educated individuals described their jobs as perhaps less complex than did the younger and more educated subjects.

A point of discussion concerns the socioeconomic group differences and whether these group differences reflect real job differences. An alternative explanation could be that the lower socioeconomic group did not fully comprehend the specific questions on the PAQ referring to these dimensions and were less apt to use the high endpoint of the rating scales for those elements. Many of the dimensions on which socioeconomic differences did emerge were based on fairly complex questions imbedded in the PAQ. Since the socioeconomic differences were based on relatively small samples these findings must be viewed as tentative.

Job evaluation has always been an issue of great importance to managers, workers, labor unions, and various governmental bodies. It is a process for determining the pay and dollar value of jobs and placing jobs in categories or grades that all receive the same basic wage. Recently, a movement has begun to reconsider the way that workers are compensated and job evaluation has taken on new meaning and importance. It has been proposed that people who perform comparable jobs should receive similar compensation. This has become known as the comparable worth movement and has been raised most frequently in the context of claims that women are generally underpaid compared to men. In this reading, Treiman and Hartman introduce the topic of comparable worth and link job analysis and pay schemes. In the second portion of the reading, McCormick makes a strong appeal for using traditional job analysis to set wage rates. Further, he contends that prevailing wage rates are not simply the result of caprice or discriminatory decisions. Instead, he suggests that current wage rates represent an implicit statement of job values.

The controversy surrounding comparable worth is likely to be with us for some time to come. There is a great deal of money and power at stake. The principle of comparable worth got a big boost in the state of Washington several years ago when it was decided that female state employees in particular job titles deserved to be paid at a rate similar to those of men with comparable jobs. More recently, a court of appeals overturned that decision and set the principle back substantially. Various political factions are strongly opposed to the concept as well. The political and philosophical aspects of this debate will guarantee its continued presence in the personnel arena.

■ READING 4 ■

Women, Work, and Wages
Equal Pay for Jobs of Equal Value

Donald J. Treiman and Heidi I. Hartmann

Committee on Occupational Classification and Analysis

Assembly of Behavioral and Social Sciences

National Research Council

At the request of the Equal Employment Opportunity Commission (EEOC), the Committee on Occupational Classification and Analysis undertook a study of the issues involved in measuring the comparability of jobs. What bases—skill, effort, responsibility, tasks—exist for comparing jobs? Can they be adequately measured? Specifically, the committee was charged with assessing formal systems of job evaluation and other methods currently used in the private and public sectors to establish the comparability of jobs and their levels of compensation.[1] The EEOC is concerned with the validity of the principles used to establish compensation—in particular, with whether methods of job analysis and clas-

Source: *Women, Work, and Wages: Equal Pay for Jobs of Equal Value* by D.J. Treiman and H.I. Hartmann, Eds., 1981, Washington, D.C.: National Academy Press. Reprinted from "Women, Work, and Wages," 1981, with the permission of the National Academy Press, Washington, D.C.

[1]Job evaluation systems typically are used to order jobs hierarchically on the basis of judgments regarding their relative skill, effort, responsibility, etc., and on this basis to group them for pay purposes. For a description of formal job evaluation systems, see Chapter 4 and also the committee's interim report to the Equal Employment Opportunity Commission (Treiman, 1979).

sification currently used are biased by traditional stereotypes or other factors.

The committee undertook its investigation at a time when compensation systems are being intensively questioned, especially by women. The issue of the "comparable worth" of jobs is being raised in complaints, grievances, public discussions, lawsuits, and legislative initiatives. Women who are nurses, librarians, government employees, and clerical workers have assessed their skills and the requirements of their jobs and have argued that their jobs are underpaid relative to jobs of comparable worth—that is, jobs requiring similar levels of skill, effort, and responsibility and similar working conditions—that are held mainly by men. For many women, the slogan "equal pay for work of equal value" has replaced the slogan "equal pay for equal work," which is embodied in the Equal Pay Act of 1963. More generally, the issue raised is that of pay equity in a labor market that is highly segregated by sex. While the opportunity to move out of segregated job categories may be welcome to many women, many others, who have invested considerable time in training for their jobs, demand wage adjustment in "women's jobs" rather than opportunities to work in other jobs.

A number of lawsuits have been initiated by women who assert that, because Title VII of the 1964 Civil Rights Act makes discrimination in compensation for employment illegal, jobs of comparable worth are required to be compensated equally and that failure to meet this requirement constitutes discrimination. Some of these lawsuits involve job evaluation systems. Nurses working for the city of Denver, for example, claimed that the classification system used by the city's Career Service Authority to assign jobs to pay classifications was discriminatory. Nursing service directors were grouped, for pay purposes, in a pay class that was 86 percent female (including, for example, beginning nurses and dental hygienists) rather than in a pay class comprised of professional jobs, held mainly by men, that were alleged by the plaintiffs to be of equivalent responsibility (for example, hospital administration officers and directors of environ-

mental health). Of a total of 74 administrative pay classes, in 65 classes all job incumbents were men and in six classes all incumbents were women; only three of the classes had incumbents of both sexes (Kronstadt, 1978). The nurses lost their case in district court, and their appeal to the U.S. Court of Appeals for the Tenth Circuit was unsuccessful (*Lemons* v. *Denver*).

Librarians, too, have challenged the use of classification systems that result in lower pay for what they regard as jobs with requirements similar to those of other nonteaching positions. In 1971 librarians at the University of California found that they were in the lowest of the university's 25 nonteaching academic pay series and that their salaries were about 25 percent lower than the salaries of those in comparable nonteaching academic positions filled mainly by men (Galloway & Archuleta, 1978). In San Francisco, employees of the city and the county compared the pay rates of classes of jobs held mainly by men with the pay rates of classes of jobs held mainly by women. They found salaries of the jobs held mainly by men to be 74 percent higher than salaries of jobs held mainly by women. When comparisons were restricted to jobs requiring equal education and experience, the salary advantage of the jobs held mainly by men ranged from 21 percent for selected professional jobs (for example, recreation instructor or real property appraiser compared with librarian) to 64 percent for selected clerical jobs (for example, storekeeper compared with clerk typist) (Women Library Workers and the Commission on the Status of Women, 1978).

Some groups have relied on job evaluation systems to support their claims of comparable worth. Examples include a number of cases brought by the International Union of Electrical, Radio and Machine Workers, alleging that electrical manufacturing companies had put jobs held exclusively by women into lower pay grades than jobs held exclusively by men, even when the jobs were judged to be of equal value on the basis of the companies' own job evaluation plans that were used as the principal bases of pay differentiation within the companies (see the discussion in Chapter 3).

Similarly, women clerical workers at the University of Northern Iowa filed a complaint because craft workers (primarily men) were paid a premium of 50 percent over the salary range dictated by a job evaluation plan used by the university. Justified by the university as a business necessity to compete in the local labor market, the premium had the effect of paying men more on the average and women less on the average than their jobs were worth according to the university's own criteria (*Christensen v. Iowa*).

In the state of Washington, the state government employees' union requested that a study be undertaken, using job evaluation techniques, to compare jobs held mainly by men (for example, traffic guide, construction coordinator, electrician) with those held mainly by women (for example, secretary, clerk typist, nurse practitioner). The study found that for jobs rated equally by the job evaluation system, those held mainly by men were paid 20 percent more on the average than those held mainly by women; the difference occurred largely because the state's pay scales had been developed by using area wage surveys (Remick, 1980). Similar studies, relying on job evaluation techniques, are being carried out to analyze civil service classifications in a number of states.

CURRENT LEGAL CONTEXT

The status of claims of comparable worth under federal law is at present uncertain. Two major federal laws cover employment discrimination: the Equal Pay Act of 1963 and the Civil Rights Act of 1964. The Equal Pay Act of 1963 (an amendment to the Fair Labor Standards Act) addresses the issue of equal pay for men and women doing equal work. The act describes equal work as that requiring equal skill, effort, and responsibility being performed under similar working conditions.[2]

Under the Equal Pay Act, job pairs such as janitor and maid, nurse's aide and orderly, and selector-packer and selector-packer-stacker have been found to be sufficiently similar as to be considered equal, and equal pay has been ordered.[3] The word "equal" in this context has been interpreted to require that the jobs so compared be very similar in work content.

Title VII of the 1964 Civil Rights Act, as amended, prohibits discrimination because of race, color, religion, sex, or national origin in all employment practices, including hiring, firing, promotion, compensation, and other terms, privileges, and conditions of employment.[4] The Equal Pay Act was partially incorporated into Title VII via the Bennett Amendment, which states: "It shall not be an unlawful employment practice under this title for any employer to differentiate upon the basis of sex in determining the amount of the wages or compensation paid or to be paid to employees of such employer if such differentiation is authorized by the provisions of [the Equal Pay Act]." Until a recent Supreme Court decision, the interpretation of this language had been in dispute. Some interpretations had held that

---

[2]The Equal Pay Act states (29 U.S.C. §206(d)(1) (1970)):

No employer having employees subject to any provisions of this section shall discriminate within any es-

tablishment in which such employees are employed, between employees on the basis of sex by paying wages to employees in such establishment for equal work on jobs the performance of which requires equal skill, effort and responsibility, and which are performed under similar working conditions, except where such payment is made pursuant to (i) a seniority system (ii) a merit system (iii) a system which measures earnings by quantity or quality of production, or (iv) a differential based on any other factor other than sex: Provided, that an employer who is paying a wage rate differential in violation of this subsection shall not in order to comply with the provisions of this subsection, reduce the wage rate of any employee.

[3]From June 1964 through the end of fiscal 1977 there were 7,878 compliance actions involving equal pay, and more than $147 million was found to be owed to more than 253,000 employees. Almost $16 million was found to be owed to 19,382 employees in 1977 alone, and nearly 13,000 employees benefited from $7 million in restored income (U.S. Department of Labor, Employment Standards Administration, 1978).

[4]Title VII states in part (42 *U.S. Code* S20003-2(h)):

Sec. 703 (a) it shall be an unlawful employment practice for an employer—(1) to fail or refuse to hire or to discharge any individual, or otherwise to discriminate against any individual with respect to his compensa-

jobs being compared to establish claims of pay discrimination against women must meet an Equal Pay Act test of similarity. An alternative interpretation had been that the Bennett Amendment was meant to incorporate only the defenses available to an employer that are enumerated in the Equal Pay Act: that is, if an employer can show that pay differences stem from seniority, merit, differences in productivity, or differences in any factor other than sex, then those differences in pay are not illegal.

In June 1981 the U.S. Supreme Court ruled, in *County of Washington et al.* v. *Gunther et al.* (80-429), in favor of the latter interpretation:

> The Bennett Amendment does not restrict Title VII's prohibition of sex-based wage discrimination to claims for equal pay for 'equal work.' Rather, claims for sex-based wage discrimination can also be brought under Title VII even though no member of the opposite sex holds an equal but higher paying job, provided that the challenged wage rate is not exempted under the Equal Pay Act's affirmative defenses as to wage differentials attributable to seniority, merit, quantity or quality of production, or any other factor other than sex (Syllabus, i−ii).

The Court made no explicit judgment regarding the validity of the concept of comparable worth as a basis for assessing pay equity between jobs, noting that such a judgment was not relevant to the dispute. Despite this, the Court appears to distinguish between cases in which plaintiffs ask the courts to judge the rel-

ative worth of jobs and cases in which plaintiffs demand that, where employers have made judgments regarding relative job worth (e.g., through the use of job evaluation procedures), they adhere to them in setting pay rates.[5]

Recently one district court has directly supported the comparable worth contention—that jobs should be paid in proportion to their relative worth. In April 1981 the U.S. District Court for Western Pennsylvania, in *Martha L. Taylor et al.* v. *Charley Brothers Company and Teamsters Local 30* (78-138), held that the employer, a wholesale grocer, had discriminated against women by assigning them to a separate department from men and paying them substantially less than those in an all-male department doing jobs that were different in their content but similar in their requirements (paragraph 19): "Defendant Charley Brothers intentionally discriminated against . . . women in Department 2 by paying them substantially less than the men in Department 1 because they worked in a department populated only by women, and not because the jobs they performed were inherently worth less

---

[5]The pertinent part of the decision reads (*County of Washington* v. *Gunther*: 18):

> Petitioner argues strenuously that the approach of the Court of Appeals places 'the pay structure of virtually every employer and the entire economy . . . at risk and subject to scrutiny by the federal courts.' Brief for Petitioners, at 99-100. It raises the spectre that 'Title VII plaintiffs could draw any type of comparison imaginable concerning job duties and pay between any job predominantly performed by women and any job predominantly performed by men.' *Id.*, at 101. But whatever the merit of petitioner's arguments in other contexts, they are inapplicable here, for claims based on the type of job comparisons petitioner describes are manifestly different from respondents' claim. Respondents contend that the County of Washington evaluated the worth of their jobs; that the county determined that they should be paid approximately 95 percent as much as the male correctional officers; that it paid them only about 70 percent as much, while paying the male officers the full evaluated worth of their jobs; and that the failure of the county to pay respondents the full evaluated worth of their jobs can be proven to be attributable to intentional sex discrimination. Thus, respondents' suit does not require a court to make its own subjective assessment of the value of the male and female guard jobs, or to attempt by statistical technique or other method to quantify the effect of sex discrimination on the wage rates.

---

tion, terms, conditions, or privileges of employment, because of such individual's race, color, religion, sex, or national origin; or (2) to limit, segregate, or classify his employees or applicants for employment in any way which would deprive or tend to deprive any individual of employment opportunities or otherwise adversely affect his status as an employee, because of such individual's race, color, religion, sex, or national origin.

The act covers all private employers of 15 or more persons, labor unions with 15 or more members, all educational institutions, federal, state, and local governments, employment agencies, and joint labor-management committees that provide apprenticeship or training. Complaints can be filed by individuals who believe they have been discriminated against or can be initiated by the Equal Employment Opportunity Commission, the federal agency charged with the enforcement of Title VII.

than the jobs performed by the men, all in violation of Title VII." A job evaluation undertaken by the plaintiffs provided the basis for the judgment that the pay differences were not due to the fact that the jobs the women performed were inherently worth less.

Although the major legislation on employment discrimination in the United States has no language explicitly incorporating the principle of equal pay for work of equal value,[6] the concept is widely endorsed abroad. Over 80 member nations of the International Labour Organisation have ratified Convention 100, which encourages each member to "promote . . . and ensure the application to all workers of the principle of equal remuneration for men and women workers for work of equal value." Great Britain's 1970 Equal Employment Opportunity Act provides for equal remuneration for men and women employed in "like work" or "work of same or a broadly similar nature" or "work rated as equivalent, having been given an 'equal value' in a job evaluation study" (International Labour Office, 1975:12). Canada's Equal Pay and Equal Opportunity Law, which went into effect in spring 1978 for the federal government and publicly chartered industries such as the railroads, airlines, and broadcasting companies, calls for equal pay for work of equal value. Work of equal value is not explicitly defined, but the criteria to be applied in the comparisons are the "composite of skill, effort, and responsibility" as well as working conditions.[7] The Canadian Human

Rights Commission, which expects the "composite of skill, effort, and responsibility" to be determined by the use of job evaluation techniques, has established a set of guidelines to assess those job evaluation systems currently in use. Initial efforts at enforcement, however, have not gone beyond cases similar to some of the broader cases brought under the U.S. Equal Pay Act. The Canadian commission has recommended, for example, that female nurses be paid at the same rate as male hospital technicians, a case similar to one in the United States in which female nurse's aides were judged to do work equal to that of male orderlies (Perlman & Ennis, 1980). In Australia, where minimum wages are set for most organizations by state and federal wage boards, the Federal Tribunal adopted a policy of equal pay for work of equal value in 1975. Since that time, the average earnings of full-time female workers have increased substantially relative to those of male workers (Gregory & Duncan, 1981). In all these examples of private and public actions in the United States and abroad, the comparable worth issue raises questions about compensation practices.

THE ISSUES

In this context the committee interprets the charge from the EEOC to study the validity of compensation systems and methods for determining the relative worth of jobs as requiring an investigation of whether and to what extent existing pay differences between jobs are the result of discrimination.

Many people argue that the wages set by the market determine precisely what jobs are worth to both employers and employees, but this position has been explicitly challenged by those who argue that existing wage differences incorporate discriminatory elements. As noted in the committee's interim report (Treiman,

---

[6]It is interesting to note, however, that there is an instance of federal legislation using comparable worth language. The Civil Service Reform Act of 1978, in the section on Merit System Principles (5 USC 2301.(b)(3)), states: "Equal pay should be provided for work of equal value. . . ."

[7]The language of both the American Equal Pay Act and the Canadian Equal Pay and Equal Opportunity Law derives from principles used in job evaluation. Skill, effort, responsibility, and working conditions are the job features most often measured in job evaluation plans. These job features are chosen because they are widely regarded as compensable; that is, these are the aspects of jobs that make them worthy of compensation and that differentiate levels of compensation. In factor point job evaluation plans, compensable features are called factors. Each job is given a numerical rating on each factor, and the scores are

added for a total job worth score (Treiman, 1979). Most interpretations of the U.S. law in effect require that two jobs have equal scores on every dimension to be considered equal under the law, whereas the word "composite" in the Canadian law is presumably meant to indicate that jobs can be considered equal if their total scores are equal.

1979), most job evaluation plans, which provide the bases for many employers' compensation programs, use market wage rates to determine the value of features they identify as contributing to job worth (typically, skill, effort, responsibility, and working conditions). That is, how much each feature contributes to the job worth score (the weight of each factor) is determined by studying, with the aid of statistical techniques, how those features appear to be compensated by market wage rates. But if market wage rates incorporate any bias based on sex, race, or ethnicity, then alternative methods for determining job comparability, or ways to remove such bias, are needed. Therefore, our investigation of job comparability required us to examine the bases for wage differentials.

We did not limit the scope of our investigation to particular legal postures, rules, or definitions. As we suggest above, the state of the law regarding comparable worth cases remains in flux. The same can be said for the legal definition of "equal" under the Equal Pay Act and of "discrimination" under Title VII.

The committee and individual members have used various definitions of discrimination to guide and shape our work. Because of this process and because there is no hard-and-fast agreement among committee members—or among legislators or the public—about the precise meaning of discrimination, or about the proper ways of identifying discrimination, we do not offer a single, absolute definition of discrimination. All members of the committee do agree that an essential element of the kind of discrimination we are concerned with here is inequitable treatment based on a person's sex, race, or ethnicity. On that basis we developed working definitions of employment discrimination and wage discrimination.

Employment discrimination exists when one class of people is denied access to higher-paying jobs solely or partly on the basis of social characteristics. If, for example, women or minority men are denied access to managerial positions solely or partly because of their sex or minority status—that is discrimination. This pattern of disparate treatment is not easy to detect and is often difficult to measure or prove, but when provable it is illegal under Title VII of the 1964 Civil Rights Act. As a result of denial of access to better-paying jobs, women and minorities earn lower wages on the average than do men and nonminorities.

Wage discrimination exists when individuals of one social category are paid less than individuals of another social category for reasons that have little or nothing to do with the work they do. There are two major types of wage discrimination:

1. One type of wage discrimination occurs when one class of people is paid less than another class for doing exactly or substantially the same job: for example, male and female machine assemblers (or truck drivers, secretaries, elementary school teachers, professors, etc.) working side by side, doing jobs that are essentially indistinguishable from one another, producing similar results. This kind of wage discrimination is relatively easy to detect and is illegal under the legislation enacted in the early 1960s.

2. A second type of wage discrimination, on which this committee focused intently, arises when the job structure within a firm is substantially segregated by sex, race, or ethnicity, and workers of one category are paid less than workers of another category when the two groups are performing work that is not the same but that is, in some sense, of comparable worth to their employer. The committee grappled with precisely what the phrase "in some sense" involves, and the more technical portions of this report focus at length on how measures of comparable worth might be used. This type of discrimination is difficult to detect, and its legal status is unclear.

Five aspects of our study should be kept in mind by the reader. First, in discussing wage discrimination, particularly of the second type, we say nothing about the question of

intent. How pay inequities have come about
—through willful exclusion, conscious underpayment, or inadvertent use of practices that
have discriminatory effects—is not addressed
in our discussion. Our use of the word "discrimination" does not necessarily imply intent.

Second, primarily because we have focused
on the second type of wage discrimination,
which appears to affect women more than minority men (see Chapter 2), our discussion of
sex discrimination is more complete than our
discussion of discrimination against minorities. This does not reflect any judgment on our
part about the relative importance of sex discrimination and discrimination based on race
or ethnicity.

Third, we have not attempted to survey all
the methods used to determine rates of pay in
the United States. There is a wide variety of
compensation systems, ranging from extremely informal to highly formal codified
plans, in use today. Each of these plans reflects
what employers (and sometimes employees) regard as the compensable features of jobs and
helps determine what the jobs are worth to
them. Because formal systems of job evaluation make explicit the bases for the comparison
of jobs and job worth, our review of compensation practices is limited to formal job evaluation plans.

Fourth, we make no judgments regarding
the relative value of jobs to employers or to society or the appropriate relationships among
the pay rates for various jobs. The concept of
intrinsic job worth—whether it exists, on
what it should be based, whether there is a just
wage—has been a matter of dispute for many
centuries. We do not believe that the value—
or worth—of jobs can be determined by scientific methods. Hierarchies of job worth are always, at least in part, a reflection of values.[8]
Our concern in this report is limited to assessing whether and to what extent current
practices of assessing the worth of jobs and as-

signing relative pay rates incorporate discriminatory elements. For this purpose we accept
the criteria of job worth developed by those
who use job evaluation plans and ask such
questions as whether the criteria are adequately
measured by the features of jobs identified and
the measurement techniques used and, in particular, whether elements of discrimination
enter the process and, if so, how they can be
removed. While many measurement problems
are involved in comparing the worth of jobs
within an establishment, we do not believe
that these problems are insurmountable in
principle. They are surmountable, with proper
attention to changes in job content and developments in the methodology of job analysis,
scaling, and the like.[9]

Fifth, we have confined our discussion to
the use of job evaluation plans within individual firms. Because employers use many different job evaluation plans, because the economic
circumstances of employers and industries differ, and because we do not believe that there is
a hierarchy of job worth that could or should
be applied to the entire economy, we look only
at the comparable worth approach as it could
be used to adjust the pay rates of jobs within
individual firms.[10]

This report has been concerned with two
questions: To what extent does the fact that
women and minorities are on the average paid
less than nonminority men reflect discrimination in the way jobs are compensated? If wage
discrimination exists, what can be done about
it?

On the basis of a review of the evidence, our
judgment is that there is substantial discrimination in pay. Specific instances of discrimina-

___

[8]It is of interest to note, however, that there is a general
consistency, although not an exact correspondence, in the
relative pay rates of jobs in different societies (Treiman,
1977;108–111), which suggests that some features of jobs
are valued quite universally.

[9]The Committee on Occupational Classification and
Analysis prepared a report for the Department of Labor on
the *Dictionary of Occupational Titles*, addressing many issues
concerning the measurement of jobs (see Miller et al.,
1980).

[10]This is not to say that we see any difficulty in the application of job evaluation procedures on an industrywide
basis, as is currently done in the steel industry. But this is
a decision properly left to those in the industry, employers
and employees. When compensation is organized on an
industrywide basis, job evaluation procedures, as part of
the compensation system, would be expected to be similarly organized.

tion are neither easily identified nor easily remedied, because the widespread concentration of women and minorities into low-paying jobs makes it difficult to distinguish discriminatory from nondiscriminatory components of compensation. One approach, which needs further development but shows some promise, is to use existing job evaluation plans as a standard for comparing the relative worth of jobs.

This chapter summarizes the evidence leading to these conclusions. In reviewing this material three considerations should be kept in mind.

First, discrimination, as the term is used in this report, does not imply intent but refers only to outcome. Wage discrimination exists insofar as workers of one sex, race, or ethnic group are paid less than workers of another sex, race, or ethnic group for doing work that is of "comparable," that is, equal, worth to their employer.

Second, the report has focused most intensively on sex discrimination because the issue of comparable worth arises largely in connection with job segregation, the propensity for men and women and for minority and nonminority workers to hold different sorts of jobs, and job segregation is more pronounced by sex than by race or ethnicity. Moreover, while most available data are at the national level, minorities, because of their numbers and geographical distribution, are more likely to be concentrated in particular occupations at a local level. We have therefore not been able to examine differentials by race or ethnic group with the same procedures we used to examine differentials by sex. In addition, most of the available studies of patterns of employment within firms refer to differences between men and women. Finally, the available analyses relating to the relative worth of jobs pertain almost entirely to sex discrimination. In this context, the fact that we focus mainly on discrimination based on sex should not be interpreted to mean that the committee has judged discrimination based on race or ethnicity to be of lesser importance.

Third, we have not been able to make any assessment of what the social and economic consequences may be of implementing wage policies based on the principle of equal pay for jobs of equal worth. This is an extremely complex question, with no clear answers, which goes well beyond the charge to the committee. We do, however, want to call attention to the need to give careful thought to the possible impact of implementation of a policy of equal pay for jobs of equal worth on the economic viability of firms as well as on employment opportunities for women and minorities.

THE EXTENT AND THE SOURCES OF PAY DIFFERENTIALS

It is well established that in the United States today women earn less than men and minority men earn less than nonminority men. Among year-round full-time workers, the annual earnings of white women in the late 1970s averaged less than 60 percent of those of white men, while the earnings of black men averaged 70–75 percent of those of white men.

Such differential earnings patterns have existed for many decades. They may arise in part because women and minority men are paid less than white men for doing the same (or very similar) jobs within the same firm, or in part because the job structure is substantially segregated by sex, race, and ethnicity and the jobs held mainly by women and minority men pay less than the jobs held mainly by nonminority men. Since passage of the Equal Pay Act of 1963 and Title VII of the 1964 Civil Rights Act, legal remedies have been available for the first source of wage differentials. Although the committee recognizes that instances of unequal pay for the same work have not been entirely eliminated, we believe that they are probably not now the major source of differences in earnings.

With respect to the second source of wage differentials, the disparate distribution of workers among jobs and the concentration of women and minority men in low-paying jobs, the data are clear. Women and minorities are differentially concentrated not only by occupation but also by industry, by firm, and by division within firms. Moreover, the evidence shows that this differential concentration has persisted, at least with respect to women, over a substantial period of time. In the face of this differential concentration, then, the question of whether pay differentials are discriminatory can be stated quite simply: Would the low-paying jobs be low-paying regardless of who held them, or are they low-paying because of the sex, race, or ethnic composition of their incumbents?

To be able to state the question simply, however, is not to be able to answer it simply. In the committee's judgment, a correct response recognizes that both elements account for observed earnings differentials. Our economy is structured so that some jobs will inevitably pay less than others, and the fact that many such jobs are disproportionately filled by women and minorities may reflect differences in qualifications, interests, traditional roles, and similar factors; or it may reflect exclusionary practices with regard to hiring and promotion; or it may reflect a combination of both. However, several types of evidence support our judgment that it is also true in many instances that jobs held mainly by women and minorities pay less at least in part *because* they are held mainly by women and minorities. First, the differentials in average pay for jobs held mainly by women and those held mainly by men persist when the characteristics of jobs thought to affect their value and the characteristics of workers thought to affect their productivity are held constant. Second, prior to the legislation of the last two decades, differentials in pay for men and women and for minorities and nonminorities were often acceptable and were, in fact, prevalent. The tradition embodied in such practices was built into wage structures, and its effects continue to influence these structures. Finally, at the level of the specific firm, several studies show that women's jobs are paid less on the average than men's jobs with the same scores derived from job evaluation plans. The evidence is not complete or conclusive, but the consistency of the results in many different job categories and in several different types of studies, the size of the pay differentials (even after worker and job characteristics have been taken into account), and the lack of evidence for alternative explanations strongly suggest that wage discrimination is widespread.

IDENTIFYING AND ELIMINATING PAY DISCRIMINATION

The identification and correction of particular instances of pay discrimination are, however, not easy tasks. One procedure that has been suggested is to compare the actual rates of pay of jobs with the relative worth of jobs; wage discrimination would be suspected whenever jobs are not paid in accordance with their relative worth. This relative (or comparable) worth approach in turn requires a generally acceptable standard of job worth and a feasible procedure for measuring the relative worth of jobs. In our judgment no universal standard of job worth exists, both because any definition of the "relative worth" of jobs is in part a matter of values and because, even for a particular definition, problems of measurement are likely.

One approach to the relative worth of jobs avoids the issue of values by equating the worth of jobs with existing pay rates. In this approach, no comparable worth strategy is needed to adjust the pay rates of jobs, because the pay rates themselves reflect the relative worth of jobs. The belief that existing pay differentials between jobs provide a valid measure of the relative worth of jobs depends on the view that the operation of labor markets is freely competitive and that pay differentials primarily reflect differences in individual productivity and are not substantially influenced by discrimination. While there is a good deal of controversy about the nature of labor markets, in our view the operation of labor markets can be better understood as reflecting a variety of institutions that limit competition with respect to workers and wages and tend to perpetuate whatever discrimination exists. As a result of these institutional features of labor markets, existing wage rates do not in our judgment provide a measure of the relative worth of jobs that avoids discrimination.

Several of these institutional features are inherent to the current operation of labor markets and cannot easily be altered. Substantial investment in training makes it difficult for workers to shift from one occupation to another in search of higher pay. Moreover, even within specific occupations, workers are not generally free to sell their labor to the highest bidder; they are constrained by geographical location and imperfect information as well as by institutional arrangements designed to encourage the stability of the work force by putting a premium on seniority. Nor do employers generally seek labor on the open market; a large fraction of all jobs are filled through internal promotions or transfers. Finally, both the supply of and demand for labor and the pay rates offered are strongly affected by still other forces—particularly union contracts and governmental regulations. Whenever jobs are relatively insulated from market forces, traditional differences in pay rates tend to be perpetuated over time. Hence, insofar as differences in pay between jobs ever did incorporate discriminatory elements, they tend to be perpetuated.

JOB EVALUATION PLANS

Although no universal standard of job worth exists, job evaluation plans do provide standards and measures of job worth that are used to estimate the relative worth of jobs within many firms. In job evaluation plans, pay ranges for a job are based on estimates of the worth of jobs according to such criteria as the skill, effort, and responsibility required by the job and the working conditions under which it is performed. Pay for an individual, within the pay range, is set by the worker's characteristics, such as credentials, seniority, productivity, and quality of job performance. Job evaluation plans vary from firm to firm; both the criteria established and the compensable factors and relative weights used as measures of the criteria differ somewhat from plan to plan.

In our judgment, job evaluation plans provide measures of job worth that, under certain circumstances, may be used to discover and reduce wage discrimination for persons covered by a given plan. Job evaluation plans provide a way of systematically rewarding jobs for their content—for the skill, effort, and responsibility they entail and the conditions under which they are performed. By making the criteria of compensation explicit and by applying the criteria consistently, it is probable that pay differentials resulting from traditional stereotypes regarding the value of "women's work" or work customarily done by minorities will be reduced.

But several aspects of the methods generally used in such plans raise questions about their ability to establish comparable worth. First, job evaluation plans typically ensure rough conformity between the measured worth of jobs and actual wages by allowing actual wages to determine the weights of job factors used in the plans. Insofar as differentials associated with sex, race, or ethnicity are incorporated in actual wages, this procedure will act to perpetuate them. Statistical techniques exist that may be able to generate job-worth scores from which components of wages associated with sex, race, or ethnicity have been at least partly removed; they should be further developed.

Second, many firms use different job evaluation plans for different types of jobs. Since in most firms women and minority men are concentrated in jobs with substantially different tasks from those of jobs held by nonminority men, a plan that covers all jobs would be necessary in order to compare wages of women, minority men, and nonminority men. The selection of compensable factors and their weights in such a plan may be quite difficult, however, because factors appropriate for one type of job are not necessarily appropriate for all other types. Nevertheless, experiments with firm-wide plans might be useful in making explicit the relative weights of compensable factors, especially since they are already used by some firms.

Finally, it must be recognized that there are no definitive tests of the "fairness" of the choice of compensable factors and the relative weights given to them. The process is inherently judgmental and its success in generating a wage structure that is deemed equitable depends on achieving a consensus about factors and their weights among employers and employees.

The development and implementation of a job evaluation plan is often a lengthy and costly process. The underdeveloped nature of the technology involved, particularly the lack of systematic testing of assumptions, does not justify the universal application of such plans. In the committee's judgment, however, the plans have a potential that deserves further experimentation and development.

▪ MINORITY REPORT ▪
By Ernest J. McCormick

The report of the Committee on Occupational Classification and Analysis deals generally with the issue of alleged discrimination in pay in the form of inequitable treatment based on sex or race. In connection with the report there are two issues with which I am in disagreement and that make it impossible for me to concur with portions of the report. Because of my disagreement on these issues I am writing this minority report.

Criterion for Determining Job Values

One of the critical issues of this minority statement relates to the standard or the criterion that should be used in judging the "worth" of jobs. Before discussing such standards, however, it would be appropriate to differentiate between two frames of reference in which alleged discrimination is discussed. One frame of reference concerns the matter of "equal pay for equal work," which deals with pay for jobs that are the same or very similar in content. The other reference point concerns the concept of equal pay for "comparable" work or work of "comparable worth" or "comparable" or "equal value." (The committee report deals largely with the "comparable worth" frame of reference.)

The Equal Pay Act of 1963 and Title VII of the Civil Rights Act of 1964 both provide for equal pay for equal work and state that it is discriminatory for men and women performing equal work to be paid differently. On legal and rational grounds there is no justification for such discrimination. The report of the committee strongly supports the objectives of ensuring equal pay for equal work as construed in the frame of reference of equal pay for jobs that are similar in content, and I fully concur in the portions of the report that deal with this concept. My concern deals primarily with the question of the standards or criteria that might be relevant for evaluating the "comparability" of jobs.

The committee report is sprinkled with direct references or implications relating to alleged discrimination in the case of certain jobs in which women tend to dominate (these are sometimes called "women's jobs") as contrasted with those in which men tend to dominate (these are sometimes called "men's jobs"). It is alleged that the pay scales for some women's jobs are lower than they "should be," and that such rates are as low as they are because employment in them is dominated by women. Such alleged discrimination is sometimes referred to as institutional discrimination, the theory being that cultural and other factors have resulted in the "tracking" of women into such jobs, with accompanying pay scales below what they "should be." The argument that differences in the pay of women's jobs and men's jobs reflect a form of discrimination has given rise to the concept of equal pay for comparable work (or for work of comparable value or equal value), the implication being that there is some concept of comparability of jobs that would make it possible to justify the establishment of equal pay for jobs that are different in content but comparable in terms of the concept of worth or value. This argument immediately raises the question as to the basis on which jobs might be considered comparable in worth (or noncomparable).

In the report of the committee there are numerous statements that either directly, or by implication or inference, take issue with the principle that the prevailing rates of pay in the labor market should serve as the primary basis for the establishment of pay scales for jobs in specific situations. Furthermore, the committee report implies that the determination of the comparability in worth between jobs should be independent of current wages and salaries found in the labor market. It is with these portions of the report that I am in disagreement, since it is my firm conviction that current wages and salaries are indeed one indication of the underlying relationship between jobs. This relationship between worth and pay, albeit imperfect, is a product of real, impartial forces (as well as of the various possible biases that trouble the committee) and thus cannot rationally be ignored.

It is my contention that there is no conceptually appropriate, economically viable, or practical basis for determining the comparability of jobs without considering the value system that underlies the wages and salaries paid to all jobs throughout the entire occupational structure of our economy. Stated differently, I am convinced that the comparable worth or value as reflected in the going rates of pay assigned to jobs will over time closely correlate with the underlying hierarchy of values that has evolved in our world of work. This hierarchy of values generally reflects the fact that job values are influenced by a variety of factors such as skill, effort, responsibility, type of work activity, and working conditions. Furthermore, this value system is essentially a function of the supply of, and the demand for, individuals who possess the relevant job skills, who have the ability to apply the relevant effort, who are capable of assuming the relevant responsibilities, who can perform the work activities in question, and who are able and willing to work under the working conditions in question. To ignore the value system because it does not produce results that fit certain preconceptions of job worth (whether for or against any class) reflects, in my opinion, a biased frame of reference.

The committee report views the labor market as one that tends to undervalue "women's jobs" relative to "men's jobs" and concludes that the market is discriminatory and therefore should be disregarded in establishing rates of pay. Such a view of the labor market seems to me to be naive and unrealistic. The labor market is the generic term for a value system rooted in the hierarchy of skills, effort, responsibility, and work activities (and to some extent working conditions) that comprise jobs, and the supply and demand forces that operate as organizations and workers compete in our economy. As a matter of interest, statements of female or minority "undervaluation" seem to be based upon the concept that there is a value system but that some types of individuals in certain jobs are not paid according to the underlying system. If there is no available hierarchy of worth, there is no objective basis upon which to make claims of bias. Accordingly, I am convinced that the labor market must be the arbiter of basic rates of pay and that there is no other logical, economic, or practical basis for determining the values of jobs, be it in terms of "equal" or "comparable" worth.

There are two general approaches that an organization can follow in relating pay scales for its jobs to those of corresponding jobs in the labor market. In the first place, if the jobs in question have identical counterparts in the labor market, the prevailing pay rates (or pay ranges) can be used directly for setting pay scales within the organization. In the second place, an organization can use some type of job evaluation system for setting the compensation rates for its jobs.[11] The most effective job evaluation system usually is one that accurately examines the content of jobs (skills, effort, responsibilities, activities, working conditions, etc.) and yields relative job values (usually point values) that correspond closely with (i.e., are correlated with) prevailing rates in the labor market. In effect, this means that job evaluation systems (or the procedures for deriving relative job values) should be based on, or related to, those job characteristics that gave rise to prevailing market values. To develop a job evaluation system that did not first

---

[11] The committee's interim report (Treiman, 1979) provided an extensive discussion of job evaluation, and I will not discuss the process of job evaluation in this minority report.

examine (and compare) the content of jobs and, second, relate the job content to a value system that underlies our entire economy is not realistic, practical, or economically or socially desirable.

The Use of Structured Job Analysis Procedures

The other point that underlies the preparation of this minority report is clearly related to the matter of determining the "comparability" of jobs either to determine their equality (or inequality) or to determine their comparability in the framework of "comparable worth." Such comparisons are basic to the processes of resolving questions about the equity of pay at various levels at which such questions might be raised, such as within an organization, when a complaint is brought to the attention of a regulatory agency or in the courts of law.

In this regard the committee lamented the problems of making such comparisons but chose to virtually ignore the very substantial amount of research and experience over more than two decades relating to the systematic, quantitative analysis of human work that has been demonstrated to be of substantial value in making comparisons for many types of jobs. The most directly relevant research and experience deals with what usually are called structured job analysis procedures. Actually, the committee did include a passing, very cursory reference (in Chapter 4) to such procedures in saying: "Moreover, methods of systematic job analysis, such as structured job analysis and task analysis, ought to be explored for their applicability to job evaluation—in particular, the job component method of job evaluation (McCormick & Ilgen, 1980:Ch. 18), which uses structured job analysis." Not only has the committee chosen to ignore structured job analysis procedures as they have direct relevance to the issue of comparability, but they also have failed to recognize the importance of such procedures to the fundamentals of job analysis per se, which is the foundation for all job evaluation systems.

The committee report has alluded to the role that job analysis serves in the job evaluation process. Actually, job analysis can be the Achilles heel of any job evaluation technique. Clearly, the impact of unreliable, invalid, and biased job analysis information on the job evaluation process could lead to an "unfair" pay plan. Again, the committee failed to acknowledge the value of structured job analysis procedures in the realm of job analysis in general and specifically in the application of such procedures to job evaluation. The bibliography to this minority report includes a limited sample of some of the research literature regarding the systematic analysis of human work, particularly that relating to structured job analysis procedures. Many of these listed works clearly demonstrate the practical utility of structured job analysis procedures and support the contention that, for certain purposes—such as comparing jobs with each other in quantitative terms—such procedures are superior to conventional verbal descriptions. Several researchers have clearly shown how data obtained with structured job analysis questionnaires can be used for such key personnel administrative functions as job evaluation.

Structured job analysis procedures have two possible applications that are directly relevant to the interests of the committee, these two applications being closely related. One application deals with the actual comparison of jobs in terms of similarities and differences, and the other deals with establishing pay rates for jobs that would minimize possible differentials based on sex or race. Basically, structured job analysis procedures provide for the documentation of the content of jobs in terms of a set of job elements. These elements typically are descriptive of work tasks ("job-oriented" elements) or of basic human job behaviors ("worker-oriented" elements) and are listed together in a job analysis questionnaire. In the analysis of jobs with such a questionnaire, the person making the analysis rates each element in terms of its relevance to the job, or, in certain instances, simply indicates whether the element does or does not apply to the job. (The reader interested in a further explanation of the nature of structured job analysis questionnaires is referred to Appendix A.)

As indicated previously, one relevant application of structured job analysis procedures is that of comparing jobs in terms of their similarities and differences. At a simple job-to-job level, two or more jobs can be compared even by a visual review of the ratings given to the jobs on the various job elements being used, as illustrated by the following hypothetical example:

of possible discrimination. In this regard the use of job-oriented questionnaires (task inventories) would be most appropriate in connection with the equal work concept if "equal work" is viewed in the framework of the specific tasks of the positions or jobs in question. If the equal work concept were interpreted as embracing similarities in the basic human behaviors involved in jobs, however, the worker-oriented type of structured job analysis questionnaire would be appropriate.

Job Element	Job A	Job B	Job C	Job D
a	1	1	1	3
b	4	4	3	1
c	0	0	0	2
d	3	3	3	0
—	—	—	—	—
n	2	2	2	4

Note: Ratings: 0 = low; 5 = high.

Jobs A and B are identical, job C is almost the same as jobs A and B, but job D differs markedly from the other three. The fact that data for the job elements are quantified makes it possible to compare jobs in quantitative terms. Most typically, some statistical index of similarity is derived for each pair of jobs. In turn, such indexes frequently are used for grouping jobs into groups that have reasonably similar profiles of job element values. In the use of task inventories in the U.S. Air Force, for example, such procedures are used to identify "job types," that is, groups of positions that are reasonably similar in the combinations of tasks that are performed (Christal, 1974). As another example, Taylor and Colbert (1978) obtained data with a "worker-oriented" type of structured job analysis questionnaire used to study jobs in an insurance company, and they found 13 job families, each family being characterized by a group of jobs with very similar behavioral components.

The possibility of being able to use statistical procedures for comparing positions or jobs in terms of their similarities, and of grouping them into job types or job families, would seem to be substantially relevant in instances

The second possible application of data from structured job analysis questionnaires that would be relevant to the charge of the committee is with regard to their use in job evaluation. Their use for this purpose is distinctly different from conventional job evaluation methods in that the judgmental evaluation process is eliminated, the job values being derived statistically. Such a procedure is called the job component job evaluation method (Jeanneret, 1980; McCormick, 1979:317–21; McCormick & Ilgen, 1980:375–78). The procedure as typically carried out involves the following steps:

1. The analysis of a sample of jobs in terms of an appropriate structured job analysis questionnaire with job elements consisting of tasks or basic human behaviors, and usually working conditions. The individual job elements, or statistically related groups thereof, can be considered as job components.

2. The derivation, for this sample of jobs, of money values for the individual components, in particular indexes of

the extent to which the individual components contribute to the going rates of pay for the jobs. (This is a statistical procedure.)

3. The analysis with the structured job analysis questionnaire of specific jobs for which evaluations are to be made.

4. The derivation of an index of the total monetary value for each such job. This is done by "building up" the total value for each job from the indexes of the relevance of the individual components to the job, in combination with the money values of the components as previously derived from the original sample of jobs as described in steps one and two. (A more specific description of the job component method of job evaluation can be found in Appendix B.)

In line with the comments made earlier, if the concept of equal work is interpreted in terms of specific work activities such as tasks, the job-oriented type of questionnaire (a task inventory) would be required in the job component method of job evaluation. Certain applications of this approach serve as illustrations, such as the study by Miles (1952) in the case of office jobs and the study by Tornow and Pinto (1976) in the case of managerial jobs. A variation of this general approach is suggested by Christal (1974).

If the concept of equal work were interpreted as applying to the similarity of basic human behaviors in jobs (as contrasted to work tasks), the worker-oriented type of structured questionnaire would be relevant. In this regard, for example, Jeanneret (1972) used such a questionnaire to place various utility company jobs in several pay grades and then compared the average actual pay of men and women in each of the "new" pay grades. In this instance he found a salary difference of $108 a month in favor of men. In studies completed for another utility company and for a savings and loan organization, similar comparisons also revealed appreciable salary differences (Jeanneret, 1978). (In these companies the

salaries of women were subsequently adjusted.) The general indication from such studies is that a worker-oriented type of structured job analysis questionnaire can, as Jeanneret (1978) expresses it, "document the content of jobs without regard to sex of the incumbents . . . and fairly evaluate jobs without regard to the sex of the incumbents."

If the objective of a job evaluation plan is to derive estimates of equal pay for comparable work (as opposed to equal pay for equal work) the worker-oriented type of structured job analysis questionnaire definitely would be the more appropriate. Thus, it is believed that such structured job analysis questionnaires could serve as the basis for determining the "comparability" of jobs if ultimately the law or the courts would provide the basis for "equal pay for comparable work" as contrasted with "equal pay for equal work."

In summary, I would like to emphasize the point that there have been significant developments in the past couple of decades in the development and use of systematic methods of analysis of human work and in the use of such methods for various practical purposes such as the quantitative comparison of jobs with each other, the identification of job types or job families, and job evaluation. There seems to be no question but that the nature and scope of these developments have substantial potential relevance to the objectives of the committee. In view of this I feel that the committee report is seriously deficient since it refers to such work with only a casual one-sentence comment. In my opinion the failure of the committee to include more adequate discussion of structured job analysis procedures reflects the fact that the staff and most members of the committee were not sufficiently familiar with the developments in this area over the past couple of decades and therefore failed to appreciate the possible relevance of such procedures to the objectives of the committee.

The two issues raised in this minority report would seem to be compatible with each other. The job component method of job evaluation is of course based on the use of going rates of pay as the standard or criterion for determining the money values of various types of work behaviors, but at the same time the use of structured job analysis procedures in this process seems to make it possible to "document the content of jobs without regard to sex of the incumbent . . . and fairly evaluate jobs without regard to sex of the incumbents" (Jeanneret, 1978).

APPENDIX A: STRUCTURED JOB ANALYSIS QUESTIONNAIRES

A structured job analysis questionnaire consists of a specific list of job elements that can be used in the analysis of jobs. There are various types of job elements that can be used in structured job analysis procedures, although there are two types that are particularly relevant. In the first place, some structured job analysis questionnaires, commonly called task inventories, provide for the analysis of jobs in terms of each of a number of tasks that might be performed by individuals within a given occupational area. Examples of such occupational areas are health services, office operations, automobile mechanics, and engineering. Examples of tasks that might be included in task inventories are: types straight copy from rough draft; removes and replaces spark plugs; takes orders for meals from customers; and estimates costs of building materials from building plans and specifications. Task inventories have been referred to as "job-oriented" questionnaires in that they provide for describing jobs in terms of the output or end-result of tasks. In the usual task inventory it is typically the practice for the job incumbent to indicate, for each task, whether he or she performs the task or not, and in addition, to indicate something about the degree of involvement with each task, such as the frequency of performance or the time spent on the task.

Task inventories frequently are used as the basis for identifying "job types" that consist of jobs or positions with relatively similar combinations of tasks. This sometimes is carried out with a hierarchical grouping technique that in-

volves the derivation of a statistical index of the degree of similarity of the tasks performed for every possible pair of jobs or positions in the sample being used. Such statistical indexes conceivably could be relevant in comparing the similarity of jobs about which some discrimination issue has been raised. Furthermore, the possibility of identifying job types by statistical procedures might also have some relevance in connection with charges relating to discrimination.

It should be pointed out that the use of any given task inventory would be restricted to the specific occupational area for which it was prepared. It is expected that there are certain types of occupational areas for which task inventories might not be feasible.

The second type of structured job analysis questionnaire provides for the analysis of jobs in terms of more generalized, basic human job behaviors that transcend or cut across occupational areas. Such questionnaires are referred to as "worker-oriented" questionnaires in that they provide for analyzing jobs in terms that describe, or imply, the basic human behaviors involved in work activities. One such questionnaire, reported by McCormick (1979, pp. 147–49) and McCormick, Jeanneret, and Mecham (1972) provides for analyzing jobs in terms of each of 187 job elements. Some examples (in paraphrased form) are: uses visual displays (as a source of job information); uses measuring devices; arranges or positions objects in a specific position or arrangement; operates keyboard devices; conducts interviews with others; works under high-temperature conditions. In the analysis of a job with this questionnaire the analyst uses an appropriate rating scale to indicate the involvement of the job incumbent with each job element. Various types of rating scales are used, such as the degree of importance, the amount of time involved, the "extent of use" of various kinds of materials, and so forth.

This particular questionnaire has been subjected to a form of factor analysis (specifically, principal components analysis) that identifies the job elements that tend to "go together" in jobs and that form what are called job dimensions. Each such job dimension can be thought of as being based primarily on the group of job elements that tend to occur in common across jobs in general. Some examples of job dimensions are: interpreting what is sensed; processing information; performing handling and related activities; exchanging job-related information; being alert to changing conditions; and potentially hazardous situations. Collectively, these job dimensions can be viewed as reflecting the "structure" of human work in terms of the basic types of human behavior that are involved in work activities. With the analysis of a job using the structured job analysis questionnaire in question it is possible to derive a score for the job on each dimension. Such scores represent a "profile" for the job, and can be used as quantitative indexes of the dimensions.

APPENDIX B: THE JOB COMPONENT METHOD OF JOB EVALUATION

The job component method of job evaluation is based on the use of a structured job analysis questionnaire in the analysis of jobs. There are various ways in which data from such questionnaires can be used in the derivation of money values of jobs, but the basic procedure referred to earlier is the one dealt with in this appendix. In actual use in deriving indexes of job values the method involves two steps. In the first place the jobs are analyzed with the structured job analysis questionnaire being used. In the second place a statistical equation is used to derive an index of the total value for each job. The equation incorporates a weight for each job "component." The job components may be individual job elements, or combinations of elements based on factor analysis, the factors usually being called job dimensions. In deriving a total value for a job the "weight" for each component is multiplied by the value of that component for the job, resulting in an arithmetic "product," for each component. These products for all components are

then added together to derive a total value for the job.

The central basis for the job component method of job evaluation is in the derivation of the weights for the individual components. For this purpose data for a sample of jobs are used. Each job is analyzed with the structured job analysis questionnaire, producing a value for each component for each job. In addition, information on the rate of pay for each job is obtained. Regression analysis is then used for the total sample to determine the statistical contribution of each component to the rates of pay for the jobs in the sample. From this analysis it is possible to derive the appropriate weight for each component. These weights can be thought of as reflecting the money "values" of the individual components in the labor market; that is, how much the individual components are "worth" in the labor market. If, collectively, data on the "values" of the job components of a structured job analysis questionnaire predict going rates of pay with acceptable accuracy for a sample of jobs, these money values can then be used as the basis for the estimation of total rates of pay for other jobs.

In a sense, then, the central objective of the job component method of job evaluation is to develop regression equations that, by and large, reflect the approximate contributions of different job components to the market values of jobs. In the operational use of this method a regression equation based on a broad, varied sample of jobs from various industries and geographical areas has been found to be reasonably applicable in various situations. However, it would be expected that, in the long run, the derivation of job values would be more accurate if the money values of the various job components were derived from data on samples of jobs of different major types and within particular labor market areas.

Although the job component method of job evaluation has not as yet been used extensively, research and experience with it offer substantive evidence that could be used in many situations to provide the basis for the establishment of equitable rates of pay for jobs.

SECTION TWO

Selection

Some of the traditional activities of personnel psychologists are developing, administering, and interpreting tests that might be used to make hiring or promotion decisions. The entire field of testing has undergone a radical transformation since the passage of the Civil Rights Act of 1964. In the years since this Act established the Equal Employment Opportunity Commission, regulations have been issued that define what can and cannot be done with respect to personnel testing. In this section we will consider the history of traditional psychological testing, the ethical pressures that confront the practicing psychologist, and how past research should be used to shape the use of tests in the future.

In this reading, Hale gives an overview of how testing techniques and theory have developed in the field of employment selection. His description clearly demonstrates that even if equal employment opportunity laws had not been passed in the late 1960s, testing would have been under substantial pressure to "prove" itself. Of course, concern for equal employment has added to that pressure.

■ READING 5 ■

History of Employment Testing

Matthew Hale

INTRODUCTION

Employment testing, broadly defined, is probably as old as employment itself. Yet employment tests as we know them today—standardized, objective, and validated examinations based on job analyses—are relatively recent. Not until the late 19th century did the U.S. government adopt standardized tests as a way to select civil servants, and only in the second and third decades of this century did private industry use employment tests on anything more than an experimental basis. Employment testing, however, has grown from tentative beginnings early in the century to become a commonplace feature of business and government. By the 1960s, most private businesses, according to several surveys, gave one form of test or another to at least some job candidates; the federal government filled more than 80 percent of all positions by competitive examination; and every state and major city in the United States conducted civil service examinations. Only recently has the use of employment tests begun to decline.

The development of employment testing in the United States, from the first civil service examinations of the 19th century to the assessment centers of the 1970s, is closely linked to the emergence of modern industrial society. Two elements of this development deserve special mention: first, employment testing arose as an answer to problems of rapid growth in industrial society and as a way to rationalize a chaotic labor market; and second, employment tests, because they were assumed to reward merit and eliminate special privilege, reflected a general movement in the 20th century toward "democratizing" American society.

Twentieth-century society, characterized by an increasingly heterogeneous and transient population, large-scale industry, and rapidly expanding bureaucracy, presented problems that neither traditional nor commonsense methods of organization could solve. In response to these problems, Americans embarked at the turn of the century on what Robert Wiebe has called a "search for order": an attempt, through rational and scientific planning, to impose organization and efficiency on a society growing too fast for traditional bonds to hold it together (Wiebe 1967). One manifestation of this search was the use of newly developed ability tests for employee selection. The employer might be able to select job candidates better than the psychologist could, as

Source: *Ability Testing* vol. 2 (pp. 3–38) by W. Garner and A. Wigdor, 1982, Washington, D.C.: National Academy Press. Reprinted from "Ability Testing: Uses, Consequences, and Controversies, Part II: Documentation Section," 1982, with permission of the National Academy Press, Washington, D.C.

one critic of testing claimed early in the century, but only if the employer was particularly skilled in judging people and only if the employer's establishment were small. Large enterprises, on the other hand, required a systematic, scientific approach to hiring. Reformers, entrepreneurs, and personnel managers promoted testing as just such an approach; testing, they argued, could overcome the problems of scale, rationalize employee selection, and ensure progress and efficiency.

Not only were businesses larger by the 20th century, they also required employees with new, specialized skills. Many Americans believed that, in a simpler age, most people could do most jobs (this was the explicit rationale of the spoils system in government), but that, in the modern era, many jobs required special skills or training. Critics pointed to inefficiency in the workplace and high rates of labor turnover as evidence that traditional hiring practices failed to produce a competent work force. Employment tests were seen as a solution. Indeed, dissatisfaction with the "human material" in the labor pool repeatedly spurred the development and application of tests, whether the concerns were over accident-prone trolley drivers or inefficient telephone operators in the 1910s, indecisive or marginally competent managers in the 1940s, or teachers weak in grammar and arithmetic in the 1970s and 1980s. Employment tests, their promoters argued, could identify people with skills or talent and screen out those who lacked the attributes necessary for particular positions.

Many Americans regarded tests not only as a way to identify the most efficient and competent workers, but also as a way to promote democracy by rewarding merit rather than privilege. The acceptance of tests in the Progressive years (and later) reflected the widespread conviction that men—and sometimes women—were to be judged on their individual skills and ability (or, in this case, on test scores assumed to measure skills and ability) rather than on appearance, class, heritage, or personal connections. Particularly in the case of civil service examinations, tests were seen as a means of guaranteeing equal opportunity as well as social efficiency.

Very recently, of course, the impact of employment tests on minority groups and the role of tests in perpetuating discrimination, have become major issues. It is impossible to assess this impact historically because the major barriers to equal employment opportunity in the past have been legal and extralegal constraints rather than tests. The civil service examinations, for example, were open to all, but in the early years the hiring official could specify the sex of candidates for specific positions. Many blacks may have scored low on certain employment tests because of their cultural background or because of poor education (if they had taken the tests at all), but in most cases they would not have been eligible for the job even if they had done well. Tests, however, did offer an alternative to the racial and ethnic stereotyping typical of hiring practices throughout the century. Whatever the actual effect of tests, most advocates of testing regarded employment tests as opening jobs to the talented rather than closing them to the underprivileged. Ironically, a tool that was originally seen by its supporters as ensuring selection on the basis of merit rather than privilege has come to be perceived by many as a barrier to social justice.

CIVIL SERVICE TESTING, 1883–1915

In the United States, the federal government was the first to experiment in a systematic way with employment tests. In 1814, the Army instituted examinations for surgeons, and shortly thereafter the Naval Academy and West Point began to administer tests to prospective students. Certain positions in the federal bureaucracy had testing requirements before the Civil War. The Treasury Department, for example, sporadically conducted examinations for entry into some accounting positions. Candidates were required to write an ordinary business letter, to show themselves acquainted with "the four rules of arithmetic," and "to evince some knowledge of the generally re-ceived principles of accounting." And in 1853 Congress required pass-examinations for a large proportion of clerical positions in the District of Columbia. On the whole, however, the spoils system operated without restraint. Government positions, from Cabinet posts to the lowest postal clerkships, were considered prizes for the politically deserving (Van Riper 1958:52–53).

The scandals that shook federal, state, and city governments in the years that followed the Civil War precipitated a movement for reform in government. One of the primary objectives of this movement was to replace the spoils sys-tem in civil service with a merit system based on the British method of appointment by com-petitive examination. In 1871 President Grant set up a civil service commission that con-ducted examinations for positions in the New York City Customs House and Post Office and in several federal offices in Washington. The experiment proved short-lived, falling before pressure from spoilsmen in 1875, but it served as a model for the Civil Service Commission, established in 1883 in the wake of the assassi-nation of President Garfield by a disappointed office seeker. The heart of the new system was the principle of open competitive examina-tions, which, presumably, would ensure ap-pointment by merit. The model was largely British, but Congress hoped to escape the aca-demic bias of the English system by requiring that the tests be "practical in character." The tests were designed to allow candidates with eighth-grade educations to compete success-fully with college graduates on the basis of merit and experience, not school learning. From the beginning, Congress had hoped to legislate against the creation of a mandarinate in the federal service, and the stipulation that the civil service tests be practical frequently set them apart from psychological testing in pri-vate industry (Van Riper 1958, ch. 5).[1]

Initially, only slightly over 10 percent of all federal positions were filled by examination; most of these were clerical positions in Wash-ington and in the nation's largest customs houses. The system, however, grew at a rapid rate until by the end of Theodore Roosevelt's presidency the figure had reached 60 percent. One innovation that allowed the rapid expan-sion of the system was its extension to certain scientific and technical positions through the nonassembled examination, which substituted ratings based on training and experience for written examinations. By the early 20th cen-tury, the Civil Service Commission admin-istered hundreds of tests to assess proficiency in specific trades and professions; the most common examinations were measures of "gen-eral intelligence," which were used in the se-lection of clerks and messengers and which tested such areas or skills as grammar, arith-metic, general information, and care and accu-racy. In the year ending June 1911, according to the Commission's annual report, 105,000 candidates were examined. Of these, 77,000 candidates passed, and 23,000 received posi-tions (U.S. CSC 1912:29; see also, U.S. Con-gress 1976).

At the same time, civil service reformers ex-tended the merit system to state and local gov-ernments. New York (1883) and Massachu-setts (1884) adopted the merit system with competitive civil service examinations on the federal model shortly after the passage of the Civil Service Act. Before the end of the cen-tury, the cities of New York, Albany, Syra-cuse, Chicago, and Seattle, among others, also adopted the merit system (Shafritz 1975:43). The pace of civil service reform picked up early in the 20th century, when Progressive reform-ers adopted efficient government and the rec-ognition of individual merit as major goals. Between 1905 and 1911, Wisconsin, Illinois, Colorado, and New Jersey introduced merit systems; by 1911 6 states, 217 cities, 20 coun-ties, and 7 villages had in part or whole adopted competitive systems of appointment to public service (Lee 1979:22, U.S. CSC 1911:161).

---

[1]See also U.S. Civil Service Commission (1911, 1912, 1924) for information on the development of the examina-tion system.

INDUSTRIAL TESTING BEFORE WORLD WAR I

Leaders of industry in the meantime increasingly turned their attention to the efficient management of personnel. Attempting to rationalize the workplace, employers introduced time cards, job clocks, and other innovations. By the early 20th century many looked with interest on the work of such efficiency experts as Frederick W. Taylor, who used time-and-motion studies to determine the one best way of performing a task and who advocated piece rates to spur production. In a few cases, mental and physiological tests were adopted as aids in the selection of personnel. Taylor recommended that certain workers be tested before they were hired—the use of reaction-time tests for selecting women in one factory, he suggested, had almost quadrupled productivity and he argued that similar efforts in other factories might produce the same results. At about the same time, several leading corporations, including General Electric and Westinghouse, developed testing and evaluation programs along academic lines in their engineering schools (Nelson 1975, Eilbirt 1959, Haber 1960, Noble 1977). On the whole, however, it was not until the second decade of the century that industrial managers looked seriously at systematic methods of employee selection.

By the 1910s, a turndown in the economy impelled many employers to rethink their hiring policies. Traditionally, hiring had simply been a question of recruiting enough able bodies through newspaper advertisements, fliers, and similar promotional literature. In most businesses, employee recruitment and selection were the prerogative of the individual supervisors. But high rates of labor turnover and industrial accidents—constant themes in the trade and progressive literature of the period—suggested to many that the modern industrial world required a skilled and efficient workforce that time-honored hiring practices could no longer guarantee. A manager at Bell Telephone Company, for example, claimed that one of three of the company's 16,000 operators quit or was dismissed within the first half year of work; another manager blamed human error for 80 percent of the railroad accidents in the United States, in which more than 10,000 people were killed in 1911 (Hale 1980, ch. 10).[2]

To many employers, especially those hiring workers whose jobs required a high degree of care or responsibility, waste and inefficiency in the workplace pointed directly to poor selection procedures. A systematic science of selection, they argued, would go far toward eliminating the disorders of scale—manifested in high rates of labor turnover, strikes, absenteeism, and industrial accidents—that beset modern industry. Indeed, it soon became a central tenet of the new profession of personnel management that all labor problems would be eliminated "when a scheme has been devised which will make it possible to select *the right man for the right place*" (Link 1919:293).

During the 1910s, numerous pseudoscientific systems of employee selection claimed to offer just such schemes. For many managers, racial and ethnic background served as a guide for hiring. For example, a text for a correspondence course (American School of Correspondence 1919, Vol. 2:215) suggested:

> It is well known that certain foreign peoples are naturally adapted to certain kinds of work. For instance, Finns, Croatians, and Austrians make good miners; Italians and Swedes are good railroad builders; Russians, Lithuanians, and Poles are good foundry and steel mill workers; Jews, French, and Irish do not take well to monotonous or repetitive work but are particularly adapted to any work requiring action, artistry, and enthusiasm. For all-round rough work, Norwegians, Greeks, Russians, and German Poles are generally recommended.

A particularly popular system was the Blackford Plan of character analysis, devised by Katherine Blackford and popularized in the 1910s in a series of books, including *The Job,*

---

[2] On labor turnover, see Bureau of Labor Statistics (1917), Eilbirt (1959), Gaudet (1960).

the Man, the Boss, published in 1919. Most psychologists of the day scorned the plan, but many practical businessmen took seriously Blackford's remarks on the character traits of blonds versus brunettes and her advice on reading physiognomy and handwriting. At the same time, a few businessmen turned to systems of mental testing already worked out by psychologists and vocational counselors.

From the 1890s, a growing number of psychologists, led by Francis Galton in England, James McKeen Cattell in the United States, Alfred Binet in France, and Emil Kraepelin in Germany, concentrated on the measurement of individual differences. In doing so, they turned their attention away from the general facts of perception and cognition, which were the central concerns of 19th-century experimental psychology. Their predecessors had regarded differences in human aptitude as interesting only insofar as they threw light on the general rules of mind. More practical-minded men like Cattell argued that the measurement of differences, whether in reaction times or in ability to remember nonsense syllables, made possible an applied psychology that could contribute to the progress of civilization as effectively as had engineering. Tests of individual traits conducted in the laboratory or with pencil and paper, Cattell suggested, could serve education, psychotherapy, and vocational guidance (Boring 1942, ch. 18, 19, Young 1923:1–47).

The concern of Cattell and other testers for vocation was typical of the period; vocation had become a central theme of the Progressive years. During this period, according to many social critics, the demands of industrial society had stripped work of its meaning. In the modern world, so the argument went, young boys and girls no longer fell naturally into their proper places in society, but were condemned to live out their lives as misfits. The toll that this situation imposed on society was enormous, for it expressed itself in industrial unrest and personal breakdown. A number of reformers—above all Frank Parsons of Boston—championed scientific vocational guidance as the answer to these social ills. As Par-

sons and fellow vocational reformers saw it, society was an organism in which each individual had a proper place, determined by his or her special aptitudes and interests. "Men work best," Parsons wrote in 1894, "when they are doing what Nature has especially fitted them for." The function of scientific vocational guidance was to fulfill society's responsibility to put men "as well as timber, stone, and iron in the places for which their natures fit them" (Parsons 1894:69, xvi).[3]

Operating out of the Boston Vocation Bureau early in the twentieth century, Parsons analyzed the aptitudes and interests of young men and women by an eclectic approach that combined interviews, questionnaires, and self-analysis (Parsons 1908:3, Brewer 1942, ch. 5). By 1909, he had enlisted the aid of the German-born and -trained psychologist Hugo Münsterberg of Harvard, a pioneer in applied psychology, to administer psychological tests to his clients and to assist him in his diagnoses (Münsterberg 1910:32–34). Münsterberg widely publicized his work with Parsons. Before long other leading psychologists, including H. L. Hollingworth of Barnard and W. D. Scott of Northwestern, had thrown themselves enthusiastically into the design of vocational tests.

Members of the vocational guidance movement, who had strong roots in education and traditional counseling, soon lost interest in mental testing, but at least a few employers and personnel managers recognized that the work of the vocational psychologists had relevance to their own needs. As Hollingworth wrote (1916:79):

> The first definite contribution of vocational psychology is . . . not so much toward the guidance of the individual worker as for the guidance of the employer who may be required to select from a number of applicants those whose general intellectual equipment is most adequate.

By the early 1910s, psychologists were at work developing tests for industry. In 1911, Münsterberg devised a test to eliminate in-

---

[3]On Parsons, see Mann (1954:126–144), Davis (1969).

competent ship captains at the request of the director of the Hamburg-American shipping line. In the following year the progressive American Association for Labor Legislation, which was financed in part by John D. Rockefeller, asked Münsterberg to develop tests for identifying accident-prone trolley drivers. Münsterberg's tests were unwieldy—although they or modifications of them were used in a number of American and European cities for a decade—and they proved highly controversial (Hale 1980, ch. 10, Münsterberg 1913, ch. 8, 9). Many contemporary psychologists challenged their validity, but as Scott (1913:283) wrote:

> The significant point of it all is that simple tests have been devised and applied in certain typical economic situations and that there is a positive correlation between the standing in the tests and the standing in the practical work.

Almost immediately, other psychologists offered their services to industry. Scott pioneered tests for salesmen for American Tobacco, National Lead Company, Western Electric, and other firms, and he developed the first tests for factory workers for the Joseph and Feiss Company of Cleveland. Edward Thorndike of Columbia University developed tests of salesmanship ability for Metropolitan Life, and Hollingworth and others devised tests for clerks and typists (Baritz 1960:38–39, Viteles 1932, ch. 5, Link 1923:34, Feiss 1915:5–16, Scott 1915). By 1915, according to Hollingworth, tests for 20 types of work had been developed and to one extent or another tried out (1915:919).

Work at the Carnegie Institute of Technology in Pittsburgh also indicated the growing interest of industrial managers and psychologists in employment testing. Administrators at Carnegie, where 50 percent of the students were training for careers in industry and management, recognized a need for "increasing the reliability of selection among applicants for employment." To meet this need, they brought in Walter V. D. Bingham from Dartmouth in 1915 as head of a new Division of Applied Psychology (Bingham 1923a:180–

181, 1923b:141–159, 1952). The most pressing demand for assistance, according to Bingham, came from sales managers and executives of large manufacturing concerns whose primary responsibility was marketing. How, managers wanted to know, could they select salesmen whose traits of mind and personality most suited them to the job? To conduct research on this question, Bingham set up a Bureau of Salesmanship Research, financed initially by 27 nationally based firms, and he hired Scott to direct it. This cooperative venture, which survived for a decade, not only proved of direct service to industry in developing tests, but it also served as a model for later enterprises.

By 1915, the battle lines on testing were drawn. Enthusiasts like Münsterberg and Scott championed their science. Thorndike wrote with enthusiasm that in two hours of testing a psychologist could diagnose an educated adult's intellectual ability better than could "two teachers or friends who have observed him in the ordinary course of life each for a thousand hours" (Thorndike 1913:139). Early testers claimed that their methods were faster than traditional methods; they also asserted that they were more accurate. Most industrial managers, however, remained skeptical. In response to Münsterberg's description of his trolley driver tests, for instance, a Philadelphia railway man asserted in a trade journal that "the traffic manager will be able to judge of his men a good deal better than Münsterberg or any other of those people who give new names to familiar facts" (see Hale 1980:156). Those who took the tests, apparently, were often no more impressed. Mary Gilson, employment manager at Joseph and Feiss, later recalled that "the girls thought it was a lot of nonsense to have run a needle up a metal alley or do some other 'high jinks'" (see Baritz 1960:39). In this case the women may have had a point. According to the industrial psychologist Henry C. Link, the correlation between productivity and test scores at Joseph and Feiss after five years proved to be 0.002. The tests had no value, Link suggested, beyond a rough ability to distinguish left-handedness (1923:34).

TESTING DURING WORLD WAR I

During World War I, the U.S. Army launched an unprecedented experiment in group testing.[4] For years the military had used academic-style tests to aid in selecting officer candidates, and, in the early years of World War I, European nations, in particular Germany, used psychological tests to select motor transport drivers, pilots, and other specialists (Dorsch 1963:149–150). None of these efforts in military testing, however, approached the scope of the program that the United States launched after the American entry into the war.

War had hardly been declared when in April 1917, Robert M. Yerkes of Harvard, then President of the American Psychological Association, offered the services of his science to the war effort. At Yerkes's urging, the newly founded National Research Council (NRC) of the National Academy of Sciences set up a Committee for Psychology made up of leading psychologists, which immediately set to work on the problem of applying behavioral science to the wartime emergency. Yerkes and others recognized that the selection and classification of recruits was the major personnel problem facing a nation without a large standing army and with no traditions of conscription. To this end, they organized a Committee on the Psychological Examination of Recruits, which included such famous testers as Yerkes, Bingham, and Lewis Terman of Stanford, who had recently adapted Binet's intelligence test for American use.

Working under the Army Surgeon General (because the Army believed that psychological testing was a medical question rather than one of personnel management), the committee undertook the task of classifying "recruits on the basis of intellectual ability, with special reference to the elimination of the unfit and the identification of exceptionally superior ability"

(Yerkes 1921:299). Committee members quickly put together the famous Army Alpha test, which was modeled after a number of pre-war intelligence tests and which included multiple-choice and true-false questions testing grammar, vocabulary, arithmetic, "common sense," general knowledge, and similar skills or areas. When the testers found in early trials that a large number of recruits could not read or write English, they developed the Army Beta, a test for illiterates that used pictures and diagrams. By early 1918, the tests were being given in recruiting stations around the nation. Within slightly more than a year, according to the official statistics, 1,726,966 men had been tested (Yerkes 1921:99).

Scores on the Alpha or Beta tests became part of each recruit's personnel records. They were available to commanding officers for use in assigning individuals to specific duties, in selecting noncommissioned officers and other special personnel, and in balancing the "intelligence" of military units. The extent to which the results were actually used for these purposes cannot be accurately determined. Many commanders believed that traditional methods of promotion and selection were more reliable than the tests; considerable testimony, however, suggested that test scores did in fact play an important role in many decisions and that many officers came out of the war impressed with the potential of mental testing. One result of the testing program, however, can be identified: Almost 8,000 recruits were recommended for immediate discharge as mentally incompetent, and approximately the same number were assigned to special labor duty (Yoakum & Yerkes 1920:12–13).[5]

Shortly after the organization of the Committee on the Psychological Examination of Recruits, members of the NRC Committee for Psychology organized a Committee on Classification of Personnel (Baritz 1960:46–47, U.S. Adjutant General's Office 1919), which worked out of the office of the Army Adjutant General. The goal of this committee, which

---

[4]The most complete account of the military testing program in World War I is Yerkes (1921). See also Camfield (1969), Kevles (1968), Samelson (1977), Napoli (1975).

[5]For a discussion of the actual use of the testing program in World War I, see Samelson (1977:278–280).

included Scott, Bingham, and John B. Watson, the founder of behaviorism, was to assign military personnel to specialized tasks and to rate officers for appointment and promotion. The ordinary methods of industry, they believed, were too slow and unwieldy for the wartime emergency; they hoped instead to develop "a measuring device which can be used *without trade knowledge on the part of the examiner*, for rating in objective, quantitative terms the degree of trade ability possessed by the person under examination" (Chapman 1923:49, 1921). For this purpose they put together batteries of tests based on oral questions about individual trades, questions based on photographs, and sample tasks. These tests were eventually used to rate almost half the personnel in the Army on their abilities, education, and experience. The work of the Committee on Classification, according to a recent historian, represented the first attempt by a large organization, public or private, "to determine the capabilities of all its individual members and to assign them accordingly" (Van Riper 1958: 252). Yerkes and Clarence Yoakum wrote that the committee's work "ultimately touched and more or less profoundly modified almost every important aspect of military personnel" (Yoakum and Yerkes 1920:ix).

The Yerkes and Scott committees, always on the verge of open rivalry, represented two different approaches to employment testing, and they foreshadowed a split that emerged in the 1920s and the following decades. Scott and Bingham argued for tests of proficiency in or aptitude for a specific trade; Yerkes contended that "general intelligence," which another psychologist defined as *the capacity to learn those things of most general use to civilized man*" (Dunlap 1923:74), was the "best available single indication of a person's occupational usefulness" (in Baritz 1960:65). In the massive analysis of the Army testing program written for the National Academy of Sciences (NAS), Yerkes and his colleagues found what they considered striking differences among the levels of intelligence of men in different occupations. The implication was that occupations could be ordered hierarchically by the degree of intelligence demanded and that the most appropriate selection tests for a given occupation were tests of "general intelligence." That the significant correlation might have been between a high level of education (and therefore a high social status) and a high occupational status was not seriously considered.

Another important result of the Army testing program was its apparent confirmation of racial stereotypes, and therefore, ironically, its validation of employment practices that most psychologists considered prescientific. In a sample of 162,526 soldiers tested, the NAS report found a wide variation in the scores of men born in different countries, the highest scores belonging to recruits from northern and western Europe, the lowest from eastern and southern Europe. Especially striking were the low scores of blacks, most of whom, like a large number of the foreign-born, took the Beta examinations. "The intellectual status of the Negro," according to the report, was "greatly inferior to that of the white" (Samelson 1977:280, Yerkes 1921:564, 693–699, 705–742).[6] These data proved a boon to postwar eugenicists and nativists, who took them as proof of their racial views. They led to a major public debate between psychologists and social commentators like Walter Lippmann over the validity of intelligence testing and the roles of heredity and environment in the development of general intelligence, and they provided ammunition to anti-immigrationists, who successfully pushed through a restrictionist immigration policy in the 1920s.

Psychologists may have disagreed over the relative values of tests of "general intelligence" and of specific aptitudes, and over the relation between intelligence and ethnicity, but almost all emerged from the war convinced that wartime testing techniques would prove invaluable to industry and education. "Great will be our good fortune," Yerkes wrote in 1919, "if the lesson in human engineering which the war has taught us is carried over directly and effectively into our civil institutions and

---

[6]For a criticism of Yerkes' conclusions by a contemporary psychologist, see Viteles (1928).

activities" (Yoakum and Yerkes 1920:viii). He need not have worried, for, as Cattell observed, the war put psychology "on the map of the United States" and precipitated a boom in testing that continued for half a decade (in Samelson 1977:275).

TESTING IN THE 1920s AND 1930s

After the war, the National Research Council and the Army Surgeon General were flooded with requests for information on testing (Baritz 1960:48). The success of the military program alone does not explain the newfound interest of private industry and employment managers in the possibilities of testing. In the final year of the war and in the immediate postwar years, American industry faced an unprecedented level of disruption in the labor market created by a sluggish economy, frequent and often violent strikes, many of which had radical overtones, and the inevitable difficulties that went along with demobilization. Above all, at least in the minds of personnel managers, high rates of absenteeism and turnover disrupted the economy and undermined industrial efficiency. Turnover, which one federal group called "a national menace," was in fact occurring at a startlingly high rate (Federal Board for Vocational Education 1919:9). The U.S. Bureau of Labor Statistics reported that in Detroit the annual turnover rate, defined as the ratio of the total number of separations to the average number of employees, was 300 percent in two of every five firms and 200 percent in four of five. Rates of turnover in other cities were almost as high (Federal Board for Vocational Education 1919:42–49). Some firms, like the Ford Motor Company, successfully cut turnover by raising wages and installing welfare programs for employees, but almost all managers agreed that the careful selection of workers was a prerequisite to reducing turnover to an acceptable level. As in the Progressive years earlier in the century, managers looked to a wide variety of schemes to aid in hiring; the wartime success of the military program made psychological

testing a more popular alternative than ever before.

Many professional psychologists, recognizing opportunity when they saw it (and fearing that the market would be taken over by character analysts, graphologists, and other charlatans), enthusiastically offered their services to industry. In 1919, the NRC replaced its Committee for Psychology with a Division for Anthropology and Psychology. The new division promoted personnel psychology and employment testing through the organization of the Personnel Research Foundation and the *Journal of Personnel Research*, soon renamed the *Personnel Journal*.

In the same year, Walter Dill Scott set up the first independent psychological consulting service for industry, the Scott Corporation, which grew directly out of the work of the Committee on Classification of Personnel. Scott's enterprise was short-lived, but in 1921 James McKeen Cattell, with the financial backing of most of the leaders of the science, organized the Psychological Corporation, which for more than 50 years has provided expert consulting in employment testing and other aspects of applied psychology. Other organizations also took up the cause. The Carnegie Institute's Bureau of Salesmanship Research, renamed the Bureau of Personnel Research after the war, continued its work on testing; the Life Insurance Sales Research Bureau, founded as a cooperative enterprise by the Carnegie Institute in 1922, assisted members of the life insurance industry in hiring and rating salesmen (Baritz 1960:51–53, Bingham 1923b:182, Yerkes 1923:172–178, Cattell 1923:165–171, Flinn 1922:7–13).

The psychological profession as a whole reflected this increased concern with the problems of industrial efficiency. By 1920, according to Lewis Terman, more than half of the members of the American Psychological Association worked primarily in applied psychology, and 25 of the 400 members were carrying out studies in industrial psychology (Terman 1919:1–4). Henry Link complained in 1923 that "the use of psychological tests in industry is most conspicuous because it is so rare"

(1923:32), but this was not for lack of enthusiasm on the part of psychologists.

Link was speaking of carefully constructed, validated testing programs; in this respect he was correct. In 1921, approximately 32 companies, one survey reported, used employment tests "in a patient and experimental manner." On the other hand, hundreds of companies bought ready-made tests, like the Army Alpha, which was applied with the same indiscriminate enthusiasm as the Blackford Plan and other pseudoscientific schemes (Baritz 1960:67).[7] However much psychologists pleaded for caution, they in fact only encouraged personnel managers to adopt tests as a panacea when, like Cattell, they proclaimed that the direct application of tests already in existence could save certain industries millions of dollars a year (Cattell 1923:169).

Among the more careful attempts at instituting a testing program were Link's at the Winchester Repeating Arms Company, which was called a model of thoroughness and accuracy, E. L. Thorndike's for the Metropolitan Life Insurance Company, Millicent Pond's for the Scovill Manufacturing Company's apprentice school for toolmakers and machinists, Morris Viteles' for the Philadelphia Yellow Cab and Rapid Transit Company, and Bruce V. Moore's for the Westinghouse Educational Department (Borow 1944:71, Moore 1921, Kornhauser and Kingsbury 1924). These and similar programs were significant because the men and women who administered them attempted to analyze the requirements of the jobs for which they were testing and to apply statistical methods to correlate test scores with success on the job—whether defined as high ratings by supervisors, high productivity, or long tenure. These testers often differed over the relative value of tests of "general intelligence," proficiency and trade tests, and tests of aptitude, but they agreed that all programs had to be validated. "The chief problem of employment psychology," Link wrote, "is to determine the value of particular tests when applied to particular tasks. The first step is to *test tests* rather than applicants" (Link 1919:20). Most important, testers agreed that no testing program could by itself be successful. To contribute to rational employment practices, a program had to be part of a general selection process that included such other practices as interviews, application blanks, references, and personal history forms.

The U.S. Civil Service Commission by this time was particularly interested in the new developments in testing. As early as 1917, the Commission's Chief Examiner, George R. Wales, approached Thorndike and Scott for information on their work; after the Armistice, the Commission, with the assistance of Yerkes, administered the Army Alpha test to a sample of its own clerical workers. Although the tests were judged no better than the established civil service tests, they convinced the Commission that the techniques of psychological testing had much to offer. The Commission hired a series of expert psychologists, including Watson and L. L. Thurstone, to assist in streamlining existing tests and developing new ones. By 1922, short-answer, objective tests were introduced for several positions. In 1923 the Commission set up a Research Section in the Office of the Chief Examiner and appointed as its head L. J. O'Rourke of the Air Service Psychological Research Laboratory, an advocate of the latest techniques of mental testing and advanced statistical methods. Under O'Rourke's leadership, the Research Section began immediate work on a broad program of general research, concentrating on measures of "general adaptability" for a wide range of positions and developing shortened examinations for clerks, policemen, firemen, postal workers, and others. In the years that followed, civil service researchers became major contributors to the development of job-specific tests (Van Riper 1958:309–310, Filer & O'Rourke 1923, Kavruk 1956, U.S. Civil Service Commission 1924:xl–xlvii).

Most employers had neither the patience nor the money to adopt testing programs along the lines that Link and other psychologists outlined, especially because psychologists so often

---

[7]For a criticism of the Blackford plan by contemporary psychologists, see Paterson and Ludgate (1922).

disagreed among themselves over the proper techniques and because careful validation programs, when instituted, often showed a low correlation between test scores and job success. In the early 1920s, the Atlantic Refining Company, for example, instituted a program of testing supervisors. After a year, the company found that the correlation between the results of their test and salaries was 0.37, which it considered unacceptably low. As a result, the program was abandoned (Baritz 1960:71–72).[8] Numerous other firms, according to observers at the time, also discovered that the results of their testing programs were not useful. One psychologist estimated that about 90 percent of the companies that began to use tests after World War I found that they did not work (Baritz 1960:71–72). By 1925, according to Morris Viteles, only 4.5 percent of a sample of companies used psychological tests in hiring (Scott et al. 1961). The postwar boom in testing had peaked by 1925.

The decline in employment testing was attributable to more than the failure of many testing programs. The marked upturn in the economy in the early 1920s and the sudden drop in both rates of turnover and concern over turnover also contributed to the decline. Equally important, perhaps, was the growing disenchantment of many industrial psychologists with employment tests (Borow 1944:70–71, Baritz 1960:72–73). Employment psychologists in the 1910s assumed that specific aptitudes or skills were the primary factors in job success, productivity, and—according to some—job satisfaction. By the 1920s, however, psychologists and personnel managers fell increasingly under the sway of functionalists and small-group theorists, who were redefining American sociology. The social context, these sociologists argued, was more important in determining behavior than were the individual traits of the people who made up the society. This theory received startling confirmation toward the end of the decade in the work of industrial sociologists at the Hawthorne Works of the Western Electric Company.

The Hawthorne experiments, which have been called "the first major social science experiment," radically shifted the direction of personnel work and, as the historian Loren Baritz has written, "became standard material for students of industrial sociology and human relations" (1960:77). For more than a decade, scientists from the National Research Council, Massachusetts Institute of Technology, Harvard Business School, and Western Electric closely monitored the work practices of employees in the Hawthorne Works. Their conclusions overturned the individual-centered approach of a previous generation of social theorists. There is no need here to describe the experiments in detail, but it should be emphasized that their results—which are still in dispute—convinced many industrial psychologists and personnel managers that social relations within the workplace were more important than individual aptitudes or indeed skills, in determining performance on the job and productivity. According to F. J. Roethlisberger, who participated in the study, the famous bank-wiring room studies of the Hawthorne project demonstrated "no direct relation between performance . . . and capacity to perform as measured by dexterity or intelligence tests" (Roethlisberger & Dickson 1939:445–446). Elton Mayo of Harvard, one of the early leaders of the work, concluded: "The belief that the behavior of an individual within the factory can be predicted before employment upon the basis of a laborious and minute examination by tests of his technical and other capacities is mainly, if not wholly, mistaken" (1945:111; also see Baritz 1960:94).

The Hawthorne experiments, which became widely publicized in the early 1930s, seemed to confirm the conclusions that economic conditions were forcing on personnel managers and industrial psychologists. The use of individual tests for specific skills, particularly clerical and typing skills, remained in practice, but, according to one estimate, 16 percent of

---

[8]On the decline of testing in the mid-1920s, see especially Baritz (1960:58–76), Napoli (1975:90), Borow (1944:70–71).

the firms that used intelligence tests for selection abandoned them in the first years of the Depression (Baritz 1960:128–129). When mental aptitude tests were given, they were more and more used to eliminate candidates who appeared to be obviously unfit than to find the right person for the right slot. As difficulties with labor grew in the 1930s and as unions gained strength, managers concentrated on personnel counseling—that is, satisfying employees who were already there—instead of on selection techniques. Where managers did use tests, they increasingly emphasized interest and personality inventories, with which they hoped to identify workers who would fit in well with the industrial "team" and who would find their work satisfying.

With millions looking for work, tests of vocational interest and aptitude took on a new importance. In the early 1930s, the Minnesota Employment Stabilization Research Institute set up an occupational analysis clinic that diagnosed thousands of unemployed with an elaborate battery of vocational tests; soon organizations in other areas followed the Minnesota example. In 1933 the National Occupational Conference set up a clearinghouse for information on guidance, promoted research on the measurement of differences in attitudes relevant to vocational success, and commissioned Walter Bingham's classic study *Aptitudes and Aptitude Testing*, which appeared in 1937 (Borow 1944: 71–73, Bingham 1937). In 1934 the newly reorganized U.S. Employment Service established an occupational research program that launched a study of the psychological aptitudes required to perform specific jobs. The worker-analysis section of the program began a major project validating aptitude tests then in use in industry, devising new trade tests, and developing an array of research tools and statistical aids. Its report, edited by William Stead (Stead et al. 1940), was the major source of validation studies in the 1940s. As a result of this work, by World War II the Employment Service was able to assist "in the selection of employees by apti-

tude tests at the specific request of many war plants" (Borow 1944:73).[9]

The use of tests in industry was low in the first years of the Depression. In 1932, the U.S. Bureau of Labor Statistics, which surveyed 224 establishments with a total of 387,826 employees in a wide range of industries, reported that only 14 establishments (6.3 percent) used any kind of intelligence, aptitude, or proficiency tests. Many of the tests were relatively simple. Some companies tested for ability to read English; two publishing firms tested men in the composing room for knowledge of arithmetic, spelling, and geography; a furniture firm tested mechanical efficiency in cabinetmakers; and another company gave intelligence tests, including the Otis test, which had been the basis of the Army Alpha tests, to candidates for executive and supervisory positions. Some firms required aptitude tests for employees who would be using expensive equipment, and a New England firm required an intelligence test for all applicants seeking office positions and a mechanical ability test for factory workers. All of the firms that used tests were happy with them (U.S. Bureau of Labor Statistics 1932:1008).

Walter Dill Scott reported very different results in a 1930 survey of the nation's largest firms: he found that 46 percent of the 195 responding firms gave stenographic or clerical tests, 27 percent gave trade tests, and 17 percent gave "intelligence" tests (Scott et al. 1961:566). A survey of over 2,000 firms by the National Industrial Conference Board (NICB) (1936:23–24) yielded results closer to those of the U.S. Bureau of Labor Statistics. Only 7.3 percent of the firms responding had any kind of testing program. The most common tests were intelligence and aptitude tests for clerical workers, followed by tests for wage earners and trade tests. The difference between Scott's figures and the NICB figures points to the unreliability of the survey methods, but it

---

[9]On the U.S. Employment Service, also see Adams 1969, Stead and Masincup 1942:xxx–xxxviii.

also reflects Scott's concentration on best-known firms.

A striking trend of the 1930s and 1940s was the increasing use of personality inventories in employment. This trend reflected an effort among personnel managers for stability in the workforce during times of considerable labor unrest; it also reflected the emphasis that post-Hawthorne industrial management placed on such intangibles as the willingness of an individual to work as a member of a team.

Even before World War I, effective personality and interest tests had been the dream of certain testers, particularly Münsterberg, whose German training had alerted him to the "whole personality" of the worker. During the war, Robert S. Woodworth put together a personality development scale, first given in standardized form to recruits to screen out those who would be particularly susceptible to shell shock and other wartime disorders. The scale proved unsuccessful—the same patients who had obtained a median score of 36 hysterical symptoms before Armistice were found to have a median score of 1 after—but Woodworth's work served as a basis for the Thurstone Personality Scale, the Allport Ascendance-Submission Test, and other scales that were adopted for industrial purposes in the 1930s (see especially National Industrial Conference Board 1941:30–37). Shortly after the war, Bruce V. Moore developed interest tests for the Westinghouse Electric Educational Department. According to Moore, these tests could be used together with ratings by interviewers and supervisors to distinguish students who would be successful in design engineering from those who would be successful in sales (Moore 1921).

By the early 1930s, a number of personnel managers began to administer personality and interest inventories to prospective employees in order to cut down rates of turnover and ensure a more cooperative workforce. In a depressed economy, much interest focused on salesmen, whose major job qualification—sales ability—was tied closely to personality. Eugen J. Benge, director of personnel for U.S. Gypsum in Chicago and a veteran of the Carnegie Bureau of Salesmanship Research, for example, developed a scale to rate prospective salesmen on their performance in interviews and on the information they supplied in application forms (he gave high scores to married men between 30 and 34 years old). Benge also devised a test for "dominance," "people interest," "judgment," and sales information. Benge claimed that the use of this scale in selecting employees, which was popular in the 1930s and 1940s, increased sales production and reduced turnover (1939:13–14).

By the end of the 1930s, a small group of firms used personality inventories to identify stable, loyal, and productive workers. The most common inventories were the Bernreuter Personality Inventory, which was claimed to measure neurotic tendencies, self-sufficiency, introversion-extroversion, dominance-submission, sociability, and confidence, and the Humm-Wadsworth Temperament Scale, which rated candidates on "general adjustment" and "constructive control of basic temperamental drives" (NICB 1941:35, Wadsworth 1941:58–60). Guy M. Wadsworth, one of the developers of the Humm-Wadsworth, spelled out the intention of his test in 1941:

> The worker is, first of all, a person who must fit into the social community in which he works. . . . As recent industrial relations readily attest, the livability of the supervisor-employee relationship is a problem of primary magnitude. We should know something of the prospective employee as a *person*, before he goes out on the job.

Wadsworth claimed that his test could be used to identify those workers who would "enter into the working relationships cooperatively" and to screen out "chronic hot-heads" (Wadsworth 1941:19, 59).

Employers generally echoed the promotional rhetoric of the test designers when they justified personality inventories. A personnel manager at the Atlantic Refining Company, for example, claimed that skill was much less important than "'personality' and 'interest' factors" for typists (NICB 1939:15). A manager of the Woodward Governor Company of

Rockford, Illinois (1941), reported that he could easily find job candidates who were highly skilled, but he wanted ones who would stick. With the assistance of the Personnel Institute of Chicago, the company developed a test that, it was believed, judged ability, strength of character, the power to resist temptation, and "oomph." Another firm, Cherry-Burrell (1941), an equipment supplier for the milk industry in Chicago, tested for the ability to get along with fellow workers.

TESTING IN WORLD WAR II AND THE POSTWAR YEARS

World War II, which, like World War I, placed extraordinary demands on the personnel systems of industry and government alike, further stimulated the growing interest in testing.[10] The U.S. Army and Navy had dropped their general testing programs in 1919 and retained only a modified personnel classification system left over from Scott's work. As war neared, however, military policymakers and civilian psychologists recognized the need for renewing the testing and classification program; well before American entry into the war, they began a coordinated program to adapt the advances in psychological testing and personnel management to military purposes. The first step was taken in 1940, when the National Research Council, at the request of the War Department, set up a Committee on Classification of Military Personnel. To head the committee, the NRC selected Walter V. Bingham, who soon assumed the title of Chief Psychologist of the Army. Under Bingham's direction, a personnel research section was established in the Office of the Adjutant General, and staff and civilian psychologists set out to develop a testing program.

Bingham later reported that his "welcome was in sharp contrast to experiences of World

War I" (Bingham in Boring et al. 1952, Vol. 4:23)—an indication that the prestige of psychology and employment testing had grown in the previous decades. Under Bingham, new tests were developed to select officer candidates, to determine mechanical and clerical aptitude, to measure aptitude for specific skills such as radiotelegraphy, and to measure knowledge of specific trades. The staff of the personnel research section also developed the Army General Classification Test, which, according to Bingham, made "no pretense of measuring *native* intelligence," but rather was used as "a rough indication of trainability," dividing recruits into five broad categories: very rapid learners, rapid learners, average learners, slow learners, and very slow learners (Bingham in Boring et al. 1952, Vol. 4:22, Bingham 1941, U.S. Adjutant General's Office 1943). By the end of the war, more than 9,000,000 recruits, or one seventh of the male population of the United States, had taken the test. Unlike the earlier Army Alpha and Beta tests, whose results were often ignored, the Army General Classification Test formed the backbone of Army selection and classification procedures (Napoli 1975:182–183, Partington & Bryant 1946:111).

Early in the war, the College Entrance Examination Board (CEEB), which by the 1930s had become a large-scale and respected enterprise in educational testing, offered its services to the military. John M. Stalnaker, Associate Secretary of the Board, was appointed chairman of the NRC Committee on Service Personnel—Selection and Training, and he subsequently took a position in the Navy. Assuming that tests used to select college students would be appropriate for selecting officers, Stalnaker and testing experts from the CEEB put together the V-12 and the A-12 tests for officer candidates in the Army and Navy (Fuess 1950:162–178). The CEEB, under contract, administered and scored the tests throughout the war.

One of the most successful testing programs in World War II was the Army Air Forces' selection procedures for pilot and air crew trainees (Flanagan 1948, Thorndike 1949, Napoli

---

[10]Unless otherwise noted, the description of employment testing during World War II comes from the following sources: Hunter (1946), Bingham (1944), Baritz (1960, ch. 8).

1975:183 – 187). Before the war, the air forces had relied on medical examinations, psychiatric interviews, and educational records to select candidates for pilot training. Because of a shortage of qualified medical examiners and because of the success of other Army testing programs, however, the air forces began psychological testing in 1941, and John C. Flanagan of the University of Pittsburgh was appointed to head the new Psychological Research Agency in the medical division. Under Flanagan's direction, Air Force psychologists and consultants developed a battery of mental and physiological tests that predicted the success of pilot cadets in the training program. It was later estimated that these tests saved the Air Force $1,000 for every dollar spent on pilot training (Lawshe and Balma 1946:7). Before the war was over, the testing program was expanded to include other members of flight crews.

A major concern of the military was to devise effective ways of assessing the qualities of leadership and reliability. The Office of Strategic Services (OSS) conducted the most striking experiment in testing for these qualities, primarily at Station S in northern Virginia. The plan was modeled on German and British programs in which military psychologists set up retreats where candidates for positions of high responsibility took batteries of tests, but the OSS added to this plan an emphasis on situational tests. Between 1943 and 1945, more than 5,000 candidates for the OSS passed through three-day testing sessions at Station S or one-day sessions at other sites. The candidates assumed false identities and cover stories and were then subjected to specially designed mental and personality tests. Central to this program were the situational tests, including such exercises as the famous "brook" test, in which a group of men were to transport a delicate range-finder, "skillfully camouflaged as a log," and a box of percussion caps, camouflaged as a rock, across an eight-foot brook, using only a few short boards, three lengths of rope, and a barrel without a bottom. During this and other exercises, OSS psychologists observed and rated the recruits. Men were then selected for overseas duty on the basis of the ratings of the assessors (U.S. OSS 1948, ch. 3).

The OSS tests departed from previous tests in the United States. Borrowing from the group interaction theory of Kurt Lewin, who was one of the people responsible for developing the program, OSS psychologists adopted what they called an "organismic" approach, which stressed tests for general "effectiveness," and rejected the "elementalistic" approach of earlier tests, which sought to measure specific traits. By observing how a candidate reacted to a specific situation that simulated the work for which he was training, OSS psychologists hoped to assess the candidate's ability to perceive and interpret a situation properly and "to coordinate his acts and direct them in the proper sequence toward the proper objects." In the situational tests, the psychologist did not measure discrete skills (although these were also tested at Station S), but set up "tasks and situations which cannot be properly solved without organization, since it is the power to organize, as much as any other power, that he wishes to measure." The program, according to the OSS report, *Assessment of Men*, was "the first attempt in America to design and carry out selection procedures in conformity with the so-called *organismic* (Gestalt) principles." The effectiveness of the program has been questioned, but the psychologists involved were convinced that it offered a model for selecting people for positions of responsibility in the civilian as well as the military world (U.S. OSS 1948:3, 38–39).

Wartime conditions also fostered interest in testing in private industry. As in World War I, war disrupted the labor market; it necessitated the hiring of people, including women and blacks, who had not traditionally been in the job market; and it led to high rates of turnover and absenteeism. At Sears Roebuck, for example, 17,000 employees entered military service during the war years, representing nearly one half the company's total male personnel in 1941 (Worthy 1951:8). In an RCA plant in Camden, New Jersey, 22 percent of a group of 212 workers hired in 1944

had left within a month and more than 50 percent had left by six months. Both companies
instituted tests to stabilize their workforce
(Bolanovich 1948).

In the immediate postwar years, new techniques of machine scoring, developed in the
1930s, made the mass use of tests more eco-
nomical. Psychological consulting services and
the U.S. Employment Service, at the same
time, promoted ready-made tests for many different occupations. In 1947, 560 commercial
tests were available, and from 1949 to 1954
the sale of test blanks tripled (Baritz
1960:156, Habbe 1948:3, Whyte 1954:118).
A large testing industry had also arisen to service companies that found it too expensive or
time-consuming to develop their own programs. Such new firms as Klein Institute for
Aptitude Testing and Rohrer, Hibler and
Replogle, which in the late 1960s employed
91 Ph.D.s in psychology, joined established

organizations like the Psychological Corporation in developing tests and evaluating personnel (*Business Week* 1965:74, Whyte 1954:
118–119, Klaw 1950:107). Also during the
war and afterward, the U.S. Employment Service made standard tests available to companies at no cost if they would report their results
to the Service. In 1949 approximately 300
companies made use of these services (Baritz
1960:156).

Surveys by Walter Dill Scott and the National Industrial Conference Board indicated
an increase in testing in private industry in the
late 1940s and early 1950s. In a survey published in 1940, Scott reported that 26 percent
of a sample of "best-known" companies gave
intelligence tests for selection and promotion;
in a 1947 survey, the figure had increased to
38 percent and in 1953 to 56 percent. From
1947 to 1953, the use of tests of all types grew
from 66 percent to 75 percent (Scott et al.

FIGURE 1 Use of Tests for Selection and Placement by Well-Known Companies

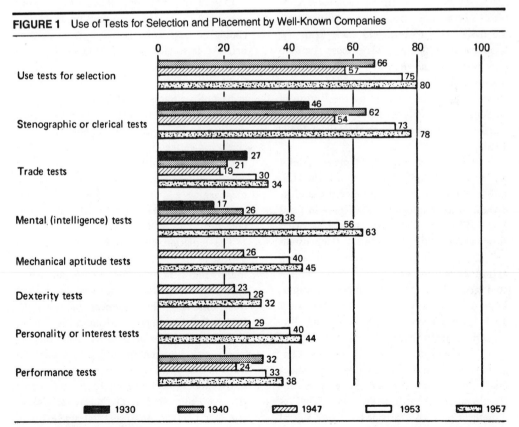

Source: Scott et al. (1961:566).

1961:566). (Scott did report that testing in general, and clerical, trade, and performance tests in particular, declined from 1940 to 1947. Perhaps the return to the labor market of veterans trained in clerical, skilled, and semiskilled work reduced the need for these job-specific tests.) Results of Scott's surveys from 1930 to 1957 are given in Figure 1. In 1946 the NICB, in a broader survey, found testing less prevalent than Scott had: 16.8 percent of 3,498 firms responding in the survey used tests of one form or another. Although the figures were lower than Scott's, they were almost twice those reported by the NICB in the 1930s (NICB 1947:13, 32).

The use of tests in private industry grew steadily through the 1950s and 1960s. In a NICB survey of 1954, 37 percent of respondents claimed to use one form or another of test, generally in selecting or promoting employees. By 1964, the number had increased sharply to 80 percent. In the 1964 survey, insurance companies, banks, and utilities were the most likely to test, and trade firms the least (NICB 1964a,b,c). The most common tests were clerical, followed by intelligence, mechanical ability, personality, and interest. Other surveys, for example by the Bureau of National Affairs (BNA), reported even higher percentages (Bureau of National Affairs 1958, 1963).

In the postwar years, state merit systems also expanded rapidly. In the 1930s, the U.S. Employment Service had promoted examinations in state employment services—in fiscal years 1934, 65,000 persons took written examinations in 38 states (Hohenstein 1956:274)—and several states, including Maine, Michigan, and Connecticut, enacted civil service laws. The most important stimulus to state civil service testing, however, was a 1939 amendment to the Social Security Act. To combat inefficiency and political abuse in the state administration of federal funds, Congress required in this amendment that states establish and maintain merit systems for employees in social security programs. This requirement was soon extended to other federal grant programs. The State Technical Advisory

Board of the Social Security Administration (later replaced by the Office of Merit Systems of the Department of Health, Education, and Welfare) assisted states in developing "practical written tests," and its illustrative booklet provided material used in many state examinations (Aronson 1973:134–141, Adkins 1956:260–61). The results of the testing requirement and of federal assistance were striking. By 1949, all but two states had merit systems for public assistance and public health programs. By the 1960s, states with comprehensive merit systems for the first time outnumbered states with systems limited primarily to federally funded programs (Hohenstein 1956:296, Aronson 1973:142).

ASSESSING MANAGERIAL POTENTIAL

One of the most important trends during the postwar years was the increasing use of psychological tests to select management personnel. At least since Bruce Moore's work for Westinghouse in 1919, leading corporations had experimented with psychological testing as part of programs for selecting managers, either from college recruits or from their own workforce. Until the 1940s, however, relatively few companies used tests in any systematic fashion to identify managerial talent. Most relied on personnel records if the potential manager were already a member of the company and references and interviews if he were not.

The situation changed in the 1940s and 1950s, as managers came to play an increasingly prominent role in the corporate structure. By the 1930s, several social commentators, following the argument in Adolf A. Berle's and Gardiner C. Means's *The Modern Corporation and Private Property*, had come to distinguish between ownership and management and to stress the key role of management in the modern, technical world. In 1941 James Burnham suggested in *The Managerial Revolution* that a class of engineers, salesmen, minor executives, and social workers ran the United

States. Others argued that a key elite, directing a select group of corporations, was the "dominant force" in society. Whatever the case, the message was the same: American industry and the American economy were held together by a core of talented managers (or not so talented, according to some critics); the American future depended on the recruitment of talent into managerial ranks.

At the same time, as many observers were proclaiming a managerial revolution, the number of managers grew markedly. In the late 1950s, Frederick Harbison of Princeton reported an average increase of 32 percent in the supervisory ranks of two thirds of a group of companies that he had studied for several years. According to another estimate, the number of nonproduction workers increased 52 percent from 1947 to 1957, while the number of production employees increased only 1 percent; according to still another, the number of professional and technical employees in business increased 200 percent from 1947 to 1957 (Spencer 1959). This rapid increase in managers and professionals precipitated what many called a crisis in talent. From the mid-1940s to the present, the shortage of technical and managerial talent has been a constant theme of industrial analysts. "The unavailability of competent men to make organizational decisions," Felix Lopez wrote in 1967, "represents a crisis in the survival and growth, not just of individual organizations, but of whole societies" (Lopez 1970:4, Hinrichs 1969:425).

During the 1940s, many managers, aware of the military programs for testing officer candidates, hoped to apply tests to the solution of their own problems in selecting management personnel. In 1941, a Lockheed personnel man (Irwin 1942:105) suggested:

> One of the key advantages of testing is its help in the selection of leaders and supervisors, men with the capacity to get along well with those under them, command their respect, and cooperate to get the job done thoroughly and pleasantly.

One of the earliest and most comprehensive testing systems was inaugurated during the war years by Sears Roebuck, which had been particularly affected by loss of personnel to the military. With the help of L. L. Thurstone of the University of Chicago, Sears installed a comprehensive testing program, including tests of intelligence, personality, and vocational interest, to assist in the selection of a reserve group of managers from its own ranks (Worthy 1951:8–17, Emmet & Jeuck 1950: 555–558). The standard Sears executive battery, it was claimed, could uncover outstanding mental qualities that might be obscured in certain situations, and it could detect "a basic instability or a deep-seated temperamental maladjustment that might not become evident except in periods of stress" (Worthy 1951:16). By the end of 1950, the tests had been administered to 10,000 people.

In their testing programs, companies like Sears demonstrated an interest in selecting managers with appropriate personal traits as well as skills. Indeed, personality inventories became increasingly popular in the selection of both managers and nonmanagers. In the 1940s, two editions of the National Industrial Conference Board's *Experience with Psychological Tests* devoted considerable space to discussions of the Humm-Wadsworth scale and other personality measures (National Industrial Conference Board 1941, 1948). By the 1950s, the Minnesota Multiphasic Personality Inventory (MMPI), developed to identify certain types of mental illness, and the Bernreuter Personality Inventory, which had sold a million copies by 1953, were in even wider use (Hathaway 1964, Whyte 1954:119). According to Walter Dill Scott, 44 percent of a sample of the best-known firms used personality inventories in 1953, up from 29 percent in 1947; a *Fortune* survey published a year later revealed that 63 percent of a sample of corporations, including General Electric, Sears Roebuck, and Westinghouse, used personality tests in selecting managers (Whyte 1954:117).[11]

Many professional psychologists and personnel managers had long questioned the use of

---

[11]On the use of projective tests in employment, see especially Kinslinger (1966).

these inventories, and by the mid-1950s they came under open attack. The social critic Walter Whyte launched the attack in his article, "The Fallacies of 'Personality' Testing," published in *Fortune* in 1954 and later included in *The Organization Man*. According to Whyte, the tests screened for the traits of tranquility, contentment, and stability, and they eliminated extremes of any sort. They were designed, he argued, to create an organization of yes-men. "If the tests were rigorously applied across the board today," he wrote, "half of the most dynamic men in business would be out walking the streets for a job" (Whyte 1954: 118). To the annoyance of many of the testers, he included a section on how to cheat on the most common inventories then in use. Several other attacks followed Whyte's, most notably Martin Gross's *The Brain Watchers* in 1962. By the mid-1960s, personality testers were on the defensive.

The attacks of Whyte, Gross, and others anticipated congressional hearings in 1964 on the use of personality inventories by the government. To be sure, the U.S. Civil Service Commission, committed to job-specific, practical tests, had never adopted personality inventories. In 1965, John W. Macy, Jr., then Civil Service Commissioner, testified to Congress that, "measured against technical standards or against standards of acceptability, present personality tests and inventories do not justify use as selection methods" (Macy 1965a,b). Other federal agencies, however, used personality inventories as screening devices. The Peace Corps, for example, administered the MMPI to all trainees to identify those who possibly had latent mental disorders or "personality deficiencies" (Shriver 1965:876, Carp 1965:917). "From the beginning," one psychologist wrote, "the Peace Corps selection and training have been dominated by psychological findings as has no other Government agency, not even the Air Force" (Amrine 1965:869). The State Department gave the MMPI in the early 1960s to personnel who were to be stationed overseas, and the Defense Department required personality inventories for certain people in sensitive positions. City

police forces also experimented with the use of personality inventories (Amrine 1965:867, Lopez 1970:14–16). Interest in personality testing had already peaked, however, in part because validation studies generally showed them to be poor predictors of success, and in part because, according to critics, they violated the rights to privacy of those tested.

By the mid-1950s, personnel managers in several leading corporations sought more effective ways of assessing managerial potential. One obvious model was the multiple assessment technique applied by the OSS in World War II. In 1956, American Telephone and Telegraph initiated a Management Progress Study to test the value of the OSS approach in selecting managers. In this program, new college-educated employees and noncollege first-level managers participated in three-day retreats, during which they took what has become a standard battery of tests, including group and in-basket exercises, paper-and-pencil ability tests, personality questionnaires, and projective tests. The theory was to adopt a "holistic" approach to testing on the grounds that "a complex of personal characteristics is more predictive of progress than any single characteristic." In a follow-up study eight years later, Douglas Bray and Donald L. Grant reported that the assessors "were clearly able to identify those more likely to advance in their organizations" (1966:1, 18).[12]

Long before the results of this follow-up study were published, a number of businesses had put assessment centers into practice in the selection of managers. As a result of the Management Progress Study, the technique of assessment centers spread rapidly through the Bell System and soon was adopted by IBM, Standard Oil (Ohio), Sears Roebuck, Kodak, and other leading corporations. By the early 1970s, approximately 1,000 companies in the United States operated some kind of assessment center; these centers had become, according to a recent observer, "one of the more phenomenal success stories of applied psychology

---

[12]On assessment centers, also see *Business Week* (1965), Huck (1973).

and organizational psychology and personnel administration" (Hinrichs 1978:596).

TESTING AND EQUAL EMPLOYMENT

The success of assessment centers in the 1970s coincided with widespread criticism of employment tests by members of the public, government agencies, and the courts. Many tests, claimed these critics, discriminated against certain groups protected by the Civil Rights Act of 1964, particularly blacks, and stood in the way of equal opportunity for employment As discussed in other sections of this report the Civil Rights Act of 1964, and the interpretation of that act by the courts and the Equal Employment Opportunity Commission, made employment testing a public issue in the 1970s. Employers have been asked to prove, often in court, that their tests are valid and job-related—a task that, given the high standards of proof required, has often been difficult. This situation has led to an increased emphasis on techniques of validation and on job-specific tests, and it has induced many companies, especially small businesses, to curtail testing programs or to abandon them entirely. For the first time since the 1920s, the use of employment tests appears to be on the decline (Siegel 1968, McCormick & Tiffin 1975:173, Petersen 1974).

SUMMARY

From its origins early in the century, modern employment testing has grown into a major business, practiced by a wide variety of employers and promoted by scores of test developers and consulting firms. Employment testing began as a tool for rationalizing hiring practices—in this respect, it reflected a 20th century drive for order and progress through the application of science to social problems. Tests, enthusiasts claimed, could provide an objective measure of human potential where the commonsense judgments of individual employers were sure to create chaos. Tests, it was also assumed, promoted fair competition for jobs and therefore equal opportunity.

Throughout the century, the practice of employment testing increased in scope and sophistication as well as in size. Before World War I, the Civil Service Commission maintained an extensive program of "practical" testing, for the most part based on written examinations assessing job-specific knowledge and experience. A few businessmen, concerned with high rates of labor turnover, experimented with the work of early psychological testers, including tests designed to measure aptitude and "trainability." It was the U.S. Army in World War I, however, that introduced testing on a modern scale—particularly group testing and short-answer, objective examinations.

In the years immediately after the war, employment testing enjoyed a short-lived boom. Many businessmen hailed tests as ensuring industrial efficiency and enthusiastically applied them to the selection of employees. By the late 1920s, however, the postwar testing boom had collapsed, in part because tests had failed to live up to the expectations of many who had adopted them. More important in the long run was the work of psychologists and personnel management specialists in the 1920s and 1930s, who for the first time seriously attempted to develop techniques for testing tests and for correlating success on tests with success on the job.

During the Depression, testers concentrated more on vocational testing than on employment testing. Late in the 1930s, however, the use of tests for employee selection was once again on the increase, and, stimulated by the military testing program of World War II, employment testing emerged as a central feature of personnel management in the postwar years. From the 1940s on, with the introduction of machine scoring and the availability of ready-made tests, both from private test developers and the federal government, the use of tests grew rapidly. In general, the pattern of testing was similar to what it had been since the 1920s: white-collar workers were the most frequently tested, and clerical and stenographic tests, followed by intelligence tests, were most frequently given. Large companies tested more often and more extensively than small companies. The 1940s and 1950s, however, saw a new development: a sharp increase in the use of interest and personality inventories, which many personnel managers hoped would ensure satisfied and loyal as well as efficient workers. The vogue of personality inventories for the most part died down in the 1960s, but another development of the 1940s —the use of tests to identify management potential—has proved more durable and remains an important element in personnel selection and promotion practices.

The recent concern for equal employment opportunity has dampened the enthusiasm for the testing of the 1950s and 1960s. As in the 1920s, the use of testing in the 1970s was apparently on the decline. In the earlier period, the promotion of tests as a panacea for all industrial ills led to disillusionment and the abandonment of testing by a number of companies. The failure of many tests to yield useful results, however, did not prevent psychologists and personnel specialists from directing their attention to careful test construction and validation. Indeed, it may have fostered these activities. In the same way, some businesses in the 1970s have cut back or abandoned testing programs, particularly programs whose validity was hard to demonstrate. Others, however, in the interest of developing more valid tests, have supported large-scale programs of research, not only in testing but in all aspects of personnel selection and promotion. Whether these programs will succeed in developing more effective, and legally acceptable, procedures of personnel selections waits to be seen.

One of the reasons why testing came under fire in the early 1960s was that people felt they were being abused by tests and that their privacy was being assaulted. This point was made forcefully in The Brain Watchers *by Martin Gross and* The Organization Man *by William H. Whyte, Jr. More recently, Steven Jay Gould has taken up the attack on the misuse of intelligence tests in* The Mismeasure of Man. *London and Bray address these and other issues by considering the various loyalties that should govern the personnel psychologist involved in testing. These loyalties are directed toward the profession, employers, and employees.*

Ethical Issues in Testing and Evaluation for Personnel Decisions

Manuel London and Douglas W. Bray
American Telephone and Telegraph Company, Morristown, New Jersey

Personnel decisions such as selection, promotion, and transfer are major events in individuals' careers. These decisions are often made with the aid of tests, interviews, behavioral exercises, performance appraisals, and other techniques developed by industrial/organizational psychologists. These psychologists, therefore, must be concerned with questions of fairness, propriety, and individual rights as well as with other ethical issues. For example, does collecting information for a personnel decision invade an individual's privacy? Who should have access to such information and how long should it be retained? What obligations do psychologists have to their employers, other employees, and job applicants? Should nonpsychologists have access to psychological techniques in making personnel decisions? What conflicts arise between the rights of psychologists and those of the individuals and organizations they serve?

This article addresses these and other questions by setting forth values and obligations related to evaluation for personnel decisions. The goal is to summarize some of the challenging, often conflicting ethical issues facing psychologists and others in human resources work and to suggest resolutions. We begin by reviewing some of the many sources that prescribe ethical practices relevant to personnel decisions. We then discuss ethical obligations of industrial/organizational psychologists to their profession, the job applicants and employees they evaluate, and their employers. Ethical obligations of employers to job applicants and employees in relation to the personnel policies under which psychologists must function are also discussed.

STANDARDS FOR ETHICAL PRACTICE

The American Psychological Association (APA) has published several documents delineating ethical guidelines. The *Standards for Educational and Psychological Tests* was prepared by a joint committee of three professional organizations—the American Psychological Association, the American Educational Research Association, and the National Council on Measurement in Education. The latest version,

Source: *American Psychologist*, 35, No. 10 (October 1980), pp. 890–900. Copyright 1980 by the American Psychological Association. Reprinted by permission of the publisher and author.

published in 1974, covers standards for both test developers and test users. The word *test* is used generically in the *Standards* and throughout this article to refer to any assessment device or aid that provides a systematic basis for making inferences about people. Sections of the *Standards* applicable to test users describe the knowledge a test user is expected to have, how tests should be chosen, and procedures for test administration, scoring, and interpretation. The sponsoring organizations have recently voted to revise these standards in light of legislative developments related to "truth in testing." That such professional guidelines require periodic revision demonstrates that ethical practice in psychology is not governed by hard-and-fast rules, but must adapt and respond to changes in the needs and interests of those served by psychologists.

The APA's *Ethical Standards of Psychologists* (1977) includes many principles applicable to test development and use. Psychologists are expected, for example, to value objectivity and integrity while providing services that maintain the highest standards of their profession. Regarding competence, "psychologists with the responsibility for decisions involving individuals or policies based on test results [are expected to] have an understanding of psychological or educational measurement, validation problems, and other test research" (p. 2). Another relevant passage states, "Psychologists will not condone practices that . . . result in illegal or otherwise unjustifiable discrimination on the basis of race, age, sex, religion, or national origin in hiring, promotion, or training" (p. 2). These standards also deal with the potential conflict between a psychologist's professional allegiance and commitment to his or her employer: "As employees . . . psychologists seek to support the integrity, reputation, and proprietary rights of the host organization" (p. 5). Other standards deal with advertising psychological services, the client's right to know the nature and purpose of tests and test results, and guarding the confidentiality of information acquired in the process of psychological assessment.

Another APA publication, *Standards for Pro-*

viders of Psychological Services (1977), specifies minimally acceptable levels of quality for providers of psychological services. Standards relevant to the industrial/organizational psychologist deal with the psychologist's obligation to support the legal and civil rights of the user of psychological services and with the establishment of a system to protect the confidentiality of psychological records. The user of such services includes job applicants and employees as well as the organization employing the psychologist.

A supplementary document to the *Standards for Providers of Psychological Services* was recently prepared by APA's Committee on Standards for Providers of Psychological Services (1979) and the Division of Industrial and Organizational Psychology (Division 14) and has been endorsed by the APA Council of Representatives. Entitled *Standards for Providers of Industrial and Organizational Psychological Services*, these "specialty standards" cover psychological functions performed by persons representing themselves as industrial/organizational psychologists. Included are topics such as safeguarding the legal and civil rights of the service user, anticipating and resolving conflicts of interest arising from dual user relationships (e.g., individuals and organizations), maintaining accurate, current, and pertinent documentation of the essential psychological services provided, and establishing a system to protect confidentiality of records.

Another pertinent set of standards was published separately by the Division of Industrial and Organizational Psychology (1975). Entitled *Principles for the Validation and Use of Personnel Selection Procedures*, the document is "the official statement of the Division concerning procedures for validation research, personnel selection, and promotion" (p. 1). The principles cover methods for establishing criterion-related validity, construct validity, and content validity as well as procedures for implementing validation studies (e.g., preparing reports and manuals, generalizing to other samples, and applying personnel selection procedures in making decisions).

A task force of researchers and practitioners

of assessment center methodology has recently agreed on *Standards and Ethical Considerations for Assessment Center Operations* (Note 1; see also Moses & Byham, 1977).[1] These standards specify guidelines for "minimal acceptable practices" in training assessors, in informing participants about what to expect, and in using assessment center data. Other ethical issues related to the quality of assessment center information deal with the relevancy of assessment center exercises for what is being predicted, how individuals are selected to attend an assessment center, and how participants are treated at the center.

Enforcement of ethical standards is difficult unless the organization promulgating the standards can influence the behavior of its members. Psychologists who violate the ethical standards of the American Psychological Association are subject to sanction and disciplinary action by the Association's Committee on Scientific and Professional Ethics and Conduct as well as by state association ethics committees, professional review committees, and state boards of examiners. Complaints from clients, employers, or others can be made to these committees for review and appropriate action. If an ethical violation has occurred, such action ranges from requesting that the psychologist rectify the situation to revoking the psychologist's membership in the Association. APA's code of ethics has been incorporated into the laws of over 20 states and therefore governs the professional conduct of all psychologists licensed in those states, even those who do not belong to APA.

In general, professional standards are meant to be technical guidelines, not laws (with the exception of those incorporated in legislation). A document that does have legal implications is the *Uniform Guidelines on Employee Selection Procedures* (Equal Employment Opportunity Commission et al., 1978, 1979). Adopted jointly by the Equal Employment Opportunity Commission, the Civil Service Commission,

the Office of Personnel Management, the Department of Labor, and the Department of Justice, it is a revision and integration of earlier guidelines. The current guidelines "incorporate a single set of principles which are designed to assist employers, labor organizations, employment agencies, and licensing and certification boards to comply with requirements of Federal law prohibiting employment practices which discriminate on grounds of race, color, religion, sex, and national origin" (p. 38296). Dealing primarily with methods of test validation, the guidelines can be applied by the sponsoring federal agencies when adverse impact against a protected group is evident and in some cases when adverse impact is not evident.

Numerous federal and state laws and executive orders also prescribe standards for equal employment opportunity. These include the Equal Pay Act of 1963, Title VII of the Civil Rights Act of 1964, the Age Discrimination in Employment Act of 1967, the Equal Employment Opportunity Act of 1972, the Vocational Rehabilitation Act of 1973, and the Vietnam Era Veterans Readjustment Act of 1974.

Other laws not related to equal employment opportunity also have implications for personnel research and practice. The Freedom of Information Act of 1976 and the Privacy Act of 1974, for example, concern the handling of government information, including the personnel records of public employees. The Privacy Protection Study Commission, headed by David Linowes, has urged that private employers adopt "fair information practice policies" that limit the type of data companies collect from employees and job applicants. Pending legislation, if enacted, will severely restrict the collection and use of personnel data. Though the specific provisions of these and other laws and regulations are beyond the scope of this article, it is clear from this brief discussion that legal requirements influence the personnel practices of both public and private employers.

The standards reviewed above have had an impact on personnel research and practice in at least three ways. First, the professional stan-

---

[1]Assessment centers use a combination of evaluation methods, including in-baskets, group discussions, business games, interviews, and psychological tests, to observe and evaluate individuals under standardized conditions.

dards and federal guidelines clearly delineate appropriate procedures for developing and validating evaluation devices. The values implied by these standards are that high-quality information should be used to make decisions about people and that psychologists are responsible for developing procedures that result in the most accurate decisions. Second, equal employment legislation has placed emphasis on the meaning and extent of unfair discrimination and how it can be avoided by affirmative action programs. Third, growing concerns for individual privacy and freedom of information are beginning to raise new research questions and challenges. For example, what is the impact on employees of suddenly having access to their supervisors' view of their potential for advancement? Does such access affect supervisors' ratings? To what extent does informing individuals about the purpose of an evaluation affect the results? How can confidentiality of information be guaranteed and invasion of privacy avoided while providing information to those who make personnel decisions?

The danger in promulgating ethical principles lies in acceptance of theories as truth without supporting evidence. As equal employment opportunity issues came to the forefront, for instance, many psychologists assumed that differential validity was a pervasive phenomenon that should be investigated by separate validation of tests on different subgroups. The most recent *Uniform Guidelines* (EEOC et al., 1978, 1979), however, requires users to produce evidence of validity only when adverse impact has been demonstrated. Adverse impact is defined in these guidelines in terms of differential rates of selection, not in terms of differential validity. This "bottom line" approach was agreed to only after substantial research and theoretical arguments in the literature negated the prevalence of differential validity (e.g., Boehm, 1977; Schmidt, Berner, & Hunter, 1973) and clarified the meaning of test bias (Schmidt & Hunter, 1974).

Unfortunately, the fields of law and personnel have a history of demanding deduction over induction. It seems that one must have a theory before gathering "relevant" data (or how

would one know that these data were "relevant"?). We must be wary of this approach in identifying and resolving ethical issues. Theories that serve as a basis for ethical principles should be formed by observing interrelationships rather than vice versa. If the available evidence is not sufficient to establish guidelines for specific ethical problems, research questions must be formulated and answered before resolutions are suggested.

Another caveat is that a law or standard does not exist for all situations. Laws and standards are frequently ambiguous and are subject to change. Many ethical questions require personal judgment at least until cases accumulate that provide a body of collective experience to guide ethical practice in similar situations. According to Mirvis and Seashore (1979), "The challenge of being ethical lies not simply in the application of moral prescriptions but in the process of creating and maintaining research relationships in which to address and moderate ethical dilemmas that are not and cannot be covered by prescription" (p. 768). These dilemmas are resolved by creating roles within a network of multiple roles and possible concomitant conflicting expectations. This requires recognizing the intersection of role systems and resolving problems "through collaborative effort and appeal to common, transcendent goals" (Mirvis & Seashore, 1979, p. 769).

The existence of multiple roles raises the question of who is accountable for evaluating personnel: Psychologists develop, validate, and implement selection devices, and employers establish personnel policies and practices, often in consultation with psychologists. The ethical obligations of both psychologists and employers are discussed in the following sections.

ETHICAL OBLIGATIONS OF PSYCHOLOGISTS

Organizational staff members who are responsible for formulating and applying evaluation procedures have ethical obligations to their profession, to the people they evaluate, and to their employers. These obligations are reviewed below.

Psychologists' Obligations to the Profession

Organizations often employ individuals with advanced degrees in personnel-related fields. Psychologists who are members of APA or who are licensed by a state to practice psychology are expected to abide by the standards and principles for ethical practice set forth by APA, regional professional organizations, and/or state statutes. However, nonpsychologists involved in evaluation are not formally responsible for adhering to these standards. Nevertheless, the federal *Uniform Guidelines on Employee Selection Procedures* sets standards for all personnel experts in organizations subject to federal regulations regarding equal employment opportunity. Moreover, many personnel experts who are not psychologists should still be considered professionals. They often belong to professional organizations (e.g., the American Society for Personnel Administration), and they should be expected to follow many of the same standards that apply to psychologists. Desirable behaviors for ethical conduct generally include keeping informed of advances in the field, reporting unethical practices, and increasing colleagues' sensitivity to ethical issues.

Maintaining professional competence is necessary for effective application of evaluation techniques. The *Standards for Educational and Psychological Tests* devotes a section to qualifications of test users. Test users must have a general knowledge of measurement and validation principles and the limitations of test interpretation as well as an understanding of the literature relevant to the evaluation devices they use. The *Ethical Standards of Psychologists* emphasizes the need for continuing education, being open to new procedures, and remaining abreast of relevant federal, state, and local regulations concerning practice and research. In addition, the *Ethical Standards* states that understanding the traditions and practices of other professional groups also contributes to ethical practice.

Knowledge of unethical professional behavior among colleagues presents a dilemma for all professionals, including those in personnel. The *Ethical Standards of Psychologists* suggests that efforts first be made to rectify unethical conduct directly with the individuals involved. If that fails, the next step is to bring the unethical activities to the attention of appropriate authorities such as state or APA ethics committees.

Reports of unethical behavior become especially problematic when competing psychologists are involved. In some cases, a psychologist may benefit from the censure of another psychologist. This raises a difficult question. Is it unethical to derogate another's behavior when the claim cannot be substantiated? The answer depends to some extent on the motivation or intention of the accuser. The intention to be malicious or derive personal gain would probably be considered by many to be unethical, especially when the accusation is unjustified and the accuser is aware that the accusation cannot be substantiated.

While it is necessary to curtail false claims of unethical practice, it is also necessary to diminish reticence to "turn in" a colleague when it is justified. Fortunately, APA's investigations of unethical conduct are confidential, thereby protecting the parties involved. Perhaps psychologists will be more willing to report unethical behavior as standards prescribing ethical practice and procedures for dealing with unethical conduct are clarified and become more widely known. In addition, increasing colleagues' sensitivity to ethical practice may diminish unethical behavior and increase the likelihood that such behavior will be reported.

Research is necessary to identify conditions that encourage reports of unethical actions and discourage false claims. One general hypothesis is that increased competition and poor economic conditions prompt individuals to behave unethically as well as to perceive unethical behavior in others—whether or not the behavior in question is actually unethical. Such a finding would suggest the need to establish special regulations governing professional practice under adverse conditions. Other research should investigate the conditions under which different unethical behaviors are most likely to arise and the conditions that contribute to their discovery.

Psychologists' Obligations to Those Who Are Evaluated

Social and legal influences mandate that career decisions be made with a concern for accuracy and equality in employment opportunity (Division of Industrial and Organizational Psychology, 1975). A concern for the person who is affected by career decisions, however, leads to a number of ethical principles that go beyond improving and maintaining accuracy and ensuring equal employment opportunity. These principles include guarding against invasion of privacy, guaranteeing confidentiality, obtaining employees' and applicants' informed consent before evaluation, respecting employees' right to know, imposing time limitations on data, minimizing false positive and false negative decisions, and treating employees with respect and consideration. Each of these is discussed in this section.

Questions of invasion of privacy arise in the use of certain types of tests. Gross (1962) has argued that personality tests in particular violate personal privacy and encourage conformity and lying. He wonders why someone should be required to share private thoughts as a condition of employment and why people are penalized for responding truthfully. Guion (1965) responds to these arguments by stating, "It is a clear invasion of privacy to ask an applicant to reveal details of thought or emotion that are not relevant to performance on the job for which he is considered" (p. 376). Ewing (1977) recommends that employees or applicants not be required or pressured to take a personality test or any other examination, for that matter, which constitutes, in their opinion, an invasion of privacy, regardless of the test's validity. This is an extreme view that

must be balanced against the value of accurate employment and placement decisions to the organization, society, and individuals themselves.

Confidentiality refers to the release of information about an employee. Confidentiality of evaluation results is essential when promises of confidentiality are made to employees or applicants prior to evaluation. As stated in the *Ethical Standards of Psychologists*, "Information received in confidence is revealed only after most careful deliberation and when there is clear and imminent danger to an individual or to society, and then only to appropriate professional workers or public authorities" (p. 4).

The *Standards for Educational and Psychological Tests* states that "test scores should ordinarily be reported only to people who are qualified to interpret them" (p. 68). This standard was designed to protect examinees from ridicule and harassment and to prevent misuse of test results. But should individuals be able to take an IQ test or some other measure simply to see how well they do, and should these individuals be required to go through a psychologist to take the test? The answer depends on the purpose of the test and on who controls its administration. People do not have a right to take a test simply because it exists. A more difficult problem is whether individuals should be denied access to a test because prior knowledge of test items may decrease the test's validity. The solution depends on how the test is used. People do not necessarily have a right to test results if these results do not affect them in any way and they have not been promised access to the scores. They have the right to know the results of evaluations, however, when these evaluations are used in making decisions about them, despite a conflict with the traditional practice of avoiding contamination of test validity by not revealing test scores.

Some organizations routinely provide evaluation results to employees in the hope that knowledge of results will improve performance. Other organizations maintain a policy of secrecy or leave it up to individual supervisors to decide whether to provide feedback. Legislation now guarantees public employees access to this information, and pending legislation, if enacted, will do the same in the private sector. Research on the effects of access on the quality of information and the behavior and attitudes of the employee is necessary.

Recent legislation in New York requires that college and graduate school entrance tests and correct answers be made public within 30 days after the results are distributed. It also requires testing services to provide a graded answer sheet to students requesting it. California has passed a similar law. The possibility that other laws may one day affect employment tests cannot be ignored. The *Standards for Educational and Psychological Tests* designates that the individual whose future is affected by a career decision is among those with a "right to know" the tests results used to make the decision. "In some instances," the document asserts, "even scores on individual items should be made known" (p. 69). Further, it suggests that the security of test content can be protected by supplying the information to qualified people who are sympathetic to the individual's interests. These standards do not, however, require that the test items be made public.

An alternative to the "truth in testing" disclosure legislation was proposed by the Association for the Advancement of Psychology, psychology's congressional lobby in Washington ("AAP Pushing 'Truth in Testing,'" 1979). Their idea is to establish a national commission on educational and occupational testing. One of its functions would be to provide Congress with facts about testing and the testing industry before federal legislation is passed. If made permanent, the commission would maintain a central data bank of test scores from government, private industry, and academic sources. Qualified scholars and scientists would be allowed access to test data, but confidentiality of test results would be guaranteed.

A recent court case dealt with the conflict between protection of the confidentiality of test results and the rights of interested parties to know whether fair practices prevailed in a particular situation. The case arose in 1971 when the Detroit Edison Company rejected

several employees who had applied for position vacancies in one of its facilities (American Psychological Association, Note 2; Roskind, Note 3). The rejections were based on the failure of the employees to obtain a minimal grade on a battery of aptitude tests consisting of two widely used and validated examinations. The tests had been administered by the company's Industrial Psychology Division, which was headed by an APA member with a license to practice psychology in the state of Michigan. Company psychologists administering the tests gave the employees written and verbal assurances that their scores would remain confidential and that only an overall interpretation of performance would be released to management. The union filed a grievance on behalf of the unsuccessful bidders. After numerous hearings, the grievance was placed before the American Arbitration Association. At that time, the union formally requested that the company supply the union with the tests, answer sheets, and scores of all employees who had applied for the job.

During the course of the subsequent arbitration and National Labor Relations Board proceedings, the company offered to supply the requested information if the employees consented, but the union refused to seek their consent. The board ordered the company to disclose the information, and this order was enforced by the Sixth Circuit Court. The American Psychological Association (Note 2) filed an amicus curiae brief in support of the company's position prior to that court's decision and again as the case reached the Supreme Court. The brief argued that the actual test batteries should not be made available to the union and that the court should uphold the confidentiality of the psychologist-client relationship despite the fact that the psychologist was retained by the company. In March 1979, the Supreme Court ruled that Detroit Edison had the right to refuse to turn over to the union copies of the tests, overturning the lower court's ruling. The Court also held that the company was not guilty of an unfair labor practice for refusing to reveal individual employee test scores without the written consent of the employees ("Justices Uphold Utility's Stand," 1979). Thus the Supreme Court recognized the right of the test user to maintain the security of the test.

Another issue pertaining to the confidentiality of evaluations such as recommendations deals with protecting the identity of individuals providing the information. Specifically, should employees have access to recommendations written about them? A similar question was answered by Congress in 1974 when it enacted a law giving students the right to inspect their records (Ewing, 1977). Now students choose whether or not to waive this right before asking someone to complete a recommendation form. Allowing employees to decide whether or not to waive their right to access to recommendations and other information in their personnel files may be a viable solution to employee complaints about confidential information they believe may be used against them. Here, as in other areas, there is a conflict between the rights of the individual and the validity of information obtained. An important research question is whether those named as references will supply negative information if they know the applicant will have access to it.

An especially difficult ethical problem involves maintaining the confidentiality of test results within an organization. Typically, many individuals outside the personnel staff have legitimate access to the information. For instance, a manager who is responsible for filling a position vacancy by promotion from within the company may use information about an employee's job experience and performance. Such information is often used without the knowledge of the employee. This raises the issue of informed consent—that is, of informing candidates about the intended use of test results prior to their taking the test. Tests given by an organization for one purpose are often used later for additional purposes. Thus, a score on an employment test may be used later for selection to a training program, assignment to a specific type of work, or promotion to a higher level. A person has the right to be told every potential use of the test results. This does not mean that the individual has to

be informed every time a decision is made. Rather, it simply means that he or she should be aware of the types of decisions that may depend in part on the test results.

If information collected early in an employee's career is to be used later to make decisions about that employee, the salience of the information should be checked when the decisions are made. Both the *Standards for Educational and Psychological Tests* and the *Ethical Standards of Psychologists* state that test score information that has become obsolete because of lapse of time should be removed from data files. The idea is to prevent such information from being misused or misconstrued to the disadvantage of the person being evaluated. But how old must data be before they are of little use? One study demonstrated that assessment center ratings predict advancement eight years later (Bray, Campbell, & Grant, 1974). Further research indicated that the same ratings retained predictive validity 16 years after they were collected (Bray & Howard, Note 4). In some cases, destroying data in personnel files may be illegal, as when such information is discoverable in a lawsuit. It is reasonable to remove old evaluative information that has not been used for personnel decisions, particularly if it has been updated. Before destroying data used to make personnel decisions, however, it is desirable to determine their likely utility for making future predictions and for serving as evidence of the rationale for prior decisions. Data with such utility should not be indiscriminately destroyed.

Another concern is the obligation of the psychologist to those who are erroneously rejected for employment or advancement (i.e., false negatives). Some such errors are inevitable, since there is no foolproof selection method. The psychologist should, however, attempt to minimize the problem by considering alternative routes to qualification. A method too expensive for screening all candidates might be affordable for a smaller number of rejectees who are motivated to try again.

Regarding false negatives, the *Uniform Guidelines on Employee Selection Procedures* states that "users should provide a reasonable opportunity for retesting and reconsideration . . . [while taking] reasonable steps to preserve the security of . . . [their] procedures" (Equal Employment Opportunity Commission et al., 1978, p. 38300). Similarly, the *Standards for Educational and Psychological Tests* states that the "person tested should have more than one kind of opportunity to qualify for a favorable decision" (p. 72). This is meant to be applied with discretion in individual cases. Extenuating circumstances might warrant that a decision be made on the basis of characteristics other than those measured by a particular evaluation technique, as long as such circumstances are not based on the personal biases of the decision maker. Retesting may be desirable as a means of checking the results when it does not alter the validity of the scores or endanger the security of the test.

When individuals do not pass the initial screening, one strategy is to give them an on-the-job trial period or at least a trial period in job training, where such training exists. In one organization, people who achieved the cutoff score on a certain aptitude test qualified for promotion. Those who did not were given the opportunity to experience some of the training needed for the next higher job. If they succeeded in this training, they qualified for promotion. Thus, rather than relying on a subjective decision or on retesting, the organization obtained a better although more costly sample of the behavior actually required on the job.

False positives present another dilemma. The individual who has failed to perform as expected is subject to embarrassment and possibly ridicule, and the organization is faced with loss of productivity. Too often, individuals who fail do so because they were not given sufficient training to deal with increased responsibility or new tasks. Strategies to handle false positives include remedial assistance and changing job assignments by demotion or lateral transfer. In the latter case, a lingering stigma of failure may be avoided by providing special training or relevant job experiences in preparation for career advancement.

Ethical treatment of employees during and after evaluation is another obligation of psy-

chologists. How employees or applicants are treated when they are evaluated can influence the results of the evaluation and their acceptance of the ensuing decision. In general, evaluation procedures should be standardized to guarantee equal treatment and to enable examinees to do their best (American Psychological Association et al., 1974). Standard procedures should include personal and considerate treatment, a clear explanation of the evaluation process, and direct and honest answers to examinees' questions.

Psychologists' Obligations to the Employer

Ethical obligations to the employer go beyond the basic design and administration of decision-making procedures. These obligations include conveying accurate expectations for evaluation procedures, ensuring high-quality test data, implementing and periodically reviewing the adequacy of decision-making procedures, respecting the employer's proprietary rights, and balancing vested interests of the employer with government regulations, with commitment to the psychology profession, and with the rights of those evaluated for personnel decisions.

The personnel expert should inform the employer of what to expect regarding the costs and benefits of a particular evaluation device or decision-making procedure. Test reports and manuals should be prepared in accordance with the standards set forth by the APA and its Division of Industrial and Organizational Psychology. Moreover, the rationale for decision criteria such as cutoff scores should be provided to employers along with the likely effects of such criteria if they are adopted.

Psychologists must attempt to provide high-quality information for personnel decisions, namely, reliable, valid, and fair data. However, psychologists are often unable to use the most rigorous scientific methods to ascertain a test's reliability and validity because of limited resources, time pressure, or other constraints imposed by the employer. For instance, it may not be possible to conduct a predictive validity study without simultaneously using the test to make a selection decision or without contaminating the criterion by distributing test scores to those who evaluate job performance. The psychologist is obligated to the employer to clarify exactly what can be expected from the types of test development and validation the employer is willing to fund.

Fairness relates to the absence of discrimination on the basis of race, sex, national origin, or other characteristics not related to the job. The law has responded to this issue in the form of legislation and judicial rulings. In general, a reasonably reliable and valid test that does not exhibit differential validity may still be unfair if it results in a substantially smaller proportion of favorable personnel decisions for one or more protected classes than for the majority group. (A substantially smaller proportion is defined in the *Uniform Guidelines* as less than 80 percent of the majority group selection rate, but this criterion does not necessarily define unfairness.) Therefore, in addition to determining that an evaluation device is reliable and valid, a psychologist must ascertain that it is free from bias.

Personnel procedures should be developed with the policies and goals of the organization in mind to the extent that these policies and goals do not conflict with ethical practice. For example, selection procedures and cutoff scores can be formulated on the basis of the number of applicants the organization expects to hire during a given period of time (Guion, 1965). However, the expected number of false positives and false negatives should be appraised so that the employer and the psychologist can decide whether the costs of these errors are worth the benefits derived from the use of a particular test. The personal and societal costs must be considered in addition to the monetary costs, and it is the psychologist's duty to bring these costs to the employer's attention.

Psychologists who develop evaluation devices are not always responsible for administering them. They are nevertheless responsible for prescribing methods for their use, which may include training nonprofessional employees to administer, score, and interpret tests.

Employees requiring such training range from managers who use appraisals to make personnel decisions to clerks on the personnel staff. Decision-making procedures should be monitored to ensure that the instructions supplied in manuals or provided during training are being followed. This is especially important when the interpretation of evaluation results requires judgment. Also, arrangements should be made for periodic research on the accuracy of the selection procedure and its appropriateness to the situation.

The advent of new knowledge, changes in job requirements, and recent legislation and judicial rulings may require adjustments in the use of evaluation techniques. For example, procedures will have to be established for providing feedback to candidates. Psychologists have an obligation to their employers as well as to their profession to keep abreast of such requirements and to inform the employers when changes are relevant. In addition, psychologists should oppose guidelines, rulings, and policies that are not in keeping with professional practice.

Psychologists must respect the proprietary rights of the employer as long as it is possible to maintain standards of ethical practice. Many organizations insist that their selection methods remain confidential, and in some cases they maintain this policy even when under review by government agencies. Companies in a competitive environment that invest heavily in personnel methods may be reluctant to publicize the details of their procedures. Moreover, organizations may fear that information given out about their procedures will lead to difficult questions even if the procedures are perfectly proper. The APA expects in-house psychologists and independent psychologists serving as consultants to support the proprietary rights of their employer as long as the employer does not demand or use unethical practices (*Ethical Standards of Psychologists*, 1977). Therefore, psychologists working in industry may be constrained from publishing data regarding test development and validation or other research results sponsored by the employer.

Another ethical issue arises when psychologists are constrained from conducting research because the results may in some way be detrimental to their employer. In the process of establishing a procedure to select high-potential employees for special developmental experiences, for instance, the psychologist may desire to document how these decisions were made in the past. The psychologist may be prevented from collecting these data, however, because the data may be discoverable in future court proceedings against the employer. The psychologist would thereby not be able to evaluate the marginal improvement of the new selection device over the old procedure. In such a case, the psychologist must abide by the wishes of the employer, try to persuade the employer otherwise, or change jobs. The ethical issue must be resolved by the psychologist. The issue becomes salient when the psychologist believes that proper practice has been hindered. Indeed, this is the crux of many ethical issues in psychology. Ethical responsibility is a personal and individual issue. Although the situation may be constructed by the employer, the psychologist perceives and interprets the situation and must deal with restrictions that he or she believes contribute to unethical practice.

Balancing obligations to the employer, the profession, and those evaluated for personnel decisions is difficult. When ethical problems arise in an organization, the *Ethical Standards of Psychologists* advises that psychologists first "attempt to effect change by constructive action within the organization before disclosing confidential information acquired in their professional roles" (p. 5). Thus, maintaining ethical standards is paramount, although the need "to support the integrity, reputation, and proprietary rights of the host organization" (p. 5) is recognized.

The potential for conflict among the professional's obligations to the employer, the profession, and employees is perhaps most likely in the area of confidentiality. Management's need to know must be satisfied while keeping promises to employees and applicants that evaluation results will remain confidential and while ensuring that the contents of evaluation

devices are not disclosed to the extent that they are invalidated.

OBLIGATIONS OF EMPLOYERS

Boards of directors, presidents, and other executive officers should adhere to the same standards as psychologists and other personnel experts when setting organizational policies regarding personnel decisions. Psychologists in a position to advise policymakers must be cognizant of these standards. Policymakers must recognize and safeguard the ethical obligations of psychologists and other personnel experts to their profession and to the employees of the organization. This requires establishing a climate that is conducive to ethical practice. As laws and court rulings dealing with equal employment opportunity, freedom of information, and individual privacy proliferate, organizational climates will of necessity become more open. Employees will routinely be informed about the purposes of evaluation and the meaning of results. Only data that are necessary and job related will be recorded, and information will be destroyed as it becomes obsolete.

Several companies, noting the above trends, have voluntarily limited access to data files or discontinued collecting vast amounts of information about their employees (Stessin, 1978). Equitable Life Assurance Society, for example, includes only nine items of essential job-related information in its personnel files. International Business Machines has pared its personnel data files to a bare minimum and has removed sensitive materials from records available to line managers. Cummins Engine Company insists that supervisors who collect information about employee behavior and performance make the fact known to subordinates and be willing to discuss the contents of these files upon request. At least half of the Fortune 500 industrial companies have initiated new policies of employee access to their own personnel records and new rules of data confidentiality in the last few years (Westin, 1978).

Many companies have their own business

code of ethics that safeguards information which may be used for career decisions. Typical statements, excerpted from three different codes of ethics, are as follows:

> Employees are not permitted to make disclosures to outside organizations or individuals of confidential employment information pertaining to other employees . . . without specific advance written approval of the Employee Relations Division.

> The privacy of your [the employee's] personnel and payroll records will be respected and you have the right to examine these records yourself.

> Records containing personnel data about customers and employees are confidential. They are to be carefully safeguarded. They should be disclosed only to authorized personnel.

Some business codes express a commitment to equal employment opportunity. For example, a multinational corporation asserts in its code of ethics that it assumes the responsibility to "recruit, hire, train, and promote employees to all levels and for all jobs on the basis of equal employment opportunity." A policy statement on nondiscrimination and equal employment opportunity issued by another company promises to "recruit, compensate, upgrade, promote, transfer, train, and maintain working conditions without discrimination because of race, religion, color, age, sex, or national origin or because of designated physical handicap or status as a disabled veteran of the Vietnam era."

Though such policies are often motivated by equal employment opportunity legislation, some companies have taken a broader perspective. One corporation states in its code of ethics, "The requirement that we operate within the law is just the beginning of ethical disciplines we must accept and follow." Another company has established a Corporate Ethics Committee that serves as the final authority with regard to the company's policies on business conduct. Some organizations voluntarily prepare "social audits" that report the results of equal employment opportunity and affirmative action programs along with the results of pro-

grams to meet other social responsibilities (Blake, Frederick, & Myers, 1976).

One implication of these policies is that creative solutions are necessary to solve personnel problems. As a consequence, organizations may be more willing now than ever before to sponsor research and try out new ideas. For example, while a substantial amount of research has been conducted on how interviewers and other personnel experts make selection decisions, little research has been done on how managers make promotion, transfer, and other decisions about employees. Some organizations have policies and codes of ethics governing these decisions. Other organizations have no standard procedures and rely totally on the ability and integrity of the managers making the decisions. Research on how managers collect and combine information to make decisions about people will help generate ethical policies and procedures.

Another example of a situation that calls for a creative solution stems from the effect early federal guidelines on employee selection had on the need to validate all selection methods (although the focus was and still is on paper-and-pencil tests, which are easily quantifiable). The guidelines provoked the question, Is it possible to validate all personnel decisions? If validation requires a statistical relationship between predictors and criteria, the answer to this question is no. The costs of time and money and the limited number of people about whom the same type of decision is made make a predictive or concurrent validity study impractical in many situations. The federal government is beginning to admit that alternative validation strategies, such as content and construct validity, may be desirable.

SUMMARY AND CONCLUSION

A review of existing standards for psychologists reveals a variety of sources prescribing ethical psychological practice. We note, nevertheless, that standards do not exist for all situations, and research may be necessary to establish strategies for dealing with certain ethical issues. Areas for research are suggested when resolutions to ethical issues are not available. The obligations of psychologists and employers in maintaining ethical principles are linked in several ways. One link is the conflict between the psychologist's attempt to use rigorous scientific methods and the rights of employers and those evaluated. Guarding against invasion of privacy, obtaining informed consent, guaranteeing confidentiality, and respecting the individual's right to know must be balanced against the need for high-quality evaluative information. Whereas in some cases it may be necessary to sacrifice scientific rigor in favor of individual rights, in most cases it is a matter of discovering and adjusting to new psychological practices that integrate the goals of psychologists and the rights of those they serve. Another dominant theme is the educational function served by psychologists in accurately communicating the nature and purpose of psychological procedures to those evaluated and to employers who rely on their results. The psychologist must respect the employer's proprietary rights while influencing personnel policies to ensure opportunities for ethical practice. Also, balancing the vested interests of employers, employees, and the profession extends beyond personnel decisions to their impact on the organization and the individuals affected by them.

This review clearly indicates that the times are changing. What was considered ethical several years ago is not necessarily considered ethical today. A growing concern for human rights has placed career decision-making procedures and associated psychological research and practices in the public domain. At one time organizations felt they had a right to hire, transfer, and fire whomever they wished for the good of the business, but recent union agreements and civil suits have markedly altered the situation. Just as more and more organizations are beginning to abide by and respect the need for equal employment opportunity (whether they are forced by regulatory agencies or not), so the emphasis on

freedom of information and individual privacy is awakening employees and employers to new concerns.

These changes have led to what may seem to be an ever growing morass of edicts, laws, and implicit values constituting ethical standards. Moreover, these standards are often ambiguous, contradictory, and far from intuitively obvious. Many researchers, practitioners, and administrators are wondering how to cope with this turbulent environment. If psychologists maintain a reactive stance and allow legislation and judicial rulings to define ethical practice, then the outlook is depressing. If psychologists creatively resolve ethical issues and deal with conflicting rights, however, then the outlook is challenging. We suggest the need for research on conditions leading to unethical conduct. Research is also needed on ways to enforce ethical principles, particularly when these principles are promulgated in the profession but not supported by legislation.

In general, personnel decisions should be closely monitored to be sure they are fair and conform to professional and legal standards as well as to the organization's own principles of ethical business practice. Admittedly this is difficult, since many personnel decisions are not well documented. It is essential, therefore, that the organization's policy on ethics be communicated and that decision makers take meaningful corrective action when such policies are violated.

Finally, we must recognize that today's ethical standards are frequently tomorrow's laws. Professional standards are often incorporated into laws and used as the basis for judicial rulings. When published professional standards are insufficient, Congress and the courts do not hesitate to impose their own. Consequently, psychologists must play active roles in lobbying and writing legislation. Recognizing that ethical prescriptions and legal requirements are intertwined and are likely to become more so should be impetus enough for adopting ethical personnel practices and conducting research that will influence legislation.

During the period following the passage of the Civil Rights Act of 1964 and the implementation of the Equal Employment Opportunity Guidelines (now called the Uniform Guidelines for Employee Selection Procedures), many industrial and organizational psychologists assumed that tests discriminated against members of minority groups. This assumption led many to accept research results uncritically. After operating for several years in this mode, some psychologists began to question that assumption. It eventually became apparent that it was more difficult than originally thought to demonstrate that tests were more valid for one group than another. Thus, the concept of "differential validity" was the subject of some debate.

Recently, Frank Schmidt and Jack Hunter have escalated the attack on the concept of differential validity by combining statistical logic with the analysis of hundreds of validity studies conducted in government and private sector settings. The result of this logic and analysis appears in this reading. The positions that Schmidt and Hunter take in this paper are the subject of a great deal of debate. As an example, the Lawyers Committee for Civil Rights Under the Law presented testimony to the House of Representatives (December 14, 1984) bitterly opposing the inferences that Schmidt and Hunter draw. The Lawyers' Committee suggests that fair employment will be set back irrevocably if validity is assumed. In essence, they argue that just as differential validity should not have been assumed in earlier practice, neither should nondifferential validity be assumed today. They argue that the question of validity should not be begged in either direction. Like the comparable worth debate, the issues raised by Schmidt and Hunter will remain current for many years to come.

■ READING 7 ■

Employment Testing
Old Theories and New Research Findings

Frank L. Schmidt, *U.S. Office of Personnel Management and George Washington University*
John E. Hunter, *Michigan State University*

This article contains two messages: a substantive message and a methodological message. The substantive message is this: (a) Professionally developed cognitive ability tests are valid predictors of performance on the job and in training for all jobs (Hunter, 1980; Schmidt, Hunter, & Pearlman, 1981) in all settings (Lilienthal & Pearlman, in press; Pearlman, Schmidt, & Hunter, 1980;

Source: *American Psychologist*, October 1981, pp. 1128–1136. Copyright 1981 by the American Psychological Association. Reprinted by permission of the publisher and author.

Schmidt, Gast-Rosenberg, & Hunter, 1980; Schmidt, Hunter, & Caplan, 1981; Schmidt, Hunter, Pearlman, & Shane, 1979; Sharf, Note 1; Timmreck. Note 2; Schmidt, Hunter, Pearlman, & Caplan, Note 3); (b) cognitive ability tests are equally valid for minority and majority applicants and are fair to minority applicants in that they do not underestimate the expected job performance of minority groups; and (c) the use of cognitive ability tests for selection in hiring can produce large labor cost savings, ranging from $18 million per year for small employers such as the Philadelphia police department (5,000 employees; Hunter,

Note 4) to $16 billion per year for large employers such as the federal government (4,000,000 employees; Hunter, Note 5).

The methodological message is this: In the last 10 years the field of personnel selection has undergone a transformation in viewpoint resulting from the introduction of improved methods of cumulating findings across studies. Use of these methods has shown that most of the "conflicting results" across studies were the result of sampling error that was not perceived by reviewers relying on statistical significance tests to evaluate single studies. Reviews in our field were also subject to systematic distortion because reviewers failed to take into account the systematic effects of error of measurement and restriction in range in the samples studied. The real meaning of 70 years of cumulative research on employment testing was not apparent until state-of-the-art meta-analytic procedures were applied. These methods not only cumulate results across studies but correct variance across studies for the effect of sampling error and correct both mean and variance for the distorting effects of systematic artifacts such as unreliability and restriction of range.

Tests have been used in making employment decisions in the United States for over 50 years. Although occasional use has been made of personality tests, and content-validated job knowledge and job sample tests have been used with some frequency, the most commonly used employment tests have been measures of cognitive skills—that is, aptitude or ability tests. Examples include tests of verbal and quantitative ability, perceptual speed, inductive and deductive reasoning, and spatial and mechanical ability. A great deal of new knowledge has accumulated over the last 10 years on the role of cognitive abilities in job performance and in the employment-selection process. In the middle and late 1960s certain theories about aptitude and ability tests formed the basis for most discussion of employee selection issues and, in part, the basis for practice in personnel psychology. At that time, none of these theories had been tested against empirical data. However, they were plausible at face value, and some were accepted by personnel psychologists as true or probably true. Two important events occurred during the 1970s: (a) new methods were developed for quantitatively integrating research findings across studies to provide strong tests of theories, and (b) these methods were used to cumulate the empirical research evidence needed to determine whether these theories were true or false. We now have this evidence, and it shows that the earlier theories were false.

THE THEORIES AND THE RESEARCH EVIDENCE

The Theory of Low Utility

The first theory holds that employee selection methods have little impact on the performance and productivity of the resultant workforce. From this theory, it follows that selection procedures can safely be manipulated to achieve other objectives, such as a racially representative workforce. The basic equation for determining the impact of selection on workforce productivity had been available for years (Brogden, 1949; Cronbach & Gleser, 1957), but it had not been employed because there were no feasible methods for estimating one critical equation parameter: the standard deviation of employee job performance in dollars (SDy). SDy indexes the magnitude of individual differences in employee yearly output of goods and services. The greater SDy is, the greater is the payoff in improved productivity from selecting high-performing employees.

During the 1970s, a method was devised for estimating SDy based on careful estimates by supervisors of employee output (Hunter & Schmidt, in press; Schmidt, Hunter, McKenzie, & Muldrow, 1979). Applications of this method showed that SDy was larger than expected. For example, for entry-level budget analysts and computer programmers, SDy was $11,327 and $10,413, respectively. This means that a computer programmer at the 85th percentile in performance is worth $20,800 more per year to the employing organization than a computer programmer at the 15th percentile. Use of valid selection tests substantially increases the average performance level of the resultant workforce and therefore substantially improves productivity. For example, use of the Programmer Aptitude Test in place of an invalid selection method to hire 618 entry-level computer programmers leads to an estimated productivity improvement of $54.7 million ($68 million in 1981 dollars) over a 10-year period if the top 30 percent of applicants are hired (Schmidt, Hunter, McKenzie, & Muldrow, 1979). Estimates have also been made of the impact of selection on national productivity. Based on extremely conservative assumptions, Hunter and Schmidt (in press) calculate that the gross national product would be increased by $80 to $100 billion per year if improved selection procedures were introduced throughout the economy.

These findings mean that selecting high performers is more important for organizational productivity than had been previously thought. Research has established that mental skills and abilities are important determinants of performance on the job. If tests measuring these abilities are dropped and replaced by the interview and other less valid procedures, the proportion of low-performing people hired increases, and the result is a serious decline in productivity in the individual firm and in the economy as a whole. The rate of growth in productivity in the United States has slowed markedly in recent years—from about 3.5 percent to zero or even negative rates. One possible reason for this decline is the decline in the accuracy with which employers sort people into jobs. In response to pressures from the federal government, American employers have substantially reduced the use of valid tests of job aptitudes in making hiring and placement decisions. Many companies have abandoned the use of such tests entirely. Over a period of 8–10 years, this change would manifest itself in lower productivity gains. Consider two examples. Seven or eight years ago, the General Electric Company (GE) responded to government pressure by dropping all tests of job aptitude and "getting their numbers right" in the hiring process. Like many firms, GE has a policy of promoting from within. About two

years ago, several plants realized that a large percentage of the people hired under the new selection standards were not promotable. GE had merely transferred the adverse impact from the hiring stage to the promotion stage. These plants have now resumed testing (Hawk, Note 6). Some years ago, U.S. Steel selected applicants into their skilled trades apprentice programs *from the top down* based on total score on a valid battery of cognitive aptitude tests. They then lowered their testing standards dramatically, requiring only minimum scores on the tests equal to about the seventh-grade level and relying heavily on seniority. Because their apprentice training center kept excellent records, they were able to show that (*a*) scores on mastery tests given during training declined markedly, (*b*) the flunk-out and drop-out rates increased dramatically, (*c*) average training time and training cost for those who *did* make it through the program increased substantially, and (*d*) average ratings of later performance on the job declined (Braithwaite, Note 7).

The theory that selection procedures are not important is sometimes presented in a more subtle form. In this form, the theory holds that all that is important is that the people hired be "qualified." This theory results in pressure on employers to set low minimum-qualification levels and then to hire on the basis of other factors from among those who meet these minimum levels. This is the system U.S. Steel adopted. In our experience, minimum levels on cognitive ability tests are typically set near the 15th percentile for applicants. Such "minimum competency" selection systems result in productivity losses 80 percent to 90 percent as great as complete abandonment of valid selection procedures (Mack, Schmidt, & Hunter, in press). For example, if an organization the size of the federal government (4,000,000 employees) were to move from ranking on valid tests to such a minimum competency selection system with the cutoff at the 20th percentile, yearly productivity gains from selection would be reduced from $15.6 billion to $2.5 billion (Hunter, Note 5), an increase in labor costs of $13.1 billion per year required to maintain the same level of output. In a smaller organization such as the Philadelphia police department, the loss would be $12 million per year, a drop from $18 million to $6 million (Hunter, Note 4).

The problem is that there is no real dividing line between the qualified and the unqualified. Employee productivity is on a *continuum* from very high to very low, and the relation between ability test scores and employee job performance and output is almost invariably linear (APA, 1980; Hunter & Schmidt, in press; Schmidt, Hunter, McKenzie, & Muldrow, 1979). Thus a reduction in minimum acceptable test scores at any point in the test-score range results in a reduction in the productivity of employees selected. A decline from superior to average performance may not be as visible as a decline from average to poor performance, but it can be just as costly in terms of lost productivity. The finding that test-score/job-performance relationships are linear means that ranking applicants on test scores and selecting from the top down maximizes the productivity of employees selected. This finding also means that any minimum test score requirement (test cutoff score) is arbitrary: No matter where it is set, a higher cutoff score will yield more productive employees, and a lower score will yield less productive employees. On the other hand, it means that if the test is valid, all cutoff scores are "valid" by definition. The concept of "validating" a cutoff score on a valid test is therefore not meaningful.

Most of the productivity loss in minimum competency selection systems comes from majority, not minority, group members. Minimum competency systems usually reduce standards for all applicants. Since most people hired are majority group members, the cumulative productivity loss from hiring less productive members of the majority group is much greater than the loss due to less productive minority workers.

The usual purpose of minimum competency systems is to eliminate discrepancies in minority and majority employment rates. However, despite the productivity losses, such systems typically merely reduce this discrepancy; they do not eliminate it. On the other hand, selection systems based on top-down hiring within each group completely eliminate "adverse impact" at a much smaller price in lowered productivity. Such systems typically yield 85 percent to 95 percent of the productivity gains attainable with optimal nonpreferential use of selection tests (Cronbach, Yalow, & Shaeffer, 1980; Hunter, Schmidt, & Rauschenberger, 1977; Mack et al., in press). However, such selection systems raise a host of legal, social, and moral questions (Lerner, 1977, 1979).

The Theory of Subgroup Validity Differences

This theory holds that because of cultural differences, cognitive tests have lower validity (test-criterion correlations) for minority than for majority groups. This theory takes two forms. The theory of single-group validity holds that tests may be valid for the majority but "invalid" (that is, have zero validity) for minorities. Although it was erroneous (Humphreys, 1973), the procedure adopted by psychologists to test for single-group validity involved testing black and white validity coefficients for significance separately by race. Since minority sample sizes were usually smaller than those for the majority, small-sample single-group validity studies produced a high frequency of white-significant, black-nonsignificant outcomes. Four different cumulative studies have now demonstrated that evidence for single-group validity by race does not occur any more frequently in samples than would be expected solely on the basis of chance (Boehm, 1977; Katzell & Dyer, 1977; O'Connor, Wexley, & Alexander, 1975; Schmidt, Berner, & Hunter, 1973).

The theory of differential validity holds that population validities are different for different groups, but are not necessarily zero for any group. This theory was tested by applying a statistical test of the difference between observed sample validities. Individual studies obtained varying results. More recent studies have cumulated findings across studies. The first such review was done by Ruch (Note 8), who found that differential validity occurred in samples at only chance levels of frequency. Two more recent reviews claim to have found somewhat higher frequencies: Boehm (1977) found a frequency of 8 percent and Katzell and Dyer (1977) reported frequencies in the 20–30 percent range. But is has been shown (Hunter & Schmidt, 1978) that the data preselection technique used in these studies results in a Type 1 bias—rejecting the hypothesis of no difference when it is true—which creates the false appearance of a higher incidence of differential validity. Two more recent studies that avoid this Type 1 bias have found differential validity to be at chance levels (Bartlett, Bobko, Mosier, & Hannan, 1978; Hunter, Schmidt, & Hunter, 1979). Bartlett et al. (1978) analyzed 1,190 pairs of validity coefficients for blacks and whites and found significant black-white differences in 6.8 percent of the pairs, using an alpha level of .05. Hunter et al. (1979) found the frequency of differential validity among the 712 pairs with a positive average validity to be 6 percent. Similar results have been obtained for Hispanic Americans (Schmidt, Pearlman, & Hunter, 1980). Thus the evidence taken as a whole indicates that employment tests are equally valid for all groups (Linn, 1978). The earlier belief in differential validity apparently resulted from excessive faith in individual small-sample studies in which significant difference occurred by chance.

The Theory of Test Unfairness

This theory holds that even if validity coefficients are equal for minority and majority groups, a test is likely to be unfair if the average test score is lower for minorities. There are numerous statistical models of test fairness, and these differ significantly in their properties (Cole, this issue; Jensen, 1980, chap. 10; Hunter & Schmidt, 1976; Hunter et al., 1977). However, the most commonly accepted model of test fairness is the regression model (Cleary & Hilton, 1968). This model defines a test as unfair to a minority group if it predicts lower levels of job performance than the group

in fact achieves. This is the concept of test fairness embedded in the Uniform Guidelines on Employee Selection Procedures (Equal Employment Opportunity Commission, Civil Service Commission, Department of Labor, & Department of Justice, 1978; Ledvinka, 1979). The theory of test unfairness is based on the assumption that the factors causing lower test scores do not also cause lower job performance. The accumulated evidence on this theory is clear: Lower test scores among minorities are accompanied by lower job performance, exactly as in the case of the majority (Bartlett et al., 1978; Campbell, Crooks, Mahoney, & Rock, 1973; Gael & Grant, 1972; Gael, Grant & Ritchie, 1975a, 1975b; Grant & Bray, 1970; Jensen 1980, chap. 10; Schmidt, Pearlman, & Hunter, 1980; Ruch, Note 8; Tenopyr, Note 9). This finding holds true whether ratings of job performance or objective job sample measures of performance are used. Tests predict job performance of a minority and the majority in the same way. The small departures from perfect fairness that exist actually favor minority groups.

These findings show that employment tests do not cause "adverse impact" against minorities. The cumulative research on test fairness shows that the average ability and cognitive skill differences between groups are directly reflected in job performance and thus are *real*. They are *not* created by the tests. We do not know what all the causes of these differences are, how long they will persist, or how best to eliminate them. For many other groups in the past, such differences have declined or disappeared over time. But at the present time, the differences exist and are reflected in job performance.

The Theory of Test Invalidity

This theory holds that cognitive employment tests are frequently invalid for all (majority and minority alike). This theory takes two forms. The first subtheory holds that test validity is situationally specific—a test valid for a job in one organization or setting may be invalid *for the same job* in another organization or setting. The conclusion is that a separate validity study is necessary in each setting. The second form of this theory holds that test validity is job specific—a cognitive test valid for one job may be invalid for another job. The conclusion is that a separate validity study is necessary for every job.

Subtheory 1: Is Validity Situationally Specific? The empirical basis for the subtheory of situational specificity was the considerable variability in observed validity coefficients from study to study even when jobs and tests appeared to be similar or identical (Ghiselli, 1966). The older explanation for this variation was that the factor structure of job performance is different from job to job and that the human observer or job analyst is too poor an information receiver and processor to detect these subtle but important differences. If so, empirical validation would be required in each situation, and validity generalization would be impossible (Albright, Glennon, & Smith, 1963; Ghiselli, 1966; Guion, 1965).

A new hypothesis was investigated during the 1970s. This hypothesis is that the variance in the outcomes of validity studies within job-test combinations is due to statistical artifacts. Schmidt, Hunter, and Urry (1976) showed that under typical and realistic validation conditions, a valid test will show a statistically significant validity in only about 50 percent of studies. As an example, they showed that if true validity for a given test is constant at .45 in a series of jobs, if criterion reliability is .70, if the prior selection ratio on the test is .60, and if sample size is 68 (the median over 406 published validity studies—Lent, Aurbach, & Levin, 1971b), then the test will be reported to be valid 54 percent of the time and invalid 46 percent of the time (two-tailed test, $p = .05$). This is the kind of variability that was the basis for the theory of situation-specific validity (Ghiselli, 1966; Lent, Aurbach, & Levin, 1971a).

If the variance in validity coefficients across situations for job-test combinations is due to statistical artifacts, then the theory of situational specificity is false, and validities are generalizable. We have developed a method for testing this hypothesis (Pearlman et al., 1980; Schmidt, Gast-Rosenberg, & Hunter, 1980; Schmidt & Hunter, 1977; Schmidt, Hunter, Pearlman, & Shane, 1979). One starts with a fairly large number of validity coefficients for a given test-job combination and computes the variance of this distribution. From this variance, one then subtracts variance due to various sources of error. There are at least seven sources of error variance: (a) sampling error (i.e., variance due to $N < \infty$); (b) differences between studies in criterion reliability; (c) differences between studies in test reliability; (d) differences between studies in range restriction; (e) differences between studies in amount and kind of criterion contamination and deficiency (Brogden & Taylor, 1950); (f) computational and typographical errors (Wolins, 1962); and (g) slight differences in factor structure between tests of a given type (e.g., arithmetic reasoning tests).

Using conventional statistical and measurement principles, Schmidt, Hunter, Pearlman, and Shane (1979) showed that the first four sources alone are capable of producing as much variation in validities as is typically observed from study to study. Results from application of the method to empirical data bear out this prediction. To date, distributions of validity coefficients have been examined for 152 test-job combinations (Lilienthal & Pearlman, in press; Pearlman et al., 1980; Schmidt, Gast-Rosenberg, & Hunter, 1980; Schmidt & Hunter, 1977; Schmidt, Hunter, & Caplan, 1981; Schmidt, Hunter, Pearlman, & Shane, 1979; Schmidt, Hunter, Pearlman, & Caplan, Note 3; Linn, Harnisch, & Dunbar, Note 10). The first four artifacts listed above accounted for an average of 72 percent of the observed variance of validity coefficients. About 85 percent of the variance in validities accounted for by artifacts is accounted for by simple sampling error. Corrections for sampling error alone lead to the same conclusions about validity generalizability as corrections for the first four artifacts (Pearlman et al., 1980; Schmidt, Gast-Rosenberg, & Hunter, 1980). Had it been possible to partial out variance due to all seven rather than to only four artifacts, all observed variance would probably have been accounted for.

These findings are quite robust. Callender and Osburn (1980) have derived alternative equations for testing validity generalizability and have shown that these produce identical conclusions and virtually identical numerical results. These findings effectively show the theory of situational specificity to be false. If one looks at the estimated distributions of operational (or true) validities (that is, validities corrected for the effects of criterion unreliability; cf. Schmidt, Gast-Rosenberg, & Hunter, 1980), one finds that in 84 percent of 152 test-job combinations, even the validity value at the 10th percentile is positive and substantial enough in magnitude to have practical value in improving workforce productivity. These findings show that cognitive test validities can typically be generalized with confidence across settings and organizations, and there is no factual basis for requiring a validity study in each situation.

Subtheory 2: Is Test Validity Job Specific? Job differences might moderate the validity of a given test in one of two ways. First, the test could be valid for all jobs but more valid for some jobs than for others. Second, the test could be valid for some jobs but invalid for others. The latter is the moderating effect postulated by the theory of job-specific validity. But sampling error and other artifacts can falsely cause a test to appear to be invalid. Just as sampling error can produce the appearance of inconsistency in the validity of a test for the same job in different settings, sampling error in validity coefficients can cause tests to appear to be valid for one job but invalid for another job.

The first large-sample tests of this hypothesis were recently completed. Based on an analysis of data from almost 370,000 clerical workers, Schmidt, Hunter, and Pearlman (1981) show that the validities of seven cognitive abilities were essentially constant across five different task-defined clerical job families.

All seven abilities were highly valid in all five job families. They next examined the validity patterns of five cognitive tests determined on a sample of 23,000 people in 35 highly heterogeneous jobs (for example, welders, cooks, clerks, administrators). Validities for each test varied reliably from job to job. But the variation was small, and *all tests were valid at substantial levels for all jobs.*

This finding has now been replicated and extended to the least complex, lowest-skill jobs. The U.S. Employment Service has conducted over 500 criterion-related validity studies on jobs that constitute a representative sample of jobs in the *Dictionary of Occupational Titles* (U.S. Department of Labor, 1977). In a cumulative analysis of these studies, Hunter (1980) showed that cognitive abilities are valid for all jobs and job groupings studied. When jobs were grouped according to complexity of information-processing requirements, the validity of a composite of verbal and quantitative abilities for predicting on-the-job performance varied from .56 for the highest-level job grouping to .23 for the lowest. These values were larger for measures of success in job training. Thus, even for the lowest-skill jobs, validity is still substantial. These studies disconfirm the hypothesis of job-specific test validity. There is no empirical basis for requiring separate validity studies for each job; tests can be validated at the level of job families. These cumulative analyses of existing studies show that the most frequently used cognitive ability tests are valid for all jobs and job families.

In conclusion, our evidence shows that the validity of the cognitive tests studied is neither specific to situations nor specific to jobs.

The Theory That Criteria of Success in Training Are Insufficient

This theory holds that a test valid for predicting success in training programs may be invalid for predicting performance on the job because training success may or may not be related to job performance. This theory was only recently subjected to a strong test. Earlier tests of the theory compared individual validity co-efficients computed on small sample sizes and were therefore methodologically unsound. As a result, the validity coefficients for different abilities for a given job were very unstable because of sampling error. For this reason, tests frequently appeared to be valid for training-success measures but not for job-performance measures, or vice versa. Further, validities for training-success measures showed only low correlations with validities for job-performance measures.

The problem of unstable validity estimates was overcome in a recent massive cumulative study based on a sample of almost 370,000. This study showed that all eight cognitive abilities examined were valid for both training and job-performance criteria. Further, even the relative degrees of validity were similar: The two sets of validities correlated .77 (Pearlman et al., 1980). These findings show that the cognitive tests valid for predicting performance in training programs are also valid for predicting later performance on the job. Further, the more valid the test is for predicting training success, the more valid it is apt to be as a predictor of later performance on the job. When employers select people who will do well in training programs, they are also selecting people who will do well later on the job (cf. Tenopyr, this issue).

CAN PAST MISTAKES BE CORRECTED?

All of the theories discussed above have been incorporated, implicitly or explicitly, in the federal Uniform Guidelines on Employee Selection Procedures (EEOC et al., 1978) and preceding guidelines. As a result, every one of these theories has been incorporated into EEO case law to one degree or another. Recent research findings show these theories to be false. Is it possible to eradicate these false theories from the field of EEO? We believe so, for two reasons. First, in court cases in which defendants have clearly presented and explained the empirical evidence showing that these theories are false, defendants have won. Judges can be

educated to the facts. The *Pegues* case is a good example. Second, the federal government is currently planning to revise and update the Guidelines to be consistent with current research knowledge and professional practice.

RELATION BETWEEN RESEARCH KNOWLEDGE AND SOCIAL POLICY CONSIDERATIONS

Not one of the advances in research knowledge summarized in this paper changes the fact of group differences in average levels of employment-related abilities. The differences in ability test scores mean that there is still a serious social problem. The research findings of the 1970s show that we can no longer entertain the belief that the problem is in the tests and that it can be solved by modifying or eliminating the tests. Instead, we must face the problem, which is that some groups of individuals are not acquiring the cognitive skills needed in a modern society to the same degree as others, and we must focus on ways of improving acquisition of those skills. For example, research in educational psychology has shown (not surprisingly) that a major educational determinant of student learning is *time on task* — the amount of time the student actually spends attempting to learn the material (cf. Berliner, 1979). However, it has also been found that minority students report spending *less* time on homework, on the average, than majority students (Sewell, Hauser, & Featherman, 1976; Wiley, 1973). The implications are obvious.

Social policy decisions about how best to attack this problem must be made. No options, including racial or ethnic quotas, need be ruled out in advance of open discussion. But the solution to the problem cannot begin until the problem is faced in an intellectually honest way. It is not intellectually honest, in the face of empirical evidence to the contrary, to postulate that the problem is biased and/or invalid employment tests. Empirical facts must be acknowledged. On the other hand, admitting that the problem is not in the tests does not mandate the conclusion that employment tests should be used in the manner that maximizes economic output. How (and whether) valid and fair tests should be used is a question of social policy (Haney, this issue; Novick, this issue; Tenopyr, this issue).

Even honestly faced, the problem is a complex one. Opposing goods must be carefully weighed; these include the trade-off between maximal economic productivity and living standards on one hand, and social goals such as proportional minority representation in the occupational structure on the other. Further, even after priorities are set, not all means are equally effective in attaining goals. For example, preferential selection systems, based on top-down hiring within each group and using valid tests, increase minority employment faster and at much less economic cost than random selection from among applicants who are above minimum qualifications levels.

STATE-OF-THE-ART META-ANALYSIS

In each empirical research area reviewed in this article, the same pattern of analysis of the literature prevailed across time. In the beginning, individual studies were interpreted as showing conflicting results. There were sporadic reports that tests valid for whites did not appear to be valid for blacks. There were sporadic reports that tests that had been shown earlier to be valid for a given job were found to be invalid for the same job in a new setting. Narrative reviews responded to this situation by arguing that there must be unknown variables causing the apparent situational specificity of findings (Schmidt & Hunter, 1978). However, use of correct methods of cumulating results across studies showed these conflicting findings to be the result of sampling error. That is, these sporadic findings were flukes resulting from the small samples forced on investigators by the limitations of field studies. The use of significance tests within individual studies only clouded discussion in the review studies because narrative reviewers falsely believed that significance tests

could be relied on to give correct decisions about single studies. Sampling error can never be detected or corrected in single studies. The only answer to the detection of sampling error is a cumulative analysis of results across studies in which the variance of results across studies is corrected for sampling error (Hunter & Schmidt, Note 11).

In similar fashion, narrative reviews tended to make systematic errors in the interpretation of quantitative results because reviewers did not correct outcome measures for either error of measurement or restriction in range. The estimate of the validity coefficient in employment studies is erroneous if it is not corrected for error of measurement of job performance. (For theoretical purposes, correlations should be corrected for unreliability in the predictor variable [i.e., ability] as well.) Furthermore, there is typically considerable restriction in range resulting from the necessity of basing studies on incumbent populations instead of on applicant populations, and failure to correct for this artifact results in (often severe) underestimation of validities. Thus, state-of-the-art procedures of meta-analysis must correct for systematic distortions such as unreliability and restriction in range as well as the unsystematic effects of sampling error.

We share with Glass (1976) the belief that narrative reviews have been disastrous for the attainment of cumulative knowledge in all areas of psychology. We strongly urge the use of meta-analysis, the quantitative cumulation of results across studies. Glass has advanced one method of meta-analysis. Concurrent to Glass's work, we and our associates developed a related quantitative meta-analysis procedure. Our procedure can be regarded as an extension of Glass's method designed to deal with the distorting effects of artifacts such as sampling error, measurement unreliability, and range restriction while integrating findings across studies (Pearlman et al., 1980; Schmidt & Hunter, 1977; Schmidt, Hunter, Pearlman, & Shane, 1979). Originally developed to integrate employment test validities across studies, this procedure has since been generalized for application to other research areas (Hunter

& Schmidt, Note 11; Hunter, Schmidt, & Jackson, Note 12).

At one time in the history of psychology and the social sciences, the pressing need was for more empirical studies to examine a problem. But now large numbers of research studies have been carried out on many research questions. The need today is increasingly becoming, not one for additional empirical data, but one for some means of making sense of the vast amounts of data that have accumulated. Unless we can do this, there is little hope of producing the cumulative, generalizable knowledge essential for theory development. Meta-analysis provides a solution to this problem. Furthermore, the need for meta-analysis goes beyond the theoretical aspirations of science. It is crucial to the solution of social problems as well. The continuing inability to produce cumulative knowledge and general principles may now be leading to widespread disillusionment with psychological research and consequent reductions in research funding by governmental and other bodies ("Cuts Raise New Social-Science Query," 1981).

How can a funding agency continue to support research in an area where researchers maintain that further studies are needed on an issue for which hundreds of studies already exist? Since most of the "conflicting results" are actually due to sampling error, it is incumbent on us to put our house in order.

Alternatives to Traditional Testing

The history of employment testing is saturated with discussions of traditional paper-and-pencil tests. As a result of the unfulfilled promise of paper-and-pencil tests and the common observation that minority group members did poorly on these tests, the last decade has seen increased interest in nontraditional measurement devices to aid in hiring and promotion decisions. In addition to the limitations of paper-and-pencil tests, it is obvious that many jobs require skills and abilities that are not easily measured by this method of testing. In this section, readings will be presented that consider some of these nontraditional devices.

Most of us have had the experience of realizing that we were not well suited for a particular activity. That activity might have been a class or a job or a leisure activity. If we were lucky, we came to this realization before we had invested our time in the activity. If less fortunate, we did not realize that there was a mismatch until after we had become involved in the activity. The difference between realizing before or after becoming involved invariably reduces to a matter of information exchange. Had we known some critical pieces of information, we would have certainly avoided the activity completely, or dropped out of it sooner.

Recently, a concept known as a realistic job preview (RJP) has been introduced as a method of employee selection. The purpose of an RJP is to provide the job applicant with sufficient information to voluntarily exit the selection loop rather than take a job for which he or she is ill-suited. In this reading, Dean and Wanous describe how the technique was used in hiring bank tellers and what the results of the process were.

■ READING 8 ■

Effects of Realistic Job Previews on Hiring Bank Tellers

Roger A. Dean, *Washington and Lee University*
John P. Wanous, *The Ohio State University*

There is a growing body of field experiments assessing the effects of realistic job previews (RJPs) on newcomers to organizations (Wanous, 1980). A recent review calculated that the turnover rates for realistic job previews versus other previews (or no preview) are 19.8 percent versus 25.5 percent, a 5.7 percentage point difference (Reilly, Brown, Blood, & Malatesta, 1981). This was based on 11 field studies of over 4,500 participants in a variety of organizations (military, service, educational, and manufacturing). In practical terms this difference in turnover rates seems to suggest that an organization *not* using an RJP will have 28.8 percent higher turnover on the average (i.e., $5.7 \div 19.8 = .288$).

The average difference may be misleading, because there is considerable variance among

studies. This has led some to suggest that more attention should be paid to the design of the RJP itself by considering it as a special case of "persuasive communication" (Popovich & Wanous, 1982). Thus, increased attention should be paid to such factors as the source of an RJP, the message content, the medium used, and the characteristics of the audience (job candidates). Practically speaking, however, it is extremely difficult to examine all four of these persuasive factors in a field experiment.

One theoretical concern of this study was to assess the effects of different types of message content on job performance. Although previous RJP research found no effect on performance (Wanous, 1980), it has been hypothesized that a specific, not general, RJP might affect job performance by increasing initial role clarity (Wanous, 1978).

A second theoretical issue concerns the psychological mechanisms that have been hypothesized to explain the effects of RJPs on

Source: *Journal of Applied Psychology*, 69, no. 1 (1984), pp. 61–68. Copyright 1984 by the American Psychological Association. Reprinted by permission of the publisher and author.

turnover. Those currently offered are: (*a*) an expectation vaccination effect, (*b*) a self-selection effect, (*c*) a gratitude-for-being-honest effect, and (*d*) a role-clarifying effect (see Wanous, 1980, for a review). The latter three "effects" are probably contingent on the RJP first "vaccinating" expectations (see McGuire, 1964). Without expectation vaccination, it is difficult to imagine how the other purported effects could occur. This is because the message of an RJP must first be received and comprehended (i.e., expectations vaccinated) by job candidates if they are to (*a*) self-select a job, (*b*) feel grateful, or (*c*) have initial role clarity (see Wanous, 1980, p.43). To test this, two RJPs were designed. One contained mostly general statements about the job and organization, whereas the other contained both general and specific statements. If the Wanous (1978) hypothesis is correct, the general preview should reduce turnover, whereas the specific preview should reduce turnover *and* increase performance.

From a practical perspective several issues were important. First and foremost the bank wanted the RJP to reduce turnover, resulting in cost savings. This was crucial because the year prior to this study the bank hired 600 tellers to maintain a workforce of 1,400, resulting in a $1,680,000 cost, based on a replacement cost estimate (see Discussion) of $2,800 per teller. Second, the bank was interested in any other beneficial effects that RJPs might have, such as increased commitment, decreased thoughts of quitting, reduced absenteeism and tardiness, or possibly increased job performance.

METHOD

Research Site and Subjects

This experiment was conducted in a large bank employing about 1,400 tellers. Participants were candidates for the teller job who had not previously worked as a teller and had not previously worked at this particular bank. Excluding job candidates who had previous experience is important because the RJP is only designed for those without extensive job/organizational knowledge. Including experienced job candidates would contaminate the results. A total of 249 teller candidates were randomly assigned into a job preview group, were hired, and began training.

Design of the Experiment

Three types of job preview groups were compared, (*a*) an RJP booklet containing both specific and general information, (*b*) an RJP booklet containing mostly general information, and (*c*) a "no-preview" condition. A particular job preview condition was randomly chosen for each hiring period of three to four weeks, during which a "training class" was completed (about 15 to 20 persons). Thus, all those in a training class received the same preview in order to prevent contamination of results by having tellers who received different job previews. A total of 16 training groups were included for study: (*a*) four specific RJP groups ($n = 63$), (*b*) five general RJP groups ($n = 91$), and (*c*) seven no-preview groups ($n = 95$).

Due to severely depressed economic conditions that caused low hiring rates, it took about 16 months to obtain the present sample. Follow-up data on turnover were monitored for the first 43 weeks of employment for all tellers. This extended the data gathering period another 10 months.

The RJPs were given to teller applicants after they had completed a job application form and were judged to be potentially qualified by an interviewer. All of these initial "screening" interviews were conducted at the main office of the bank, even for those who had initially applied at a branch office. If a candidate passed this interview, assignment was made to one of the three job preview groups. Those receiving an RJP were told to read the booklet and return for testing at a later time. The no preview persons were simply told to return for testing at a later time. All job candidates returned for testing. Thus, there was no self-selection at this point. In fact, virtually all were given job offers, except for two candidates. Job offer acceptance rates were virtually identical across groups, ranging from 69.0 percent to 71.6 percent. Again, there were no differences in self-selection.

The first day of employment was devoted to orientation and completion of the first of two research questionnaires. The second questionnaire was mailed to tellers who were still with the bank after eight weeks (three weeks of training plus five weeks of job experience).

Measures

To test the effects of previews on initial expectations, the Job Descriptive Index (JDI; Smith, Kendall, & Hulin, 1969) was used in an "expectations" format for the first day questionnaire, and its traditional "descriptive" format at eight weeks. The alpha reliabilities for the JDI expectations and descriptions formats, respectively, are as follows: Work (.63, .69), Pay (.65, .78), Supervision (.66, .79), Coworkers (.80, .78), and Promotions (.80, .84). Because this is a service organization, a sixth JDI-type scale called Customers was developed. It had 12 adjectives (annoying, friendly, easy to work with, unreasonable, rude, grateful, discourteous, tough to please, helpful, pleasant, impatient, and expecting too much). The internal consistency (alpha) of this scale was .81 for expectations and .79 for descriptions.

Other attitude scales included in both questionnaires were the following: (a) the Organizational Commitment Questionnaire (OCQ, alpha = .74) developed by Porter, Steers, Mowday, and Boulian (1974), (b) a three-item scale measuring one's desire to remain employed at the bank (alpha = .87). (c) a three-item scale measuring one's perception of the bank's honesty and concern for newcomers (alpha = .64).

Branch managers were mailed a questionnaire at the same time the eight-week survey was conducted. Managers supplied information to calculate the quality of job performance (number of days without errors ÷ number of days scheduled). This was *not* a "supervisory rating," rather it was an actual counting taken from bank records, thus its reliability is probably close to perfect. It is an important measure, since the bank gives it high weight in performance appraisals.

Design of the RJPs

To ensure that job candidates were given complete, relevant, and unbiased information, three different sources of data were used. First, several groups of tellers ($n = 100$, approximately) of varying tenure were interviewed. The purpose was to gain informal knowledge about the teller job, so that a subsequent questionnaire could have at least part of it written in the "language" of those in this particular organization (i.e., an "empathic" questionnaire, Alderfer & Brown, 1972). As a result of these interviews, three issues/concerns were uncovered—(a) how to get a pay raise, (b) how to receive a promotion, and (c) how to move into branch management. The interviewees were asked to supply their own ideas of how these might occur, and bank managers were asked the same three questions. After identifying all the conceivable "theories" (or instrumentalities) about how to obtain these three results, questionnaire items for each were constructed. These three scales became the "empathic" part of a diagnostic questionnaire administered in the bank prior to the RJP experiment. The data from the diagnostic questionnaire were used as one basis for designing the RJP.

The other part of the diagnostic questionnaire was the Job Diagnostic Survey (Hackman & Oldham, 1980). The primary strategy for analyzing these diagnostic survey data ($n = 850$) was to search for inflated newcomer expectations. The means of JDS data were assessed for differing tenure groups, but few differences emerged on the job characteristics scales. Only receiving "feedback from agents" (customers) was significantly inflated for newcomers. A number of satisfaction items, however, declined with tenure, for example, general satisfaction, growth need satisfaction, and satisfaction with pay and supervision (Dean,

1981), as has been found previously (Wanous, 1980).

The results concerning how to obtain a pay raise, to get a promotion, or become a manager were also compared across groups of differing tenure. Comparing the means of these path-goal scales is relatively meaningless, because not all paths to the goal are feasible—or compatible. For example, someone endorsing the item "do nothing, because promotions are based on seniority" is unlikely to also endorse an item such as "work well because good performance is usually rewarded." (This particular aspect of these three scales made calculating an internal consistency reliability coefficient useless, too.)

Instead of assessing the means of these three scales, the correctness of a teller's perception was calculated as follows. Two senior managers from each of three departments (employment, training and development, and operations) were asked to complete these three scales by answering with their view of actual bank practice (not "official policy"). After they had done this individually, they were assembled for a group meeting to resolve their differences, and come to a consensus on the "correct" answer.

The senior managers' consensus of the correct answer was subtracted (absolute value) from each teller's answers. This yielded a "coefficient of correctness" where zero meant "perfectly correct." A teller's coefficient of correctness for each scale was then correlated with length of organizational tenure. Negative correlations indicate increasing accuracy (lower scores) with increasing tenure: $r = -.14$ ($p < .001$) for pay raises, $r = .05$ (ns) for promotions, and $r = -.21$ ($p < .001$) for moving into management. Thus, statements about pay raises and career opportunities were included in the RJP booklets.

Several personnel executives (head of personnel research and the senior vice president of personnel) also provided information. Thus, the information pool from which to construct the RJPs included first-hand knowledge of the job from observation by the researchers, interviews with tellers, questionnaire responses, and the executives' inputs. Combining this information was done by the researchers and then checked with several managers at the bank. No rigid decision rules were used to form the RJPs, but validity was protected by using multiple data sources and having several

TABLE 1 Comparison of Realistic Job-Preview (RJP) Booklets

Topic	Specific RJP	General RJP
Training	Training described. Final exam at the end of training mentioned. Failure rate during training reported.	No mention of training content nor of failure rate.
Work	Banking transactions described. Accuracy important and it is checked daily. Working under pressure, e.g., Mondays and Fridays. Manager schedules work one week in advance. Working on your feet. Working may become routine and repetitive.	Banking transactions described.
Customers	Courtesy is always required. Rude customers encountered.	Courtesy is always required.
Career opportunities	Promotion criteria specified. Average promotion rates for each job given. How to move into branch management. (college degree needed)	The various teller positions described.
Compensation	Pay rates specified. Employee benefits described. How pay increases are determined.	Pay rates specified. Employee benefits described.
Summary of major points	Summary included—one-half page long, titled "It's not for everyone."	No summary included.

sources double-check the final previews. Table 1 highlights the differences (see Dean, 1981, for complete details).

RESULTS

Effects on Initial Expectations

Table 2 shows the results of job preview effects on Day 1 expectations. However, before discussing the results for the six scales shown in Table 2, it is important to explain what is meant by "predicted results" and how they were determined. For three of the six scales the specific RJP group should have the lowest expectations, and there should be "no differences" among groups in the remaining three scales. This prediction is based on an assessment that the two preview booklets described Work, Promotions, and Customers differently. Thus, if job candidates read and comprehended the booklets, their expectations should be lower on these three scales—a direct reflection of the differences in booklet content. In contrast, the booklets were judged sufficiently similar (both said the same thing, or both said nothing) on the other three scales. Thus, the prediction is that no differences will be found for Pay, Supervision, and Co-workers. The complexity of specifying which scales should, or should not, show differences

occurs because the RJPs were specific to this job, whereas the JDI is a general instrument.

To substantiate the researchers' content analysis, a sample of 50 college students from an introductory organizational behavior class was asked to read both booklets. Students formed triads to discuss the similarities and differences between the booklets. They were asked to consider each item of the JDI scales and judge whether it would likely be answered similarly or differently—and the direction of the difference. The mean number of items judged to be answered lower in the specific RJP was as follows: (a) Work (18 items) = 6.8; (b) Pay (9 items) = 1.1; (c) Promotions (9 items) = 5.3; (d) Co-Workers (18 items) = .2; (e) Supervision (18 items) = 2.4; (f) Customers (12 items) = 8.4.

The only direct comparison that could be made was between the two RJP booklets, because their content was known. Making predictions about differences between either of the two RJPs and the no-preview group is much more difficult. However, much previous research on the initial expectations of newcomers (Bray, Campbell, & Grant, 1974; Dunnette, Arvey, & Banas, 1973; Hoiberg & Berry, 1978; Wanous, 1976) strongly suggests the expectations of no-preview tellers will be inflated relative to those created by the specific preview. Whether it is reasonable to expect differences between the general-preview

TABLE 2 Effects of Job Previews on Initial Expectations

Type of Initial Expectation	Job-Preview Group						Overall F Among Groups	Comparisons among Preview Groups			
	Specific (N=57–59)		General (N=73–76)		No Booklet N=55–64)			Predicted Differences Among Groups	Specific versus General	Specific versus No Booklet	General versus No Booklet
	M	SD	M	SD	M	SD					
Work itself	35.36	6.68	39.11	6.95	38.46	5.93	3.04	Specific group lowest	Specific lower*	Specific lower†	No difference
Pay	17.89	4.69	18.47	4.89	19.56	4.01	1.92	No difference	No difference	Specific lower†	No difference
Promotions	19.14	6.56	21.20	5.54	20.81	4.90	2.37†	Specific group lowest	Specific lower*	Specific lower†	No difference
Supervision	43.05	4.93	43.46	5.24	41.25	6.65	2.85†	No difference	No difference	Specific higher†	General higher*
Co-workers	47.34	5.82	48.64	6.44	46.40	8.09	1.85‡	No difference	No difference	No difference	General higher†
Customers	19.76	7.74	23.24	8.54	22.41	8.05	3.17*	Specific group lowest	Specific lower*	Specific lower†	No difference

Note: The sample sizes are reported as ranges, due to missing questionnaire data.
*p<.05. †p<.05<.10. ‡ ns.

group and the no-preview group is questionable. This is because the greatest specificity (and therefore the most negative information) was incorporated into the specific RJP.

Turning back to the results shown in Table 2, it can be seen that all six of the predicted differences between specific and general groups are supported. Omega-squared coefficients (Hays, 1963) were calculated for the three significant differences. They were as follows: Work (.042), Promotions (.032), and Customers (.043). Although these are not large, they do represent significant differences. It also must be remembered that all six predictions were confirmed when specific and general preview groups are compared, that is, the three nonsignificant differences were as predicted. Comparing the specific RJP and the no-preview groups shows a similar but weaker pattern. The final column in Table 2 shows that relatively few significant differences were found between the general and no-preview groups.

Effects on Job Attitudes

No significant differences were found among the three groups at either Day 1 or eight weeks on the OCQ scale means. When tellers were asked their interest in remaining at the bank at eight weeks, the specific RJP group had the lowest interest ($p < .05$), opposite of predictions. When tellers were asked for their perceptions of the bank's honesty and concern for them, the specific RJP group was significantly ($p < .05$) lower than the other two groups, at both Day 1 and eight weeks, again the opposite from what would be expected.

Effects on Job Survival and Job Performance

Table 3 shows the job-survival rates for three separate time periods, which were selected because they represent organizationally relevant stages of assimilation into the bank. The first three weeks are always devoted to formal, off-the-job training. Following training the new teller begins work in a branch but typically does not attain a level of job proficiency "up-to-standard" until about 20 weeks of on-the-job experience (see Discussion), that is, Week Number 23. Therefore, the 20-week period after training has been labeled "competence acquisition." In order to have an equal time period for comparison purposes, the second 20-week period after training is examined separately and called "performing at standard."

There were no overall differences among the three job-preview groups in job survival rates, contrary to what was predicted. When each time period is assessed separately, significantly *more* tellers survive during training who were in the no preview group. Because of the small differences between the two RJP groups, they

TABLE 3 Job Survival Rates for Specific Time Periods

| Time Period | Preview Booklet | | | | Preview Groups Combined (n = 154) | | No Preview (n = 95) | | Significance Tests (All Three Groups) | Significance Tests (Preview vs. No Preview) |
| | Specific (n = 63) | | General (n = 91) | | | | | | | |
	No.	%	No.	%	No.	%	No.	%		
Training period (Weeks 0–3)	48/63	76.2	71/91	78.0	119/154	77.3	85/95	89.5	$x^2(2, N = 249) = 6.03$, $p < .05$	$x^2(1; N = 249) = 5.95$, $p < .05$.
Competence acquisition (Weeks 4–23)	39/48	81.3	62/71	87.3	101/119	84.9	68/85	80.0	ns	ns
Performing at standard (weeks 24–43)	34/39	87.2	50/62	80.6	84/101	83.2	59/68	86.6	ns	ns
Overall job survival (first 43 weeks)	34/63	54.0	50/91	54.9	84/154	54.5	59/95	62.1	ns	ns

were combined, and the results are shown in a separate column of Table 3. Realistic job previews appear to increase the *rate* of *early* turnover but have no impact on overall job survival. Because it took 16 months to gather these data and because unemployment rose steadily, the date of hiring could affect the turnover results. This could occur because those hired later in the period might be less likely to leave. To check for this possibility, the month someone was hired (1 to 16) was correlated with the length of job tenure (in weeks, up to a maximum of 43). The correlation was .03 (*ns*), thus the effect of increasing unemployment was *not* confounding these results.

To test the hypothesis that the specific RJP might increase job performance, the performance quality index was compared at eight weeks (specific RJP $M = 96$ percent, $SD = 7.4$ percent; general RJP $M = 96.6$ percent; $SD = 4.9$ percent; no preview $M = 94.1$ percent, $SD = 8.1$ percent). These differences were not significant, thus no support was found for the hypothesis.

Effects on the Rate of Leaving

Table 4 shows an analysis of only the tellers ($N = 106$) who left during the first 43 weeks after entry. Because of the small differences between the two RJP groups, they were again combined in a separate column. If a person received an RJP and ultimately left the organization, they were more likely to do so during training. Conversely, those in the no-preview group (who ultimately left the bank) were more likely to do so during the first 20 weeks on the job. There were no differences in turnover rates among groups during the second 20 weeks of employment on the job.

DISCUSSION

The results here provide only mixed support for current conceptions of the RJP. The strongest finding was that the specific RJP clearly "vaccinated" (lowered) expectations as intended. Because the RJP information was se-

lectively received, this should be reassuring to practitioners.

The vaccination effect found here was quite durable. This is because a new training class only began about once every month. Thus, several days—or even weeks—might occur between the RJP and the Day 1 questionnaire. Using booklets does allow a job candidate to take the RJP home and provides the opportunity to reread the material. Another possible explanation of this durability is that a printed medium is typically superior to audiovisual methods when the content of a message is complex (Chaiken & Eagly, 1976).

In contrast to the strong support for expectation vaccination, other results found here show little or no support for the predictions made. The RJP did not appear to have any positive effect on job survival, performance, or other job attitudes. This raises the legitimate question of whether current conceptions of the RJP should be revised in light of these data or whether other factors can explain the pattern of results found here.

There are probably two reasons for the continued inability of RJPs to affect performance. First, the RJP may not have contained sufficient information about how to do one's job successfully and may have focused too heavily on how to "get ahead" in the bank. Even if the specific RJP were to be redesigned, a second consideration is even more serious. The effect of three weeks' training will always "overwhelm" any possible effects due to reading an RJP booklet. The amount of incremental job performance information in a booklet must be extremely small in comparison to that obtained through training. Because this is likely to be a serious problem for almost any organization having a training program, researchers should not expect RJPs to affect job performance, no matter how well they might be designed.

Perhaps the most unusual findings of this study concern turnover rates. Leavers from the combined specific and general RJP groups left at an accelerated rate, that is, during training compared to those in the no preview group. No preview leavers, however, departed faster

TABLE 4   Rates of Leaving the Organization for "Leavers" Only

| Time Period | Preview Booklet | | | | Preview Groups Combined (n = 70) | | No Preview (n = 36) | | Significance Tests (All Three Groups) | Significance Tests (Preview vs. No Preview) |
| | Specific (n = 29) | | General (n = 41) | | | | | | | |
	No.	%	No.	%	No.	%	No.	%		
Training period (Weeks 0–3)	15/29	51.7	20/41	48.8	35/70	50.0	10/36	27.8	$x^2(2, N = 106) = 4.91$, $.05 < p < .10$.	$x^2(1, N = 106) = 4.85$, $p < .05$.
Competence acquisition (Weeks 4–23)	9/29	31.0	9/41	22.0	18/70	25.7	17/36	47.2	$x^2(2; N = 106) = 5.57$, $.05 < p < .10$.	$x^2(1, N = 106) = 4.95$, $p < .05$.
Performing at standard (Weeks 24–43)	5/29	17.2	12/41	29.3	17/70	24.3	9/36	25.0	ns	ns

during the first 20 weeks after training, during the acquisition-of-job-competence period. Since this appears to be the first time this has occurred in RJP experimentation, it deserves discussion.[1]

A tempting explanation of the differences in turnover rates among the leavers is that a delayed "self-selection effect" took place. No self-selection had taken place prior to the beginning of training, no doubt a reflection of the severely depressed local economic conditions. Thus it is possible that skeptical newcomers in the RJP groups only needed the additional experience and information obtained during training to conclude that it was time to leave. In contrast, the no preview recruits may have needed the additional experience after training to confirm skeptical feelings that were first aroused during training. Although this is a reasonable explanation, there is no direct evidence supporting it, for example, exit interviews with the early leavers.

From the bank's perspective the rate of turnover does have important cost implications, because "early" turnover generally costs less than late turnover. Based on two different internal audits of bank teller replacement costs, the following were estimated: hiring, $150; orientation, $50; off-the-job training, $1500;

on-the-job training, $250; and lost production until a teller "makes standard," $850. Standard is reached after 20 weeks on the job, or at the end of 23 weeks when training is included. Replacement costs total to $2800 for a teller who leaves after 23 weeks. Thus, those who leave earlier do not cost the full $2800. In fact, those who leave during training cost about $950 ($150 for hiring, $50 for orientation, and about $750 for training). Training costs were estimated at $750, because some tellers left earlier than others during the three-week period. If a teller left between Weeks 4 to 23, the replacement cost is higher, because the full training cost is lost ($1500 rather than $750), the OJT cost of $250 is incurred, and about half of the lost production cost ($850/2 = $425) is added. Thus, a teller leaving during Weeks 4 to 23 costs $1425 more than one during training, for a total of $2375.

Extreme caution should be exercised in using these cost estimates, however. First, the two internal audits disagreed in several important aspects, for example, how long it takes to reach standard. Second, costs are figured on a per person basis, but this average cost is dramatically affected by the number of tellers processed in a given year. Because of fixed costs, the average cost usually goes down when more tellers are hired. (This was one reason the two audits differed.) Third, the turnover rates found during this study were certainly affected by the local economic depression, so they may not be generally representative. Considering

---

[1] We say "appears" because previous RJP experiments have not always assessed attrition for multiple time periods. Those that have, however, have not reported this type of result.

these three cautions, perhaps the most conservative conclusion is that early turnover costs less—up to the point when a teller "reaches standard." So, although the RJPs had no effect on overall job survival, they probably saved the bank some replacement costs.

Overall job survival was unaffected for three reasons. First, annual hiring dropped from 600 to 300 during the two years of this research. This, in effect, curtailed the variance in turnover, making it more difficult to detect differences between groups due to a job preview. Second, this particular type of low-level job may not be amenable to an RJP. Reilly et al. (1981) found RJPs were more effective for complex jobs. Perhaps the RJP cannot add much new information to a low-complexity job because there is little that can be added. Finally, RJPs may only be able to add small amounts of information to service jobs with high "visibility," like being a bank teller.

The interview is one of the most widely used non-paper-and-pencil test techniques for hiring and promotion. Many of the literally thousands of studies of the employment interview show that the reliability and validity of these interviews are questionable. Latham and Saari suggest a new method of interviewing called the situational interview and demonstrate both its reliability and its validity. The new technique seems to draw its strength from the fact that it begins with a job analysis. This is in stark contrast to many interviews that seem to have little or nothing to do with the job in question. This article provides an excellent description of how the employment interview can be structured around relevant applicant experiences.

■ READING 9 ■

The Situational Interview

Gary P. Latham and Lise M. Saari, *University of Washington*
Elliott D. Pursell and Michael A. Campion,
Weyerhaeuser Company, New Bern, North Carolina

The interview is used as a selection device by virtually every company in the United States. In fact, *The Wall Street Journal* (Lancaster, 1975) reported that a majority of companies have phased out pencil-and-paper tests and rely solely on the interview for making hiring decisions.

The widespread use of the interview in favor of tests has occurred despite the fact that the interview is considered as much a test by government agencies as is a standardized test of intelligence or any other decision-making process that affects an individual's employment status in an organization. Nevertheless, companies appear to believe that the probability of being investigated by a government agency for wrongdoing in the areas of selection, promotion, layoff, and termination is reduced if only the interview is used as the decision-making instrument. What makes the reliance on the interview for making selection decisions alarming is that the interview often lacks relia-

bility and validity (Mayfield, 1964; Ulrich & Trumbo, 1965; Wagner, 1949).

One reason why the interview often lacks reliability is that interviewers seldom ask the same questions of different applicants. Moreover, when the same questions are asked, interviewers frequently disagree on the desirability or appropriateness of the interviewee's responses. Lack of reliability is a serious problem in that it can attenuate validity (Thorndike, 1949).

A theoretical approach on which valid interviews might be based is Locke's (1968) theory of goal setting. The underlying assumption of this theory is that intentions are related to behavior. If what people say correlates highly with what they do, the advantage of using the interview for making selection decisions is obvious. The interview would approximate a sample of actual job behavior, and the need for expensive written aptitude tests would be reduced, as would the cost of developing job simulation exercises (e.g., in-baskets). However, a potential problem with the interview that is generally not a concern with aptitude tests or job simulations is the social desirability response or faking. Many interviewees can

Source: *Journal of Applied Psychology*, 65, 1980, pp. 422–427. Copyright 1980 by the American Psychological Association. Reprinted by permission of the publisher and author.

quickly discern from the wording of a question the answer the interviewer wants to hear.

In an attempt to overcome some of these issues, Maas (1965) developed an interview procedure based on Smith and Kendall's (1963) recommendations for developing behavioral expectation scales. In brief, Maas's procedure involved having interviewers who were familiar with the job in question brainstorm traits that should be exhibited by effective job incumbents. Examples of on-the-job behaviors were then written by the interviewers to illustrate a high, average, and low degree of each trait. A second group of judges, unaware of which examples were written for a given trait or level (high, average, or low) reallocated the examples into traits and levels. Only examples with high agreement as to trait and level were retained. The anchors or illustrations for each level were then reworded as "expectations."

Interviewers subsequently rated each job candidate on each trait by making analogies from the candidate's interview responses to the behavioral anchors on the appraisal instrument. In a study of college orientation counselors, the interobserver reliability was .58. In a second study the interobserver reliability was .69. These coefficients were significantly higher than those that were obtained using rating scales benchmarked with adjectives (e.g., very good).

There are several limitations to Maas's study. First, the criterion-related validity of the procedure is not known. Second, the emphasis in the interview was on traits. It is doubtful whether such an interview would satisfy requirements for content validity. Moreover, the brainstorming of traits may leave much to be desired from the standpoint of a systematic job analysis. Third, the manner in which the questions for assessing each trait were formulated was not reported. Fourth, despite the reallocation procedure, the interobserver coefficients obtained from the interviewers were not high by conventional standards for evaluating a test. This may not be surprising in light of the approach used for the job analysis and the emphasis that was put on traits. Moreover, it is questionable whether the anchored examples should have been worded in

terms of expected on-the-job behavior rather than actual interviewee behavior indicative of subsequent job behavior. Finally, the interviewers were college students interviewing applicants for a college job. Thus, the generalizability of the results to industrial organizations is not known.

The present research differs from that reported by Maas in that we were concerned with the validity as well as the reliability of our interview technique. In addition, a systematic *job analysis* was used to develop the performance appraisal instrument as well as the selection interview. With regard to the latter, the job analysis information was used to develop the actual interview questions rather than to benchmark the answers. Job experts benchmarked answers for scoring an interviewee's responses in terms of comments that they had heard in interviews that they believed identified employees who subsequently became poor, average, or excellent performers on the job. Studies 1 and 2 report the results of two concurrent validity studies that were conducted in an industrial setting in the northwestern United States for both an entry-level job and a first-line supervisory position. Study 3 reports the results of a predictive validity study for entry-level workers in a company in the rural South.

STUDIES 1 AND 2

Method

Sample. Study 1 was conducted on unionized hourly sawmill workers. Forty-nine of these individuals were randomly selected from 207 employed in a company facility. Of the 49 people interviewed, all were male and 44 were white. The mean age was 29.4 years ($SD = 2.5$).

The participants in Study 2 were 63 first-line foremen, all white males. Their mean age was 43.3 years ($SD = 10.6$), and the mean number of years they had worked on the job was 5.4 ($SD = 4.5$).

Procedure. A job analysis was conducted using the critical-incident technique (Flanagan, 1954). The results for the foremen have been reported in detail elsewhere (Latham, Fay, & Saari, 1979). In brief, four performance criteria or behavioral observation scales (BOS; Latham & Wexley, 1977) were developed. Each BOS contained from 4 to 13 behavioral items that were rated on a five-point Likert-type scale.

The job analysis for the hourly workers yielded nine criteria or BOS. Each BOS contained from 2 to 12 behavioral items. Because these criteria were developed independently of the first two authors (Pursell, Note 1), the appraisal format differed from that used for evaluating the job performance of foremen. First, each behavioral item was rated on a six-rather than a five-point scale. Second, after rating an individual on all items defining a given criterion or BOS, the rater made a global rating on a nine-point scale as to the overall effectiveness of the individual on that criterion.

The situational interviews for the hourly workers and the foremen were developed by three–five company supervisory people. These were superintendents who had experience in interviewing and supervising both hourly workers and foremen. The superintendents examined the critical incidents collected in the job analysis. These incidents reflected job areas such as attendance, safety, interaction with peers, work habits, and so forth. Each superintendent picked one incident that he believed exemplified the criterion under consideration and turned the incident into a question. Each question was read aloud to the group. Through group consensus, one or at most two interview questions were selected. Restricting each criterion to one or two questions was necessitated by the 60-minute time limit that the company believed could be devoted to conducting one interview.

An example of a critical incident describing ineffective behavior of an hourly worker was:

The employee was devoted to his family. He had only been married for 18 months. He used whatever excuse he could to stay home. One day the fellow's baby got a cold. His wife had a hangnail or something on her toe. He didn't come to work. He didn't even phone in.

This incident was rewritten by the superintendents in the form of the following question:

Your spouse and two teenage children are sick in bed with a cold. There are no relatives or friends available to look in on them. Your shift starts in three hours. What would you do in this situation?

Each member of the group was then asked to independently benchmark a 5 answer, that is, "things you have actually heard said in an interview by people who subsequently were considered outstanding on the job"; a 1 answer, that is, "things that you have actually heard said in an interview by people who as a result got hired but turned out to be very poor performers"; and a 3 answer, that is, "answers that you have actually heard said in an interview by people who as a result got hired and turned out to be mediocre performers." For job experts who did not have extensive interviewing experience (e.g., line managers), these instructions were modified to read "think of people you know who are outstanding, poor, and mediocre on the job. How do you think they would respond to this question if they were being interviewed?"

Each person then read his answers to the other group members. After group discussion, consensus was reached on the answers to use as benchmarks. The three benchmarks for the above question were: I'd stay home—my spouse and family come first (1); I'd phone my supervisor and explain my situation (3); and since they only have colds, I'd come to work (5).

The reallocation step used by Maas was not used in the present study due to time constraints. The situational interview for hourly workers contained 17 questions; the interview for foremen contained 10 questions. A concurrent validity study was then conducted on each interview.

To ensure the cooperation of the hourly union workers who were interviewed, we stressed that it was hoped that the results of the study would bring about the selection of employees who would do their fair share of the work and not become a burden to them. We also emphasized that the results would not affect them directly because their answers would not be placed in their personnel files; but again, it was stressed that the test results would indirectly affect them in the sense that they would be affected by the performance of "losers who were hired but seldom fired around here." Similar comments were given to the foremen; however, no assurance was given that their test results would not be examined closely by upper management. When questions concerning this issue were raised, the personnel administrator stated, "Come on, you guys are big boys; you know you wouldn't be going through all this if it didn't count." This statement was given deliberately, according to her, to simulate the test anxiety experienced by job applicants.

In conducting the interview, one person read the question and two or more interviewers recorded the answer. The interviewee was told that the question would be repeated on request.

Twenty superintendents scored the interviews. Code numbers rather than names were used so that the supervisors' scoring of the interview could not be biased by knowledge of the interviewee's identity. The superintendents worked in pairs. Each answer was scored independently and then through discussion one rating was agreed on. Both the independent ratings and the consensus ratings were recorded.

Prior to having supervisors appraise the job performance of the hourly workers, the second author generated 15—20 minutes of group discussion with them on ways to minimize rating errors such as contrast effects, halo, similar to me, and so forth. The superintendents who completed the BOS on foremen in Study 2 received an eight-hour in-depth training course for minimizing rating errors in observing and evaluating others. This training program has been described in detail elsewhere (see Latham, Wexley, & Pursell, 1975).

On completion of this discussion and training, both the supervisors ($n = 8$) who evaluated the job performance of hourly workers and the superintendents ($n = 20$) who evaluated

the job performance of the foremen worked alone when completing the performance appraisal forms. None had knowledge of anyone's performance in the situational interview.

Results

The mean interjudge reliabilities of the independent ratings for both the hourly worker and foreman interviews were significant, $r(15) = .76$, $p < .05$ and $r(8) = .79$, $p < .05$, respectively. The internal consistencies of the hourly worker and foremen interviews were also satisfactory ($\alpha = .71$, $p < .05$ and $\alpha = .67$, $p < .05$, respectively). Internal consistency was desirable in this instance because of the moderately high intercorrelations among the BOS ($M = .58$). The intercorrelations do not necessarily imply halo error because industries, like universities, strive for homogeneity by discharging individuals who perform poorly in one or more areas. Moreover, the criteria are logically related. For example, the criteria for evaluating foremen tap different aspects of supervisory behavior as opposed to skills that are logically unrelated (e.g., physical versus cognitive abilities). Multidimensional criteria are necessary because the measures do not overlap one another completely, and more importantly they facilitate accountability and control by the organization and feedback and development for the individual.

The results of the hourly worker interview validation in Study 1 indicated that the interview scores correlated significantly with each of the nine performance criterion areas on the BOS, correlation coefficients ranging from .28 to .51 ($ps < .05$); the interview scores correlated significantly with the sum of the nine "overall (global) ratings" that followed each performance criterion, $r(47) = .50$, $p < .05$; and the interview scores correlated significantly with the total BOS scores, $r(47) = .46$, $p < .05$. Partialing out experience did not reduce these correlations significantly, the latter two correlations dropping to .46 and .41, respectively.

The validation results for the foreman situational interview in Study 2 indicated that the interview scores correlated significantly with three of the four BOS. These were $r = .28$ for Safety, $r = .35$ for Work Habits, and $r = .31$ for Organizational Commitment (all $ps < .05$). The interview scores did not correlate with performance of the criterion Interaction With Subordinates. The intercorrelations among the four BOS ranged from .52 to .79. The interview scores also correlated significantly with the composite BOS score, $r(61) = .30$, $p < .05$. When experience was partialed out, this correlation was reduced to $r(61) = .29$, $p < .05$.

STUDY 3

Although well-conducted concurrent studies can provide useful estimates of validity, there is a possibility that test scores may be affected by additional job knowledge, different motivation levels, or added maturity of job incumbents versus applicants. For this reason the predictive validity of the situational interview was determined in a third study. This study was conducted with an organization in the rural South that has a strong Affirmative Action policy. Therefore, an additional purpose of this study was to determine the effectiveness of the situational interview in selecting females and blacks.

Method

Sample. The situational interview was administered to 56 applicants for entry-level work in a pulp mill, all of whom were subsequently hired. Of this number, 30 were female and all were black. The mean ages of the females and blacks were 31.5 years ($SD = 8.9$) and 30 years ($SD = 6.9$), respectively.

Procedure. The procedures for developing both the interview questions and the performance appraisal instrument were identical to those described for foremen in Study 1. Ten situational questions were developed.

Results

The mean interobserver reliabilities ($df = 8$) of the ratings on the situational interview were

.87 and .82 (all $ps < .05$) for blacks and females, respectively. Similarly, the internal consistency (Cronbach's alpha) of the situational interview was .70 for blacks and .78 for females (all $ps < .05$).

The employees' job performance was evaluated after they had been on the job for 12 months. None of the supervisors who evaluated the employees were aware of how well any employee had performed in the situational interview. Prior to making their evaluations, the supervisors received the same training for minimizing rating errors (Latham et al., 1975) used in Study 2. A composite job performance rating was calculated for each employee. The correlation between performance in the interview and performance on the job 12 months later was .39 for females and .33 for blacks ($ps < .05$).

GENERAL DISCUSSION

The results of these three studies provide further support for the theoretical proposition (Locke, 1968) that intentions correlate with behavior. Previous support for this assumption has been confined primarily to the motivational literature (cf. Latham & Yukl, 1975). The present findings are particularly impressive in light of the low reliability and validity of other interview methods, and the comparability of the validity coefficient for job performance of supervisors with that which is typically reported for assessment centers ($r = .33$; Cohen, Moses, & Byham, Note 2). Assessment centers generally last a minimum of one entire day, and many are conducted for three days. A situational interview can be conducted within an hour. This is not to imply that a situational interview should be used in place of an assessment center or other selection tests. However, it is likely that including this technique in an assessment center or with other test batteries would significantly improve the validity of the selection process.

The effectiveness of the situational interview is readily explainable. First, the interview questions are derived from the results of a systematic job analysis. A representative sampling of job situations is incorporated in the interview questions. Thus, the content validity of the procedure appears to be satisfactory as judged by job experts.

Second, the face validity of the procedure is ensured by asking only job-related questions. This appears to increase the motivation of the interviewee to take the test seriously.

Third, focusing on the interviewers' experience with a wide range of interviewee responses, and choosing among these responses to develop a scoring key to anchor 1, 3, and 5 answers, may have increased the interobserver reliability and validity of the procedure. The instructions to interviewers emphasized that these benchmarks were only illustrations or aids for scoring an answer. Interviewers were to use their judgment of what constituted a 1, 2, 3, 4, or 5 answer. The similarity between the answers given by each interviewee and one of the three benchmarks to each question, however, was striking. In short, the job experts who developed the scoring key turned out to be truly expert in predicting almost exactly how people would respond to each interview question.

Fourth, both the selection and the performance appraisal instruments were based on overt employee behavior rather than traits or economic constructs. Traits are generally ambiguous and thus unpredictable. Economic constructs are frequently affected by factors over which the job performer has little or no control. For effective selection it is necessary to develop predictors that are not only realistic samples of behavior but are as similar to the criteria as possible (Wernimont & Campbell, 1968). An interview by nature can usually tap only behavioral intentions. The present research has shown that when the intentions measured are job-related they can serve as valid indicators of on-the-job behavior. Nevertheless, the generalizability of these results cannot be assumed; the effectiveness of a situational

interview must be demonstrated through proper validation.

The situational interview might be improved by combining it with an approach used by Ghiselli (1966), which focuses on *past* behavior rather than *future* intentions. Job candidates could be asked what they have done in the *past* in situations similar to those posed by the interviewer. Such information has the potential for being verified by former employers who are willing to answer straightforward job-related questions. A possible problem with this approach, however, is that it may discriminate against people who have not been given the opportunity to engage in certain behaviors in the past. Thus, checks for adverse impact would need to be conducted. When adverse impact is not a problem, it would appear likely that the two methods would significantly increase the validity of the interview as a selection device.

A possible limitation of the present research is that the validation of the situational interview in two of the three studies was confounded with a training program to minimize rating errors. However, on the basis of the positive results obtained for hourly workers in Study 1, in which only a warning was given to avoid rating errors when evaluating job performance, it is doubtful that much of the variance in the validity coefficients is explainable by this training. For example, Levine and Butler (1952) and Wexley, Sanders, and Yukl (1973) found that a lecture of warning to minimize rating errors had little or no effect on rater behavior. It is likely that the need for extensive rater training was minimized in the present studies by the similarity of the interviewee answers with the benchmark answers. Nevertheless, Pursell, Dossett, and Latham (1980) have found that training raters to minimize rating errors when making performance appraisals can increase the validity coefficients of predictors significantly.

Employers are always looking for the "extra edge" in employment decision making. That extra edge might represent a reduction in cost or an improvement in validity. As an example of the former, ridiculous and unsubstantiated claims are often made for the validity of handwriting analysis as a selection device. The advantage proposed is that it costs a great deal less than standard psychological testing. In fact, little or no validity can be demonstrated for graphoanalysis (as handwriting analysis has been labeled by its practitioners), so the cost becomes irrelevant. Another example of the attempt by the employer to gain some extra edge is the use of methods for uncovering dishonesty—either present or potential. One of the most common techniques considered for measuring dishonesty is the polygraph or lie detector. Many employers would like to predict employee honesty in an attempt to reduce pilferage and other illegal employee activities. In spite of the absence of any compelling theory or data that would support the use of polygraphs, the claims for validity continue. In this article, Sackett and Decker review the scientific literature on the use of the polygraph in employment settings.

■ READING 10 ■

Detection of Deception in the Employment Context: A Review and Critical Analysis

Paul R. Sackett, *University of Kansas*
Phillip J. Decker, *University of Missouri—St. Louis*

An extensive body of literature exists on the topic of the detection of deception and investigation of theft using various techniques, including interpretation of physiological responses and questionnaires. Very little of this literature has appeared in psychological journals. Most reports are contained in polygraph trade publications or law enforcement publications. Lykken (1978b) discussed the lack of involvement by psychologists in this field, labeling it a case of "policemen rushing in where science fears to tread."

Regardless of who has done the research or its quality, the vast majority of polygraph examinations are conducted in the employment context rather than the criminal investigation context (U.S. Senate, 1974). However, virtually all reported research has dealt with actual or simulated criminal investigations. The only studies dealing with the detection of deception in the employment context concern the development and use of paper-and-pencil surrogates for the polygraph. The one review paper focusing on assessing honesty in employment (Ash, 1976) fails to deal adequately with the differences between the criminal investigation context and the employment context.

The primary purpose of this paper is to identify a number of issues relevant to the use of the polygraph and other devices designed to identify deception or predict theft in the employment context. This paper is not intended as a comprehensive description of "lie detection" procedures and techniques, nor as an evaluation of such techniques in the context of criminal investigations. References to detailed treatments of these topics will be made where appropriate.

Source: *Personnel Psychology, 32,* 1979, pp. 487–504.

Of the instruments available for the detection of deception and the prediction of honesty, three are typically used in industrial settings: polygraphs, voice stress analyzers, and paper-and-pencil questionnaires. Each will be discussed in turn, with the major focus being placed on the polygraph. Many of the issues discussed regarding the polygraph will also be applicable to the other techniques for detecting deception.

THE POLYGRAPH

Objective measurement of physiological symptoms of stress began in the late 18th century (Reid & Inbau, 1977). The first use of a scientific instrument in an effort to detect deception occurred in 1895 (Lombroso, 1912) and subsequent refinement culminated in 1926 with the basic instrument known today as the polygraph (Keeler, 1930; Larson, 1921). The polygraph is a portable machine which measures and records pulse rate, relative blood pressure, rate and depth of respiration, and galvanic skin response (GSR). The polygraph is used to detect deception using various questioning procedures, among the most common being the peak of tension, control question, relevant-irrelevant question (Reid & Inbau, 1977), and the guilty-knowledge techniques (Lykken, 1974).

Extent of Use

Legal restrictions on the use of the polygraph vary considerably in the public and private sectors. Controls were placed on Federal Government use of polygraphs in 1968 (U.S. House of Representatives, 1976). The use of polygraphs as a condition of employment in private industry is restricted in 15 states (U.S. Senate, 1974). At least 19 states have some licensing requirements for polygraph operators (Belt & Holden, 1978).

Belt and Holden (1978) surveyed 143 large retail, life insurance, transportation, banking, financial, and industrial organizations to determine the extent of polygraph use. Twenty percent indicated current use of polygraphs.

Commercial banks and retailers were the most common users of the polygraph. Thirty-five percent of the companies use the polygraph for pre-employment screening, 35 percent use the polygraph for periodic surveys of employee honesty, and 90 percent use the polygraph for investigation of specific thefts or other irregularities. Firms using the polygraph emphasize speed of obtaining results as a major advantage of its use, while moral and ethical implications are deemphasized. Firms not using the polygraph emphasize moral and ethical implications as a major reason for their decision.

Belt and Holden's findings provide some substantiation for the American Polygraph Association's claim that approximately 25 percent of major corporations are using the polygraph (Corporate Lie Detector Comes under Fire, 1973). The findings also indicate a small but sustained growth rate in the use of polygraphs in industry, and there is a greater tendency to find use of polygraphs in industries located in states which legally prescribe licensing and training requirements for polygraph operators.

Reliability and Validity

Before discussing validity evidence, a brief summary of the reliability of polygraph examiners' judgments is in order. Interrater reliability in examining polygraph charts has been summarized by a number of authors (Ash, 1976; Barland & Raskin, 1973), with reliability coefficients typically in the .80s and .90s resulting. It should be noted that interrater reliabilities have typically been computed among examiners trained at the same school. Raskin and Barland (Note 1) studied agreement between psychologists and law enforcement and privately trained examiners and found significantly lower agreement between psychologists and privately trained examiners than between psychologists and law enforcement examiners, with judgments made solely on the basis of polygraph charts.

Whether the opportunity to observe the examinee's behavior, as opposed to chart interpretation alone, raises or lowers reliability is an open question. The additional information gained by observing the examinee may augment the physiological response data and increase reliability; alternatively, subjective factors such as stereotypes, first impressions, etc., may enter into the decision, thus decreasing reliability. These opposing viewpoints as to the merits of behavioral observation apply to validity as well as to reliability.

It should be noted that the results of validity studies in the polygraph literature are uniformly reported in percent accuracy terms, rather than in correlational terms. Thus the terms *validity* and *accuracy* will be used synonymously in this paper.

A number of factors have been found to affect validity or have been posited by writers in the field as factors affecting validity. Among these are characteristics of the examiner, the examination procedure, the physiological measures used, the subjects, and the experimental paradigm. Each will be discussed briefly.

Some authors (e.g., Horvath & Reid, 1971) report greater accuracy for more experienced examiners, while others (e.g., Raskin & Barland, Note 1) report no difference. Raskin & Barland (Note 1) also report reliability differences due to the type of training received.

A number of different examination techniques exist, and while some efforts at comparing the techniques have been made (e.g., Podlesny, Raskin & Barland, Note 2; Podlesny & Raskin, 1977), the relative effectiveness of the various techniques is not completely understood. Other relevant characteristics of the examination include the amount of time available for the test, pressure to make a guilty-not guilty decision rather than allowing inconclusive results, and the time devoted to a pretest interview.

Orne, Thackray, and Paskewitz (1972), Podlesny and Raskin (1977), and Raskin, Barland, and Podlesny (Note 3) provide reviews of the range of physiological measures which have been used. Tied to the measurement of physiological variables is the use of these variables in making a judgment. Some writers (e.g., Reid & Inbau, 1977) advocate a subjective combination of information from polygraph charts and verbal and behavioral cues gathered by observation of the examinee. Others (e.g., Barland & Raskin, 1975) use a more objective procedure, based solely on polygraph charts. Recently, Lieblich, Ben-Shakhar, Kugelmass, and Cohen (1978) have described a sophisticated decision-theoretic objective approach to polygraph decisions. The method of reaching a judgment can certainly be expected to have an impact on the accuracy of the decision reached.

Differences in the motivation of subjects in laboratory and "real life" settings may affect validity. It is taken as fact by proponents of the polygraph that "real life" examinations are more accurate than laboratory studies (Ash, 1976). The reasoning is that the consequences to the individual of being detected in a laboratory study are minimal; thus, strong physiological reaction to any questions asked in the course of the examination is less likely. In a real-world setting the individual's motivation is presumably enhanced, thus increasing the chances of correctly distinguishing between deceptive and nondeceptive individuals. This reasoning discounts the possibility, mentioned by Lykken (1978a), that serious consequences in a real life setting may cause innocent individuals to produce responses indicative of a high amount of stress. This notion receives some support from data reported by Raskin, Barland and Podlesny (Note 3) who found an increased risk of false positives among individuals who were well educated, had no prior history of criminal activity, and who were very concerned about their reputation in the community.

Two distinct paradigms for studying polygraph accuracy have been used (Orne, Thackray, & Paskewitz, 1972). The first, labeled the "guilty information" paradigm, involves a situation in which the subject is given a piece of information (e.g., picks one card from a deck) and attempts to prevent the examiner from determining which piece of information he/she has. Generalizability to real world settings is severely limited in that all subjects have "something to hide." The examiner knows that they have one of a finite set of pieces of information, and the task is to determine which by examining the polygraph charts corresponding to questions of the form "Answer no to each question: was the card a three, a five," etc. There is no analog to this situation in the criminal investigation or employment context. The second, labeled the "guilty person" paradigm, involves the determination of which of a number of individuals are and are not guilty of a crime. "Mock crime" scenarios have been developed for use in laboratory settings (e.g., Kubis, Note 4). Uses of the polygraph in criminal investigations and in the employment context all deal with this type of problem.

Thus, one is not validating "the" polygraph test, but rather the specific combination of the above variables used in the particular study. No single figure representing the validity of the polygraph will be forthcoming. Following a review of validity evidence, a single figure will be used to illustrate the consequences of generalizing to an employment context.

Abrams (1973) reviews a large number of laboratory studies of validity. Abrams reports a mean accuracy in laboratory studies of 81 percent. There are very few field studies of polygraph accuracy which are of sufficient quality to warrant discussion. A major reason for this is the fact that the actual state of affairs regarding an individual's guilt or innocence—known as "ground truth"—is seldom known. If it were, the need for devices such as the polygraph would be eliminated. This problem with obtaining an objective criterion limits opportunities to study polygraph validity in the field. Two procedures for validating field examinations have been used. The first is verification of the examiner's judgment due to later confession by the examinee or by another party, thus exonerating the examinee (Horvath, 1977). The second procedure involves the presentation of all of the evidence in a case to a panel of lawyers and/or judges, asking for a judgment about the actual guilt of the individual (e.g., Bersh, 1969). Consensus by this panel is then used as the criterion of guilt or innocence.

Two crucial issues in evaluating field studies are the sequential independence of examina-

tions and the base rate of guilt in the sample of examinees. Abrams (1973) reviews five studies involving situations such as identifying which of a number of dormitory residents was responsible for a theft. Identifying the guilty individual out of 25–100 examinees and reporting 100 percent accuracy is not an appropriate test of validity. First, with 1 to 4 percent of the sample guilty, labeling all examinees innocent would result in an accuracy rate of 96–99 percent without using the polygraph. Second, examining 100 individuals under these circumstances is very different from making guilty-not guilty judgments about 100 individuals accused of 100 different crimes (or 100 hire-reject decisions about job applicants). In the first instance, information gathered from one examinee which is strongly indicative of guilt is bound to impact on decisions made about later examinees. This contaminant is eliminated in the second instance. A fair requirement for a test of polygraph validity is that the examiner use only data gathered from the examinee in the course of the examination as the basis for a decision. Prior knowledge of probability of guilt or innocence creates a bias unless this probability is explicitly acknowledged. Accuracy should be viewed as an increment over a pre-specified chance rate of detection.

Lykken (1979) reviews three field studies which meet the requirements of having acceptable criteria and independence of examinations, namely studies by Bersh (1969), Barland and Raskin (Note 5), and Horvath (1977). Bersh (1969) had a panel of four prosecuting attorneys read case materials from a number of criminal investigations. A deception-no deception judgment had been made at the time of the investigation by a polygraph examiner. The attorneys examined the complete file for each case, minus the polygraph report, and each made an independent judgment as to whether deception was or was not indicated. The majority opinion of the attorneys agreed with the polygraph examiners' decision in 88 percent of the cases. Lykken pointed out that Bersh's polygraph examiners had access to whatever evidence was available prior to the examination and were able to interview the subject beforehand, thus making it impossible to determine the independent contribution of the polygraph results alone to this accuracy figure. Barland and Raskin (Note 5) also used a panel agreement criterion with criminal suspects. The polygraph examination was conducted by one examiner, and the judgment made by a second examiner. The judgment was based only on the polygraph charts themselves, and an accuracy rate of 86 percent was reported. However, with a 78 percent base rate of guilt, relatively high accuracy could be obtained simply by labeling all individuals guilty. With a base rate of 50 percent, accuracy would be expected to drop to 71 percent. Horvath (1977) also reports an investigation of accuracy based solely on polygraph records. His base rate was 50 percent, and the investigation was based on a reexamination by ten polygraph examiners of the charts of criminal suspects who either later confessed to the crime or were cleared by the later confession of another individual. The examiners agreed with the criterion in 64 percent of the cases ($p <$ .001).

Raskin and Podlesny (1979) have identified five additional studies which have used verified guilt or innocence in examining the accuracy of decisions based solely on the interpretation of polygraph charts obtained using the control question technique. They report an average accuracy of 90 percent in identifying guilty subjects and 89 percent in identifying innocent subjects. Several issues regarding these studies deserve mention. First, the method by which the polygraph charts were selected for inclusion in the study was not specified in a number of the studies, leaving open the question of the representativeness of the sample. Second, the method of verifying guilt or innocence was not specified in a number of the studies. Lykken (1978a) has suggested that individuals who later confess may not be representative of all guilty individuals and may be more easily identifiable. Nonetheless, these studies do indicate that there are circumstances under which a high degree of accuracy can be obtained. Raskin and Podlesny (1979) suggest

that the fact that the examiners in these studies were trained to rely on chart interpretation rather than observing behavioral symptoms may account for differences between the accuracy figures in these studies and those cited by Lykken.

It is apparent that widely divergent accuracy figures have been obtained. The role of examiner characteristics, examination procedure, subject characteristics, the equipment used and the physiological measures recorded, the criterion of guilt or innocence, among others, in accounting for these differences cannot be determined without systematic variation of these factors. For purposes of the points to be developed in the next section regarding a comparison of employment and criminal investigation uses of the polygraph, an upper limit figure of 90 percent accuracy will be used. In most cases a figure this high cannot be expected.

Comparison Between the Criminal Investigation and Employment Contexts

Three different uses of the polygraph can be differentiated. The first is pre-employment screening, which commonly seeks information regarding past theft, health concerns (e.g., a history of workman's compensation claims), alcohol, drug, or gambling problems, willingness to make a long-term commitment to the job, and others. The examination typically constitutes a "final hurdle" before hiring. The second use is in periodic checks of all current employees. Identifying individuals stealing from the company is a major purpose of this type of investigation (in addition to its value as a deterrent). The third use involves an investigation into a specific theft in an organization, and can be seen as comparable to a criminal investigation context. Information about a specific act is sought in this type of examination, while seeking information about certain general types of actions typifies the first two.

Ash (1976) makes a comparison between the validity evidence for the polygraph and Ghiselli's (1973) average validity figures of .2 for aptitude tests and near zero for personality tests with job performance as the criterion. The next sections of the paper will show that this comparison is thoroughly inappropriate. In doing so, we will raise three issues important to generalizing from the criminal investigation context to the employment context.

The first issue is that an overall accuracy figure may not be the appropriate index to use in evaluating the polygraph. This was first pointed out by Skolnick (1961) and reemphasized by Lykken (1974). Skolnick suggested that what should be used is not the unconditional probability of a correct judgment, but a conditional probability, namely, the probability of actual guilt, given an examiner judgment of guilt. This argument presumes that the false labeling of an innocent individual as guilty is an outcome to be avoided. This conditional probability is dependent upon the base rate of guilt in the sample. Assuming unconditional accuracy of 90 percent and a base rate of 50 percent in a sample of 100 individuals, the distribution in Table 1 is expected. Of the 50 individuals judged guilty by the polygraph examiner, 45, or 90 percent, are actually guilty. Changing the base rate to 10 percent produces the distribution in Table 2. Of the 18 individuals judged guilty by the polygraph examiner, 9, or 50 percent, are actually guilty. As the base rate decreases from 50 percent, the lower the conditional probability that an individual judged to be guilty is in fact guilty. In cases where the base rate is 10 percent, with an unconditional accuracy of 90 percent, half the individuals judged guilty by

the polygraph will actually be innocent. If the unconditional accuracy of the polygraph were 80 percent, retaining the 10 percent base rate, 69 percent of those judged guilty would actually be innocent.

Even if unconditional accuracy were as high as 90 percent, the use of the polygraph in situations with a low base rate of guilt will result in a relatively large number of honest individuals being erroneously labeled dishonest. Following the terminology used by Leiblich et al. (1978), this will be labeled a "false alarm," while failing to identify a dishonest individual will be labeled a "miss."

Employers and applicants are likely to have extremely divergent views on the importance of avoiding false alarms and misses. In a selection context, an employer is likely to place a high value on identifying individuals with a history of theft, drug or alcohol problems, and the like, and may be willing to erroneously categorize a relatively large number of applicants in order to insure that the smallest possible number of "dishonest" individuals are selected. The employer is essentially interested in accuracy defined as the conditional probability that a guilty individual is judged guilty. The perspective of the job seeker is likely to be quite different. While acknowledging the value of screening out dishonest individuals, he/she is unlikely to accept a procedure which is incorrect as often as it is correct in labeling an individual as dishonest. The job seeker is interested in the conditional probability that an individual judged guilty actually is guilty.

The definition of accuracy is value-laden and

TABLE 1 Expected Distribution of Polygraph Judgments with an Accuracy of 90 Percent and a Base Rate of Guilt of 50 Percent

	Actual Situation		
	Not Guilty	Guilty	
Polygraph Judgment			
Guilty	5	45	50
Not guilty	45	5	50
	50	50	

TABLE 2 Expected Distribution of Polygraph Judgments with an Accuracy of 90 Percent and a Base Rate of Guilt of 10 Percent

	Actual Situation		
	Not Guilty	Guilty	
Polygraph Judgment			
Guilty	9	9	18
Not guilty	81	1	82
	90	10	

situation dependent: employers and applicants may espouse the need to consider different conditional probabilities, and these different conditional probabilities yield widely different accuracy estimates in situations with a base rate quite discrepant from 50 percent. A crucial issue in determining the usefulness of the polygraph in the employment context involves the determination of the base rate to be expected in each of the three uses of the polygraph in the employment context.

With regard to pre-employment screening, Lykken (1978a) presumes a base rate of 5 percent in developing his argument against the use of the polygraph. Ash (1976) cites a figure of 40 percent as the percent of employees who will be dishonest. A number of factors are likely to influence the base rate found in different situations. First, the smaller the magnitude of admitted wrongdoing considered necessary to predict that an individual will be dishonest, the higher the base rate of dishonesty one will find. Second, the population of applicants for positions at different levels and in different industries may be quite different and have different base rates of dishonesty. Finally, if the percentage of individuals rejected by a polygraph examination is used as an estimate of the base rate, individuals mistakenly identified as dishonest overestimate the true base rate. Obtaining information about the base rate in the specific situation is indicated if one is to evaluate the impact of polygraph use in that situation. In some selection situations, if not most, the base rate will be relatively low.

A low base rate may also be expected in many instances where periodic screening of current employees is practiced. In contrast, the base rate is much higher in situations where only individuals suspected of a specific theft are polygraphed. Thus base rate of guilt is an important difference between pre-employment and periodic screening in an employment context and the use of the polygraph in a criminal context, where the proportion of guilty individuals among those arraigned as criminal suspects and polygraphed is relatively high.

A second objection to generalizing an accuracy figure from a criminal investigation context to an employment context lies in the nature of the decision made on the basis of the polygraph examination. Accuracy figures from criminal investigations refer to a single judgment, e.g., that the individual is or is not the guilty person. Contrast this with a pre-employment polygraph examination of the type in which the examiner is making a series of judgments, for example, that the individual does or does not have a history of filing questionable workmen's compensation claims, alcoholism, drug abuse, theft, or "job hopping." Independent of any decrease in accuracy due to attempting to cover all these areas in too brief a time period, accuracy will be lower due simply to the fact that multiple judgments are made. Assuming a 90 percent unconditional accuracy for each judgment, an individual having none of the above characteristics would have only a .59 chance of being judged accurately ($.59 = .95$). The multiple judgment problem is not an issue in the periodic screening of current employees if such screening involves only one topic, such as theft. It is also not an issue in the investigation of a specific theft.

A third objection to generalizing an accuracy figure to the employment context lies in an important distinction between identification and prediction as the goal of polygraph examinations. In criminal investigations, in periodic screening of current employees, or in the investigation of a specific theft, the goal is the identification of the individual(s) responsible for an act. In pre-employment screening, however, it is implicitly assumed that an individual who has stolen in the past (or who has used drugs, or whatever other characteristics are felt to be crucial) will steal from the organization (or will be frequently absent, or whatever criterion is being predicted). The generalization of an accuracy figure from a criminal investigation to a pre-employment context assumes that past behavior is a perfectly valid predictor of future on-the-job behavior. The accuracy figure for identification should be multiplied by the best estimate one has of the strength of the past behavior-future behavior relationship to obtain a more realistic picture of the value of the polygraph in pre-employment screening.

By failing to articulate this identification-prediction distinction in generalizing from criminal investigation to pre-employment screening, the potential for a true predictive validation of pre-employment screening polygraph decisions has been overlooked. While certainly an expensive undertaking, polygraph examinations may be administered without using the results in the selection decision, and validated against the criterion of interest, be it absence, turnover, or theft. The fact that a large number of thefts are undetected is a major difficulty in such an undertaking.

The uses of the polygraph discussed thus far represent two conceptually distinct approaches to the reduction of industrial loss due to theft. The first approach involves pre-employment screening to predict which individuals are likely to steal from the company. The alternative to a polygraph examination is an investigation into the applicant's background by other means, such as reference and credit checks. Such investigations are considered to be time consuming and to have a good chance of producing inaccurate or incomplete information. The second approach involves attempts at preventing theft by employees through the use of various mechanisms. Periodic polygraph screening may be valued as much for its deterrent value as for its value as a mechanism for actually identifying individuals stealing from the company. Alternate preventive approaches involve attempts at tighter security through employee surveillance and increased accountability. Also under the category of preventive mechanisms come a number of factors more typically of concern to the industrial/organizational psychologist, such as the organization's reward and control systems, and organizational climate. The identification of the characteristics of an organization in which theft is likely to occur, and interventions to alter these characteristics may be a viable alternative to focusing completely on individual factors in attempting to reduce theft.

Reactions to Polygraph Examinations

The questions raised in this paper have focused on the accuracy of polygraph examinations. It should be noted that a number of objections to the polygraph can be made on ethical, social, and constitutional grounds. Among these are objections that the polygraph is an invasion of privacy and an infringement on the dignity of man, that it reverses the principle that one is innocent until proven guilty by requiring individuals to prove their innocence, and that it violates 5th amendment rights against self incrimination. Proponents of the polygraph reply that individual rights must be weighed against employer losses, and that individuals have an obligation to society to cooperate in attempts to identify dishonest individuals (Shattuck, Brown, & Carlson, Note 6). The stand one takes regarding the polygraph may be largely determined by whether one's sympathies lie with the individual or the employer.

Another issue of interest is the attitude of applicants and employees toward the polygraph examination. Ash and Wheeler (Note 7) report that 86 percent of applicants thought the examination was fair, 96 percent were willing to take the test to get a job, and 88 percent were willing to routinely take an exam as a condition of employment. They interpret these results as indicating that resistance to the polygraph has been overestimated. However, all participants completed the attitude questionnaire after the polygraph examination. Thus, the questionnaire may have been viewed as part of the selection procedure, and applicants may have felt that expressing negative attitudes toward the examination would affect their chances for employment. Further research is needed in a setting in which no negative outcome may be anticipated by the subjects due to expression of negative attitudes.

Bias in Polygraph Examinations

Title VII of the Civil Rights Act of 1964 prohibits discrimination in employment decisions on the basis of race, color, religion, sex, and national origin. Two potential sources of bias in polygraph examinations have been identified. The first involves possible racial, ethnic, or sexual differences in physiological reactivity to psychological stress. Kugelmass and Lieblich (1968) have shown that persons of Eastern mediterranean origin show GSR nonreactivity more often than other ethnic groups. Relying on different physiological measures for different subgroups may result in differential accuracy across subgroups. It should be noted that ethnic differences in GSR *level* (e.g., Johnson and Corah, 1963; Lazarus, Tomita, Opton, & Kodama, 1966) do not constitute a threat to polygraph accuracy, since the subjects' responses to irrelevant or control questions are compared with their responses to relevant questions.

Second, and perhaps of greater interest, is the potential for factors such as first impressions, prejudices, and stereotypes to consciously or unconsciously affect the overall judgment made by the examiner. Orne, Thackray, and Paskewitz (1972) have suggested that "the manner in which questions are asked can certainly influence the physiological response. The interrogator wishing to obtain a record with physiological evidence of deception is likely to be able to do so. In view of the work of Rosenthal (1966) on experimenter bias, it seems extremely likely that the interrogator could unwittingly communicate some aspects of his conviction to the subject" (p. 751). There are no published field studies reporting information on the percent of deceptive and nondeceptive judgments among the various protected classes. Such information should be readily available and deserves to be reported.

There is one appelate court case confirming the EEOC's right of access to polygraph records *(Circle K Corporation v. EEOC)*. The information sought by the EEOC is instructive: "a list of all applicants and present employees subjected to the polygraph examination, their racial/ethnic identity and whether they were accepted or rejected; documentation of the nature, standardization and validity of the polygraph test, and a list of questions asked of each

applicant; qualifications of the examiners who administered the tests . . ." (p. 1054). The EEOC was granted access to this information, but a case involving discrimination on the basis of the polygraph examination has not come to trial. There have, however, been a number of cases in which the subjective nature of the decision made in an employment interview has been identified as having the potential for discrimination (e.g., *Hester* v. *Southern Railway Co., Causey* v. *Ford Motor Co.*). On the other hand, one interview case has upheld the employer's right to subjective evaluation unless there is evidence of bias *(Salton* v. *Western Electric)*. Thus, an examination based solely on the interpretation of polygraph charts may be on stronger legal grounds than one involving both charts and an evaluation of the examinee's verbal and nonverbal behavior.

Countermeasures

Some literature exists concerning techniques to avoid detection in a polygraph examination (see Barland & Raskin, 1973). Countermeasures may be attempted on the spur of the moment or be the product of some research and assistance before the examination. Different polygraph examination techniques are more or less susceptible to different countermeasures. Two mental countermeasures which have been examined are dissociation—attempting to suppress responses by focusing on some neutral object or through—and imagery—attempting to produce responses to irrelevant questions by focusing on some exciting or arousing topic. Kubis (Note 8) taught subjects to use a "modified yoga" technique to control responses and found that subjects in this group could be detected as easily as control subjects. However, other subjects taught to use "exciting imagery" to control responses were detected only at chance levels. Voluntary muscle contractions to create a response to an irrelevant question constitute another class of countermeasures. The problem is for a subject to pick a muscle group whose manipulation would not be seen by a polygrapher. Kubis (Note 8), for example, has shown that pressing toes to the floor can be used effectively as a countermeasure, lowering detection to below chance levels. Other potential countermeasures reviewed by Barland and Raskin (1973) include hypnosis and drug use. Much of the countermeasure literature is anecdotal; little research on the effectiveness of these measures has been done.

VOICE ANALYSIS

The use of voice stress analysis dates from about 1970. What voice stress analyzers actually measure is not clear from the scientific literature (U.S. House of Representatives, 1976). Manufacturer-supplied literature indicates that inaudible stress related frequency modulations resulting from minute oscillations of the voice mechanism are measured by these instruments (Dektor, Note 9; Law Enforcement Associates, Note 10; see also Horvath, 1978). Unlike the polygraph, voice analysis can be used covertly by the analysis of tape recorded conversations. Most reported studies have been analyses of tape recorded polygraph interrogations (e.g., Barland, 1975; Horvath, 1978; Kubis, Note 4). Two states specifically restrict voice analysis as a condition for employment; 12 states require that at least three physiological symptoms of stress be measured —thus effectively banning voice analysis (Business buys the lie detector, 1978; Rice, 1978). Because of the recent development of voice analyzers, no solid data are available on their degree of use. In one document supplied by a voice analyzer manufacturer (Dahm, Note 11) at least 423 of their machines had been sold by 1974 and these machines had been used in over 39,000 examinations.

A review of early attempts at the detection of deception by voice analysis is provided by Myers and Merluzzi (Note 12). Research using the voice analysis instruments prevalent in industry today, however, is very sparse. Fifteen studies with instruments currently in industrial use have been done. Twelve of these are studies provided by the manufacturers of the instruments; none of these are published (Rice, 1978). The three independent studies will be reviewed here.

Kubis (Note 4) conducted a laboratory study involving simulated crime situations where ground truth was known. Kubis reported a polygraph accuracy of 76 percent, a voice analysis accuracy of 38 percent, and an accuracy of 65 percent with judgment of behavior alone, where chance was 33 percent. A small proportion of the subjects in this study were interrogated without polygraph apparatus attached. Voice analysis accuracy of these recordings was 53 percent, compared with 19 percent in analysis of recordings of subjects simultaneously monitored by a polygraph. Barland (1975) carried out a study investigating both polygraph and voice analysis accuracy with suspects involved in actual criminal investigations. The criteria used in his research were judgments by a panel of judges and attorneys who reviewed all case information. Polygraph accuracy was 78 percent while voice analysis accuracy did not exceed chance levels. The most recent investigation was that of Horvath (1978) in which voice analysis accuracy was compared to accuracy of GSR measured by a standard field polygraph in a laboratory situation with ground truth known. The accuracy of voice analysis was 24 percent, which does not exceed a chance level; GSR accuracy was 68 percent. Thus, in both lab and field studies, its only potential value would seem to be its role as a "fear inducer" in eliciting confessions or as a deterrent.

PENCIL-AND-PAPER MEASURES

There are several paper-and-pencil measures designed specifically to predict employee theft, each including questions on attitudes toward theft, theft admissions, and various biographical indices (Rosenbaum, 1976). All claim high correlations with polygraph examination results, emphasize their racial neutrality, and purport to identify a large proportion of applicants who would later steal. The Reid Report has the most supporting validation data (Ash, 1970, 1971, 1972, 1975). For example, Ash (1971) has validated the Reid Report against the polygraph. Recommendation to hire, hire with qualifications, or not hire were made separately based on polygraph examinations and on the Reid Report. The hit rate was 65 percent (Pearson $r = .43$). Terris (Note 13) has developed a measure assessing only theft-related attitudes which he has used to predict theft admissions made during polygraph examinations. The correlation between theft-related attitudes and theft admissions was .56. One problem with several studies (e.g., Ash, 1970; Terris, Note 14) is that the survey was given before the polygraph examination. The purpose of these instruments is quite transparent to the examinee, and therefore if the examinee had forewarning of the polygraph examination (which is likely) it seems that the responses to the questionnaires would be affected. Anticipation of an impending polygraph examination or recent completion of a polygraph examination is very likely to affect questionnaire response, thus eliminating independence of predictor and criterion.

Biographical information alone has been used as a predictor for later theft. Rosenbaum (1976) constructed weighted application blanks to predict documented employee theft in two separate studies. In the first, five predictors were identified out of 35 items resulting in a correlation of .47. Later cross-validation with independent samples resulted in correlations of .63 and .21. In the second study, 10 predictors were identified out of 60 items resulting in a correlation of .30 with documented theft. Cross-validation with independent samples resulted in correlations of .17 and .49. The predictors included such diverse items as "wears eyeglasses," "number of dependents," "no middle initial," and "is black."

Before any endorsement of the prediction of theft with pre-employment questionnaires can be made, further research is needed. Specifically, predictive validation with future theft, rather than admissions of past theft as the criterion, evidence of validity where subjects completing the paper-and-pencil instrument are not also polygraphed, and stronger evidence that biographical data holds up under cross validation are needed. Evaluation of the predictive power of each separate component of the measures—biographical data, attitudes, and admissions of theft—would also be a useful contribution.

SUMMARY AND CONCLUSIONS

Despite evidence that as many as 25 percent of major firms are using the polygraph, the published evidence of its value deals exclusively with the criminal investigation context. Three different uses of the polygraph in the employment context have been identified, namely, pre-employment screening, periodic screening of current employees, and investigation of a specific theft. While there is evidence from the criminal investigation context that polygraph judgments are accurate well beyond a chance rate, there are sufficient differences between some employment uses of the polygraph and the criminal investigation context to seriously limit the generalizability of accuracy figures from one context to the other.

A number of the issues identified in this paper are of importance for evaluating the use of the polygraph in pre-employment screening. First, with a low base rate of guilt/dishonesty in a situation where all judgments are independent (e.g., one is not seeking to identify one guilty individual from among several suspects) a large proportion of those judged guilty will actually be innocent. A low base rate can be expected in many instances in pre-employment screening. Second, when multiple judgments are made about an individual, as in a pre-employment examination into theft, alcoholism, drug use, and other areas, the probability of error is much greater than when a single judgment is made. Third, in contrast with both criminal investigation uses and other employment uses of the polygraph, pre-employment screening does not stop with the identification of individuals with some wrongdoing in their past. Rejecting such individuals involves an implicit prediction that such individuals will be dishonest as employees. Unlike other uses of the polygraph, in pre-employment screening one is faced with errors of identification and errors of prediction. Fourth, the partly subjective nature of most polygraph judgments raises the possibility of bias against classes protected by Title VII. No empirical evidence either supporting or refuting this suggestion has been offered to date.

The effects of each of these issues on polygraph accuracy have been discussed separately; the potential for these problems to occur jointly and severely restrict accuracy should be noted. In light of these problems we seriously question pre-employment use of the polygraph.

The second use of the polygraph in the employment context involves the periodic screening of current employees, usually to identify individuals stealing from the company. The base rate issue is of great concern in this context: in situations where a low percentage of examinees have actually been stealing, a large proportion of those judged deceptive are likely to be innocent. The consequences to an innocent individual of being judged deceptive —loss of job and damage to reputation—are of such magnitude that polygraph errors must be minimized. Given the expected false alarm rate with a low base rate, we are opposed to the dismissal of an individual based solely on a polygraph examination where guilt is not admitted by the examinee. The deterrent value alone of periodic screening may make screening worthwhile to the employer, though the effects of the threat of such screening on individual satisfaction and organizational climate are unknown.

The third use of the polygraph in the employment context involves the investigation of a specific theft. Research findings from a crim-inal investigation context are directly applicable here. As opposed to other employment uses of the polygraph, decisions made about the different suspects are not completely independent in that the identification of the guilty individual(s) clears other suspects. The polygraph may be a useful investigative tool, but, given the research on the accuracy of polygraph decisions, it should not be relied on as unquestionable evidence of guilt.

In addition to the polygraph, other devices for assessing honesty have been examined. The research on voice analysis instruments indicates an inability to detect deception at greater than chance levels. Thus, their value would appear to be limited to a "fear inducing" role, the threat of examination serving as a deterrent to theft. Paper-and-pencil instruments show some evidence of validity, but require additional research. Most pressing is the need for a study where these instruments are used alone, rather than in conjunction with polygraph examinations, to predict future theft.

We have attempted to raise a number of issues regarding the assessment and prediction of honesty which hopefully will be of interest to both researchers and practitioners alike. A number of areas worthy of future investigation have been identified, including potential bias, the effects of examiner experience and training, the effectiveness of various counter-measures, the potential for examinee training to "beat" the polygraph, and the need for more systematic investigation of paper-and-pencil measures, among others. Given the widespread use of these instruments in industry, such research is urgently needed.

In the last several decades, different types of predictors have been explored in an attempt to develop the most valid devices for hiring and promotional decisions. In addition, success has been defined in many different ways. In this reading, Schmitt et al. review the literature and come to some conclusions about what the most reasonable methods might be for selecting individuals given different definitions of successful performance. In addition, they consider the effect of varying experimental designs on the observation of validity.

■ READING 11 ■

Meta-Analyses of Validity Studies Published between 1964 and 1982 and the Investigation of Study Characteristics

Neal Schmitt, Richard Z. Gooding, Raymond A. Noe, and Michael Kirsch, *Michigan State University*

With the development of meta-analytic procedures (Glass, McGaw, & Smith, 1981; Hunter, Schmidt, & Jackson, 1982) and their application to personnel selection (for examples, see Pearlman, Schmidt, & Hunter, 1980; Schmidt, Gast-Rosenberg, & Hunter, 1980; Schmidt & Hunter, 1977; Schmidt, Hunter, & Caplan, 1981; and Schmidt, Hunter, Pearlman, & Shane, 1979), several problems in the use of tests in employee selection have disappeared or seem considerably less important than previously thought. Most significantly, the body of research generated by Hunter, Schmidt, and their colleagues suggests that test validity generalizes across situations within broad occupational families (see Hunter, Note 1). Most of their validity generalization work involved the use of unpublished studies of measures of cognitive ability. However, Hunter and Hunter (Note 2) have completed meta-analyses on "alternate" predictors as well as cognitive ability tests. In that

analysis of entry level jobs, they found no predictor with validity higher than that of cognitive ability tests. In this paper, we present the results of a meta-analysis completed on validation studies published in the *Journal of Applied Psychology* and *Personnel Psychology* between 1964 and 1982. No previous systematic meta-analytic work has been done on these published studies (some were included in work by Reilly & Chao, 1982; Boehm, 1982; and Hunter & Hunter, Note 2). We use our analyses to address several questions we believe are of interest to personnel researchers.

Besides materials published by Hunter, Schmidt and their colleagues, two other review efforts are relevant to the results summarized in this paper. Reilly and Chao (1982) examined the validity of eight categories of alternate predictors. Their conclusion was that only biodata and peer evaluation were supported as having validities approximately equal to those of standardized tests. In another review, Boehm (1982) examined nearly the same studies reviewed in this paper (namely, studies

Source: *Personnel Psychology*, 37, 1984, pp 407–421.

published in the same two journals between 1960 and 1979). Her focus was on a determination of the changes, if any, which have occurred in the volume of published research, the types of research design, occupations investigated, predictors and criteria used, and obtained validities. The overall average validity across all studies reviewed by Boehm was approximately .22 which represents no change from the results of earlier reviews for proficiency criteria (Ghiselli, 1973). However, she did not report average validities for any of the subgroups of studies she examined.

In this paper, using meta-analytic procedures outlined by Hunter, Schmidt, and Jackson (1982), we analyze the validities of various subgroups of studies in an attempt to answer five questions. First, we look at validities from studies in which the research design was concurrent, purely predictive, or predictive with selection. In concurrent studies, measures of predictors and criteria are collected from job incumbents. In a purely predictive design, predictor data are collected from job applicants and hiring decisions are made with no knowledge of the predictors. A very common situation in validation research is that in which predictor information is collected from job applicants and also used as the basis for selection producing range restriction (Thorndike, 1949). Concurrent and predictive studies in which the tests were used to make hiring decisions should yield test validities which are lower. Recently, Barrett, Phillips, and Alexander (1981) referred to four criticisms of the concurrent design that supposedly make its use less than desirable. These include "missing persons", restriction of range, motivational and demographic differences between present employees and job applicants, and confounding by job experience. However, their review of existing data indicated that these differences have a minimal impact on the magnitude of the validity coefficient. For example, an empirical comparison of concurrent and predictive validity coefficients of the General Aptitude Test Battery suggests that the two research designs yield virtually identical coefficients (Bemis, 1968). Further, Schmitt and

Schneider (1983) suggest the possibility that there may also be conditions in which range enhancement occurs (obviously this would only be a problem when applying range restriction corrections to concurrent validity coefficients). On the other hand, several authors (Lee, Miller, & Graham, 1982; Linn, 1983; Linn, Harnisch, & Dunbar, 1981) have affirmed the appropriateness of corrections for range restriction and even their conservative nature in some instances. Examination of validities for different research designs in this paper is directed toward determining the extent to which the level of the observed validity coefficients are associated with the type of research design used in the validation effort.

A second question addressed in this paper is whether validity coefficients vary by the criterion employed in the study. In this connection, it has been standard practice for industrial psychologists to express a preference for "objective" criteria such as productivity, tenure, or salary increases and promotions while settling for "subjective" performance ratings. While a great deal of attention is currently being focused on the determinants of performance ratings (see Ilgen & Feldman, 1983; Landy & Farr, 1980; Wexley & Klimoski, 1984), no previous examination of differences in observed validity coefficients has been undertaken.

Our third question concerns the relative size of validity coefficients for various types of predictors. Similar questions have been addressed by Lent, Aurbach, and Levin (1971), Hunter and Hunter (Note 2) and Reilly and Chao (1982). The dates of the published studies (1964–1982) were set so as to ensure inclusion of all work since the Lent et al. effort and to cover the period of time since EEO concerns became important in personnel selection. Our review includes only published work whereas the Hunter and Hunter effort included much unpublished data. Finally, the Reilly-Chao review focused on predictors which may be considered alternatives to traditional paper-and-pencil measures. Of these three reviews, only the Hunter and Hunter work included the use of meta-analytic techniques to summarize the validity data.

Fourth, for those categories in which a sufficient number of studies exist, we examined predictor-criterion combinations. This examination is particularly relevant to construct and content validity questions and represents an examination of the importance of the Wernimont and Campbell (1968) distinction among tests that are signs or samples. Wernimont and Campbell suggested that development of predictors which were intended to be actual job samples should result in increased validity coefficients. In other words, if our predictor and criterion measures are both from the same content domain, correlations should be maximized.

The final study characteristic used to subgroup validity coefficients is the occupational group which served as research participants. This, of course, represents one of the major concerns of the initial validity generalization research (Schmidt & Hunter, 1977; Hunter, Note 1). Hunter's recent work (Note 1) on virtually all jobs in the Dictionary of Occupational Titles, suggests that validities are similar within broad job categories, but that there are practically meaningful differences across these categories.

To summarize, our purpose in this paper was to apply meta-analytic methodology to examine validities as a function of five study characteristics: (a) validation research design; (b) the type of criterion used; (c) the type of predictor used; (d) predictor-criterion combinations; and (e) the occupational group studied.

Sample

All studies reporting criterion-related validity studies in *Personnel Psychology* and *Journal of Applied Psychology* between the years of 1964 and 1982 were the source of the meta-analysis reported in this paper. A total of 99 articles were reviewed; 65 came from the *Journal of Applied Psychology* and 34 from *Personnel Psychology*. References to these papers are available from the senior author.

Procedure

Each of the 99 papers was reviewed and the appropriate data coded. Specifically, of interest to this study, validity coefficients, study design, occupational group(s), predictor type(s), and criterion type(s) were coded for each study. An effort was also made to code criterion reliabilities, and the standard deviations of selected and applicant populations and/or the selection ratio but these data were available on a very small proportion of the studies. When appropriate, cross-validated correlations or validities corrected for shrinkage were recorded.

Intercoder reliability for the various information extracted from the papers was assessed by examining the coding of a subset of 25 papers by three of the authors. Independent agreement exceeded 90 percent for all variables; subsequent discussion of the cases involving disagreement clarified the coding standards and produced agreement in all cases. The remaining studies were coded by the second author. A list and description of the coding categories is available from the senior author. A total of 840 cases or validity coefficients were coded. Most of the subgroups included sizable numbers of validity coefficients (in excess of 30). As has been true in other meta-analytic studies of validity coefficients, many of the 840 coefficients coded were nonindependent observations in the sense that several validity coefficients were computed from data collected on a single group of subjects with several intercorrelated performance criteria (see Hunter, Schmidt, & Jackson, 1982). For each independent sample within a study, validities of the various measures within a single predictor category for a single criterion category were averaged to produce a "summary" validity coefficient. This produced a total of 366 coefficients. It should be noted that while these summary validities were conceptually independent validity coefficients, they were not necessarily statistically independent in the sense that criteria intercorrelations were not zero. Analyses of both the total set of validities and the 366 summary validities were conducted; only the latter are reported in this paper. There was little difference between the results of these two analyses; total analyses are available upon request from the senior author.

In averaging the validity coefficients, each coefficient was weighted by its sample size. In addition, the variance of the coefficients (σ_r^2), the variance due to sampling error (σ_e^2), variance remaining after subtracting variance due to sampling error (σ_ρ^2) and the percent of remaining or unexplained variance were computed using formulas available in Hunter, Schmidt, and Jackson (1982).

No attempt was made to correct the variance of the coefficients for other artifacts such as differences in range restriction or criterion unreliability (Schmidt & Hunter, 1977). Data that would have made these corrections possible were unavailable in the large majority of studies. In studies in which the distributions of these artifacts are assumed or constructed based on available literature or best guesses indicate that most of the variability in validity coefficients can be explained by sampling error. For example, of the percentage of variance in validity coefficients accounted for in one validity generalization study (Schmidt, Hunter, & Caplan, 1981), approximately 90 percent was accounted for by sampling error whereas an additional 10 percent was accounted for by criterion reliability, test reliability, and range restriction distributions. Similar results were reported in Pearlman et al. (1980) and Schmidt, Gast-Rosenberg, and Hunter (1980). Consequently removal of artifacts other than sampling error would appear to have little or no effect on conclusions concerning the variability of validity coefficients.

RESULTS

Study Design

In Table 1, we present data relevant to the question concerning the design of a validation study. The average overall observed validity is .28, consistent with previous reviews (Ghiselli, 1973; Boehm, 1982). There appear to be minimal differences across study designs in the average validity coefficient and contrary to conventional wisdom, the concurrent designs actually produce validity coefficients which are slightly superior to predictive designs, especially those predictive designs in which the predictor instruments were used to make hiring decisions. This direct restriction of range, then, may have more serious deflating effects on observed validity coefficients than does the indirect restriction that is assumed to have occurred through attrition and promotion in the typical concurrent study.

Sample sizes vary considerably which suggests that there be concern about averaging the sample size weighted validity coefficients, but the correlation between sample size and validity was .03. It is true, however, that sample sizes in the concurrent studies were smaller and this is reflected in the fact that a greater proportion of the variance in validity coefficients is explained by sampling error. Not surprisingly given the variety of tests, criteria, and occupational groups in these studies, sampling error did not account for much of the variability in validity coefficients.

According to Hunter, Schmidt, and Jackson (1982, pp. 47–48), a moderator variable is

TABLE 1 Validity Coefficients as Function of Validation Study Design

Design	Number of Validities	Sample Range	Sample Total	$\bar{r}$	σ_r^2	σ_e^2	σ_ρ^2	Percent Unexplained
Concurrent	153	22–520	17838	.341	.03703	.00670	.03011	82
Predictive	99	19–68616	90552	.296	.00668	.00091	.00577	86
Predictive with selection	114	19–14738	124960	.259	.02140	.00079	.02061	96
Total	366	19–68616	233350	.280	.01750	.00133	.01617	92

TABLE 2 Validity Coefficients as Function of Various Occupational Groups

Occupational Group	Number of Validities	Sample Range	Sample Total	$\bar{r}$	σ^2_r	σ^2_e	σ^2_ϱ	Percent Unex-plained
Professional	81	19–2411	18610	.319	.02393	.00351	.02042	85
Managerial	93	24–8885	43188	.335	.01943	.00170	.01773	91
Clerical	36	25–1091	9690	.385	.02284	.00270	.02014	88
Sales	50	22–14738	31732	.170	.00845	.00149	.00696	82
Skilled labor	46	34–3964	37658	.177	.01519	.00115	.01404	92
Unskilled labor	60	47–68616	92472	.314	.00633	.00053	.00580	92
Total	366	19–68616	233350	.280	.01750	.00133	.01617	92

indicated when the average correlation varies across subgroups and the corrected variance averages lower in the subsets than for the whole data. For the data summarized in Table 1, there are small differences in average validity coefficients, but the variances of the subgroups certainly are not smaller than the variance of the total. As a further effort to assess the effect of study design on the size of observed validity coefficients, three dichotomous variables were created by coding each study design 1 and the remaining studies, 0. These dichotomous variables were correlated with the validity coefficients. Correlations were .16, .00, -.17 for concurrent, predictive, and predictive with selection respectively. While the

.16 and -.17 correlations are statistically significant, the correlations are certainly not large. Validity does not appear to be underestimated when researchers use concurrent strategies; if there is any difference at all, it seems that concurrent strategies result in higher estimates of validity coefficients than do predictive strategies especially those predictive studies which involve some use of the selection instruments to eliminate potentially low performing employees.

Occupational Group

The results summarizing validation studies over various occupational groups are presented

TABLE 3 Predictors and Criteria Used with Various Occupational Groups

	Professional Number of Validities	Managerial Number of Validities	Clerical Number of Validities	Sales Number of Validities	Skilled Labor Number of Validities	Unskilled Labor Number of Validities
Predictor						
Special aptitude	9	4	8	1	7	2
Personality	21	17	1	6	11	6
General mental ability	8	18	12	3	5	7
Biodata	23	4	9	31	13	19
Job Sample	8	3	3	0	4	0
Assessment center	3	15	0	3	0	0
Supervisor/peer evaluations	4	24	0	3	0	0
Physical ability	0	1	0	0	6	15
Criterion						
Performance rating	43	31	12	15	17	22
Turnover	5	0	9	11	12	11
Achievement/grades	8	11	3	4	14	3
Productivity	7	0	0	20	0	3
Status change	4	33	0	0	0	9
Wages	13	17	0	0	0	3
Work samples	0	1	12	0	2	9

TABLE 4 Validity Coefficients as a Function of Type of Predictor

Predictor	Number of Validities	Sample Range	Sample Total	$\bar{r}$	σ^2_r	σ^2_e	σ^2_ρ	Percent Unexplained
Special aptitude	31	19–1091	4315	.268	.02083	.00619	.01464	70
Personality	62	24–3964	23413	.149	.01109	.00253	.00856	77
General mental ability	53	24–8885	40230	.248	.01908	.00117	.01791	94
Biodata	99	22–14738	58107	.243	.01831	.00151	.01680	92
Work sample	18	19–1091	3512	.378	.01139	.00377	.00762	67
Assessment center	21	35–8885	15345	.407	.00250	.00095	.00155	62
Supervisor/peer evaluations	31	30–1979	6620	.427	.03046	.00313	.02733	89
Physical ability	22	55–588	3103	.315	.04865	.00575	.04290	88
Total	366	19–68616	233350	.280	.01750	.00133	.01617	92

in Table 2. As in Table 1, the average validity coefficients computed for the subgroups involve a wide variety of test-criterion relationships, hence it is not surprising that sampling error does not account for a large portion of the variability in observed coefficients. There are, furthermore, sizable differences in the magnitude of the coefficients for different subgroups with the Sales and Skilled Labor groups having coefficients below .20 and the other groups having coefficients above .30. The average within group corrected variance, σ^2_ρ, was lower than the variance of coefficients for the total set of coefficients but dichotomous occupational group variables did not correlate highly ($<.16$) with the validity coefficients.

Some of the differences across occupational groups in validity coefficients could also be due to the particular type of predictor or criterion used in validation research. Table 3 is a summary of the number of instances a particular criterion or predictor was used for each occupational group.

Studies of Sales and Skilled Labor groups most frequently involved the use of personality and biodata as predictors and, relative to other groups, more frequently used turnover as a criterion. The generally lower validities associated with the prediction of turnover and the use of personality measures (see Tables 4 and 5) may account for the lower validities for the Sales and Skilled and Unskilled Labor groups.

Further breakdowns of the validity coefficients for predictor-criterion relationships by occupational subgroups were also done. Data from these analyses are not reported here

TABLE 5 Validity Coefficients as a Function of Type of Criterion

Criterion	Number of Validities	Sample Range	Sample Total	$\bar{r}$	σ^2_r	σ^2_e	σ^2_ρ	Percent Unexplained
Performance ratings	140	22–520	17559	.260	.03051	.00693	.02358	77
Turnover	48	37–68616	127021	.246	.01104	.00033	.01071	97
Achievement/grades	43	19–453	7156	.270	.03971	.00516	.03455	87
Productivity	30	50–3590	14869	.208	.00584	.00185	.00399	68
Status change	46	30–8885	52686	.359	.01303	.00066	.01237	95
Wages	33	47–443	5470	.378	.02278	.00443	.01835	81
Work samples	24	77–1091	8244	.401	.02638	.00205	.02433	92
Total	366	19–68616	233350	.280	.01750	.00133	.01617	90

(though available upon request) because for many of the predictor-criterion-occupational subgroup categories, the number of validity studies available was simply too few. Especially noteworthy was the fact that little information concerning physical ability measures is available even for skilled and unskilled occupational groups in which they may be useful. Also, there are few studies for any occupational subgroup which involve the use of production criteria.

Predictor Type

Average validity coefficients for various types of predictors are presented in Table 4. There are substantial differences in the average validity coefficients with personality measures being associated with the lowest validities and work samples, assessment centers, and supervisor and peer evaluations most highly correlated with criteria. The average within predictor type variance σ_e^2 was slightly lower than the variance of coefficients for the total set of coefficients. Two of the dichotomously scored predictor type variables did correlate with the validity coefficients ($r = -.27$ and .15, $p < .01$, for personality and physical ability measures, respectively). It is also noteworthy that average validities for special aptitudes and general mental ability are lower than those for predictors we classified as work samples, supervisor or peer evaluations, and assessment centers.

Criterion Type

In Table 5, average validity coefficients obtained with various criteria are listed. A concern among industrial psychologists has been the extensive use of performance rating criteria and the relative lack of use of more "objective" criteria. Due to their sensitivity to various biases, performance ratings may either inflate validity estimates or result in the inappropriate weighting of certain predictors. Performance ratings yield slightly better validity coefficients than do turnover criteria and productivity criteria but much lower validity coefficients than those associated with work samples, wages, and status changes. Feature correlations

in the form of dichotomously scored criterion type variables were all less than .10 except for the work sample correlation ($r = .18\ p < .01$). While these results yield no information concerning appropriate/inappropriate weighting of predictors when one uses various criteria, the results certainly do not support the belief that use of so-called subjective criteria will result in inflated validity coefficients. If anything, use of performance rating criteria results in lower validity coefficients than does the use of other criteria.

Predictor-Criterion Relationships

A question relevant to concerns about construct validity is whether validities for certain predictor-criterion relationships are higher than others. Certainly, personnel researchers will use those predictors which research, training, and experience indicate will be most useful in the prediction of given criteria, but are there any substantial differences? In Table 6, we summarize the data concerning predictor-criterion relationships.

Several points concerning the data summarized in Table 6 are worth noting. First, performance ratings are best predicted by assessment centers and supervisor-peer evaluations, both of which are themselves, rating predictors. Validity coefficients for biodata and work samples are also relatively high while those associated with paper-and-pencil tests (special aptitude, personality, and general mental ability) are lower. It is also true that studies involving work samples, assessment centers, and supervisory or peer evaluations as predictors were relatively few in number and the total sample size associated with these average validities, low.

Studies using turnover as a criterion have almost exclusively used biodata as a predictor presumably because of the notion that past behavior with respect to job or life changes is the best predictor of future behavior. Of those studies available, this seems to be true; though all validity coefficients for turnover criteria tend to be low. These low validities may occur because of the nature of the turnover criterion, but may also be due to the fact that our predic-

TABLE 6 Average Validity Coefficients for Various Predictor-Criterion Combinations

Predictor	Number of Validities	Total Sample	$\overline{r}$	σ^2_r	$\sigma^2_\bullet$	σ^2_ϱ	Percent Unexplained
Performance ratings							
Special aptitude	14	838	.162	.02841	.01584	.01257	44
Personality	32	4065	.206	.03531	.00722	.02809	80
General mental ability	25	3597	.220	.01563	.00629	.00934	60
Biodata	29	3998	.317	.03566	.00587	.02979	84
Work sample	7	384	.319	.01081	.01471	—	0
Assessment center	6	394	.428	.00259	.01016	—	0
Supervisor/peer evaluations	12	1389	.315	.03140	.00701	.02439	78
Turnover							
Personality	5	15927	.121	.00104	.00030	.00074	71
General mental ability	8	12449	.141	.01877	.00062	.01815	97
Biodata	28	28862	.209	.01444	.00089	.01355	94
Physical ability	3	852	.154	.00762	.00336	.00426	56
Achievement/grades							
Special aptitude	8	1093	.275	.03622	.00625	.02997	83
Personality	6	980	.152	.01406	.00584	.00822	58
General mental ability	5	888	.437	.02209	.00369	.01840	83
Biodata	9	1744	.226	.07841	.00465	.07376	94
Work sample	3	95	.314	.01876	.02566	—	00
Assessment center	3	289	.312	.00692	.00846	—	00
Physical ability	4	976	.281	.00327	.00348	—	00
Productivity							
Biodata	19	13655	.203	.00362	.00128	.00234	65
Status change							
Personality	7	561	.126	.03139	.01208	.01931	61
General mental ability	9	21190	.282	.00880	.00036	.00844	96
Biodata	6	8008	.332	.00144	.00059	.00085	59
Assessment center	8	14361	.412	.00151	.00038	.00113	75
Supervisor/peer evaluations	9	4224	.512	.01537	.00116	.01421	92
Physical ability	3	245	.613	.00028	.00477	—	—
Wages							
Personality	10	1720	.268	.00903	.00501	.00402	45
Biodata	7	1544	.525	.01571	.00238	.01333	85
Work sample	4	1191	.438	.00547	.00219	.00328	60
Assessment center	4	301	.237	.00531	.00184	—	00
Supervisor/peer evaluations	4	301	.206	00737	.01219	—	00
Work sample							
Special aptitude	3	1793	.280	.00423	.00142	.00281	66
General mental ability	3	1793	.426	.00660	.00112	.00548	83
Work sample	3	1793	.353	.01126	.00128	.00998	89
Physical ability	11	959	.419	.08924	.00784	.08140	91

Note: All predictor-criterion combinations for which less than three coefficients were available were ignored.

.00737

tor instruments do not reflect the wide range of potential determinants of turnover such as organizational commitment, perceptions of the labor market, and job satisfaction (Mobley, Griffeth, Hand, & Meglino, 1979). Further analyses of the biodata might be helpful since only 6 percent of the variability in validity co-

efficients was explained by differences in the sample sizes across studies. Measures of achievement/grades are best predicted by general mental ability tests and least well by personality tests. Perhaps the widest variety of predictors have been used to predict achievement and grades hence the number of studies and total sample size for any given predictor category is relatively low. Somewhat surprisingly, the only selection instrument used frequently to predict productivity has been biodata and, as with turnover, the validity coefficients are modest.

Status change appears to be best predicted by supervisor/peer evaluations and assessment center ratings. Personality measures yield very low coefficients though total sample size is small. General mental ability correlates relatively low with status change though the average validity coefficient is about the same as that for the total set of coefficients.

Wages are best predicted by biodata and work samples and least well predicted by assessment centers and supervisor/peer evaluations. All results for wages are based on a small number of validity coefficients and low total sample size, however.

Work samples have been predicted most frequently by physical ability measures (though total sample size is only 959) with relatively good results ($\bar{r}_{xy} = .419$). In reviewing Table 6, it is evident from the amount of unexplained variance in validity coefficients that there may be other moderators of the observed validity coefficient besides the type of predictor or criterion.

DISCUSSION AND CONCLUSIONS

Throughout Tables 1–6, it is evident that validities exhibit considerable variability after corrections for sample size variability. While Hunter, Schmidt, and their colleagues have usually reported that 50 to 100 percent of the variance in validities can be explained by sample size differences, the results of our meta-analyses do not indicate that much more than 25 percent of the variability is due to sample size differences. It may very well be that our data sources are more variable in that (*a*) different predictors are used even within a predictor category; (*b*) the researchers in our studies varied more in the way data were collected and analyzed; or (*c*) the organizational settings of the published studies which were our source of

data were more variable. The latter is purely speculative, but the fact remains that our corrections for sample size variability explained a relatively small portion of the total variability in validity coefficients.

Another obvious fact is that for many predictor-criterion relationships, we still lack adequate data with which to draw conclusions even when using meta-analysis of all available data. For some predictor-criterion relationships it would make little sense to collect data. For example, the turnover-general mental ability relationship does not seem interesting unless one has a theoretical rationale based perhaps on the complexity of the job and the relative speed with which persons with varying levels of mental ability become bored and leave. Productivity should be correlated with a wider range of predictor variables. There is of course a much larger body of unpublished literature which Hunter and Schmidt and their colleagues have summarized especially on cognitive paper-and-pencil measures (see Hunter, Note 1; Hunter and Hunter, Note 2). Unpublished literature on less widely used and nontraditional selection instruments does not seem to be as large and some potentially useful methods such as miniaturized training sessions, situational interviews, and unassembled examinations have not been frequently studied (Reilly & Chao, 1982).

As noted above, there is little evidence that concurrent studies of test validity yield different results than predictive studies. This suggests that motivational effects and/or job experience effects that are generally cited as reasons for not employing concurrent validation strategies (Guion, 1965) may not be that important. Alternatively, job experience may enhance the range of job performance and test scores in concurrent studies thus artificially inflating validity coefficients. This hypothesis has been suggested elsewhere (Schmitt & Schneider, 1983) and conflicts with the more popular belief that job experience and/or selection and attrition serve to restrict the variance of predictor and criterion in concurrent studies. Obviously data concerning the standard deviation of selection instruments and criteria collected at various times before and after employment are required to evaluate what degree of range restriction or enhancement occurs.

The use of performance ratings as criteria in validation studies does not serve to inflate observed validity coefficients. The lower observed validity coefficients for performance rating criteria counterindicate the concern that these coefficients are inflated because of various biases whereas more "objective" criteria would not be affected by these biases. One reason performance rating criteria yield lower validities may be because their reliability is lower than the reliability associated with criteria such as tenure, wages, or status changes.

Results concerning different types of predictors are consistent with previous literature reviews (Ghiselli, 1973; Guion & Gottier, 1965) which indicate that personality tests have low validity. The data are not consistent with Hunter and Hunter's conclusion (Note 2) that cognitive ability tests are superior to other predictors. The data summarized in this paper indicate that work samples, assessment centers, and supervisor/peer evaluations yield validities which are superior to those of general mental ability and special aptitude tests which are closest to those labeled ability measures by Hunter and Hunter (Note 2). There are likely several reasons for the difference between our work and that of Hunter and Hunter, but at least one occurs to the authors. Our data consist solely of published work in two journals over the past two decades while the work summarized by Hunter and Hunter (Note 2) included a large portion of unpublished data. Much of the published research was directed to the development and study of alternate predictors; more traditional tests were included only as standards of comparison or because they were available in many of these studies. In much of the work which served as the source of validity coefficients for Hunter and Hunter, the paper-and-pencil ability measures were carefully developed and standardized measures. As noted above, the studies which we reviewed may also have been more variable along several dimensions than those which were the source of the Hunter analyses.

Several other conclusions are similar to those stated by previous authors doing meta-analytic work on validation studies (Hunter, Schmidt, & Jackson, 1982; Callender & Osburn, 1980). Data for accurate assessment of the effect of artifacts in personnel selection studies is largely unavailable. Authors simply do not report the predictor or criterion standard deviations of applicant and incumbent groups nor do they report the selection ratio or the reliability of the measures they use. Second, use of credibility values for the various average validities obtained in this paper indicates one should have reasonable confidence in obtaining nonzero validity coefficients using various selection instruments and criteria for all job families. Our results are not as consistent with previous validity generalization work if one considers the amount of variability in validity coefficients accounted for by sampling error. Even when validities were averaged for a single occupational group for a single criterion-predictor relationship (analyses available from senior author), large portions of the validity variance remained in many cases. Finally, as is evident by examining our tables there are a wide variety of predictor-criterion relationships for which we have very little data and for which initial results are encouraging. Rather than squelching validity research, meta-analytic work should serve to redirect and stimulate both the actual validation studies and their detailed reporting.

One final note of caution in the use of the meta-analytic procedures outlined by Hunter, Schmidt, and Jackson (1982) is appropriate. In those cases where the number of validities was small (<6), we nearly always found that corrections for differences in sample size accounted for most of the validity coefficient variability. Whenever the number of studies was greater, the corrections did not account for nearly as large a proportion of the validity variance. This suggests that these corrections are likely inappropriate or misleading when the number of different validities over which one is averaging is small.

SECTION FOUR

Performance Measurement

The description and measurement of performance is a hot topic. Several years ago, a move was made by both private and public sector employers to base pay on performance rather than simply on loyalty or seniority. The only problem was that there were substantial difficulties in measuring performance with any confidence. The most common form of performance measurement, the supervisory rating, seemed riddled with various types of rating errors. There were plenty of home remedies for reducing these errors, but the bottom line was that there was no compelling theory of rating to guide application or research. In this section, we will pick up the story of performance evaluation—particularly performance rating.

Supervisory rating scales were introduced in the industry in the late 1920s. They were called graphic ratings because the most common response format was a line or scale of some kind that represented merit, with instructions to mark on that line or scale (or graph) the position of one or more people who were being considered. Despite the enormous amount of research conducted on rating scales, it is best characterized as undisciplined and without direction. Although Wherry did careful work in his research for the Army in the late 1940s, this research and his model of rating were little known outside his circle of friends and acquaintances. In 1980, Jim Farr and I published a review of most of the published research that had been conducted on supervisory rating scales. As a result of that review, we developed a model of the rating process and suggested while some aspects of the rating process had been over-researched, other areas had been ignored. This reading is a summary of that review. Perhaps the most important conclusion in this review is the fact the actual appearance or format of the rating scale may be the least important aspect of the rating process.

■ READING 12 ■

Performance Rating

Frank J. Landy and James L. Farr
Pennsylvania State University

The measurement of performance in industrial settings has occupied the attention of psychologists for 50 years. Performance description and prediction play an important role in all personnel decisions. Criteria are necessary for validation studies and training evaluation; indices of effectiveness or relative worth are necessary for administrative decision making with respect to current employees; performance-related information is necessary for feedback and employee counseling; there is even some indication that the process of performance evaluation may function as a reward and be capable of inducing feelings of satisfaction in some employees (Landy, Barnes, & Murphy, 1978).

Unfortunately, realizing the importance of performance measurement and actually measuring performance accurately are two different matters. In some ideal sense, complete performance measurement would include the combination of objective, personnel, and judgmental indices (Landy & Trumbo, 1980). Unfortunately, it is difficult to obtain objective indices of performance for many job titles. In addition, personnel information is applicable to a small portion of the employee population in any organization (e.g., 5 percent of the employees may have 100 percent of the accidents, less than 8 percent of the employees may have more than one unexcused absence per year, tardiness records are not well kept, etc.).

Consequently, most individuals concerned with performance measurement depend on judgmental indices of one type or another. Guion (1965) reported that 81 percent of the published studies in the *Journal of Applied Psychology* and *Personnel Psychology* between 1950 and 1955 used ratings as criteria. Blum and Naylor (1968) sampled articles from the *Journal of Applied Psychology* for the period from 1960 to 1965 and found that of those using criterion measurement, 46 percent measured performance via judgmental indices. Landy and Farr (1976) reported that 89 percent of

Source: *Psychological Bulletin*, 87, no. 1 (1980) pp. 72–107. Copyright 1980 by the American Psychological Association. Reprinted by permission of the publisher and author.

196 police departments in major metropolitan areas used supervisory ratings as the primary form of performance measurement. Finally, Landy and Trumbo (1980) reported that a literature review of validation studies in the *Journal of Applied Psychology* between 1965 and 1975 revealed that ratings were used as the primary criterion in 72 percent of the cases. By any standard, judgmental measurements of performance are widely used.

In spite of the widespread use of judgmental indices of performance, there has been a constant dissatisfaction with these measures on the part of both researcher and practitioner. The source of this dissatisfaction has been the vulnerability of these measures to both intentional and inadvertent bias. As a consequence, an enormous amount of research has been conducted in an attempt to improve the validity of judgmental indices of performance. These studies have covered a wide variety of issues, such as rater and ratee individual differences, types of formats, conditions surrounding the judgmental process, and so forth. In this article, we review the outcomes of this research.

We limit the scope of this review to a consideration of one particular form of performance judgment—the performance rating. We choose to concentrate on this method for three reasons: (*a*) As indicated in earlier reviews (Guion, 1965; Landy & Farr, 1976; Landy & Trumbo, 1980), the rating is by far the most ubiquitous form of performance judgment; (*b*) research on various aspects of rating is more common than research on any other judgmental index of performance, and (*c*) other judgmental methods, such as ranking, pair comparison estimation, and other forms of worker-to-worker comparison, imply a qualitatively different discrimination process. Thus, the review deals primarily with a consideration of rating methods. In addition, since Wherry (Note 1) completed an exhaustive review of performance rating research prior to 1950, we deal predominantly with the literature appearing subsequent to that review. Other reviews have appeared since 1950 (e.g., Barrett, 1966b; J. P. Campbell, Dunnette,

Lawler, & Weick, 1970; Lopez, 1968; Miner, 1972; Smith, 1976), but these have generally been more narrowly focused than is the present review.

We exclude detailed consideration of several broader issues in the measurement of job performance. These include such issues as the dynamic nature of criteria (B. M. Bass, 1962; Ghiselli & Haire, 1960; Prien, 1966), the composite criterion versus multiple criteria controversy (Dunnette, 1963; Guion, 1961; Schmidt & Kaplan, 1971), and the relationship of ratings to more general theories or models of human performance (James, 1973). These are excluded because they deal with all forms of criterion measures, not just ratings of performance. Their inclusion would necessitate extensive space that is not available, and their discussion would not be appropriate here. The relationships between performance rating and broader organizational questions of selection, training, counseling, and job satisfaction are generally not addressed. Works by Barrett (1966b), Lopez (1968), and Miner (1972), among others, address many of these relationships.

The literature in the area of performance rating is fragmented. Some do research on different rating formats, whereas others examine characteristics of raters and ratees. This insularity has tended to obscure the fact that performance rating is best thought of as a system comprising many different classes of variables. The rating instrument and the characteristics of raters and ratees are only parts of that larger system. At a general level, that system might include the following classes of variables: (*a*) the roles (rater and ratee), (*b*) the vehicle (the rating instrument), (*c*) the rating context (the type of organization, the purpose for rating, etc.), (*d*) the rating process (administrative constraints, individual rater strategies, etc.), and (*e*) the results of the rating (raw and transformed performance information, actions based on that information, etc.). Our review deals with research results bearing on those major classes of variables. Figure 1 is a graphic representation of how those components might

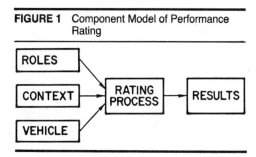

FIGURE 1   Component Model of Performance Rating

interact. Although Figure 1 might be heuristi-cally helpful in structuring the body of the re-view, it is not particularly illuminating with respect to the specific influences affecting the judgment that one person makes of another's performance. Consequently, after reviewing the available research evidence, we present a more elaborate model of the performance rat-ing process that should be more theoretically useful than Figure 1.

There are some unique constraints on the performance rating literature. Consider the phenomenon in question. Typically, a supervi-sor is asked to consider the past performance of one or more subordinates. The period of past performance is typically one year. During that period of time, the supervisor and the subordi-nate have interacted frequently and probably know each other reasonably well. Most re-search on the topic of performance rating has considered the adequacy of rating in this type of context. For that reason, we have excluded from consideration studies dealing with the evaluation of applicants in interview situa-tions. This literature has been well covered elsewhere and is not directly relevant to tradi-tional performance rating. We conceive of the prototypic performance rating as a retrospec-tive synthesis by one individual of the efforts or performance of another. Thus, we are deal-ing with an appraisal of a long string of actions rather than a single one; in addition, we are dealing with a constellation of activities rather than with single physical or mental operations in isolation. We have included in the review studies of simulated work settings that have experimentally manipulated variables of inter-est to performance rating, if the behaviors of the ratees were observable rather than repre-sented only by a pencil-and-paper task.

Since the research on performance appraisal is predominantly in the form of field studies, we are unable to make comparisons from one study to another with respect to the dimen-sions of performance examined. Each organiza-tion has a different idea of what may be impor-tant in assessing their people; consequently, each rating instrument is ultimately unique. This is unfortunate, since there is every reason to believe that different types of performance may be evaluated more or less accurately than others. For example, interpersonal skills might be more accurately evaluated than creativity. However, this is a source of variation over which we have no control as reviewers. These are the structural boundaries of the review.

ROLES

Rater Characteristics

The research on rater characteristics pro-vides relatively few general conclusions. Since most studies examine only one or a few charac-teristics, it is likely that unmeasured or unre-ported variables have had some effect on the re-sults of any single study. This results in a chaotic pattern of findings in many instances. Nevertheless, some generally consistent effects can be described. Sex of the rater does not gen-erally affect ratings, although female raters may be more lenient. Raters usually give higher ratings to same-race ratees, although this may be moderated by the degree of contact that members of each race have with each other. Rater age and education have been stud-ied too infrequently to make general state-ments about their effects.

Psychological characteristics of raters have not been systematically researched, but it ap-pears (and has been empirically demonstrated to some extent) that cognitive complexity may be an important variable to examine. There is a large body of research in other content areas which suggest that cognitive complexity affects information processing and evaluation.

Rater experience appears to positively affect the quality of performance ratings, but the mechanism or mechanisms responsible (e.g., more training or experience with the rating form, better observation skills, better knowledge of the job requirements, etc.) is not known. The general job performance of the rater is related to rating quality, with better performers also providing higher quality ratings. Production-oriented (as opposed to interaction-oriented) raters seem to be less lenient and to pay more attention to planning activities.

Comparisons of different types of raters suggest that in general, one should expect only low to moderate correlations among raters of different types (e.g., peer, supervisory, self, etc.). It cannot be stated that any one type of rater is more valid than any other, although peer ratings appear to be especially useful for predicting promotions. Peer ratings appear to be more lenient than supervisory ratings. As Borman (1974) and others have suggested, the best conclusion may be that different types of raters have different perspectives on performance that influence their ratings. Lawler (1967) and Blood (1974) have noted that these differences may provide valuable information for the diagnosis of organizational problems.

Raters require knowledge of the individual ratee and of the requirements of the ratee's job to adequately evaluate job performance. The relevance of the rater-ratee interaction is apparently more important than simply the amount of interaction.

Ratee Characteristics

The research on the effects of ratee characteristics on performance ratings offers some general conclusions. It appears that the sex stereotype of an occupation interacts with the sex of the ratee, such that males receive more favorable evaluations than do females in traditionally masculine occupations but that no differences or smaller differences in favor of females occur in traditionally feminine occupa-

tions. Ratees tend to receive higher ratings from raters of their same race, although this may not occur in highly integrated situations. Race and performance level of the ratee appeared to interact in complex ways. Further research is needed to determine if performance ratings have the same meaning for ratees of different races. Other personal characteristics of ratees have been studied too infrequently to yield conclusions about their general effects.

Experimental studies of the effect of the performance level of the ratee on performance ratings generally support the validity of the ratings. Performance level and ability have been found to have the strongest effect on ratings in these studies, although other ratee variables also significantly affect ratings. Raters may evaluate favorable performance more accurately than unfavorable, but not for all performance dimensions. Performance variability also appears to influence rating accuracy and reliability. Contrast effects may be important in performance ratings and need further investigation. Tenure and performance ratings are generally positively but weakly correlated, although situational variables may moderate this relationship.

Interaction of Rater and Ratee Characteristics

Rater sex and ratee sex do not appear to interact in their effects on evaluative judgments. Research in actual work settings is needed, however. Both male and female raters may have common sex role stereotypes that affect judgments. Raters often give more favorable ratings to same-race ratees, although situational factors may moderate this effect. It was suggested that the similarity of rater and ratee on background and attitudinal factors may affect ratings, although no direct results are available that bear on this question.

VEHICLE

An enormous amount of effort has been spent exploring the potential effects of various rating formats over the years. The hypothesis has been that the vehicle that is used to elicit information has an effect on the accuracy and utility of that information. In our examination of the literature bearing on this hypothesis, we deal with methods of direct rating (in which the rater actually assigns a number to a ratee representing some level of performance), methods of derived rating (in which the rater makes a series of discrete judgments about the ratee, from which a performance rating can be derived), and technical issues, such as response categories and rating scale anchors.

After more than 30 years of serious research, it seems that little progress has been made in developing an efficient and psychometrically sound alternative to the traditional graphic rating scale. Nevertheless, we have learned some things about rating formats in general. In spite of the fact that people may have preferences for various physical arrangements of high and low anchors, of graphic numbering systems, and so forth, these preferences seem to have little effect on actual rating behavior. The number of response categories available to the rater should not exceed nine. If a continuous rather than discrete response continuum is contemplated, it would be wise to conduct some pilot studies to determine how many response categories are perceived by the potential raters. There is some advantage to using behavioral anchors rather than simple numerical or adjectival anchors. This advantage is probably increased in the absence of good dimension definitions. Finally, it is important that rigorous item selection and anchoring procedures be used in the development of rating scales, regardless of the particular format being considered. It may be that new techniques, such as the BARS or the mixed standard, will show improvements over more traditional methods, if more rigorous developmental procedures are used.

CONTEXT

Included in this section are studies that have examined the effects of factors that are not explicitly related to the nature of the rater, ratee, or rating instrument but that may be consid-

ered as part of the context in which the rating occurs.

Ratings for administrative purposes will be more lenient than those for research purposes. Unfortunately, since most of the published research was done in the research purposes context, too little information is currently available to draw firm conclusions about impact of purpose for rating. Although it does not appear that the variances of the ratings are affected by the purpose component, more definitive tests of this relationship are needed.

RATING PROCESS VARIABLES

Another class of variables affecting performance ratings are those factors related to the process by which ratings are obtained, exclusive of the rating instrument itself. Included here are such variables as rater training, rater anonymity, and sequence of traits and ratees.

Rater training has generally been shown to be effective in reducing rating errors, especially if the training is extensive and allows for rater practice. Questions still remain about the longitudinal effects of such training, about the effect of rater training on the validity of ratings, and about the optimal content of such training programs.

Identified raters, as opposed to anonymous raters, appear to give equivalent ratings. There appears to be no reduction in halo error when all ratees are evaluated on one trait, then all ratees are evaluated on the next trait, and so forth. Serial position appears to have some effect on ratings, but no general pattern has emerged from the research to date.

RESULTS OF RATING

After one gathers ratings of performance, decisions must still be made concerning the manner in which these data might be analyzed to produce accurate and reliable performance descriptions. It is possible that various analytic techniques are more successful at reducing or eliminating rating errors than other techniques. In this section, we review the research that addresses this issue.

The research on dimensional combination strategies resulting from data reduction algorithms has been equivocal. A substantial amount of research still must be done before it will be possible to specify what those performance factors represent—behavioral patterns of ratees or cognitive constructs of raters. The research on the combination of multiple ratings is also equivocal. If distinct patterns of rating exist among raters (i.e., policies), the presumed gains in reliability may represent a hollow victory. On a practical basis, it seems unlikely that techniques based on multiple ratings will prove useful in applied settings, although they may be of value in cataloging sources of error. The research by Myers (1965), Ritti (1964), and Landy and Vance (1978) suggests a possible avenue for continued research in data analysis procedures.

PROCESS MODEL OF PERFORMANCE RATING

Many researchers in the area of performance rating have concluded that a model of some

sort is necessary before any significant advances can be made in understanding judgmental performance measures (DeCotiis, 1977; Jenkins & Taber, 1977; Kane & Lawler, 1978; Schwab et al., 1975; Zedeck, Jacobs, & Kafry, 1976). Figure 1 was presented earlier as a first or primitive representation of the rating process. On the basis of our review, as well as on some theoretical influences that are described below, we propose that Figure 2 is a more refined, coherent, and catholic representation of the system of performance rating. In Figure 2, we have tried to be more specific about the subsystems that form the larger rating system. Thus, the context component of Figure 1 has been broken into three components: position characteristics, organization characteristics, and the purpose for rating. Similarly, the rating process component now comprises two subsystems: the cognitive process of the rater (observation, storage, recall, and judgment) and the administrative rating process of the organization. With this general evolution in mind, we now discuss specific components of the model.

The model assumes that there are certain characteristics brought to the rating task that are properties of the rater and ratee, respectively. For example, the rater brings to the

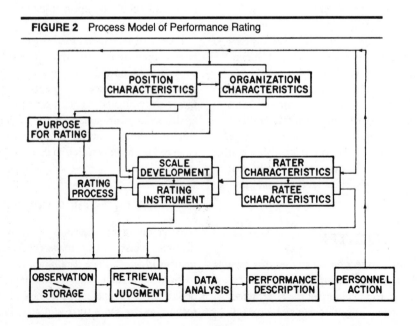

FIGURE 2   Process Model of Performance Rating

task "sets" or biases that may be related to age, sex, race, leadership style, personal relationship to ratee, and so forth. In addition, the ratee possesses certain characteristics, in addition to level of performance on the dimension under consideration, that may influence the judgment. In addition to the main effects that these respective rater and ratee characteristics represent, there are undoubtedly interactions of rater and ratee characteristics. Thus, in addition to the fact that black ratees may receive lower ratings than white ratees and in addition to the fact that black raters may be harsher in rating than white raters, there is also the possibility of an interaction of the race of the rater and the race of the ratee in performance judgment. The same would be true of other rater —ratee characteristics. The model also implies that the characteristics of the rater and ratee have an influence on the selection and/or development of the rating instrument. These characteristics might include education, previous experience with performance rating, and tenure in the organization.

The most immediate context in which rating occurs is defined by the particular organization and the particular position under consideration. Organizational size moderates such critical variables as span of control, seasonal variation in workforce, levels of turnover, part-time to full-time employee ratio, and so forth. It has also been proposed that organizations differ with respect to the climate that is perceived by their members. In addition to differences among organizations, there are distinct differences among positions within those organizations. Positions differ with respect to level within the organizational hierarchy; they also differ with respect to line versus staff and blue collar versus white collar designations. We propose that position and organizational characteristics jointly affect both the choice and/or development of a rating instrument and the purpose for which rating is done. It is not uncommon to see ratings used to make administrative decisions at one level in an organization but used for counseling at another level. In addition, supportive organizations often use ratings for employee development, whereas

punitive organizations might use the same information for employee terminations. It is appalling to note how little systematic research has addressed the impact of position and organizational characteristics on performance rating.

The purpose component of the model is of central importance.[1] Employee counseling usually requires an instrument different from that to be used simply for administrative purposes. In addition, the purpose for the rating also affects the rating process. As an example, employees are often permitted to examine supervisory comments in development or training contexts, but they are usually not permitted similar access in the context of salary decisions. Finally, the purpose for ratings is assumed to have a substantial effect on the cognitive process of the rater. As indicated in the earlier review, ratings done for research purposes differ substantially from those done for administrative purposes.

A conceptually independent variable in the system is the vehicle or instrument actually used to gather the performance information. Through a process of scale development or selection, an instrument is identified that presumably is capable of helping raters make distinctions among ratees with respect to various categories of behavior. The scale development may involve developmental groups, as in the case of the BARS methodology, or item analysis derived from a study of current employees, as in the case of summated ratings or forced-choice inventories. Regardless of the method of development, an instrument will be selected or constructed to produce judgments about performance. This instrument will have certain phenotypic characteristics—type and number of anchors, number of response categories, spatial orientation, and so forth. As indicated previously, these characteristics will be directly influenced by the rating context (including position characteristics, organizational characteristics, and purpose for rating) and the

[1] We are grateful to Shelly Zedeck for suggesting that this is an explicit component of the model rather than a derivative component.

characteristics of the rater and ratee. The final instrument will have a major impact on the cognitive operations of the rater.

The component-labeled rating process refers to the constraints placed on the rater by requests or demands. For example, ratings gathered once a year will have different characteristics than those gathered twice a year; ratings gathered on the same day for all ratees will have different characteristics than those gathered on the anniversary of the date of hire for each ratee; ratings done in a noisy, public, distracting environment will have different characteristics than those done in a quiet, private, distraction-free environment; ratings that will eventually be seen by the ratee will have different characteristics than those that will not be seen by the ratee; rating sessions preceded by brief training modules will yield ratings that have different characteristics than those produced "cold," and so forth. As indicated earlier, the rating process is not developed in isolation. It will inevitably be influenced by the purpose for rating and the instrument used for the rating.

The cognitive operations of the rater are thought to fall into two temporal categories. In the first category we find observation and storage. Usually, the rater is asked to retrieve and use that information at some later time. These cognitive operations are influenced by a multitude of variables: the purpose for the rating, the administration rating process, the instrument used, and interacting rater-ratee characteristics.

After performance judgments are made by the rater, a decision must be made concerning how to treat that information. As we have seen in the literature review, these decisions may have substantial effects on error variance estimates. One might use influences identified in previously discussed rater, ratee, position, or organizational components as covariates or moderators. The way in which the data are treated must be considered as a potential source of variance in the resulting performance description. The long-standing argument regarding composite versus multiple criteria is evidence of the importance of this component

in a general performance measurement system (Landy & Trumbo, 1980). If information is improperly combined and inaccurately fed into the personnel decision system, it will inevitably have negative effects on that system.

The component-labeled performance description implies that the data analytic procedure yields a result that is fed back to appropriate sources. These sources might be personnel departments engaged in validation studies or training evaluation studies. They might include administrative officers engaged in salary or workforce planning for the coming year. They might include ratees who receive performance feedback interviews from supervisors. In a sense, each of these sources engages in a personnel action either actively or by default — selection systems are maintained or changed, salaries or workforce levels are maintained or changed, employees are told of strengths and weakness or ignored. These actions, or lack thereof, influence the characteristics of both raters and ratees. If layoffs result from rating data, both raters and ratees will be changed by virtue of that action. Rater biases or sets and ratee behavior will most likely both change. Presumably, accurate performance data fed back in a nonpunishing manner will help individuals eliminate weakness and maintain strengths.

The feedback loop from personnel action to purpose for rating has an important implication. It implies that we must consider how the purpose for rating is perceived by the rater; it is the resulting personnel action that will clearly inform the rater of the purpose for rating rather than the organization's stated purpose, if the two are at odds.

As can be seen from the descriptions of the model in Figure 2, there is a good deal of research still to be done if we are to understand the nature of performance ratings in any nontrivial way. The model is strongly process oriented and must be eventually supported by more substantive propositions concerning where rater biases come from, why certain rating processes minimize rating error, whereas other procedures exaggerate those errors, and so forth. One substantive approach that may be useful to use in conjunction with the process model previously described is implicit personality theory. We now describe how this approach complements and supports our process model.

IMPLICIT PERSONALITY THEORY

For a substantive theoretical framework to be of value in understanding a behavioral phenomenon, such as rating of performance, it should be able to unify the various manifestations of the phenomenon; it should have the capacity to explain conflicting results, to bring order to disorder. The major theme in the research that has been conducted in the area of performance rating has been that variables of major importance can be found in the rating scales themselves. Individual differences in raters were only occasionally investigated. Even when these differences were examined, they tended to be second-level or demographic differences, such as sex or experience, rather than first-level direct influences, such as cognitive operations or feelings toward the stimulus object.

It is our feeling that implicit personality theory research is rich with implications for understanding rating behavior. Bruner and Tagiuri (1954) considered implicit personality theory to be assumed relationships among traits. This is close to the definition of halo in performance rating that one might infer from reading the literature that we have reviewed in the earlier sections of this article. Cronbach (1955) expanded this definition to include not only the covariation among traits but also the means and variances of the traits, implying some relationship between implicit personality theory and leniency and central tendency errors.

In some senses, performance ratings may represent specific instances of implicit personality theories of raters—assumed values on performance dimensions that are independent of actual behavior of the ratee on those dimensions. The work of Passini and Norman (1969) and Norman and Goldberg (1966) is interesting in that respect. They were able to demonstrate that the correlation among traits could be accounted for through constructs of the rater rather than through co-occurrences of behavior patterns in ratees.

An earlier study by Koltuv (1962) demonstrated that implicit personality theories were most likely to operate in situations in which there was low familiarity of rater with ratee. Thus, one might reasonably conclude that the means, variances, and covariances of performance ratings will depend to a certain extent on the degree of familiarity of rater with ratee. This will not come as a surprise to anyone who has conducted research in the performance rating area; nevertheless, it represents a more general phenomenon, since it has been found in settings other than that of performance ratings. In addition, the finding takes on more cognitive overtones when it is embedded in other findings in the implicit personality theory research. For example, implicit personality theories seem to operate more often in trait evaluations than in behavioral evaluations (D. J. Schneider, 1973). Particularly, trait labels seem to lead more often to implicit assumptions. Together, these findings suggest that rating scales should be behaviorally anchored with no trait labels at all. It may be that the labels that introduce the scales create response sets that the definitions and anchors are unable to eliminate. It would be easy enough to test this hypothesis by examining the intercorrelations of ratings made with labels and without labels; although the presence or absence of definitions has been examined, and the presence or absence of behavioral anchors has been examined, little attention has been paid to dimension labels, which invariably read as trait names.

There has been also the suggestion in implicit personality theory research that we seek less information about persons we dislike or about individuals from different strata. This is similar to the Differential Accuracy Phenomenon (DAP) described by M. E. Gordon (1970, 1972) that led him to conclude that low performers are described less accurately than high performers; in addition, the number of levels in the organization that separate the rater and ratee seem to affect the accuracy of the performance judgment (Whitla & Tirrell, 1953; Zedeck & Baker, 1972).

The interesting aspect of implicit personality theory as a heuristic device for examining performance ratings is that it brings a new outlook to some old and vexing questions. It requires us to view rating errors in a new light. These errors become behavioral phenomena governed by individual differences. Landy et al. (1976) suggested that rating errors are not simply properties of scales or instruments. Errors are governed by many parameters, and some of these parameters may be cognitive differences among raters. One might apply Kelly's (1955) notions of personal constructs to performance rating and come to the same conclusion. As another example, Tajfel and Wilkes (1963) found that subjects made more extreme judgments on dimensions that they provided themselves rather than on those given to them. What would happen if we were to allow raters to choose a subset of dimensions from a larger number of dimensions? Would halo be reduced? Would central tendency be reduced? Would new errors appear? The point we are trying to make is that we have a substantive body of research more clearly tied to interpersonal evaluation than currently exists in the performance evaluation literature. This body of research appears under the rubric of implicit personality theory. We feel that advances can be made in understanding rating behavior, if we view rating as a specific instance of the more general phenomenon of person perception.

UNIFIED APPROACH TO PERFORMANCE RATING

As indicated earlier, many researchers in the field of performance rating have recognized the need for models or frameworks to apply to the rating context. These models should integrate the various potential influences on performance descriptions into a single system. The process model that we propose in Figure 2 might be thought of as a superstructure of rat-

ing behavior. As such, it is primarily taxonomic in nature. Nevertheless, taxonomies represent a significant step in theory building. By identifying major components of the system, hypothesis generation and testing is facilitated. Through the application of substantive models related to the process in question, higher level theories emerge. We feel that such is the case with the combination of our process model, implicit personality theory research, and Wherry's deductive propositions regarding variance components in ratings.

It is clear from even a cursory examination of the rating process that all information must ultimately pass through a cognitive filter represented by the rater. Multiple raters simply imply multiple filters that combine in some particular manner. Thus, one must understand the way in which environmental changes or constancies affect this cognitive operation called judgment. Organismic characteristics such as the sex, race, or age of the rater are peripheral. The more important questions relate to how cognitive operations are affected by group membership. The phenotypic characteristics of a rating format are theoretically less important than the interaction of these characteristics with cognitive operations that are involved in recording judgments concerning the behavior of others. Even data analytic procedures, such as factor analysis of multiple rating dimensions, presume that rater observations and the resulting ratings are veridical.

There are, of course, considerations beyond theory building. For the purposes of application and administration, it is useful to know the effect of contextual factors on ratings. Forewarned of certain systematic interactions between rater and ratee characteristics, practitioners are better able to develop equitable decision systems. The administrative implications of Wherry's model of rating variance are important. His propositions make it possible to determine what price is being paid for decreases in particular types of rating error (Wherry, 1952). For example, the use of a rating scale with multiple items to be rated for each performance dimension increases the reliability of the performance rating for that dimension (due to random error reduction) but does not increase the relative proportion of true score to bias. Also, the addition of multiple raters, each evaluating the ratee on several performance dimensions, will reduce overall and areal bias in the composite rating only if the raters' irrelevant contacts with the ratee are at least somewhat different. If these contacts are the same, then there will be no reduction in bias. In addition to the administrative implications, Wherry clearly emphasized the importance of the cognitive operations of the rater, an emphasis only recently appearing in the applied literature on rating.

There is an enormous amount of work to be done, both inductive and deductive, in tying the propositions of person perception to the components of the process model. The propositions of Wherry regarding variance partitioning represent a procedure for accomplishing the initial steps of this integration.

Future Research Needs

The literature review suggests some global conclusions that can be drawn on the basis of available evidence. In one sense, rater and ratee characteristics are fixed—they cannot be changed as easily as can the format of a rating scale. Since little is known concerning the dynamics by which demographic characteristics, such as race and sex, affect ratings, it is difficult to imagine training programs that would eliminate specific biases peculiar to group membership. On the other hand, there is some indication that training in the use of a particular rating format is of value in reducing common rating errors. We must learn much more about the way in which potential raters observe, encode, store, retrieve, and record performance information, if we hope to increase the validity of ratings.

Given the superficiality of our knowledge of the cognitive processes of raters, we probably have gone as far as we can in improving rating formats. We know that the rater should have a clear understanding of the rating task, that the number of response categories should be limited, that the anchors on the scale should be rigorously developed, and that those anchors should be more than simple descriptive labels, such as poor, average, outstanding, and so forth. Nevertheless, even when all of these suggestions are taken into account, evidence suggests that their effect may be minimal. Data reviewed earlier indicate that about 4 to 8 percent of the variance in ratings can be explained on the basis of format. When one considers that the designs that yielded these estimates were seldom sensitive enough to identify true levels of performance, even this effect may be an overestimate. Thus, at least for the time being, we suggest a moratorium on format-related research.

Research in the area of statistical control of common rating errors has been sparse but encouraging. There are two distinct lines of research that might be fruitful. The first is the development of schemes for deriving residual performance scores—scores with rater–ratee context factors partialed out. Although this is a mechanical solution that implies no increase in the understanding of the rating process, it offers the possibility of simultaneously providing the practitioner with better numbers and the researcher with hypotheses. A second research line suggested by data analytic procedures is using ratings or judgments to derive cognitive maps or sets of raters. This would require some sophisticated designs directed toward understanding how individual raters construe their reality (Kelly, 1955).

Finally, our process model implies that the rater's experience with ratings affects the validity of those ratings. We know little or nothing about the effects that decisions based on current ratings have on future ratings. It is reasonable to assume that there are such effects. We can demonstrate that ratings for research purposes have different properties than ratings for administrative purposes. This implies that there is a feedback loop of some sort. Research in this area is long overdue. It is time to stop looking at the symptoms of bias in rating and begin examining potential causes.

The Uniform Guidelines for Employee Selection, published in 1978, made it abundantly clear that when performance information was used to make personnel decisions, those ratings were considered a "test" in the functional sense and would be subject to scrutiny just as any other test might be if the ratings turned out to have an adverse impact on members of a minority group. In fact, there had been many court cases before the Uniform Guidelines were issued that had examined the impact of ratings on personnel decisions. Cascio and Bernardin have reviewed these court cases and come to some conclusions regarding the do's and don'ts of performance ratings from the legal perspective.

■ READING 13 ■

Implications of Performance Appraisal Litigation for Personnel Decisions

Wayne F. Cascio, *Florida International University*

H. John Bernardin, *Virginia Polytechnic Institute and State University*

Over the last 50 years or so, industrial/organizational psychologists have learned a great deal about performance appraisal systems and about the performance appraisal process. At the risk of greatly oversimplifying, one portion of this knowledge is summarized into eight prescriptive categories. We then examine how these prescriptions have been violated in court cases that reached the Federal Appeals or Supreme Court level, recognizing, of course, that the actual number and severity of violations is probably far higher. In a concluding section we consider the implications of this body of case law for I/O scientists and practitioners.

Prescriptions for Performance Appraisal Systems

1. Appraisal of job performance must be based upon an analysis of job requirements as reflected in performance standards. Graphically:

Job Analysis   Performance Appraisal
↘   ↗
Performance Standards

2. Appraisal of job performance only becomes reasonable when performance standards have been communicated and understood by employees.

3. Clearly defined individual components or dimensions of job performance should be rated, rather than undefined, global measures of job performance.

4. Performance dimensions should be behaviorally based, so that all ratings can be supported by objective, observable evidence.

5. When using graphic rating scales, avoid abstract trait names (e.g., loyalty, honesty) unless they can be defined in terms of observable behaviors.

6. Keep graphic rating scale anchors brief and logically consistent.

7. As with anything else used as a basis for employment decisions, appraisal

Source: *Personnel Psychology, 34,* 1981, pp. 211–225.

systems must be validated, and be psychometrically sound, as well as the ratings given by *individual* raters.

8. Provide a mechanism for appeal if an employee disagrees with a supervisor's appraisal.

Adverse Impact and Appraisal

Unfair discrimination occurs in a variety of ways and there are a number of methods for seeking redress through the courts. Cascio (1978) presents a listing of possible sources for suits involving allegations of employment discrimination. The vast majority of suits involving performance appraisal that reached the U.S. Court of Appeals are filed under Title VII of the 1964 Civil Rights Act.

Although it is sound personnel practice to validate all decision-making methods, validation is legally required only if there is evidence of adverse impact on individuals or groups covered by Title VII of the 1964 Civil Rights Act. Several methods have been used to operationalize the term "adverse impact." One of the most common methods is to compare the selection rates of minority and nonminority groups for the position in question. The 80 percent rule is suggested by the *Uniform Guidelines* as a "rule of thumb" for assessing adverse impact despite the obvious problem with such a criterion when dealing with small numbers of people. The *Guidelines* do make it clear that the 80 percent rule is *not* meant to be the sine qua non in determining adverse impact.

In *McDonnell Douglas Corp.* v. *Green (1973)*, the court specified four criteria for establishing a prima facie case of unfair discrimination. These criteria have been cited often in subsequent cases, and include the following elements: *(a)* complainant belongs to a racial minority; *(b)* she/he applies for and is qualified for a job for which the employer is seeking applicants; *(c)* she/he is rejected despite the qualifications; and *(d)* after the rejection, the position remained open and the employer continued to seek applicants from persons of the complainant's qualifications. The courts might also look at population statistics for the rele-

vant geographical area (e.g., Standard Metropolitan Statistical Area data) in order to compare percentages of occupants in given positions. Finally, adverse impact could also be defined simply in terms of evidence that the employer *deliberately* denied equal opportunity for individuals or groups covered under Title VII. Horstman (1978) reviewed court cases with respect to the definitions of adverse impact that are imposed. She found that there was little consistency in the definitions applied and that extraneous factors apparently play a major role in the proceedings of the cases.

RELEVANT CASE LAW

For the sake of parsimony, only pertinent sections of legal rulings will be cited in order to illustrate their impact on the prescriptions presented above.

1. Job Analysis and Performance Standards

In *Patterson* v. *American Tobacco Co.* (1976, 1978), the Court affirmed a finding of discrimination in the selection of supervisors and ordered the company to develop written job descriptions and objective criteria for appointments. Prior to 1968 each department in the company maintained its own seniority roster, and departments were rigidly segregated by race. The company had no formal, objective, written standards for promotions to supervisory positions. Instead, a system of "unwritten qualifications" was used to deny black employees access to higher paying jobs. A similar pattern of personnel practices was also struck down in *Sledge* v. *J.P. Stevens & Co.* (1978).

In *Robinson* v. *Union Carbide Corp.* (1976), the statistical evidence showed substantial adverse impact against blacks in supervisory positions. The Company said it relied on nondiscriminatory data for promotion—foremen were asked to recommend qualified persons for vacant positions. The Court ruled that while the "foreman's recommendation is the indispensable single most important factor in the promotion process, [he is] given no written instructions pertaining to the qualifications necessary for promotion . . . Standards determined to be controlling are vague and subjective. . . . There are no safeguards in the procedure designed to avert discriminatory practices." Similar issues were considered in *Rowe* v. *General Motors Corp.* (1972), *EEOC* v. *Radiator Specialty Co.* (1979), and in *Meyer* v. *Missouri State Highway Commission* (1977), where a female toll bridge collector was never promoted to shift captain. The manager of the bridge hired, fired, and promoted individuals to the position of shift captain. However, since the job of shift captain was "unclassified", there was no written description of job duties or minimum qualifications for the job. "Informal procedures" were used in making promotions (the manager summoned chosen individuals to his office and asked if they wanted the position of shift captain). Personnel practices such as these never have, and probably never will, stand the test of judicial scrutiny.

2. Communication of Performance Standards

In *Donaldson* v. *Pillsbury Co.* (1977), a female sought relief for wrongful discharge based on race and sex and asked for class action certification. Among other things, she claimed that since she had never been given a job description and never told of policies regarding personal phone calls or other work standards, her subsequent discharge was unlawful. The Eighth Circuit Court of Appeals ruled that similar grievances by others *were* sufficient to constitute a class action, and remanded the case back to the District Court, which it found had excluded certain evidence which might have affected the findings.

Similarly, in *Weahkee* v. *Perry* (1978), an American Indian sued the chairperson of E.E.O.C. alleging discharge based on racial discrimination. Weahkee claimed he was not given specific instructions as to where to put work priorities when investigating complaints in his job as a complaint investigator for E.E.O.C. Moreover, when given an unsatisfactory evaluation, he was not told how he could

improve, and then he was discharged. The District court ordered judgment for Weahkee, but the Appeals Court reversed, and sent the case back to the District Court for further evidence and findings on issues of fact. In both *Donaldson* and *Weahkee*, clear communication of job requirements and performance standards may well have made formal legal action unnecessary.

3. Define and Rate Individual Performance Dimensions

There are two landmark cases on this point, both dealing with the use of global, undifferentiated paired comparisons—*Albemarle Paper Co.* v. *Moody* (1975) and *Watkins* v. *Scott Paper Co.* (1976). In *Albemarle*, the company conducted a concurrent validity study without benefit of any job analyses, among other deficiencies. In gathering criterion data, supervisors were instructed to judge which employee was the better of the two when names were presented in a paired comparison format. Employees in different jobs were compared, and supervisors were given no bases on which to determine the "better" employee of each pair. The Supreme Court found that supervisory ratings based on such "vague and inadequate standards" are subject to a plethora of interpretations of doubtful job relatedness.

In *Watkins*, as in *Albemarle*, the paired comparison system in use did not require supervisors to judge specific skills or work functions. "Nowhere in the record is there any suggestion that the supervisors were asked to determine something other than which of the two employees was 'better'." As in *Albemarle*, the use of a global paired comparison technique which used no focused or stable body of criteria was rejected. Several of the suggestions the Court made for the company relate to the appraisal process:

(1) "Formulating guidelines that explain the manner in which job-related, objective criteria such as absenteeism and number of reprimands are evaluated, (2) formulating guidelines that explain the relative importance of subjective criteria found to be job-related, and (3) devising a

procedure by which Scott can recognize situations where first line supervisors' recommendations might be subject to racial bias."

Other types of appraisal systems that are factorially heterogeneous are also subject to challenge, e.g., when "quantity" and "quality" of work are combined into a single rating dimension as in *James* v. *Stockholm Valves & Fittings Co.* (1977).

4, 5, and 6. Performance Dimensions Should Be Behaviorally Based. Avoid Abstract Trait Names in Graphic Rating Scales. Keep Graphic Rating Scale Anchors Brief and Logically Consistent.

At *Stockholm Valves* employees were evaluated by supervisors using a form composed of seven undefined dimensions: quantity and quality of work, job or trade knowledge, ability to learn, cooperation, dependability, industry, and attendance. In examining these dimensions we are reminded of the study done in the early 1960s in which 47 executives were asked to define the word "dependability" (Bass & Barrett, 1981). The 47 executives produced 75 *different* definitions of "dependability"! Yet today, many appraisal systems still present the dimension "dependability," and leave its definition to the rater. While several of the *Stockholm Valves* dimensions are potentially behaviorally based, abstract traits such as cooperation, dependability, and industry are less defensible, unless they can be defined in terms of observable behaviors. However, when we examine the anchors for each of these dimensions, they are not behaviorally based and they are open to diverse interpretation. On each factor, employees were rated "unsatisfactory," "poor," "average," "superior," or "exceptional." Among other problems that caused a violation of Title VII, the Court noted the following: *(a)* incumbent foremen (predominantly white) play a critical role in the selection of new foremen or supervisors, *(b)* recommendations are largely discretionary and there are no adequate safeguards against racial bias, *(c)* no written guidelines specify necessary qualifica-

tions, and *(d)* criteria for promotion are subjective. On these last two points in *Gilmore* v. *Kansas City Terminal Railway Co.* (1975), supervisors were asked to evaluate their subordinates' promotability and to consider "aptitude, ability, and work habits" in doing so. However, the supervisors were given no criteria for effective "aptitude, abilities or work habits." Again, the court ruled in the plaintiff's favor.

As in *Stockholm Valves,* given evidence of adverse impact resulting from the use of ratings, unless each appraisal dimension can be supported by objective, observable evidence, its continued use may well be prohibited. However, there is another issue here, and that is, even if an otherwise legitimate performance appraisal system is *used* improperly it may be struck down. Thus in *U.S.A.* v. *City of Chicago* (1978), a racial discrimination case involving fire department promotions, appraisal ratings made in a lower level job were used as criteria in a concurrent validation study where the tests were intended for use in a higher level job. The court noted,

> The only way a correlation between pre-promotion efficiency ratings and test scores could comply with the E.E.O.C. Guidelines would be if the employer could establish that requirements of the lower level job and the job for which the test is being administered are identical. No such showing was made in this case.

In *Marquez* v. *Omaha District Sales Office, Ford Division of the Ford Motor Company* (1971), performance appraisals had been designated formally as an important factor in employee promotions. Mr. Marquez had excellent appraisals for 15 years, together with consistent ratings from his supervisors as promotable to the next higher level job. Nevertheless he was kept at his same position, and for no reason which appears on the record or in his employment files, his name was removed from the list of promotable employees. No reason was given for the removal of his name and the company was found guilty of racial discrimination.

Similarly, in *Cleverly* v. *Western Electric Co.* (1979), an age discrimination case, a personnel decision to discharge an employee was contradicted by the weight of evidence in 14 years' worth of performance appraisal data. Cleverly had received satisfactory performance ratings and steadily increasing salary during his 14 years of service to the company. When discharged, he was told that one reason for the discharge was to make way for younger engineers in the department, and his discharge occurred just six months prior to the vesting of his pension. The company was found guilty of age discrimination and Cleverly was awarded back pay. As in Chicago and Marquez, an otherwise lawful appraisal system was used improperly.

7. Validate Appraisal Systems and Raters

For those cases involving performance appraisal that reached a U.S. Court of Appeals, rarely are any empirical data presented to justify either the system itself or the ratings given by individual raters. The importance of such data surfaced early in *Rowe* v. *General Motors Corp.* (1972), *Brito* v. *Zia Co.* (1973), *Bolton* v. *Murray Envelope Corp.* (1974), and *Wade* v. *Mississippi Cooperative Extension Service* (1976). In *Zia*, for example, unsatisfactory performance appraisal ratings were used as the basis for layoffs of 12 Hispanic and three native American workers. When challenged, the company was unable to introduce any evidence of the validity of its appraisal system. No records of performance were maintained, and thus no specific performances were documented to justify the ratings. Employees were not evaluated according to their "average daily amount of acceptable performance," and were not even observed on a daily basis. The appraisal system was struck down because Zia could provide "no empirical data demonstrating that the appraisal system was significantly correlated with important elements of work behavior relevant to the jobs for which the appellants were being evaluated."

It should be pointed out that the type of validity evidence required for performance ratings is linked to the *purposes* for which the ratings are made. For example, if appraisal of past performance is to be used as a predictor of future performance (i.e., promotions), validation evidence must be presented to show first that the ratings of past performances are in fact valid, and second, that the ratings of past performance are related to *future* performance in another job (*U.S.A.* v. *City of Chicago*, 1978). At the very least, this latter step should entail a job analysis indicating the extent to which the two jobs in question overlap. Given evidence of adverse impact, if appraisal of past performance is to be used for the purpose of making personnel decisions such as merit pay, layoffs, or demotions, defendants must show that the appraisals are valid measures of past performance. This need to validate apparently also applies to appraisal when the data are only used for the empirical validation of some predictor as, for example, in the Supreme Court case of *Albemarle* v. *Moody* (1975).

Validity data of any kind are rare indeed for appraisal systems since one of the principal reasons for using "soft" criteria is the nonexistence of "hard" criteria such as error rates, production rates, etc. Moreover, it appears that the relationships between ratings and "hard" criteria are weak (e.g., Cascio & Valenzi, 1978; Hausmann & Strupp, 1955).

To put this issue in perspective, Cascio and Valenzi (1978) hypothesized that overall variance in supervisory ratings is composed of four elements: (a) systematic, job-relevant variance that is contained in objective performance indices; (b) systematic, job-relevant variance that is not reflected in strictly objective indices of performance; (c) systematic, but job-irrelevant variance that may or may not be contained in strictly objective measures of performance; and (d) error variance. Consistent with previous research findings, and despite the use of behaviorally anchored rating scales, less than 25 percent of the variance in supervisors' ratings was accounted for by objective indices. In terms of their model, therefore, it appears that overall variance in supervisory ratings is composed mainly of one or more of the last three elements.

The problem of validating ratings is further illustrated by the following quote from the *Uniform Guidelines*:

. . . ratings should be examined for evidence of racial, ethnic or sex bias. All criteria need to be examined for freedom from factors which would unfairly alter scores of members of any group. The relevance of criteria and their freedom from bias are of particular concern when there are significant differences in measures of job performance for different groups (*Federal Register*, 43, 166, August 25, 1978).

The first two sentences of this quotation imply that there is some way to distinguish true sources of variance from error variance due to biasing factors. In other words, if mean differences are found on some rating scale as a function of race or sex, the *Guidelines* imply there is a method of determining whether the mean differences were due to bias in the system (e.g., prejudiced raters) or actual differences in performance as a function of race or sex. In fact, such a distinction cannot clearly be made in almost any appraisal circumstance. As we have seen in this review, however, the courts continually call for safeguards against such racial, ethnic, or sex bias (e.g., *Robinson* v. *Union Carbide*; *Watkins* v. *Scott Paper*; *James* v. *Stockholm Valves*). We address this issue more fully in a final section of the paper.

The third sentence from the *Uniform Guidelines* quote above (i.e., "relevance of criteria") in fact has been the focus of attention when significant race/sex differences in appraisal ratings exist.

Thus in *U.S.A.* v. *City of Chicago* (1978), in remanding the case back to the District Court, the Appeals Court noted:

> On remand, the district court should follow this approach in analyzing the legality of the efficiency ratings. This district court should first make specific findings on whether whites received higher efficiency rating scores than minorities. If such a disparity exists, the district court should make additional findings on whether defendants have met their burden of establishing job relatedness. This determination should involve more than face validity; an inquiry into whether the efficiency ratings accurately predict performance in the job being tested for will be required (16EPD 8141, p. 4651).

In order to demonstrate this, Chicago relied on two criterion-related validity studies. In the first study, test results were correlated (inappropriately, as was pointed out earlier) with pre-existing performance appraisals of each candidate's performance in positions held before taking the promotional exam. In the second study, performance ratings were correlated with ratings given in drill tests. The relevance of drill tests as criteria was evaluated by the Appeals Court as follows:

> Indeed, the district court recognized that drill tests 'do not clearly distinguish between the individuals' performance and that of the unit under his direction.' Moreover, even if the performance of the drill test leader could be effectively isolated, drill test scores would still be an inadequate validation device absent a showing that the drill tests measured the major responsibilities of the promotional positions (126 EPD 8141, FN.9).

And further,

> Defendants contend on appeal that the correlation between efficiency ratings and drill tests demonstrates that the promotional exams are construct valid. A construct valid study is one in which examinations are structured to measure the degree to which job applicants have identifiable characteristics that have been determined to be important in job performance (*Washington* v. *Davis, supra* at 247, n. 13). This argument does not help defendants, however, because there has been no attempt to determine from a job analysis what traits are necessary for job performance. E.E.O.C. Guidelines, 29 C.F.R. 1607.5(a). Thus the drill tests fail to demonstrate either criterion validity or construct validity because they fail to predict performance in promotional ranks (16 EPD 8141, FN.10).

In short, there is no doubt that performance criteria are subject to the same standards as written tests (as they should be), that the courts in general are quite sophisticated in evaluating their job relatedness, and that the development of criteria must receive the same careful attention to detail as the development of "predictors".

8. Provide a Mechanism for Appeal

One of the few things we do know for certain with respect to appraisal systems is that they must be acceptable to those being rated if they are to work in practice. An appeal procedure does not guarantee that employees will agree with their ratings or even agree with the rating system. But it does help to know that ratings assigned (usually by the immediate supervisor) are reviewable, that the rater is answerable to a higher authority, and that employees have the right to present their side of the story before pursuing more formal, legal means for redress. Personnel practices which permit one person's appraisal to carry complete weight in personnel decisions, as in *Rowe, Robinson, Meyer, Watkins, Stockholm Valves,* and *Wade* are unlikely to be permitted unless they can be supported by documented, objective, reliable evidence for each dimension rated. In most cases, this is difficult, if not impossible, to demonstrate.

IMPLICATIONS OF CASE LAW CITED

Clearly this body of case law has implications for a wide variety of personnel decisions. In this section we consider five such implications.

1. Appraisal Systems Must Meet the Uniform Guidelines Like Other Tests

It is apparent from *Brito* v. *Zia,* and *U.S.A.* v. *City of Chicago* that, once adverse impact is shown, performance appraisal systems must be validated in some manner, that they must be psychometrically sound, and that arguments for face or even content validity are unacceptable. *Zia* focused on particular raters and their rating behavior, work habits, and attitudes. In this context, we must thus validate raters as well as appraisal systems. The *Guidelines* state that criteria should represent: "important or critical work behavior(s) or work outcomes . . ." (*Federal Register, 43,* 166, August 25, 1978).

We invoke the term "content domain sampling" here as preferable to "content validity" because we wish to distinguish inferences about the adequacy and representativeness of the content of the rating form *vis a vis* the content of the job (content domain sampling) from the appropriateness of inferences made about the rating scores (content validity). Both are clearly important. While the use of a behaviorally-based rating form may be *necessary* in order to provide a job-relevant rationale for personnel actions, the use of such a (content domain sampled) form is certainly not *sufficient* for defense of the appropriateness or reasonableness of the actions taken. In short, the validity of the rating scores themselves must also be demonstrated. Arvey (1979) has written that "organizations that have made reasonable efforts to develop criterion measures through carefully developed job analysis, have checked the reliabilities of these measures, and have performed statistical tests to detect differences between ratings of minority and majority groups will likely survive court challenges of these measures" (p. 119). We disagree. While behaviorally anchored rating scales, for example, would certainly be looked upon more favorably than trait-oriented scales, mean differences on the two scales as a function of race or sex would be a more critical issue in any court proceeding (cf., *Brito* v. *Zia,* 1973; *U.S.A.* v. *City of Chicago,* 1978). Thus, we prefer to reserve the term "validity" for inferences about scores, rather than contents of appraisal forms.

What then should be done if racial differences are found in appraisal results? To be sure, this is an outcome the individual differences literature would predict more often than not (cf. Humphreys, note 1). Assuming that such differences are found in ratings and the ratings result in adverse impact against a group or individual covered under Title VII, some type of validation evidence must be presented to justify the ratings (parenthetically, if the ratings are used only as criteria in a validation study where adverse impact occurs as a function of the predictor, evidence for the validity of the ratings is also likely to be required).

The most basic issue at this point is the purpose of the appraisal, for as Jacobs, Kafry, and Zedeck (1980) have noted, different purposes require different information to be collected, which in turn requires different methodologies for performance appraisal. Appraisals may be used either as predictors (e.g., in personnel decisions to promote, to train, or to transfer) or as criteria (e.g., in personnel research, in establishing objectives for training programs, as a basis for employee feedback and development, merit pay decisions, disciplinary decisions, layoff decisions). Criterion-related validity strategies seem most appropriate when appraisals are used as predictors, especially when unbiased criteria are or become available (e.g., dollar-valued productivity measures). When appraisals are used as criteria, a construct-oriented strategy seems more appropriate (e.g., Campbell, 1976). The first step is to demonstrate that an adequate content domain sampling procedure has been followed. Thus, a showing of job-relatedness would depend on the adequacy with which the appraisal instrument sampled the content domain(s) of the job, the extent to which critical tasks or work behaviors were assessed, the extent to which any special circumstances were considered in developing the content domains, and the extent to which definitions of psychological constructs were supported by research evidence (American Psychological Association, Division of Industrial-Organizational Psychology, 1980).

Some of the best evidence for the validity of ratings regardless of purpose would be correlations with important, uncontaminated, nonjudgmental criteria (e.g., sales volume). As stated above, however, this type of data is more often than not unavailable. Thus, we must turn to other methods in order to validate the appraisal system and individual raters.

Bernardin (1979) has proposed two methods for validating raters. One approach is to have raters evaluate any variables that are in fact verifiable along with those which are not verifiable. For example, raters could be asked to rate absenteeism or error rates for ratees and these ratings could be correlated with objective data on these two variables. A high correlation would indicate that the raters are basing their evaluations on observed individual differences. Inferences can then be made regarding ratings on nonverifiable dimensions. With this procedure, individual raters can also be examined for error in ratings (e.g., leniency and severity errors). One obvious criticism of this approach is that the validity of ratings on verifiable dimensions such as absenteeism or error rates may have little or no relationship to the validity of ratings on nonverifiable dimensions. Some research has shown accuracy or validity in ratings may be generalizable across dimensions (Borman, 1977; Mullins & Force, 1962). When one considers the impact of rater motivation on the validity of ratings (e.g., Landy & Farr, 1980), the generalizability of validity within raters and across dimensions is plausible.

The second approach to "validating" raters is to correlate observations of ratee behavior with appraisals. For example, raters could do their evaluations at the regularly scheduled time. However, during the observation period, the raters or, preferably, the ratees would also maintain records of exhibited work behaviors. These incidents of behavior should be as descriptive and nonevaluative as possible. There should be no mention of traits or dimensions, merely behaviors and contexts. Once a fair number of these incidents is recorded for each ratee and, preferably, from more than one observer's perspective, subject matter experts thoroughly familiar with the positions under study would receive randomly ordered lists of these now "anonymous" incidents (behaviors at this point are no longer linked to individual ratees). Ratings of effectiveness and importance could then be derived for each incident and descriptive statistics could be compiled for each incident, for each ratee, and from each rater. A ratee's overall rating for each observation period would be compiled by taking the mean or median effectiveness rating for the group of incidents applicable to him/her, perhaps using importance ratings as multipliers. These ratings could then be correlated with ratings made on the formal evaluation form by each rater. After a test of level differences as a function of rater, a differential accuracy measure (Cronbach, 1955) could then be used to derive an accuracy coefficient for each rater. A high correlation would represent high agreement between a rater's order of evaluations for his/her ratees and subject matter experts' order of evaluations for behaviors exhibited by the same ratees. Thus, with this procedure, a form of construct validity is revealed for each rater's ratings.

While validating raters is indeed a difficult task, such data may be essential if adverse impact has resulted from personnel decisions based on ratings or when significant mean differences are found as a function of race, sex, or age when ratings are used as criteria in a test validation study. The presentation of summary statistics on ratings such as convergent or discriminant validity, halo error, or reliability appears to be of limited significance in court cases on appraisal. Rather, the emphasis has been on particular raters and justification for their ratings.

2. Encourage Internal Review of Appraisal Systems

After reading the testimony of company officials in many of these cases, one gets the uneasy feeling that *(a)* top management was totally unaware of what kind of appraisal system was in effect at lower levels, or *(b)* the employer was well aware of the (illegal) appraisal system in use but was unaware of what was wrong with it. Like drivers who try unsuccessfully to alibi their way out of a traffic ticket are all too painfully aware (". . . but officer, I didn't know this was a one-way street"), ignorance is no excuse. One lesson which top managers understand well is that mistakes in the personnel area can be costly. However, improvement in appraisal systems requires a method as well as the motivation to improve. Personnel professionals might well use the eight prescriptions cited earlier as a checklist and encourage organizations to take proactive steps to correct deficiencies rather than reactive steps to cover them up or explain them away.

Knowing the issues involved in appraisal litigation helps in diagnosing existing systems, and in convincing line managers of their vulnerability.

3. Fit Practice to Purpose

The lesson from *Chicago, Cleverly* and *Marquez* is clear. Appraisal systems which pass muster in every respect, but which either are disregarded in personnel decisions (such as lay-off or promotion), or are used improperly (appraisals made at lower levels used as validation criteria for higher level jobs), will be subject to challenge.

4. Expand Research on Rater Training and Rater Accuracy

As Bernardin and Buckley (1981) and Spool (1978) have shown, we know little about how to train people to observe performance-related behavior. The effects of training to avoid constant errors such as halo and leniency has had mixed results (Bernardin & Pence, 1980; Thornton & Zorich, 1980). There can be little question, however, that some dimensions are more difficult to rate accurately than others, especially when embedded within particular political, social, and emotional contexts. Finally, the characteristics that differentiate easy from difficult dimensions should be investigated. At the outset, however, we must recognize that we don't know what truth is in performance appraisal.

5. Let's Get Back to Basics

One of the important lessons to be learned from this review of litigation in performance appraisal is that appraisal systems are often found wanting because in translating theory into practice we have ignored the fundamental principles that make performance appraisal scientifically sound (i.e., the eight prescriptions noted earlier). Nevertheless, it is clear that factors other than those cited above will, on occasion, influence the ultimate decision of the courts. For example, the scrutiny a decision system receives will depend to a large extent on the overall impact of the system and the affirmative action posture of the employer (Herring, note 2; Horstman, 1978; Kleiman & Faley, 1978; Schneier, 1978). In their review of 66 court cases, most of which were settled at the District Court level, Feild and Holley (Note 3) found that the type of organization of the defendant was the best predictor of case outcome. That is, if a charge was filed against an industrial organization, verdicts were more likely to be found in favor of the plaintiff compared to cases involving a nonindustrial employer. Feild and Holley (Note 3) also cited the importance of job analysis, written instructions for raters, a behavioral rating format, and an employee review process as important determinants of the outcomes of cases.

It is clear from case law that high levels of adverse impact in promotion, facilitated by sex or race differences on an appraisal instrument, would be difficult to defend even with a very sophisticated rating format. And, unfortunately, we know all too well that more sophisticated formats are no less subject to rating biases than the simpler types (Landy & Farr, 1980). Prescriptions for scientifically sound, court-proof appraisal systems are not difficult to offer (e.g., job relevance, user acceptability, sensitivity, reliability, practicality). As we have seen, however, the implementation of credible, workable appraisal systems requires diligent attention by organizations to the fundamental principles, plus an enduring commitment to make them work in practice.

The Landy and Farr review that was reprinted earlier illustrated the results of letting research get out of control. For over 40 years, there was no general theme guiding the rating research. As a result, everyone studied scale format. The newest and most exciting theme in performance rating research is the cognitive theme. It is becoming increasingly apparent that the way raters collect, process, store, and retrieve performance information has a substantial effect on the accuracy and consistency of performance ratings. As a result, a great deal of research that might be labeled "cognitive" is going on in the performance rating area. Banks and Murphy warn that unless we consider ways of controlling and guiding that cognitive research, it will become as irrelevant and unfocused as the research that has preceded it. They suggest ways for making sure that current research using the cognitive paradigm maintains some practical value.

■ READING 14 ■

Toward Narrowing the Research-Practice Gap in Performance Appraisal

Cristina G. Banks,
Department of Management,
The University of Texas at Austin
Kevin R. Murphy,
Department of Psychology
Colorado State University

Organizations continue to express disappointment in performance appraisal systems despite advances in appraisal technology. Appraisal reliability and validity still remain major problems in most appraisal systems, and new (and presumably improved) appraisal systems are often met with substantial resistance. In essence, effective performance appraisal in organizations continues to be a compelling but unrealized goal.

Problems associated with performance appraisal are documented in volumes of articles in scientific and trade journals. Both research-ers and practitioners have analyzed performance appraisal problems and have suggested several and generally different remedies.[1] For example, practitioners suggest that organizations need to increase management's commitment to the appraisal system, increase communication between supervisors and subordinates regarding tasks to be performed, improve appraiser feedback skills, and clarify performance objectives and criteria. Researchers, on the

---

[1]The terms *researcher* and *practitioner* describe roles rather than individuals, since many psychologists working in the area of performance appraisal are involved in both research and application. Thus the same individual may employ different strategies, or may be concerned with different issues in performance appraisal research and practice.

Source: *Personnel Psychology*, 38, 1985, pp. 335–344.

other hand, stress the need to sharpen observational skills, reduce rating errors, use better formats, and utilize information more effectively. The fact that researchers and practitioners focus on a different set of appraisal problems and hence, advocate different solutions, suggests a lack of coordination in solving appraisal problems. More important, this divergence in focus indicates that researchers' solutions may not speak to practitioners' problems.

In recent years, researchers have suggested analyzing the cognitive processes underlying performance appraisal as a method of improving appraisal judgments. This approach, which has taken performance appraisal researchers by storm since Feldman's (1981) seminal article, allows researchers to tap a wealth of research in social and cognitive psychology that is applicable to performance appraisal. In particular, this approach promises to generate a better understanding of *how* performance judgments are formed and retained for use in appraisals. Several studies using the cognitive processing approach have appeared recently (Balzer, 1983; Banks, 1979, 1982; Barnes-Farrell & Couture, 1983; Cooper, 1981a; DeNisi, Meglino & Cafferty, 1984; Lord, 1985, in press; Murphy & Balzer, 1983; Murphy, Balzer, Kellam, & Armstrong, 1984; Murphy, Balzer, Lockhart, & Eisenman, 1985; Murphy, Garcia, Kerkar, Martin, & Balzer, 1982; Murphy, Martin, & Garcia, 1982). These studies have examined a variety of issues, ranging from ways in which raters decide what to observe to distortions in memory for behavior.

Despite the potential promise of cognitive research in appraisal, this shift in the focus of performance appraisal research may have ominous implications for performance appraisal practice. By investigating appraisers' cognitive processes, researchers appear to be drifting even farther from concerns which are most clearly voiced by practitioners. Thus, although research on cognitive processes in performance appraisal may advance our understanding of human judgment, it has not yet led to significant advances in the practice of performance appraisal. Indeed, very few applications of this

approach have been suggested or applied: the cognitive processing approach will improve the practice of performance appraisal only to the extent it is applied in the field. A clear divergence between the concerns of performance appraisal researchers and the concerns of practitioners suggests that advances in cognitive research may have little impact on practice.

The purpose of this paper is to describe why the existing gap between research and practice is likely to become *wider* as a result of the widespread use of the cognitive processing approach, and to suggest what can be done to narrow the gap. In this paper, we address conceptual and methodological problems associated with cognitive processing research which make applications of this research difficult. To increase the usefulness of this research, we suggest how one aspect of the appraisal process, observation of reliable and valid ratee information, may lead to improved performance appraisals by designing studies that capitalize on the technical strengths of both researchers and practitioners. We believe that only through the joint effort of researchers and practitioners can useful products be generated and adopted in organizations.

PRODUCTS GENERATED FROM PERFORMANCE APPRAISAL RESEARCH

Over the past 35 years, researchers have developed several products to assist performance appraisal in organizations. Contributions fall within three general categories: appraisal formats, rater training programs and strategies, and appraisal processes. Researchers developed numerous *formats* such as checklists, rating scales, narratives, and work samples that help to structure the appraisal (see Bernardin & Beatty, 1983, or Carroll & Schneier, 1982, for detailed descriptions of formats). Formats aid actual appraisals by determining the type and number of dimensions assessed, the types of judgments made (frequency of behaviors versus evaluation of behaviors), appraisal length, and comprehensiveness. Some researchers argue that particular formats also guide appraisal judgments (e.g., Bernardin & Smith, 1981). *Rater training programs* were designed to promote proper utilization of appraisal systems and to improve rating skills. Some of these training programs incorporate learning principles such as practice, feedback, and active participation (Spool, 1978) and emphasize behavioral observation (Boice, 1983; Thornton & Zorich, 1980). Various *processes* were developed to assist the appraisal process. Examples of these processes are the critical incident method (Flanagan, 1954), diary-keeping (Bernardin & Walter, 1977), participation in format development (Friedman & Cornelius, 1976), and goal setting (Latham & Locke, 1979). These processes, as well as others, consist of a set of techniques appraisers can use to help them generate valid ratee data.

These products are useful in an ideal sense because they promote (but do not guarantee) systematic, job-related, and relatively error-free evaluation. However, these products have not been adopted widely (cf., DeVries, Shullman, Morrison, & Gerlach, 1981); for the most part, the appraisal systems actually used in organizations have failed to draw upon this body of research. For example, despite the advances made in training programs, few training programs in industry employ learning principles or emphasize observations; most involve proper use of appraisal forms (Feldman, 1983; in press). Thus, while the products developed by performance appraisal researchers help form accurate appraisals in theory, they are not perceived as useful (and therefore are not applied) in practice.

We believe that the products generated from current cognitive processing studies will be perceived as even *less* useful than those developed in the past. There are two reasons for this belief. The first reason is that cognitive processes captured in laboratory studies are likely to be substantially different from cognitive processes in actual appraisals. Several factors contribute to the potential lack of generalizability of laboratory research on appraisal. First, cognitive process research designs routinely eliminate or control for contextual factors such as competing tasks, time pressures,

and delay between ratee behavior and appraisal; these factors are thought to have substantial effects on actual appraisals. Second, laboratory studies eliminate or control for interpersonal and effective processes, which also have considerable impact on actual appraisals (Dipboye, 1985). Third, laboratory studies focus on the judgment process (evaluation of ratee performance), whereas appraisals in organizations include both the judgment process and a rendering process (the marking of the appraisal form). Because laboratory studies eliminate or control for motivational factors such as personal and political agendas, financial need, and avoidance of conflict in laboratory studies, the ratings recorded by subjects in these experiments are likely to correspond with their evaluation of the (often videotaped) "ratee." In contrast, raters in organizations are often strongly motivated to record ratings which differ significantly from their evaluations (Mohrman & Lawler, 1983). In particular, raters are often motivated to avoid giving low ratings regardless of how poorly the ratees perform. Cognitive processing research may tell us about evaluation but will not necessarily tell us much about rendering behavior when motivational factors are present.

A less obvious problem with cognitive processes captured in the laboratory concerns the type of information available to appraisers. Laboratory studies are often constructed so that appraisers are not forced to differentiate between relevant and irrelevant ratee information. Typically, most of the information presented is relevant and, as a result, the appraiser's task is to attend to as much information as possible. Quite the opposite is true in organizational settings: appraisers need to suppress information that is irrelevant or unreliable. Accurate appraisal in organizations is likely to depend heavily on one's ability to *suppress* irrelevant information as well as *select* relevant information; accurate appraisal in the laboratory may depend primarily on accuracy in observing (Murphy, Garcia et al., 1982). In sum, we believe the cognitive processes studied in the laboratory do not simulate well enough the circumstances of actual appraisals to improve significantly the quality of appraisals in organizational settings. Although cognitive research has generated a good deal of information about processes involved in evaluating others, this knowledge has not yet proved useful in practice.

The second reason for our lack of faith in the applicability of the cognitive processing approach is the difficulty of accessing cognitive processes. Since these processes are not observable, we must assume that elicitation techniques capture representative portions of relevant mental processes. However, how do we measure error in the data we elicit? Should we treat all verbal statements and other measurable outcomes as valid indicators of appraisers' cognitive processes? Unfortunately, the cognitive processing approach deals with variables that are simply difficult to measure and for which research methodologies are primitive. If the relevant cognitive processes *are* measurable, they may be exceedingly difficult to manipulate and change permanently. Lifelong biases, decision strategies, prejudices, world views, experiences, and feelings are likely to be highly resistant to change. Even if we learned a great deal about appraisers' cognitive processes, we may not be able to improve them significantly.

NARROWING THE GAP

At this point, the reader may be wondering what, if anything, can we gain from the cognitive processing approach? We argue that *given a particular focus,* cognitive processing studies can yield highly useful information for both researchers and practitioners. The focus we prefer examines appraisers' cognitive processes in settings that simulate the essential features of appraisal in organizations, using methods that take organizational constraints into account. This focus and underlying rationale is presented below.

The goal for both researchers and practitioners is to develop measures of job performance that are reliable, valid, job-related, standardized, and based on criteria known to both ap-

praiser and ratee. A central aspect of achieving this goal is the identification and use of valid ratee information in that appraisal. Toward this end, researchers are likely to be concerned with what information appraisers attend to in evaluating ratee performance, while practitioners are likely to be concerned with basing evaluations on job-related information. Fortunately, practitioners' concern for greater use of valid ratee data is addressed by cognitive processing research. One of the central components of cognitive process models of performance appraisal (e.g., Cooper, 1981b; Feldman, 1981; Landy & Farr, 1980) is *behavior observation.* Cognitive researchers have examined raters' ability to observe and select valid and relevant behavioral information in conducting appraisals (Banks, 1982; Lord, in press; Murphy, Garcia et al., 1982; Murphy et al., 1984; Murphy et al., 1985). To the extent this research can identify circumstances in which raters accurately observe and make sensible and reliable decisions about what to observe, the practitioners' goal of providing a base of valid behavioral information for appraisals will be met.

One of the clearest manifestations of the present gap between appraisal research and appraisal in organizations is the role of observation in research versus practice. Researchers have believed for many years, probably since the development of the critical incident technique (Flanagan, 1954), that observation of job behavior is critical for appraisal reliability and validity. Observation of actual ratee behavior is assumed to be a determinant of appraisal accuracy, based on the assumption that such observations are objective, verifiable, and can be tied closely to job analysis information (Dunnette, 1966). Recently, preliminary links have been established between observation and appraisal accuracy (Bernardin, 1981; Bernardin & Walter, 1977; Murphy, Garcia et al., 1982; Thornton & Zorich, 1980). Despite the evidence supporting the importance of observation, relatively few organizations have incorporated observation-driven methods and techniques (e.g., behavior diaries, behavior observation scales) to improve the accuracy of their ratings. Why is there a gap when researchers have argued so strongly for its importance?

The gap becomes obvious when we consider in what *manner* observation will lead to greater accuracy. In order to improve appraisal accuracy, observations must be frequent, unbiased, and representative. Researchers often design laboratory studies in which appraisers have access to all information, most of the information presented is relevant, and appraisers' time is devoted exclusively to the appraisal task. Under these circumstances, observation is almost assured to be frequent, and because ratee behavior is likely to be internally consistent, almost any sampling strategy will result in unbiased and representative sampling. In contrast, observation in organizations is fraught with distortions and inadequacies: observation is infrequent and noisy, and appraisers lack focus due to competing pressures, motivations, and demands. Perhaps it is not surprising, then, to find that adoption of techniques aimed at increasing observational accuracy is rare. Researchers' recommendations may work well under laboratory conditions but become impractical or inapplicable in practice because of inherent shortcomings in the quality of observations in organizational settings.

Specific Recommendations

Instead of applying laboratory-generated and, to some extent, laboratory-bound methods, researchers need to generate methods of observation and cognitive aids that ensure valid input data (e.g., ratee job behaviors) *given organizational constraints*. This strategy suggests more attention needs to be focused on the problem of separating relevant from irrelevant information and on obtaining valid information when observation is infrequent. Specifically, appraisers need to learn to discriminate between relevant and irrelevant information and then select relevant information for use in appraisals. Recent empirical studies underscore the importance of separating the two (Banks, 1982; Murphy et al., 1985). In addition, appraisers need to learn how to employ

work sampling to obtain valid data when observation is necessarily infrequent.

Given these needs, training programs should not train appraisers merely to observe; rather they should train them *how to decide what to observe* (Banks & Roberson, 1985). Researchers could contribute most by determining what are the best *methods* of encouraging appraisers to use relevant as opposed to irrelevant information in appraisals and to systematically collect valid ratee information through work sampling. For example, it would be useful to compare different memory (or "forgetting") aids to determine which ones allow appraisers to retain relevant information and suppress irrelevant information. Another example is a systematic analysis of work sampling approaches for jobs that vary in task complexity and concreteness.

If the role of the researcher now is to determine the best *method* of achieving utilization of relevant information, then the practitioner's role becomes one of specifying the *content* of appraisals. First, practitioners could determine what aspects of performance are *measurable*. That is, they can identify which aspects of performance can be observed validly. In a way, we are suggesting an anthropological approach to specifying the content of appraisals. If managers are viewed as a culture, they may be studied in such a way to develop characterizations of effective and ineffective performance. Practitioners who are most familiar with job activities would be the best candidates for developing these characterizations.

In a related vein, a second contribution practitioners can make is development of effective prototypes of performance in organizations. We use the term "prototype" here to refer to a specific, coherent behavioral definition of satisfactory or superior performance. Thus, a prototype is a description of what the typical satisfactory or superior worker *does*. Observable and measurable aspects of performance gleaned from the work described above can be organized into prototypes of performance for specific jobs. These can be used subsequently to help appraisers develop stable and consistent performance schemas. Practitioners can help shape appraisers' prototypes by comparing individual schemas with a preferred prototype. In addition, practitioners could also identify instances in which stereotypes and biases are most intrusive or most strongly held. Revision of firmly entrenched stereotypes may be extremely difficult; practitioners may be able to identify which stereotypes can or cannot be changed.

A final contribution practitioners can make is separating the multiple functions of performance appraisal data. There are statistical as well as practical reasons for minimizing multiple use of appraisal data. When the same appraisal data is used for multiple personnel decisions (e.g., pay increases, training interventions, suitability for promotion), error associated with these judgments will be greater than the error expected if judgments were made on independent sets of data. This is because errors associated with each judgment combine rather than cancel each other out, thus dramatically underestimating the probability of error with each assessment. Basically, the error associated with the set of unrelated judgments taken together is greater than the error indicated by the alpha level (Hays, 1981). As a result, this strategy might present a highly unreliable picture of the ratee. Practitioners should heed these measurement guidelines whenever possible. To avoid this problem, practitioners could help by developing different performance prototypes for each purpose. For example, prototypes involved in assessing candidates for promotion might concentrate on behaviors which are required for more advanced jobs, whereas prototypes used in salary administration should focus on behavior required in the ratee's own job.

Capability versus Willingness

Most performance appraisal interventions and technologies, including those described herein, are designed to increase the rater's ability to accurately evaluate ratees. However, as we have noted earlier, raters are rarely motivated to provide accurate appraisals and may, in some cases, be strongly motivated to pro-

vide inaccurate appraisals (e.g., refusing to give low ratings). Research on performance appraisal has consistently failed to distinguish between evaluation and rating behavior. Cognitive process research is clearly relevant to evaluation but may be only tangentially relevant to rating behavior. The interventions we describe could increase raters' ability to make accurate discriminations but will not have a significant impact on rating behavior unless raters are willing, as well as able, to rate accurately.

We believe that the problem of increasing the rater's willingness to provide accurate ratings falls largely outside of the domain of cognitive process research. The same, however, can be said of almost all of the intervention and rating technologies developed to date. The distinction between capability and willingness is especially useful, since it helps clarify what sort of problems can or cannot be addressed with specific interventions, and also suggests appropriate criteria for evaluating these interventions. We believe that the problem of making someone a better rater and the problem of obtaining better ratings from that person are conceptually and practically distinct. Although it makes sense to attack the problem of capability first, organizations must also consider factors which affect each rater's willingness to record faithfully the judgments he or she has made.

CONCLUSION

Performance appraisal researchers are now at the crossroads of making significant strides in achieving a better understanding of the appraisal process; in theory, this information should contribute to increasing appraisal effectiveness in organizations. By adopting the cognitive processing approach, researchers have the opportunity to tap a wealth of information relevant to the appraisal context. Regretably, this current line of research is likely to widen the already existing gap between research and practice in performance appraisal unless researchers and practitioners coordinate their efforts. We suggest that one way to achieve coordination is for both to undertake the task of determining how to increase appraisers' use of valid input data in appraisal decisions. Researchers could identify methods and other aids that will best facilitate appraisers' selection of valid ratee information. Practitioners could determine the content of appraisals and specify how job behaviors could be assessed most accurately in organizational settings.

An analogy might illustrate how we envision coordination between researchers and practitioners. If the goal is to hit a nail on the head, then we need to find a hammer and locate the nail. Researchers can provide the hammer by determining what *methods* would be most effective for hitting the target. Practitioners can locate the nail by determining what *nails* can be observed best and which ones to hit. Appraisers simply hit the nail. We argue that collaboration between researchers and practitioners is essential to build a stronger and more appealing structure for performance appraisal.

SECTION FIVE

Training

Training and learning have always been inextricably bound together. In fact, training might be thought of as the administrative structure for organizational learning. Training is what you do *to* someone or what someone *experiences*. It is hoped that learning is the result. In the past decade, learning theory has undergone some substantial changes. For 20 years, the behaviorists controlled learning research. This stranglehold has been broken with the introduction by people like Bandura of the notions of social learning and self-control rather than stimulus control. In the industrial training literature, these newer influences have appeared in the form of either a combination of reinforcement theory with feedback systems or in the form of modeling as a representation of social learning theory. In this section, we will consider one example of each of those newer influences in training research.

When individuals are promoted into supervisory positions, it is usually because they have done well in the technical aspects of some lower level job. Unfortunately, many of these new supervisors are ill-prepared for dealing with the interpersonal demands of their new position. As a result, training in such skills is necessary. Traditionally, this type of training has been superficial and minimally effective. Latham and Saari describe a training program directed toward improving supervisory interpersonal skills that combines instruction, observation, discussion, and feedback. It is based on social learning principles and seems to be successful. One particularly appealing aspect of the reading that you should note is the care that Latham and Saari have given to evaluating the effectiveness of the training program. This makes their claim for the technique all the more compelling.

■ READING 15 ■

Application of Social-Learning Theory to Training Supervisors through Behavioral Modeling

Gary P. Latham and Lise M. Saari
University of Washington

In 1968, Locke proposed a cognitive theory of human behavior stating that there is a relationship between an individual's intentions or goals and subsequent behavior. Since then, debates on the necessity of taking into account cognitions for predicting, controlling, and understanding behavior have flourished in industrial-organizational (I-O) psychology (e.g., Gray, 1979; Locke, 1977, 1979; Hamner, Note 1; Karmel, Note 2; Steers, Note 3). Such exchanges are reminiscent of the arguments among experimental psychologists 40 years ago (e.g., Guthrie, 1935; Hull, 1936; Skinner, 1938; Tolman, 1932).

Campbell and Stanley (1966) have argued that when competent scientists

advocate strongly divergent points of view, it seems likely on a priori grounds that both have observed something valid about the natural situ-

ation, and that both represent a part of the truth. The stronger the controversy, the more likely this is. (p. 3)

They argue that we should not expect crucial experiments to yield clear-cut outcomes. A mature focus in science "avoids crucial experiments and instead studies dimensional relationships and interactions along many degrees of the experimental variables" (Campbell & Stanley, 1966, p. 3).

In recognition of this thesis, and our desire for I-O psychologists not to spend another 40 years rehashing arguments already put forth by experimental psychologists, we believe that a rapprochement between the cognitivists and the behaviorists in I-O psychology is an appropriate step for the advancement of knowledge in our field. Social-learning theory, as proposed by Bandura (1977), provides a theoretical structure to facilitate this rapprochement.

Social-learning theory explains human behavior in terms of a continuous reciprocal interaction among cognitive, behavioral, and

Source: *Journal of Applied Psychology*, 64, 1979, pp 239–246. Copyright 1979 by the American Psychological Association. Reprinted by permission of the publisher and author.

environmental determinants. As stated by Bandura (1977),

> in the social learning view, people are neither driven by inner forces nor buffetted by environmental stimuli. Rather, psychological functioning is explained in terms of a continuous reciprocal interaction of personal and environmental determinants. (p. 11)

Inherent in this viewpoint is the acknowledgment that arguments as to whether behavior is due solely to cognitive or to environmental variables are nonsensical. To show that behavior is determined only by cognitions, one would have to find a control group consisting of individuals who cannot think. Similarly, to provide empirical support for the argument that behavior is due to environmental consequences alone, one would have the impossible task of forming a control group for which there was no environment.

Social-learning theory specifically acknowledges that human thought, affect, and behavior are influenced by observation as well as by direct experience. It states that people use symbols to create, to communicate, to analyze conscious experience, and to engage in foresightful action. Moreover, the theory states that people do not merely react to external influences but actually select, organize, and transform stimuli that impinge on them.

Both operant (Skinner, 1938) and social-learning theories agree that behavior is affected by its consequences, but the two theories differ on whether a reinforcer strengthens preceding responses or whether it facilitates learning anticipatorily through its effects on attentional, organizational, and rehearsal processes. Laboratory experiments (see Bandura, 1977) have shown that learning is achieved more effectively by informing observers in advance the consequences of engaging in a specific behavior than by waiting until the behavior is demonstrated and then administering the reinforcer. This is particularly true in observational learning in which anticipation of a reinforcer influences not only what is observed but what goes unnoticed. Observer attentiveness to and learning from the model is increased when he

or she knows that the consequence of a model's behavior is either a valued outcome or the avoidance or removal of a punishing stimulus. This use of modeling as a basis of learning, a technique that is critical to much of social-learning theory, is the foundation of the present study.

Impressive empirical support for social-learning theory has been obtained in well-controlled studies conducted in experimental, developmental, and clinical settings. (See Bandura, 1977, for a review of the literature.) Nevertheless, the theory has not been widely embraced by I-O psychologists. Goldstein and Sorcher (1974) explained the potential value of behavioral modeling procedures for first-line supervisory training, but they offered limited empirical support for the techniques they used. In a recent symposium (Kraut, 1976), four authors presented results from what were essentially pilot studies on the application of behavioral modeling procedures to industrial training programs. These are the only studies to our knowledge that have been published. None of the studies used multiple internal and external criteria (Campbell, Dunnette, Lawler, & Weick, 1970) to systematically test the effects of the training over an extended time period using a true (Campbell & Stanley, 1966) experimental design. This is unfortunate because few training programs have shown that they bring about a relatively permanent change in behavior (Campbell et al., 1970); this is particularly true regarding leadership training (Stogdill, 1974).

The purpose of the present research was to examine the effects of a behavioral modeling program developed by Sorcher (Goldstein & Sorcher, 1974) to increase the effectiveness of first-line supervisors in dealing with their employees.

The nine training modules developed by Sorcher parallel the results of a job analysis (Latham, Fay, & Saari, in press) identifying effective and ineffective supervisor performance in this organization. The training program was designed to include the components of effective modeling as outlined by Bandura (1977); that is, the training episodes included attentional processes, retention processes, motor reproduction processes, and motivational processes.

METHOD

Sample

One hundred first-line male supervisors were employed by an international company located in the Northwestern United States. All of them knew that they would receive the training. Since it was impossible to train all 100 people simultaneously, we were able to randomly select 40 supervisors and randomly assign them to either the training ($n = 20$) or the control group ($n = 20$). However, the people assigned to these two groups did not know that they had been labeled as a control or an experimental group. They assumed that for logistical reasons, they were either among the first or the last to receive the training. The mean age of these supervisors was 43.34 years ($SD = 10.6$). The mean number of years they had worked in a supervisory capacity was 5.42 ($SD = 4.54$).

Procedure

The training group was divided into two groups of 10 to facilitate individualized instruction. Each group met for two hours each week for nine weeks. The sessions focused on (a) orienting a new employee, (b) giving recognition, (c) motivating a poor performer, (d) correcting poor work habits, (e) discussing potential disciplinary action, (f) reducing absenteeism, (g) handling a complaining employee, (h) reducing turnover, and (i) overcoming resistance to change.

Each training session followed the same format: (a) introduction of the topic by two trainers (attentional processes); (b) presentation of a film that depicts a supervisor model effectively handling a situation by following a set of three to six learning points that were shown in the film immediately before and after the model was presented (retention processes); (c) group discussion of the effectiveness of the model in

demonstrating the desired behaviors (retention processes); (d) practice in role playing the desired behaviors in front of the entire class (retention processes; motor reproduction processes); and (e) feedback from the class on the effectiveness of each trainee in demonstrating the desired behaviors (motivational processes).

In each of the practice sessions, one trainee took the role of supervisor and another trainee assumed the role of an employee. No prepared scripts were used. The two trainees were simply asked to recreate an incident, relevant to the film topic for that week, that had occurred to at least one of them within the past 12 months. The spontaneity of each practice session was designed to parallel that which occurs on the job.

The learning points shown in the film were posted in front of the trainee playing the role of supervisor. For example, the learning points on handling a complaining employee included the following: (a) Avoid responding with hostility or defensiveness, (b) ask for and listen openly to the employee's complaint; (c) restate the complaint for thorough understanding; (d) recognize and acknowledge his or her viewpoint; (e) if necessary, state your position nondefensively; and (f) set a specific date for a follow-up meeting. These guidelines provided one of the key components of coding and retention.

Each person who played the role of a supervisor had no idea what the hourly employee was going to say to him. He responded as well as he could using the learning points as goals or guidelines. The rest of the group provided feedback on his effectiveness in using the learning points to deal with the situation. The original learning points and their sequencing were developed by Sorcher (see Goldstein & Sorcher, 1974).

The primary function of one trainer was to select and supervise the practice session of each pair of trainees. The primary function of the second trainer was to supervise the feedback given by peers so as to maintain and/or enhance the confidence and self-esteem of the person receiving the feedback. This was done by coaching individuals on how to make evaluative comments that were constructive rather than critical, namely, by having the trainee restate negative comments in a positive manner (e.g., "encourage the hourly employee to talk" rather than "you talk too much").

At the conclusion of each of the nine training sessions, the supervisors were given copies of the learning points for that session. They were instructed to use the supervisory skills that they had learned in class with one or more employees on the job within a one-week time period. In this way, transfer of learning from the classroom to the job was facilitated. The supervisors were asked to report their successes and/or failures to the class the following week. In instances in which a supervisor reported difficulty in demonstrating one or more behaviors, he was asked to explain the situation to the class, to select one individual from the class to assume the role of an hourly employee, and to show exactly what took place. The other trainees then gave him feedback, which he used to practice the desired behavior(s) a second time. In rare instances in which a supervisor said that he was "absolutely stuck," another trainee was asked to show the group how he would handle that supervisor's situation.

In several instances the learning points developed by Sorcher were not rigidly followed. In situations in which there was group consensus among the trainees that a learning point from one session should be added to another session, the learning points were rewritten. In only one instance were the learning points deleted, namely, for overcoming resistance to change. The trainees agreed on the appropriateness of the model's behavior but not on the learning points that described his behavior. Again, the learning points were rewritten by the supervisors to fit their situation.[1]

To further ensure that the supervisors would be reinforced for demonstrating on the job the

behaviors that were taught in class, their superintendents attended an accelerated program of two training sessions per week for four weeks. For the role plays in each of these training sessions, one superintendent assumed the role of foreman while a second superintendent played himself. This training emphasized to superintendents the importance of praising a supervisor, regardless of whether he was in the training or control group, whenever they saw him demonstrate a desired behavior. This procedure enhanced the motivational processes of the training.

RESULTS

The dependent variables included reaction, learning, behavioral, and performance criteria. Trainee reactions to the program were collected immediately and again eight months after training; the learning measures were collected six months after training; the behavioral criteria were collected three months after training; and performance appraisals were conducted one year after the training. These time intervals were selected primarily on the basis of administrative convenience for the company personnel who collected the data.

Reaction Measures

Participation in the training program was mandatory. Attendance records were monitored regularly by the vice president with the prior knowledge of the trainees. In situations in which an absence was unavoidable, a make-up session was held. Thus, it may not be surprising that many foremen were initially unreceptive to the program. The lack of receptiveness was evident at the initial training classes when the supervisors stared at the floor with observable frowns.

In the practice sessions, the trainees who were asked to take the role of an hourly worker frequently behaved in an extremely uncooperative manner. This was done to show the trainers "the way things really are" and why this program was a waste of their time. By the third session, however, this behavior had

---

[1]The revised learning points for overcoming resistance to change are as follows: Clearly describe the details of the change; explain why the change is necessary; discuss how the change will affect the employee; stress the positive aspects of the change; listen openly to the employee's concern about the change; ask the employee for his or her help in making the change work; if necessary, plan a specific follow-up meeting.

changed. Supervisors playing the role of an employee announced publicly to the group that "This program really works; there is no way I can outmaneuver him when he sticks to those damn learning points." Concerns initially expressed to the effect that the company was trying to get everyone to act exactly the same way gave way to such comments as, "Did you notice that none of us are doing the same thing and yet we are all following these key points?" Other representative comments included,

> Most training isn't worth ____; it works in the classroom, but not on the job. With this program, it is just the opposite. It is much easier to do on the job what we learned here than it is to do it in front of all of you.

Other people simply thanked us privately for giving them the confidence to do their job. These individuals included foremen who had been supervisors for 20 years. Still other foremen reported how the program had helped them improve their relationships with their wives and/or children. This latter information, albeit anecdotal in nature, suggests the generalizability of the training to interpersonal effectiveness off the job.

A reaction questionnaire was given immediately after the final training session. The questionnaire contained five questions each with a five-point Likert-type scale. The questions dealt with the extent to which the training (a) helped you do the job better; (b) helped you interact more effectively with employees, (c) peers, (d) supervisors; and (e) the degree to which you would recommend this training to other supervisors. The internal consistency of this scale was adequate ($\alpha = .70$). The mean response for the five items was 4.15 ($SD = .59$). These attitudes were supported behaviorally by the fact that 6 of the 20 trainees were on vacation during one or more of the nine weeks that the training was conducted. All six individuals voluntarily attended the training class held during their vacation.

The reaction questionnaire was administered again eight months later. All the questionnaires were returned. The mean response

for the five items was 4.29 ($SD = .51$). There was no significant difference in the reaction to the program immediately after and eight months after the training program had been conducted, indicating that the initial positive reactions to the program were sustained over time.

Learning Measures

The learning measures consisted of a test containing 85 situational questions. The questions were developed from critical incidents obtained in the job analysis (Latham et al., in press) of supervisory behavior. The incidents were turned into questions by asking, "How would you handle the following situation?" Prior to administering the test, superintendents behaviorally anchored 1 (poor), 3 (mediocre), and 5 (excellent) answers for each question so that the trainees' responses could be objectively scored from 85 to 425 points. An example of a question with its benchmark answers is given below.

> You have spoken with this worker several times about the fact that he doesn't keep his long hair confined under his hard hat. This constitutes a safety violation. You are walking through the plant and you just noticed that he *again* does not have his hair properly confined. What would you do?

The benchmarks (not shown to the trainees) were "send the worker home (1), call the shop steward and give the worker a written warning (3), or explain the rationale as to why the behavior cannot continue, and ask for his ideas on how to solve the problem (5)."

The test was completed on the job, under uniform conditions, with a personnel representative present as a monitor. Code numbers were used for identification purposes so that superintendents who scored each test could not be biased by knowledge of a respondent's identity or whether he had received the training.

The mean score ($M = 301$, $SD = 36.55$) of the training group was significantly higher ($t = 2.29$, $df = 38$, $p < .05$) than that of the control group ($M = 273.36$, $SD = 37.06$). It should be noted that the learning test did not contain questions restricted solely to the nine areas covered in the training, but, rather, it examined all possible interpersonal situations that had been identified in the job analysis. Thus, performance on this test was considered an external criterion measure. The results indicated that the trainees had acquired the knowledge necessary to transfer the principles learned in class to different types of job-related problems.

Behavioral Measures

The behavioral measures consisted of tape-recorded role plays of supervisors resolving supervisor–employee problems. For these role plays, brief scripts were developed for each of the nine training topics. For example, the scripts for overcoming resistance to change were as follows:

> You have just called in the employee sitting in front of you to inform him that you are switching him from the day shift to the night shift. You suspect that he may not want to make this switch. Show how you would handle this situation;

and

> Your supervisor has just called you into his office. You have heard that he wants you to work the night shift. You resent this very much. Show how you would handle this situation.

The scripts were randomly assigned to the supervisors. None of these situations had been previously described to the supervisors during training, and none of them were the same as those depicted on the training films. The individuals who played the role of an employee were people who had been through the training program. However, they did not role play with supervisors from their own training class. This was done to prevent them from knowing whether the person in the role of supervisor was from another training class or had yet to receive training. The pairing of role players was randomly determined.

The 20 supervisors in the training group were given the appropriate set of learning points to use during the role play. This is because the trainees were encouraged to keep the learning points with them at all times on the job.

Of the 20 foremen in the control group, 10 were given the learning points. This was done to determine whether knowledge alone of what one is "supposed to do" is sufficient to elicit the desired behavior. The learning points or goals are straightforward. For example, in giving recognition, foremen are instructed to "describe to the employee what was done that deserves recognition, express your personal appreciation, and ask the employee if there is anything you can do to make the job easier." If giving the foremen the learning points as guidelines to follow was as effective as requiring them to attend the nine training sessions, considerable time and expense would be saved for the company.

The tape recordings were evaluated by 15 superintendents who worked in groups of 3. The superintendents were blind as to the identity of each supervisor and whether the supervisor had received training. To eliminate the possibility of judges recognizing a person's voice on a tape, superintendents in one area of the company evaluated the tape recordings of supervisors from another area of the company.

Approximately eight taped role plays were randomly assigned to each set of judges. The rating for each role play was determined by each of the judges working independently and then through group consensus agreeing on a single rating. This procedure is recommended by those who conduct assessment centers (Moses & Byham, 1977) because it allows for a thorough discussion of a supervisor's performance rather than a mechanical calculation of the average of the independent ratings.

The superintendent ratings were compared with those of a second set of judges, consisting of the two trainers and the personnel manager. These individuals were aware of the identity of each supervisor and whether he had received training. However, all judges (blind and informed) had received intensive training in minimizing rating errors. This training program has been described elsewhere (Latham, Wexley, & Pursell, 1975).

The rating scale consisted of the learning points taught in class, each with a five-point scale on which the judge rated the quality of the performance. In addition, the individual playing the role of the hourly worker was rated on eight five-point bipolar adjectives (e.g., helpful–frustrating). This was done to determine whether the role plays of hourly workers were significantly different among the three conditions in terms of difficulty level. The internal consistency of the scale was satisfactory ($\alpha = .95$).

No significant difference was found among the ratings of the hourly workers in the training group, the control group who received the learning points, or the control who did not receive the learning points. Moreover, there was no significant difference between the ratings of the blind and the informed judges.

Planned t tests indicated that the ratings of the trained group ($M = 4.11$, $SD = .67$) were significantly higher than those of the control group with ($M = 2.70$, $SD = .66$), $t(28) = 5.38$, $p < .05$, and without the learning points ($M = 2.84$, $SD = .66$), $t(28) = 4.86$, $p < .05$. There was no significant difference between the ratings assigned to the two control groups. The same rank ordering of means and the same levels of statistical significance were obtained with the ratings assigned by the informed judges. Thus, it would appear that symbolic and motor rehearsal enhanced learning as is suggested by social-learning theory.

These measures were classified as internal criteria in that they only assessed skill levels in performing the specific behaviors for which the training program was designed to teach. The critical question was whether the training program brought about a relatively permanent change in the foremen's behavior on the job.

Job Performance

Superintendents evaluated the supervisors on behavioral observation scales (Latham & Wexley, 1977) one month before and one year after the training. Thirty-five behavioral items (Cronbach's $\alpha = .95$) that comprised the scales had been developed on the basis of the job

analysis of effective/ineffective supervisor behavior (Latham et al., in press). The supervisor's superintendent indicated on a five-point scale for each item the extent to which he had observed the supervisor demonstrate the behavior. Because the superintendents knew who had received training, they received intensive instruction on minimizing rating errors (Latham et al., 1975) when appraising others.

There was no significant difference on the premeasures between the experimental group and the control group. Two-tailed t tests on the postmeasure indicated that the training group ($M = 3.47$, $SD = .42$) performed significantly better, $t(38) = 2.51$, $p < .05$, on the job than the control group ($M = 2.98$, $SD = .68$).

The job performance of the supervisors was also examined using the company's traditional performance appraisal instrument. This instrument contains 12 behavioral items (Cronbach's alpha = .87) each with a five-point scale. The correlation between the two appraisal instruments was .72 ($p < .01$). The data on this second instrument were examined because the superintendents did not know that these ratings would be used to evaluate the effectiveness of the training program nor that the researchers had access to them.

Again, there was no significant difference between the training and the control group on the premeasure, but there was a significant difference on the postmeasure ($M = 3.80$, $SD = .43$; $M = 3.30$, $SD = .47$, training, control groups, respectively), $t(38) = 2.68$, $p < .05$. Together, the results from these two instruments indicate that supervisors who received training performed more effectively on the job than those in the control group.

Control Group

One year after the training had taken place, the 20 foremen in the control group received the same training as the original training group. Subsequent to their training, there was no significant difference between the two groups on any of the four criterion measures. It is important to note that the change in the control group's behavior did not occur until after the training, despite the fact that prior to training, the superintendents were instructed to praise them for engaging in the behaviors that were taught in the classroom.

DISCUSSION

The typical approach to the evaluation of a training program is to review the program with one or two vice presidents, various managers in the field, and perhaps a group of prospective trainees. If the program "looks good," the company uses it until someone in a position of authority decides that the program has outlived its purpose. All of this is done on the basis of opinion and judgment. In the end, no one really knows whether the training attained the objectives for which it was designed.

What distinguished the present program from most approaches to training was the method by which it was evaluated. Measurement criteria for evaluating the program were established prior to training. The use of multiple criteria indicated that the trainees liked the program and, hence, had the motivation to learn the leadership principles; they acquired and retained the knowledge taught; they were able to demonstrate the behaviors under controlled standardized conditions; and their performance subsequently improved on the job. These are highly significant findings because few training programs have shown empirically that they do anything other than please the trainee, and this positive reaction frequently dissipates over time. Finally, it is important tc point out that the use of a control group, crucial for proper evaluation, was not a difficult concept to employ with the company. In a situation in which it is impossible to train everyone simultaneously, there is no reason not to use a control group. In a situation in which everyone is to be trained, it is not difficult to convince an organization of the value of random assignment to two groups.

The practical significance of this study is that it supports earlier applications of this approach to training for first-line supervisors (Burnaska, 1976; Byham, Adams & Kiggins, 1976; Moses & Ritchie, 1976; Smith, 1976). These studies taken together indicate that

leadership skills can be taught in a relatively short time period (i.e., 18 hours), providing that the trainees are given a model to follow, are given a specific set of goals or guidelines, are given an opportunity to perfect the skill, are given feedback as to the effectiveness of their behavior, and are reinforced with praise for applying the acquired skills on the job. These features of the program follow from the theoretical framework of social-learning theory.

The theoretical significance of this research is that it demonstrates that the integration of both cognitive and behavioristic principles within the context of social-learning theory brings about a relatively permanent change in supervisory behavior in what to supervisors is the most difficult part of their job, managing people. Future researchers may want to compare the overall components of this training with one or more of its subparts (e.g., goal setting plus reinforcement with no model, reinforcement only, etc.), but the evidence from other disciplines in psychology indicates that the whole is superior to any of its individual subparts (Bandura, 1977; O'Connor, 1972). More profitable time might be spent by I-O psychologists in examining different areas in which the theory can be extended, applied, and/or modified for understanding behavior in organizational settings. It is time to move from truncated theory building in which we look only at cognitive or only at environmental variables.

At a theoretical level, behavioral modeling works because of reciprocal interactions among cognitive, behavioral, and environmental variables (Bandura, 1977). It is true that supervisors' behaviors are influenced by their environment, but the environment is partly of their own making. By their actions, supervisors play a role in creating the social milieu and other circumstances that arise from daily transactions with subordinates. The relative influence of these three variables—cognitive, behavioral, and environmental—varies under different circumstances. Behavioral modeling allows the trainees to try new behaviors, to experience different consequences, and to accurately perceive the outcomes.

One hallmark of the behaviorists is careful observation. Komaki and her colleagues have combined observational technology with feedback to demonstrate that training alone is not sufficient to effect a permanent change in behavior. This reading describes the efforts to carefully identify the components of safe behavior, and develop a training and feedback system that would encourage safe work behavior among the employees of a vehicle maintenance department. It is particularly instructive to consider the design that was employed to carry out the research. A baseline, two training periods, and two training plus feedback periods consumed 45 weeks of observational time. This is an enormous investment of energy. Nevertheless, the payoff is the ability to see more clearly what the causal links are in the training chain. Try to remain aware of the great detail and effort that went into this study when you are reading it.

Effect of Training and Feedback: Component Analysis of a Behavioral Safety Program

Judi Komaki, Arlene T. Heinzmann, and Loralie Lawson
San Jose State University

Behavioral programs, particularly those employing nonmonetary consequences such as feedback, have been found effective as motivational strategies and readily acceptable to employees and employers (Adam, 1975; Catano, 1976; Cooper, Thomson, & Baer, 1970; Hegarty, 1974; Kim & Hamner, 1976; Leamon, 1974; Nadler, Mirvis, & Cammann, 1976; Panyan, Boozer, & Morris, 1970; Quilitch, 1975; Sulzer-Arazoff, 1978; "Performance Audit, Feedback, and Positive Reinforcement," 1972).

In many behavioral programs employees are first prompted as to what constitutes desired performance. This is effected through such an-tecedent events as the provision of written rules, verbal instruction, suggested standards, and/or extensive training. Consequences such as feedback are then provided following performance.

Many behavioral programs consolidate the antecedent and consequent components into one treatment package, as exemplified by a recent study of Komaki, Barwick, and Scott (1978). In this case, the researchers introduced a combination training and feedback program to improve worker safety in a food manufacturing plant. Employees received information about desired performance in the form of explanations, presentations of safe and unsafe practices, rules, and desired standards. Following their performance, employees were given feedback through the public posting of departmental performance levels on graphs several times a week.

Source: *Journal of Applied Psychology*, 65, 1980, pp. 261–270. Copyright 1980 by the American Psychological Association. Reprinted by permission of the publisher and author.

Although the results of behavioral programs such as this have been positive, the fact that the two components were introduced simultaneously raised several important questions. Was it necessary to provide feedback? Perhaps workers improved because they finally knew what to do. Why not just provide training, a predominant improvement strategy? Despite constant reference to these issues by both researchers and practitioners, few comparisons have been made between these antecedent and consequent components.

As a result, the present study addresses two questions: (a) Is training alone sufficient to substantially improve and maintain performance on the job? and (b) is it necessary to provide feedback to maintain performance? It differs from previous studies in that it includes a component analysis, that is, an analysis of a treatment package in terms of its components. The training component was presented alone, and its effects were assessed before the introduction of the second feedback component. The study also differs from previous studies because data were collected three to four times a week for almost a year, thereby making it possible to evaluate the effect of these different components over an extended period of time. A unique perspective was attained by extending the results of the previous study (Komaki et al., 1978) to a more skilled subject population working in the public sector and by including on-site personnel in the feedback process.

METHOD

Subjects and Setting

This study was conducted in the vehicle maintenance division of a large western city's department of public works. The department had one of the highest accident rates in the city, recording 84.2 lost-time accidents per million man hours. The only units with higher accident rates were in the police department and water pollution control plant. It should be noted, however, that the accident rate was comparable to the average rates of other vehicle and equipment maintenance units in the nation (National Safety Council, 1978). The city safety officer selected the vehicle maintenance division within the Department of Public Works because of the interest expressed by its superintendent, the accessibility of the work sites, and its high accident rate relative to other divisions in the department. Prior to the study, an average of three lost-time accidents had occurred each month.

The vehicle maintenance division is responsible for equipment repair and maintenance of the majority of the city's rolling stock. It is organized into four sections: (a) Sweeper repair constructs and repairs equipment, provides welding services, and maintains the city's line of street sweepers: (b) preventive maintenance fuels, washes, and lubricates vehicles; (c) light equipment repair provides a ready line of police cars and other light vehicles (pick-up trucks, motorcycles); and (d) heavy equipment repair maintains vehicles weighing three-fourths of a ton and over. The sections are located in the main corporation yard, a one-square-block area that includes shop facilities, washing and fueling sections, vehicle storage areas, and administrative offices, and in the police garage, located one mile (1.6 km) from the main yard.

In the sweeper repair, preventive maintenance, light equipment repair, and heavy equipment repair sections, there were a total of 55 employees (7, 37, 7, and 4, respectively). The work groups differed widely in terms of seniority level and age. The heavy equipment repair section included the oldest (M age = 53.5 years) and most experienced men (M seniority = 31.8 years). In contrast, the light equipment repair section, with a mean age and mean experience level of 32 and 11.5 years, respectively, consisted of the youngest and the most recently trained employees. In both sweeper repair and preventive maintenance the workers varied in age (range = 23 to 50 years) and seniority level (range = 6 months to 29 years). Employees belong to an operating engineers' union and are responsible to section supervisors, who, in turn, report to the division superintendent. Salaries range from $866 to

$1,275 per month. With the exception of the 24-hour garage facility, employees work weekdays.

Measure

Definitions of Safe Performances. To generate safety items, accident logs from the previous five years were examined. When it was found that an accident occurred after a worker fell off a jack stand, for instance, an item was included regarding the proper use of jacks and jack stands. Supervisors were also asked to suggest items they believed to be important. Throughout the development stage, both supervisors and workers were invited to eliminate punctilious items.

There were four general categories of items: proper use of equipment and tools, use of safety equipment, housekeeping, and general safety procedures. Some examples of safety items in the vehicle maintenance division are:

Proper use of equipment and tools. When reaching upward for an item more than 30 cm (1 foot) away from extended arms, use steps, stepladder, or solid part of vehicle. Do *not* stand on jacks or jack stands.

Use of safety equipment. When using brake machine, wear full-face shield or goggles. When arcing brake shoes, respirator should also be worn.

Housekeeping. Any oil/grease spill larger than 8 x 8 cm (3 x 3 inches) in an interior walking area (defined as any area at least 30 cm (1 foot) from a wall or a solid standing object) or an exterior walking area (designated by outer white lines parallel to the wall and at least 30 cm (1 foot) from the wall) should be soaked up with rice hull or grease compound.

General safety procedures. When any type of jack other than an air jack is in use (i.e., vehicle is supported by jack or off the ground), at least one jack stand should also be used.

Because of differences in jobs, equipment, and individual supervisors' concerns about safety, items were tailored to each section. In the sweeper, preventive, heavy, and light sections, there were a total of 22, 15, 21, and 18 items, respectively. Many of the general procedures and housekeeping items were similar to one another, however.

Each item was described so that observers would have minimal difficulty in making reliable judgments. Supervisors were encouraged to describe desired practices in objective terms (e.g., remain within 6 m of gas pumps when fueling) instead of noting that workers "should be more careful" or "should not rush." For items with an observable result, the outcome of behavior (e.g., oil spill) was indicated rather than the act (e.g., spilling oil).

Observational Procedures. Trained raters, identified as interested in the area of safety, served as non-participant observers. They coded each item as safe, unsafe, or not observed in full view of the workers. If, for instance, an employee in light equipment repair was seen working under a vehicle, it was observed whether or not he was wearing eye protection. If he was, that item was recorded as "safe"; if he was not, the item was recorded as "unsafe." If no work was being done under a vehicle during the observation period, the item was marked "unobserved." The percentage of incidents performed safely was calculated as the number of safe items observed divided by the number of total incidents observed (the number of items checked as being either safe or unsafe) and multiplied by 100.

Each observation lasted for a total of 60 minutes. Observers spent five minutes in each of three shops in the sweeper repair section (15), five minutes in each of four locations in the preventive maintenance section (20), 10 minutes in the heavy equipment repair section (10), and 10 minutes in one location and five minutes in a second location of the light equipment repair section (15).

Observations took place from four to five times (4.2) each week for the first three phases. During the last two phases, observations were conducted as before but took place on the average of three times (3.0) a week. The exact times varied; no observation was carried out at the same time of day on any two consecutive visits.

A total of 165 observations were conducted

over a 45-week period of time. Interrater reliability was assessed 21 times, for an average of one reliability check every 7.5 observations. This entailed independent recording by a second observer who accompanied the primary observer. A percentage agreement method was used in which the number of agreements was divided by the number of agreements plus disagreements and multiplied by 100. An agreement was tallied when both raters categorized an item in an identical manner. Primary and secondary observers consistently obtained high percentages of agreement throughout the study, averaging 94.8 percent overall.

To minimize the possibility of observer bias, approximately half (52 percent) of the observations were made by three persons (out of seven) who were not told about the order or the timing of the phases. A total of 15 (out of 21) interrater reliability checks was conducted with at least one of the naive observers. Agreement here was also consistently high, with an average of 94.4 percent, indicating that the changes were not likely to be a function of observer bias.

Behavioral Analysis

A behavioral analysis, that is, an assessment of the antecedents and consequences of behavior, was conducted to determine factors that led to unsafe practices and hindered safe acts. The existing safety program was first examined. There was an established 12-member central safety committee that provided direction and formulated policy and a safety officer, who was responsible for planning, supervising, and coordinating the citywide accident prevention program. Each department head set up and maintained a written safety program for his or her staff and designated a safety coordinator and a departmental safety committee. In the public works department the eight-member safety committee met monthly. In keeping with city rules and regulations, the safety committee made and followed through on inspections of the premises, reviewed accident investigation reports, and made arrangements for the distribution of safety materials and bulletins (e.g., Occupational Safety and Health Act (OSHA) regulations. "Wear safety goggles" reminders). Other than the monthly involvement by these few workers on the committee and the posting of these materials, however, safety was rarely mentioned on a day-to-day basis.

The behavioral analysis also revealed that newly hired workers received no formal safety training, there were few consequences for safe or unsafe practices, and unsafe acts were sometimes inadvertently reinforced. Even when employees did take the time to act in a safe manner, little or nothing was said or done by supervisors and co-workers. At the same time, when workers performed unsafely, they rarely experienced an injury (relative to the number of unsafe acts) and sometimes were reinforced by completing tasks more rapidly.

Design and Procedures

A multiple-baseline design with a reversal component was employed with a total of five phases: baseline, Training Only 1, Training and Feedback 1, Training Only 2, and Training and Feedback 2. Baseline data were collected in all four sections, and the second and third phases were introduced in a staggered sequence. After the 26th and 36th weeks, the fourth and fifth phases were introduced. The duration and sequence of each phase are outlined in Table 1.

Training Only. At the beginning of the second phase, workers attended a safety training session that lasted from 30 to 45 minutes during their regular workday. To assess their knowledge of safety regulations, the men were shown a series of 35-mm transparencies and were requested to write down what they thought was wrong or unsafe in each scene. Each slide protrayed an unsafe condition or practice as described in the observational code. The slides had been taken by the city safety officer in the employees' own work areas, showing equipment they used, with a fellow worker as a model. One slide, for instance, showed an employee working under a vehicle without eye

TABLE 1 Duration and Sequence of Experimental Phases across Sections

| | Section in Vehicle Maintenance Division | | | | | | | |
| | Sweeper Repair | | Preventive Maintenance | | Light Equipment Repair | | Heavy Equipment Repair | |
Experimental Phase	Dura-tion*	Se-quence†	Dura-tion*	Se-quence†	Dura-tion*	Se-quence†	Dura-tion*	Se-quence†
Baseline	9		10		11		11	
Training only 1	5	10	6	11	8	12	8	12
Training and feedback 1	11	15	9	17	6	20	6	20
Training only 2	10	26	10	26	10	26	10	26
Training and feedback 2	10	36	10	36	10	36	10	36

*Length of phase in weeks.
†Week after which the phase was introduced.

protection. (Note: The pictures of employees were carefully posed, and this announcement was made to the viewers.)

Following the assessment of safety knowledge, the employees were encouraged to discuss the hazards portrayed, as well as to suggest other safety rules that had not been mentioned. The unsafe scenes were then shown again, followed by scenes that pictured the condition corrected or the act performed in a safe manner. The employee working under the vehicle now wore eye protection, for instance. As each safe scene was shown, the safety rule was stated. After the second showing of the slides, the men were given a copy of the safety rules that were later posted in their respective departments. Employees were encouraged to pay special attention to rules that were overlooked most often (from three to eight, depending on the section).

Training and Feedback 1. At the beginning of the Training and Feedback 1 phase, the slides and the safety rules were reviewed. Then the section supervisor explained that he would be making a randomly timed daily safety observation and that he would post the results on a graph. The supervisor used the graph to point out the mean safety level during the baseline and Training Only 1 phases and drew attention to the line demarcating the section's goal. The goal of the sweeper and preventive sections was set at 75 percent and that of the heavy and light sections at 90 percent.

The supervisor emphasized that the goal was realistic and had been set in conjunction with the superintendent, based on their previous safety performance. He made it clear that performance at the 100 percent level was neither expected nor required. After the meeting the graph was posted where all the employees would be able to see how they were doing in comparison with their previous performance and the goal.

Prior to this meeting, supervisors learned how to observe and provide feedback. Using the same observational procedures as the observers, they practiced observations with one of the experimenters until they agreed consistently on over 90 percent of the items. Thereafter, the experimenter conducted periodic interrater reliability checks with each supervisor. They consistently agreed, averaging 96.8 percent and 99.3 percent for Phases 3 and 5, respectively. Each supervisor used the information he himself had collected in providing feedback to his subordinates. Independent observers continued to collect data throughout the study.

Training Only 2. In the fourth phase, the supervisors ceased conducting observations and providing feedback. The list of written rules remained posted.

Training and Feedback 2. During the fifth and final phase, feedback was again provided. Depending on the section, supervisors or co-workers conducted the observations and posted the safety level on section graphs.

RESULTS

Figure 1 shows the percentage of incidents performed safely on a weekly basis as recorded by the independent observers. Tables 2 and 3 present summary data for the four sections during the five experimental phases and the results of the autoregressive integrated moving averages (ARIMA) analysis. An ARIMA analysis is designed for time-series data and removes any existing serial dependencies within the data through a series of transformations. It can be used to assess whether there is a significant and immediate change in level from one phase to another and whether there are changes in trends from one phase to another that lead the data to drift in a different direction. (For further details, refer to Box & Jenkins, 1970; Glass, Wilson, & Gottman, 1975; Jones, Vaught, & Weinrott, 1977.)

Component Analysis. To determine the relative effectiveness of the components, a visual inspection was made, and the data that were collected during the 165 observation sessions were analyzed using an ARIMA analysis. The results of the ARIMA analysis essentially confirmed the interpretations based on a visual inspection of the data. When comparisons were made between the baseline and the Training Only 1 phases, there were no significant level or drift changes. During baseline, employees were performing safely from one third to two thirds of the time. Following the Training Only 1 phase, the percentage of safe incidents increased in all sections, albeit slightly, for an overall increase of 9 percent.

When comparisons were made between baseline and the Training and Feedback 1 phases, however, significant level changes were found in three out of four sections, sweeper, $t(77) = 2.41$, $p < .05$, preventive, $t(71) = 3.90$, $p < .01$, and heavy, $t(65) = 3.11$, $p < .01$, with the fourth section in the same direction. During the Training and Feedback 1 phase, performance increased significantly. All sections improved their safety level for an average increase of 16 percent over the Information Only 1 phase and 26 percent over baseline. During this phase all sections were performing safely at least two thirds of the time with two sections (light, heavy) performing consistently at the 90 percent level.

Plausible alternative hypotheses (history, maturation, statistical regression) were ruled out because the two phases were introduced to the sections at different points in time and improvements occurred after, and not prior to, the introduction of these phases. History was ruled out as a source of internal invalidity because it is not likely that an extraneous event would have the same impact in separate sections at different times. If maturation were responsible, performance would be expected to improve as a function of the passage of time; however, improvements occurred, with few exceptions, after the introduction of Phase 3. The effects of statistical regression were ruled out because regression effects would be seen in any series of repeated measurements and not just after the introduction of the two phases.

Reactivity of measurement was also not likely to be a plausible explanation for the improvements obtained because the observers were present during all phases. Therefore, improvements in performance during any one phase could not be due to the reactivity of the measure per se. Questions concerning reactivity and external validity, however, were not so straightforward. Although the issue of the generality of improvements was not addressed directly in the present study, support was provided by accident records, which showed that injuries were reduced by a factor of seven from the preceding year. Since the observers were present during a relatively small percentage of working hours, it is unlikely that improvements were confined to these times.

Employee Knowledge. As expected, employees demonstrated that they could readily identify unsafe conditions and actions and could suggest appropriate remedies. The mean percentage of items correctly identified in each section ranged from 93 percent in light to 78

FIGURE 1   Percentage of Incidents Performed Safely by Employees in Four Vehicle Maintenance Sections under Five Experimental Conditions

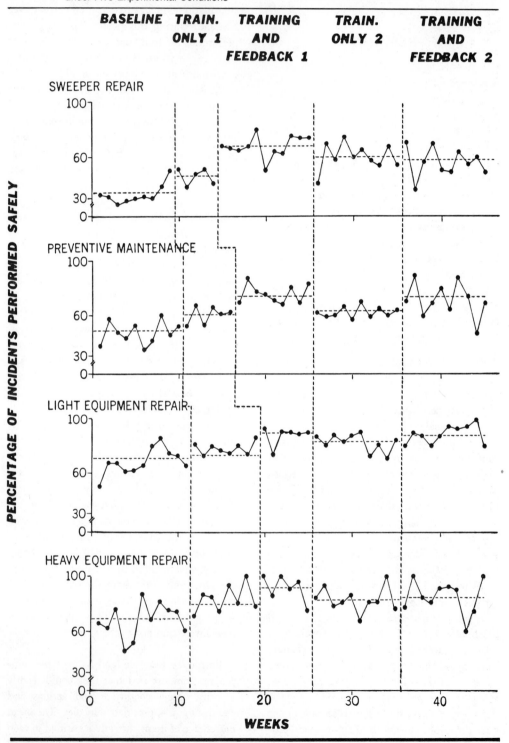

TABLE 2   Mean Safety Level and Standard Deviations in the Vehicle Maintenance Division during the Five Experimental Phases

	Section in Vehicle Maintenance Division							
	Sweeper Repair		Preventive Maintenance		Light Equipment Repair		Heavy Equipment Repair	
Experimental Phase	M*	SD	M*	SD	M*	SD	M*	SD
Baseline	34.4	17.5	49.2	17.7	70.8	14.7	68.6	18.5
Training only 1	46.1	21.0	61.3	17.1	73.8	13.9	84.3	16.6
Training and feedback 1	68.4	21.2	76.2	13.7	89.6	13.0	92.3	13.4
Training only 2	60.1	21.8	64.2	12.7	83.7	13.1	83.2	17.8
Training and feedback 2	58.8	17.7	74.6	16.1	88.9	11.6	84.1	15.3

*Percentage of incidents performed safely divided by the number of observations in each phase.

percent in heavy. Approximately 80 percent of the workers scored 80 percent or better, with only 11 percent scoring below 70 percent.

Workers' Reactions. The responses of individual workers were generally favorable. During the training sessions, workers in all sections made suggestions about additional safety items, with some pointing out how fellow workers had been injured in the past. When feedback was provided, the workers frequently referred higher level personnel to their graphs. The graphs, although easily accessible, were never mutilated. When two adjoining sections (light, heavy) each received feedback, an informal competition arose, with workers checking to see which section had scored higher.

Maintenance. The final phases of the 10½-month study indicate the long-term effects of a feedback program. During the Training Only 2 phase, the safety level declined below that of the previous information and feedback phase by an average of 9 percent. During the final phase, however, workers in two sections (preventive, light) again improved when feedback was provided three to four times per week. In the other two sections, feedback was provided on the average of only one or two times a week, and performance leveled off at the previous Training Only 2 percentage.

TABLE 3   Results of the Autoregressive Integrated Moving Average Analysis

	Section in Vehicle Maintenance Division											
	Sweeper Repair			Preventive Maintenance			Light Equipment Repair			Heavy Equipment Repair		
Comparison	Level Change*	Drift Change†	df	Level Change*	Drift Change†	df	Level Change*	Drift Change†	df	Level Change*	Drift Change†	df
1 versus 2	0.25	−1.76	54	.25	.69	65	.18	−.59	70	1.01	.79	70
1 versus 3	2.41‡	−1.81	77	3.90§	−.56	71	1.44	−.31	65	3.11§	−.72	65
1 versus 4	2.16‡	−1.46	63	2.23‡	−.72	68	1.82	−1.63	71	1.81	−.01	71
1 versus 5	1.89	−2.16‡	57	3.29§	−.65	62	.69	.88	65	1.70	−.03	65
2 versus 3	2.37‡	.65	69	1.38	−1.13	64	1.09	.15	57	1.20	−1.80	57
3 versus 4	−.82	.12	78	−2.03‡	−.07	67	−.25	−.84	58	−.17	1.12	58
4 versus 5	−.55	−.51	58	2.48‡	−.23	58	.15	2.30‡	58	.34	−.28	58

*Probability of the observed change as determined by a t-test comparison.
†Probability of the observed trend change as determined by a t-test comparison.
§ $p < .01$.   ‡ $p < .05$.

Supervisory Participation. During the initial phases supervisors willingly made suggestions about safety incidents and readily mastered the collection and posting of data. However, the consistency with which they collected and posted data declined during the final feedback phase. The percentage of time that feedback was provided in the final phase ($M = 62.6$ percent, range = 36 percent to 83 percent) was lower than in the initial feedback phase ($M = 81.6$ percent, range = 55 percent to 98 percent). What this meant in practice was that during the final phase, supervisors rarely provided feedback on a daily basis, and for some weeks in some sections feedback was provided only once or twice each week. In contrast, during the initial feedback phase, supervisors provided feedback at least three and as many as five days each week. It was subsequently found that the supervisors' consistency in data collection and posting was positively related to the frequency of interactions with the experimenters. Supervisors who observed at least 90 percent of the available days interacted relatively frequently with the experimenters (on the average of three or four times a month), whereas the rate of interaction was less than once a month with a supervisor who was less consistent.

Management Support. Although the division superintendent continued to give verbal support, he was inconsistent in communicating this support to workers and supervisors. On occasion he personally facilitated the implementation of the program; however, he did not make the effort to attend all of the safety sessions. He volunteered to learn how to observe and to recognize supervisors and workers informally for their participation in the program. Unfortunately, these activities never materialized.

Accident reduction. The overall program appeared to have a beneficial effect on the number of accidents. During the eight-month period of the program (Phases 2–5), the number of lost-time accidents declined to .4 accidents per month. For the same time period (April through November) during the years immediately preceding and following the program, there were 3.0 and 1.8 lost time accidents per month, respectively.

DISCUSSION

The results of the present study underscore the importance of consequent control. When employees received training in the form of a slide presentation, verbal explanations, and written rules, performance improved slightly. It was not until feedback was provided that performance significantly improved. Thus, it was concluded that training alone is not sufficient to substantially improve and maintain performance even though desired practices are objectively defined and examples are tailored to specific job situations.

The relative importance of these two components is particularly relevant to the occupational safety field, in which the traditional emphasis is on antecedent control strategies. In-house attempts to improve safety rely almost exclusively on the provision of safety training and the posting of rules and reminders (e.g., Anderson, 1975; Laner & Sell, 1960; Leslie & Adams, 1973; Milutinovich & Phatak, 1978; "Operator Training," 1975). The assumption is that workers who know what to do will automatically conduct themselves in a safe manner for extended periods of time regardless of the consequences on the job. The results of the present study suggest that although proper training is essential, safety training alone is inadequate, that more attention should be devoted to the provision of consequences for desired performance, and that feedback is an effective and readily accepted motivational strategy.

The results of the present study also highlight the key role that supervisory and managerial personnel play in any successful program. Although the acquisition and maintenance of supervisory and managerial support is a commonly acknowledged problem, a review of the literature reveals few well-controlled studies demonstrating the efficacy of programs designed to sustain the involvement of these personnel (Campbell, Dunnette,

Lawler, & Weick, 1970; Katzell, Bienstock, & Faerstein, 1977). The same principles that have been shown to be effective with lower level personnel could profitably be used with middle and upper level personnel. Further research on this neglected, but important segment of the work population would be of great value.

The findings during the final feedback phase suggest that the frequency with which consequences are provided may be a critical factor. Although it is widely accepted that consequences should be provided frequently and that less reinforcement is necessary once the behaviors have been established, this study was not designed to determine exactly how often feedback should be provided to maintain performance in a given situation. Studies involving schedules of reinforcement in work settings have not been directly concerned with how to maintain performance over extended periods of time (Latham & Dossett, 1978; Yukl & Latham, 1975; Yukl, Latham, & Pursell, 1976). A systematic investigation of the frequency of feedback would benefit future programs in work settings.

A common feature of many behavioral programs is the clarification of performance objectives (Mager, 1962). In the present study, for example, safe practices were defined before baseline, employees were told about the definitions during the training phase, and the criterion of acceptance was set during the feedback phase. Whereas the latter event would not be singled out in most behavioral programs, a distinction has been made in the industrial/organizational psychology literature between the act of providing feedback and the act of setting standards, as the recent goal-setting literature attests. Various studies have been conducted regarding the impact of goal setting and the relative effect of different types of goals: hard versus easy, specific versus general, participa-

tive versus assigned in work settings (refer to reviews by Latham & Yukl, 1975; Steers & Porter, 1974). Another continuing issue regards the relative effect of feedback and goal setting (Locke, 1980), recalling dubious paradigm debates of the past. Although it has been found that feedback facilitates the effect of goal setting (Erez, 1977; Kim & Hamner, 1976), no studies have adequately addressed the question of whether feedback alone would improve performance in the absence of goal setting. Instead, evidence for the latter has been based on indirect extrapolations rather than reports of studies that found no improvement when feedback alone was introduced. To resolve this issue, it is highly recommended that the terms be operationally defined and that data be collected regarding these frequently confounded components.

Still another research issue regards the content and mode of the feedback provided. In the present study, anecdotal reports revealed that the posting of the safety level on prominently displayed graphs provided natural opportunities for management, supervisors, and workers to interact in a positive manner about safety. It would be worthwhile to determine the role of this interaction. It would also be interesting to assess the effects of such variables as providing information regarding employee behaviors rather than accident indices, presenting information on a group rather than an individual basis, maintaining a continuing written record rather than a noncumulative tally, and publicly rather than privately posting feedback.

In addition to raising a variety of intriguing questions for further research, the present study demonstrates the importance of consequent control strategies and the potential of the behavioral approach in improving safety practices and reducing accidents over an extended period of time.

SECTION SIX

Motivation

In work settings, it is commonly observed that the difference between success and failure depends not on whether an individual *can* do the job but whether that individual is *willing* to do the job. In other words, the question is not one of ability but rather of motivation. A generally accepted definition of motivation is that it concerns the initiation, direction, intensity, persistence, and termination of behavior. That's a lot to be concerned with. It is no wonder, then, that there are many theories of motivation. Some of these theories stress the environmental control over action; others emphasize internal mechanisms such as the existence of goals, the perception of fairness, or the estimated probability of reward to be gained from a particular action. In this section, we will consider some recent approaches to motivation.

Beginning 40 years ago, and continuing for 20 years, an important theory of human motivation was that of Abraham Maslow. In 1964, Vroom began a revolution in theories of work motivation that has not yet ended. After the revolution began, there was a scramble to develop new theories and, as a result, we went from one or two theories to a dozen or so. That trend has slowed dramatically. As Guest points out in this reading, current research and theory is combining existing theories rather than developing new ones. In addition, there seems to be a movement away from general theories that might explain every aspect of behavior toward more specific theories that might account for limited and specific behavioral events. In this article, Guest provides a broad overview of what is happening currently in work motivation research.

■ READING 17 ■

What's New in . . . Motivation

David Guest

We hear less than we used to about motivation at work. No writers on the subject seem to have captured the imagination of managers in the way Maslow, McGregor, and Herzberg did and yet more material on motivation is in fact being published now than ever.

The subject of employee motivation may appear to have lost some of its glamour and novelty to managers, but this has been more than compensated for by gains in utility. Three general trends can be identified which help to explain this. First, there has been a shift away from presenting simplified theories and promising general solutions to the "problem" of motivation towards more careful, more narrowly focused and generally more valid work. The second trend has been to favour consolidation and elaboration of existing theory—improving methods of testing theories in work settings—rather than the development of new theory. And the third trend, and one which most managers would welcome, is a shift away from the development of general theories of

motivation at work to a concern for approaches such as job design, leadership, participation and goal setting which can be pursued in different ways according to the underlying motivation theory that informs them.

For management, therefore, many of the most interesting developments lie in the strategies designed to overcome organisational problems by utilising motivation theory.

Meanwhile, new gurus have emerged; they may have moved into different fields, but they are still talking, albeit more indirectly, about motivation at work. Two of the best examples are Ouchi with *Theory Z* (1981), and Peters and Waterman with their more recent best seller *In Search of Excellence* (1982). At the heart of the management strategy which emerges from these studies is some sort of consensus about the need to obtain the involvement, the commitment—the motivation—of employees to their work and to their organisation. The message is over-simplified, but it captures something of the magic of management and most managers are intrigued to know what makes for success. In North America, one

Source: *Personnel Management*, May 1984, 147–151.

by-product has been a marked increase in the importance attached to the broad personnel management field and more particularly to utilising the behavioural sciences, including motivation theory, to ensure effective human resource management. It is an opportunity which does not yet seem to have been recognised or seized to anything like the same extent by personnel management in the UK.

Since developments in motivation cover such a broad field, this relatively brief and inevitably rather sketchy review will examine some of the recent—and in some cases not so recent but nevertheless interesting—work that has yet to make an impact in mainstream management literature.

NEEDS, GOALS, AND ORIENTATIONS

The attempt to classify work-related motives or goals has continued. Research conducted in the 1960s and early 1970s showed little or no support for the theories of Maslow and Herzberg and they have therefore ceased to be a significant focus for further work. Perhaps the most useful work of that time was conducted by Alderfer who adapted Maslow's general classification of needs to the organisational setting. He found three rather than Maslow's five distinct set of needs: the concern for "existence" (including pay and security), for "relatedness" (covering all the social aspects of work) and for "growth" (reflecting job content and personal development).

Power, Achievement and Affiliation

However, while Alderfer has attracted little attention recently (perhaps because his ERG theory seems to offer nothing distinctive or new), there has been a rekindling of interest in the work of Murray, a psychologist working in the 1930s who suggested that people have a set of needs, many of which are latent until stimulated by the environment. Four which have potentially important implications in work settings are the needs for achievement, power, affiliation, and autonomy. McClelland (1975),

among others, has conducted extensive research on the first three. Unfortunately the problem of devising acceptable measures of these needs has yet to be satisfactorily resolved, leading to caution in the interpretation of research.

Nevertheless, interesting findings are emerging about the appropriate priorities among these needs for different levels in the management hierarchy. In general terms, it is argued that high need for achievement is particularly important for success in many junior and middle management jobs where it is possible to feel direct responsibility for task accomplishment, but in senior management positions a concern for institutionalised (as opposed to personal power) becomes more important. A strong need for affiliation is not helpful at any level.

The idea that different kinds of motive may be important at different levels in the management hierarchy, and the implied need for flexibility, are useful insights with implications for selection, promotion, and career development decisions. However, those making a bid for power should take note of one of McClelland's findings. In a 20-year follow-up of Harvard graduates who had scored high on the need for power, 58 percent had high blood pressure or had died of heart failure.

Orientation to Work

Sociologists have approached motivation through the study of orientations to work. An orientation is a persisting tendency to seek certain goals and rewards from work which exists independently of the nature of the work and the work context. The initial and by now well-known work by Goldthorpe and his colleagues on *The Affluent Worker* highlighted the "instrumental orientation" of their sample of blue-collar workers, that is, a general view of work as a means to an end, a context in which to earn money to purchase goods and leisure. Unfortunately there has been a tendency to draw a general conclusion from this single study that British blue-collar workers are similarly only likely to be motivated by money.

The orientation approach overlaps quite considerably with the work of Murray and McClelland. Both emphasise the importance of the social environment outside work as the context for the development of motives, an encouraging and important move away from the emphasis of Maslow and others on instinctive needs; and both accept that motivation is subject to modification. This becomes important, for example, in the face of consistent research findings that frustrated career orientations are a major problem in industry. The management of career expectations provides an opportunity to test the feasibility of modifying orientations. At present it is all too common to find that recruitment and management development practices continue to encourage unrealistic expectations of promotion. If they are faced with a motivation problem as a result of this, personnel managers may have only themselves to blame.

EXPECTANCY THEORY

Expectancy theory continues to provide the dominant framework for understanding motivation at work. The basic formulation of expectancy theory, which will be familiar to many readers, argues that high effort or motivation will exist when an employee perceives a link between effort, performance, and rewards. In other words, there is a positive pay-off in exerting effort because it leads to higher performance which in turn leads to higher rewards. Whether it actually results in higher performance depends on the extent to which the employee possesses the necessary knowledge and skills and has an accurate appreciation of the appropriate role requirements.

The basic formulation of expectancy theory has been established for some time. Many managers have been put off by its complexity and by its failure to specify the kind of rewards that will prove attractive. For academic researchers, however, its clear propositions have proved irresistible and it has generated a vast amount of detailed research.

A number of reviews have drawn this research together. The most recent lead to the following general conclusions:

1. The predictions about motivation derived from expectancy theory usually hold true at a statistically significant level. In other words, workers do display more effort when they perceive a link between effort, performance, and reward.
2. The predictive power of the theory is greater when the nature of the task and the demands placed on an employee are clear and unambiguous.
3. Expectancy theory assumes that an employee engages in information processing and decision making. This seems more likely to hold true for decisions regarded by jobholders as important or which for some reason attract their attention. For routine day-to-day events at work, habit, derived from previous experience, may well be a more yp ical basis for motivated behaviour. In other words, workers will not always go through the expectancy theory process before displaying motivation.
4. The research reinforces the view that motivation is an extraordinarily complex process.

As expectancy theory has become more popular, it has attracted criticism—of its underlying assumptions, theoretical propositions, and their measurements; but most important from management's point of view is the practical usefulness of the theory. The nub of the problem concerns the feasibility of testing the theory in work settings where individuals often have limited freedom to make choices due to constraints imposed by their roles, by technology and by established procedures. Only when such tests have been conducted will it be possible to make a more confident assessment about the value of the theory. One way of circumventing this problem is to apply the theory to occupational and organisational choice (Wanous, Keon, & Latack, 1983). The most recent evidence suggests that expectancy theory is an excellent predictor of motivation in this setting. By taking account of the extent to which particular occupations or organisations provide individuals with valued rewards, this research neatly complements the earlier comments about the importance of considering orientations in selection.

Despite a number of problems, expectancy theory still offers an extremely useful basis for understanding and seeking to influence motivation. Many managers may find it most useful as a conceptual and diagnostic framework. In other words, expectancy theory:

Points to the key variables to examine to understand motivation and performance;

Is helpful in diagnosing the causes of problems in motivation and performance;

Points to the steps that need to be taken to improve motivation, *i.e.,* improving the perceived link between effort, performance, and attractive rewards—feasibility or, in cost-benefit terms, desirability of such changes permitting. While it may not make sense to alter technology, at least in the short term, or to incur the wrath of the trade unions, it may be possible to influence perceptions and information feedback.

More specifically, expectancy theory indicates that if management wants a highly motivated workforce it should:

Systematically identify goals and values within the workforce and survey attitudes and perceptions;

Provide rewards on an individual basis, tied to performance, rather than on a general basis. An overall pay rise, for example, will have little motivational impact;

Make the selective provision of rewards public, so that all employees can see a link between good performance and higher rewards. This will influence expectations; *and*

Make sure subordinates have the knowledge, skills and understanding necessary to their role to translate motivation into high performance.

If workers are motivated by the opportunity to achieve attractive rewards, then key tasks for the supervisor are to ensure that subordinates perceive that attractive rewards are available and to clear and clarify the path along which they must pass to achieve these rewards. The supervisor should, for instance, encourage subordinates to value goals which are complementary to organisational goals, and identify and try to remove blocks to goal attainment, such as lack of resources or of skills or understanding of role (in which case the supervisor should provide coaching and explanation).

Expectancy theory predicts that job redesign, which should improve effort-performance-reward links, will have a powerful motivating effect on those with a strong "higher order need" strength, that is, those who value the intrinsic rewards associated with doing an interesting and challenging job.

A final illustration of the application of expectancy theory is Klanderman's work examining the conditions under which union members are likely to engage in militant activity. He shows that members are more likely to participate in strikes, demonstrations, and protests if they perceive that such action is likely to lead to valued goals.

GOAL THEORY

Locke has developed a relatively simple, and for many people an intuitively appealing, theory of motivation built around the influence of goals. The theory proposes that motivation and performance will be higher when individuals are set specific goals, when goals are difficult but accepted, and when there is feedback on performance. This approach overlaps with some aspects of expectancy theory and even, as a technique, with behaviour modification, but Locke has resisted attempts at integration. There is even more obvious overlap with "management by objectives" (MBO).

Goal theory has generated a considerable body of research, and interest in it shows no signs of abating. The results are generally highly supportive, indicating that individuals are motivated by having a specific goal and they perform better when they are aiming for difficult goals which they have accepted (Latham & Locke, 1979). Participation in goal setting seems to help for some employees, especially at lower levels in the organisation, but mainly as a means of gaining acceptance in the setting of higher goals. Feedback on goal attainment is essential, more particularly in gaining acceptance of subsequent more difficult goals, but it will often have to incorporate social feedback, on the performance and reactions of others, as well as task feedback.

The research on MBO shows that its impact has often been disappointing. This is partly because it has not been effectively "sold" and operated; partly because it has often failed to meet the requirements of goal theory; and partly because difficult goals are not reinforced. The management implications are clear. Higher motivation and performance are likely where specific, difficult but accepted goals are set and feedback is arranged. When goal setting becomes encumbered by bureaucratic constraints, as can sometimes happen with ineffectively operated MBO schemes, then its impact can be swiftly dissipated.

BEHAVIOUR MODIFICATION

Strictly speaking, behaviour modification is not a theory of motivation, but rather a technique concerned with creating the circumstances to ensure appropriate behaviour. It has continued to enjoy some popularity, partly as a reaction to some of the more complex cognitive features of motivation theory.

Typical applications of behaviour modification in industry involve four stages:

1. Pinpoint—specify the behaviour to be changed in precise behavioural terms.
2. Record—establish basic data on current performance.
3. Identify influences on behaviour; these may include prompting, guidance, modelling.
4. Arrange for reinforcement of the desired performance. This typically takes

the form of 'social' reinforcement from the supervisor such as praise and careful feedback of results.

One of the most interesting features of this approach is its emphasis on a clear specification of the kind of behaviour sought. Too often attempts to improve motivation are very vague about this. There are some well-known examples of success in obtaining improved performances through behaviour modification. However, recent writing has tended to highlight its limitations. These include the difficulty of precisely specifying behaviour for nonroutine jobs where "correct" behaviour is hard to predict; the danger of narrowing behaviour to focus only on reinforced tasks; the assumption that extrinsic rather than intrinsic rewards are crucial; and the potentially limited effect of verbal praise, which is nevertheless probably the most feasible form of reinforcement in industry. It seems therefore that in most circumstances we cannot dispense with the concept of motivation.

REACTANCE THEORY

Most approaches to motivation at work go some way towards behaviour modification in suggesting that motivation can be best understood in terms of individual responses to external stimuli, that employees behaviour is, to a considerable extent, moulded by influences such as management policies and practices and the attitudes of co-workers. The key concern is therefore to develop management practices which will have the most positive effect on employee behaviour. However, in much the same way as strategic approaches to the study of organisations emphasise organisational choice and the opportunity for an organisation to exert influence on, rather than merely being controlled by, its environment, so an alternative approach within psychology suggests the same may be true of individuals.

This alternative perspective suggests that individuals are not passive receivers and responders (Staw, 1977). Instead they actively strive to make sense of their environment and to reduce uncertainty by seeking to control factors influencing rewards. Equity theory research, for example, shows how employees can strive for fairness by adjusting their effort or performance in relation to the input/output ratios of other people. There is a growing body of work on "ingratiation," the process whereby subordinates manipulate their superiors' opinion of them to increase their chance of obtaining valued rewards. This helps to explain how some employees appear to be more skillful in obtaining promotion or allocation to attractive work. Some of the research on leadership, most notably the study by Rosen, suggests that subordinate behaviour and reactions influence leadership style as much as leadership style influences subordinates' behaviour (Rosen, 1969). Finally, the evidence from goal theory and from research on the path-goal approach to leadership shows the preference for a reasonably predictable and controllable environment.

Brehm's reactance theory argues that when freedom and control is threatened, an individual is motivationally aroused to reassert freedom and control—the experience of reactance. The work on commitment, intrinsic motivation, and equity shows that *if* individuals expect to control outcomes for themselves, they devalue outcomes chosen for or imposed on them. Reactance is most likely to occur among employees who perceive that their control is threatened. Therefore middle managers, threatened from below by autonomous work groups or quality circles, are just as susceptible as shopfloor workers. The danger is that any employee who, after many attempts to reassert control, finds that he cannot control factors influencing his rewards may experience "learned helplessness", a process of giving up and ceasing to try. This is more likely when he cannot identify influences on his rewards.

A further important feature of this approach is its analysis of the way in which individuals strive to reduce uncertainty and impose structure and meaning by attributing explanations to events. A first step has been to identify the main types of variable which people use to explain success or failure and four have consistently emerged as the most important. These are ability, effort, luck, and task difficulty. For example, in explaining how they received a large bonus, some workers may attribute it to luck, others to their own efforts. The first are unlikely to display higher effort, since they believe the reward was not subject to their own control; the second, on the other hand, believe the reward was due to effort and may therefore continue to display high motivation. A second step in this research has been to determine what influences the explanation or "causal attribution" that is made. There is some evidence of individual differences in "locus of control". Those with a strong internal locus of control are more likely to believe that they personally control events, whereas those with an external locus of control believe they are controlled by the external environment (Weiner, 1974).

For managers and others concerned to increase motivation, it would appear to be essential to understand the types of attributions made by employees and the influences on them. In this respect, feedback processes and the way in which imformation is communicated becomes vital. The more that workers perceive that they are responsible for and can influence their rewards, the greater the likelihood of continued high levels of motivation.

At this point, reactance theory links into expectancy theory. The perceptions of effort-performance-reward links are susceptible to change through feedback and through careful communication of new information. Attribution theory therefore has an important part to play in explaining changes in levels of motivation and in the persistence of high levels of motivation in some workers but not others.

MOTIVATION AND MANAGEMENT POLICY

Taking some of the main implications of the expectancy and reactance theories together, certain policy choices emerge. On the one hand it may be possible to obtain high and productive motivation through judicious staff selection, by using reactance principles to obtain high commitment to organisational goals, by using goal setting techniques, by careful job design to provide personal or group control over effort-performance-reward links, and by adopting facilitative leadership. On the other hand management may attempt to impose tight control using conventional control systems such as technology, authority structures, and careful allocation of punishment and reward. The result will be a passive, compliant but possibly resentful workforce; the day-to-day work will be done but there will be little enthusiasm, initiative or commitment. Recent research on motivation has helped to make these choices clearer. There are risks in both approaches, but the changing nature of organisational work with its demands for greater autonomy, flexibility, and commitment should encourage many managers to consider how they can use the insights from the more recent work on motivation.

The behaviorists propose that the term motivation *implies some underlying, unobservable force that is unnecessary in accounting for differences in behavior. Instead, they suggest that one need only examine the various rewards and punishments in the environment and the individual's history of receiving those rewards or punishments to understand why a person behaves in a particular way. Luthans, Paul, and Baker consider the behavior of retail sales personnel in a department store. They demonstrate that aspects of this behavior can be controlled by specific rewards that are presented when desired behavior occurs. The authors make a good case for the behaviorist position. Their data seem quite clear. On the other hand, consider Figures 1 and 2 carefully. Look at what happens to behavior on the very first day of the intervention—day 20. The behavior changes in the correct direction; it changes immediately and dramatically. This is because people were told that the intervention would begin on that day. Keep in mind that they did not receive any concrete rewards on day 20—just the promise of them. Thus, it seems as if Luthans, Paul, and Baker are making just as strong a statement (although they may not have intended to) about the role of cognitive variables in motivated behavior. As you read this article, try to pick out points that help distinguish the traditional behaviorist approach from the newer cognitive approach.*

■ READING 18 ■

An Experimental Analysis of the Impact of Contingent Reinforcement on Salespersons' Performance Behavior

Fred Luthans, *Department of Management, University of Nebraska–Lincoln*
Robert Paul, *Department of Management, Kansas State University*
Douglas Baker, *Department of Management, University of Nebraska–Lincoln*

The theoretical background and application of behavioral techniques in work settings have received some attention over the past several years (Bobb & Kopp, 1978; Hamner & Hamner, 1976; Jablonsky & DeVries, 1972; Luthans & Kreitner, 1975; Luthans & White, 1971; Mawhinney, 1975; Nord, 1969; Schneier, 1974). Although the exact meaning and scope of this behavior management approach is still open to question, it is based on operant learning theory and assumes that employee behavior is a function of environmental contingencies. Most approaches focus on the use of contingent reinforcement to improve employee performance behavior. Despite its growing popularity in theoretical discussions

Source: Journal of Applied Psychology, 66(3), 1981, pp. 314–323. Copyright 1981 by the American Psychological Association. Reprinted by permission of the publisher and author.

and in actual practice (e.g., several management consulting firms specialize in an operant approach), very little systematic research has been conducted to date. For example, one comprehensive review of the training literature from 1967 to 1976 found no scientific evaluations of behavior modification as an industrial training technique (McGhee & Tullar, 1978). A broader based review of behavior modification in business settings (Andrasik, 1979) did reveal about 20 applications, but these fared poorly when analyzed with respect to the reviewer's criteria of reliability of measurement (30 percent performed reliability assessments), systematic intervention (60 percent sufficiently met this criterion), and follow-up (only 20 percent performed postintervention assessments). An even broader based review uncovered 63 published articles that reported some aspect of the application of behavior modification to performance problems in organizational settings (Snyder, 1978). Again, however, this review concluded—after an analysis of the literature—that the majority of these studies did not meet the minimal criteria for acceptable research methodology as proposed by Campbell and Stanley (1963).

This does not mean there have been no systematic analyses of the operant approach to human resource management. In particular, Adam (1972, 1975) and Adam and Scott (1971) analyzed the impact of operant conditioning procedures on quality control. Hermann, de Montes, Dominguez, Montes, and Hopkins (1973) examined the impact of contingent reinforcers on punctuality. Nord (1970), Pedalino and Gamboa (1974), Kempen and Hall (1977), Orpen (1978), and Stephens and Burroughs (1978) analyzed the impact of behavior modification techniques on absenteeism. Ottemann and Luthans (1975) analyzed the impact that supervisors trained in behavior modification have on the productivity of their departments. In addition, there has been a series of studies that examined the impact of reinforcement schedules on employee performance (Berger, Cummings, & Heneman, 1975; Latham & Dossett, 1978; Yukl & Latham, 1975; Yukl, Latham, & Pursell,

1976; Yukl, Wexley, & Seymore, 1972). Finally, two studies by Komaki and her colleagues have examined the impact of contingent reinforcement on employee performance (Komaki, Waddell, & Pearce, 1977) and safety (Komaki, Barwick, & Scott, 1978). All of these researchers reported that the operant approach generally has had a favorable impact on the dependent variables measured. With the possible exception of the Komaki et al. study (1977), however, there has been a decided lack of systematic research evaluating the effectiveness of operant techniques for improving employee performance per se.

In addition to the scarcity of systematic research on the operant approach in work settings, there is in general a lack of field studies that use observational measures. Field research in organizational behavior has relied primarily on indirect data from questionnaires. There is growing criticism of behavioral data derived from questionnaires (Davis & Luthans, 1979; Koch & Rhodes, 1979; Schriesheim & Kerr, 1977; Schriesheim, Kinicki, & Schriesheim, 1979). Instead of quickly dismissing observational measures as having as many or more problems than do questionnaires in organizational behavior research, we must remember that observation techniques are being perfected in other areas such as ethology and eco-behavioral science (Barker, 1965; Willems & Raush, 1969). As Kerlinger (1973) and Weick (1968) have pointed out, there are problems with observational methods, but there are not as many problems as most researchers believe, nor are these problems insurmountable. In Weick's article on observational methods used in behavioral research, he offered some specific guidelines that can lead to reliable and valid collection of data. A small number of management studies have successfully employed observational techniques in data collection (see McCall, Morrison, & Hannan, 1978, for a review of observational studies of managerial work). Mintzberg (1973) noted that organization members do not change their routine of operations just because an observer is present. Telephones are answered, meetings are attended, and events take place just as they normally would. In addition, where frequency or rate of behavior is important, as in the present study, observational measures may be the only alternative for data collection (Heyns & Lippitt, 1954).

The purpose of this study is to make a systematic analysis of the impact of behavioral technology on employee performance behavior in a nonmanufacturing environment. A control group experimental design with observational measures was used. The study took place in a large metropolitan retail store that offered a full line of products and merchandise in about 100 departments. Each phase of the experiment (baseline, intervention, postintervention) was 20 working days long for a total of 12 weeks.

METHOD

Subjects

The sample consisted of 16 randomly selected departments, 8 of which were randomly assigned to the experimental group and the other 8 to the control group. The store was departmentalized according to the type of merchandise handled, and each department had a manager and five or six salespersons. The total subject population comprised 82 salespersons from these departments (41 in the experimental group and 41 in the control group). All of these subjects had completed the store's standard orientation and job training programs, had been repeatedly told what was expected of them in terms of performance standards such as waiting on customers and keeping shelves stocked, and had been employed by the store for at least six months. This common background for both the experimental and the control subjects was deemed important so that changes in behavior could not be attributed to orientation/training, to performance expectations, or to the steep learning curve that new employees typically exhibit.

Measurement

Work sampling techniques used extensively in industrial engineering and observational measures suggested by behavioral science research methodology were employed in the study. This approach consisted of directly observing the behavior of the subjects, classifying their behavior according to predetermined categories, and systematically recording the observations.

The starting point for determining the behavioral categories was to find similar behavior that was readily identified by direct observation and considered relevant to the performance of these departments. Following these guidelines, the behavior identified in the present study was derived from a variety of sources. Information was first gathered from written job descriptions. With this background, direct observations in the naturalistic setting were then conducted to confirm or modify behavioral components. In addition, managerial personnel and staff specialists in the personnel department were brought in to further refine the categories. From this process the following five categories of salespersons' performance behavior were determined:

1. *Selling*. This behavior included conversing with customers, showing merchandise to customers, assisting customers with fitting and selection, ringing up the sale, and filling out charge slips.

2. *Stockwork*. All behavior concerning arrangement and display of merchandise, folding and straightening merchandise stacks or racks, tagging, replenishing stacks or racks, and packing and unpacking merchandise were part of this category.

3. *Miscellaneous*. Included here was all other work-related behavior that could not be classified as selling or stockwork. This included such behavior as directing customers to other departments, checking credit ratings of customers, handling returns, receiving instructions, and business-related conversations with supervisors or coworkers.

4. *Idle time*. This category included behavior that obviously did not contrib-

ute to the requirements/goals of the department, such as socializing with co-workers or just standing/sitting around.

5. *Absence from the work station.* The individual was not in his/her assigned work area.

After these behavioral categories were derived, observational recording forms were designed in order to assure accurate collection of the data. The design of the observation form was guided by the objectives of the study, the amount of detail required, the number of behavioral categories, and the number of people to be observed. The resulting form contained one department's behavioral activities for one day. The behavior was recorded by placing a check mark in the appropriate box for each salesperson in that department, for the time that the observation was made, and for the behavioral category that was appropriate.

In order to avoid, as much as possible, errors in systematic measurement, the observational data were obtained at random times throughout the working day and as many times as feasible. The constraints on the number of observations that could actually be made by the two observers used in the study included the physical layout of the building, the departmental location, and the time constituting a work shift. It was deemed feasible to make two observations per hour per day on each of the 16 work groups. An observational trip was begun at a random time during every 30-minute block of time. The number of observations and subjects was held constant throughout the study. This resulted in a total of 256 observations per day and a total of 15,360 total observations in the experiment.

Procedure

The first phase (four weeks) of the experiment consisted of obtaining observational measures in both the experimental and the control groups to establish the baseline rate for the five categories of behavior (selling, stockwork, miscellaneous, idle time, and absence from the work station). These observational measures were continued in the second and third phases of the experiment. In the second phase (intervention), Weeks 5–8, contingent reinforcement was applied to the experimental group. In the third phase (postintervention), Weeks 9–12, the reinforcement was withdrawn from the experimental group. Hence a true experimental design (baseline-intervention-return to baseline) compared with a control group was used in the study.

The 82 subjects in the 16 departments were initially told during the first phase that a customer survey was underway and that there would be observers in their departments from time to time. Postexperimental questioning of the subjects verified that they were unaware of the true purpose of the observers during this baseline phase. During the second phase, the subjects in both groups were told that the observers were gathering data on their performance. Both groups were given the same performance standards.

In developing the intervention for the study, a more precise interpretation of the performance standards was needed. Although general performance standards—such as waiting on customers right away and always keeping shelves stocked—were impressed on sales employees from their initial orientation onward, a more specific, operational definition of these standards was needed in order to administer contingent positive reinforcement. On the basis of the five critical categories of behavior that were being measured by the observers, the following performance standards were derived and then carefully explained to salespersons in both the experimental and the control groups at the beginning of the second phase of the study:

1. The salespersons, except when on excused absence, should be present in the department (within three feet [.9 m] of displayed merchandise) during assigned working hours.

2. When a customer comes to the department, she/he should be offered assistance. When a customer requests assistance, he/she should be assisted within five seconds. When a customer requests assistance while the salesperson

is assisting another customer, she/he should be acknowledged and promised aid momentarily. Such help should be given within five seconds of the completion of the in-process customer service.

3. The display shelf should be filled to at least 70 percent of its capacity (assuming merchandise is available during store hours).

To obtain an estimate of the first and second performance standards, the observer noted the presence or absence of each subject in the department for each random visit. If the subjects were absent, this was recorded, and if the subjects were in the department at the time of the visit, their behavior was recorded (i.e., selling, stockwork, miscellaneous, or idle time). At the end of each one-week observation period, the percentage of time devoted to each category of behavior by each salesperson was calculated. This calculation involved dividing the number of observations in each behavioral category by the total number of random visits to the department. To estimate the third performance goal of the number of merchandise racks and counters that were filled to at least 70 percent of their capacity, a similar procedure was used. The observer noted the number of racks and counters that met the 70 percent inventory level requirements during each random visit. This number was divided by the total number of racks and counters available in the department. At the end of the week, these percentages were averaged to get a representative proportion of storage spaces meeting the "70 percent filled" standard.

Specifically, the intervention consisted of contingent rewards of time off with pay or equivalent cash in addition to an opportunity to compete in a drawing for a company-paid one-week vacation for two for attaining the performance standards. The selection of these particular rewards resulted from discussion with the individual experimental subjects to determine what they really valued. The company agreed to the rewards. The number of hours off with pay or equivalent cash was on a

graduated scale so that as more of the desired behavior was exhibited, the amount of the reward was increased. For example, one hour per week was awarded for a record of 10 percent (or lower) absence from the work station, and two hours per week were awarded for a good absence record and for reaching the standard for the sales activity. Finally, if all the performance standards were achieved, to at least minimum specification, a half day off with pay or equivalent cash was awarded each week. In addition, for each week that an experimental subject achieved all standards of performance, his/her name was entered into the vacation drawing, thus increasing the probability of selection at the end of four weeks. Upon completion of the four-week intervention, the company "paid off" on their promised vacation for two, and the contingent reinforcement ceased. In the four weeks following the intervention, observers continued to record the behavior for both the experimental and the control groups exactly as they had in the preceding eight weeks of the experiment.

RESULTS

For more simplified computational and graphic presentation, the behavioral categories of selling, stockwork, and miscellaneous were collapsed into a single category termed aggregate retailing behavior. Similarly, absence from the work station and idle time were combined. As can be seen in Figures 1 and 2, the baseline frequencies for the control group and the experimental group are quite similar. Table 1 shows that the baseline means between the control group and the experimental group are not significantly different. Immediately on the first day of the contingent reinforcement, however, the experimental group had a dramatic increase in aggregate retailing behavior. The mean number of retailing behavior for the experimental group during this intervention period was 433.2 and, for the control group, only 362.2. This difference was significant, $t(14) = 17.0$, $p < .001$. The higher frequency of retailing behavior carried over into the

FIGURE 1   Aggregate Retailing Behavior

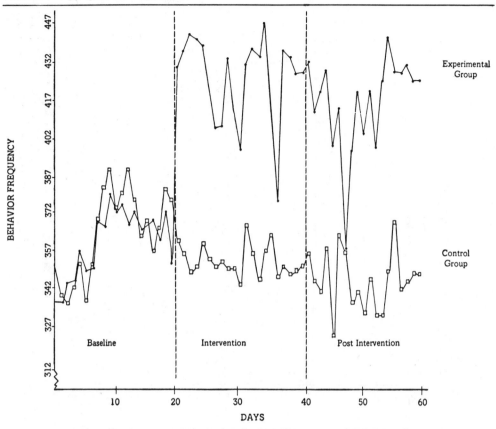

postintervention period, when the experimental group had a significantly higher mean number of retailing behavior than did the control group, $t(14) = 14.7, p < .001$.

An equally dramatic effect was noted for absence from the work station and idle time. The control and the experimental groups were quite similar during the baseline period (Table 1 shows no significant difference). As soon as the contingent reinforcement was introduced, however, there was a huge decline in the average incidence of absence from the work station and idle time. The mean for the control group during the intervention period was 293.8, whereas the mean for the experimental group dropped to 225.4. This was a highly significant difference, $t(14) = 14.9, p < .001$. The mean for the experimental group was also significantly lower in the postintervention

phase than was the mean for the control group, $t(14) = 19.4, p < .001$.

DISCUSSION

The results indicate a significant change in the frequency of salespersons' performance behavior in the predicted direction after the contingent reinforcement was introduced. The dramatic change in the performance behavior of the salespersons in this study was almost immediate and was maintained over time. In fact, the effects carried over even after the intervention period. The behavior did not return to baseline frequencies following the removal of the reinforcement intervention.

There are a number of possible reasons why the reversal did not occur. Although reversals have a major advantage in that they help to

FIGURE 2   Absence from the Work Station and Idle Time

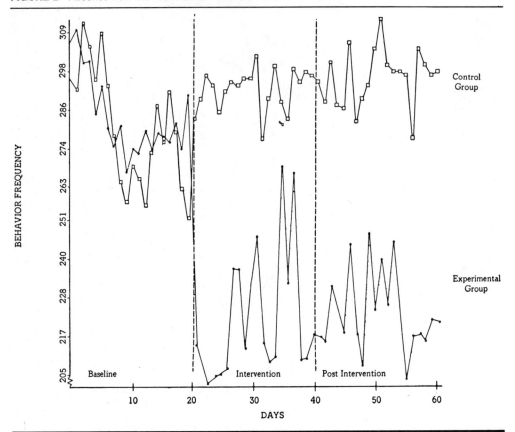

TABLE 1   Means, Standard Deviations, and *t* Tests for Experimental and Control Groups

Phase of Experiment	Absence from the Work Station and Idle Time			Aggregate Retailing Behavior		
	Experimental Group		Control Group	Experimental Group		Control Group
Baseline						
M	286.0		282.6	370.4		373.4
SD	12.5		17.5	12.9		17.1
t value*		.68			.6	
Intervention						
M	225.4		293.8	433.2		362.2
SD	20.6		6.2	17.7		6.0
t value*		14.9†			17.0	
Postintervention						
M	226.7		297.2	424.6		354.8
SD	13.2		9.5	18.		11.1
t value*		19.42†			14.7	

Note. N = 8 departments for the experimental and for the control groups.
*The two-tailed *t* values are for the relationship between experimental and control groups in each phase of the experiment.
†*p* < .001.

overcome the problem of intersubject variability and can provide powerful evidence for cause-and-effect conclusions (Kazdin, 1973; Komaki, 1977), they assume that behavior changes made under the conditions of the intervention are capable of being reversed when the intervention is withdrawn (i.e., when there is a return to baseline conditions). In other words, when reversals are used in behavioral change experiments, the assumption is that the behavior is transient. This assumption, of course, does not always hold. Two important considerations seem to affect the degree of reversibility of targeted behavior: the extent to which the behavior in question becomes learned and the extent to which environmental consequences other than the intervention work to maintain the targeted behavior (Luthans & Bond, 1977). In the present study, learning is not so much the explanation for why the reversal did not occur as is the latter possibility of other contingencies in the environment taking over to maintain the behavior at intervention levels of frequency. As Miller (1973) pointed out, "If the original environment had a consequence that was too weak to initiate a behavioral change but that is strong enough to maintain such a response once initiated, the behavior should not be expected to revert" (p. 535). This may have been the case in this study's work environment. The injection of the contingent reinforcement may have been necessary to get the salespersons' performance behavior tracking in the desired direction, but then other existing, natural reinforcers (e.g., a supervisor's praise, positive customer reactions, or even self-reinforcing contingencies such as the feeling of a job well done) in the environment took over to maintain the behavior when the intervention was withdrawn. In other words, in relatively complex work settings such as was found in this field experiment, it would not be surprising that the performance behavior did not reverse when the intervention was withdrawn.

There is some previous support for this explanation. In a series of seven case studies that used a reversal to evaluate the impact of a contingent reinforcement intervention on various individual employee's behavior in different work settings, it was found that in all cases the behavior was significantly changed by introducing the intervention, but in only four of the seven cases did a reversal occur (Luthans & Bond, 1977). In these case studies, and especially when compared with more highly controlled laboratory and institutional (mental hospitals and schools) studies in which reversals have traditionally been used, there does seem to be a definite relationship between the degree of environmental complexity in the study and the reversibility of the targeted behavior.

It is recognized that the alternative explanation for why the behavior in this study did not reverse after withdrawing the intervention is that the intervention did not actually cause the behavior to change in the first place. As in any field study, there are possible confounding effects resulting from a lack of control, and as Locke (1980) recently pointed out, one could formulate alternative, cognitively based explanations for the results of operant studies such as this one. Such alternate explanations of the results of this study cannot automatically be dismissed. Nevertheless, because of the random selection and assignment of the subjects to experimental and control groups, the use of a control group for purposes of comparison, and other specific controls used in this study should have minimized the threats to internal validity (Cook & Campbell, 1976) and supported the conclusions. In this study, the contingent reinforcement had a positive impact on the salespersons' behavior.

In particular, the internal validity criteria were met as follows: (a) *history and demand characteristics* (both experimental and control subjects knew during the intervention phase of the experiment that the observers would be recording data on their specific performance behavior), (b) *maturation* (all the subjects had at least six months of experience, and the experiment was relatively short in duration), (c) *testing* (no tests were used), (d) *instrumentation* (as Figures 1 and 2 show, the effects of the intervention were immediate instead of gradual, as instrumentation would indicate, and the observers were unaware both that the intervention had started and of which subjects were in the control group and which were in the experimental group; that is, they did not change their recording of behavior in order to meet demand characteristics), (*e*) *statistical regression* (there was random assignment to experimental and control groups), (*f*) *selection* (again it was random), (*g*) *mortality* (no subjects dropped out during the experiment), (*h*) *interaction with selection* (there was random assignment to experimental and control groups), (*i*) *diffusion or imitation of treatment* (although the control subjects knew during the intervention phase that the observers would be recording their specific performance behavior, they were not told that anyone would be receiving contingent reinforcement), (*j*) *compensatory equalization of treatment* (there was random assignment to groups, and only the experimental group received the contingent reinforcers), (*k*) *compensatory rivalry* (Figures 1 and 2 show that the control group's performance remained stable across all three phases of the experiment), and (*l*) *resentful demoralization* (the control group's performance did not go down).

In summary, this study does provide needed systematic evaluation of the impact of behavioral techniques on the performance behavior of employees in nonmanufacturing work settings. Replications of this type of experiment, especially those using observational measures, and research on other types of behavioral interventions in other work settings are recommended.

The single strongest force in motivation theory from 1970 through 1980 was expectancy theory. Vroom had popularized the concept in 1964 and by 1970 everyone was testing one or another of the propositions of expectancy theory. As is commonly the case, the first wave of research was very positive and enthusiastic. The research seemed to confirm the logic of the theory. Then things began to go a bit sour and predictions were not being confirmed as frequently. This trend is a common one in the development of new theories because the most ardent advocates are usually in the forefront of the research effort. The devil's advocates don't come along for several years. After the negative results began to appear with greater frequency, researchers began to point out that when hypotheses were tested in a between-subjects design, predictions seemed less likely to hold. On the other hand, when within-subjects designs were used, predictions were more likely to be confirmed. In a between-subjects design, the subject's responses to a series of possible outcomes are compared to the responses of other subjects to those same outcomes. In a within-subjects design, the subject's responses about one set of outcomes are compared to that same subject's responses to another set of outcomes. In this reading, these mixed results for expectancy research are reviewed and some explanations are provided that may account for the failures of tests of expectancy theory.

■ READING 19 ■

Between-Subjects Expectancy Theory Research: A Statistical Review of Studies Predicting Effort and Performance

Donald P. Schwab, Judy D. Olian-Gottlieb,
and Herbert G. Heneman III
Graduate School of Business and Industrial Relations Research Institute
University of Wisconsin–Madison

Expectancy theory (Vroom, 1964) is a process theory of work motivation that has received considerable theoretical and empirical attention. Although numerous variations of the theory have been proposed (Campbell & Pritchard, 1976), the core of all formulations is the proposition that motivation (force) to perform is a function of (a) the expectancy that changes in effort will result in changes in performance, (b) the instrumentality of performance changes for the attainment of outcomes (such as pay increases), and (c) the valences of the outcomes. Also, in most formulations,

Source: *Psychological Bulletin*, 86, 1979, pp. 139–147. Copyright 1979 by the American Psychological Association. Reprinted by permission of the publisher and author.

these variables are combined in a multiplicative fashion as follows: Force to perform $= f$ [expectancy $\times \Sigma$ (instrumentalities $\times$ valences)].

A substantial amount of research has been stimulated by expectancy theory. Almost all of it has used a between-subjects design in which a measure of force to perform is correlated with a measure of effort or performance for a sample of individuals. Some reviewers have objected to this orientation and have suggested that a within-subject design would be more appropriate for testing the theory (e.g., Mitchell, 1974). To date, however, there has been almost no such research on the prediction of effort or performance.

As the body of empirical literature on this theory has proliferated, so also have reviews summarizing and interpreting that literature (e.g., Campbell & Pritchard, 1976; Connolly, 1976; Heneman & Schwab, 1972; House, Shapiro, & Wahba, 1974; Mitchell, 1974; Mitchell & Biglan, 1971; Wahba & House, 1974). Although some of these reviews are essentially uncritical descriptions of the theory and research findings (e.g., House et al., 1974), all have made at least some suggestions aimed at improving the conduct of future research.

The suggestions that have been made can be viewed from two related perspectives. One is primarily theoretical in orientation. From this perspective, reviewers can be viewed as encouraging their empirically oriented colleagues to test expectancy theory qua theory. Thus, as examples, Heneman and Schwab's (1972) admonition to include assessments of expectancy in force measures and Mitchell's (1974) plea to perform within-subject studies can be viewed as attempts to make the measures and procedures of empirical investigations isomorphic with the theory.

An alternative perspective is to view these suggestions as aimed at increasing the theory's ability to predict effort or performance. The focal point of such an orientation is in increasing variance explained rather than in the elegance of the theoretical formulation per se. The reviews mentioned here have generally made suggestions regarding the measurement of the constructs specified in the theory. These recommendations, however, have in every case been based on casual assessments of previous research; that is, none of the reviews have empirically determined if variance explained differs as a function of the measurement procedures used.

The present review involves a statistical analysis of the results obtained in previously published between-subjects studies of expectancy theory. Studies included in our statistical analysis were those that examined the amount of variance explained in measures of effort or performance by measures of force to perform. These variance-explained values reported in the previous studies became our dependent variable. Independent variables chosen for the statistical analysis were various characteristics of (*a*) the measures of performance or effort and (*b*) the force measures that were used in the previously published research. Thus, the present study aims to account for variation in the strength of the relationship observed in other studies between force to perform and performance or effort as a function of characteristics of the effort, performance, and force-to-perform measures.

Three issues were examined regarding characteristics of the performance and effort measures. The first of these involved distinguishing between use of effort and use of performance as criterion measures. The conception of force is clearly aimed at predicting the effort expended toward some behavior. The actual behavior (job performance in the case at hand) is seen as a multiplicative function of force to perform and ability to perform (Vroom, 1964). Thus, from a theoretical perspective, one might argue, *ceteris paribus*, that more variance would be explained in studies using effort as the dependent measure than in studies using some measure of performance.

There is, however, reason to suspect that measures of effort might not be more predictable than measures of performance. Specifically, as Campbell and Pritchard (1976) have stated, "Organizational psychology is without any clear specification of the meaning of effort and consequently there is no operationalization of the variable that possesses even a modicum of construct validity" (p. 92). Thus, one might anticipate difficulty in predicting effort from force on pure measurement grounds.

A second dependent variable issue pertained to whether the measure was internal (self-reports) or external (others' ratings and rankings or productivity indexes) to the subject. Mitchell (1974) has argued that internal measures are more appropriate because effort is difficult to observe and hence measure externally. Moreover, it is generally agreed that when self-ratings are used simultaneously for both the dependent and the independent variables, the resultant correlations are inflated. Thus, we hypothesized that more variance would be explained when self-ratings were used to measure effort or performance than when alternative measures were employed.

A third issue regarding the dependent variable was concerned with performance measures that were external to the subject. These measures have typically been ratings or rankings of performance provided most often by the subject's work supervisor. There have also been a number of instances in which investigators had access to quantitative productivity measures (units produced, sales volume, etc.). We hypothesized that more variance would be explained with the latter measures because of the reliability problems that frequently occur with performance ratings or rankings.

It was also possible to examine a number of issues dealing with characteristics of the force measure used. One important issue had to do with the number of outcomes (i.e., consequences of performance) assessed. Both Heneman and Schwab (1972) and Mitchell (1974) have suggested that a theoretical orientation would require that a large number of such outcomes be included in any test of the theory. This would be necessary to ensure that all outcomes of potential relevance to subjects are included in the measure of force to perform. No harm would come from this strategy because outcomes of no importance (with zero valence) would fall out of the force equation. For example, an outcome such as *improved recreational facilities* might not be important to most subjects. They would be expected to assign such an outcome zero valence, and hence it would not enter their force-to-perform equations. Nevertheless, including such an outcome would presumably enhance the force-to-perform estimates of those subjects for whom this outcome has some nonzero valence.

Again, however, psychometric issues potentially conflict with theoretical precision. Outcomes of little importance to subjects may contribute to unreliability of measurement and hence to reduced predictability. The potential conflict between theoretical and psychometric considerations suggests that a nonlinear relationship between number of outcomes and variance explained might be hypothesized. Up to a certain point increases in the number of second-level outcomes may increase variance explained because the marginal increment in total valence is large relative to the reliability decrement. We hypothesized, however, that beyond some point the marginal increment would be offset by the reliability decrement, resulting in a reduction in the variance explained.

The data permitted the examination of two issues involving the measurement of valence of second-level outcomes. One of these issues has to do with the verbal anchoring of the valence measures. Vroom (1964) defined valence as indicating anticipated satisfaction with, or desirability of, second-level outcomes. Both Connolly (1976) and Mitchell (1974) noted that many studies have anchored their valence scales with *importance*, which potentially represents an alternative construct. Connolly (1976) argued that unless the use of importance can be justified in variance-explained results, "There is a good argument for returning to the original conception of valence as anticipated satisfaction, or a close analog such as attractiveness, desirability, or anticipated utility" (p. 40). The second issue regarding valence has to do with the numerical anchors used. Again Mitchell (1974) has argued that theoretical purity requires that the anchors range from positive to negative values instead of using just the positive values that are frequently reported. Both of these valence issues (importance versus desirability and positive to negative versus positive only) were examined in the present study, although directional hypotheses were not specified a priori.

The final issues considered in the present study pertain to the measurement of expectancy. In their review Heneman and Schwab (1972) pointed out that most of the initial studies failed to measure expectancy at all or confounded expectancy with measures of instrumentality. They urged that future research include unconfounded measures of expectancy. This plea has apparently been heeded because a number of investigations have now been reported that include expectancy measures unconfounded with instrumentality. Moreover, Campbell and Pritchard (1976) concluded that measures of expectancy, considered singularly, tend to be positively correlated with measures of effort and performance. Thus, it was hypothesized that variance-explained values would be greater when the force measure included an expectancy term than when it did not. It was also hypothesized that more variance would be explained when this measure was not confounded with instrumentality. A related issue was the measurement of expectancy in those studies that included an unconfounded measure. Vroom (1964) defined expectancy as the subjective probability that an outcome (e.g., performance) will follow a specified level of effort. Thus, a theoretically correct measure of expectancy would assess it in likelihood terms, although in a number of studies it has been measured in alternative ways (e.g., having subjects compare the importance of personal effort relative to other potential determinants of performance; Schwab & Dyer, 1973). Following this theory we hypothesized that more variance would be explained when expectancy was measured in subjective-probability or likelihood terms.

METHOD

Dependent Variable and Population

The dependent variable was the amount of variance explained in a measure of effort or performance by a measure of force. These values were easily obtained in studies that reported results in correlational terms by computing coefficients of determination (r^2 or R^2). The R^2 values were corrected for number of independent variables using Nunnally's (1967) correction formula. In two studies the results were not directly presented in correlational terms, but it was possible to derive the correlation from the information presented (Lawler, 1966; Turney, 1974).

A number of decisions about choice of the dependent variable were made. Many studies reported a variety of analyses; for example, performance might be correlated with a number of alternative force formulations. In these instances, data were used only from the model that most closely approximated the multiplicative force model specified earlier. In addition, we included only the force measure that used the total number of outcomes assessed in the study. In the four studies that used cross-lagged correlation analysis (Kopelman & Thompson, 1976; Lawler, 1966; Lawler & Suttle, 1973; Sheridan, Slocum, & Richards, 1974), only the predictive results (force at time one, effort or performance at time two) were used. In all instances only one model of force was included from each study. However, an observation corresponding to each relationship between the force measure and alternative measures of effort or performance was included from those studies that had multiple measures of effort or performance.

A total of 32 published studies (using effort or performance measures as criteria) were found in which the results were reported in such a manner that a variance-explained value was presented or could be derived. Using the decision rules specified previously, a total of 160 observations were extracted from the 32 studies. For analysis purposes we viewed this $N = 160$ as the population of variance-explained values in between-subjects studies.

Independent Variables

The studies were reviewed to obtain the necessary independent variable information. Since the information was relatively straightforward, little ambiguity occurred in reviewing the studies and coding the data. The following independent variables were used in the present study: (*a*) whether effort or performance was measured, (*b*) whether the effort/performance measure was self-reported or externally assessed, (*c*) whether the externally assessed measure was based on objective data (e.g., sales volume and productivity) or subjective appraisal, (*d*) number of second-level outcomes (trichotomized into categories of approximately equal numbers of observations consisting of 1–9 outcomes, 10–15 outcomes and 16 or more outcomes), (*e*) whether valence was scaled positive to negative or only positive, (*f*) whether the verbal anchor for valence was importance or desirability, (*g*) whether an expectancy measure was included in the force measure, (*h*) whether the expectancy measure was unconfounded with instrumentality, and (*i*) whether expectancy was measured as a likelihood estimate.

Analysis

All independent variables were dummy coded (Cohen, 1968). The frequency with which each category appeared in the studies reviewed is shown in Table 1. Table 1 shows, for example, that 28 of the observations had an externally assessed productivity measure, that 29 had a self-report measure of effort, and so forth. Frequencies within each general category (dependent variable, number of outcomes, valence characteristics, and expectancy characteristics) sum to the total ($N = 160$) because they are made up of mutually exclusive and exhaustive sub-categories. The mean variance explained was calculated for each of the categories shown in Table 1. In addition, the variance-explained values were regressed on various combinations of the dummy categories. This analysis was performed to assess how much of the variability in the results of previous research could be accounted for by the procedural characteristics of the studies. All multiple coefficients of determination reported in subsequent tables are significant ($p < .05$). However, significance levels are not reported in the tables because we view this analysis as

TABLE 1 Frequency Distribution of Independent Variables

Variable	f
Dependent variable	
Productivity	28
Self-report effort	29
Self-report performance	15
Other-report effort	13
Other-report performance	75
Number of outcomes	
≤9	46
10–15	61
≥16	53
Valence characteristic	
Importance	
Negative–positive	1
Positive only	58
Desirability	
Negative–positive	72
Positive only	29
Expectancy characteristic	
Unconfounded	
Likelihood estimate	27
Other	69
Confounded	51
None	13

Note. N = 160.

describing the population of between-subjects, variance-explained estimates of effort and performance. Some inferential implications of this study are considered in the discussion.

RESULTS

The first analysis involved an examination of the variance-explained values from the 160 observations in terms of the characteristics of the variables used to measure effort and performance. Table 2 reports the average variance explained between measures of force and the

TABLE 2 Variance Explained as a Function of Type of Effort or Performance Measure

Dependent Variable	*M* Variance Explained
Productivity	.13
Self-report effort	.13
Self-report performance	.10
Other-report effort	.03
Other-report performance	.07
R^2	.08

TABLE 3 Variance Explained as a Function of Number of Outcomes

Number of Outcomes	M Variance Explained
≤ 9	.08
10–15	.14
≥16	.05
R^2	.12

five classifications of the dependent variables employed in the studies reviewed. As hypothesized, force and self-report measures of effort and performance are more highly related than are force and others' assessment of effort or performance. For example, measures of force account for 10 percent of the variance on the average in self-report measures of performance and for 7 percent in performance measures assessed by others. Table 2 also shows, as hypothesized, that quantitative measures of productivity are more predictable than others' ratings or rankings of performance or effort. On the other hand, effort was less predictable than performance only for others' ratings and rankings. Overall, method of categorizing the measures of effort and performance accounted for 8 percent of the variability in the variance-explained values.

Table 3 shows the variance that force measures account for in measures of performance and effort as a function of the number of outcomes assessed. As hypothesized, highest average variance is explained in studies with an intermediate number of outcomes (14 percent), somewhat less variance is explained in studies with nine or less outcome (8 percent), and the least variance is explained in studies with 16 or more outcomes (5 percent). Twelve percent of the variability in the results of the studies reviewed is accounted for by this categorization of the number of outcomes.

Preliminary analysis found that the numerical (negative to positive versus positive only) and verbal (desirability versus importance) anchoring procedures for valence measures were not independent (see Table 1). As a consequence, four categories were established for valence, as shown in Table 4. It can be seen that desirability scalings on the average have yielded higher variance-explained estimates than have importance scalings. Thus, Vroom's (1964) original definition receives some empirical support in terms of the verbal anchors. On the other hand, Table 4 shows that positive-only anchors, especially when combined with desirability anchors, have resulted in the highest average variance explained. All told, the scaling of valence accounts for 10 percent of the variability in the results obtained in the expectancy research reviewed here.

Table 5 shows average variance explained as a function of the measurement of expectancy. Contrary to the hypothesis, greatest average variance is explained in studies that did not include a measure of expectancy (12 percent) or that confounded this measure with instrumentality (14 percent). Moreover, slightly less variance is explained in studies that used a likelihood estimate (5 percent) than in those that used alternative procedures (6 percent) among studies that did include an unconfounded measure. Twelve percent of the varia-

TABLE 4 Variance Explained as a Function of Valence Characteristics

Characteristic	M Variance Explained
Importance	
Negative–positive	.05
Positive only	.08
Desirability	
Negative–positive	.07
Positive only	.16
R^2	.10

TABLE 5 Variance Explained as a Function of Expectancy Characteristics

Characteristic	M Variance Explained
Unconfounded measure	
Likelihood estimate	.05
Other	.06
Confounded measure	.14
None	.12
R^2	.12

bility in the results of the studies reviewed is accounted for by the categorization of the procedures used to assess expectancy.

A final equation was generated by regressing the variance explained in previous expectancy studies on all of the independent variables simultaneously. The signs of the regression coefficients in this equation were the same as in the equations generated to obtain R^2 values in Tables 2–5. The R^2 for this last equation was .42. Thus, 42 percent of the variability in the results of the studies reviewed is accounted for by the categorizations of the dependent variables and force measures.

DISCUSSION

At the outset it is important to recognize that our analysis was necessarily constrained by the measures and procedures used in the studies reported in the literature. Thus, as an example, Heneman and Schwab (1972) called for comparisons of results obtained using additive versus multiplicative combinations of force measures. Schmidt's (1973) criticism of multiplicative analyses aside, the present study was forced to consider multiplicative models because of those studies included in this review, only the Dyer and Weyrauch (1975), Oliver (1974), Pritchard and Sanders (1973), and Schwab and Dyer (1973) studies reported additive (or additive plus interactive) combinations of all force components in addition to the multiplicative mode of combination.

An additional issue that could have been investigated, but was not, is the distinction between models that contrast results obtained using so-called intrinsic versus extrinsic outcomes. House et al. (1974), Wahba and House (1974), and Mitchell (1974) have all urged that such distinctions be made, and, indeed, a number of studies have purportedly done so (e.g., Mitchell & Albright, 1972; Oliver, 1974). However, such distinctions seem arbitrary in view of Dyer and Parker's (1975) demonstration that one social scientist's extrinsic outcome is another's intrinsic outcome and vice versa. As a consequence, we considered

only the models in each study that included all outcomes.

Nevertheless, the issues that were investigated in the present review accounted for a substantial portion of the variance in the results of between-subjects expectancy theory studies designed to predict effort or performance. This was accomplished by categorizing several characteristics regarding the operationalization of the dependent variable and of force to perform. We found that self-report measures were more highly related to measures of force than were measures provided by other evaluators. This finding has been observed by other reviewers and probably reflects spurious method covariation. Objective measures of performance were also associated with greater variance explained than were measures obtained from other evaluators. There are at least two possible explanations for the higher predictability of objective measures. One possibility is that quantitative measures are more reliable than measures provided through an appraisal process. An alternative explanation has to do with the possible boundary conditions of the theory. Dachler and Mobley (1973) have suggested that the theory may only be predictive in situations in which outcomes are objectively linked to behaviors. It may be that in situations in which performance is objectively measured, the organization is more likely to use contingent reward systems (particularly those involving monetary rewards).

The composition of the force measure used was also related to the results obtained by previous researchers. Studies that used 10–15 second-level outcomes obtained stronger relationships between force and performance or effort than did studies that used either fewer or more outcomes. Additionally, studies that scaled valence only positively and that used desirability–undesirability verbal anchors resulted in more variance explained than alternative formulations of valence. Studies that did not measure expectancy at all or that confounded expectancy with instrumentality measures obtained stronger results than those that measured expectancy in a more theoretically correct fashion.

It is obvious from these results that maximum variance explained in between-subjects predictions of performance or effort has not been obtained by making force measures adhere to the theory. Indeed, every finding regarding the measurement of force could be interpreted as contrary to the theory except for the verbal anchoring of valence. Models have yielded the strongest results without a theoretically appropriate expectancy measure, with a moderate number of second-level outcomes, and with valence scaled only in a positive direction.

It is tempting to infer from these findings the likely results that would be obtained if one were to conduct a between-subjects study of performance or effort based on expectancy theory. The major probable constraint on inference, however, stems from the fact that multiple observations were taken from many of the studies reviewed. This clustering of observations within studies results in the probable underestimation of the standard error of estimates and hence in the overestimation of the corresponding F values (Kish, 1957). Unfortunately, since the nonindependence of dependent values within clusters, if any, is confounded with the impact of the independent variables investigated, we know of no way to identify the magnitude of the problem and still retain all 160 observations.

We attempted to obtain some information regarding the appropriateness of generalization by replicating the analyses performed on the population in two independent subsamples drawn from the population. These samples were obtained by randomly choosing one observation per study, subject to the constraint that an observation could appear only once in the two samples. This procedure resulted in subsamples of $n = 31$ and $n = 27$ (six studies had only one observation). Variance explained was used as a dependent variable, as were two transformations aimed at generating a dependent distribution approximating normality. The first was Fisher's r to z transformation, and the second was a transformation derived

according to procedures suggested by Hinkley (1977).

Generally speaking, the direction of results from these analyses was similar to the direction of results obtained on the population of observations. Self-report dependent variables were more predictable than others' reports in both samples, as in the population. Productivity was more predictable than others' reports in one sample, but the two were about equally predictable in the other. The intermediate number of outcomes was associated with highest average variance explained in one sample. In both samples, as in the population, lowest variance explained on the average occurred in the category with 16 or more outcomes. Also as in the population, valence scaled only positively resulted in greater variance explained in both samples. Moreover, in both samples the average variance explained was greater in studies that did not measure expectancy or that confounded this measure with instrumentality.

However, none of the coefficients of determination generated on the variance-explained values or on the transformed values were statistically significant ($p < .05$) in either sample. This lack of significance is probably due to the small sample sizes that were necessary to achieve independence of observations, as well as due to the large numbers of independent variables (relative to sample size). Thus, inferences drawn about the probable outcomes of future research findings from the results obtained here must be made cautiously.

Despite these qualifications, there is a nagging suspicion that expectancy theory overintellectualizes the cognitive processes people go through when choosing alternative actions (at least insofar as choosing a level of performance or effort is concerned). The results of the present review are consistent with this suspicion. At the very least, whether for theoretical or measurement reasons, our results indicate that complicated measures of force have not aided prediction in between-subjects investigations.

The concept of fairness has always had a place in the work setting. When a worker feels that his or her efforts are not being suitably rewarded, some sort of action is required. Sometimes, that action may be a simple readjustment of ways of thinking. On other occasions, the worker may actually alter his or her behavior to make the situation "fairer." The notion of fairness or justice is directly addressed in equity theory.

Research on equity theory has produced mixed results. In this reading, Vecchio suggests that one of the reasons for the mixed results may be that not everyone has a well-developed sense of fairness or justice. It would seem to logically follow that those with little or no concept of justice would behave differently than those with a very well-developed concept of justice. Vecchio gathers data to look at the relationship between moral development and equity motivation.

■ READING 20 ■

An Individual-Differences Interpretation of the Conflicting Predictions Generated by Equity Theory and Expectancy Theory

Robert P. Vecchio

Department of Management, University of Notre Dame

Although a number of theories based on the concept of social equity have been advanced (Blau, 1967; Homans, 1961; Jacques, 1961; Patchen, 1961; Sayles, 1958; Walster, Berscheid, & Walster, 1973), Adams's theory of equity (1963a, 1965) has received the greatest attention in the empirical organizational literature. Studies of individuals' reactions to inequity in terms of quantity and quality of performance have dealt with four situations: underpayment on an hourly basis of compensation, underpayment on a piece-rate basis of

compensation, overpayment on an hourly basis, and overpayment on a piece-rate basis. For the first of these four situations, the theory's performance predictions are that an individual will try to restore equity by reducing his or her inputs through lowered quantity and quality of performance. For underpayment on a piece-rate system, it is predicted that individuals will restore equity by holding their inputs constant and raising their outcomes through the generation of larger quantities of low-quality work (relative to that of equitably paid individuals). Because overpayment on an hourly rate results in fixed outcomes, equity restoration can best be brought about in this situation by increased effort on the part of the individual (i.e., increased inputs manifested as greater

Source: *Journal of Applied Psychology*, 66(4), 1981 pp. 470–481. Copyright 1981 by the American Psychological Association. Reprinted by permission of the publisher and author.

quality and/or quantity of performance). The theory predicts that the fourth condition, overpayment on a piece-rate basis, will result in lower quantity but higher quality of performance relative to that of equitably paid individuals (as a result of overcompensated individuals trying to increase their inputs to restore equity). An inverse relationship between quantity and quality of performance is assumed to be typical for most piece-rate systems because of a limited amount of time and effort that must be devoted to either enhancing the quality of a single unit of output or generating more units of output (Lawler, 1968a, p. 608; Weiner, 1970).

Because the predictions for the inequity condition of overpayment on a piece-rate basis of compensation are counter to the predictions generated by expectancy theory for quantity and quality (Porter & Lawler, 1968; Vroom, 1964), considerably more research and discussion have been devoted to investigating this condition of inequity relative to the other conditions (for comprehensive reviews of equity theory see Adams & Freedman, 1976; Berkowitz & Walster, 1976; Carrell & Dittrich, 1978; Goodman & Friedman, 1971; Lawler, 1968a; Mowday, 1979; Pritchard, 1969). This

difference in investigative effort is probably due to the various similarities and ambiguities of predictions generated by expectancy theory relative to equity theory across the other three inequity conditions (see Table 1). The remainder of this article will further consider the conflicting predictions generated by equity theory and expectancy theory for the inequity condition of overpayment on a piece-rate compensation scheme.

THE PROBLEM

Expectancy theory holds that persons seek to maximize their positive outcomes. Equity theory, in contrast, posits that individuals seek to balance their inputs against their outcomes. A difficulty arises when the maximum-gain hypothesis of expectancy theory is pitted against equity theory's hypothesis of maximization of wage equity. The possibility that increasingly large piece-rate rewards would have, in the terminology of expectancy theory, a decreasing valence for individuals is incompatible with expectancy theory as commonly formulated.

In an effort to cope with early findings that were supportive of equity theory, Vroom (1964) suggested that ". . . the valence of a given level of wages to a worker is dependent not only on its amount but on the extent to which it is believed to be deserved. Explaining [equity] findings in terms of the [expectancy] model requires the additional assumption that [individuals] prefer equitable payment and tend to perform at a level which maximizes the equity of their wages" (p. 260). Because of the greater generality of expectancy theory and the conceptual difficulty for equity theory to explain an observed correlation between subjects' need for money and productivity (Lawler, Koplin, Young, & Fadem, 1968; Lawler & O'Gara, 1967), Lawler (1968a, 1968b) proposed that equity theory be incorporated within the framework of expectancy theory. Quoting Lawler (1968a), "If expectancy theory is stated so that it explicitly includes feelings of equity as one of the determinants of the valence, then it can explain the data obtained" (p. 609). The relegation of equity theory to the

TABLE 1 Predicted Directions of Performance Relative to Equitably Paid Individuals According to Theory, Payment Condition, and Method of Compensation

	Hourly Rate		Piece Rate	
Performance	Expectancy Theory*	Equity Theory	Expectancy Theory	Equity Theory
	Overpayment			
Quantity	—	↑†	↑	↓
Quality	—	↑†	↓	↑
	Underpayment			
Quantity	—	↓	↑	↑
Quality	—	↓	↓	↓

*Expectancy theory does not make rigid predictions for these situations because the (effort—reward) belief may take the value of 0 (Lawler, 1971, p. 96).
†These predictions may also be inversely related, depending on whether the task requirements result in an inverse relationship between quality and quantity.

position of a corollary within the expectancy paradigm, however, represents a superficial resolution of the conflict (i.e., equity theory could also be reformulated to incorporate expectancy theory in order to account for the data, Lawler, 1968a). As noted by Mowday (1979), it is premature to incorporate equity theory into expectancy theory. The critical issue lies deeper.

The origin of the opposite predictions generated by expectancy theory and equity theory for the overpayment piece-rate condition are traceable to the assumptions each theory maintains about human nature. As Vroom (1964) noted, the revivification of the principles of Epicurus by the philosophers Jeremy Bentham and J.S. Mill has influenced, and continues to influence, conceptualizations of the nature of human motivation.

Expectancy theory's "hedonism of the future" reflects the impact of the hedonistic principle. Equity theory, on the other hand, appears to be somewhat more exempt from the influence of the hedonistic doctrine. The demonstration of the superiority of equity theory over expectancy theory for predicting production-related behavior in certain situations (Adams, 1963b; Adams & Jacobsen, 1964; Adams & Rosenbaum, 1962; Andrews, 1967; Lawler et al., 1968; Lawler & O'Gara, 1967) confirms the contention that philosophical hedonism and its psychological derivatives cannot easily explain certain aspects of human behavior.

Explanations of human behavior that do not conform to the hedonistic principle have been subsumed under the heading of pro-social or altruistic behavior. In comparison with theories of human motivation based on hedonistic principles, the research generated by theories of altruism has been sparse. Also, hedonism and altruism are often viewed, erroneously, as a dichotomy.

According to Opshal and Dunnette (1966), ". . . there are distinct differences in the way different kinds of people respond to feelings of inequity. The incorporation of such variables into [equity] theory may increase its explanatory power. As it stands the theory ignores in-

dividual differences" (p. 113). The only study to explore the relation of various personality dimensions to inequity reduction (an underpayment study; Lawler & O'Gara, 1967) concluded that the results of "a personality test do argue that personality factors are important in determining which mechanisms will be chosen and that they must be considered in any comprehensive theory of [inequity] reduction" and that when it "comes to understanding the role of personality and the importance of outcomes, it appears that further elaboration is needed if the theory is to handle individual differences in reactions to an inequity situation" (p. 410).

A MODEL OF MORAL MATURITY

Relevant to an explanation of the equity phenomenon is research conducted in the area of individual value systems. As originally noted by Vroom (1964), equity theory assumes that individuals are guided by a moral system in which the fair distribution of rewards is a fundamental tenet. Much of the research conducted in the area of moral behavior has dealt with socialization because of the difficulty of defining a generally acceptable system of moral values as a yardstick for assessing degree of morality among adults. One system of moral development that has attempted to deal with the conceptualization and measurement of adult morality, however, has been put forth by Kohlberg (1963, 1968).

Extending Piaget's (1948) four-stage theory of moral development in children, Kohlberg (1963, 1968) proposed a six-stage theory of moral growth. Typically, an individual is assumed to pass through each stage in a progressive sequence, although regression is possible, from childhood through adulthood. The six stages may be divided into three major levels of moral maturity, with two stages within each level (see Table 2). At the first level, labeled preconventional, the child or adult is aware of cultural rules of right and wrong but interprets these rules in terms of the hedonistic consequences of an action. The second or conventional level is characterized by the individual's

---

TABLE 2   Classification of Moral Judgment into Levels and Stages of Development
(Adapted from Kohlberg, 1969)

Level I   Premoral

Moral value resides in external happenings or in quasi-physical needs rather than in persons and standards.

Stage 1.   Obedience and punishment orientation. Egocentric deference to superior, power, prestige, or a trouble-avoiding set.

Stage 2.   Instrumental relativist. Naively egoistic orientation. Right action is that which instrumentally satisfies the self's needs and occasionally others' needs. Awareness of relativism of value to each actor's needs and perspective. Naive egalitarianism.

Level II   Conventional

Moral value resides in performing good or right roles in maintaining the conventional order and the expectencies of others.

Stage 3.   Interpersonal concordance: "Good boy" or "nice girl" orientation. Orientation to approval and to pleasing and helping others. Conformity to stereotypical images of majority or natural role behavior and judgment by intentions.

Stage 4.   Law and order orientation. Authority and social-order maintenance orientation. Orientation to "doing duty" and to showing respect for authority and maintaining the given social order for its own sake. Regard for earned expectations of others.

Level III   Principled

Moral value resides in conformity to sharable standards, rights, or duties.

Stage 5.   Social contract: Contractual legalistic orientation. Recognition of an arbitrary element or starting point in rules or expectations for the sake of agreement. Duty defined in terms of contract, of general avoidance of violations of the will or rights of others, and of majority will and welfare.

Stage 6.   Conscience or universal ethical principles orientation. Orientation not only to actually ordained social rules but to principles of choice involving appeal to logical consistency. Orientation to conscience as a directing agent and to mutual respect and trust.

---

desire to fulfill the expectations of family, group, or nation. The attitude at this level is one of conformity to expectations and social order. The postconventional or principled level of moral maturity is identifiable by the individual's application of autonomous moral principles. It should be noted that Kohlberg's scheme is not a static trait theory but instead emphasizes the significance of the reciprocal interaction of person and environment during socialization.

The assignment of an individual to one of Kohlberg's (1963, 1968) stages of moral reasoning is based on that individual's responses to the Kohlberg Moral Judgment Scale. The scale consists of several short stories that are presented to an individual. Each story poses a classic moral dilemma that is followed by questions designed to elicit the respondent's resolution of the dilemma as well as her or his supporting reasons for the resolution selected. One dilemma, for example, concerns an impoverished husband who must steal a life-saving drug in order to save his dying wife. After being presented with the dilemma, the respondent answers questions regarding the rightness or wrongness of the husband's actions, a husband's duty to relatives and to nonrelatives, and the appropriate punishment (if any) for the husband. Following a manual developed by Kohlberg (Note 1), several judges score the responses. Interrater reliabilities have typically been found in the .70s and .80s (Kohlberg, 1963). A study by Haan, Smith, and Block (1968) obtained an interrater reliability of .82 with 510 respondents.

Evidence that supports the validity of Kohlberg's (1963, 1968) scheme is available from a variety of studies. Kohlberg (Note 2) reported that of eight Stage 6 subjects who participated in Milgram's (1963) obedience study, six subjects quit the experiment. Of 24 subjects who were assessed by the scale to be at the conventional level of morality, only three refused to continue. Using a sample of college students and Peace Corps volunteers ($N = 957$), Haan,

Smith, and Block (1968) investigated the political-social behavior, family background, and personality correlates of individuals who are representative of each stage of Kohlberg's model. Among the more interesting findings of the Haan et al. study was a curvilinear relationship between stage of moral development and participation in social protests. Of those respondents who participated in the 1965 Berkeley Free Speech Movement Sit In to the point of being arrested, the percentages within stages were as follows: for men, Stages 1 and 2, 60 percent; Stage 3, 18 percent; Stage 4, 6 percent; Stage 5, 41 percent; Stage 6, 75 percent; for women, Stages 1 and 2, 33 percent; Stage 3, 9 percent; Stage 4, 12 percent; Stage 5, 57 percent; Stage 6, 86 percent. Although morally conventional individuals are apparently less willing to engage in protests, significant percentages of both preconventional and principled individuals exhibit a positive stance toward protest activities, but they do so for different reasons. Morally preconventional individuals, it was concluded, viewed protest activities as an opportunity to better their own status through a power conflict with the status quo. On the other hand, morally principled individuals who actively participated in protests were probably concerned with issues of human rights and liberties. The implication of these findings is that an increase in empathy is associated with moral development. A restatement of this implication would read: Advanced stages of moral development are associated with greater concern for others who are further removed in both time and space.

AN EMPIRICAL DEMONSTRATION OF THE RELEVANCE OF MORAL MATURITY FOR EMPLOYEE BEHAVIOR

Returning to the issue of the opposite predictions of expectancy and equity theories in terms of individual differences, it is obvious that research in individual differences in value orientation is applicable. Clearly, certain individuals behave in closer accord with a set of moral principles than do other individuals. The behavior of less principled, self-serving individuals has been the focus of theories derived from hedonism, whereas the behavior of individuals who seek equity in social settings has received less attention. By implementing the tautology inherent in the principle of reinforcement, however, the hedonistic view can claim to explain prosocial behavior in terms of the reinforcement of altruistic responses during early socialization. It is reasonable to assume that individual differences in response to inequitable settings are partly a function of early socialization experiences. By using individual differences in value orientation as a moderator of behavior in inequitable situations, however, it is possible to account for the opposite predictions generated by expectancy and equity theory and to generate predictions for individual responses to inequity.

With respect to the aforementioned overpayment piece-rate condition, the predictions for individual response to inequity are as follows: (a) The predictions deduced from equity theory, that is, greater individual efforts toward maximizing quality and minimizing quantity, will be more strongly supported by those individuals who can be characterized as morally mature (in Kohlberg's [1963, 1968] scheme); and (b) the predictions deduced from expectancy theory, that is, greater individual efforts toward maximizing quantity and minimizing quality, will be more strongly supported by those individuals who can be characterized as less morally mature. Therefore, individual value orientation will serve as a moderator of efforts to restore equity, such that the correlation of moral maturity and quantity will be more negative for overpaid employees (relative to that for equitably paid employees), whereas the correlation of moral maturity and quality will be more positive for overpaid employees (relative to that for equitably paid employees). Succinctly stated, the underlying rationale of these hypotheses is one of predicting employee behavior (enhancement of quality versus quantity of performance) in response to a salient situational attribute (extent of overpayment inequity) from knowledge of employee predisposition (outcome maximization versus equity maximization).

METHOD

The study's design incorporated many of the methodological features of the better (and more recent) equity studies. Several aspects of the present design and procedures were most notably borrowed from Lawler and O'Gara (1967).

The subjects were 40 undergraduate students (34 men and 6 women) who were hired through advertisements placed in a campus newspaper and signs posted in a student center. The ads stated that undergraduates were needed to fill a short-term, part-time job dealing with attitude assessment. It was specifically stated that the job involved only two and one-half hours of work and would be completed in just one afternoon. The ads also noted that two distinct tasks were involved in the job. Rate of pay was not advertised.

When the students reported for the job (to a site on campus), a male experimenter explained to them that the job, a project sponsored by the university's Department of Management, consisted of two separate tasks. One of the tasks was described as an interviewing project requiring students to help gather information concerning their fellow students' opinions on controversial campus-life issues. The intent of this task, it was explained, was to help the university's administration to manage the institution more effectively by being aware of student sentiment on topics concerning "student life." The other task was described as a separate project that also dealt with student attitudes, but this second task required the job applicant to complete an anonymous questionnaire. It was also explained that the rates of pay for the two tasks were quite different. For completing the questionnaire, the applicant would be paid a "flat rate" of $1.00 from a separate research fund. For the interviewing task, however, compensation would be determined on a piece-rate basis.

Half of the students were randomly selected to complete the questionnaire before working on the interview task. The remaining students completed the interview task prior to answering the questionnaire.

The interview task was described to the job applicants in detail. In essence, the applicants were instructed to interview students on campus for a two-hour period. Each applicant was presented with 40 interview sheets. Each sheet required the interviewer to record some general information about the interviewee (e.g., age, major, sex) as well as each interviewee's responses to four "campus-life" questions. The four questions (dealing with student feelings about campus regulations restricting opposite-sex dorm visitation after certain hours, the disproportionately small number of women on campus, etc.) had been selected on the basis of discussions with several students that dealt with identifying truly controversial issues related to campus life. Each student was also instructed on the matter of how to conduct interviews. Specifically, the experimenter presented the student with a "Guide for Conducting Interviews" and briefly explained the Guide to him or her. The Guide encouraged the student not to ask "leading" or suggestive questions of the interviewee, not to show approval or disapproval of respondent's remarks, to record the respondent's remarks in sufficient detail, and so on.

For a randomly selected group of half of the students, the pay rate was given as 40 cents per interview. Furthermore, these students were informed that the rate was the normal rate for this job and that other interviewers had also been paid at this rate (Equitable Payment Condition). The other half of the students were informed that "although the established rate of pay for this task is 40 cents per interview, and we have in the past paid some workers the 40 cents per interview rate—in fact just yesterday we paid some people at that rate—you will be paid at the rate of 75 cents per interview" (Overpayment Condition). No explanation was provided to the students as to how their pay rate was determined. The experimenter explained the pay rate in a manner that suggested that he was simply following orders.

The rates of 40 cents and 75 cents per interview were, in fact, determined after (a) examining the pay rates used in previous overpayment equity studies, (b) considering the rate of inflation since some of the early equity studies were conducted, (c) pretesting the interview task to determine a likely hourly rate of performance, and (d) considering the established university hourly pay rate for student workers.

Following the description of the pay scheme, each student was asked to complete a job application form. In addition to asking the usual questions (sex, age, previous employment history, etc.), this form contained two further questions designed to assess the effectiveness of the inequity induction. The first of these (a "filler" item) asked a simple yes-no question, "Has your rate of pay been explained to you by the project director?" The second question asked, "Compared with other student interviewers on this project, I am being . . ." The response format for this question was a nine-point scale, with 1 = "equitably paid" and 9 = "overpaid." It was reasoned that an assessment of the effectiveness of the inequity induction should *precede* the interview task (rather than follow the task, as has commonly been the case in prior research) because of the possibility that some subjects would reduce inequity via their efforts on the interviewing task. As will be discussed later, a post-interview assessment of perceived inequity was also taken.

Each student was then told, "Because this is a new job and we are attempting to structure it as best as possible, we would appreciate it if you would answer a few questions about the job when you have finished the interviewing. We are sorry that we cannot explain to you more precisely the goals of the project, but as you must realize, this might introduce some bias into your data collection. Because the interview consists of four open-ended questions, we are employing as many interviewers as possible in order to avoid any bias that a single interviewer might introduce." The present time was then noted for the student, and she or he was told to return at a specific time (two hours later).

Upon returning from the interview task,

each student was requested to fill out an opinion form that asked the following nine-point questions: (a) "At the time you were hired, how well or poorly qualified did you think you were to do the job?" (very unqualified = 1, very qualified = 9); (b) "How much do you need the money from the job?" (not at all = 1, very much = 9). The next section of the form consisted of five nine-point semantic differential items that asked the respondent to describe the interviewing job. The adjectives were boring-interesting, unimportant-important, simple-complex, underpaid-overpaid (an "embedded"; postinterviewing manipulation check), and unchallenging-challenging. Also, each student was asked to indicate what the rate of pay per interview, in his or her opinion, should be. Lastly, each student responded to two 11-point Kunin-type (Kunin, 1955) faces scales 1 = very unhappy, 11 = very happy). The first faces scale asked for an overall assessment of how satisfied the student was with the pay, and the second asked how satisfied she or he was with the work itself. The students were thanked for taking time to complete the postinterview opinion form (i.e., they were not paid for completing it).

Those students who had not already completed the aforementioned anonymous questionnaire did so after completing the opinion form. The questionnaire contained a variety of attitude statements plus the Kohlberg Moral Judgment Scale (1963). Rather than use the entire Kohlberg scale (which is too lengthy for present purposes by virtue of posing a wide variety of moral dilemmas, such as breaking promises and disregarding property rights), it was previously decided to use a moral dilemma that centers on empathy (i.e., the case of the husband stealing a drug to save the life of his wife). This case required the respondent to indicate, in response to a series of questions, whether the act of stealing was conscionable and, if not, under what circumstances might it have been so. Further, it inquired as to whether the respondent was empathic with respect to the feelings of closely related others, acquaintances, unrelated others (i.e., strangers) and with respect to life in general (e.g., animal life). The scoring of individual responses to the case was based on a detailed manual developed by Kohlberg (Note 1). Kohlberg contends that about 50 percent of most individuals' moral reasoning is identifiable with a single moral stage, regardless of the moral dilemma involved.

After the students completed both tasks, they were paid by check for their services. Following this payment, the experimenter questioned each student to determine the extent of his or her prior knowledge of the job. From this friendly probing, it was possible to establish that some of the later subjects were recommended to apply for the job by earlier subjects. If the earlier subject (recommender) was someone who was equitably paid (i.e., paid 40 cents per interview), then no problem existed with respect to individual expectations. If an earlier subject (recommender) was in the overpaid condition, however, then the more recent subject's data were judged invalid, regardless of the more recent subject's payment assignment. The problem posed by this second situation may be simply stated as follows: If a subject applies for a job for which a friend has been handsomely paid, then the overpayment inequity induction is substantially weakened (if it can exist at all); whereas, if the same subject who applies at the suggestion of the handsomely paid friend is paid 40 cents per interview, then the equitable payment condition becomes one of relative underpayment. Because of this problem of "contamination," additional subjects were used until a total of 40 "pure" subjects was obtained. This contamination problem, a topic not discussed in any of the previous equity literature but likely to have existed to some unknown degree in other studies, necessitated the discarding of data for eight subjects. It was decided not to probe the subjects prior to using them because probing would be interpreted as a threat to their obtaining the job, which would make them more defensive and far more likely to lie about any prior knowledge. Because the contaminated subjects were few in number, it was decided that a statistical comparison of their performance with the performance of the pure subjects was not feasible.

The central hypothesis of this study deals with the utility of moral maturity for predicting individual response to inequity. The measurement of moral maturity, as noted earlier, was accomplished within the Kohlberg system. Each subject's responses to a moral dilemma were scored, in accordance with the Kohlberg manual (Kohlberg, Note 1), by the author and a research assistant. Both scorers had extensive prior experience in scoring Kohlberg protocols by virtue of a previous study that involved the scoring of nearly 200 protocols. The obtained interrater correlation for the present study was .91 ($p < .001$). For purposes of the following analysis, the Kohlbergian (moral maturity) scores of the raters were averaged for each subject and then weighted by 10.

Because of the existence of several extreme performance values (outliers), the performance data were put through a natural log transformation (this transformation did not substantially alter the following results). Within equity conditions, correlations of moral maturity with the performance variables were then calculated. For quantity of performance, the correlations for overpaid and equitably paid subjects were − .34 and .30, respectively, whereas for quality of performance, the correlations for overpaid and equitably paid subjects were .07 and − .43, respectively. The differences between correlations for each dependent variable were tested for significance using the Fisher r-to-Z transformation. The result of the test for the quantity dependent variable was significant ($Z = 1.94$, $p \cong .05$), whereas the result for the quality dependent variable did not achieve statistical significance ($Z = 1.55$).

In order to have a fuller appreciation of these results (i.e., to see whether ordinal or disordinal interactions exist), the regressions for these data are displayed in Figure 1. From this figure it is apparent that the more morally mature subjects were the most differentially affected by the occurrence of inequity in a work setting.

FIGURE 1 Moral Maturity × Equity Condition (plots of regression lines)

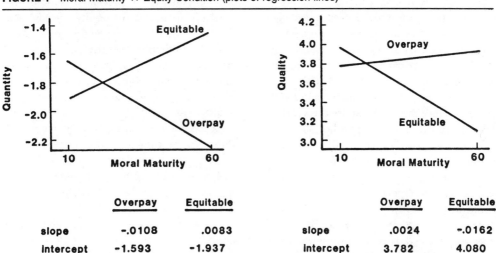

	Overpay	Equitable		Overpay	Equitable
slope	-.0108	.0083	**slope**	.0024	-.0162
intercept	-1.593	-1.937	**intercept**	3.782	4.080

Further analyses identified a significant difference in the reported satisfaction with pay for the interviewing task as a function of payment condition (*M* equitable payment = 8.850, *SD* = 1.089; *M* overpayment = 9.850, *SD* = 11.502; $F = 5.198$, $p < .05$). Also, the subjects' recommended pay rate per interview (an item on the postinterviewing opinion form) differed significantly from the received rate of pay for the overpayment condition but not for the equitable payment condition (*M* overpayment = 64.25, *SD* = 11.502, $Z = 4.18$, $df = 19$, $p < .01$; *M* equitable payment = 42.35, *SD* = 9.03, $Z = 1.163$, $df = 19$, *ns*). The evidence that overpaid subjects recommended a significant decrease in the rate of pay (whereas equitably paid subjects did not recommend a rate that was significantly different from what they received) represents a new and intuitively appealing approach to documenting the effectiveness of equity inductions.

The fact that overpaid subjects recommended a significant decrease in the rate of pay appears to contradict the finding that overpaid subjects reported greater satisfaction with their pay. Unfortunately, there is not a readily available explanation for this apparent inconsistency. This result suggests the need for more

systematic conceptual work regarding emotion and motivation within the equity framework.

DISCUSSION

The current evidence reaffirms the reliability of the overpayment main effects (i.e., reduced quantity and increased quality of performance). This is especially important given that the context of the present study was one of overpayment as a consequence of outcomes and not one that used attacks on the subject's self-esteem to create a sense of overpayment.

The present study did not replicate Lawler et al.'s (1968) finding of strong positive correlations between need for money and performance. The present correlations for need for money and performance, by equity condition, were as follows: − .06 for quantity-equitable; − .02 for quality-equitable; .12 for quantity-overpaid; and − .11 for quality-overpaid. These same correlations (in the same order) for the Lawler et al. study (Session 1 data) were .09, .25, .51, and .80, respectively ($n = 40$). Because the Lawler et al. assessment of need for money involved the combination of worker responses to an open-ended question and a seven-point scale of need for money, any comparison of the correlations across studies must be a guarded one. It is interesting to note, however, that an equity study that examined the relation of need for money and performance, and that also used a single-item measure of need for money (Garland, 1973), failed to replicate the Lawler et al. finding ($r = .03$).

Because a degree of ambiguity surrounds both expectancy theory and equity theory, it is always possible to generate, post hoc, an additional outcome that will reconcile their conflicting predictions (Campbell & Pritchard, 1976). In a response to Lawler's (1968b) suggestion of "incorporating" equity theory within the expectancy framework, Adams (1968) urged that simple "either-or" testing of expectancy theory and equity theory would be less fruitful than would identifying conditions that arouse equity (or justice-maximizing) motives versus gain-maximizing motives. The present study contributes to this search by identifying an important individual-differences variable that predisposes an equity-maximizing response to inequitable situations.

Further inquiry into the equity phenomenon that would be based on the present study must be mindful of two sets of problems: (*a*) limitations of the present study and (*b*) difficulties associated with investigating equity theory in conjunction with expectancy theory. Regarding the first set of problems, the most obvious limitation is the problem of generalizing from a student population to the labor force. Short-term simulations that enable us to predict actual behavior, however, do permit the identification of, at a minimum, a predisposition to act. Whether the predisposition is actualized in a traditional work setting is, of course, a function of many additional moderators. Given the present author's desire to utilize the current research design to its fullest, the use of a student sample is not incongruent with a goal of maximizing internal validity. Although the obtained results were overall in the predicted direction, the power of the statistical analyses was limited by the sample size (unfortunately, the sample is necessarily an expensive item, as well as a labor-intensive factor, for any overpayment equity study). A further limitation on the interpretation of the present results is the previous finding of the transitory nature of the equity phenomenon (Lawler et al., 1968). The present study, however, perhaps implies that the "permanence" of the inequity effect may vary as a function of employee moral maturity. In other words, a future study that would be worth conducting would address the hypothesis that the equity effect has a longer lasting effect on employees with a strong conscience (i.e., greater moral maturity) than on those with a weak conscience. It should be noted, however, that the opposite prediction is also logically defensible (i.e., individuals who strongly value equity will experience greater dissonance, and the resulting motivational force to restore equity would in turn shorten the inequity effect). Therefore, the design of studies of the inequity effect's permanence must be sensitive to the possible existence of these two processes.

The difficulties associated with studying equity theory in conjunction with expectancy theory stem primarily from their distinctly different theoretical origins. Because expectancy theory has never been concerned with social comparison processes (and the issue of cognitive dissonance) and equity theory has never been concerned with instrumentality concepts, it is particularly difficult to achieve an interface for these theories. Nonetheless, the search for an integration of these theories may be a worthy endeavor. Until such an integration can be achieved (if it is possible), tolerance of theoretical pluralism is required (Feyerabend, 1963). That is to say, the existence of a variety of motivation theories should not be viewed as representing a primitive stage in the quest for a "One True Theory."

Also, the utility of individual value systems for predicting task performance (either as a main effect or through interactions with other variables) is a comparatively new research topic that is worthy of further exploration. Perhaps the concepts and measures of adult moral maturity proposed by Hogan (1973) and by Christie and Geis (1970) may provide innovative directions for future research. With the exception of Machiavellianism, the usefulness of measures of adult moral maturity for studying behavior in work settings is a topic that has been largely ignored.

In summary, the present investigation provided empirical support for a proposed moderator of inequity resolution. Because an "act" cannot be separated from its "agent" and all acts therefore must be selfishly motivated, the infinite-regress aspect of cognitive hedonism can, as always, provide an alternative interpretation of the present findings (i.e., equity has a low or negative valence for morally immature individuals and a comparatively higher valence for morally mature, emphatic individuals). Therefore, the present study also contributes to the expectancy literature by identifying individuals who, by inference, are likely to attach a high valence to equity.

If expectancy theory was the "in" motivational theory of the 70s, goal-setting theory is the "in" theory of the 80s. For 20 years, Locke and his colleagues have been doing research to demonstrate the facilitating effect that specific, challenging goals have on effort. In this reading, the results of these studies are reviewed. In addition, the authors consider the effect of various other variables such as participation in setting the goals and the use of money as an incentive or a reward.

■ READING 21 ■

Goal Setting and Task Performance: 1969–1980

Edwin A. Locke, *College of Business and Management and Department of Psychology, University of Maryland*

Karyll N. Shaw, *College of Business and Management, University of Maryland*

Lise M. Saari, *Department of Psychology, University of Washington*

Gary P. Latham, *Graduate School of Business Administration, University of Washington*

In this article we summarize research relating to *(a)* the effects of setting various types of goals or objectives on task performance and *(b)* the factors (other than the goals themselves) that influence the effectiveness of goal setting.

All-encompassing theories of motivation based on such concepts as instinct, drive, and conditioning have not succeeded in explaining human action. Such theories have been gradually replaced by more modest and limited approaches to motivation. These approaches do not presume to explain all motivational phenomena; their domains are more restricted. The study of goal setting is one such limited approach.

The concept of goal setting falls within the broad domain of cognitive psychology and is consistent with recent trends such as cognitive behavior modification (Meichenbaum, 1977). The present interest of researchers in goal setting has two sources, one academic and the other organizational. The academic source extends back in time from Ryan (1970) and G. Miller, Galanter, and Pribram (1960), through Lewin, to the Wurzburg School and the associated concepts of intention, task, set, and level of aspiration (see Ryan, 1970, for a summary). The organizational source is traced from Management by Objectives programs, now widely used in industry (see Odiorne, 1978, for a summary), back to the Scientific Management movement founded by Frederick W. Taylor (1911/1967). These two trains of thought converge in the more recent work of Locke (1968), Latham (Latham & Yukl, 1975b), and others who have studied the effects of goal setting on task performance. Goal

Source: *Psychological Bulletin*, 90(1), 1981, pp. 125–152. Copyright 1981 by the American Psychological Association. Reprinted by permission of the publisher and author.

setting is also an important component of social learning theory (Bandura, 1977), which has become increasingly influential in recent years. Even the literature on organizational behavior modification can be interpreted largely within a goal-setting framework (Locke, 1977).

Research on goal setting is proliferating so rapidly that recent reviews (Latham & Yukl, 1975b; Locke, 1968; Steers & Porter, 1974) are now outdated. To provide a longer term perspective than just the last six years, our review includes research published since 1968. Studies that are explicitly clinical and social-psychological in nature are not included (for a detailed review of the latter, see Fishbein & Ajzen, 1975).

THE CONCEPT OF GOAL SETTING

A goal is what an individual is trying to accomplish; it is the object or aim of an action. The concept is similar in meaning to the concepts of purpose and intent (Locke, 1969). Other frequently used concepts that are also similar in meaning to that of goal include performance standard (a measuring rod for evaluating performance), quota (a minimum amount of work or production), work norm (a standard of acceptable behavior defined by a work group), task (a piece of work to be accomplished), objective (the ultimate aim of an action or series of actions), deadline (a time limit for completing a task), and budget (a spending goal or limit).

Earlier attempts by behaviorists to reduce concepts like goal and purpose to physical events have been strongly criticized (e.g., see Locke, 1969, 1972). Goal setting might be called "stimulus control" by a modern behaviorist, but the key question then becomes, What is the stimulus? If it is only an assigned goal (an environmental event), then the importance of goal acceptance is ignored; an assigned goal that is rejected can hardly regulate performance. If goal acceptance is considered relevant, then the regulating stimulus must be a mental event—ultimately the individual's

goal. The environment, of course, can influence goal setting as well as goal acceptance, an issue that is dealt with in some of the recent research.

The basic assumption of goal-setting research is that goals are immediate regulators of human action. However, no one-to-one correspondence between goals and action is assumed because people may make errors, lack the ability to attain their objectives (Locke, 1968), or have subconscious conflicts or premises that subvert their conscious goals. The precise degree of association between goals and action is an empirical question that is dealt with in the research we review here. We also examine the mechanisms by which goals affect action, the effects of feedback, participation, and money on goal-setting effectiveness, the role of individual differences, and the determinants of goal commitment.

GOAL-SETTING ATTRIBUTES[1]

Mental processes have two major attributes, content and intensity (Rand, 1967). The content of a goal is the object or result being sought. The main dimensions of goal content that have been studied so far are specificity or clarity (the degree of quantitative precision with which the aim is specified) and difficulty (the degree of proficiency or level of performance sought). The terms *task difficulty* and *goal difficulty* are often used interchangeably, but a distinction between them can be made.

A task is a piece of work to be accomplished. A difficult task is one that is hard to do. A task can be hard because it is complex, that is, requires a high level of skill and knowledge. For example, writing a book on physics is a harder task than writing a thank you note. A task can also be hard because it requires a great deal of effort: digging the

---

[1]Our view of what constitutes a goal attribute differs from that of Steers and Porter (1974) who, for example, called participation an attribute of goals. We treat participation as a mechanism that may *affect* goal content or goal acceptance.

foundation for a pool takes more effort than digging a hole to plant a flower seed.

Since a goal is the object or aim of an action, it is possible for the completion of a task to be a goal. However, in most goal-setting studies, the term *goal* refers to attaining a specific standard of proficiency on a task, usually within a specified time limit. For example, two individuals are given the same task (e.g., simple addition), but one is asked to complete a large number of problems within 30 minutes, and the other, a small number. The harder goal would be achieved by expending greater effort and attention than would be expended to achieve the easy goal. Harder goals, like harder tasks, also can require more knowledge and skill than easier goals (e.g., winning a chess tournament versus coming in next to last). To summarize the distinction between the terms, goal difficulty specifies a certain level of task proficiency measured against a standard, whereas task difficulty refers simply to the nature of the work to be accomplished.

Although greater task difficulty should lead to greater effort (Kahneman, 1973; Kaplan & Rothkopf, 1974; Shapira, Note 1), the relation of task difficulty to performance is problematic. If more work is translated into a goal to get more done, task difficulty may be positively related to performance (Sales, 1970). On the other hand, if harder tasks require more ability or knowledge, most people will, at least initially, perform less well on them, even if they try harder, than they would on easier tasks (e.g., Shapira, Note 1).

An experiment by Campbell and Ilgen (1976) demonstrated that the distinction between task and goal difficulty has practical utility. They manipulated both dimensions independently. On chess problems difficult goals led to better performance than easy goals; training subjects on hard problems (tasks) led at first to poorer performance but later to better performance than training subjects on easier problems (tasks). Presumably the harder goals led to greater effort than the easier goals, and training on the harder chess problems led to the acquisition of more skill and knowledge than training on easier ones.

Although there has been extensive research on the effects of goal specificity and difficulty on performance, little attention has been paid to two other dimensions of goal content: goal complexity (the number and interrelation of the results aimed for) and goal conflict (the degree to which attaining one goal negates or subverts attaining another).

The second attribute of goals, intensity, pertains to the process of setting the goal or of determining how to reach it. Intensity would be measured by such factors as the scope of the cognitive process, the degree of effort required, the importance of the goal, and the context in which it is set. Goal intensity may be related to goal content; for example, a more intense psychological process is needed to set complex goals and to figure out how to attain them than the process needed to set and attain simple goals. Goal intensity has not been studied as such, although a related concept, goal commitment, has been measured in a number of experiments.

RELATION OF GOAL DIMENSIONS TO PERFORMANCE

Goal Difficulty

In an earlier review of the goal-setting literature, Locke (1968) found evidence for a positive, linear relation between goal difficulty and task performance (assuming sufficient ability), and more recent studies have supported these findings. Four results in three experimental field studies demonstrated that harder goals led to better performance than easy goals; Latham and Locke (1975) with logging crews; Yukl and Latham (1978) with typists; and a simulated field study by Bassett (1979). In a separate manipulation, Bassett also found that shorter time limits led to a faster work pace than longer time limits.

Twenty-five experimental laboratory studies have obtained similar results with a wide variety of tasks: Bavelas (1978), with a figure-selection task; Bavelas and Lee (1978) in five of six experiments involving brainstorming, figure selection, and sum estimation tasks; Campbell and Ilgen (1976) with chess; Hannan (1975) with a coding (credit applications) task; LaPorte and Nath (1976) with prose learning; Latham and Saari (1979b) with brainstorming; Locke and Bryan (1969b) with simple addition; Locke, Cartledge, and Knerr (1970) in four studies, three with reaction time and one with simple addition; Locke, Mento, and Katcher (1978) with perceptual speed; London and Oldham (1976) with card sorting; Masters, Furman, and Barden (1977) in two studies of four- and five-year-old children working on a color discrimination task; Mento, Cartledge, and Locke (1980) in two experiments using a perceptual speed task; Rothkopf and Billington (1975) and Rothkopf and Kaplan (1972) in more complex prose-learning studies than that of LaPorte and Nath (1976); and Sales (1970), using anagrams. In Sales's study, task rather than goal difficulty was manipulated by means of varying the work load given to the subjects. Presumably subjects developed implicit goals based on the amount of work assigned to them. Ness and Patton (1979) also found that a harder task led to better weight-lifting performance than an easier task when subjects were deceived as to the actual weights.

Four studies found conditional support for a positive relation between goal difficulty and performance.[2] Becker (1978) with an energy conservation task, Erez (1977) with a clerical task, and Strang, Lawrence, and Fowler (1978) with a computation task, all found that only subjects who had high goals and who received feedback regarding their performance in relation to those goals performed better than subjects with low goals. This pattern of results seems also to have been present in Frost and Mahoney's (1976) first study using a reading

task (see their Table 1, p. 339). Subjects with high and moderately high goals who apparently received frequent feedback performed better than those with average goals, whereas the opposite pattern was obtained for subjects given no feedback during the 42-minute work period (interaction $p = .11$; t tests were not performed).

Six experimental laboratory studies found no relation between goal level and task performance. Bavelas and Lee (1978) allowed only 15 minutes for an addition task and gave subjects no information either before or during the task of how fast they needed to go to attain the goal. Frost and Mahoney (1976) found negative results with a jigsaw puzzle task, although their range of goal difficulty was limited: from medium to hard to very hard (actual probabilities of success were .50, .135, and .026, respectively). The same narrow range of difficulty (very difficult to moderately difficult) may explain the negative results of Oldham (1975) using a time sheet computation task. Moreover, not all subjects accepted the assigned goals in that study, and it is not clear that ability was controlled when Oldham (1975, pp. 471–472) did his post hoc analysis by personal goal level. Organ (1977) also compared moderate goals with hard goals using an anagram task. However, since no group average even reached the level of the moderate goal, the hard goal may have been totally unrealistic.

The fifth negative study, by Motowidlo, Loehr, and Dunnette (1978), using a complex computation task, examined the goal theory-expectancy theory controversy. Goal theory predicts that harder goals lead to better performance than easy goals, despite their lower probability of being fully reached. In contrast, expectancy theory predicts (other things being equal) a positive relation between expectancy and performance, the opposite of the goal theory prediction. Motowidlo et al. found a positive relation between expectancy and performance, which is in agreement with expectancy theory. One possible confounding factor is that the subjects in the Motowidlo et al. study did not make their expectancy ratings conditional

---

[2]Partially or conditionally supportive studies were distinguished from nonsupportive studies as follows: A study was called partially supportive if the treatment was significant for one subsample of the full sample of subjects or for one of several experimental treatments or criteria. If an entire sample or study found no significant effects, it was called nonsupportive.

upon trying their hardest to reach the goal or to win (pointed out by Mento et al., 1980, based on Yates & Kulick, 1977, among others). Thus, low expectancy ratings could mean that a subject was not planning to exert maximum effort, whereas high ratings would mean the opposite. This would yield a spurious positive correlation between expectancy and performance. Furthermore, Motowidlo et al. did not provide their subjects with feedback regarding how close they were coming to their goals during task performance. (The importance of this factor is documented below.) The two studies by Mento et al. (1980), which avoided the errors of the Motowidlo et al. study and incorporated other methodological improvements, found the usual positive relation between goal level and performance and no relation between expectancy and performance.

Forward and Zander (1971) used goals set by groups of high school boys on a team-coding task as both independent and dependent variables. Success and failure as well as outside pressures were covertly manipulated to influence goal setting, which occurred before each trial of the task. Under these somewhat complex conditions, goal discrepancy (goal minus previous performance level) was either unrelated or negatively related to subsequent performance.

The results of the experimental studies were, to varying degrees, supported by the results of 15 correlational studies. Andrews and Farris (1972) found that time pressure was associated with high performance among scientists and engineers. Hall and Lawler (1971), with a similar sample, found no relation between time pressure and performance but found a significant relation between both quality and financial pressure (implied goals?) and work performance. Ashworth and Mobley (Note 2) found a significant relation between performance goal level and training performance for Marine recruits. Blumenfeld and Leidy (1969), in what also could be called a natural field experiment, found that soft-drink servicemen who were assigned higher goals serviced more machines than those assigned

lower goals. Hamner and Harnett (1974) found that subjects in an experimental study of bargaining who expected (tried?) to earn a high amount of money earned more than those who expected (tried?) to earn less money. Locke et al. (1970), in the last of their five studies, found a significant correlation between grade goals on an hourly exam and actual grade earned.

The majority of the correlational studies found only a conditional positive relation between goal difficulty and performance and/or effort. Carroll and Tosi (1970) found a positive relation only for managers who were mature and high in self-assurance; Dachler and Mobley (1973) found it only for production workers (in two plants) with long tenure (one or two years or more); Dossett, Latham, and Mitchell (1979), found it in two studies of clerical personnel, but only for those who set goals participatively; Hall and Hall (1976) found it for the class performance of second through fourth grade students in high-support schools; and Ivancevich and McMahon (1977a, 1977b, 1977c) found it for skilled technicians who had higher order (growth) need strength, were white, and had higher levels of education.

Negative results were obtained by Forward and Zander (1971) with United Fund campaign workers, Hall and Foster (1977) with participants in a simulated management game, and Steers (1975) with first-level supervisors.

All the correlational studies are, of course, open to multiple causal interpretations. For example, Dossett et al. (1979) implied that their results may be an artifact of ability, since ability was considered when setting goals in the participative groups but not in the assigned groups. In fact, none of the correlational studies had controls for ability. Also, many relied on self-ratings of goal difficulty or performance. The Yukl and Latham (1978) study found that only objective goal level, not subjective goal difficulty, was related to typing performance. None of the correlational studies measured the individual's personal goal level, a measure that Mento et al. (1980) found to be the single best motivational predictor of performance. Their measures of subjective goal difficulty did not explain any variance in performance over and above that explained by objective and personal goal levels.

Goal Specificity

Specific Hard Goals versus "Do-Best" Goals or No Goals. Previous research found that specific, challenging (difficult) goals led to higher output than vague goals such as "do your best" (Locke, 1968). Subsequent research has strongly supported these results, although in a number of studies, no distinction was made between groups told to do their best and those assigned no specific goals. The latter were typically labeled *no goal* groups. We have not found any differences in the results obtained by studies in which no goals are assigned and those in which subjects are explicitly told to do their best. No goal subjects, it appears, typically try to do as well as they can on the assigned task.

Twenty-four field experiments all found that individuals given specific, challenging goals either outperformed those trying to do their best or surpassed their own previous performance when they were not trying for specific goals: Bandura and Simon (1977) with dieting; Dockstader (Note 3) with key punching; Dossett et al. (1979) in two studies, one using a clerical test and the other performance evaluations for clerical workers; Ivancevich (1977) with maintenance technicians; Ivancevich (1974) in two plants with marketing and production workers (for one or more performance criteria); Ivancevich (1976) with sales personnel; Kim and Hamner (1976) with telephone service jobs; Kolb and Boyatzis (1970) with personality change in a T-group; Latham and Baldes (1975) with truck loading; Latham and Kinne (1974) with logging; and Latham and Yukl (1975a) with woods workers who participated in goal setting; Latham and Yukl (1976) with typing; Latham, Mitchell, and Dossett (1978) with engineering and scientific work; Migliore (1977) with canning (press department) and ship loading (two studies); Nemeroff and Cosentino (1979) with performance appraisal activities; Umstot, Bell and

Mitchell (1976) with coding land parcels; Wexley and Nemeroff (1975) with managerial training; and White, Mitchell, and Bell (1977) with card sorting. The studies by Adam (1975) with die casters, Feeney with customer service workers ("At Emery Air Freight," 1973), and Komaki, Barwick, and Scott (1978) with pastry workers are also included in this group. Although these investigations claimed that they were doing behavior modification, the major technique actually used was goal setting plus feedback regarding goal attainment (Locke, 1977).

A negative result was obtained by Latham and Yukl (1975a) with one sample of woods workers. Either individual differences or lack of organizational support may have been responsible for this failure. (Ivancevich, 1974, also cited differences in organizational support as the reason for obtaining better results in one of his plants than the other.)

The generally positive results of the field studies were supported by the results of 20 laboratory studies: Chung and Vickery (1976; their KR condition included implicit goal setting) with a clerical task; Frost and Mahoney (1976) with a reading task (but only for subjects given frequent feedback) and with a puzzle task; Hannan (1975) with a coding task; Kaplan and Rothkopf (1974) and LaPorte and Nath (1976) with prose learning; Latham and Saari (1979a) with brainstorming; Latham and Saari (1979b) with brainstorming again, but only for subjects who set goals participatively (though this may have been an artifact since the authors reported that the assigned goal subjects may not have understood the instructions clearly); Locke and Bryan (1969a) with a driving task; Locke et al. (1978) with perceptual speed (comparing the hard-goal versus do-best groups only); Mossholder (1980) using two assembly tasks; Organ (1977) with anagrams; Pritchard and Curtis (1973) with card sorting; Reynolds, Standiford, and Anderson (1979) with learning prose; Rosswork (1977) with a sentence construction task used with sixth graders; Rothkopf and Billington (1975) and Rothkopf and Kaplan (1972), again with learning prose; Strang, Lawrence, and Fowler

(1978) with arithmetic computation (but only for hard-goal subjects who had feedback); and Terborg and Miller (1978) with tinker-toy assembly.

A negative result was obtained by Organ (1977) on a proofreading task. Evidently the goals set were moderate rather than hard, since they were set at the median scores for pretest subjects and were surpassed by subjects in all conditions. Moderate goals are not predicted to lead to higher performance than do-best goals. Locke et al. (1978), for example, found that although hard-goal subjects exceeded the performance of do-best subjects, moderate-goal subjects did not.

Seven correlational field studies also supported or partially supported the superiority of specific hard goals over do-best goals or no goals: Blumenfeld and Leidy (1969) with soft-drink servicemen; Brass and Oldham (1976) and Oldham (1976) with foremen; Burke and Wilcox (1969) with telephone operators; Ronan, Latham, and Kinne (1973) with pulp-wood producers; Steers (1975) with supervisors (but only those high on need for achievement); and Terborg (1976) with students studying programmed texts.

Clear versus Unclear Goals or Intentions. Relatively few studies have been concerned with the effect of goal clarity on performance. Two experimental studies (Kaplan & Rothkopf, 1974; Rothkopf & Kaplan, 1972) found that specific prose-learning goals led to more learning than generally stated goals. Carroll and Tosi (1970) found that goal clarity correlated with increased effort only for managers who were mature and decisive and who had low job interest and low support from their managers. Ivancevich and McMahon (1977a, 1977b, 1977c) found that goal clarity correlated with performance mainly for technicians who were black, less educated, and high on higher order need strength. These correlational studies seem to provide no consistent pattern, which is not surprising in view of the problems inherent in concurrent, self-report designs.

The borderline and negative results of Hall

and Hall (1976) and Hall and Foster (1977) with respect to goal difficulty and performance may have been because their goals did not consist of clear objectives but of the self-rated strength of the subjects' intentions to perform well.

The findings of these studies involving vague intentions can be contrasted with the organizational studies by Miller, Katerberg, and Hulin (1979), Mobley, Horner, and Hollingsworth (1978), and Mobley, Hand, Baker, and Meglino (1979). They found significant longitudinal correlations between the specific intention to remain in or leave the organization and the corresponding action.

Conclusions

Overall, 48 studies partly or wholly supported the hypothesis that hard goals lead to better performance than medium or easy goals; nine studies failed to support it. Fifty-one studies partially or wholly supported the view that specific hard goals lead to better performance than do-your-best or no goals; two studies did not support it. Combining these two sets of studies, we found that 99 out of 110 studies found that specific, hard goals produced better performance than medium, easy, do-your-best, or no goals. This represents a success rate of 90 percent.

Most of these studies (at least the experimental ones) were well designed; they included control groups, random assignment, negligible attrition, controls for ability, objective performance measures, and a great variety of tasks and situations. Thus, considerable confidence can be placed in them in terms of both internal and external validity.

MECHANISMS FOR GOAL-SETTING EFFECTS

Given that goal setting works, it is relevant to ask how it affects task performance. We view goal setting primarily as a motivational mechanism (although cognitive elements are necessarily involved). The concept of motivation is used to explain the direction, amplitude (effort), and duration (persistence) of action. Not surprisingly, all three are affected by goal setting. One additional, indirect mechanism is also described.

Direction

Most fundamentally, goals direct attention and action. Perhaps the most obvious demonstration of this mechanism is the study by Locke and Bryan (1969a) in which drivers were given feedback regarding five different dimensions of driving performance but were assigned goals with respect to only one dimension. The dimension for which a goal was assigned showed significantly more improvement than the remaining dimensions. Similarly, Locke et al. (1970) found that subjects modified their speed of reaction (to make it faster or slower) on a simple reaction-time task in the direction of their overall objective. Reynolds et al. (1979) found that subjects spent more time reading prose passages that were relevant to their goals (consisting of questions inserted in the text) than to reading parts that were not relevant. Terborg (1976) found that subjects with specific goals spent a greater percentage of the time looking at the text material to be learned than did subjects with nonspecific goals or no goals. (Terborg labeled this measure *effort* in his study.) Rothkopf and Billington (1979) found that subjects with specific learning goals, as compared with subjects with no specific learning goals (do-your-best instructions), spent an equal or greater amount of time inspecting passages with goal-relevant material and significantly less time looking at incidental passages.

Effort

Since different goals may require different amounts of effort, effort is mobilized simultaneously with direction in proportion to the perceived requirements of the goal or task. Thus, as Kahneman (1973) and Shapira (Note 1) have argued, more effort is expended on hard tasks (which are accepted) than on easy tasks. Sales (1970) found that higher work loads produce higher subjective effort, faster heart rates, and higher output per unit time than lower work loads. Latham and Locke (1975) and Bassett (1979) found that people work faster under shorter than under longer time limits. In summary, higher goals produce higher performance than lower goals or no goals because people simply work harder for the former (Locke, 1968; Terborg, 1976; Terborg & Miller, 1978; for earlier documentation see Locke & Bryan, 1966).

This hypothesis of a positive linear relation between motivation or effort and performance (also stated in Locke, 1968, and Yates & Kulick 1977), contradicts the Yerkes-Dodson inverted-U "law," which asserts that performance is maximal at moderate levels of motivation. Although it is true that with any given subject, performance eventually will level off as the limit of capacity or ability is reached (Bavelas & Lee, 1978; Kahneman, 1973), this is a separate issue from that of motivation. Of course, subjects may abandon their goals if they become too difficult, but the hypothesized function assumes goal commitment. Performance may also drop if subjects become highly anxious, especially on a complex or underlearned task. But a state of high anxiety should not be labeled *high motivation* in the positive sense because it represents a state of conflict rather than of single-minded goal pursuit.

Persistence

Persistence is nothing more than directed effort extended over time; thus, it is a combination of the previous two mechanisms. Most laboratory experiments on goal setting have not been designed to allow for the measurement of persistence effects, since time limits typically have been imposed; field studies to date have measured only the end results of goal setting rather than how they were obtained. LaPorte and Nath (1976) allowed some subjects unlimited time to read a prose passage. Those asked to read the passage to get 90 percent of 20 postreading questions correct spent more time on the passage than subjects asked to get 25 percent of the post-reading questions correct. Rothkopf and Billington (1979) found that more time was spent on goal-relevant than on incidental passages. More studies of this type would be highly desirable.

Strategy Development

Whereas the first three mechanisms are relatively direct in their effects, this last mechanism is indirect. It involves developing strategies or action plans for attaining one's goals. Although strategy development is motivated by goals, the mechanism itself is cognitive in essence; it involves skill development or creative problem solving.

Bandura and Simon (1977), for example, found that dieting subjects with specific quotas for number of mouthfuls eaten changed their eating patterns (e.g., by eating more low-calorie foods that did not count in their quotas). They also engaged in more planning (e.g., by saving part of their quota for a dinner out). Latham and Baldes (1975) observed that some of the truck drivers assigned specific hard goals with respect to truck weight recommended minor modifications of their trucks to help them increase the accuracy of their judgments of weight.

In Terborg's (1976) study, the subjects who set specific goals were more likely to employ relevant learning strategies (e.g., writing notes in the margins) than those who did not set goals. A unique aspect of Terborg's (1976) design was that he was able to obtain separate measures of direction of effort (which he called "effort") and of strategy use (which he called "direction"). He found that when these mechanisms were partialed out, there was no relation between goals and task performance. This supports the argument that these are some of the mechanisms by which goals affect performance.

In a similar vein, Kolb and Boyatzis (1970) found that behavior change in a T-group was greatest for participants who developed plans for evaluating their performance in relation to their goals. Such plans evidently were developed only for behavior dimensions that the subjects were trying to change.

Bavelas and Lee (1978) made detailed analyses in three experiments to determine the strategies subjects used to attain hard goals. They found that subjects would frequently redefine the task in a way that would permit them to give "looser" or lower quality answers. For example, subjects asked to list very large numbers of "white, hard, edible objects" were more likely to list objects that were white but not very hard or hard but not very edible than were subjects given easier goals. Similarly, with appropriate training, subjects given hard addition goals would more often estimate rather than calculate their answers as compared to subjects with easy goals.

Subjects given hard goals in Rosswork's (1977) study simply wrote shorter sentences to meet their quota, which was expressed in terms of total sentences written. The subjects in Sales's (1970) study who were given a high workload made more errors, presumably by lowering their standards, than those given a low workload. Christensen-Szalanski (1980) found that subjects who were given a short time limit in problem solving used less complex and less adequate strategies than subjects given a longer time limit. Strategy development is especially important in complex tasks. If the requisite strategies are not developed, the increased motivation provided by the goals will not be translated into effective performance.

We now examine the influence of feedback, money, and participation on the effectiveness of goal setting.

Knowledge of Results (Feedback)

In early goal-setting studies, attempts were made to separate the effects of feedback (i.e., knowledge of results [KR]) from the effects of goal setting to determine whether KR directly influenced performance or whether its effects were mediated by goal-setting activity (Locke, 1967; Locke & Bryan, 1968, 1969a, 1969b; Locke, Cartledge, & Koeppel, 1968). In the most carefully controlled of these studies, all subjects with specific goals also received knowledge of their performance in relation to their goals; individuals in the KR conditions

FIGURE 1   Model for Analyzing Goal-KR Studies. (KR = knowledge of results.)

	KR	No KR
Specific hard goal	1	2
No specific goal or do-best goal	3	4

received knowledge of their actual scores presented in such a way as to preclude their use in setting goals. Such knowledge of scores did not lead to better performance than no knowledge of scores. The evidence from these and related studies indicated that knowledge of scores was not sufficient to improve task performance. However, since groups with goals and no KR were not included, these studies did not test the possibility that KR may be a necessary condition for goals to affect performance. Few studies relevant to this hypothesis had been conducted at the time of the Latham and Yukl (1975b) review.

A number of such studies have since been completed in both the laboratory and the field. Figure 1 illustrates the conditions of interest. Cell 1 represents specific, hard goals combined with KR; Cell 2, specific, hard goals without KR; Cell 3, KR with no specific goals (or do-best goals that are equivalent to no assigned goals); and Cell 4, neither specific goals nor KR.

The studies reviewed here included at least three of the four cells in Figure 1. Table 1 summarizes the results of these comparisons.

Two types of studies are evident in Table 1. The first set consists of comparisons between Cells 1, 3, and 4. Consistent with Locke's (1968) mediating hypothesis, these studies indicate that although KR alone is not sufficient to improve performance (3 = 4), KR plus goals results in performance increases (1 > 3).

In a study of overweight clients in a weight clinic, participants who kept daily records of all the food they consumed but did not set goals to reduce food intake did not alter their eating habits and performed no differently than a control group who kept no records and set no specific goals (Bandura & Simon, 1977). However, participants who set goals based on their daily records significantly decreased food consumption compared with the KR-only group.

Dockstader (Note 3) found no apparent effect of KR alone on the performance of key punch operators, but those provided with KR and a performance standard significantly exceeded their own previous performance and that of the KR-only group.

Latham et al. (1978) found no differences between engineers and scientists with do-best goals who were provided with feedback concerning their performance on certain appraisal criteria and those who received no feedback; however, the subjects who set or were assigned

TABLE 1   Studies Comparing the Effects of Goals and KR on Performance

Study	Comparison Performed			
	1 versus 2	1 versus 3	2 versus 4	3 versus 4
Bandura & Simon (1977)		1 > 3		3 = 4
Dockstader (Note 3)		1 > 3		3 = 4
Latham, Mitchell, & Dossett (1978)		1 > 3		3 = 4
Nemeroff & Cosentino (1979)		1 > 3		3 = 4
"At Emery Air Freight" (1973)	1 > 2		2 = 4	
Komaki, Barwick, & Scott (1978)	1 > 2		2 = 4	
Becker (1978)*	1 > 2		2 = 4	
Strang, Lawrence, & Fowler (1978)*	1 > 2		2 = 4	
			2 < 4†	

Note: KR = knowledge of results. 1 = specific, hard goals combined with KR; 2 = specific, hard goals without KR; 3 = KR with no specific goals (or do-best goals); 4 = neither specific goals nor KR.
*Included both hard and easy goal plus KR conditions. The performance of easy-goal subjects was no better than that in the control condition.
†Results differed, depending on performance criterion utilized.

specific, hard goals in response to the feedback performed significantly better than those in the do-best and control groups.

Nemeroff and Cosentino (1979) found that supervisors who were provided with feedback concerning their behavior during performance appraisal sessions but who did not use the KR to set specific goals did not improve subsequent performance. Those supervisors who set specific goals in response to the feedback performed significantly better on the 12 behaviors for which they set goals and conducted significantly more successful appraisal interviews.

This first set of studies demonstrates that KR without goals is not sufficient to improve performance $(3 = 4)$, but given KR, goals are sufficient for performance to be improved $(1 > 3)$. Thus, goals seem necessary for KR to improve performance.

The second set of studies consists of comparisons between Cells 1, 2, and 4. In what was called a "positive reinforcement" program ("At Emery Air Freight," 1973), employees in the customer service department and on the shipping docks were given a group-performance goal, progress toward the goal was posted, and each employee also kept a personal record of performance. Performance levels increased markedly, but when KR was removed and self-reports were not kept, employee performance returned to baseline levels "or was almost as bad" ("At Emery Air Freight," 1973, p. 45), even though the performance target remained in effect $(1 > 2, 2 = 4)$.

In another behavior modification program (actually a goals and KR study; see Locke, 1980), Komaki, Barwick, and Scott (1978) examined safe behavior in the making and wrapping of pastry products. The authors introduced a specific, hard safety goal and displayed performance results on a graph in view of all the workers. Substantial performance improvements occurred, but when the KR was eliminated in a reversal phase, performance returned to baseline levels.

In a study of residential electricity use, Becker (1978) manipulated specific goals and KR. Families included in his study represent Cells 1, 2, and 4 of Figure 1; he also included easy-goal groups with and without KR. The

only families whose conservation performance improved significantly from baseline levels were those with hard goals plus KR. All other groups performed no better than a control group. Strang et al. (1978) conducted a laboratory study utilizing a design similar to Becker's (Cells 1, 2, and 4 plus the same two easy-goal conditions as above). Subjects worked on an arithmetic computation task. The performance of subjects with hard goals and feedback was significantly better than that of the goals-only subjects $(1 > 2)$. Using time to finish as a criterion, there were no differences between the performance of the goals-only subjects and that of control group subjects $(2 = 4)$. In terms of number of errors, however, the control group's performance was significantly better than that of the goals-only group $(4 > 2)$, suggesting that goals without KR may even inhibit accurate performance.

The results of this second group of studies indicate that goals without KR are not sufficient to improve performance $(2 = 4)$, but given goals, KR is sufficient to effect performance improvement $(1 > 2)$. Thus, KR seems necessary for goals to affect performance.

Although her study is not included in Table 1 because she used a correlational analysis, Erez (1977) was the first to suggest that KR is a necessary condition for the goal—performance relation. In her laboratory study, subjects worked on a number comparison task. At the end of one performance trial, they set goals for a second trial. Half of the subjects were provided with KR at the end of the first trial and half were not. Erez used a multiple regression analysis to identify the unique contribution of the Goal × KR interaction. The regression equation included Stage 1 performance, the two main effects variables (goals, KR), and the Goal × KR interaction. When all four variables were placed in the regression simultaneously, the interaction effect was significant, but beta weights for goals and KR were not significantly different from zero. The goal-performance correlation in the KR group was .60 and in the no-KR group, .01. These findings led Erez to conclude that KR is necessary for goals to affect performance.

Kim and Hamner's (1976) study of goals

and feedback was not included in this analysis because they acknowledged that their goals-only group actually may have received informal feedback. Thus, their study only includes two cells: Cell 1, with different groups having different amounts and types of feedback, and Cell 4, which comprised the "before" scores of the various groups. In this study, as in the one by Frost and Mahoney (1976, Task A), providing explicit or frequent feedback clearly facilitated performance.

Integrating the two sets of studies points to one unequivocal conclusion: neither KR alone nor goals alone is sufficient to improve performance. Both are necessary. This view of goals and feedback as reciprocally dependent seems more useful and more accurate than Locke's (1968) earlier position, which viewed goals as mediating the effects of feedback on performance. Together, goals and feedback appear sufficient to improve task performance (given the obvious contextual variables such as adequate ability and lack of external blocks to performance). The studies demonstrate that action is regulated by both cognition (knowledge) and motivation.

Table 1 demonstrates that not a single study was designed to allow all of the four possible comparisons. In other words, no study involved a complete 2×2 design with KR/no-KR and specific, hard goals/"do-best" goals, or no goals as the variables. Even the studies reported did not always involve total control over the variables; for example, spontaneous goal setting among KR-only subjects was not always prevented. Such a complete, controlled study is now being conducted by two of the present authors. It is predicted that Cell 1 (see Figure 1) will show better performance than the remaining cells, which should not differ among themselves. This would parallel the results of Becker (1978) and Strang et al. (1978) using KR/no-KR and hard/easy goal conditions.

Other issues remain to be explored regarding the role of KR. For example, Cummings, Schwab, and Rosen (1971) found that providing KR can lead to the setting of higher goals than not providing KR; this indicates that subjects may underestimate their capacity without correct information about their previous performance. Related to this, Greller (1980) found that supervisors incorrectly estimated the importance of various sources of feedback to subordinates. These issues deserve further study.

One issue that does not seem to deserve further study is that of feedback as a reinforcer. The findings and arguments of Annett (1969), Bandura (1977), and Locke (1977, 1980) speak convincingly against the thesis that feedback conditions behavior. It seems more useful and valid to treat feedback or KR as information, the effect of which depends on how it is processed (e.g., see Locke, Cartledge, & Koeppel, 1968).

A recent article (Ilgen, Fisher, & Taylor, 1979) specifies several dimensions along which KR can vary: amount, type, frequency, specificity, timing, source, sign, and recency. Experimental studies of these dimensions could reveal the most effective form in which to provide KR in conjunction with goals. Unfortunately, the studies to date have not been systematic enough to allow any conclusions about these dimensions.

Our major conclusion, that both goals and KR are necessary to improve performance, provides a clear prescription for task management. Not only should specific, hard goals be established, but KR should be provided to show performance in relation to these goals. The "At Emery Air Freight" (1973), Komaki et al. (1978), Latham and Kinne (1974), and Latham and Baldes (1975) studies emphasize how inexpensive such goals-plus-KR programs can be in field settings relative to their benefits.

GOAL ACCEPTANCE, COMMITMENT, AND CHOICE

Goal acceptance and commitment are similar though distinguishable concepts. Goal commitment implies a determination to try for a goal (or to keep trying for a goal), but the source of the goal is not specified. It could be an assigned goal or a participatively set goal or a goal that one set on one's own. Goal acceptance implies that one has agreed to commit oneself to a goal assigned or suggested by another person. Both acceptance and commitment presumably can exist in varying degrees. Since most studies have used assigned goals, the two concepts can often be used interchangeably.

Most recent studies of goal setting have used goals as an independent variable. However, since it is assumed that assigned goals must be accepted before they will affect task performance, it is also relevant to examine the determinants of goal commitment or acceptance. Generally, attempts to measure degree of goal commitment in a manner that will differentiate between experimental treatments and/or relate to task performance have failed. None of the experimental conditions in the studies by Latham and Saari (1979a, 1979b), Latham et al. (1978), Yukl and Latham (1978), or Dossett et al.'s Study 1 (1979) affected self-report measures of goal acceptance. Dossett et al.'s (1979) Study 2 found an initial difference, with assigned goals showing greater acceptance than participatively set goals, a prediction contrary to expectations. However, this difference disappeared by the end of the experiment. Frost and Mahoney (1976), London & Oldham (1976), Mento et al. (1980, two studies), Oldham (1975), and Yukl & Latham (1978) found no relationship between measures of goal acceptance and performance. Organ (1977) found that goal acceptance correlated with performance within some of his assigned goal subgroups, but the pattern of correlations was uninterpretable theoretically.

There are several possible reasons for these negative results. First, the measures of goal acceptance (which consisted typically of direct, face-valid questions such as, "How committed are you to attaining the goal?") may not have been valid. Some evidence that the measures of goal acceptance may be at fault was obtained in a study by Hannan (1975) in the credit application evaluation task noted earlier. He measured goal acceptance not by a rating scale but by the degree of difference between the subject's external (i.e., assigned or participatively

agreed upon) goal and his or her personal goal (as determined from a questionnaire given after external goals were set). Hannan found that participation did lead to greater goal acceptance (though it had no main effect on performance) than assigning goals and that the effects of participation became progressively stronger as the difficulty of the external goal increased. The goal acceptance measure was related to one measure of performance. Hannan also found that personal goals predicted performance better than assigned goals, as did Mento et al. (1980). These findings suggest that indirect measures of goal acceptance may be more valid than direct measures.

Second, in most of the studies where acceptance was measured, nearly all subjects showed complete or substantial goal commitment; thus the range of scores was quite limited. Small differences on the scales typically used may not reflect genuine differences in psychological states.

Third, due to limitations in introspective ability, most (untrained) subjects may not be able to discriminate small differences in psychological commitment (see Nisbett & Wilson, 1977; but see also Lieberman, 1979, for a more sanguine view of the usefulness of introspection). Recall that in the studies by Latham et al. (1978) and Pritchard and Curtis (1973) described earlier, there appeared to be significant commitment effects for monetary incentives based on actual performance, but these were not reflected in the direct goal commitment questions.

The solution to the last two problems may be to modify the design of the typical goal-setting experiment. Designs that encourage a wide range of goal commitment, such as those with a choice of various possible goals, with commitment to each being measured after choice, may reduce the introspective burden and increase the variance of the answers on the commitment scale. Within-subject designs, which involve assigning different goals (under different conditions) to the same subjects at different times, might also make the commitment responses more accurate by providing a clearer frame of reference for the subject. In addition, when a subject is less than fully committed to a given goal, it is important to determine what other goals he or she is committed to. For example, a subject who is not fully committed to a moderately difficult goal could be trying for a harder goal, an easier goal, or no specific goal. Each alternative choice would have different implications for performance.

Different degrees of goal commitment might be induced by varying types or degrees of social influence (e.g., approval, disapproval). Such influences undoubtedly have profound effects on goal choice and commitment among certain individuals, but a detailed discussion of the social-psychological literature is outside the scope of this review.

Goal acceptance or commitment can be considered a form of choice (i.e., the choice between accepting or rejecting a goal that was assigned or set participatively). In this sense these studies tie in with the more traditional studies of what is called "level of aspiration," which allowed subjects to freely choose their own goals after each of a series of trials on a task (e.g., see Frank, 1941; Hilgard, 1958). The factors that affect goal acceptance and goal choice are basically the same. They fit easily into two major categories, which are the main components of expectancy theory (Vroom, 1964).

Expectations of Success

Other things being equal, individuals are more likely to accept or choose a given goal when they have high rather than low expectations of reaching it (Mento et al., 1980). Such expectations evidently stem from self-perceptions about ability on the task in question (Mento et al., 1980). Presumably these perceptions are inferences from past performance. Past performance has consistently been found to predict future goals (Cummings et al., 1971; Lopes, 1976; Wilsted & Hand, 1974; Ashworth & Mobley, Note 2). Individuals are more likely to become more confident and to set higher goals after success and to become less confident and to set lower goals after fail-

ure (Lewin, 1958), although failure may lead to higher goals in pressure situations (Forward & Zander, 1971; Zander, Forward, & Albert, 1969) or even due to self-induced pressure (Hilgard, 1958). Generalized self-confidence may also affect goal acceptance and choice.

Values

When the perceived value of attaining or trying for a goal is higher, the goal is more likely to be accepted than when the perceived value is low (Mento et al., 1980). The valued outcomes involved may range from intrinsic rewards like the pleasure of achievement to extrinsic rewards following performance, such as money, recognition, and promotion. Instrumentality in expectancy theory is the belief that goal acceptance or goal attainment will lead to value attainment. Theoretically, goal choice and goal acceptance should be predictable from the expectancies, values, and instrumentalities the subject holds with regard to the various choices (Dachler & Mobley, 1973).

This is clearly a maximization-of-satisfaction model, which is not without its critics (e.g., Locke, 1975). Nevertheless, treating expectancy theory concepts as factors that predict an individual's goal choices does suggest a way of integrating the expectancy and goal-setting literatures (Dachler & Mobley, 1973; Mento et al., 1980).

Although external factors such as rewards and pressures presumably affect the individual through their effects on expectancies, instrumentalities, and values, it is worth emphasizing *pressures* because they have played a major role in most of the goal-setting studies. For example, the typical laboratory goal-setting study simply involves asking the subject to try to reach a certain goal. The subject typically complies because of the demand characteristics of the experiment (probably reducible to beliefs regarding the value of extra credit and the desire to help the experimenter).

Similarly, in field settings subjects are typically asked to try for goals by their supervisor. The supervisor, of course, is in a position to reward or punish the employee; furthermore, employees know they are being paid to do what the organization asks them to do. Ronan, Latham, and Kinne (1973) found that goal setting among woods workers was only effective when the supervisor stayed on the job with the employees. The mere presence of the supervisor could be considered a form of pressure in this context. In the studies by Forward and Zander (1971) and Zander et al. (1969), competitive or community pressures led to setting goals that were unrealistically high.

Although pressure is something that social scientists generally have been against, Hall and Lawler (1971) argued that if used appropriately (e.g., by combining it with responsibility), it can facilitate both high commitment and high performance. Pressure, of course, also can be self-imposed as in the case of the Type A personality who appears to be a compulsive goal achiever (Friedman & Rosenman, 1974).

SUMMARY, CONCLUSIONS, AND DIRECTIONS FOR FUTURE RESEARCH

Based on the findings to date, the following conclusions about goal setting seem warranted:

1. The beneficial effect of goal setting on task performance is one of the most robust and replicable findings in the psychological literature. Ninety percent of the studies showed positive or partially positive effects. Furthermore, these effects are found just as reliably in field settings as in the laboratory.

2. There are at least four mechanisms by which goals affect task performance: by directing attention and action, mobilizing energy expenditure or effort, prolonging effort over time (persistence), and motivating the individual to develop relevant strategies for goal attainment. The latter two mechanisms are most in need of further study.

3. Goals are most likely to affect performance under the following conditions:

Range and Type of Goals. Individuals with specific and hard or challenging goals outperform individuals with specific easy goals, do-best goals, or no assigned goals. People with specific moderate goals show perfor-

mance levels between those of people with easy and hard goals but may not perform better than individuals with do-best goals. A common problem with easy-goal subjects is that their goals are so easy that once they are reached, they set new, higher goals to have something to do, which means that they are no longer genuine easy-goal subjects. Perhaps easy-goal subjects should be told not to try to exceed their goals or not to set new goals when the easy goals are reached.

The wider the range of goal difficulty, the more likely goal setting is to affect performance (cf., Frost & Mahoney, 1976, with Locke et al., 1978). It is probable that longer time spans will progressively increase the difference between subjects with hard goals and those without hard goals.

One aspect of goal setting that has not received much attention to date is the usefulness of setting intermediate goals or subgoals as an aid to attaining longer term or end goals. Locke and Bryan (1967) found that on a two-hour addition task, setting 15-minute subgoals led to slightly poorer performance than setting just end goals. Bandura and Simon (1977), however, found that setting weekly goals for weight loss only led to weight loss when daily goals (or multiple goals within days) were set as well. There is probably an optimal time span for the setting of goals depending on both the individual and the task situation. Subgoals could conceivably facilitate performance by operating as a feedback device; they might also serve to maintain effort over long time spans. On the negative side, they might limit performance if the subgoals were treated as performance ceilings. More studies are clearly needed on this topic.

Goal Specificity. Goals seem to regulate performance most predictably when they are expressed in specific quantitative terms (or as specific intentions to take a certain action, such as quitting a job) rather than as vague intentions to "try hard" or as subjective estimates of task or goal difficulty.

Ability. Individuals must have the ability to attain or at least approach their goals. (In complex tasks they must choose appropriate strategies, as noted previously.) Exerting more effort will not improve task performance if improvement is totally beyond the individual's capacity. Goal-setting studies should carefully control for ability (such as by a work sample pretest) to isolate the variance in performance due to goals from that due to ability. If ability is not controlled, it becomes error variance when testing for a motivation effect. The most practical way to set goals may be to base them on each individual's ability on the task in question as measured by a preexperimental work sample. This usually insures ready goal acceptance and makes it easy to control for ability when comparing different goals.

Knowledge of Results (Feedback). Knowledge of performance in relation to the goal appears to be necessary if goals are to improve performance, just as goals are necessary if feedback is to improve performance. Feedback is probably most helpful as an adjunct to goal setting when the task is divided into trials and feedback is provided after each one, although the ideal frequency is not known. Feedforward, telling the subjects how fast they will need to work on a future trial as compared with their speed on an immediately preceding trial may be a partial substitute in some cases (e.g., see Mento et al., 1980, Study 1). Knowledge and feedback, of course, may have purely cognitive (learning) effects on performance (see Locke et al., 1968, for a discussion of this issue), but these are not the concern of this review. Clearly more research is needed on feedback, especially research based on the issues raised by Ilgen et al. (1979), such as timing, frequency, source, interpretation, and so on.

Monetary Rewards. Money may be an effective method of improving performance in relation to a given goal (presumably through increased commitment), but the amounts involved must be large rather than small (e.g., three dollars rather than three cents in a typical laboratory experiment).

Further research on money and goal setting could be tied into Deci's work on intrinsic and extrinsic motivation. Deci and Porac (1978) suggested that money rewards that encourage

the attainment of competence on a task (reaching a challenging goal?) may enhance rather than decrease interest in the task.

Participation and Supportiveness. There is no consistent evidence that participation in setting goals leads to greater goal commitment or better task performance than assigned goals when goal level is controlled, though it sometimes leads to setting higher goals than the supervisor would have assigned. One study found that participation facilitated the acceptance of hard goals (Hannan, 1975).

Supportiveness may be more important than participation, although this concept needs to be defined more clearly. Latham and Saari (1979b) defined it as friendliness, listening to subjects' opinions about the goal, encouraging questions, and asking rather than telling the subject what to do. More exploration of the nature and effects of supportiveness in goal setting is clearly warranted.

Individual Differences. No reliable individual difference factors (other than ability) have emerged in the goal-setting literature, probably because most of the studies have used assigned goals. Thus, situational constraints have prevented personal styles and preferences from affecting performance. In free-choice situations individual personality traits may play a more substantial role. Subjects high in need for achievement should prefer to set moderate goals, whereas those low in this motive should be more likely to set easy or very hard goals. Individuals with high self-esteem should be more likely to accept and try for challenging goals than those with low self-esteem. However, it is not clear whether a generalized self-esteem measure would show as great an effect as a more task-specific measure of perceived competence. Mento et al. (1980; based on Motowidlo, 1976) found that self-perception of ability added unique variance to performance even when expectancy, valence, and goal level were controlled.

Goal Acceptance and Choice. A basic assumption of goal setting research is that the individual accepts (is actually trying for) the goal that was assigned or was set. Personal goals usually predict performance better than related measures such as assigned (or objective) goal difficulty or subjective goal difficulty. Direct measures of goal acceptance have been found to be generally unrelated to either experimental treatments or task performance. For example, rewards such as money may affect performance, with goal difficulty controlled, even though goal acceptance questions do not indicate increased commitment. Indirect measures, such as the difference between the personal and the assigned goal, show more promise. However, better experimental designs (e.g., within-subject designs and designs allowing free choice of goals) may show effects even using direct questions.

Goal choice and acceptance are influenced by numerous factors, including pressure, all of which may work through influencing the individual's expectancies, values, and perceived instrumentalities. Support on the part of higher management for goal-setting programs in organizations seems critical for their success, as is the case for most social science interventions (e.g., see Hinrichs, 1978; Ivancevich, 1974; Woodward, Koss, & Hatry, Note 6). In an organizational context support may include ensuring or securing the commitment of middle and lower managers. It is likely that the degree of continuing support for goal-setting programs will determine the duration of their effects. The Latham and Baldes (1975) study with truck drivers has continued to be successful for the past seven years (reported in Latham & Locke, 1979, Figure 1, Footnote b).

Other Issues. Not mentioned in the above discussion was how the type of task affects goal-setting effectiveness. Obviously, individuals must have some control over task pace, quality, method, and so on for goal setting, or any other motivational technique, to affect performance. We do not agree with those who claim that goal setting might work only on certain types of tasks. However, it will undoubtedly be the case that the four mechanisms noted earlier are differentially important in different tasks. For example, where more effort leads to immediate

results, goals may work as long as they lead the subject to work harder. On the other hand, where the task is complex, hard goals may only improve performance if they lead to effective strategies.

Regarding the relation of goals to rewards, an intriguing finding by Masters et al. (1977) was that children who were told to evaluate their performance after each trial block while speaking into a tape recorder (e.g., "I did very good [sic];" "I didn't do very good [sic]") all reached assymptote on the task regardless of their assigned goals. Self-reward ultimately vitiated what had been highly significant goal effects. This finding is clearly worthy of future study.

Competition in relation to goal setting also requires further study. Both Latham and Baldes (1975) and Komaki et al. (1978) found that goal setting plus feedback led to spontaneous competition among subjects. White et al. (1977) found that telling subjects that their performance would be compared to that of others ("evaluation apprehension," in their terminology) had a powerful effect on task performance independent of a separate goal manipulation. However, spontaneous goal setting within the evaluation apprehension condition was not measured. It is likely that competition could lead people to set higher goals than they would otherwise (other people's performances become the goals) and/or lead to greater goal commitment (Locke, 1968).

Another issue that has not been investigated is whether hard goals combined with high pressure might lead to a conflict situation and therefore high anxiety. It has been shown that anxiety disrupts performance on complex tasks when it leads subjects to worry rather than concentrate on the task (Wine, 1971). As noted earlier, conflicts may also occur among different goals, although this has not been studied. Conflicting pressures in goal setting may vitiate the usual goal-performance relationship (Forward & Zander, 1971). Nor has the issue of individual versus group goal setting received much attention. (Group goals are discussed in Zander, 1971.)

A final note is in order with respect to the

practical significance of the technique of goal setting. In a review of all available experimental field studies of goal setting, Locke et al. (1980) found that the median improvement in performance (e.g., productivity, quality) that resulted from goal setting was 16 percent. In one company the use of goal setting on just one job saved a company $250,000 (Latham & Baldes, 1975). Combined with the use of monetary incentives, Locke et al. (1980) found that goal setting improved performance by a median of more than 40 percent—a finding of great practical significance.

A model for the use of goal setting in field settings has been developed by Latham and Locke (1979). White and Locke (in press) have documented the high frequency with which goals actually regulate productivity in business settings. Locke (1978) has argued that goal setting is recognized explicitly or implicitly in virtually every theory of and approach to work motivation.

Leadership

Historically, most research on leadership has been limited to a concern for the effect of a leader's behavior on a follower's behavior. This suggests that leadership is little more than applied motivation theory. A broader view of leadership suggests a more complex problem —the reciprocal effect that leaders and followers have on each other. Currently, leadership research and theory are in disarray and there is no one compelling paradigm or theory. Research is haphazard and often unimaginative. The dichotomy between unidirectional theories (i.e., the effect of leaders on followers) and reciprocal theories remains quite clear. In this section, readings related to both approaches will be presented. There seems little doubt that the psychologist should be interested in the reciprocal effects. On the other hand, there is much to be gained in the reciprocal approach from understanding some of the propositions of the unidirectional approach and incorporating the most compelling of them. Leadership will remain one of the most substantial untapped resources in organizational performance. As you read the following articles, try to identify the strong points of each approach that you might combine to form your own theory of leadership.

In the unidirectional school of leadership research, there have really only been two approaches that have received more than limited attention. The first was developed by researchers at Ohio State University in the 50s and emphasized certain leader traits, such as a concern for the well-being of subordinates or a concern for structure and predictability on the work group. The second approach was popularized by Fiedler and was the driving force in leadership research from the mid-1960s to the mid-1970s. It was known as contingency theory because it proposed that the "best" leadership style depended (or was contingent) on the particular situation in which the leader found herself. In this reading, Fiedler describes his contingency approach and proposes a method for creating a better match between the leader and the situation.

Consider the possibility that you have just been appointed a leader of a student group that has been through several months of internal dispute. Consider further that you have no more expertise than anyone else in the group and that it is not clear what the group should attempt to accomplish in the next year. What type of leadership style should you adopt? Fiedler provides a blueprint for choosing the style in this situation.

■ READING 22 ■

Engineer the Job to Fit the Manager

Fred E. Fiedler

What kind of leadership style does business need? Should company executives be decisive, directive, willing to give orders, and eager to assume responsibility? Should they be human relations-oriented, nondirective, willing to share leadership with the men in their group? Or should we perhaps start paying attention to the more important problem of defining under what conditions each of these leadership styles works best and what to do about it?

The success or failure of an organization depends on the quality of its management. How to get the best possible management is a question of vital importance; but it is perhaps even more important to ask how we can make better use of the management talent which *we already have.*

To get good business executives we have relied primarily on recruitment, selection, and training. It is time for businessmen to ask whether this is the only way or the best way for

getting the best possible management. Fitting the man to the leadership job by selection and training has not been spectacularly successful. It is surely easier to change almost anything in the job situation than a man's personality and his leadership style. Why not try, then, to fit the leadership job to the man?

Executive jobs are surprisingly pliable, and the executive manpower pool is becoming increasingly small. The luxury of picking a "natural leader" from among a number of equally promising or equally qualified specialists is rapidly fading into the past. Business must learn how to utilize the available executive talent as effectively as it now utilizes physical plant and machine tools. Your financial expert, your top research scientist, or your production genius may be practically irreplaceable. Their jobs call for positions of leadership and responsibility. Replacements for these men can be neither recruited nor trained overnight, and they may not be willing to play second fiddle in their departments. If their leadership style does not fit the job, *we must learn how to engineer the job to fit their leadership style.*

Source: Reprinted by permission of the *Harvard Business Review*, 43(5), 1965. Copyright © 1965 by the President and Fellows of Harvard College; all rights reserved.

231

In this article I shall describe some studies that illuminate this task of job engineering and adaptation. It will be seen that there are situations where the authoritarian, highly directive leader works best, and other situations where the egalitarian, more permissive, human relations-oriented leader works best; but almost always there are possibilities for changing the situation around somewhat to match the needs of the particular managers who happen to be available. The executive who appreciates these differences and possibilities has knowledge that can be valuable to him in running his organization.

To understand the problems that a new approach would involve, let us look first at some of the basic issues in organizational and group leadership.

STYLES OF LEADERSHIP

Leadership is a personal relationship in which one person directs, coordinates, and supervises others in the performance of a common task. This is especially so in "interacting groups," where men must work together cooperatively in achieving organizational goals.

In oversimplified terms, it can be said that the leader manages the group in either of two ways. He can tell people what to do and how to do it, or share his leadership responsibilities with his group members and involve them in the planning and execution of the task.

There are, of course, all shades of leadership styles in between these two polar positions, but the basic issue is this: the work of motivating and coordinating group members has to be done either by brandishing the proverbial stick or by dangling the equally proverbial carrot. The former is the more orthodox job-centered, autocratic style. The latter is the more nondirective, group-centered procedure.

Research evidence exists to support both approaches to leadership. Which, then, should be judged more appropriate? On the face of it, the first style of leadership is best under some conditions, while the second works better under others. Accepting this proposition immediately opens two avenues of approach. Management can determine the specific situation in which the directive or the nondirective leadership style works best, and then select or train men so that their leadership style fits the particular job, or determine the type of leadership style which is most natural for the man in the executive position, and then change the job to fit the man.

The first alternative has been discussed many times before; the second has not. We have never seriously considered whether it would be easier to fit the executive's job to the man.

NEEDED STYLE?

How might this be done? Some answers have been suggested by a research program on leadership effectiveness that I have directed under Office of Naval Research auspices since 1951. This program has dealt with a wide variety of different groups, including basketball teams, surveying parties, various military combat crews, and men in open-hearth steel shops, as well as members of management and boards of directors. When possible, performance was measured in terms of objective criteria—for instance, percentage of games won by high school basketball teams; tap-to-tap time of open-hearth shops (roughly equivalent to the tonnage of steel output per unit of time); and company net income over a three-year period. Our measure of leadership style was based on a simple scale indicating the degree to which a man described, favorably or unfavorably, his least-preferred co-worker (LPC). This co-worker did not need to be someone he actually worked with at the time, but could be someone the respondent had known in the past. Whenever possible, the score was obtained before the leader was assigned to his group.

The study indicates that a person who describes his least-preferred co-worker in a relatively favorable manner tends to be permissive, human relations-oriented, and considerate of the feelings of his men. But a person who describes his least-preferred co-worker in an unfavorable manner—who has what we have come to call a low LPC rating—tends to be managing, task-controlling, and less concerned with the human relations aspects of the job. It also appears that the directive, managing, and controlling leaders tend to perform best in basketball and surveying teams, in open-hearth shops, and (provided the leader is accepted by his group) in military combat crews and company managements. On the other hand, the nondirective, permissive, and human relations-oriented leaders tend to perform best in decision- and policy-making teams and in groups that have a creative task—provided that the group likes the leader or the leader feels that the group is pleasant and free of tension.

Critical Dimensions

But in order to tell which style fits which situation, we need to categorize groups. Our research has shown that "it all depends" on the situation. After reviewing the results of all our work and the findings of other investigators, we have been able to isolate three major dimensions that seem to determine, to a large part, the kind of leadership style called for by different situations.

It is obviously a mistake to think that groups and teams are all alike and that each requires the same kind of leadership. We need some way of categorizing the group-task situation, or the job environment within which the leader has to operate. If leadership is indeed a process of influencing other people to work together effectively in a common task, then it surely matters how easy or difficult it is for the leader to exert his influence in a particular situation.

Leader-Member Relations. The factor that would seem most important in determining a man's leadership influence is the degree to which his group members trust and like him, and are willing to follow his guidance. The trusted and well-liked leader obviously does not require special rank or power in order to get things done. We can measure the

leader-member relationship by the so-called sociometric nomination techniques that ask group members to name in their group the most influential person, or the man they would most like to have as a leader. It can also be measured by a group-atmosphere scale indicating the degree to which the leader feels accepted and comfortable in the group.

The Task Structure. The second important factor is the "task structure." By this term I mean the degree to which the task (*a*) is spelled out step by step for the group and, if so, the extent to which it can be done "by the numbers" or according to a detailed set of standard operating instructions, or (*b*) must be left nebulous and undefined. Vague and ambiguous or unstructured tasks make it difficult to exert leadership influence, because neither the leader nor his members know exactly what has to be done or how it is to be accomplished.

Why single out this aspect of the task rather than the innumerable other possible ways of describing it? Task groups are almost invariably components of a larger organization that assigns the task and has, therefore, a big stake in seeing it performed properly. However, the organization can control the quality of a group's performance only if the task is clearly spelled out and programmed or structured. When the task can be programmed or performed "by the numbers," the organization is able to back up the authority of the leader to the fullest; the man who fails to perform each step can be disciplined or fired. But in the case of ill-defined, vague, or unstructured tasks, the organization and the leader have very little control and direct power. By close supervision one can ensure, let us say, that a man will correctly operate a machine, but one cannot ensure that he will be creative.

It is therefore easier to be a leader in a structured task situation in which the work is spelled out than in an unstructured one which presents the leader and his group with a nebulous, poorly defined problem.

Position Power. Thirdly, there is the power of the leadership position, as distinct from any personal power the leader might

EXHIBIT 1   A Model for Classifying Group-Task Situations

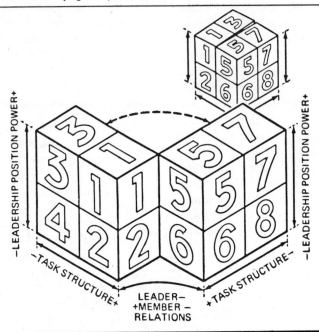

have. Can he hire or fire and promote or demote? Is his appointment for life, or will it terminate at the pleasure of his group? It is obviously easier to be a leader when the position power is strong than when it is weak.

Model for Analysis

When we now classify groups on the basis of these three dimensions, we get a classification system that can be represented as a cube; see Exhibit 1. As each group is high or low in each of the three dimensions, it will fall into one of the eight cells.

From examination of the cube, it seems clear that exerting leadership influence will be easier in a group in which the members like a powerful leader with a clearly defined job and where the job to be done is clearly laid out (Cell 1); it will be difficult in a group where a leader is disliked, has little power, and has a highly ambiguous job (Cell 8).

In other words, it is easier to be the well-esteemed foreman of a construction crew working from a blueprint than it is to be the dis-

liked chairman of a volunteer committee preparing a new policy.

I consider the leader-member relations the most important dimension, and the position-power dimension the least important, of the three. It is, for instance, quite possible for a man of low rank to lead a group of higher-ranking men in a structured task—as is done when enlisted men or junior officers conduct some standardized parts of the training programs for medical officers who enter the Army. But it is not so easy for a disrespected manager to lead a creative, policy-formulating session well, even if he is the senior executive present.

Varying Requirements

By first sorting the eight cells according to leader-member relations, then task structure, and finally leader position power, we can now arrange them in order according to the favorableness of the environment for the leader. This sorting leads to an eight-step scale, as in Exhibit 2. This exhibit portrays the results of a

EXHIBIT 2 How the Style of Effective Leadership Varies with the Situation

LEADER-MEMBER RELATIONS	GOOD	GOOD	GOOD	GOOD	POOR	POOR	POOR	POOR
TASK STRUCTURE	STRUCTURED		UNSTRUCTURED		STRUCTURED		UNSTRUCTURED	
LEADER POSITION POWER	STRONG	WEAK	STRONG	WEAK	STRONG	WEAK	STRONG	WEAK

series of studies of groups performing well but (*a*) in different situations and conditions, and (*b*) with leaders using different leadership styles. In explanation:

The *horizontal* axis shows the range of situations that the groups worked in, as described by the classification scheme used in Exhibit 1.

The *vertical* axis indicates the leadership style which was best in a certain situation, as shown by the correlation coefficient between the leader's LPC and his group's performance.

A positive correlation (falling above the midline) shows that the permissive, nondirective, and human relations-oriented leaders performed best; a negative correlation (below the midline) shows that the task-controlling, managing leader performed best. For instance, leaders of effective groups in situation categories 1 and 2 had LPC-group performance correlations of − .40 to − .80, with the average between − .50 and − .60; whereas leaders of effective groups in situation categories 4 and 5 had LPC-group performance correlations of .20 to .80, with the average between .40 and .50.

Exhibit 2 shows that both the directive, managing, task-oriented leaders and the non-directive, human relations-oriented leaders are successful under some conditions. Which leadership style is the best depends on the favorableness of the particular situation for the leader. In very favorable or in very unfavorable situations for getting a task accomplished by group effort, the autocratic, task-controlling, managing leadership works best. In situations intermediate in difficulty, the nondirective, permissive leader is more successful.

This corresponds well with our everyday experience. For instance:

Where the situation is very favorable, the group expects and wants the leader to give directions. We neither expect nor want the trusted airline pilot to turn to his crew and ask, "What do you think we ought to check before takeoff?"

If the disliked chairman of a volunteer committee asks his group what to do, he may be told that everybody ought to go home.

The well-liked chairman of a planning group or research team must be nondirective and permissive in order to get full participation from his members.

The directive, managing leader will tend to be more critical and to cut discussion short; hence he will not get the full benefit of the potential contributions by his group members.

The varying requirements of leadership styles are readily apparent in organizations experiencing dramatic changes in operating procedures. For example:

The manager or supervisor of a routinely operating organization is expected to provide direction and supervision that the subordinates should follow. However, in a crisis the routine is no longer adequate, and the task becomes ambiguous and unstructured. The typical manager tends to respond in such instances by calling his principal assistants together for a conference. In other words, the effective leader changes his behavior from a directive to a permissive, nondirective style until the operation again reverts to routine conditions.

In the case of a research planning group, the human relations-oriented and permissive leader provides a climate in which everybody is free to speak up, to suggest, and to criticize. Osborn's brainstorming method in fact institutionalizes these procedures. However, after the research plan has been completed, the situation becomes highly structured. The director now prescribes the task in detail, and he specifies the means of accomplishing it. Woe betide the assistant who decides to be creative by changing the research instructions!

Practical Tests

Remember that the ideas I have been describing emanate from studies of real-life situations; accordingly, as might be expected, they can be validated by organizational experience. Take, for instance, the dimension of leader-member relations described earlier. We have made three studies of situations in which the leader's position power was strong and the task relatively structured with clear-cut goals and standard operating procedures. In such groups as these the situation will be very favorable for the leader if he is accepted; it will be progressively unfavorable in proportion to how much

EXHIBIT 3   How Effective Leadership Styles Vary Depending on Group Acceptance

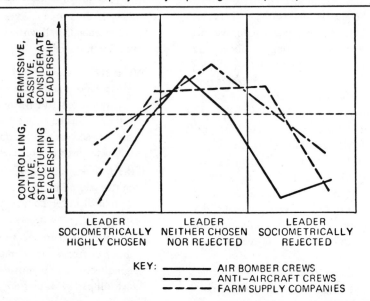

a leader is disliked. What leadership styles succeed in these varying conditions? The studies confirm what our theory would lead us to expect:

The first set of data comes from a study of B-29 bomber crews in which the criterion was the accuracy of radar bombing. Six degrees of leader-member relations were identified, ranging from those in which the aircraft commander was the first choice of crew members and highly endorsed his radar observer and navigator (the key men in radar bombing), to those in which he was chosen by his crew but did not endorse his key men, and finally to crews in which the commander was rejected by his crew and rejected his key crew members. What leadership styles were effective? The results are plotted in Exhibit 3.

A study of anti-aircraft crews compares the 10 most chosen crew commanders, the 10 most rejected ones, and 10 of intermediate popularity. The criterion is the identification and "acquisition" of unidentified aircraft by the crew. The results shown in Exhibit 3 are similar to those for bomber crew commanders.

Exhibit 3 also summarized data for 32 small-farm supply companies. These were member companies of the same distribution system, each with its own board of directors and its own management. The performance of these highly comparable companies was measured in terms of percentage of company net income over a three-year period. The first quarter of the line (going from left to right) depicts endorsement of the general manager by his board of directors and his staff of assistant managers; the second quarter, endorsement by his board but not his staff; the third quarter, endorsement by his staff but not his board; the fourth quarter, endorsement by neither.

As can be seen from the results of all three studies, the highly accepted and strongly re-

jected leaders perform best if they are controlling and managing, while the leaders in the intermediate acceptance range, who are neither rejected nor accepted, perform best if they are permissive and nondirective.

Now let us look at some research on organizations in another country. Recently in Belgium a study was made of groups of mixed language and cultural composition. Such teams, which are becoming increasingly frequent as international business and governmental activities multiply, obviously present a difficult situation for the leader. He must not only deal with men who do not fully comprehend one another's language and meanings, but also cope with the typical antipathies, suspicions, and antagonisms dividing individuals of different cultures and nationalities.

At a Belgian naval training center we tested 96 three-man groups, half of which were homogeneous in composition (all Flemish or all Walloon) and half heterogeneous (the leader differing from his men). Half of each of these had powerful leader positions (petty officers), and half had recruit leaders. Each group performed three tasks: one unstructured task (writing a recruiting letter); and two parallel structured tasks (finding the shortest route for ships through 10 ports, and doing the same for 12 ports). After each task, leaders and group members described their reactions—including group-atmosphere ratings and the indication of leader-member relations.

The various task situations were then arranged in order, according to their favorableness for the leader. The most favorable situation was a homogeneous group, led by a well-liked and accepted petty officer, which worked on the structured task of routing a ship. The situation would be especially favorable toward the end of the experiment, after the leader had had time to get to know his members. The least favorable situation was that of an unpopular recruit leader of a heterogeneous group where the relatively unstructured task of writing a letter came up as soon as the group was formed.

There were six groups that fell into each of these situations or cells. A correlation was then

EXHIBIT 4   Effective Leadership Styles at the Belgian Naval Training Center

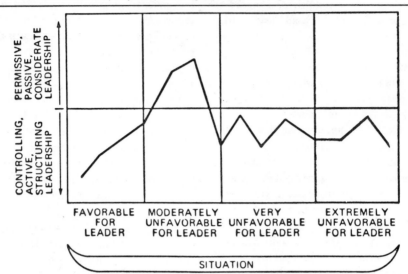

computed for each set of six groups to determine which type of leadership style led to best team performance. The results, indicated in Exhibit 4, support the conclusions earlier described.

Of particular interest is the fact that the difficult heterogeneous groups generally required controlling, task-oriented leadership for good performance. This fits the descriptions of successful leader behavior obtained from executives who have worked in international business organizations.

CONCLUSION

Provided our findings continue to be supported in the future, what do these results and the theory mean for executive selection and training? What implications do they have for the management of large organizations?

Selection and Training

Business and industry are now trying to attract an increasingly large share of exceptionally intelligent and technically well-trained men. Many of these are specialists whose talents are in critically short supply. Can industry really afford to select only those men who have

a certain style of leadership in addition to their technical qualifications? The answer is likely to be negative, at least in the near future.

This being the case, can we then train the men selected in one leadership style or the other? This approach is always offered as a solution, and it does have merit. But we must recognize that training people is at best difficult, costly, and time-consuming. It is certainly easier to place people in a situation compatible with their natural leadership style than to force them to adapt to the demands of the job.

As another alternative, should executives learn to recognize or diagnose group-task situations so that they can place their subordinates, managers, and department heads in the jobs best suited to their leadership styles? Even this procedure has serious disadvantages. The organization may not always happen to have the place that fits the bright young man. The experienced executive may not want to be moved, or it may not be possible to transfer him.

Should the organization try to "engineer" the job to fit the man? This alternative is potentially the most feasible for management. As has been shown already, the type of leadership called for depends on the favorableness of the situation. The favorableness, in turn, is a product of several factors. These include leader-member relations, the homogeneity of the group, and the position power and degree to which the task is structured, as well as other, more obvious factors such as the leader's knowledge of his group, his familiarity with the task, and so forth.

It is clear that management can change the characteristic favorableness of the leadership situation; it can do so in most cases more easily than it can transfer the subordinate leader from one job to another or train him in a different style of interacting with his members.

Possibilities of Change

Although this type of organizational engineering has not been done systematically up to now, we can choose from several good possibilities for getting the job done:

1. *We can change the leader's position power.* We can either give him subordinates of equal or nearly equal rank or we can give him men who are two or three ranks below him. We can either give him sole authority for the job or require that he consult with this group, or even obtain unanimous consent for all decisions. We can either punctiliously observe the channels of the organization to increase the leader's prestige or communicate directly with the men of his group as well as with him in person.

2. *We can change the task structure.* The tasks given to one leader may have to be clarified in detail, and he may have to be given precise operating instructions; another leader may have to be given more general problems that are only vaguely elucidated.

3. *We can change the leader-member relations.* The Belgian study, referred to earlier, demonstrates that changing the group composition changes the leader's relations with his men. We can increase or decrease the group's heterogeneity by introducing men with similar attitudes, beliefs, and backgrounds, or by bringing in men different in training, culture, and language.

The foregoing are, of course, only examples of what could be done. The important point is that we now have a model and a set of principles that permit predictions of leadership effectiveness in interacting groups and allow us to take a look at the factors affecting team performance. This approach goes beyond the traditional notions of selection and training. It focuses on the more fruitful possibility of organizational engineering as a means of using leadership potentials in the management ranks.

In contrast to the trait theories (such as the one from Ohio State) or contingency theories such as Fiedler's, some researchers have emphasized the reciprocal nature of the leader-follower relationship. The basic proposition is that a follower's behavior affects the leader's behavior. The behavior of that leader, in turn affects the subsequent behavior of the follower. One version of this reciprocal approach is known as the vertical dyad linkage (VDL) model. This is an overly complex term for a relatively simple concept. Leaders are usually higher on the organization chart than followers—thus the characterization of vertical. *Any given leader has a specific relationship with each and every follower—thus the term* dyad *(a two-person group). Finally, the theory proposes that the behavior of each member of the dyad affects the other—thus the term* linkage. *In this reading, Graen and Schiemann describe the basic reciprocal model and present some data that support it.*

■ READING 23 ■

Leader–Member Agreement: A Vertical Dyad Linkage Approach

George Graen, *University of Cincinnati*
William Schiemann, *Georgia Institute of Technology*

The purpose of this investigation was to test a hypothesis derived from the vertical dyad linkage model of leadership development. Briefly, this model describes the processes by which a leader and a member develop various behavioral interdependencies between their respective roles. These interdependencies have been found to vary in quality from something approaching a "partnership" (i.e., reciprocal influence, extra-contractual behavior exchange, mutual trust, respect and liking, and common fate) at the high pole to something approaching an "overseer" (i.e., unidirectional downward influence, only contractual behavior exchange, role-defined relations, and loosely coupled fates) at the low pole (Cashman &

Graen, in press; Dansereau, Graen, & Haga, 1975; Graen, 1976).

The general hypothesis of interest in this study is that the agreement between a leader and a member regarding the meaning of certain mutually experienced events and situations will covary with the quality of their dyadic interdependencies. According to this hypothesis, dyads with higher quality interdependencies will demonstrate higher agreement than dyads with lower quality interdependencies.

On what dimensions might we look for these differences? One important dimension should be members' job problems. If a leader and a member have a high-quality dyadic relationship, the leader should be more aware of the problems confronting the member on the job. Hence, their perceptions should be more alike regarding the severity of job problems

Source: *Journal of Applied Psychology*, 63(2), 1978, pp. 206–212. Copyright 1978 by the American Psychological Association. Reprinted by permission of the publisher and author.

than those of a leader and a member in a low-quality relationship. Another important set of variables suggested by the model is that describing the relationship itself. Such variables include sensitivity of the leader to the member's job and attention, information, and support given the member by the leader. Despite the subjectivity of these relational variables, if the quality of the interdependencies is high, leader and member should agree more accurately about these variables than those locked into lower quality relationships.

Previous attempts to document leader–member agreement have produced results suggesting that such agreement is seldom achieved (Graham & Oleno, 1970; Heller, 1971; Parker, Taylor, Barrett, & Martins, 1959; Templer, 1973; Thornton, 1968; Tucker, Cline, & Schmitt, 1967). However, all of these studies failed to use a dyadic approach to the problem but relied instead upon unit or work groups approaches (Graen, Dansereau, & Minami, 1972). To the extent that leadership is based within the dyad and to the extent that vertical dyads typically vary in quality with organizational units or work groups (assumptions of the vertical dyad linkage model), the procedures of an average leadership approach (averaging across vertical dyads within units) may effectively disguise high leader–member agreement at the dyadic level. Moreover, the vertical dyad linkage model of leader–member exchange hypothesizes that the higher the quality of the exchange, the greater will be the vertical dyad linkage agreement.

Hence, our basic concern centers on the validity of this proposition. Do high-quality dyads actually produce greater agreement on the dimensions predicted by the model? Second, can we measure this agreement? Third, what measure is more appropriate?

METHOD

Sample and Settings

Two independent samples were employed to develop and test the measure of leader–mem-

ber agreement. The first sample was composed of three semi-autonomous service departments of a large midwestern university, and the second was composed of three service departments of a medium-sized university in the southcentral United States. Within each of the three departments from the midwestern university, the entire managerial staff, from department head to first-level supervisor, was included in the study. In contrast, within the university in the southcentral United States such an exhaustive sampling was not feasible even though major portions of two departments were included. For purposes of this study, the 109 managerial dyads from the midwestern university were designated the initial sample and the 41 managerial dyads from the university in the southcentral United States were designated the check sample. Each sample was assessed at three-month intervals for three consecutive periods. The initial sample was assessed under the direction of the authors and its data were analyzed first. In contrast, the check sample was assessed under the direction of Tom Johnson at a distant location and was analyzed to check on the generality of the findings from the initial sample.

Instruments

Three different sets of instruments were employed in this study: (a) quality of leader–member exchange assessed via judgments of the members, not the leaders, (b) severity of member's job problems based on judgments of members and leaders, and (c) various relational measures of aspects of the dyad also based on judgments of members and leaders. All of these three sets of instruments were used to collect data from participants at three points in time during the course of one year.

Leader–Member Exchange Measure. This measure was originally developed by Dansereau et al. (1975), and extended and validated by Graen and Cashman (1975). The refined measures of this construct have been shown to be internally consistent (Kuder-Richardson-20 estimates at three successive quarterly intervals of .76, .80, and .84) and stable (Heise test-retest, stability coefficients of .90, .89, and .80 between first and second quarter, second and third quarter, and first and third quarter, respectively, and .91 true reliability) on a sample of 109 managerial dyads. In addition, multimethod, multisource analysis revealed that leader and member estimates showed reliable convergent validity both within two different assessment methods as well as between the two different methods (Graen & Cashman, 1975). Furthermore, this analysis demonstrated that peers of members (horizontal dyads) showed reliable agreement with both leader and member estimates regarding the quality of leader–member exchange. Based on these validation results, it appeared that approximately 25 percent of the dyads were of low quality (out exchanges), 25 percent were of high quality (in exchanges), and the remaining 50 percent were of medium quality (middle exchanges). Hence, for purposes of comparison, dyadic exchange was trichotomized into three distinct exchange groups based upon the above results. The items in this measure as judged by members are presented in Exhibit 1, which follows. Member rather than leader scores were used in this analysis to index leader–member exchange quality.

Severity of Member's Job Problems. This set of instruments was developed originally by Dansereau et al. (1975). In a later pilot study, problem issues from the Dansereau et al. study were tested and several modifications were made for the present study. These instruments assess the degree of severity of 21 separate problems for a member. Within a patterned interview, the participant is asked to consider the severity of each problem as an obstacle confronting his or her effective performance and to estimate its severity in terms of whether it is "not a problem," "a minor problem," "somewhat of a problem," or "a major obstacle." The 21 potential problems are shown in Exhibit 2, which follows. At each of the three points in time, severity estimates were collected from each member (regarding the member's particular situation) by one interviewer and from each leader (concerning each particular member) by a different interviewer. In no case did the same interviewer collect information from both parties to a dyad.

Relational Measures. These measures were used to collect perceptual judgments regarding such issues as the interpersonal sensitivities of the leader to the member, the job needs of the member, and the supervisory treatment of the member. All of these sets of

---

EXHIBIT 1   Leader–Member Exchange Quality

1. How flexible do you believe your supervisor is about evolving change in your job duties and responsibilities?
2. Regardless of how much formal organizational authority your supervisor has built into his position, what are the chances that he would be personally inclined to use his power to help you solve a problem in your work?
3. How often do you take your suggestions regarding your work to your supervisor?
4. To what extent can you count on your supervisor to "bail you out" at his expense when you really need him?

EXHIBIT 2   Job Problems

1. Not enough authority to do my job right.
2. Bureaucratic red tape, delays, etc.
3. Lack of managerial competence within the department.
4. Job leaves no time for personal life.
5. Budget limits.
6. Civil service rules.
7. Lack of upward mobility within the department.
8. Lack of consensus among my colleagues.
9. Inadequate staff to get this job done right.
10. Resistance to change in the administration.
11. Breakdown in cooperation within the department.
12. Strains in my working relationship with supervisor.
13. Too many organizational layers stifle communication between top and bottom.
14. Resistance to change among my colleagues.
15. Lack of flexibility in organizational procedure.
16. Lack of evaluation of my job performance.
17. Unproductive, time-consuming meetings.
18. Personal backbiting among colleagues.
19. Inadequate physical facilities.
20. Unsure of what my supervisor wants me to do in this job.
21. Department is oriented to dealing with crisis; lack of planning.

measures were administered orally to both leaders and members. As was the case with problems, no interviewer collected information from both parties to a dyad. For each item, both leader and member were asked to estimate the same aspect but to do so from their respective positions. Sensitivity items inquired about the extent to which a leader was helpful with respect to the work situation as well as personally, the amount of performance feedback, job latitude, and the like. Job needs items asked about information, influence, and support given and received. A sample of the 32 exchange items used with leaders is shown in Exhibit 3, which follows:

EXHIBIT 3 Relational Measures

---

1. To what extent do you help him know what he should be doing in his job?

    a great deal   some   little   not at all

2. To what extent has he been able to define his job for himself?

    completely   somewhat   little   not at all

3. How often do you let him know what you expect from him?

    always   usually   seldom   never

4. Does he usually know how satisfied you are with what he does? (In your opinion, does he know where he stands with you?)

    always   usually   seldom   never

5. Within the present framework of his job, to what extent does he have the power necessary to bring about the changes which he would like?

    great deal   some   little   none

6. To what extent does the structure of your job allow you to help him make changes in his job . . . (regardless of whether you are personally for or against such change)?

    great deal   some   little   none

The details of the data collection procedure are contained in Graen and Cashman (1975).

Analysis

The analytical procedures employed to develop a measure of leader–member agreement included (a) item analysis to check on item-distribution characteristics, (b) internal consistency analysis to estimate the homogeneity of item grouping, (c) comparison of alternative discrepancy scoring procedures, (d) stability analysis of scales, (e) change analysis, (f) hypothesis testing, and finally (g) replication of a through f on the check sample. Two different methods of discrepancy scoring were explored. One method was that of "profile similarity" (d^2/N). This method produces a variable that is sensitive to both the pattern and the absolute level of differences between the two parties. Following this procedure, the score difference between leader and member on each of the 53 items is squared and the squared differences are summed and divided by the number of items. This method has received a good deal of study (Cronbach & Furby, 1970; Lord, 1956; Manning & DuBois, 1962) and has been found to contain a number of psychometric shortcomings. Agreeing with Hammer and Dachler (1975), we prefer and report on an alternative method of "pattern agreement" (person correlation). This procedure correlates leader and member scores across 53 items within time. Hence, a person correlation is computed for each vertical dyad. For the purpose of analysis of variance (Bock, 1963) of leader–member exchange (trichotomized) at Time 1, the pattern agreement correlations were converted to z scores using Fisher's z transformation and converted back into correlations after the means were calculated (Winer, 1962). This scoring procedure (zr) was used within each of the three time periods to test the agreement hypotheses.

The composition of the leader–member dyads within each sample was as follows: The 109 leader and 109 member positions in the initial sample were filled by 32 different leaders and 109 different members. The 41 leader and 41 member positions of the check sample were filled by 16 different leaders and 41 different members.

RESULTS

Item Analysis and Item Homogeneity

Item analysis showed that all items possessed adequate distributional characteristics. Alpha estimates of homogeneity (Winer,

1962) of leader–member discrepancies for all items together at each of three times were .96, .97, and .96 for Times 1, 2, and 3, respectively.

Stability

The Heise (1969) test–retest reliability estimates for pattern agreement on the initial sample were .89 (Time 1–2), .90 (Time 2–3), and .81 (Time 1–3). Therefore, high stability over time was indicated. Moreover, the overall reliability coefficient estimated from test–retest correlations (Heise, 1969) on the initial sample was .71 for pattern agreement. Turning to the check sample of 41 managerial dyads, the Heise test–retest reliability estimates for pattern agreement were .84 (Time 1–2), .73 (Time 1–3), and .61 (Time 2–3). These stabilities are reasonable both from a statistical point of view and in comparison to the initial sample. The overall reliability coefficient estimated from test–retest correlations (Heise, 1969) was .96 for pattern agreement.

Change over Time

Although the stability estimates allow for very little change over time, it is of interest to present the concurrent and lagged correlations between leader–member exchange and pattern agreement. Three sets of these correlations for the initial sample are shown in Table 1. The first set of correlations (dyadic level) was computed using the vertical dyad linkage model assumption of within-unit valid variance at the dyadic level, and hence leader–member exchange was based upon dyadic-level data. In contrast, the second and third sets of correlations were computed on the basis of the average leadership style model assumption of no within-unit valid variance at the dyadic level, and thus leader–member exchange was based upon unit-averaged data. In addition, the second and third sets differed in that the second set contained a number of units with only a single member, whereas the third set contained only units with four or more members. Between corresponding correlations of the first

TABLE 1   Correlations between Leader–Member Exchange and Pattern Agreement at Two Time Periods for the Initial Sample

	Pattern Agreement	
Leader–Member Exchange	Time 1	Time 3
Dyadic level ($n = 109$)		
Time 1	.52*	.55*
Time 3	.36*	.67*
Unit average ($n = 109$)		
Time 1	.38*	.42*
Time 3	.34*	.49*
Unit average ($n = 74$) (Size 4 or longer)		
Time 1	.24	.26
Time 3	.26	.30

Note. Concurrent correlations are underlined.
*$p \le .001$, two-tailed test.

and second sets, no statistically significant difference was demonstrated, though the predictive relationship for dyadic level accounted for 30 percent of the variance while that for unit average accounted for 18 percent. Finally, none of the correlations for units of Size 4 or larger reacher either an acceptable level of statistical or practical significance. Turning to the check sample, the corresponding three sets of correlations are shown in Table 2. As with the initial sample, none of the corresponding

TABLE 2   Correlations Between Leader–Member Exchange and Pattern Agreement at Two Time Periods for the Check Sample

	Pattern Agreement	
Leader–Member Exchange	Time 1	Time 3
Dyadic level ($n = 41$)		
Time 1	.63*	.64*
Time 2	.54*	.68*
Unit average ($n = 41$)		
Time 1	.47	.53*
Time 2	.47	.54*
Unit average ($n = 18$) (Size 4 or longer)		
Time 1	.55	.44
Time 2	.56	.53

Note. Concurrent correlations are underlined.
*$p \le .001$, two-tailed test.

correlations of the first and second sets revealed a statistically significant difference, though the predictive relationship of leader–member exchange at Time 1 and pattern agreement at Time 2 accounted for 41 percent and 28 percent of the variance for dyadic level and unit average, respectively. Also in agreement with the results of the initial sample, none of the correlations for units of Size 4 or larger reached an acceptable level of significance.

Hypothesis Testing

It was hypothesized that the order of pattern agreement means would be out exchange, middle exchange, and in exchange from lowest

FIGURE 1 Patterns of Leader–Member Agreement Means

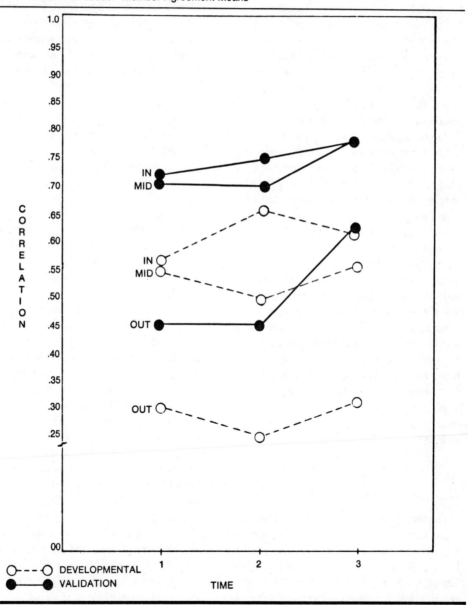

to highest agreement. Converting the standardized (zr_p) pattern agreement means back into mean correlations and plotting the correlations of these means by sample (initial and check), by dyadic leader–member exchange (out, middle, and in), and by time (first quarter, second quarter, third quarter) produced the trends shown in Figure 1. As this figure shows, the initial sample demonstrated moderate overall agreement at Times 1, 2, and 3. Overall, the check sample showed statistically ($p < .001$) higher agreement than that shown by the initial sample. The pattern of means was as hypothesized, and Neuman-Keuls tests revealed that both in-groups and middle groups were significantly different from the out-group but were not different from each other. This last set of findings applied to both samples at all three time periods.

In the weighted-means analysis of variance that was run on this design, each sample was equally weighted, and leader-member exchange was weighted proportionally for each sample. Results showed significant main effects for sample ($p < .001$), leader–member exchange ($p < .001$), and time ($p < .001$). Neither the Sample × Leader–Member Exchange, nor the Leader–Member Exchange × Time, nor the three-way interaction was significant, but the Sample × Time interaction was significant ($p < .001$). Sample estimates of strength of contribution, eta-squared (Hays, 1963), were 20 percent for sample, 21 percent for leader–member exchange, 3 percent for time, 1 percent for sample and time, 1 percent for sample and leader–member exchange, 1 percent for leader–member exchange and time, and 1 percent for the three-way interaction.

DISCUSSION

The literature on leader–member agreement shows that high dyadic agreement is not common (Graham & Oleno, 1970; Heller, 1971; Parker, Taylor, Barrett, & Martins, 1959; Templer, 1973; Thornton, 1968; Tucker et al., 1967). What distinguishes these earlier attempts from the present investigation? Typically, these earlier attempts employed the average leadership style approach, which assumes that the linkages between a leader and each of the members are homogeneous (can be treated as the same) and thus can be appropriately averaged. Moreover, these studies employed procedures of data collection, design, and analysis that were appropriate to this approach.

In contrast, the present investigation employed the vertical dyad linkage model, which assumes that the linkages between a leader and each of the members within a unit are potentially heterogeneous and hence cannot be appropriately averaged. Rather, the vertical dyad must be treated as the unit of analysis and the unit of leadership. In the present setting, organizational units were found to differ on the basis of the composition of different types of vertical dyads. Furthermore, leader–member agreement, according to this model, is predicted to vary as a function of the exchange quality of the vertical dyad linkage. Those members establishing high-quality exchanges with their leaders (in-group exchanges) can be expected to show higher agreement with their leaders than those who develop low-quality exchanges (out-group exchanges), and those who establish medium quality exchanges (middle-group exchanges) can be expected to show agreement with their leader that is between the in- and out-groups. Also according to the model, leader–member agreement is an outcome of functioning within the vertical dyad. Consequently, leaders acquire more accurate information about their in-group than their out-group members partially as a by-product of their interactions on task-relevant activities.

The strong relationships between leader–member exchange and agreement are compatible with the vertical dyad linkage model. Correlations of this magnitude for both the initial and the check samples clearly suggest the utility of this approach. However, the validity of the predictions from the model depend not only on the validity of the model but also on the appropriateness of the empirical procedures employed to test these predictions.

This study has demonstrated that leader–member agreement can be studied by employing the vertical dyad linkage model and the empirical procedures appropriate to it. The failure of previous research to produce these results may be attributable, at least in part, to the use of the average leadership style approach. Once again, the utility of approaching a leadership phenomenon by acknowledging the system in which it is embedded has been demonstrated.

In conclusion, results of our attempt to develop and test a measure of leader–member agreement were gratifying. Although the process is not by any means completed, we are confident that we have an emerging, psychometrically sound measure for indexing agreement within at least the managerial dyads of the types investigated. Obviously, further work is needed to refine, test, and understand the nomological network containing dyadic agreement. We encourage other researchers to employ this measure whenever reasonable.

Reciprocal theories of leadership are clearly more complex than the unidirectional theories. Nevertheless, when it comes to explaining why or how followers' behaviors affect leaders' behaviors, these theories are less informative. Mitchell and Wood offer a suggestion: Leaders make inferences about why followers are behaving in a particular way. Sometimes the leader assumes that follower performance is the result of internal forces such as follower motivation. Sometimes the leader assumes that the follower behavior is the result of outside forces such as the difficulty of the task or simply luck. In social psychology, the attempt by one person to explain why another person performed in a particular way (e.g., performed effectively or ineffectively) is called an attribution, *a guess about the causes for behavior. In this reading, Mitchell and Wood explore the mechanism of attribution in an attempt to explain how and why follower behavior affects leader behavior.*

■ READING 24 ■

Supervisor's Responses to Subordinate Poor Performance: A Test of an Attributional Model

Terence R. Mitchell, *University of Washington*
Robert E. Wood, *University of Maryland*

One of the most current topics in today's literature on organizational behavior is the use of attribution theory (Mitchell, 1979). Mitchell and Green (1978) and Green and Mitchell (1979) in a series of recent papers have reviewed the use of attribution theory in the area of leadership and have developed a model that shows how attributions may be used to help describe how leaders deal with poor performers. The purpose of this paper is to briefly describe this model and provide an empirical test of some of its propositions.

The attributional model presented by Green and Mitchell (1979) suggests two main links. First, leaders are presented with an incident of

Source: *Organizational Behavior and Human Performance*, 25, 1980, pp. 123–138.

poor performance (e.g., tardiness, low productivity, a missed deadline, disruptive behavior), and they try to figure out the cause of the poor performance. This process involves the sorting through of a variety of informational cues and results in an attribution. This attribution typically involves a judgment about whether something about the subordinate was the cause (e.g., his or her personality, ability, or effort) or whether the cause was external to the subordinate (e.g., a difficult task, lack of support, insufficient information). This internal/external distinction between causes is an important one, and we will return to the topic later in the paper.

The second link in the model involves the relationship between the assumed cause (attribution) and the leader's response. That is,

FIGURE 1   An Attributional Model of a Leader's Response to a Subordinate's Performance Failure

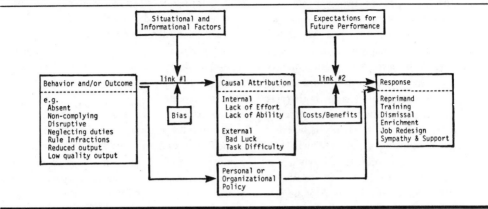

given that poor performance has occurred and a specific attribution is made, how does the leader respond to the subordinate—what does he or she do about it? The second link is especially important, because most of the literature on attribution theory has focused on the causes of attributions, while little work has concerned their consequences. A major emphasis of the model is on predicting how leaders actually respond to poor performance.

A figure that represents the model is presented in Figure 1. The reader can see that both links are somewhat more complex than described above. More specifically, there are a number of factors that influence or mediate both links. A detailed review of these factors is not possible here (see Green & Mitchell, 1979). However, the factors which were tested in the following research will be discussed more fully.

First, of primary concern for Link 1 is an attempt to explain what information the leader uses to make an attribution of causality. Kelley (1972) has suggested three factors: distinctiveness, consistency, and consensus. For our purposes, distinctiveness refers to the degree to which the subordinate performs poorly or well on other types of tasks. High distinctiveness (i.e., the subordinate performs well on other tasks but poorly on the one in question) is likely to lead to an external attribution by the supervisor (i.e., this assignment was too difficult for the subordinate). Consistency refers to how well the subordinate has done on similar

tasks. Low consistency (i.e., the subordinate has done well on this type of assignment in the past) would also lead to an external attribution by the supervisor. Finally, consensus refers to how other subordinates perform on this particular task. High consensus (i.e., everyone seems to do poorly) would also lead to an external attribution by the supervisor. In summary, high distinctiveness, low consistency, and high consensus should result in external attributions, while the reverse should result in internal attributions (i.e., the subordinate has performed poorly at other tasks, has performed poorly at this task before, and no one else seems to have trouble with this task).

A second factor of interest in the model concerns the effects or consequences of the poor performance. The poor performance (e.g., a nurse giving the wrong medication) may result in minor difficulties (e.g., a headache) or major difficulties (e.g., death). These consequences may impact on both the attribution and the response. Based upon the Green and Mitchell model and previous research (Rosen & Jerdee, 1974), we would suspect that the more severe the consequences the more likely a leader will be to make internal attributions and respond in a punitive and personal way toward the subordinate (e.g., reprimands, probation, suspension, or termination).

A third proposition from the model is that attributions are directly related to responses. When an internal attribution is made, we would suspect the leader to direct the response toward the subordinate in an attempt to change the subordinate's behavior through feedback, punishment, or training. When an external attribution is made, we would hypothesize that the leader would direct his or her response to changing the situation or task (e.g., provide more help, better information). Obviously, the intended effect in both cases is to alter the subordinate's performance. However, the point we are raising is whether the supervisor is using a model which says: task or setting → subordinate's behavior → poor performance, or whether the model is simply: subordinate behavior → poor performance. The former model starts with an external attribution while the latter uses an internal attribution as the cause.

Finally, evidence presented in Green and Mitchell (1979) suggests that supervisors in general will see poor performance on the part of their subordinates as more internally rather than externally caused. Thus, our fourth and final hypothesis is that over all conditions an internal attribution for subordinates' poor performance is more likely than an external attribution. The following two studies were designed to test these hypotheses.

METHOD OVERVIEW

Both experiments utilized the same background procedures. The first stage of the research involved some interviews designed to gather critical incidents of poor performance by nurses in a hospital setting. The second stage involved supervisors reading, making attributions, and indicating how they would respond to some of these incidents. Information about the nurses' work history (distinctiveness, consistency, consensus), likely attributions, and the consequences of the poor performance were manipulated within these cases to create different experimental conditions.

In stage one, the Directors of Nursing of seven hospitals in the Seattle area were contacted, informed of the research, and agreed to participate. From the 260 supervisors available, 17 were randomly selected for in-depth interviews. Critical incidents of poor perfor-

mance were gathered as well as information about possible causes of the poor performance (attributions) and possible responses to poor performance. The incidents served as our stimulus materials, and the information about potential causes and responses helped us to develop realistic scales on which supervisors could respond.

A little more detail about the incidents may be helpful. From the 17 interviews, 41 usable incidents were generated. Attributions were given for each incident, resulting in 81 causal explanations. The two authors separately classified these 81 causes into Weiner et al.'s (1972) four categories of effort, ability, task difficulty, and luck. The initial agreement was 81.5 percent between the two judges. Only attributions for which there was clear agreement were eventually transformed into questions to be used in the study.

Finally, we found that about half of the incidents ($N = 19$) focused on medical behaviors (e.g., improper nursing procedure on the ward) and half ($N = 22$) focused on nonmedical behaviors (e.g., absenteeism, tardiness). We decided to use only medical incidents in our stimulus materials due to their obvious relevance and importance. Within this category of medical incidents we also had to use some decision rules to determine which incidents to use as stimulus materials. We selected incidents that had the following characteristics. First, we ruled out any incidents that were too extreme or so grossly inappropriate that an organizational policy would be called into play. Second, we chose types of incidents that seemed to have a high frequency of occurrence. The incidents should have been problems with which supervisors would be familiar. Third and last, we chose incidents for which both a serious or nonserious outcome was possible since this was a variable we wished to manipulate.

EXPERIMENT 1

The first experiment utilized six episodes of poor performance. Based on consistency, consensus, and distinctiveness, three levels of work history for the nurse in question were used (good work history, no work history, and poor work history), as well as two levels of outcome severity (severe, not severe). These manipulations produced a 3 × 2 design with each case representing one cell. Each respondent read six cases which represented all six conditions and responded by giving attributions and responses.

Subjects

Twenty-three nursing supervisors from one of the hospitals participated in the study.

Procedure

The supervisors met as a group and were given the stimulus materials. We explained that the episodes they were to read were actual examples of incidents that had occurred on the hospital ward, and we wanted their judgments as to why these incidents happened and what they would do about it. Due to time restraints, the supervisors finished the questionnaire at a later time and returned their responses by mail.

Materials

Six cases were used involving poor performance on the hospital ward. For example, one episode dealt with the administration of too much of a dangerous drug, while another dealt with the failure of a nurse to put up the side railing on a patient's bed. Each case was one or two paragraphs long.

Manipulations

Each case provided a work history for the nurse in question. She was described as having done well on other tasks, done well on this task in the past, and her colleagues had also had difficulty with this task (a good work history—high distinctiveness, low consistency, high consensus), or she was described as having done poorly on other tasks, she had made similar mistakes before, and her peers

seldom made this error (a poor work history). A third condition had no work history.

The no work history was unique in that subjects did not receive any information regarding the distinctiveness, consistency, or consensus of the nurse's performance. Under this condition subjects had to make attributions and responses from a more limited information base than in the poor work history and good work history conditions. In a repeated measures design there exists the danger of carryover effects and it is possible that the availability of other incidents anchored judgments in the no work history condition. An alternative hypothesis about the impact of being in this state of information dependency is that subjects will place greater weights on other, more immediate, cues such as seriousness of outcome. An inspection of cell means in later tables shows that the size of effects for seriousness of outcome is greater in the no work history condition than in the other two conditions. This result holds, with one minor exception in a composite variable, for all reported attributions and responses directed at the nurse. Although this result does not dispel the possibility of carryover effects, which are hopefully randomized by counterbalancing, it does suggest that the main effect for the seriousness of outcome factor was working in the no work history condition and was accentuated by the absence of other cues.

The seriousness of the outcome was provided as information within the case. For example, when the wrong drug was administered, the patient suffered either mild discomfort or a cardiac arrest. There were six different cases and six different experimental conditions. The cases and conditions were counterbalanced so that for each case the manipulations appeared approximately an equal number of times. Since incidents were counterbalanced across stimulus conditions any systematic variance across incidents would increase within-cell variance and therefore reduce the likelihood of significant F ratios. A one-way analysis of variance showed no significant main effect for incident for any of the attribution or response variables discussed later. An

FIGURE 2   An Incident of Poor Performance with a Nonserious Outcome and a Good Work History

Incident 1

A patient had recently returned from surgery after a prostatectomy. Nurse Connally (R.N.) had checked the patient's condition and found him to be doing satisfactorily. However, she failed to tape down a catheter as requested in a written order by the patient's surgeon. The untaped catheter was discovered by the surgeon when he came to check the patient, and he reported this incident to you. The patient had suffered no ill effects.

Work History

Nurse Connally has been on the job for three months and this is the first time she has made an error of this type, failing to complete a physician's order. Her performance on other tasks has generally been error free. Other R.N.'s on this unit have made similar errors relating to completion of physician's orders and this type of behavior has occurred on several occasions in the last year.

example of an incident is presented in Figure 2.

Measures

There were three types of measures: Manipulation checks, attributions, and responses. One manipulation check was "How serious do you feel the actual outcome described in the incident was for the particular patient involved?" Responses were made on a "not at all serious" to "very serious" seven-point scale. The second manipulation check was, "If a work history was provided, to what extent do you feel the nurse was generally a good performer?" The responses were on a seven-point "poor performer" to "good performer" scale.

The attribution questions provided eight possible causes for the nurses' performance. Four of these were internal (e.g., the nurse was not putting enough effort into her work), and four were external (e.g., the nurse was working on a continually busy ward without support staff). The supervisors responded to each attribution on a "very likely cause" to "very unlikely cause" seven-point scale. The four internal items were summed to form an internal

composite and the four external items formed an external composite. In addition, a summary question was asked that inquired, "In general, how important do you feel the nurse's personal characteristics (such as ability, attitudes, mood, and so on) were as possible causes of her behaving the way she did?" Participants responded on an "extremely important" to "extremely unimportant" seven-point scale. A second summary question asked about the degree to which the supervisor felt the characteristics of the situation (e.g., busy ward) were as causes of the behavior.

The response questions provided 10 different actions ranging from "take no action at all" to "immediate termination." Some of these actions were directed at the nurse (such as verbally reprimand the nurse) and some were directed at the task (such as reschedule the work load). Some were positive in nature (e.g., provide counseling) and some were negative (e.g., termination). Participants indicated their response on a seven-point "very appropriate" to "very inappropriate" scale. Again, summary questions were used which asked, "To what extent do you feel this incident demands that you direct your response at the nurse and attempt to change something about her (her job attitude, level of effort, etc.)?" and a second question asked, "To what extent would you want to change something about the situation?" Seven-point scales ranging from "not at all" to "to a great extent" were used on both questions.

RESULTS: EXPERIMENT 1

Manipulation Checks

An analysis of the manipulation checks showed that the mean rating for the good work history ($\bar{X} = 6.00$) condition was significantly higher ($t = 16.0$, $p < .001$) than that for the poor work history ($\bar{X} = 1.86$). Comparison of the mean ratings for the serious ($\bar{X} = 6.94$) and nonserious ($\bar{X} = 3.80$) conditions was also significant ($t = 10.7$, $p < .001$) and in the expected direction. We can feel fairly confident that the manipulations were successful.

TABLE 1 Subjects' Ratings of the Nurse in Each Incident as a Possible Cause of the Poor Performance (Study 1)

Outcome	Work History		
	Good	Not Available	Poor
Nonserious	3.34	4.57	6.18
Serious	4.14	5.65	6.36

Note. Higher values indicate a higher rating of the nurse as a possible cause, i.e., more internal attribution.

Causal Attributions

Two hypotheses were tested for the causal attributions questions: (*a*) that work history, in terms of distinctiveness, consistency, and consensus, would have a main effect on a subject's internal attributions of causality; (*b*) that seriousness of outcome would have a main effect on subjects' internal attributions of causality.

A 2 × 3 analysis of variance was run, with the dependent variable being the subjects' overall rating of the nurse as a cause of the incident (the summary question). These results are shown in Table 1. Poor work history led to the nurse being rated higher as a possible cause of the incident being evaluated, $F(2,22) = 28.06$, $p < .001$. Also, as hypothesized, a more serious outcome resulted in a higher rating for the nurse as a possible cause of the incident of poor performance, $F(1,22) = 9.00$, $p < .01$. The interaction was not significant It is interesting to note that work history ($\omega^2 = .30$) was far more potent as an explanation for variance in the overall internal attribution than the seriousness of the outcome ($\omega^2 = .04$). The summary question asking about the degree to which the environment was seen as a cause produced a main effect for work history [$F(2,22) = 16.05$, $p < .001$]. A poor work history led to the environment being rated lower as a possible cause of the incident being evaluated. The main effect for seriousness of outcome and the interaction were both not significant.

The results using the combined scores for the four internal attributions (Cronbach alpha = .43) and the four external attribu-

tions (Cronbach alpha = .55), were consistent with the results reported above for the summary questions. For the summated scores of ratings on internal attributions, there was a main effect for work history, $F(2,22) = 20.34$, $p < .001$, and a weaker but marginally significant main effect for seriousness of outcome, $F(1,22) = 3.94$, $p < .05$. Summations for the external attributions showed a main effect for work history, $F(2,22) = 7.08$, $p < .001$, but not for seriousness of outcome, $F(1)$. Again, a poor work history and a severe outcome produced internal attributions, while a good work history and a nonserious outcome were more likely to result in external attributions.

Responses to Poor Performance

It was hypothesized that both work history of the nurse and seriousness of the outcome would influence the supervisor's ratings of the appropriateness of directing a response at the nurse. In addition, it was felt that these two factors would also influence the severity of the response.

A 2 × 3 analysis of variance, with the summary question regarding the appropriateness of directing a response at the nurse as the dependent variable, provided support for the first hypothesis. These results are shown in Table 2. A poor work history resulted in higher ratings of a response directed at the nurse, $F(2,22) = 10.72$, $p < .001$. Seriousness of outcome also had a main effect on choice of response, $F(1,22) = 7.75$, $p < .01$, while the interaction was not significant.

The summary question for an external response showed a significant effect for work history, $F(2,22) = 13.27$, $p < .001$ but no effect

TABLE 2 Subjects' Ratings of the Appropriateness of Directing a Response at the Nurse Described in the Incident (Study 1)

Outcome	Work History		
	Good	Not Available	Poor
Nonserious	4.74	5.36	6.50
Serious	5.61	6.48	6.59

for seriousness of outcome and no interaction. A positive work history was more likely to result in an external response ($\bar{X} = 4.54$) than negative work history ($\bar{X} = 2.70$).

This hypothesis was tested further by doing a more detailed analysis of the specific response questions. First, our intuitive classification of the 10 responses gave us 6 responses directed at the nurse (termination, monitor future performance, written reprimand, verbal reprimand, counseling, and in-service training), 3 at the situation (reschedule work, additional staff, and moral support) and 1 item that said "take no action." The group of six personal responses and the group of three situational responses were summed to form composites and used as dependent variables in a 3 × 2 analysis of variance. The Cronbach alphas for these two composite variables were .37 and .72, respectively.

The results for the personal responses were as predicted. There was a main effect for both the seriousness of the outcome [$F(1,22) = 5.93$, $p < .02$] and the work history [$F(2,22) = 13.75$, $p < .001$]. As expected, the more serious the outcome the more suitable was a response directed at the nurse (see Table 3). Also, the poorer the work history, the more suitable was a response directed at the nurse. Neither of these two independent variables had a significant effect on the composite of three situational responses.

Since there was an abundant literature on how attributions could be classified into internal and external categories we felt comfortable using those responses. Therefore, we factor analyzed our response questions to see if the factor structure corresponded to our initial cate-

TABLE 4 Summated Ratings of the Appropriateness of Three Responses with a Negative Impact on the Nurse Described in the Incident (Study 1)

Outcome	Work History		
	Good	Not Available	Poor
Nonserious	5.83	8.09	14.18
Serious	9.35	12.39	16.24

gorization procedure. These results showed that our three responses directed at the situation and the in-service-training response formed one factor along with the summary question for directing a response at the situation. The "take no action" item failed to load clearly on any factor. Our composite of responses directed at the nurse broke down into two factors: those that were punitive (a verbal reprimand, a written reprimand, and termination) and those that were fairly soft (counseling and monitor the nurse) in terms of their impact on subordinates. The summary question for a response directed at the nurse loaded clearly on the factor containing punitive responses.

Since the problems of termination and reprimands are difficult and unpleasant to handle in most organizations we decided to analyze these three items separately. A composite was formed (Cronbach alpha = .75) and was treated as a dependent variable in the design. The results of the 2 × 3 analysis of variance showed a significant main effect for work history [$F(2,33) = 35.16$, $p < .001$] and for seriousness of outcome [$F(1,22) = 22.59$, $p < .001$]. The cell means are shown in Table 4.

Again, these data support our hypotheses. More negative responses are chosen when the outcome is serious and the work history is poor than when the outcome is not serious and the work history is good.

Attributions and Responses

A third hypothesis suggested that internal attributions would be related to responses directed at the subordinate. To test the hypothesis we correlated the summary attribution

TABLE 3 Effects of Outcome Seriousness and Work History on Composite of Six Responses Directed at the Nurse (Study 1)

Outcome	Work History		
	Good	Not Available	Poor
Nonserious	19.74	23.95	27.29
Serious	25.44	27.04	29.00

questions with the summary response questions. The more the supervisor felt that the nurse was the cause of the incident, the more she considered it appropriate to direct her response at the nurse ($r = .55$, $p < .01$). Also, the more the supervisor felt that the situation was responsible, the more she considered it appropriate to direct her response at the situation ($r = .64$, $p < .01$). These results are as predicted.

Bias toward Internal Responses

Our last hypothesis suggested that there would be a general bias on the part of the supervisors toward using internal attributions and internal responses. To test this hypothesis, we again used the summary questions. The mean difference between the internal attribution question and the external attribution question was significant ($t = 3.63$, $p < .001$) and in the predicted direction. Over all conditions the nurse was more likely to be seen as the cause ($X = 5.07$) of the incident than the situation ($X = 4.41$). The results for the two summary response questions were similar. The t value was 10.89, ($p < .001$) and the means were 5.87 for the internal response question and 3.76 for the external response.

EXPERIMENT 2

In the first experiment we showed that information cues had an impact on both attributions and responses as did the seriousness of the outcome. It was not clear, however, that one could unambiguously argue that the order of these events was as we had hypothesized. More specifically, one could use the information cues to decide on a response and then infer one's attribution. A related problem might be that seriousness of outcome really affected the attribution and its effect on the intended behavioral response was only secondary. In order to clarify these conceptual issues we designed a simple second experiment in which attributions were directly manipulated and crossed with severity of outcome.

The procedures, materials, and subjects in the second experiment were similar to those used in the first experiment. A 2×2 design was used with one factor being the seriousness of outcome (severe or not severe). The second factor was some "additional information" supplied directly to the respondent about an appropriate attribution (internal or external).

Subjects

Twenty-three nurse supervisors from a different hospital were the respondents.

Procedures

The procedures were the same as in the first experiment.

Materials

Four cases were used instead of six.

Manipulations

The severity of outcome was manipulated the same way as in Experiment 1. The additional information variable was provided by adding a section which supplied the respondent with an attribution. For example, the internal attribution information for one of the episodes was "From your discussions with Nurse Connally and some other nurses on the ward, you believe that the failure to tape down the catheter was due to a lack of effort on Nurse Connally's part. She had not spent sufficient time or thought on her duties at the time of the incident. This lack of attention to detail had caused an error on a somewhat simple task at a time when the ward was not very busy." As before, the manipulations and cases were counterbalanced so that each combination appeared approximately an equal number of times and one-way analyses of variance showed no significant main effect for incidents for any of the attribution or response variables.

Measures

The manipulation check for seriousness of outcome was the same as in Experiment 1. The check for the attribution asked, "To what extent do you feel the incident was caused by something about the nurse?" A seven-point "not at all" to "to a great extent" scale was used. We also asked the extent to which the supervisor felt the incident was caused by something about the situation.

The attributional questions used in Experiment 1 were dropped, because the attribution was directly manipulated. The response questions were the same as in Experiment 1, with 10 separate behaviors and two summary items.

RESULTS: EXPERIMENT 2

Manipulations Checks

The manipulations appeared successful. Serious outcomes were seen as more serious than nonserious outcomes ($t = 7.09$, $p < .001$) and the nurse was seen more as the cause of the incident in the internal attribution condition than in the external condition ($t = 9.84$, $p < .001$).

Responses to Poor Performance

We had hypothesized that the internality of the attribution and the seriousness of the outcome would affect both the response and the severity of the response. A 2×2 analysis of variance supported these hypotheses for the subjects' ratings of the appropriateness of directing a response at the nurse. An internal attribution resulted in the response being directed at the nurse, $F(1,22) = 62.88$, $p < .001$, as did a serious outcome, $F(1,22) = 5.25$, $p < .03$.

The summary question for the degree to which the response should be directed at the situation produced a main effect for the attribution [$F(1,22) = 122.58$, $p < .001$] but not for the outcome seriousness or the interaction. An external attribution resulted in the response being directed at the situation ($\overline{X} = 5.20$) more than an internal attribution ($\overline{X} = 1.70$).

A factor analysis of the 10 response questions provided a factor structure very similar to

that obtained in Study 1. The three environmental responses and the summary question for a response directed at the situation formed one factor. The six responses directed at the nurse broke down into punitive and soft factors as in Study 1 with the summary question regarding appropriateness of directing a response at the nurse loading positively on both factors.

As before, the 10 specific responses were first broken down into the 6 internal responses and the 3 external responses. Composites, with Cronbach alphas of .54 and .70, respectively, were formed. The analysis of variance for the 6 personal responses produced a main effect for attribution [$F(1,22) = 58.58$, $p < .001$] and for the seriousness of the outcome [$F(1,22) = 19.43$, $p < .001$]. There was no interaction. The means show that more serious outcomes resulted in responses being directed at the nurse ($\overline{X} = 26.28$) more than nonserious outcomes ($\overline{X} = 22.96$). Also, an internal attribution produced responses directed at the nurse ($\overline{X} = 28.20$) more than external attributions ($\overline{X} = 21.04$).

When the three situational variables were used as the dependent variable there was a main effect for the attribution [$F(1,22) = 40.97$, $p < .001$] but no effect for outcome or the interaction. An external attribution resulted in the response being directed more at the situation ($\overline{X} = 12.48$) than an internal attribution ($\overline{X} = 7.27$). These results are as predicted.

Finally, as in Study 1, the three responses with a negative impact were summed and treated as a dependent variable in the 2×2 analysis. For this composite, which had a Cronbach alpha of .73, there was a significant effect for outcome seriousness and attribution. The more serious the outcome, the more negative the response [$F(1,22) = 18.36$, $p < .001$]. The more internal the attribution, the more negative the response [$F(1,22) = 48.27$, $p < .001$]. These results were as predicted.

Attributions and Responses

While attributions were manipulated in Study 2 but not Study 1 it was still possible to test whether internal attributions were related to internal responses and external attributions to external responses. Two of the manipulation check items asked to what extent the supervisor thought the nurse was the cause or the situation was the cause of the incident. These two items were correlated with the summary response questions.

The results supported the hypothesis. The more the supervisor saw the nurse as the cause the more her response was directed at the nurse ($r = .70$, $p < .01$). The more the supervisor saw the cause as external, the more her response was directed at external factors ($r = .71$, $p < .01$).

Bias toward Internal Responses

Since there were no attributions made in Study 2 this hypothesis was tested using the summary response questions only. Across all conditions, the mean appropriateness of an internal response was 5.36 and for an external response was 3.57 ($t = 4.46$, $p < .001$). These results suggest that internal responses were preferred over external ones regardless of the conditions surrounding the incident.

DISCUSSION

The purpose of the present studies was a preliminary investigation of factors which influence a supervisor's choice of behavior when confronted with incidents of poor performance. The experimental data indicate that the nursing supervisors were acting in a manner consistent with the hypotheses suggested by the attribution model presented by Mitchell and Green (1978) and Green and Mitchell (1979).

A summary of the findings is as follows. First, in their evaluation of nurses involved in an incident of poor performance, supervisors attributed causality more to the internal factors than external factors regardless of the surrounding circumstances. Second, this bias toward internal attributions was increased when the work history of the nurse was poor and when the outcome was serious. Third, the be-

haviors chosen as responses to the poor performance were related to the attributions and surrounding circumstances. The more internal the attribution, the more the response was directed at the nurse.

Before turning to a discussion of the practical implications of these findings it is important to discuss some of the limitations of the research itself. For example, we recognize that responses in the context of this study represent behavioral intentions and not actual behavior and, therefore, the correlation between attribution and response may be overstated because the actual costs of implementing a particular response are not evident. However, the fact that the responses represent alternatives available to subjects in their actual work settings could be expected to, at least partially, offset this effect. There is evidence to suggest that the more specific an attitude measure the more likely it is to be related to behavior (Hall & Hall, 1976; Jaccard, King, & Bomazal, 1977).

A related problem is the use of incidents or stories as stimulus materials. One could argue about the generalizability of such stimuli to real-world settings and whether people can realistically assess how they would react. In an attempt to respond to this criticism we have conducted a number of other studies testing the attributional model using different methodologies. Two of these studies are work simulations where supervisors are hired and then given bogus data about their subordinates' performance or work directly with confederates. In this way we have been able to actually present a supervisor with a poor-performing subordinate and observe his or her reaction. In another study we have used a film of a supervisor and a subordinate discussing an incident of poor performance as the stimulus materials. A fourth study has used role playing as the stimulus setting. A brief review of this research can be found in Mitchell, Green, and Wood (in press).

A third issue for discussion focuses on the fact that the situations presented as stimulus materials in the study were extremes and unambiguous. The outcome was very serious or not serious, the attributions, internal or external, and the consistency, distinctiveness, and consensus cues were all positive or negative when they were used. Practicing managers are seldom presented with such clear-cut cues. There may be both internal and external explanations that are plausible. The consistency, distinctiveness, and consensus cues might not mesh very well. We recognize these points and many of these issues are discussed in Green and Mitchell (1979). It was our intention in this research to demonstrate that such attributional processes occur and can have an important impact on behavior. We suspect that when we do research with situations that are less clear cut we will have (a) more uncertainty about attributions, (b) more uncertainty about responses, (c) less severe responses, and (d) a greater dependence on personal or organizational policies. We are currently investigating some of these questions.

There are some theoretical issues that should be discussed as well. First, it is obvious from our model and our research that little has been said about individual differences. While we suspect that characteristics like an internal or external locus of control will influence an individual's tendency to use internal or external attributions, we have not chosen to pursue these factors in more detail. This is partly because we believe that the variables we have described are the most important ones and partly because the use of individual differences as main effects or moderators has not been very fruitful in many areas of organizational behavior research (Mitchell, 1979). We might add, however, that when we split our samples at the median on such variables as experience as a nurse, experience as a supervisor, and number of subordinates we found no significant differences in attributions or behavior.

One final theoretical point which was consistent across both studies was that the attribution, whether it was directly manipulated or influenced through cues of consistency, distinctiveness, and consensus, was a more powerful predictor of intended response than the seriousness of the outcome. While the outcome seriousness was significant for many of the analyses it consistently controlled less variance than attributions. These data help to suggest not only what factors affect responses but their relative contribution as well.

Besides theoretical support for the model, the data have some practical implications. First, to the degree that attributions serve as a mediator of poor performance—leader response relationships, then a number of errors may be present in the process. For example, there is considerable evidence that supervisors (as observers) may err in over attributing subordinates' (actors') behavior to internal causes (Jones & Nisbett, 1972). This difference in the perception of causes of poor performance may lead to inaccurate appraisals and points of conflict.

Second, the data suggest that supervisors make attributions and responses partly as a function of the seriousness of the outcome. In work settings, these outcomes may be completely out of the subordinate's control (e.g., whether a patient falls out of bed when the railing is down). It seems to us that supervisors would be more efficient if they concentrated on trying to change the behavior that caused the incident rather than focusing on the outcome. What our analysis suggests is that when poor performance occurs but the outcome is not serious, the supervisor is more likely to overlook the problem. This strategy can lead to serious negative consequences at some later time and is clearly not an effective means of feedback. To change behavior we must focus on the behavior not the outcome.

Just as behaviorism represented an antimotivation theory approach to the phenomenon of motivated behavior, so there is a similar line of thought in leadership research. Is the concept of leadership unnecessary? Is a person called a leader nothing more than a symbol of a group process or an individual follower attribute? Are leaders necessary at all for group success? In this reading, Kerr and Jermier suggest two possibilities. The first is that certain variables may act as substitutes for leadership. The second is that certain variables can cancel the effects of a leader's behavior. Either of those propositions, if true, is sufficiently powerful to question the need for a theory of leadership in the first place. If there are such things as leadership substitutes, there may be less of a need to identify effective leaders. On the other hand, if there are such things as leadership neutralizers, there may be little value in identifying effective leaders since they will not be permitted to lead.

■ READING 25 ■

Substitutes for Leadership:
Their Meaning and Measurement

Steven Kerr, *University of Southern California*
John M. Jermier, *The Ohio State University*

A number of theories and models of leadership exist, each seeking to most clearly identify and best explain the presumedly powerful effects of leader behavior or personality attributes upon the satisfaction and performance of hierarchical subordinates. These theories and models fail to agree in many respects, but have in common the fact that none of them systematically accounts for very much criterion variance. It is certainly true that data indicating strong superior-subordinate relationships have sometimes been reported. In numerous studies, however, conclusions have had to be based on statistical rather than practical significance, and hypothesis support has rested upon the researcher's ability to show that the trivially low correlations obtained were not the result of chance.

Current theories and models of leadership have something else in common: a conviction that hierarchical leadership is always important. Even situational approaches to leadership share the assumption that while the style of leadership likely to be effective will vary according to the situation, *some* leadership style will *always* be effective *regardless* of the situation. Of course, the extent to which this assumption is explicated varies greatly, as does the degree to which each theory is dependent upon the assumption. Fairly explicit is the Vertical Dyad Linkage model developed by Graen and his associates (Graen, Dansereau, & Minami, 1972; Dansereau, Cashman, & Graen, 1973), which attributes importance to hierarchical leadership without concern for the

Source: *Organizational Behavior and Human Performance,* 22, 1978, pp. 375–403.

situation. The Fiedler (1964, 1967) contingency model also makes the general assumption that hierarchical leadership is important in situations of low, medium, and high favorableness, though predictions about relationships between LPC and performance in Octants VI and VII are qualified (Fiedler & Chemers, 1974, p. 82). Most models of decision-centralization (e.g., Tannenbaum & Schmidt, 1958; Heller & Yukl, 1969; Vroom & Yetton, 1973; Bass & Valenzi, 1974) include among their leader decision-style alternatives one whereby subordinates attempt a solution by themselves, with minimal participation by the hierarchical superior. Even in such cases, however, the leader is responsible for initiating the method through delegation of the problem, and is usually described as providing (structuring) information.

The approach to leadership which is least dependent upon the assumption articulated above, and which comes closest to the conceptualization to be proposed in this paper, is the Path-Goal Theory (House, 1971; House & Mitchell, 1974). Under circumstances when both goals and paths to goals may be clear, House and Mitchell (1974) point out that "attempts by the leader to clarify paths and goals will be both redundant and seen by subordinates as imposing unnecessary, close control." They go on to predict that "although such control may increase performance by preventing soldiering or malingering, it will also result in decreased satisfaction."

This prediction is supported in part by conclusions drawn by Kerr, Schriesheim, Murphy, and Stogdill (1974) from their review of the consideration-initiating structure literature, and is at least somewhat consistent with results from a few recent studies. A most interesting and pertinent premise of the theory, however, is that even unnecessary and redundant leader behaviors will have an impact upon subordinate satisfaction, morale, motivation, performance, and acceptance of the leader (House & Mitchell, 1974; House & Dessler, 1974). While leader attempts to clarify paths and goals are therefore recognized by Path-Goal Theory to be unnecessary and redundant in certain situations, in no situation are they ex-

plicitly hypothesized by Path-Goal (or any other leadership theory) to be irrelevant.

This lack of recognition is unfortunate. As has already been mentioned, data from numerous studies collectively demonstrate that in many situations these leader behaviors *are* irrelevant, and hierarchical leadership (as operationalized in these studies) per se does not seem to matter. In fact, leadership variables so often account for very little criterion variance that a few writers have begun to argue that the leadership construct is sterile altogether, that "the concept of leadership itself has outlived its usefulness" (Miner, 1975, p. 200). This view is also unfortunate, however, and fails to take note of accurate predictions by leadership theorists even as such theorists fail to conceptually reconcile their inaccurate predictions.

What is clearly needed to resolve this dilemma is a conceptualization adequate to explain both the occasional successes and frequent failures of the various theories and models of leadership.

SUBSTITUTES FOR LEADERSHIP

A wide variety of individual, task, and organizational characteristics have been found to influence relationships between leader behavior and subordinate satisfaction, morale, and performance. Some of these variables (for example, job pressure and subordinate expectations of leader behavior) act primarily to influence which leadership style will best permit the hierarchical superior to motivate, direct, and control subordinates. The effect of others, however, is to act as "substitutes for leadership," tending to negate the leader's ability to either improve or impair subordinate satisfaction and performance.

Substitutes for leadership are apparently prominent in many different organizational settings, but their existence is not explicated in any of the dominant leadership theories. As a result, data describing formal superior-subordinate relationships are often obtained in situations where important substitutes exist. These data logically ought to be, and usually are, insignificant, and are useful primarily as a

TABLE 1   Substitutes for Leadership

Characteristic	Will Tend to Neutralize	
	Relationship-Oriented, Supportive, People-Centered Leadership: Consideration, Support, and Interaction Facilitation	Task-Oriented, Instrumental, Job-Centered Leadership: Initiating Structure, Goal Emphasis, and Work Facilitation
of the subordinate		
1. Ability, experience, training, knowledge		X
2. Need for independence	X	X
3. "Professional" orientation	X	X
4. Indifference toward organizational rewards	X	X
of the task		
5. Unambiguous and routine		X
6. Methodologically invariant		X
7. Provides its own feedback concerning accomplishment		X
8. Intrinsically satisfying	X	
of the organization		
9. Formalization (explicit plans, goals, and areas of responsibility)		X
10. Inflexibility (rigid, unbending rules and procedures)		X
11. Highly specified and active advisory and staff functions		X
12. Closely knit, cohesive work groups	X	X
13. Organizational rewards not within the leader's control	X	X
14. Spatial distance between superior and subordinates	X	X

reminder that when leadership styles are studied in circumstances where the choice of style is irrelevant, the effect is to replace the potential power of the leadership construct with the unintentional comedy of the "Law of the instrument."[1]

What is needed, then, is a taxonomy of situations where we should not be studying "leadership" (in the formal hierarchical sense) at all. Development of such a taxonomy is still at an early stage, but Woodward (1973) and Miner (1975) have laid important groundwork through their classifications of control, and some effects of nonleader sources of clarity have been considered by Hunt (Note 2) and Hunt

and Osborn (1975). Reviews of the leadership literature by House and Mitchell (1974) and Kerr et al. (1974) have also proved pertinent in this regard, and suggest that individual, task, and organizational characteristics of the kind outlined in Table 1 will help to determine whether or not hierarchical leadership is likely to matter.

Conceptual Domain of Substitutes for Leadership. Since Table 1 is derived from previously conducted studies, substitutes are only suggested for the two leader behavior styles which dominate the research literature. The substitutes construct probably has much wider applicability, however, perhaps to hierarchical leadership in general.

It is probably useful to clarify some of the characteristics listed in Table 1. "Professional

[1]Abraham Kaplan (1964, p. 28) has observed: "Give a small boy a hammer, and he will find that everything he encounters needs pounding."

orientation" is considered a potential substitute for leadership because employees with such an orientation typically cultivate horizontal rather than vertical relationships, give greater credence to peer review processes, however informal, than to hierarchical evaluations, and tend to develop important referents external to the employing organization (Filley, House, & Kerr, 1976). Clearly, such attitudes and behaviors can sharply reduce the influence of the hierarchical superior.

"Methodologically invariant" tasks may result from serial interdependence, from machine-paced operations, or from work methods which are highly standardized. In one study (House, Filley, & Kerr, 1971, p. 26), invariance was found to derive from a network of government contracts which "specified not only the performance requirements of the end product, but also many of the management practices and control techniques that the company must follow in carrying out the contract."

Invariant methodology relates to what Miner (1975) describes as the "push" of work. Tasks which are "intrinsically satisfying" (another potential substitute listed in Table 1) contribute in turn to the "pull" of work. Miner believes that for "task control" to be effective, a force comprised of both the push and pull of work must be developed. A least in theory, however, either type alone may act as a substitute for hierarchical leadership.

Performance feedback provided by the work itself is another characteristic of the task which potentially functions in place of the formal leader. It has been reported that employees with high growth need strength in particular derive beneficial psychological states (internal motivation, general satisfaction, work effectiveness) from clear and direct knowledge of the results of performance (Hackman & Oldham, 1976; Oldham, 1976). Task-provided feedback is often: (a) the most immediate source of feedback given the infrequency of performance appraisal sessions (Hall & Lawler, 1969); (b) the most accurate source of feedback given the problems of measuring the performance of others (Campbell, Dunnette, Lawler, & Weick, 1970); and (c) the most self-evalua-

tion evoking and intrinsically motivating source of feedback given the controlling and informational aspects of feedback from others (DeCharms, 1968; Deci, 1972, 1975; Greller & Herold, 1975). For these reasons, the formal leader's function as a provider of role structure through performance feedback may be insignificant by comparison.

Cohesive, interdependent work groups and active advisory and staff personnel also have the ability to render the formal leader's performance feedback function inconsequential. Inherent in mature group structures are stable performance norms and positional differentiation (Bales & Strodtbeck, 1951; Borgatta & Bales, 1953; Stogdill, 1959; Lott & Lott, 1965; Zander, 1968). Task-relevant guidance and feedback from others may be provided directly by the formal leader, indirectly by the formal leader through the primary work group members, directly by the primary work group members, by staff personnel, or by the client. If the latter four instances prevail, the formal leader's role may be quite trivial. Cohesive work groups are, of course, important sources of affiliative need satisfaction.

Programming through impersonal modes has been reported to be the most frequent type of coordination strategy employed under conditions of low-to-medium task uncertainty and low task interdependence (Van de Ven, Delbecq, & Koenig, 1976). Thus, the existence of written work goals, guidelines, and ground rules (organizational formalization) and rigid rules and procedures (organizational inflexibility) may serve as substitutes for leader-provided coordination under certain conditions. Personal and group coordination modes involving the formal leader may become important only when less costly impersonal strategies are not suitable.

The Measurement of Substitutes for Leadership. This section will discuss the assessment of leadership substitutes through the administration of a questionnaire. Such an approach obviously will provide information about respondent perceptions, not "objective" properties, of the variables under study. It is not the intention of this paper to enter into the controversy over the relative merits of paper-and-pencil and other approaches, or the investigation of "psychological" rather than "actual" attributes. In common with most other variables in the behavioral sciences, potential substitutes for leadership can be measured in more than one way, and when feasible these ways should be employed in combination.

In seeking to devise a questionnaire to measure the potential substitutes listed in Table 1, it was initially assumed that scales already in existence would probably be adequate. This turned out not to be the case. To understand why, consider the following items, taken from scales which strongly relate to the substitutes construct:

—I feel certain about how much authority I have.

—I know exactly what is expected of me (from the "Role Clarity" scale, Rizzo, House, & Lirtzman, 1970).

—The mission of work groups is clearly defined.

—Objectives are clearly communicated and understood (from the "Goal Consensus and Clarity" scale, House & Rizzo, 1972).

—Schedules, programs, or project specifications are used to guide work.

—Group rules or guidelines to direct efforts are very clear (from the "Formalization" scale, House & Rizzo, 1972).

—How much are you required to depend on your superior for the nonfinancial resources (information, supplies, etc.) necessary for the performance of your job?

—To what extent are you able to act independently of your superior in performing your job duties? (from the "Job Autonomy/Independence from Others" scale, Wigdor, Note 4).

The problem with such items is that it is impossible to determine whether they refer to substitutes of the kind suggested in Table 1, or whether they refer to leadership itself. For example, suppose we learn that respondents must depend on the leader for information,

and cannot act independently in performing job duties. Is this a commentary on their level of training and experience, or does it tell us instead about the leader's managerial style? Similarly, if subordinates express certainty about how much authority they have, does such certainty arise from organizational formalization, or from frequent access to and communications with the leader?

Such questions should not be taken as criticism of the scales mentioned above. Since theories have not been concerned with substitutes for leadership, scales used in leadership research have not been required to distinguish leader-provided autonomy, goal and role clarity, etc., from autonomy and clarity which stem from other sources. It may become necessary in the future to make such distinctions, however, and the scales described in Table 2 have been constructed for this purpose. These scales are presented in the same order as the listing of characteristics in Table 1 to which they refer. It should be noted that the measure of Organizational Formalization is very similar to House and Rizzo's (1972) Formalization scale, and some items in the Organization Rewards Not within the Leader's Control scale derive from Wigdor's (Note 4) measure of Job Autonomy/Independence from Others. Unlike early scales, however, those in Table 2 have been written so as to permit a distinction between effects which are the result of leadership and those which stem from substitutes for leadership.

TELEVISION SCRIPT PRETEST

Administration of the Questionnaire. To learn something about scale properties, nine subscales in Table 2 were administered to 153 male and female juniors and seniors who were enrolled in a first course in organizational behavior.[2] Complete and usable information was obtained from 148 of them. The administration was intended to (a) provide information

---

[2]The Task-Provided Feedback Concerning Accomplishment, Organizational Inflexibility, Spatial Distance, and Need for Independence scales were not included in this administration.

TABLE 2   Questionnaire Items for the Measurement of Substitutes for Leadership*

(1) *Ability, Experience, Training, and Knowledge*
— Because of my ability, experience, training or job knowledge, I have the competence to act independently of my immediate superior in performing my day-to-day duties.
— Because of my ability, experience, training or job knowledge, I have the competence to act independently of my immediate superior in performing unusual and unexpected job duties.
— Due to my lack of experience and training, I must depend upon my immediate superior to provide me with necessary data, information, and advice. (R).

(2) *Professional Orientation*
— For feedback about how well I am performing I rely on people in my occupational specialty, whether or not they are members of my work unit or organization.
— I receive very useful information and guidance from people who share my occupational specialty, but who are not members of my employing organization.
— My job satisfaction depends to a considerable extent on people in my occupational specialty who are not members of my employing organization.

(3) *Indifference toward Organizational Rewards*
— I cannot get very enthused about the rewards offered in this organization, or about the opportunities available.
— This organization offers attractive payoffs to people it values. (R)
— In general, most of the things I seek and value in this world cannot be obtained from my job or my employing organization.

(4) *Unambiguous, Routine, and Methodologically Invariant Tasks*
— Because of the nature of the tasks I perform, on my job there is little doubt about the best way to get the work done.
— Because of the nature of the work I do, I am often required to perform nonroutine tasks. (R).
— Because of the nature of my work, at the beginning of each work day I can predict with near certainty exactly what activities I will be performing that day.
— There is really only one correct way to perform most of my tasks.
— My job duties are so simple that almost anyone could perform them after a little bit of instruction and practice.
— It is so hard to figure out the correct approach to most of my work problems that second-guessers would have a field day. (R)

(5) *Task-Provided Feedback Concerning Accomplishment*
— After I've done something on my job I can tell right away from the results I get whether I've done it correctly.
— My job is the kind where you can make a mistake or an error and not be able to see that you've made it. (R)
— Because of the nature of the tasks I perform, it is easy for me to see when I've done something exceptionally well.

(6) *Intrinsically Satisfying Tasks*
— I get a great deal of personal satisfaction from the work I do.
— It is hard to imagine that anyone could enjoy performing the tasks that I perform on my job. (R)
— My job satisfaction depends to a considerable extent on the nature of the actual tasks I perform on the job.

(7) *Organizational Formalization*
— Clear, written goals and objectives exist for my job.
— My job responsibilities are clearly specified in writing.
— In this organization, performance appraisals are based on written standards.
— Written schedules, programs and work specifications are available to guide me on my job.
— My duties, authority, and accountability are documented in policies, procedures, and job descriptions.
— Written rules and guidelines exist to direct work efforts.
— Written documents (such as budgets, schedules, and plans) are used as an essential part of my job.
— There are contradictions and inconsistencies among the written statements of goals and objectives. (R)
— There are contradictions and inconsistencies among the written guidelines and groundrules. (R)

(8) *Organizational Inflexibility*
— In this organization the written rules are treated as a bible, and are never violated.
— People in this organization consider the rulebooks and policy manuals as general guidelines, not as rigid and unbending. (R)

TABLE 2 (concluded)

— In this organization anytime there is a policy in writing that fits some situation, everybody has to follow that policy very strictly.

(9) *Advisory and Staff Functions*
— For feedback about how well I am performing, I rely on staff personnel inside the organization, based outside my work unit or department.
— In my job I must depend on staff personnel located outside of my work unit or department to provide me with data, reports, and informal advice necessary for my job performance.
— I receive very useful information and guidance from staff personnel who are based outside my work unit or department.

(10) *Closely Knit, Cohesive, Interdependent Work Groups*
— For feedback about how well I am performing I rely on members of my work group other than my superior.
— The quantity of work I turn out depends largely on the performance of members of my work group other than my superior.
— The quality of work I turn out depends largely on the performance of members of my work group other than my superior.
— I receive very useful information and advice from members of my work group other than my superior.
— I am dependent on members of my work group other than my superior for important organizational rewards.
— My job satisfaction depends to a considerable extent on members of my work group other than my superior.

(11) *Organizational Rewards Not within the Leader's Control*
— On my job I must depend on my immediate superior to provide the necessary financial resources (such as budget and expense money). (R)
— On my job I must depend on my immediate superior to provide the necessary nonfinancial resources (such as file space and equipment). (R)
— My chances for a promotion depend on my immediate superior's recommendation. (R)
— My chances for a pay raise depend on my immediate superior's recommendation. (R)
— My immediate superior has little say or influence over which of his or her subordinates receives organizational rewards.
— The only performance feedback that matters to me is that given me by my immediate superior. (R)
— I am dependent on my immediate superior for important organizational rewards. (R)

(12) *Spatial Distance between Superior and Subordinates*
— The nature of my job is such that my immediate superior is seldom around me when I'm working.
— On my job my most important tasks take place away from where my immediate superior is located.
— My immediate superior and I are seldom in actual contact or direct sight of one another.

(13) *Subordinate Need for Independence*
— I like it when the person in charge of a group I am in tells me what to do. (R)
— When I have a problem I like to think it through myself without help from others.
— It is important for me to be able to feel that I can run my life without depending on people older and more experienced than myself.

*Response choices to each item include:
(5) Almost always true or almost completely true,
(4) Usually true, or true to a large extent,
(3) Sometimes true, sometimes untrue or true to some extent,
(2) Usually untrue, or untrue to a large extent, and
(1) Almost always untrue or almost completely untrue.
(R) indicates reflected item.

about the subscales' internal reliabilities; (*b*) assess their degree of interdependence; and (*c*) permit at least a crude validation of responses, by examining them with reference to work units whose characteristics and mode of leader-ship were already known, and whose type and strength of leadership substitutes were systematically different. To accomplish "*c*," rather than being asked to describe past or present work experiences, respondents were asked to take on the role of one of the following television characters, and to reply to the questions from the vantage point of that character:

— Mary Richards, working for Lou Grant (*The Mary Tyler Moore Show*).

— Hawkeye Pierce, working for Colonel Sherman Potter (*M.A.S.H.*).

— Archie Bunker, working for the loading dock supervisor in his plant (*All in the Family*).

Respondents who were unfamiliar with all three characters were asked to reply from the vantage point of "a low-level assembly line worker, working for a foreman in an automobile plant."

It should be emphasized that the credibility of these data is limited. Respondents undoubtedly are differentially familiar with the various television characters, and assembly line worker "replies" were obviously based mainly on stereotypes. Furthermore, inferences had to be made with regard to questions which could not unequivocally be answered from the television scripts. These problems could have been partially resolved by asking respondents to reply from the perspectives of characters in a written case study. However, it is unlikely that a case study could create as much completeness and richness of characterization as is provided by a continuing television series.

Subscale Properties. Reliabilities and intercorrelations for the nine subscales are shown in Table 3. As can be seen from the table, all reliabilities are above .7, and five exceed .8.

Table 3 also suggests that the subscales may be considered, in this sample at least, to be essentially independent. Only one of 36 intercorrelations is greater than .5. On the other hand, 14 are below .1, and 29 are less than .3. Furthermore, all relatively high intercorrelations are readily comprehensible from a conceptual standpoint. Those which exceed .4 are:

Intrinsically Satisfying Tasks

__positively with Ability, Experience, Training, and Knowledge

__negatively with Indifference toward Organizational Rewards

__negatively with Unambiguous, Routine, and Methodologically Invariant Tasks

Ability, Experience, Training, and Knowledge

__negatively with Unambiguous, Routine, and Methodologically Invariant Tasks

Professional Orientation

__positively with Advisory and Staff Functions

TABLE 3 Subscale Reliabilities and Intercorrelations

Subscale title	Reliability*	1	2	3	4	5	6	7	8	9
				(Pretest Sample = 148)						
1. Ability, experience, training, and knowledge.	.85	1	.06	−.07	−.45	.41	−.21	.03	−.18	.15
2. Professional orientation.	.74		1	−.08	−.26	.07	.04	.45	−.20	.18
3. Indifference toward organizational rewards.	.85			1	.03	−.47	−.29	−.26	−.03	.29
4. Unambiguous, routine, and methodologically invariant tasks.	.78				1	−.56	.32	−.34	.00	−.16
5. Intrinsically satisfying tasks.	.85					1	.06	.26	.03	−.06
6. Organizational formalization.	.77						1	.17	.09	−.17
7. Advisory and staff functions.	.80							1	.14	.07
8. Closely knit, cohesive interdependent work groups.	.78								1	−.12
9. Organizational rewards not within the leader's control.	.81									1

*Reliabilities were calculated using the Kuder–Richardson Formula 8.

TABLE 4 Means and Standard Deviations, by Character

	Mary Richards (N = 27)		Hawkeye Pierce (N = 60)		Archie Bunker (N = 41)		Assembly Line Worker (N = 20)	
Subscale title	M*	SD	M	SD	M	SD	M	SD
1. Ability, experience, training, and knowledge.	4.0	.73	4.2	.69	4.1	.82	2.5	.82
2. Professional orientation.	3.1	.73	3.0	.78	2.3	.87	2.4	.67
3. Indifference toward organizational rewards.	2.2	.48	3.7	1.00	2.9	.88	3.6	.72
4. Unambiguous, routine, and methodologically invariant tasks.	2.7	.50	2.8	.69	3.4	.60	4.3	.66
5. Intrinsically satisfying tasks.	4.3	.50	3.4	.88	3.5	.82	2.2	.96
6. Organizational formalization.	2.9	.56	2.5	.69	2.8	.49	3.1	.74
7. Advisory and staff functions.	3.1	.73	2.6	.91	2.1	.68	1.9	.61
8. Closely knit, cohesive, interdependent work groups.	3.5	.55	3.3	.72	3.3	.91	3.7	.46
9. Organizational rewards not within the leader's control.	2.1	.53	3.1	.74	2.3	.62	2.3	.82

*A scale mean of 5.0 would indicate that the characteristic is perceived to be present to the maximum degree, while a 1.0 would suggest its virtual absence. The closer any scale mean comes to 5.0, the more likely it is that the characteristic will act as a substitute for hierarchical leadership.

Subscale Means and Standard Deviations. Table 4 summarizes means and standard deviations, by character, for each potential leadership substitute. Despite the crudeness of the data in Table 4, some interesting insights emerge.

For our hypothetical assembly line worker, the characteristic with the greatest potential to negate the leader's influence is the routine and unambiguous nature of the job duties (mean = 4.3). According to Table 1, whether the leader behaves in a structuring manner may in this situation be an irrelevant question. Scale means show no strong substitutes for leader-provided consideration, however, and questions relating to relationship-oriented behavior by the hierarchical superior may therefore be highly relevant.

For Mary Richards, the strongest potential leadership substitute is the intrinsic satisfaction she (presumably) obtains from the tasks she performs (mean = 4.3). Table 1 suggests that this could act as a substitute for leader-provided consideration, and on the show she does seem happy in her work despite the erratic attempts at warmth and collegiality displayed by her superior.[3] She is also seen as able

and knowledgeable (mean = 4.0), and under some circumstances might for this reason be unresponsive to leader-provided structure as well. However, Table 4 also shows that she is very interested in organizational rewards (least indifferent of the four characters described), and that her superior is seen as controlling these rewards to a high degree (more than the superior of any other character). As a consequence, hierarchical leadership is probably not irrelevant in this situation. (This point will be elaborated upon shortly.)

For Hawkeye Pierce, the strongest substitute for hierarchical leadership is his personal skill, training, and job knowledge (mean = 4.2). Table 1 indicates that these qualities should obviate the need for leader-provided structure, and he does in fact perform his work decisively and competently on the show despite the fact that his superior gives him virtually no structure. Pierce is also indifferent to organizational rewards (more so than the other characters), and in any case his superior is seen

---

[3]On one occasion her superior, encountering a situation clearly crying out for some show of supportive leadership, finally and reluctantly exhorted his staff to "keep up the fair work!"

as lacking control over such rewards. In Pierce's case, no clear alternatives to leader-provided consideration behavior appear in Table 4, perhaps because such likely substitutes for a surgeon as "professional orientation" and "intrinsic satisfaction from tasks performed" are less likely to be salient under combat conditions. Pierce might therefore welcome and benefit from relationship-oriented leader behavior. For the most part, however, it is not evident from either Table 4 or the television show that hierarchical leadership exerts much influence upon Hawkeye Pierce's performance or satisfaction.

The data pertaining to Archie Bunker should be viewed with particular caution since *All in the Family*, unlike the other shows used for this study, focuses upon the character's home rather than work environment. Table 4 scale means suggest that for Archie, as for Hawkeye Pierce, the strongest potential substitute for leadership is his own experience and job knowledge. Similarity between Pierce's and Bunker's situation is not, however, very great. Pierce's personal competence probably stems from extensive formal training, while Bunker's is the result of his having spent many years in essentially the same position. Furthermore, the job which Bunker is competent at is, according to Table 4, much more routine and methodologically invariant. An important final difference is that compared to Pierce, Bunker is much more concerned with organizational rewards, and his superior is seen as controlling rewards to a great degree. This would probably cause Bunker to be at least somewhat influenced by his hierarchical superior's leadership style.

Summarizing what has been discussed in this section of the paper, the data presented in Tables 3 and 4 suggest that in this sample at least, the nine subscales administered are essentially independent and have adequate internal reliabilities. They also yield readily interpretable data which plausibly describe the presence or absence of substitutes for leadership in the work situations of those who are (hypothetically) responding.

FIELD STUDIES

To further demonstrate the validity and reliability of the constructs developed in this paper, and to investigate their importance in actual organizational settings, two field studies were conducted. Data were gathered using the 55-item substitutes for leadership questionnaire presented in Table 2,[4] and various leader behavior-subordinate outcome measures.

Samples and Procedure. In both of the organizational studies, police officers in a large Midwestern city filled in the questionnaire during normal working hours. Police organizations provide settings to severely test the import of leader substitutes since formal rank and command control are essential elements which enhance the police supervisor's role (Wilson & McLaren, 1972). If important leader substitutes are found in these settings, their presence in other organizations could reasonably be assumed.

In the first study, 54 sworn university police officers of rank less than sergeant participated: in the second study, 113 sworn city police officers of rank less than sergeant participated. Subjects were guaranteed anonymity prior to filling in the questionnaire.

Subscale Properties. Internal reliability and correlation coefficients for the 13 subscales are presented in Table 5. Nearly all of the subscales exhibit a satisfactory level of internal consistency in both samples. Where the estimates of reliability are less than .7 for a measure in one sample (task-provided feedback, inflexibility, and organizational rewards not within the leader's control), adequate levels of reliability were obtained in the other sample. Thus, these subscales meet acceptable standards of reliability for preliminary research, and may be employed to further assess the validity of the substitutes for leadership construct.

As in the student sample discussed above, subscale intercorrelations (Table 5) are modest,

---

[4] In the university police sample the Need for Independence scale was not included.

TABLE 5 Subscale Reliabilities and Intercorrelations[†]

Subscale Title	Reliability* University Police	Reliability* City Police	1	2	3	4	5	6	7	8	9	10	11	12	13
1. AETK‡	.83	.85		-.06	-.08	-.07	.14	.16	.02	-.06	.10	-.13	-.02	.20	.14
2. PROF	.81	.81	.32		.00	.28	.20	-.01	.19	.15	.55	.33	-.24	-.28	-.05
3. INDOR	.82	.82	-.26	-.10		-.04	-.16	-.48	-.10	-.07	.00	.13	.06	.06	.05
4. ROUTIN	.74	.70	-.08	-.18	-.12		.06	-.07	.27	.27	.03	.06	-.17	-.21	-.02
5. TSKFB	.79	.67	.28	.14	-.20	.38		.21	.22	.01	.23	.18	-.18	.11	-.12
6. INSAT	.80	.72	.28	.26	-.36	-.27	.32		.23	.05	.12	.02	-.11	.20	-.09
7. ORFORM	.85	.77	-.17	.16	-.21	.39	.47	.21		.34	.30	.04	-.26	.07	-.02
8. INFLEX	.53	.70	.04	-.27	.01	.33	.14	-.12	.29		.03	.20	-.12	-.02	-.12
9. ADSTF	.80	.76	.28	.29	-.39	-.15	.02	.08	.07	.10		.27	-.17	.06	-.10
10. CLOSE	.79	.79	.09	.54	-.23	-.15	.24	.44	.36	-.03	.40		-.20	-.02	-.09
11. ORNWLC	.81	.63	.22	.05	.17	.11	-.07	-.23	-.14	-.09	-.05	-.31		-.02	.07
12. SPDIST	.85	.82	.04	.10	.31	-.23	-.04	.04	-.11	-.13	-.13	.19	-.04		.03
13. NINDEP	—	.76	—	—	—	—	—	—	—	—	—	—	—	—	—

*Reliabilities were calculated using the Kuder–Richardson Formula 8.
†City police sample above diagonal (n = 113); University police sample below diagonal (n = 49).

p<.05 if r≥.20   p<.05 if r≥.29
p<.01 if r≥.25   p<.01 if r≥.38
‡See Table 2 for Legend.

suggesting that these conceptually distinct varieties of leader substitutes tap relatively unique content domains.

In the sample of city police, only 4 of 78 correlations coefficients exceed .3, and only 2 are in excess of .4. In the sample of university police, 14 of 66 correlations exceed .3, but only 3 are in excess of .4.

Subscale Means and Standard Deviations. Table 6 presents means and standard deviations for potential leadership substitutes in both police samples. While quite similar on most characteristics, some interesting differences among groups did emerge.

For example, city police perceived their organization to be significantly more formalized and rule-inflexible ($p < .01$) than did university police. This probably reflects the fact that the university policing function is a relatively new addition to the criminal justice system in the city. Standardized rules and policies are less

TABLE 6 Means and Standard Deviations

Subscale Title	Field Studies University Police (n = 49) M	SD	City Police (n = 113) M	SD
1. AETK	4.3	.61	4.1	.64
2. PROF	2.9	.88	2.7	.76
3. INDOR	3.5	.99	3.0	.77
4. ROUTIN	2.4	.65	2.7	1.08
5. TSKFB	3.5	.75	3.6	.58
6. INSAT	3.8	.76	3.6	.62
7. ORFORM	2.9	.72	3.2	.53
8. INFLEX	2.6	.60	3.2	.63
9. ADSTF	2.7	.84	2.7	.71
10. CLOSE	3.3	.65	2.9	.60
11. ORNWLC	2.8	.80	3.5	.53
12. SPDIST	4.0	.84	3.5	.82
13. NINDEP	—	—	3.6	.60

prevalent, and are somewhat less likely to be enforced, in an organization at this stage of development. Also, the relatively small size of the university force makes coordination by rules and standard operating procedures less necessary.

University police also reported, on average, greater indifference toward organizational rewards, but higher dependence upon their formal supervisor to administer rewards. They perceived their supervisor to be more spatially distant (with less direct contact) than did city police.

A partial explanation for the finding concerning reward indifference is that university police are better educated (many with college credit toward degrees) than city police (roughly 70 percent with no college or technical school training). In general, reward packages specific to any organization tend to be less important to those who are externally mobile as a result of previous training and well-developed skills.

There was no relationship between Spatial Distance and Organizational Rewards Not within the Leader's Control in either sample (Table 5). This indicates that the leader's reward power is perceived to be essentially independent of the amount of direct contact between himself and his subordinates. The leader is apparently able to exert outcome control through reward distribution even when behavioral control through direct contact is not possible (Ouchi, 1977).

Thus supervisors among the university police, though characterized as more spatially distant from subordinates than those in the city police organization, nevertheless are perceived to be more influential with respect to organizational reward power. However, given differences in attractiveness of extrinsic rewards to subordinates between the two organizations, one might question whether university police supervisors can transform reward power into interpersonal influence any more effectively than their city police counterparts.

Predictive Validity. In a preliminary attempt to assess the criterion-related validity of the substitutes for leadership subscales, city police data were regression analyzed and interpreted. Recall that earlier in this paper it was argued that the emphasis upon hierarchical leadership variables (though they have often failed to share much criterion variance) has retarded attempts to understand subordinate behavior and attitudes.

Police departments, usually characterized by quasi-military organization where the formal leadership function is assumed to be of paramount importance (Bordua & Reiss, 1966; McNamara, 1967), are a case in point. Important leadership substitutes undoubtedly exist, but are usually excluded as predictors of subordinate morale and performance since their contribution is thought to be dwarfed by leadership variables. This portion of the study examines that assumption within the systematic framework presented above, focusing upon the relative predictive power of various substitutes for leadership as well as leader behaviors.[5]

In addition to the *leadership substitutes* discussed above, two subordinate outcomes (organizational commitment, role ambiguity) and four varieties of leader behavior were measured. Porter, Steers, Mowday, and Boulian's (1974) *Organizational Commitment* scale measures expressed willingness to strive toward internalized organizational goals and desire to remain a member. Rizzo, House, and Lirtzman's (1970) *Role Ambiguity* scale was chosen as the other criterion variable because of its demonstrated reliability and consistent relationships with job satisfaction, tension/anxiety, and performance, as well as its frequent inclusion in leadership research (Schuler, Aldag, & Brief, 1977). The KR-8 reliability coefficients for these two criterion variables were .86 and .90, respectively.

Instrumental and *Supportive leader behaviors*

---

[5]Note that sample size rules out a full-scale test of the interactive influence of several substitutes upon hierarchical leadership. Ideally cases would be selected where substitutes are abundant, then where they are scarce, and then subsamples compared. The validity coefficient where substitutes are abundant should then be relatively low, suggesting that hierarchical leadership influence upon subordinate outcomes has been neutralized.

were measured using a set of scales designed specifically for use in Path-Goal Theory hypothesis testing (Schriesheim, Note 3). The Instrumental leader behaviors which were measured included: clarification of what is expected of subordinates in their work roles (*Role Clarification* KR-8 = .92, five items); assignment of subordinates to specific tasks (*Work Assignment* KR-8 = .64, five items); and rule, procedural, and method specification relevant to task execution (*Specification of Procedures* KR-8 = .72, five items). It has been shown that these varieties of instrumental leadership are perceived distinctly by subordinates, and that they differentially relate to criteria (Bish & Schriesheim, Note 1; Schriesheim, Note 4). *Supportive leader behavior* is indicative of warmth, friendship, trust, and concern for the subordinate's personal welfare (KR-8 = .95, 11 items). These dimensions of leader behavior are discussed in House and Mitchell (1974) and House and Dessler (1974).

Table 7 displays the validity coefficients between subordinate role ambiguity and organizational commitment and selected leadership and substitutes for leadership variables. As may be seen, even in a police command bureaucracy, where the formal leader's role is traditionally afforded high significance, leader

TABLE 7   Multiple Regression Equations: Organizational Commitment and Role Ambiguity Regressed upon Leader Behaviors and Leadership Substitutes

	(City Police $n = 113$) Organizational Commitment				
	Full Model			**Reduced Model**	
Predictor	Simple r	Beta Weight	F Ratio	Beta Weight	F Ratio
AETK	.20*	.08	1.0		
PROF	.09	−.03	0.1		
ROUTIN	.10	.13	2.3		
TSKFB	.32**	.15	3.2	.19*	6.3
INSAT	.56**	.46**	28.7	.45**	32.1
ORFORM	.22	.00	0.0		
INFLEX	−.04	−.09	0.9		
ADSTF	.20*	.12	1.3		
CLOSE	.01	−.01	0.0		
NINDEP	−.15	−.09	1.1		
ILBROLCL	.39**	.22*	5.0	.22**	7.5
ILBWA	.06	−.03	0.1		
ILBSPEC	.03	−.01	0.0		
SUPPORT	.21*	−.07	0.6		
	$R = .66**$			$R = .63**$	
	Role Ambiguity				
AETK	−.07	.00	0.0		
PROF	−.06	.12	1.9		
ROUTIN	−.40**	−.29**	15.4	−.29**	18.6
TSKFB	−.28**	−.11	2.2		
INSAT	−.41**	−.24**	10.9	−.25**	13.5
ORFORM	−.53**	−.29**	13.1	−.30**	18.8
INFLEX	−.19	−.03	0.2		
ADSTF	−.08	.02	0.0		
CLOSE	−.03	−.04	0.4		
NINDEP	.11	.02	0.1		
ILBROLCL	−.55**	−.36**	17.6	−.35**	26.0
ILBWA	−.18	−.03	0.1		
ILBSPEC	−.06	.00	0.0		
SUPPORT	−.24*	−.04	0.2		
	$R = .77**$			$R = .75**$	

*p < .05
**p < .01

behaviors account for only a small portion of the criterion variance. Indeed, role clarification is the only leader behavior which exerts a significant independent effect upon the subordinate outcome variables.

High organizational commitment tends to be associated with intrinsically satisfying tasks where performance feedback is readily available as much as with leader role clarification. Similarly, the independent contributions of task and organizational variables (organizational formalization, task routinization, intrinsically satisfying tasks) toward explaining role ambiguity are not overshadowed by the leadership predictors. Again only leader role clarification provides a statistically significant, independent contribution among the leader behaviors.

As shown in the reduced models, parsimonious predictor sets may be selected which account for meaningful portions of criterion variance. When powerful leader substitutes such as intrinsically satisfying work and task-provided performance feedback exist, the leader's supportive behaviors fail to contribute significantly in predicting organizational commitment. The function of leader work assignment and specification of procedures in reducing role ambiguity may be seen to be superfluous given the importance of organizational structure and task variables, though no important substitutes for leader role clarification were found.

This latter finding may be partially explained by recognizing that information about work goals, authority and responsibility, and job performance standards may be difficult to transmit except by personal modes, while work assignment and specification of procedures can readily be transmitted by central dispatching and standard operating procedures, respectively (see Bordua & Reiss, 1966).

ELABORATION OF THE CONSTRUCT

Table 1 was designed to capsulize our present knowledge with respect to possible substitutes for hierarchical leadership. Since present knowledge is the product of past research, and since past research was primarily unconcerned with the topic, the table is probably oversimplified and incomplete in a number of respects. Rigorous elaboration of the substitutes construct must necessarily await additional research, but we would speculate that such research would show the following refinements to be important.

Distinguishing between "Substitutes" and "Neutralizers." A "neutralizer" is defined by Webster's as something which is able to "paralyze, destroy, or counteract the effectiveness of" something else. In the context of leadership, this term may be applied to characteristics which make it effectively *impossible* for relationship and/or task-oriented leadership to make a difference. Neutralizers are a type of moderator variable when uncorrelated with both predictors and the criterion, and act as suppressor variables when correlated with predictors but not the criterion (Zedeck, 1971; Wherry, 1946).

A "substitute" is defined to be "a person or thing acting or used in place of another." In context, this term may be used to describe characteristics which render relationship and/or task-oriented leadership not only impossible but also *unnecessary*.[6] Substitutes may be correlated with both predictors and the criterion, but tend to improve the validity coefficient when included in the predictor set. That is, they will not only tend to affect which leader behaviors (if any) are influential, but will also tend to impact upon the criterion variable.

The consequences of neutralizers and substitutes for previous research have probably been similar, since both act to reduce the impact of leader behaviors upon subordinate attitudes and performance. For this reason it is not too important that such summaries of previous research as Table 1 distinguish between them. Nevertheless, an important theoretical distinction does exist. It is that substitutes do, but neutralizers do not, provide a "person or thing

---

[6]This potentially important distinction was first pointed out by M. A. Von Glinow in a doctoral seminar.

acting or used in place of" the formal leader's negated influence. The effect of neutralizers is therefore to create an "influence vacuum," from which a variety of dysfunctions may emerge.

As an illustration of this point, look again at the characteristics outlined in Table 1. Since each characteristic has the capacity to counteract leader influence, all 14 may clearly be termed neutralizers. It is *not* clear, however, that all 14 are substitutes. For example, subordinates' perceived "ability, experience, training, and knowledge" tend to impair the leader's influence, but may or may not act as substitutes for leadership. It is known that individuals who are high in task-related self-esteem place high value upon nonhierarchical control systems which are consistent with a belief in the competence of people (Korman, 1970). The problem is that subordinate perceptions concerning ability and knowledge may not be accurate. Actual ability and knowledge may therefore act as a substitute, while false perceptions of competence and unfounded self-esteem may produce simply a neutralizing effect.

"Spatial distance," "subordinate indifference toward organizational rewards," and "organizational rewards not within the leader's control" are other examples of characteristics which do not render formal leadership unnecessary, but merely create circumstances in which effective leadership may be impossible. If rewards are clearly within the control of some other person this other person can probably act as a substitute for the formal leader, and no adverse consequences (except probably to the leader's morale) need result. When no one knows where control over rewards lies, however, or when rewards are linked rigidly to seniority or to other factors beyond anyone's control, or when rewards are perceived to be unattractive altogether, the resulting influence vacuum would almost inevitably be dysfunctional.

Distinguishing between Direct and Indirect Leader Behavior Effects. It is possible to conceptualize a *direct effect* of leadership

as one which occurs when a subordinate is influenced by some leader behavior *in and of itself*. An *indirect effect* may be said to result when the subordinate is influenced by the *implications* of the behavior for some future consequence. Attempts by the leader to influence subordinates must always produce direct and/or indirect effects or, when strong substitutes for leadership exist, no effect.

This distinction between direct and indirect effects of leader behavior has received very little attention, but its importance to any discussion of leadership substitutes is considerable. For example, in their review of Path-Goal theory, House and Dessler (1974, p. 31) state that "subordinates with high needs for affiliation and social approval would see friendly, considerate leader behavior as an immediate source of satisfaction" (direct effect). As Table 1 suggests, it is conceivable that fellow group members could supply such subordinates with enough affiliation and social approval to eliminate dependence on the leader. With other subordinates, however, the key "may be not so much in terms of what the leader does but may be in terms of how it is *interpreted* by his members" (Graen et al., 1972, p. 235). Graen et al. concluded from their data that "consideration is interpreted as the leader's evaluation of the member's role behavior . . ." (p. 233). For these subordinates, therefore, consideration seems to have been influential primarily because of its perceived implications for the likelihood of receiving future rewards. In this case the effect is an indirect one, for which group member approval and affiliation probably cannot substitute.

In the same vein, we are told by House and Dessler (1974, pp. 31–32) that:

> Subordinates with high needs for achievement would be predicted to view leader behavior that clarifies path-goal relationships and provides goal-oriented feedback as satisfying. Subordinates with high needs for extrinsic rewards would be predicted to see leader directiveness or coaching behavior as instrumental to their satisfaction if such behavior helped them perform in such a manner as to gain recognition, promotion, security, or pay increases.

It is apparent from House and Dessler's remarks that the distinction between direct and indirect effects need not be limited to relationship-oriented behaviors. Such characteristics of the task as the fact that it "provides its own feedback" (listed in Table 1 as a potential substitute for task-oriented behavior) may provide achievement-oriented subordinates with immediate satisfaction (direct effect), but fail to negate the superior's ability to help subordinates perform so as to obtain future rewards (indirect effect). Conversely, subordinate experience and training may act as substitutes for the indirect effects of task-oriented leadership, by preventing the leader from improving subordinate performance, but may not offset the direct effects.

Identifying Other Characteristics and Other Leader Behaviors. Any elaboration of the substitutes construct must necessarily include the specification of other leader behaviors, and other characteristics which may act as substitutes for leader behaviors. As was mentioned earlier, most previous studies of leadership were concerned with only two of its dimensions. This approach is intuitively indefensible. Richer conceptualizations of the leadership process already exist, and almost inevitably underscore the importance of additional leader activities. As these activities are delineated in future research, it is likely that substitutes for them will also be identified.

Table 8 is offered as a guide to research. It portrays a state of increased sophistication of the substitutes construct, assuming future development along lines suggested in this section. Substitutes would be differentiated from neutralizers, and direct effects of leadership empirically distinguished from indirect effects. The columns on the right are intended to represent as-yet-unexplored leader behaviors, and the dotted lines on the bottom indicate the presence of additional characteristics which may act either as neutralizers or as true substitutes for leadership.

Distinguishing between Cause and Effect in Leader Behavior. Another area where the substitutes construct appears to have implications for leadership research concerns the question of causality. It is now evident from a variety of laboratory experiments and longitudinal field studies that leader behavior may result from as well as cause subordinate attitudes and performance. It is possible to speculate

ABLE 8 Substitutes for Leadership: A Theoretical Extension

Characteristic	Relationship-Oriented, Supportive, People-Centered Leadership (Consideration, Support, and Interaction Facilitation):		Task-Oriented, Instrumental, Job-Centered Leadership (Initiating Structure, Goal Emphasis, and Work Facilitation):		(Other Leader Behaviors . . .)	
	Directly	Indirectly	Directly	Indirectly	Directly	Indirectly
Substitutes						
of the subordinate						
1. Ability				X	?	?
3. "Professional" orientation	X	X	X	X	?	?
of the task						
5. Unambiguous and routine			X	X	?	?
7. Provides its own feedback concerning accomplishment			X		?	?
8. Intrinsically satisfying	X				?	
of the organization						
12. Closely knit, cohesive work groups	X		X	X	?	?
Neutralizers						
4. Indifference toward organizational rewards		X		X	?	?
13. Organizational rewards not within the leader's control		X		X	?	?

upon the effect that leadership substitutes would have on the relative causal strength of superior- and subordinate-related variables. This paper has tried to show that such substitutes act to reduce changes in subordinates' attitudes and performance which are *caused* by leader behaviors. On the other hand, there seems no reason why leadership substitutes should prevent changes in leader behavior which *result* from different levels of subordinate performance, satisfaction, and morale. The substitutes for leadership construct may therefore help to explain why the direction of causality is sometimes predominantly from leader behavior to subordinate outcomes, while at other times the reverse is true.

Specification of Interaction Effects among Substitutes and Neutralizers. From the limited data obtained thus far, it is not possible to differentiate at all among leadership substitutes and neutralizers in terms of relative strength and predictive capability. We have received some indication that the strength of a substitute, as measured by its mean level, is not strongly related to its predictive power. Substitutes for leadership as theoretically important as intrinsic satisfaction, for example, apparently need only be present in moderate amounts (as is the case with the city police; see Table (6) to have potent substituting effects (see Table 7). Other, less important substitutes and neutralizers, might have to be present to a tremendous degree before their effects might be felt. Clearly, the data reported in this study are insufficient to determine at what point a particular substitute becomes important, or at what point several substitutes, each fairly weak by itself, might combine to collectively impair hierarchical leader influence. Multiplicative functions involving information on the strength and predictive power of substitutes for leadership should be able to be specified as evidence accumulates.

CONCLUSIONS

The research literature provides abundant evidence that for organization members to maximize organizational and personal outcomes, they must be able to obtain both guidance and good feelings from their work settings. Guidance is usually offered in the form of role or task structuring, while good feelings may stem for "stroking" behaviors,[7] or may be derived from intrinsic satisfaction associated with the task itself.

The research literature does *not* suggest that guidance and good feelings must be provided by the hierarchical superior; it is only necessary that they somehow be provided. Certainly the formal leader represents a potential source of structuring and stroking behaviors, but many other organization members do too, and impersonal equivalents also exist. To the extent that other potential sources are deficient, the hierarchical superior is clearly in a position to play a dominant role. In these situations the opportunity for leader downward influence is great, and formal leadership ought to be important. To the extent that other sources provide structure and stroking in abundance, the hierarchical leader will have little chance to exert downward influence. In such cases it is of small value to gain entree to the organization, distribute leader behavior questionnaires to anything that moves, and later debate about which leadership theory best accounts for the pitifully small percentage of variance explained, while remaining uncurious about the large percentage unexplained.

Of course, few organizations would be expected to have leadership substitutes so strong as to totally overwhelm the leader, or so weak as to require subordinates to rely entirely on him. In most organizations it is likely that, as was true here, substitutes exist for some leader activities but not for others. Effective leadership might therefore be described as the ability to supply subordinates with needed guidance and good feelings which are not being supplied by other sources. From this viewpoint it is inaccurate to inform leaders (say, in management development programs) that they are incompetent if they do not personally provide these

---

[7]"Stroking" is used here, as in transactional analysis, to describe "any type of physical, oral, or visual recognition of one person by another" (Huse, 1975, p. 288).

things regardless of the situation. While it may (or may not) be necessary that the organization as a whole function in a "nine-to-nine" manner (Blake & Mouton, 1964), it clearly is unnecessary for the manager to behave in such a manner unless no substitutes for leader-provided guidance and good feelings exist.

Dubin (1976, p. 33) draws a nice distinction between "proving" and "improving" a theory, and points out that "if the purpose is to prove the adequacy of the theoretical model . . . data are likely to be collected for values on only those units incorporated in the theoretical model. This usually means that, either experimentally or by discarding data, attention in the empirical research is focused solely upon values measured on units incorporated in the theory."

In Dubin's terms, if we are really interested in improving rather than proving our various theories and models of leadership, a logical first step is that we stop assuming what really needs to be demonstrated empirically. The criticality of the leader's role in supplying necessary structure and stroking should be evaluated in the broader organizational context. Data pertaining to both leadership and possible substitutes for leadership (Table 1) should be obtained, and both main and interaction effects examined. A somewhat different use of information about substitutes for leadership would be as "prescreen," to assess the appropriateness of a potential sample for a hierarchical leadership study.

What this all adds up to is that, if we really want to know more about the sources and consequences of guidance and good feelings in organizations, we should be prepared to study these things *whether or not* they happen to be provided through hierarchical leadership. For those not so catholic, whose interest lies in the derivation and refinement of theories of formal leadership, a commitment should be made to the importance of developing and operationalizing a *true* situational theory of leadership, one which will explicitly limit its propositions and restrict its predictions *to those situations* where hierarchical leadership theoretically ought to make a difference.

SECTION EIGHT

Employment

Two decades ago when automation began to creep into industrial operations, the worker was assured that there was no reason for concern, that the effect would be to change the nature of work but not to reduce the number of jobs available. That was not true then and it is not true now. Computer-assisted manufacturing is becoming increasingly common. Unemployment is a way of life in many European countries and in many segments of the American population. It is becoming clear that unemployment should be considered part of the human condition. The deep and disturbing recession that began in 1979 is still disrupting lives in the United States. Psychologists should have something to say about unemployment. In this section, we will consider the basic relationship between work and nonwork and how each component of this relationship can affect the other.

It is generally assumed that unemployment is bad. There are sufficient data to suggest that unemployment can have a debilitating effect on both physical and psychological well-being. Nevertheless, some types of unemployment can be seen to have a more devastating effect on people than others. In this reading, Warr suggests that there is good unemployment and bad unemployment and describes the difference between them. If this is true, and if it is inevitable that unemployment will remain a reality of the modern industrial society, then it makes sense to try to create conditions for good unemployment.

■ READING 26 ■

Work, Jobs, and Unemployment

Peter Warr
Director, MRC Social and Applied Psychology Unit, University of Sheffield, England

Psychological health depends upon the nature of the work which a person undertakes. In general terms "work" may be defined as activity directed to goals beyond enjoyment of the activity itself. That does not exclude enjoyment, it merely indicates that enjoyment is not part of the definition. Work can vary from momentary exertion through to effort sustained over a period of time. Sustained activity almost always takes place within a network of social roles and institutions. In addition to workers in paid jobs, mothers work in their domestic roles, volunteers in community projects are working, members of an amateur football team or a choir work during practice and in public performance, and a person works in the garden or in decorating the kitchen.

In examining the psychological importance of work, I am reminded of Jahoda's (1966, 1981) discussion of Freud's (1930) suggestion that work is a person's strongest tie to reality. The key feature is that work provides links with the environment which prevents us from becoming overwhelmed by fantasy and emotion. In that sense work can be beneficial even when it is not enjoyable. It is in general important in that it requires investment of self in something outside of the self. Conversely, of course, work can also be harmful. We need to learn which aspects and types enhance psychological well-being and which impair well-being. Such an approach does not deny the significance of leisure, the opportunity *not* to work. Leisure is valuable in its own right, and also because contrasts between work and leisure sharpen the value of each.

My focus in this paper will mainly be upon sustained activity which involves payment, but many of the points I raise apply also to work of other kinds. I will mainly be describing research which my colleagues and I have recently undertaken into unemployment: what happens psychologically when paid work is not possible? I will then introduce some aspects of our research into people who do have paid work, looking at variations between jobs and the way those affect psychological health. Finally, I will link the two types of investigation within an overall perspective. This will identify a common set of features which contribute to

Source: *Bulletin of The British Psychological Society*, 36, 1983, pp 305–311.

health both in paid work and also during unemployment.

PSYCHOLOGICAL ASPECTS OF UNEMPLOYMENT

Rates of unemployment have more than tripled in the last 10 years. At present the overall official figure in the United Kingdom is almost 14 percent (representing more than three million people), but the average value is greatly exceeded in certain geographical areas and among certain demographic groups (the young, the old, and the disabied, for example). Furthermore, long periods of unemployment are becoming common; more than a million people have now been out of work for more than a year. It is important to expand knowledge about the psychological consequences of unemployment, for two reasons. First, so that we can have a more informed public debate. One still hears wild talk about unemployment being very attractive to most unemployed people, or (at the other extreme) that unemployment is driving tens of thousands of people to an early grave. In this area we clearly need more facts. The second reason why research is needed is to improve psychological theory about work and well-being: which aspects of being unemployed particularly impair psychological well-being, and what personal attributes or social processes permit high levels of well-being in the absence of paid work?

My first attempt to answer questions of that kind was a follow-up of steel-workers who had lost their jobs after closure of their plant in 1976 (Warr & Lovatt, 1977; Warr, 1978). I developed and applied interview measures of anxiety, life satisfaction, and positive and negative affect, showing that those who were still unemployed six months after closure exhibited significantly lower psychological well-being than those who had obtained new jobs. My colleagues and I have since obtained similar findings from a number of cross-sectional comparisons of employed versus unemployed people. Without doubt the psychological

health of unemployed people is significantly below that of people in jobs (e.g. Stafford et al., 1980; Warr & Payne, 1982; Warr, 1983a,b). However, *longitudinal* research is particularly desirable if we are to make causal attributions: does psychological well-being change as a consequence of a change in employment status? We have obtained several longitudinal sets of data about general psychological distress, anxiety, depression, and negative self-esteem; these all yield the same pattern of changes associated with changes in employment status (Banks & Jackson, 1982; Warr & Jackson, 1983; Jackson et al., 1983). We are confident that the poorer psychological health of unemployed people is not usually a reflection of the fact that they have always had poorer health: being without a job has indeed caused the decline, and a return to paid employment sharply increases psychological well-being. Another approach to the impact of unemployment is to ask unemployed people whether their health has changed at all since job loss. We have posed that question in several studies, following it with an open-ended request for details of *how* a person's health has changed. That procedure permits us to examine reported changes in psychological health separately from changes in physical health.

In one recent study of almost 1,000 unemployed men, a fifth of the sample reported psychological deterioration since losing their job. The changes they described were increased anxiety, depression, insomnia, irritability, lack of confidence, listlessness, inability to concentrate, and general nervousness. The vast majority of people reporting such changes for the worse indicated that these were directly associated with their being unemployed (Jackson & Warr, 1984). However, it was interesting to find that 8 percent reported an *improvement* in psychological health. In almost all cases this was described as coming about because people were now free from the stresses of their paid jobs. A small minority of people may thus in certain respects benefit from becoming unemployed.

My conclusion from these and several other studies is that moving from paid work into

unemployment yields an overall very significant reduction in psychological well-being.
However, despite a substantial overall shift,
not everyone is affected negatively when they
become unemployed.

POTENTIALLY NEGATIVE FEATURES OF UNEMPLOYMENT

Let us consider next *why* becoming unemployed might yield this deterioration. Nine
features of the unemployed person's role may
bring about reduced psychological well-being,
although these are not important to the same
degree or in the same pattern in all cases. It
should be stressed that these features are not
logically entailed by the concept of unemployment. I see them as components of the current
social construction of unemployment, and I
will argue later that we must strive to alter
that social construction.

First, it is clear that unemployment is likely
to yield a reduced income. For example, our
studies of unemployed working-class men suggest that about two thirds of them now have a
household income which is half or less of their
income when employed. We also find repeatedly that financial anxiety is high, and that
worries about money strongly predict unemployed people's overall distress scores (e.g.
Jackson & Warr, 1984; Payne et al., 1984).

Second, without paid employment the variety within a person's life is likely to be relatively restricted. This is partly a question of
being required less often to leave the house
when you are unemployed, and is also a function of reduced income: you cannot afford to
go to the cinema, the club, or the football
match as often as you could when you had a
paid job. We have studied reduced variety
through reports of changes in daily activities
after loss of a job (Warr & Payne, 1983). Not
surprisingly we found that unemployed men
take on significantly more child-care activities
and meal preparation, but there is also significantly more inactivity, merely sitting around,
sleeping during the day, and watching televi-

sion. A related feature of unemployment is
that in comparison with paid work it introduces fewer goals and less "traction". Many
forms of activity are made up of interrelated
sets of tasks and goals. Committing yourself to
a certain goal also commits you to other goals
and tasks; you become drawn along by the
structure of your work. I think it is often the
case that employment introduces more traction
in this sense than is present when one is without a paid job.

A fourth potentially negative feature of
unemployment is reduced decision latitude, a
smaller scope for decision making. In one sense
of course an unemployed person has a great
deal of freedom: he or she can decide when to
get up, whether or not to go out, whether or
not to watch television, and so on. But this
freedom of choice is in most cases limited to
small repetitive decisions about daily routine.
In respect of larger decisions, for example
about lifestyle or leisure activities, the range of
realistic options available to an unemployed
person is usually quite small, since material resources are severely curtailed. In addition *psychological* resources are reduced in many cases.

Fifth, there is considerable evidence that
much of the satisfaction derived from jobs
comes from the development and practice of
skills. Not all jobs offer opportunities of that
kind, but for most people unemployment is
likely to bring a reduction in skill use and development. In one sense, of course, unemployed people have *more* opportunities to practice their skills, just as in one sense they have
greater decision latitude. However, in practice
diminished resources and a reduction in externally imposed goals are likely for most people
to lead to more limited skill use or development during unemployment.

A sixth feature is an increase in psychologically threatening activities. Unemployed people are committed to seeking jobs where they
will probably be rejected, they have to deal
with a society which often appears to view
them as second-class citizens, and they may
have to struggle to raise money through official agencies or through borrowing and selling. In general they are liable to experience a

large number of threatening life-events. Associated with this is a seventh aspect of unemployment, insecurity about the future. In one of our studies of unemployed working-class men, approximately two thirds identified as a major problem not knowing what was going to happen to them in future months (Payne et al., 1984). A high proportion felt threatened by the possibility that they might become unemployable, lose their self-respect, or have insoluble money problems. Current threats are thus compounded by a sense of insecurity about the future.

An eighth feature of unemployment is restricted interpersonal contact. It is widely believed that unemployed people have more restricted contact because of the absence of job colleagues and because of their reduced money to visit clubs, pubs, or other social settings. However, in our own studies unemployed men have reported *more* time spent with friends and neighbours since they became unemployed (e.g. Warr & Payne, 1983). That clearly needs to be followed up. It seems likely that unemployed men may spend more time with a *restricted range* of other people, so that the number of *different* contacts is reduced although the overall amount of contact is if anything increased.

Ninth, we must consider the changes in social position which accompany unemployment. By this I mean the public identity associated with a role, which contributes to a person's self-concept and self-evaluation. There is no doubt that many social positions within paid employment can strongly influence self-concept and the way a person is categorized and evaluated by others. On becoming unemployed a person loses a socially accepted position and the roles and self-perceptions which go with it. And the newly acquired position is widely felt to be inferior. Unemployed people tend to feel that they have moved into a position of lower prestige, and they may sense a normative expectation that their aspirations ought to be reduced in keeping with this apparently subordinate position.

The causal processes which yield reduced psychological health in unemployment may be quite complex. For example, the listlessness and depression reported by many of our subjects is itself a causal influence as well as an outcome. Loss of a job may yield several of the features I have described, and together these may create depression, inability to concentrate, and a general listlessness. Those psychological processes may in turn influence some or all of the nine features, for example leading to reduced variety and restricted interpersonal contact. The causal links are thus cyclical, from environment to person, from person to environment, and so on in interactive fashion.

MEDIATING VARIABLES

So far I have been considering the *general* psychological impact of unemployment. Next I would like to examine eight variables which might mediate the effects.

First, employment commitment. Most unemployed people are locked into a strong commitment to obtain another job. This aspect of the so-called "work ethic" may be referred to as "employment commitment," and we have measured it in most of our investigations (e.g. Warr et al., 1979; Jackson et al., 1983). Contrary to some popular opinion, we repeatedly find that employment commitment is extremely high among unemployed people: they really do want a job (Warr, 1982). However, there are of course variations between people in the degree to which having a job is personally salient. We have consistently found that strength of employment commitment is strongly positively associated with degree of psychological distress during unemployment: higher employment commitment goes with higher distress. This fact is logically not very surprising. But as an instance of the general importance of ego-involvement in all areas of life it raises interesting theoretical and practical questions. For example, what personal and social factors are likely to give rise to high or low levels of employment commitment? Can, and should, high levels of commitment be reduced, through counselling, teaching, or social pressures, when unemployment is so high that the probability of finding a job is negligible? We are here at the heart of the social construction of unemployment, and the strong values which determine that.

Second, age. It is clear that, at least among men, age is curvilinearly associated with the negative effects of unemployment. We have in several studies found that middle-aged unemployed men experience greater distress than those who are younger or older (e.g. Hepworth, 1980; Jackson & Warr, 1984). In part this is associated with greater financial strain among the middle-aged group, who often have more demanding family commitments.

Length of unemployment, a third possible mediating variable, is particularly interesting, since published research to date has typically failed to show that longer durations of unemployment are associated with lower psychological well-being (Warr et al., 1982). We have recently carried out an investigation which we believe has advantages over those in the literature, and a strong association between duration and lower well-being was found. It appears that psychological health drops at the point of transition. Even for those who had just become unemployed, distress scores were significantly above those in paid jobs. Well-being continues to decline through the early weeks of unemployment, but it seems that there is a levelling off around four to six months. For example, the proportion of our sample reporting a deterioration in psychological health was 12, 17, 24, and 24 percent for unemployment durations of less than one month, one to three months, four to six months, seven to 12 months, and more than 12 months respectively.

What about the combined effects of two mediating variables? I have been intrigued by the possibility that age and length of unemployment may *interact* in determining the psychological impact of being without a job. More precisely, I think there are grounds for predicting that longer unemployment will *not* be associated with greater distress for people who are at both extremes of the age distribution of the workforce. Unemployed people above 60 years of age are increasingly seeing

themselves as in "early retirement". And unemployed people below the age of about 20 are different from middle-aged unemployed people in several respects. Teenagers who are unemployed tend to have fewer financial problems than older unemployed people, for instance, because they may be living reasonably cheaply with their parents. They carry forward from school a network of friends and leisure activities, and the social stigma of unemployment may be less for them than for unemployed middle-aged people.

We have recently drawn a carefully defined sample in which lengths of unemployment were equally represented for each of 10 age bands (Jackson & Warr, 1984). We expected that greater duration of unemployment would be significantly associated with higher distress scores, for all age groups except those at the extremes. And this pattern was indeed observed. Within each of the four 10-year bands between 20 and 59, the expected significant association of distress with duration was found. However the association with duration was not present at the extremes. For teenagers and those approaching, retirement, increased duration of unemployment was not linked to greater psychological ill-health.

Turning to a fourth and a fifth mediating variable, it is clear from several of our studies that both financial strain and a low level of activity are also significantly associated with psychological ill-health during unemployment (e.g., Hepworth, 1980; Payne et al., 1984). As mentioned before, the causal pattern is probably a cyclical one, in that financial strain and inactivity are likely both to be outcomes of unemployment as well as themselves influencing other outcomes. Those two features come together when we examine social class as a sixth possible mediator. We have recently compared matched groups of middle-class and working-class unemployed people in terms of their experiences of unemployment and several aspects of well-being. We found substantially greater financial problems among the working-class sample, and also that they had greater difficulty in filling the time than did middle-class unemployed people. This difference in activity level is partly a function of the working-class sample having less money to spend, but there are suggestions in the data that the difference is also a matter of greater internal control and self-directedness among the middle-class sample (Payne et al., 1984).

Personal vulnerability is a seventh possible mediating variable. The general notion is the plausible one that some people are less able than others to withstand environmental pressures. These people (being more vulnerable) are expected to show greater negative change in response to stress. We have recently obtained some information about *physical* change after job loss which bears upon this point (Jackson & Warr, 1984). "Vulnerability" here was assessed in terms of presence or absence of a chronic health impairment. Eighteen percent of our sample reported having some chronic impairment, such as continuing arthritis, bronchitis, a heart complaint, a slipped disc, and so on. This vulnerable group (the people with chronic health problems) revealed a significant association between longer duration of unemployment and greater decline in health. In almost all cases the deterioration was reported to be in respect of a person's chronic condition: this was getting worse, and more so with longer time out of paid work. However, for the less vulnerable group (people with no chronic health problems) there was no association between duration of unemployment and reported physical deterioration. The interaction term in analysis of variance (vulnerability by duration) was highly significant. It seems likely that a similar pattern might be found for *psychological* vulnerability, and we clearly should be looking out for that.

Finally, what about sex differences in the effect of unemployment? Most of the results I have described have come from samples of men. However, we have also looked at aspects of women's unemployment, attempting to bring together a wide range of findings within an overall model. In general we have learned that for single women or others who are principal wage-earners, the pattern of effects is the same as for men. But for mothers of young children there is apparently no general associa-

tion between having a job and experiencing higher psychological well-being. Neither does there appear to be an association between paid employment and well-being for mothers in general, defined as a group irrespective of the age of their children. In so far as paid employment does yield a psychological benefit for mothers, this effect appears to be greater for members of the working class than among middle-class mothers (Warr & Parry, 1982*a,b*; Parry, 1983). I think that this last finding is contrary to some people's belief. We interpret it in terms of differences between social classes in the quality of mothers' nonoccupational environment. The daily lives of mothers without paid work tend to be more stressful and psychologically impoverished in working-class than in middle-class homes (e.g. Brown & Harris, 1978). There is thus greater scope for improvement brought about by paid employment for working-class mothers than there is scope for improvement for middle-class mothers. Over and above that, the quality of an employment relationship is of course important; I will return to that shortly.

DIFFERENCES BETWEEN JOBS

In addition to research into unemployment, the Social and Applied Psychology Unit is also carrying out parallel studies within a second design: we are investigating people all of whom are in paid employment, in order to identify those features of their jobs which enhance or diminish psychological well-being. I believe that the factors we are identifying as psychologically important in paid work turn out to be the ones which also determine the impact of unemployment.

The second set of investigations is aiming to identify and change occupational environments which are psychologically undesirable. We carry out controlled experiments to change the content of jobs, in a direction which we predict will increase employee well-being. These experiments continue for up to three years, and we carefully monitor the consequences of the changes. For example, one study set out to examine the consequences of increasing the control which lower-level production employees have over their work tasks and interrelationships (Wall & Clegg, 1981). This involved redesigning jobs, so that responsibilities were shifted from supervisors to teams of shop-floor workers. The workers were given control over setting the pace of work, the distribution of tasks between themselves, and the general organization of their time and effort.

These changes were based upon a model of psychological well-being in paid work, which emphasizes the importance of decision latitude and personal control over resources. The experimental changes increased the scope of workers' decision making, and also introduced wider opportunities for skill use, more work variety, and more constructive interpersonal contacts. Data about employee attitudes, well-being and performance were gathered before the changes and 6 and 18 months later. It was found that employee well-being increased substantially as a result of the experimental changes: overall job satisfaction became significantly greater and psychological distress significantly declined. The changes recorded through standard instruments were also apparent within the factory, where the atmosphere had become more relaxed with less conflict and less strain as people went about their jobs. Although it is not directly relevant to my present theme, work motivation and performance also increased significantly. Increases in occupational well-being and increases in work performance are not necessarily mutually exclusive.

That is one example of the Unit's change studies within organizations. These are complemented by a project investigating *individual* change. The Unit contains a psychological clinic accepting referrals from the National Health Service. The clinic receives as patients workers who have been referred by their medical practitioners as suffering neurotic problems linked to their jobs. We are carrying out experimental research into psychotherapy for these patients, aiming to restore their psychological health and occupational effectiveness, and also to learn more about the role of paid

TABLE 1   Characteristics of Psychologically "Good" and Psychologically "Bad" Jobs

	"Good" Jobs Have	"Bad" Jobs Have
1. Money	more	less
2. Variety	more	less
3. Goals, traction	more	less
4. Decision latitude	more	less
5. Skill use/development	more	less
6. Psychological threat	less	more
7. Security	more	less
8. Interpersonal contact	more	less
9. Valued social position	more	less

work in their lives and how it can enhance or impair their well-being (e.g. Shapiro et al., 1979; Brewin, 1980; Firth, 1983).

I have derived from these studies of people in the clinic and in jobs a perspective on which features of paid work are psychologically "good" and which are psychologically "bad". This is shown in Table 1, in terms of the two poles of what is in fact a continuum. I believe that it is generally the case that psychological well-being is enhanced by jobs which are defined as "good" jobs in terms of the characteristics set out there. I also believe that far too many jobs fall into the category of psychologically "bad" in respect of these features. Of course many of the features are desirable only up to a point: for example, most people want interpersonal contact, but to a degree they consider reasonable rather than excessive. And some psychological threat is inherent in the development of skills and the pursuit of challenging goals. To determine the optimum level of these variables is of course one of the tasks of occupational research.

This perspective is intentionally at a very general level. There are many possible configurations of these job properties, and we need detailed research into the ways they are combined. Indeed that is one of the functions of my own Unit, to investigate in detail the job characteristics I have identified here. We are also alert to the need to develop models in terms of individual differences in skills, attitudes, and values. Models of work, paid or unpaid, clearly need to embrace features of the individual as well as features of the environment.

GOOD AND BAD UNEMPLOYMENT

I now want to suggest that we can talk about psychologically "good" and psychologically "bad" unemployment, and that we can do this in the same terms as I have viewed jobs. This is shown in Table 2. For most people, unemployment is characterized by the right-hand column; it is that pattern of features which yields the decrement in psychological health.

It may seem strange to talk of "good" unemployment, when so much evidence points to its harmful effects. But I have argued that unemployment is harmful in part through the way it is socially constructed; the present negative consequences are not entailed by the concept itself. I have also pointed out that a small number of people appear not to suffer when they are unemployed, and that a very small minority exhibit an improvement, especially if their previous job was in the "bad" category.

I described earlier how the causal impact of unemployment was cyclical: from the environment to the person, and from the person to the environment. It follows that whether or not unemployment is psychologically harmful depends both on the nature of the environment and also on a person's style of acting upon that environment. It is possible for unemployed people to change their own unemployment from being psychologically "bad" towards the "good" pole of the continuum. Let me illustrate that through one final study from the Unit (Fryer & Payne, 1984). This involved interviews with a small sample of people who had been specially identified as coping particularly well with unemployment. Each member of the sample was found to maintain a very high level of activity, which was channelled by strongly held values towards the achievement of particular goals, usually in the domain of religious, political, or community groups. These unemployed people drew a clear distinction between work in general, to which they were strongly committed, and employment, to which they were less committed. They were very proactive, tending to create and then exploit opportunities; and they were self-directed to a high degree, being able to structure their own activities in line with their objectives and their commitment to specific tasks.

That group of people was intentionally selected to be coping well with unemployment, and their success might at least in part be attributed to their own active creation of most of those features of "good" unemployment which I have suggested. However, such active, self-directing people are relatively unusual. I am certainly not suggesting that all unemployed people could transform their situation in this way, but I am pointing out that some self-engendered movement from "bad" towards "good" unemployment is in principle possible.

TABLE 2 Characteristics of Psychologically "Good" and Psychologically "Bad" Unemployment

		"Good" Unemployment Has	"Bad" Unemployment Has
1.	Money	more	less
2.	Variety	more	less
3.	Goals, traction	more	less
4.	Decision latitude	more	less
5.	Skill use/development	more	less
6.	Psychological threat	less	more
7.	Security	more	less
8.	Interpersonal contact	more	less
9.	Valued social position	more	less

THE RECONSTRUCTION OF UNEMPLOYMENT

Let me now bring these several themes together into my conclusion. It seems to me that whatever government is in power, rates of unemployment in the next decade are likely to be much higher than those which were customary only 10 years ago. Large structural changes have taken place in industry and other employment sectors. And whatever the long-term effects of new technology, the introduction of micro-processor-based equipment is bound to reduce job opportunities in the short term. Furthermore the size of the labour force has increased substantially in recent years. As a nation we clearly need more jobs. But as psychologists I think we should go beyond that, to argue particularly for jobs which enhance rather than impair psychological health. There are a lot of "bad" jobs around, in terms of the characteristics I have identified. So the top priority is to move people out of "bad" unemployment into "good" jobs, defining these in the terms I have used here.

However, I believe that the most optimistic predictions of any political party indicate that, despite possible changes in government or in economic climate, there will still not be enough jobs to go round, at least as long as a job is expected to fill 35 or 40 hours of each week. Too many people will be unemployed whatever happens politically or economically. This is where the concept of "good" unemployment is so important; as I have argued, it is possible for psychological well-being to be high during unemployment, although for most unemployed people at present that is not the case. As well as aiming for more jobs, we need also to change values and behaviours so that unemployment comes closer to "good" unemployment as I have identified it in Table 2. This is partly an individual matter, arising from the self-directedness of individual unemployed people, but it is primarily a matter for society in general. We need structural changes and new social processes which can enhance the psychological health of unemployed people.

Ideas are starting to gain ground in terms of job sharing during a week or in alternate weeks, having a paid job for only a limited number of months in each year, undertaking work for voluntary agencies, helping community groups, attending short-term or part-time educational courses, or having access to free recreational facilities. But there is need for more intensive effort, and that must start with the recognition that unemployment will remain too high whatever happens politically and economically. At present too many people and groups are assuming that unemployment can be eradicated. It certainly could (and should) be reduced, but I believe that the level will nevertheless remain higher than is desirable. On serveral occasions I have referred to the contemporary "social construction" of unemployment. We clearly need more jobs, but what is also needed is the "social reconstruction" of unemployment. That is a huge task, involving also the reconstruction of paid jobs, but I hope that psychologists will play their part in achieving it.

Unemployment can have dramatic effects on individuals. It is clear that it will have an effect on nonwork behavior since social relations, time schedules, economic independence, and skill utilization and development are all affected. But what about the relationship between work and nonwork when the individual is fully and regularly employed? There are several different views of this possible relationship. Some researchers propose that you try to make up for bad experiences at work by seeking good experiences in nonwork settings. Others propose that you seek to have the same good experiences in nonwork settings as you do at work. Still others suggest that there is no relationship between work and nonwork behavior. In this reading, several models of the relationship between work and nonwork are considered.

■ READING 27 ■

Work and Leisure: A Task Attributes Analysis

Boris Kabanoff and Gordon E. O'Brien

School of Social Sciences, Flinders University of South Australia,

Bedford Park, Australia

Although a number of authors have stated that psychologists should study the relation among work experiences and patterns of leisure (Dunnette, 1973; Neulinger, 1974; Porter, Lawler, & Hackman, 1975; Spink, 1975), little has been done in the way of detailed empirical research. A few studies have reported the relative contribution of work and nonwork satisfaction to general life satisfaction (London, Crandall, & Seals, 1977; Orpen, 1978), but these have been unable to describe the manner in which different work experiences are associated with leisure activities. Lack of information cannot be attributed to lack of research hypotheses and theories for there are at least three major hypotheses about the relation be-tween work and leisure (Meissner, 1971; Parker, 1971, 1976; Rousseau, 1978; Seeman, 1971; Wilensky, 1960). These hypotheses may be labeled generalization, compensation, and segmentation.

Wilensky (1960) attributed to Engels the two classic hypotheses of the work/leisure field: spillover (or generalization) and compensation. Generalization implies a similarity or positive correlation between the sort of work people perform and their leisure activities. That is, a person in a routine, repetitive, un-challenging job situation should have similarly routine leisure pursuits. On the other hand, compensation represents an opposition or neg-ative correlation between work and leisure; those with routine work should choose varied, challenging activities. A more contemporary hypothesis of work and nonwork is most closely associated with Dubin's idea of a cen-tral life interest (Dubin, 1956). Dubin offers

Source: *Journal of Applied Psychology,* 65(5), 1980, pp. 596–609. Copyright 1970 by the American Psychological Association. Reprinted by permission of the publisher and author.

the axiom that social experience is inevitably segmented for most individuals in industrial society, with each social segment lived out more or less independently of the rest. This view implies that the worlds of work and leisure are psychologically separate.

All three hypotheses have received some support. Mansfield and Evans (1975) offered some evidence for the compensatory hypothesis from a sample of management and clerical personnel. Employees who said they had few opportunities to meet personal needs on the job also said that they tried to maximize opportunities to meet these needs off the job. On the other hand, using a somewhat similar method, Rousseau (1978) found that her sample tended to describe their work and leisure as being similar, thus suggesting generalization. Kornhauser (1965), in his classic study of Detroit automobile workers, also claimed to find evidence of generalization. His major finding was that the higher the occupation in respect to skill and associated attributes of variety, responsibility, and pay, the better the average mental health. Men in routine, repetitive jobs had narrow leisure interests with little evidence of self-development, self-expression, or interest in larger social purposes. Meissner (1971) studied the work and leisure of workers from one industrial plant and found evidence of a generalization from work to leisure. His results suggested that having work with little discretionary potential, that is, with limited autonomy or decision making, carried over into reduced participation in voluntary, self-directed activities outside of work.

However, Dubin (1956) found that three quarters of his sample of blue-collar workers could be described as nonwork oriented. The majority perceived the workplace as a purely formal environment that was not congenial to the development of preferred, informal relationships. Dubin concluded that most workers hold entirely different expectations of what is rewarding in work and nonwork time and argued that because of this, there is essentially no overlap between the two "worlds." Dubin's later research (Dubin, Champoux, & Porter, 1975; Dubin & Champoux, 1977) has not

elaborated on this segmentalist viewpoint, but his hypothesis has received support from several other sources. Bacon (1975) found no evidence for either compensation or generalization on the part of workers in routine jobs, and London et al. (1977) found no correlation between expressed satisfaction with work and with nonwork.

There are probably a number of reasons for the apparent inconsistency of these findings. First, the relationship between work and leisure may depend on the characteristics of the group studied. Age, sex, education, income, and work orientation may moderate the observed relationships, and such variables should be measured. These variables can affect, to a moderate extent, the perception of job attributes but might be expected to have a larger effect on the choice and availability of leisure activities. Second, some of the difficulties in identifying consistent relationships may be due to the use of general global categories for describing work and leisure. Terms such as *good quality* or *enriched* do not permit detailed analysis of the extent to which different work/leisure relationships may apply to different dimensions of work and leisure. One set of relationships may apply to the dimension of skill utilization, another set to variety, and so on. Global categories that reflect a summation of such dimensions may show no strong effects when, in principle, strong relationships could be present for specific work/leisure dimensions. Third, there are difficulties in the measurement of generalization, compensation, and segmentation. Typically there is no specification of what job attributes employees are supposed to generalize, compensate for, or segment. Sometimes the job attributes are defined, but the appropriate leisure dimension is not measured. Strict examination of the alternative work/leisure relationships requires that work and leisure be measured on similar dimensions. The main hypotheses imply that work and leisure activities may be compared but logically require that common dimensions be specified before the comparison can be made.

The present study attempts to meet these

difficulties by measuring sociological variables (age, education, sex, income, and work orientation) as well as specifying a set of five dimensions that can be used to describe both work and leisure activities. These dimensions are skill utilization, influence, variety, pressure, and interaction. To widen the generalizability of the results, a random sample from a wide range of occupational categories was used although, of course, the results will strictly be descriptions only of Australian employees.

Work/Leisure and the Locus of Control

Another innovation of the study was to measure the effect of a relevant personality variable, locus of control, on work/leisure patterns. The Internal-External Locus of Control (I-E Scale; Rotter, 1966) measures people's perceptions that the events that happen to them are contingent on their own actions, abilities, or behavior. Internal persons feel in control of their own life experiences and outcomes, whereas external persons tend to see life outcomes as being controlled by forces outside of their control such as luck, fate, or powerful others.

It has consistently been found that internals are more active, alert, or directive in attempting to control and manipulate their environment than are externals (Lefcourt, 1976; Phares, 1976), indicating a greater adaptiveness to a variety of environmental circumstances (Gilmor, 1978). If one assumes, and it seems reasonable to do so (e.g., Kelly, 1972; Meyersohn, 1972; Zuzanek, 1974), that a distinguishing feature of leisure is the opportunity it provides for a relatively high level of personal discretion and control, then it seems likely that internals should be able to make greater use of this opportunity.

It was hypothesized that persons who compensate for a low-quality working environment, that is, one lacking in positive experiences such as variety, skill, and decision making, have an active, self-directed orientation toward their leisure. Internal persons should act in the expectation that they can obtain satisfactions denied in their work by ma-

nipulating the nonwork environment to meet their needs. Thus it was expected that internals in low-quality jobs would show evidence of *supplemental compensation* (Kando & Summers, 1971) by pursuing desired goals in nonwork time. On the other hand, externals should tend to feel that factors beyond their personal control determine their leisure behavior. Given this expectation, externals should show evidence of a *passive generalization* from low-quality work to low-quality leisure. It seems likely that persons with an external locus of control orientation should experience a sense of incongruence and dissatisfaction with jobs that require them to exercise influence, use skills, and cope with a varied task environment (Andrisani & Nestel, 1976; Gilmor, 1978). Hence, externals should show evidence of *reactive compensation* (Kando & Summers, 1971), in which they will seek to minimize in their leisure the undesired experiences they encounter at work. Internals, on the other hand, should find a relatively challenging job situation as being congruent with and reinforcing of their basic control orientation. This should enhance their readiness to manipulate the nonwork context, indicating a process of *active generalization*.

Thus the present study had two major aims —to examine the validity of the three dominant models of work/leisure relationships, namely, compensation, generalization, and segmentation and to examine the direct and interactive effect of locus of control on work/leisure relationships.

METHOD

Sample

The sample was a .5 percent household sample drawn from metropolitan Adelaide using the technique of multistage cluster sampling (Kish, 1965) to obtain adequate representation of occupations and socioeconomic status. A sample frame (based on the Australian Bureau of Statistics, 1971, census sampling frame) constructed by the Flinders University Centre for Applied Social and Survey Research was

TABLE 1 Characteristics of Employed Sample

Characteristics	Percent	Characteristics	Percent
Sex		Education	
Male	63.1	Primary only	12.1
Female	36.9	Secondary (three years or less)	34.2
		Leaving (fourth year)	22.3
Age (in years)		Matriculation (sixth year)	6.6
15–19	8.9	Tertiary (no degree)	6.6
20–24	16.2	Tertiary (first degree)	6.0
25–34	24.7	Tertiary (MA or PhD)	.9
35–44	21.6	Other (trade certificate, diploma, etc.)	11.2
45–54	18.8		
55–59	6.3	Industry	
60–64	2.8	Agricultural	2.0 (8.6)
–65+	.7	Mining	1.1 (.8)
		Manufacturing	25.3 (24.4)
Occupation		Electricity, water, gas	2.9 (1.8)
Professional	15.8 (13.0)	Construction	6.3 (7.4)
Administrative/Managerial	7.0 (6.6)	Wholesale and retail trade	16.9 (19.7)
Clerical	18.6 (14.5)	Transport and storage	6.0 (4.8)
Sales/Insurance	9.6 (8.4)	Communication	3.7 (1.9)
Farm workers	.6 (9.0)	Finance, insurance and business services	7.4 (5.9)
Miners	.4 (.4)	Public administration	6.8 (4.0)
Transport/Communication	6.7 (5.3)	Entertainment/Recreation	6.2 (4.9)
Trades (skilled and unskilled)	30.7 (33.3)	Community services	14.4 (15.8)
Personal services	10.6 (7.8)		

Note. N = 1,383. Figures in parentheses are from the 1971 South Australian Year Book showing total occupational distribution, urban and rural.

used. Of 1,473 households approached, 1,123 allowed research access, resulting in a final number of 1,383 persons in current employment completing useable questionnaires. This gave a household response rate of 76 percent which was considered satisfactory.

Since the sample was drawn from a metropolitan area, occupations in the farm worker category are underrepresented. Categories for occupation and industry are those used by the Australian Bureau of Statistics (see Table 1).

Procedure

A personal interview approach was utilized, with each selected household being visited by an interviewer who completed the questionnaire if the respondent was present or left it for completion and subsequent collection. A total of 27 female interviewers were used. Preference was given to women who had previously been employed by the Australian Bureau of Statistics. Applicants were required to attend a two-day training program and participate in

pilot testing of the questionnaire. After training and selection, interviewers were allocated a quota of households selected from the sampling frame. (Further details about sample characteristics, procedure, and questionnaire design are available in O'Brien & Dowling, 1980, and O'Brien, Dowling, & Kabanoff, Note 1.)

Job Attributes

The job attributes chosen in this study are derived from an analysis of the formal job structure (O'Brien, 1968; O'Brien, Biglan, & Penna, 1972; Oeser & O'Brien, 1967). A job is a set of tasks allocated to a position in an organization. A particular job can be defined formally in terms of the structural relationships that connect its task elements to other task elements; its task elements to the position; and the position with the person who is the job occupant. Using this framework, the major job relations defined are assignment, authority, allocation, and precedence. These relations determine people's perceptions of their jobs and the perceptions can be categorized into corresponding components. The perceptual dimensions corresponding to the five structural relations are, respectively, skill utilization, influence, variety, pressure, and interaction (O'Brien, 1980).

The job attributes of influence, skill utilization, variety, pressure, and interaction were measured on five-point scales, with the influence scale having 10 items and the other attributes having 4 items for each scale. The scales achieved an acceptable level of reliability except for pressure, which was rather low ($\alpha = .33$). The other alpha values were .78 (skill utilization), .90 (influence), .74 (variety), and .62 (interaction).

Leisure Attributes

If there is incomplete agreement about how work should be described, then this problem is even more evident when it comes to describing leisure. In the present study, a task-based definition of leisure was adopted. Leisure activities were conceived of as tasks that are chosen by an actor (Kabanoff, 1980). It was assumed that the nature of the leisure tasks people choose determines the kind of actions they carry out and the satisfactions they can experience. It is arguable that since leisure activities are personally chosen and directed toward meeting individual rather than some formally prescribed goals, then a leisure activity can have as many different meanings as there are participants (Kando & Summers, 1971; Neulinger, 1974). To a degree this suggestion is valid, but this view has been challenged by other writers (Meyersohn, 1972; Zuzanek, 1974). If one strictly maintains that leisure meanings are unique to each individual, then research on patterns of leisure becomes uninterpretable. It appears preferable to describe leisure by using task dimensions that have been shown previously to have important psychological or behavioral consequences for the actor. Though it is not claimed that this provides an exhaustive or exclusive description of a particular activity, it should provide an overall activity profile

that is parsimonious and includes important behavioral dimensions. Studies that have classified activities in terms of their potential for gratifying various psychological needs can be seen to have a somewhat similar goal (e.g., Bishop, 1970; London, Crandall, & Fitzgibbons, 1977).

The survey included a list of 93 leisure activities, and respondents were asked to indicate whether they had taken part in each activity at least three times in the last year. They were asked not to check any activity in which they participated as a duty or chore. The recall method of measuring leisure participation is considerably simpler and apparently equally as accurate as the costly diary method (Bishop, Jeanrenaud, & Lawson, 1975). All of these activities were classified by independent raters using the same task attributes as were used by respondents to describe their jobs, namely, influence, variety, pressure, skill utilization, and interaction. Raters used a five-point rating scale ranging from "a great deal" (5) to "not at all" (1). The five attributes were defined as follows:

Influence or autonomy means the amount of control over the environment (including other people) that a person has when he or she is involved in any particular activity. That is, the extent to which the participant can set goals, decide how best to meet these goals, influence the actions of other people, and generally determine the course of events.

Variety denotes the amount of change or mixture of activities, behaviors, or interests involved in any activity.

Pressure means the extent to which an activity puts some stress or strain, mental or physical, on a person's capacities; that is, the extent to which an activity demands some exertion on the part of the individual for the successful completion or accomplishment of a goal.

Skill utilization means how much opportunity an activity provides for a person to employ skills and personal capacities, or the extent to which it requires an individual to learn and develop special techniques and knowledge.

Interaction is the extent to which any activity involves other people. Eighty activities used in a pilot survey were rated by 18 raters (9 male, 9 female) who achieved intraclass correlations above .90 for all five attributes. A second group of 13 raters (7 male, 6 female) who rated 13 activities achieved intraclass correlations between .50 and .70, again satisfactory. The mean scores of all 93 activities on the five attributes are contained in O'Brien et al. (Note 1). To allow for differential rates of responding, each respondent's score on the five leisure attributes was calculated as the average score over all activities nominated. For example,

$$\text{leisure influence} = \frac{\text{influence activity}_1 + \text{influence activity}_2 + \text{influence activity}_n}{n}$$

where n = number of leisure activities engaged in.

Other Measures

Included in the survey questionnaire were a number of other psychological scales and questions related to the respondents' demographic status. The scales included the standard, 29-item I-E scale (Rotter, 1966) and a 12-item work orientation scale that asked respondents to rate the importance of six intrinsic work facets (e.g., opportunities to use skills, responsibility, variety) and six extrinsic work facets (e.g., job security, pay, time for leisure). The appropriate items were then combined to give two work orientation scales. The alpha values for these scales were locus of control, .69; intrinsic orientation, .66; and extrinsic orientation, .63. The demographic information included age, sex, education, income, marital status, number of hours worked in the last week, and whether there were any children under 15 years of age in the family.

RESULTS

To examine both the direct and interactive effects of work attributes and locus of control on leisure attributes, the sample was split into approximate thirds on the five work attributes and locus of control to give a high, intermediate, and low category on each independent variable. A series of two-way analyses of variance (ANOVAS) were then carried out, individually treating the five leisure dimensions as dependent variables (Table 2).

Table 2 shows that only locus of control was consistently related to the leisure attributes.

TABLE 2 Summary of Analyses of Variance with Leisure Attributes Dependent

Source	MS	df*	F†	Percent Variance
Work influence (A)	.001	2,1252	—	—
Locus of control (B)	.226	2,1252	6.48§	1
A × B	.028	4,1252	—	—
Work variety (A)	.156	2,1253	3.24†	1
Locus of control (B)	.159	2,1253	3.29‡	1
A × B	.006	4,1253	—	—
Work pressure (A)	.015	2,1244	—	—
Locus of control (B)	.195	2,1244	3.32‡	1
A × B	.080	4,1244	—	—
Work skill utilization (A)	.230	2,1252	2.60	—
Locus of control (B)	.764	2,1252	8.63§	1
A × B	.093	4,1252	—	—
Work interaction (A)	.128	2,1251	2.22	—
Locus of control (B)	.052	2,1251	—	—
A × B	.041	4,1251	—	—

*df varies due to slight differences in amount of missing data.
†F < 1 in all rows where no value appears.
‡p < .05.
§p < .01.

There were no significant interactions. Internals are more likely to be involved in activities that require greater skill utilization, influence, variety, and pressure, but locus of control was unrelated to amount of interaction. This result is consistent with our expectations. Work variety was significantly related to leisure variety. t-test comparisons showed that the only significant difference was between the low work variety and moderate work variety groups, with the moderate group having higher leisure variety, $t(937) = 2.34$, $p < .02$. t-test comparisons also showed that both the moderate work skill utilization group, $t(984) = 3.49$, $p < .002$, and the high work skill utilization group, $t(850) = 4.47$, $p < .001$, had a higher level of leisure skill utilization than the low work skill utilization group. As Table 2 indicates, the variance accounted for by the independent variables was small. It is possible that work's effects on leisure are distinguishable only between the two extreme (high–low) groups. t-test comparisons between these two groups for the five task attributes failed to identify any significant differences, except for skill utilization as mentioned before.

Factors Associated with Different Work/Leisure Patterns

Although work attributes seem to have little direct effect on leisure attributes, it is still sensible to ask whether there are any identifiable differences between persons with different work/leisure patterns. This question places emphasis on examining what leads to the development of distinctive patterns of work/leisure behavior rather than asking only how work affects leisure. Some differences in work/leisure patterns may be attributable primarily to differences in work-associated experiences; other differences may be due to experiences or attitudes acquired outside of work.

On the basis of the relationships described earlier, it is possible to identify four a priori work/leisure patterns or "groups." These four groups are *passive generalization*—persons who are low on both the work and leisure attributes; *supplemental compensation*—persons who are low on the work attribute but high on the leisure attribute; *active generalization*—persons who are high on both the work and leisure attributes; and *reactive compensation*—persons who are high on the work attribute but low on the leisure attribute. These are four significant and distinctive work/leisure patterns, and it is possible to investigate what distinguishes persons with these different patterns.

An appropriate way of examining this question is to identify variables that discriminate among the members of these four groups. Discriminant analysis is a general technique for statistically distinguishing between two or more groups of cases that have been defined on an a priori basis (Tatsuoka, 1971). Two advantages of the discriminant technique are its capacity to treat simultaneously a number of discriminating variables and two or more groups of cases. The four work/leisure groups defined earlier were identified across each of the five attributes, and differences in group membership were analyzed using a direct discriminant procedure that treats all of the discriminating variables simultaneously rather than in stepwise fashion (Klecka, 1975). Ten discriminant variables were employed: intrinsic job orientation, extrinsic job orientation, sex, age, education, income, marital status (single/married), presence of children under 15 years of age in the family (yes/no), hours worked in the last week, and locus of control. Factor analysis of the locus of control scale identified two main factors, political control beliefs and general control beliefs (Cherlin & Bourque, 1974; Duffy, Shiflett, & Downey, 1977), but these accounted for only 21 percent of the total variance (O'Brien & Kabanoff, Note 2). Because of the weakness of the factorial structure and the reduced reliability of the two factorial subscales, a total locus of control score was used in the following analyses.

In each of the five discriminant analyses, two significant discriminant functions were identified (Table 3). The first discriminant functions provided a moderate degree of discrimination, with the median canonical correlation being .450. The second functions provided a fairly low level of discrimination, the

TABLE 3 Results of Discriminant Analysis of Four Work/Leisure Groups Showing Standardized Discriminant Coefficients and Group Centroids

	Attribute									
	Influence		Variety		Pressure		Skill Utilization		Interaction	
Variables	Function 1	Function 2	Function 1	Function 2	Function 1	Function 2	Function 1	Function 2	Function 1	Function 2
Discriminant functions					Discriminant Coefficients					
Intrinsic orientation	.411‡	−.149	−.159	−.625‡	.461†	.006	.409‡	.426	.077	−.154
Extrinsic orientation	−.298	−.352‡	−.061	.473†	−.295	−.412	−.178	−.784†	.022	.130
Age	.069	.459‡	.239†	−.204	−.349	−.385	.016	−.410	−.567	.207
Education	.269‡	.073	.021	−.191‡	.106†	−.087	.240‡	.059	.126	.232†
Income	.535‡	−.417	−.108	−.406‡	.483‡	.037	.612‡	−.402	.292	−1.019‡
Marital status	.207†	−.087	−.056	−.175†	.127	−.439‡	.049	.218	.112	−.296
Child <15	−.011	−.325	.051	.069	−.237	.369†	.076	.039	−.198	−.311
Hours worked	.105	.153‡	−.188	−.205‡	.046	−.459	.154	−.429‡	−.093	−.203
Locus of control	−.176	−.434‡	−.212	−.084	−.232	−.409†	−.273‡	−.164	−.326†	.003
Sex	.255	.602‡	.869‡	−.431	−.187†	−.108	.302	−.065	−.597	−.834‡
Canonical correlation	.541ⁱ	.318ⁱ	.505ⁱ	.439ⁱ	.295ⁱ	.242‡	.450ⁱ	.283§	.373ⁱ	.200*
					Group Centroids					
Group										
Low work/low leisure (Passive generalization)	−.585	−.181	−.368	.575	−.332	−.054	−.566	−.203	432	.102
Low work/high leisure (Supplemental compensation)	−.467	.359	.606	.225	−.138	.329	−.289	.363	.164	.299
High work/low leisure (Reactive compensation)	.266	−.465	−.648	−.234	−.048	−.373	.285	−.366	−.348	−.215
High work/high leisure (Active generalization)	.697	.214	.216	−.624	.437	.028	.556	.147	.449	−.137

* .06 > p > .05.
†p < .05.
‡p < .01.
§p < .005.
ⁱp <.001.

median canonical correlation being .283. Cooley and Lohnes (1971) recommend the use of a redundancy index to estimate the discriminating power of a set of variables. By summing together the redundancy index of all significant discriminant functions, one can represent the total criterion variance extracted (in this case represented by the group identification data), given the predictor variate. That is, the redundancy coefficient is a measure of the proportion of variance in the set of criteria accounted for by the predictors. Redundancy coefficients for these discriminant analyses were influence, .24; variety, .23; skill utilization, .16; pressure, .07; and interaction, .11. Since the redundancy coefficient can vary between 0 and 1, it is clear that the discriminant analyses provide fairly incomplete descriptions of persons in the different work/leisure categories. In view of this, the interpretations that follow must be seen as only suggestive and must be treated with some caution. Also, despite the significant degree of discrimination achieved, there was considerable overlap among groups, with the highest percentage of correctly classified cases being 51 percent (variety) and the lowest 40 percent (pressure). Given the exploratory nature of the research, both discriminant functions were interpreted (Table 4). Unfortunately, though perhaps not surprisingly, neither Table 3 nor Table 4 shows a single, consistent pattern. Nevertheless, some generally consistent trends are identifiable.

The results for the four attributes of influence, variety, pressure, and skill utilization are broadly similar, whereas the pattern for the interaction dimension is different from all of the others. Persons with a low level of influence, variety, pressure, and skill utilization in both work and leisure have a low intrinsic work motivation but a high extrinsic one. This high extrinsic motivation seems to be frustrated, in part at least, since they have a low income. Thus persons with a passive generalization pattern do not express any intrinsic attachment to work, and their extrinsic needs are probably not adequately met. Persons who have a high level of influence, variety, skill utilization, and pressure in both work and leisure are conceptually, and apparently empirically, the

opposite of those with the low/low pattern. The active generalization group shows a high intrinsic involvement in work but expresses low importance for extrinsic features of the job. Their extrinsic needs are probably to a large extent satisfied, since they have a high income.

Those who may be described as displaying supplemental compensation tend to be female, older, internal, and relatively unconcerned with extrinsic job outcomes. These results suggest that no conscious process of compensation is occurring here; rather, persons showing this pattern seem dependent not on their work role for their source of satisfaction and self-concept but on their nonwork role, perhaps as family members or parents. A somewhat different pattern seems to occur for this group for the pressure and skill utilization dimensions. Although a low extrinsic work orientation is again evident, those showing the supplementary compensation pattern tend to be younger, work shorter hours, and show some evidence of a higher intrinsic work orientation. It may be that these persons represent a "true" or conscious compensatory pattern in which intrinsic needs unfulfilled at work are pursued in leisure. It has been suggested that some persons achieve prestige in their workplace through their achievements in competitive sports or perhaps in demanding hobbies (Parker, 1971). Such an explanation may be appropriate for this group. They are younger, have more nonwork time, and are more involved in high-skill, high-pressure activities, a description that typifies competitive sports and demanding hobbies.

Those who show the high work/low leisure pattern in turn seem to be describable as the opposites of those with the low work/high leisure pattern. They seem to be centered on the economic outcomes of their work role. These persons work longer hours, have higher extrinsic work values but lower intrinsic ones, have a higher income, and are predominantly male. They also tend to be more external than those showing the supplementary compensation pattern. There is some variation across attributes for this group. Those classified as displaying reactive compensation for the influence and variety dimensions tend to be younger, whereas

TABLE 4 Verbal Description of Work/Leisure Groups Based on Discriminant Analysis

Group	Influence	Variety	Attribute: Pressure	Skill Utilization	Interaction
Low work/low leisure	Low income, low intrinsic work orientation, high extrinsic work orientation, low education, male, single	Low intrinsic work orientation, high extrinsic work orientation, male, low income, work shorter hours, younger	Low income, low intrinsic work orientation, older, high extrinsic work orientation, children <15, external	Low income, low intrinsic work orientation, male, external, low education	Male, younger, internal, high income
Low work/high leisure	Female, older, internal, low income, low extrinsic work orientation, children <15 years	Female, older, internal	Work shorter hours, low extrinsic work orientation, internal, younger, no children <15 years	Low extrinsic work orientation, work shorter hours, high intrinsic work orientation, younger, low income	Low income, male, children <15 years
High work/low leisure	Male, younger, external, high income, high extrinsic work orientation, no children <15 years	Male, younger, external	Work longer hours, single, high extrinsic work orientation, external, older, children <15 years	High extrinsic work orientation, work longer hours, low intrinsic work orientation, older, high income	Female, older, external, lower income
High work/high leisure	High income, high intrinsic work orientation, low extrinsic work orientation, high education, female, married	High intrinsic work orientation, low extrinsic work orientation, female, high income, work longer hours, older	High income, high intrinsic work orientation, younger, low extrinsic work orientation, no children <15, internal	High income, high intrinsic work orientation, female, internal, high education	Male, younger, internal, high income

those showing it for the pressure and skill dimensions tend to be older. It is possible that this relatively affluent group that is not intrinsically involved in demanding work and has an undemanding leisure pattern represents the "conspicuous consumption" pattern that has been described by some writers (Gorz, 1965; Mills, 1951).

The results for the interaction dimension are unique and seem to defy any ready interpretation. Interaction seems to be a type of activity that is not readily understood within the context of the present set of variables. Perhaps this is because the study defined and measured interaction at the individual level, whereas it has been suggested that to describe leisure interaction we must concentrate on defining the nature of people's "connectedness" with others (Cheek, 1971). That is, there may need to be a greater emphasis on the quality of involvement with others than on sheer quantity and on the social group than on the social individual.

Another significant feature of these results is the relatively higher externality of those showing the reactive compensation pattern compared with those showing supplementary compensation on three of the attributes. This provides partial support for the original hypothesis. It was hypothesized that internals in undemanding, external-type work would tend to be involved in more demanding leisure pursuits, and this seems to be the case. On the other hand, externals in demanding, internal-type jobs should tend to be involved in undemanding leisure activities, and this also tends to be the case. This may indicate some kind of conscious or even unconscious psychological balancing in which work that is incongruent with a person's dominant control beliefs is counterbalanced by leisure that is congruent with these beliefs. An alternative explanation may be that people are more likely to behave in their leisure than in their work in congruence with their "personality." For example, externals in internal-type jobs may have chosen these jobs because they place a high value on a large income, which is more likely to be derived from jobs of high influence, high skill, and high pressure. Internals in external jobs

could have chosen those jobs because they are relatively unconcerned with their work role in any case and given this chose it on the basis of some "irrelevant" (to their personality, anyway) consideration such as location, availability of time off, and so on. Clearly, in a cross-sectional study causes and effects cannot be unequivocally resolved.

A surprising feature of these results is the failure of locus of control to differentiate between the two extreme groups (i.e., low/low and high/high) despite the markedly higher externality of the low/low group (overall $M = 11.9$ versus $M = 8.6$). The likely explanation for this result is that the difference in locus of control scores for the two groups is itself largely determined by one or more of the other discriminant variables. Evidence for this interpretation is the fact that income is the main variable discriminating between these extreme groups, and income is a major correlate of locus of control for this sample. Externality may still be important for understanding the noncompensatory pattern for the low/low group given the relationship between leisure and locus of control that has already been shown.

Combined Measures of Work and Leisure Quality

Much of the debate on work/leisure relationships has been conducted at the general level of the relationship of work quality to leisure quality (e.g., Kornhauser, 1965). In the present study, five conceptually distinct attributes of work and leisure were identified and analyzed separately. It could be argued that the failure to find any major effects of work on leisure is due to some dilution of the overall concept of job and leisure quality as a result of splitting this concept up. Two overall indexes of job and leisure quality were therefore created. Job quality was defined as the sum of work influence, variety, skill utilization, and interaction, minus pressure. Scores on these five dimensions had been previously standardized into z-score form to allow for the greater number of items in the influence scale. A similar index of leisure quality was also calculated. The analyses reported above (ANOVA and discriminant analysis) were then repeated using these combined indexes. The ANOVA again showed a significant effect of I-E on leisure, $F(2, 1215) = 7.12$, $p < .001$, but no significant effect for job quality and no significant interaction. The discriminant analysis produced a result similar to the broad pattern described above. However, the advantage of the individual attributes approach is that it identified some possibly significant differences in work/leisure patterns that failed to emerge when gross indexes were used.

DISCUSSION

Three main conclusions emerge from the present study. First, the results do not support the existence of a strong relationship between people's work and leisure attributes of either a generalizing or compensatory nature. Second, locus of control is consistently related to leisure attributes and seems to moderate work/leisure patterns, at least in part. Third, it is possible to identify with some degree of consistency persons with different work/leisure patterns.

Before discussing these conclusions, it is necessary to make clear some of the limitations of this study. Since the survey was carried out at a single point in time, it is not possible to identify causal relationships. However, even allowing this does not alter the usefulness of identifying some different work/leisure patterns and the characteristics of persons with these different patterns. Terms such as *supplemental compensation* or *reactive compensation* in the present study perhaps have inappropriate causal overtones, but they were retained because they have been used previously to label the sorts of relations examined here. The significance of these results perhaps lies not so much in their limited success at explaining these patterns but rather in their demonstration of the potential value of this approach and the inadequacy of concepts such as compensation and generalization.

In general, the present results indicate a weak relationship between work and leisure attributes in the general population. The few significant relationships that were found would seem to be of small practical significance. Researchers who have posited generally deleterious effects of work on leisure (e.g., Emery, 1977; Emery & Phillips, 1976; Gardell, 1976; Kornhauser, 1965; Meissner, 1971) seem to have overstated their case. Partially supporting the conclusions of Meissner and Kornhauser, however, was the identification of a predominately male, low income, low intrinsic job involvement, low job quality group that also had low-quality leisure. However, even persons in jobs such as those described by Meissner and Kornhauser failed to show a universal generalization pattern. The simple fact that there were groups with low-quality jobs and high-quality leisure, and vice versa, questions the validity of theories such as compensation and generalization as general explanations of work/leisure patterns.

However, the present results do not necessarily support a segmentalist theory of work and leisure. The results indicate only that it is not possible to assume that leisure activity is influenced by work activity in some general, consistent pattern. The results suggest that for some persons at least, work experiences may have some causal effects on their leisure, although alternative explanations could be made of these results in terms of leisure's effects on work; a mutual, causal interaction of work and leisure; or joint determination of work and leisure by a third set of factors. The results support a conservative segmentalist hypothesis stated along the lines of "work does not hold a generally causal relationship to leisure." The results do not support a radical segmentalist hypothesis along the lines of "work experiences are unrelated to leisure experiences"; quite the contrary.

It might be argued that the failure to find strong work/leisure relationships was due to the way in which leisure was defined. However, if the leisure indexes were not reflecting actual differences in the nature of people's leisure participation, they should not have been systematically and predictably related to locus of control. In fact, locus of control was related to four of the leisure attributes and the overall index. Admittedly, the relationship was not strong, but one would not expect it to be, given the diverse nature of the criterion measure and what is known about the general strength of personality effects. Another study (O'Brien, in press) has found a task attributes-based description of leisure to predict people's satisfaction with life during retirement, which offers further evidence for the validity of this approach. The findings also provide further evidence for the validity of the locus of control concept and indicate that personality may be a significant influence on leisure behavior (Craik & McKechnie, 1977; Driver & Knopf, 1977). Perhaps due to the influence of sociology, much of the research in this area seems to have concentrated on identifying general leisure trends that are presumed to be fairly universal. The results indicate that personality variables may have marked effects on leisure activities. This is not surprising considering that leisure is a relatively free, unconstrained state that allows individual freedom of choice (Kelly, 1972; Neulinger, 1974).

A major implication of the present study is the need for a redefinition of the work/leisure problem. Rather than ask, "How does work determine leisure?" it would seem more fruitful to ask, "Which factors, personal and situational, are associated with or cause people to have different work/leisure patterns?" or "How do people balance their commitments across different life spheres?" (Kabanoff, 1980; Rapaport & Rapaport, 1974). This approach takes the "onus of cause" away from work and moves it toward an interactional model of work and leisure. Though such a model will undoubtedly be more complex than simple compensation/generalization notions, it will probably also provide a truer reflection of

events in the real world (Seashore, 1975; Spink, 1975). Such an approach does not invalidate compensation or generalization theories but incorporates them into a larger framework. It requires that work/leisure concepts be integrated with a larger set of both work and nonwork concepts including personality, family patterns (Kelly, 1978), demographic and community variables, and orientations toward work and leisure roles. The present study went part of the way in this undertaking by identifying four work/leisure patterns and relating them to a number of other variables. The limited extent to which these variables were able to explain work/leisure patterns is a further indication of the complex causes underlying these patterns. Clearly, the present conclusions must be treated as suggestive rather than definitive and in need of validation by further studies. Cross-cultural differences in attitudes toward work and leisure are also likely to be important. For the sample studied, the relative independence of work and leisure may in part reflect Australian values concerning the relative importance of work and leisure as sources of life satisfaction.

In conclusion, the present study, despite its limitations, has made a contribution both to methodology and substantive knowledge about work/leisure relations. Work-related variables do not seem to be major predictors of people's nonwork activities, although their effects vary across segments of the employed population. Future research should be directed toward identification of different work/leisure patterns and the factors that lead to the development of these different patterns. It seems clear from both earlier results and the findings of the present study that simplistic theories of generalization, compensation, and segmentation are not adequate for explaining the complexities of observed relationships between work and leisure attributes.

Job Design

One dimension on which jobs can be seen to vary is the extent to which they encourage or discourage workers to think and act for themselves. In some senses, the major thrust of assembly line production was to eliminate individual differences among worker behaviors. Consistency, reliability, and uniformity were the keys to profitability. It is obvious that there is a price to be paid for that consistency and uniformity. It seems as if that price is first paid by the worker but ultimately by the organization and the consumer. In this section, we will consider the issue of how the design of jobs (in a global sense) can affect the satisfaction and motivation of workers.

In the late 1950s, Frederick Herzberg revolutionized thinking about job satisfaction and work motivation by suggesting that satisfaction and dissatisfaction were caused by completely independent factors. Further, he introduced the notion of job enrichment as a way of increasing job satisfaction and work motivation. Although the term job enrichment had a nice ring to it, it was not clear how one would go about actually enriching jobs. In this reading, Hackman describes a way of analyzing jobs in terms of their motivational potential. By extension, knowing the components of motivation potential provides us with a scheme for enriching the job.

■ READING 28 ■

Work Redesign and Motivation

J. Richard Hackman

The term *work redesign* refers to activities that involve the alteration of specific jobs (or systems of jobs) with the intent of improving both productivity and the quality of employee work experiences. Although there are no generally accepted criteria for what is a well-designed job, there are some commonalities in work redesign projects. Typically, job specifications are changed to provide employees with additional responsibility for planning, setting up, and checking their own work; for making decisions about work methods and procedures; for establishing their own work pace; and for dealing directly with the clients who receive the results of the work. In many cases, jobs that previously had been simplified and segmented into many small parts in the interest of production efficiency are reassembled and made into larger and more meaningful wholes.

Sometimes work is redesigned to create motivating and satisfying jobs for individual employees who work more or less on their own. Such activities are usually known as "job

enrichment" (Herzberg, 1974). Alternatively, work may be designed as a *group* task, in which case a team of workers is given autonomous responsibility for a large and meaningful module of work. Such teams typically have the authority to manage their own social and performance processes as they see fit; they receive feedback (and often rewards) as a group; and they may even be charged with the selection, training, and termination of their own members. These teams are variously known as "autonomous work groups" (Gulowsen, 1972), "self-regulating work groups" (Cummings, 1978), or "self-managing work groups" (Hackman, 1978). A well-known and well-documented example of the design of work for teams is the Topeka pet food plant of General Foods. (See Walton, 1972, for a description of the innovation and Walton, 1977, for a six-year history of the Topeka teams.)

Both individual and team work redesign can be viewed as responses and alternatives to the principles for designing work that derive from classical organization theory and industrial engineering. These principles specify that rationality and efficiency in organizational operations can be obtained through the simplification, standardization,

Source: *Professional Psychology, II*(3), 1980, pp. 445–53. Copyright 1980 by the American Psychological Association. Reprinted by permission of the publisher and author.

and specialization of jobs in organizations. These principles are based on the assumption that most employees, if managed well, will work efficiently and effectively on such jobs. Research over the last several decades has documented a number of unintended and dysfunctional consequences—both for workers and for their employing organizations—of work designed in accord with classical principles (Kornhauser, 1965; Vernon, 1924; Walker & Guest, 1952). Current approaches to work redesign, then, tend to have a behavioral emphasis and attempt to create jobs that enhance work productivity without incurring the human costs that have been associated with the traditional approaches.

THEORIES OF WORK REDESIGN

Most work redesign activities are guided by one or another of the four theoretical approaches summarized below. We begin with a theory that has a very psychological focus (activation theory), move next to two "mid-range" theories (motivation-hygiene theory and job characteristics theory), and conclude with a more molar and system-focused theory (sociotechnical systems theory).

Activation Theory

As noted above, numerous human problems have been associated with work on routine, repetitive tasks. Included are diminished alertness, decreased responsiveness to new stimulus inputs, and even impairment of muscular coordination. Employees who work on highly routine jobs are often observed to daydream, to chat with others rather than work on their tasks, to make frequent readjustments of posture and position, and so on.

Activation theory can help account for such behaviors (Scott, 1966). Basically, activation theory specifies that a person's level of activation or "arousal" decreases when sensory input is unchanging or repetitive, leading to the kinds of behavior specified above. Varying or unexpected patterns of stimuli, on the other

hand, keep an individual activated and more alert, although over time the individual may adapt to even a varied pattern of stimulation.

One approach to work redesign that is based on activation theory is that of *job rotation,* that is, rotating an individual through a number of different jobs in a given day or week, with the expectation that these varied job experiences will keep the person from suffering the negative consequences of excessively low activation. The problem, it seems, is that people adapt fairly quickly even to new stimulation, and if the new task is just as boring as the old one, then no long-term gains are likely.

At present, activation theory seems most useful for understanding the consequences of jobs that are grossly understimulating (or overstimulating). Except for the pioneering work by Scott (1966) and more recent theorizing by Schwab and Cummings (1976), relatively little progress has been made in applying the tenets of activation theory to the design of jobs so that they foster and maintain high task-oriented motivation.

Motivation-Hygiene Theory

By far the most influential theory of work redesign to date has been the Herzberg two-factor theory of satisfaction and motivation (Herzberg, 1976; Herzberg, Mausner, & Snyderman, 1959). This theory proposes that factors intrinsic to the work determine how satisfied people are at work. These factors, called "motivators," include recognition, achievement, responsibility, advancement, and personal growth in competence. Dissatisfaction, on the other hand, is caused by factors extrinsic to the work, termed "hygienes." Examples include company policies, pay plans, working conditions, and supervisory practices. According to the Herzberg theory, a job will enhance work motivation only to the extent that motivators are designed into the work itself; changes that deal solely with hygiene factors will not generate improvements (cf. Katzell, 1980).

Motivation-hygiene theory has inspired a number of successful change projects involving the redesign of work (e.g., Ford, 1969; Paul, Robertson, & Herzberg, 1969). Because the message of motivation-hygiene theory is simple, persuasive, and directly relevant to the design and evaluation of actual organizational changes, the theory continues to be widely known and generally used by managers of organizations in this country. There is, however, considerable uncertainty and controversy regarding the conceptual and empirical status of motivation-hygiene theory qua theory. For a succinct treatment of the theory, see Herzberg (1968). For reviews of research assessments of the theory, see King (1970), House and Wigdor (1967), who are particularly skeptical, and Whitsett and Winslow (1967), who are particularly sympathetic.

Job Characteristics Theory

This approach attempts to specify the objective characteristics of jobs that create conditions for high levels of internal work motivation on the part of employees. Based on earlier research by Turner and Lawrence (1965), current statements of the theory suggest that individuals will be internally motivated to perform well when they experience the work as *meaningful,* they feel they have personal *responsibility* for the work outcomes, and they obtain regular and trustworthy *knowledge of the results* of their work. Five objective job characteristics are specified as the key ones in creating these conditions: skill variety, task identity, task significance, autonomy, and feedback from the job itself (Hackman & Lawler, 1971; Hackman & Oldham, 1976).

When a job is redesigned to increase its standing on these characteristics, improvements in the motivation, satisfaction, and performance of job incumbents are predicted. However, individual differences in employee knowledge and skill and in need for personal growth are posited as influencing the effects of the job characteristics on work behaviors and attitudes. Strongest effects are predicted for individuals with ample job-relevant knowledge and skill and relatively strong growth needs.

A diagnostic instrument, the Job Diagnostic Survey, has been developed to assess employee perceptions of the job characteristics listed above, selected attitudes toward the work and the organization, and individual growth need strength (Hackman & Oldham, 1975). This instrument is intended for use both in diagnosing work systems prior to job redesign and for assessing the consequences of work redesign activities.

For an overview of the theory that emphasizes its practical application to work redesign, see Hackman, Oldham, Janson, and Purdy (1975); for the most current statement of the theory, including its application to the design of work for groups as well as individuals, see Hackman and Oldham (1980). For a skeptical view of the job characteristics approach, see Salancik and Pfeffer (1977).

Sociotechnical Systems Theory

Contrasting the job-focused theories mentioned above, the sociotechnical systems approach emphasizes the importance of designing entire work *systems,* in which the social and technical aspects of the workplace are integrated and mutually supportive of one another (Emery & Trist, 1969).

This approach emphasizes the fact that organizations are imbedded in, and affected by, an outside environment. Especially important are cultural values that specify how organizations "should" function and generally accepted roles that individuals, groups, and organizations are supposed to play in society. Thus, there is constant interchange between what goes on in any given work organization and what goes on in its environment. This interchange must be carefully attended to when work systems are designed or changed (Davis & Trist, 1974).

When redesigned in accord with the sociotechnical approach, work systems are never changed in piecemeal fashion. Although jobs, rewards, physical equipment, spatial arrangements, work schedules (and more) may be altered in a sociotechnical intervention, none of these is taken as the primary focus of change activities. Instead, organization members (often including rank-and-file employees and/or representatives of organized labor as well as managers) examine *all* aspects of organizational operations that might affect how well the work is done or the quality of organization members' experiences. Changes that emerge from these explorations invariably involve numerous aspects of both the social and technical systems of the organization. Typically, however, such changes do involve the formation of groups of employees who share responsibility for carrying out a significant piece of work —the "autonomous work group" idea mentioned earlier (Cummings, 1978). Such groups are becoming an increasingly popular organizational innovation and now are frequently seen, even in work redesign projects that are not explicitly guided by sociotechnical theory.

For a summary of sociotechnical systems theory as it applies to work redesign, see Cherns (1976), Davis (1975), or the now-classic study of coal mining by Trist, Higgin, Murray, and Pollock (1963). For a critique of the theory, see Van der Zwaan (1975).

Comparison of the Theoretical Approaches

Activation theory, motivation-hygiene theory, job characteristics theory, and sociotechnical systems theory offer different approaches to work redesign. Activation theory specifically addresses the dysfunctional aspects of repetitive work, whereas motivation-hygiene theory and job characteristics theory emphasize ways to enhance positive motivational features of the work. The Herzberg model differs from the job characteristics theory in proposing a more general process for increasing motivation (i.e., identify motivators and increase them), whereas the job characteristics approach emphasizes specific diagnostic procedures to optimize the fit between people and their work. Sociotechnical systems theory contrasts sharply with the other theories in that it emphasizes the design of work for groups rather than individuals.

Another difference among the theories lies in their assumptions about how the redesign of

work should be planned and implemented. Activation and motivation-hygiene theories appear to put the burden on management to identify the problematic aspects of the work. Neither approach suggests extensive gathering of information and inputs from employees. At the other end of the continuum, sociotechnical work redesign projects involve a high degree of worker participation. Job characteristics theory emphasizes the importance of understanding workers' perceptions and attitudes toward their jobs but does not explicitly require their participation in actual planning for work redesign.

OUTCOMES OF WORK REDESIGN

How successful are work redesign activities in achieving their intended objectives? Systematic data about the matter are surprisingly sparse, given the popularity of work redesign as an organizational change technique. My own assessment of the state of the evidence is summarized briefly below; more thorough and/or analytic reviews are provided elsewhere.

1. Work redesign, when competently executed in appropriate organizational circumstances, generally increases the work satisfaction and motivation of employees whose jobs are enriched. Especially strong effects have been found for employees' level of satisfaction with opportunities for personal growth and development on the job as well as for their level of *internal* work motivation (i.e., motivation to work hard and well because of the internal rewards that good performance brings). There is little evidence that work redesign increases satisfaction with aspects of the organizational context such as pay, job security, co-workers, or supervision. Indeed, enrichment of the work sometimes prompts decreases in satisfaction with pay and supervision, especially when these organizational practices are not altered to mesh with the new responsibilities and increased autonomy of the persons whose jobs are redesigned.

2. The quality of the product or service provided generally improves. When a job is well designed from a motivational point of view, the people who work on that job tend to experience self-rewards when they perform *well*. And, for most people, performing well means producing high-quality work of which they can be proud.

3. The quantity of work done sometimes increases, sometimes is unchanged, and sometimes even decreases. What happens to production quantity when work is redesigned may depend mostly on the state of the work system *prior* to redesign (Hackman & Oldham, 1980). Specifically, productivity gains would be expected under two circumstances: (*a*) when employees were previously exhibiting markedly low productivity because they were actively "turned off" by highly routine or repetitive work, or (*b*) when there were hidden inefficiencies in the work system, as it was previously structured—for example, redundancies in the work, unnecessary supervisory or inspection activities, and so on. If such problems preexisted in the work unit, then increases in the quantity of work performed are likely to appear after the work is redesigned. If such problems were not present, then quantity increases would not be anticipated; indeed, decreases in quantity might even be noted as people worked especially hard on their enriched jobs to produce work of especially high *quality*.

4. Findings regarding employee attendance at work—absenteeism and turnover—are not clear. The research needed to draw trustworthy conclusions about turnover is not yet available; and it may be that turnover is far more powerfully affected by economic and labor market conditions than by how jobs are designed. Research findings regarding absenteeism, like those for production quantity, are inconsistent: Some studies report improvements in attendance when jobs are enriched, some report no change, and some show worse absence problems than before. It may be that *who* is absent is different for routine, simple jobs compared to complex, challenging jobs. More talented employees, for example, may show higher absence rates for routine jobs because of boredom. Less talented employees may be more unhappy (and therefore more frequently absent) for challenging jobs, because they find themselves overwhelmed by the same complexity that engages and motivates their more competent peers. This hypothesis would suggest that any overall indicator of absenteeism for total work groups could be misleading because of the differential effects of work redesign on employees who differ in competence.

Although it is now generally recognized that work redesign is not a panacea for all organizational ills, it remains difficult to arrive at a "bottom line" estimate of the costs and benefits of job changes. Simple reports of improvements in job satisfaction are not likely to significantly warm the hearts of cost-conscious line managers; and, for reasons outlined above, simple measures of production quantity or labor cost are inappropriate when used as the sole measure of the effects of work redesign.

Other outcomes, including many that may be among the most appropriate indexes of work redesign outcomes, are presently difficult or impossible to measure in terms that are comparable across organizations. What, for example, is the ultimate cost of poor quality work? Or of "extra" supervisory time? Or of redundant inspections? Or of absenteeism, soldiering, or sabotage? Until we become able to assess the effects of work redesign on such outcomes, it will continue to be difficult to determine unambiguously whether or not work redesign "pays off" in traditional economic coin.

UNANSWERED QUESTIONS AND FUTURE DIRECTIONS

Despite the recent popularity of work design as a research topic and change technique, many unanswered questions remain, especially regarding the application of work design principles in complex, ambiguous organizational situations. In the paragraphs to follow, I briefly highlight several research and conceptual issues that strike me as among the most currently pressing.

Diagnostic and Evaluation Methodologies

How are we to assess the readiness of work systems for work redesign, to ascertain precisely what changes are called for in those systems, or to measure the consequences of the changes that are made? Heretofore, most diagnostic and evaluation methodologies have relied on paper-and-pencil instruments completed by individuals whose jobs are about to be (or have been) redesigned. As Walton (1980) notes in another article in this issue, there are reasons for caution and skepticism in the use of such methods, even when they are psychometrically adequate (also see Barr, Brief, & Aldag, Note 1, for a critical analysis of the psychometric properties of existing instruments that measure perceived task characteristics). Yet there also are significant problems in relying on the perceptions of managers and consultants about people and their work when work systems are diagnosed and the effects of job changes are assessed. Research has shown, for example, that both cognitive limitations and social distortions can significantly bias what is seen by observers who have a "stake" in the organization or in contemplated changes (Hackman & Oldham, 1980, chapter 5). What, then, is to be done to improve our diagnostic and evaluation capabilities?

Researchers both at the University of Michigan (Lawler, Nadler, & Cammann, 1980) and at the University of Pennsylvania (Van de Ven & Ferry, 1980) have recently developed organizational assessment packages (some parts of which include observational and archival measures as well as paper-and-pencil instruments) that may be of considerable use in diagnosing and evaluating work redesign programs. One especially promising approach to measuring the outcomes of work redesign has been developed by Macy and Mirvis (1976) as part of the Michigan project. This methodology involves defining, measuring, and costing certain kinds of behavioral outcomes in economic terms. It appears to offer the potential for more rigorous assessment of the economic effects of work restructuring than has heretofore been possible;

ultimately, it should help reduce some of the previously noted ambiguities in comparing the outcomes of different work redesign activities.

The Role of Individual Differences

Although only one of the theoretical approaches to work redesign reviewed earlier (job characteristics theory) explicitly incorporates individual differences as a part of the theory itself, literally dozens of studies have tested the general proposition that different people react differently to enriched, challenging work. A great heterogeneity of individual difference measures has been tried, ranging from theory-specified measures of growth need strength to subcultural background to relatively esoteric personality measures. In general, results have been inconsistent (i.e., individual-differences moderators have sometimes operated as predicted and sometimes not) and of limited magnitude (i.e., the moderating effects, when obtained, have not accounted for major portions of the variation in satisfaction or performance).

That there are important individual differences in readiness for enriched work and reactions to it seems indisputable; but it also is clear that existing theories and research methods have so far failed to provide satisfactory ways of conceptualizing and measuring whatever it is that accounts for the highly variegated reactions of people to their work. How is this discrepancy to be understood? Some new thinking and some new research methods clearly are called for to resolve this conceptually interesting and practically important question.

Individual versus Team Designs for Work

The theories of work redesign reviewed earlier in this article vary in their relative emphasis on the design of work for individuals versus teams (i.e., motivation-hygiene theory is essentially an individual-focused theory; sociotechnical systems theory is oriented primarily to work teams). Presumably an individual design is more appropriate (and will be more effective) in some organizational circumstances, and a team design will be better in others. Yet except for some untested conjectures about the circumstances under which one or the other design is more appropriate (see Hackman & Oldham, 1980), there is little in the way of research and theory to guide decision making about whether an individual or a team design is relatively more appropriate for given organizational circumstances. There should be more.

The Job of the Supervisor

Relatively little research and few change programs have focused on the design of lower-level jobs in management. These jobs deserve greater attention for two reasons. First, supervisory jobs in many organizations are as poorly designed as are rank-and-file jobs selected for enrichment. Especially troublesome are restrictions on the autonomy lower-level managers have to carry out their work and limitations on the amount and the validity of the feedback they receive about their performance. Yet, in the rush to attend to the jobs held by supposedly alienated rank-and-file workers, very real problems in the design of managerial jobs often are overlooked.

Second, the jobs of lower-level managers invariably are affected, often negatively, when their subordinates' jobs are improved. Indeed, improvements in employee jobs are sometimes made directly at the expense of managerial jobs: Decision-making responsibilities and special tasks that traditionally have been reserved for management are given to workers, and the jobs of managers may be denuded to about the same extent that subordinate jobs are improved.

When this happens, supervisors may become justifiably angry at the effects of work redesign on the quality of their own life at work, with predictable effects on their continued cooperation with the work redesign activities. Moreover, constraints on the supervisory job (and limited opportunities for training and practice) may make it difficult for supervisors to learn the new behaviors that they need to ef-

fectively manage employees who work on newly enriched jobs.

Walton and Schlesinger (1979) have recently completed a detailed analysis of supervisory role difficulties when work is restructured. They offer some provocative ideas about how that role might be redesigned —and how persons might be selected and trained for it —that merit careful attention by both scholars and practitioners of work redesign.

Tensions in the Installation Process

Although the hoped-for outcomes of work redesign are generally clear in a given change project, planning about how to get there from here is often a rather murky and uncertain affair. In general, our theories about the *content* of work redesign are much better than our theories about the *process* of making the needed changes.

Among the questions at issue are the following. How responsive should changes be to idiosyncracies of the people, the setting, and the broader environment? How closely should changes be tied to one or another of the theories of work design, as opposed to a more ad hoc approach to change? How fully should the employees whose jobs are to be changed participate in the planning and execution of those changes? If one aspires to diffusion beyond the initial site of the change, how should the first site be selected (i.e., should it be an "easy" or a "difficult" change target)? How should one manage the expectations of employees and managers about the magnitude of the change and its anticipated benefits? Should expectations be kept low to avoid possible disappointment, or should they be raised to provide a hedge against possible conservatism and retreat when the time comes to actually put planned changes in place? What is the appropriate model for union-management collaboration in carrying out work redesign? How should evaluation activities be designed and carried out to provide the opportunity for midcourse corrections, but to avoid the risk of premature judgment about whether the project is a success or a failure?

There is little research evidence available about questions such as these. Worse, it is doubtful that traditional research methodologies in organizational psychology are likely to generate trustworthy data about them. Questionnaires and cross-sectional surveys seem unlikely to do the trick, for obvious reasons. And even true or quasi-experimental studies of the installation process seem not very promising, despite the repeated calls for more of them.

Why? For one thing, not many organizations are likely to allow the kinds of controls that are required for good experimental research (e.g., randomization of "subjects" across conditions or use of change processes that are not expected to be effective in "control groups"). Managers and employees in organizations, understandably, usually insist that when change is done, only state-of-the-art procedures should be used.

Even if decent experimental designs could be put in place, organizations are notorious for not "holding still" until all follow-up observations are collected. Key managers are transferred, the technology or market changes, a strike occurs or is about to, a large number of employees in one experimental unit (but not in another) depart for reasons that have nothing

to do with the manipulated variables, and so on. Indeed, if it *were* possible to obtain and maintain the kind of control needed for "good" experimental research on work redesign processes, that would be such an unusual state of affairs that one would have to worry about the generality of the findings to more typical (and more chaotic) organizational circumstances.

It appears, therefore, that building systematic understanding about the process of installing and supporting changes in the design of work may require some significant innovations in organizational research methodologies. Perhaps, for example, ways can be found to collect and report data from case studies so that they can be combined to build trustworthy and cumulative bodies of knowledge. Or perhaps certain anthropological techniques can be adapted to the study of change processes in organizations.

We do not know at present *what* methodological innovations will be developed and be found useful. But it seems beyond dispute, at least to this reviewer, that *some* such innovations will be required to generate research findings about work redesign that are more conceptually sound and practically useful than those we have at present.

Job enrichment and design are nice abstract terms. They can be made concrete in conversation by giving examples of how they might be applied. Once in a blue moon, a perfect example comes along of how a certain concept was applied successfully. It functions like a parable, educating the reader by illustration. The next two readings represent just such an example in the area of job design. They describe the reaction of one business owner to what his "gut" told him was right. He had not read any theories or books on work motivation but had an intuitive feel for motivational principles. This should serve to remind theorists that they are not creating something where nothing existed before. Instead, they are simply articulating what the cleverest among us had already recognized but had not taken the time to set down on paper.

■ READING 29 ■

Arthur Friedman's Outrage: Employees Decide Their Pay

Martin Koughan
The Washington Post

One thing for sure, Arthur Friedman will never become the chairman of the board at General Motors.

It is not just because the modish, easygoing Oakland appliance dealer does not look the part—Hush Puppies, loud shirts, and denim jackets tend to clash with the sober decor of most executive suites. And it certainly is not because he is an incompetent administrator—the Friedman-Jacobs Co. has prospered during the 15 years of his stewardship.

It is mainly because Art Friedman has some pretty strange ideas about how one runs a business.

Five years ago, he had his most outrageous brainstorm. First he tried it out on his wife Merle and his brother Morris.

"Here he goes again," replied Merle with a sigh of resignation, "Another dumb stunt."

Source: *The Washington Post*, February 23, 1975.

"Oh my God," was all that Morris could muster.

His idea was to allow employees to set their own wages, make their own hours, and take their vacations whenever they felt like it.

The end result was that it worked.

Friedman first unleashed his proposal at one of the regular staff meetings. Decide what you are worth, he said, and tell the bookkeeper to put it in your envelope next week. No questions asked. Work any time, any day, any hours you want. Having a bad day? Go home. Hate working Saturdays? No problem. Aunt Ethel from Chicago has dropped in unexpectedly? Well, take a few days off, show her the town. Want to go to Reno for a week, need a rest? Go, go, no need to ask. If you need some money for the slot machines, take it out of petty cash. Just come back when you feel ready to work again.

His speech was received in complete silence.

No one cheered, no one laughed, no one said a word.

"It was about a month before anyone asked for a raise," recalls Stan Robinson, 55, the payroll clerk. "And when they did, they asked Art first. But he refused to listen and told them to just tell me what they wanted. I kept going back to him to make sure it was all right, but he wouldn't even talk about it. I finally figured out he was serious."

"It was something that I wanted to do," explains Friedman. "I always said that if you give people what they want, you get what you want. You have to be willing to lose, to stick your neck out. I finally decided that the time had come to practice what I preached."

Soon the path to Stan Robinson's desk was heavily travelled. Friedman's wife Merle was one of the first; she figured that her contribution was worth $1 an hour more. Some asked for $50 more a week, some $60. Delivery truck driver Charles Ryan was more ambitious; he demanded a $100 raise.

In most companies, Ryan would have been laughed out of the office. His work had not been particularly distinguished. His truck usually left in the morning and returned at five in the afternoon religiously, just in time for him to punch out. He dragged around the shop, complained constantly, and was almost always late for work. Things changed.

"He had been resentful about his prior pay," explains Friedman. "The raise made him a fabulous employee. He started showing up early in the morning and would be back by three asking what else had to be done."

Instead of the all-out raid on the company coffers that some businessmen might expect, the 15 employees of the Friedman-Jacobs Co. displayed astonishing restraint and maturity. The wages they demanded were just slightly higher than the scale of the Retail Clerks union to which they all belong (at Friedman's insistence). Some did not even take a raise. One service man who was receiving considerably less than his co-workers was asked why he did not insist on equal pay. "I don't want to work that hard," was the obvious answer.

When the union contract comes across Friedman's desk every other year, he signs it without even reading it. "I don't care what it says," he insists. At first, union officials would drop in to see how things were going, but they would usually end up laughing and shaking their heads, muttering something about being put out of a job. They finally stopped coming by. It was enough to convince George Meany to go out to pasture.

The fact is that Friedman's employees have no need for a union; whatever they want, they take and no one questions it. As a result they have developed a strong sense of responsibility and an acute sensitivity to the problems that face the American worker in general that would have been impossible under the traditional system.

George Tegner, 59, an employee for 14 years, has like all his co-workers achieved new insight into the mechanics of the free enterprise system. "You have to use common sense; no one wins if you end up closing the business down. If you want more money, you have to produce more. It can't work any other way. Anyway, wages aren't everything. Doing what you want to is more important."

Roger Ryan, 27, has been with the company for five years. "I know about the big inflation in '74, but I haven't taken a raise since '73. I figure if everybody asks for more, then inflation will just get worse. I'll hold out as long as I can."

Payroll clerk Stan Robinson: "I'm single now. I don't take as much as the others, even though I've been here longer, because I don't need as much. The government usually winds up with the extra money anyway."

Elwood Larsen, 65, has been the company's ace service man for 16 years. When he went into semi-retirement last year, he took a $1.50 cut in pay. Why? Larsen does not think a part-timer is worth as much. "I keep working here because I like it. We all know that if the Friedmans make money, we do. You just can't gouge the owner."

In the past five years, there has been no turnover of employees. Friedman estimates that last year his 15 workers took no more than a total of three sick days. It is rare that anyone is late for work and, even then, there is usually a good reason. Work is done on time and employee pilferage is nonexistent.

"We used to hear a lot of grumbling," says Robinson. "Now, everybody smiles."

As part of the new freedom, more people were given keys to the store and the cash box. If they need groceries, or even some beer money, all they have to do is walk into the office, take what they want out of the cash box and leave a voucher. Every effort is make to ensure that no one looks over their shoulder.

There has been only one discrepancy. "Once the petty cash was $10 over," recalls Friedman. "We never could figure out where it came from."

The policy has effected some changes in the way things are done around the store. It used to be open every night and all day Sunday, but no one wanted to work those hours. A problem? Of course not. No more nights and Sundays. ("When I thought about it," confesses Friedman, "I didn't like to work those hours either.")

The store also used to handle TVs and stereos—high-profit items—but they were a hassle for all concerned. The Friedman-Jacobs Co. now deals exclusively in major appliances such as refrigerators, washers, and dryers.

Skeptics by now are chuckling to themselves, convinced that if Friedman is not losing money, he is just breaking even. The fact is that net profit has not dropped a cent in the last five years; it has increased. Although volume is considerably less and overhead has increased at what some would consider an unhealthy rate, greater productivity and efficiency have more than made up for it.

Arthur Friedman: A Decade Later

Frank J. Landy

Since this article about Arthur Friedman first appeared in 1975, I wondered what happened to him. Did his business eventually fail, succeed, or stay the same? As a result, I gave him a call several months ago. He told me that he sold his business shortly after the newspaper article appeared. He was tired of working and decided to take up cooking for personal fulfillment. About a year later, a friend suggested he combine his love for cooking with his business experience and open a microwave oven store. He did this in 1977. Naturally, he used the same principles of management that had been so successful in his appliance store. In his first year in business, his gross sales amounted to $1 million. He opened five more stores. Each year, the business doubled. This year, his gross sales amounted to $50 million. He handles the business as a franchise operation and now has about 90 franchisees. He still operates on location himself, however, and uses exactly the same procedures as he did before in his first appliance store. Union contracts are still signed without looking. He still keeps an open cashbox. People still set their own wages (including new employees). Furthermore, he uses the same philosophy with franchisees. Each month, they simply send him what they claim they owe him. He does not audit their books. I asked him if he had any regrets about his unique system of management. He said that his only regret was that he did not introduce it sooner with the original business.

When GM designed the Lordstown plant, it was hailed as the new wave of production facilities. It had incorporated the finest technology and industrial engineering principles available. Unfortunately, the designers had not taken into account some basic principles of human behavior. As a result, the designer's fantasy turned out to be the workers' nightmare. In this reading, Barbara Garson documents the effect of ignoring the social and emotional aspects of the worker's response to work in the design of that work. The jobs she describes are not the "enriched" jobs of Hackman or Arthur Friedman seen in the earlier readings in this section.

■ READING 31 ■

Luddites in Lordstown
It's Not the Money, It's the Job

Barbara Garson

Though labor unrest has long been commonplace in American society, more and more young workers now seem to be fed up with the whole ethos of the industrial system. Freer in spirit than their fathers, they often scorn the old work ethic and refuse to be treated like automatons, no matter how good the pay or how brief the hours. Their anguish and boredom are likely to worsen in the next few years, perhaps infecting not only those on the assembly line but also white-collar workers who resent toiling at trivia. Nowhere has the new discontent been more forcibly expressed than by the young auto workers who recently shut down a GM plant at Lordstown, Ohio.

"Is it true," an auto worker asked wistfully, "that you get to do 15 different jobs on a Cadillac?" "I heard," said another, "that with Volvos you follow one car all the way down the line."

Such are the yearnings of young auto workers at the Vega plant in Lordstown, Ohio. Their average age is 24, and they work on the fastest auto assembly line in the world. Their jobs are so subdivided that few workers can feel they are making a car.

The assembly line carries 101 cars past each worker every hour. Most GM lines run under 60. At 101 cars an hour, a worker has 36 seconds to perform his assigned snaps, knocks, twists, or squirts on each car. The line was running at this speed in October when a new management group, General Motors Assembly Division (GMAD or Gee-Mad), took over the plant. Within four months they fired 500 to 800 workers. Their jobs were divided among the remaining workers, adding a few more snaps, knocks, twists, or squirts to each man's task. The job had been boring and unbearable before. When it remained boring and became a bit more unbearable there was a 97 percent vote to strike. More amazing—85 percent went down to the union hall to vote.[1]

---

[1]The union membership voted to settle the 22-day strike in late March, but the agreement appeared to be somewhat reluctant; less than half of the members showed up for the vote, and 30 percent of those voted against the settlement. The union won a number of concessions, among them full back pay to anybody who had been

---

One could give a broad or narrow interpretation of what the Lordstown workers want. Broadly, they want to reorganize industry so that each worker plays a significant role in turning out a fine product, without enduring degrading supervision. Narrowly, they want more time in each 36-second cycle to sneeze or to scratch.

John Grix, who handles public relations at Lordstown, and Andy O'Keefe for GMAD in Detroit both assured me that work at Lordstown is no different than at the older assembly plant. The line moves faster, they say, but then the parts are lighter and easier to install. I think this may be true. It is also true of the workers. These young people are not basically different from the older men. But they are faster and lighter. Because they are young they are economically freer to strike and temperamentally quicker to act. But their yearnings are not new. The Vega workers are echoing a rank-and-file demand that has been suppressed by both union and management for the past 20 years: HUMANIZE WORKING CONDITIONS.

Hanging around the parking lot between shifts, I learned immediately that to these young workers, "It's not the money."

"It pays good," said one, "but it's driving me crazy."

"I don't want more money," said another. "None of us do."

"I do," said his friend. "So I can quit quicker."

"It's the job," everyone said. But they found it hard to describe the job itself.

"My father worked in auto for 35 years," said a clean-cut lad, "and he never talked about the job. What's there to say? A car comes, I weld it. A car comes, I weld it. A car comes, I weld it. One hundred and one times an hour."

I asked a young wife, "What does your husband tell you about his work?"

"He doesn't say what he does. Only if something happened like, 'My hair caught on fire,' or, 'Something fell in my face.'"

"There's a lot of variety in the paint shop," said a dapper 22-year-old up from West Virginia. "You clip on the color hose, bleed out the old color, and squirt. Clip, bleed, squirt, think: clip, bleed, squirt, yawn: clip, bleed, squirt, scratch your nose. Only now the Gee-Mads have taken away the time to scratch your nose."

A long-hair reminisced: "Before the Go-Mads, when I had a good job like door handles, I could get a couple of cars ahead and have a whole minute to relax."

I asked about diversions. "What do you do to keep from going crazy?"

"Well, certain jobs like the pit you can light up a cigarette without them seeing."

"I go to the wastepaper basket. I wait a certain number of cars, then find a piece of paper to throw away."

"I have fantasies. You know what I keep imagining? I see a car coming down. It's red. So I know it's gonna have a black seat, black dash, black interiors. But I keep thinking what if somebody up there sends down the wrong color interiors—like orange, and me putting in yellow cushions, bright yellow!"

"There's always water fights, paint fights, or laugh, talk, tell jokes. Anything so you don't feel like a machine."

But everyone had the same hope: "You're always waiting for the line to break down."

The Vega plant hires about 7,000 assembly-line workers. They commute to Lordstown from Akron, Youngstown, Cleveland, even as far as Pittsburgh. Actually, there is no Lordstown—just a plant and some trailer camps set among farmhouses. When the workers leave, they disperse throughout southern Ohio. GM presumably hoped that this location would help minimize labor troubles.

I took the guided tour of the plant. It's new, it's clean, it's well lit without windows, and it's noisy. Hanging car bodies move past at the speed of a Coney Island ride slowing down. Most men work alongside the line but some stand in a man-sized pit craning their necks to work on the undersides of the cars.

disciplined in the past five months for failure to meet work standards. Meanwhile, however, UAW locals at three other GM plants around the country threatened to strike on grounds similar to those established at Lordstown. In early April GM recalled 130,000 Vegas of the 1972 model because of a possible fire hazard involving the fuel and exhaust systems.

I stopped to shout at a worker drinking coffee, "Is there any quiet place to take a break?" He shouted back, "Can't hear you, ma'am. Too noisy to chat on a break." As a plant guard rushed over to separate us I spotted Duane,[2] from Fort Lewis, shooting radios into cars with an air gun. Duane had been in the Army while I was working at a GI coffeehouse. He slipped me a note with his address.

When I left the plant there were leafleteers at the gate distributing *Workers' Power.* Guards with binocular cameras closed in, snapping pictures; another guard checked everyone's ID. He copied down the names of leafleteers and workers who took papers. He took my name, too.

Duane's Military-Industrial Complex

That evening I visited Duane. He had rented a two-bedroom bungalow on the outskirts of a town that had no center. He had grown his hair a bit but, in fact, he looked neater and trimmer than when he'd been in the Army.

I told him about the incident at the gate. "Just like the Army," he said. He summarized life since his discharge: "Remember you guys gave me a giant banana split the day I ETSed [got out on schedule]? Well, it's been downhill since then. I came back to Cleveland; stayed with my dad, who was unemployed. Man, was that ever a downer. But I figured things would pick up if I got wheels, so I got a car. But it turned out the car wasn't human and that was a problem. So I figured, 'What I need is a girl.' But it turned out the girl *was* human and *that* was a problem. So I wound up working at GM to pay off the car and the girl." And he introduced me to his lovely pregnant wife, of whom he seemed much fonder than it sounds.

A couple of Duane's high-school friends, Stan and Eddie, wound up at Lordstown too.

Stan at 21 was composed and placid, a married man with a child. Eddie at 22 was an excitable youth. Duane had invited them over to tell me what it's like working at the plant.

"I'll tell you what it's like," said Duane. "It's like the Army. They even use the same words like *direct order.* Supposedly you have a contract so there's some things they just can't make you do. Except, if the foreman gives you a direct order, you do it, or you're out."

"Out?" I asked.

"Yeah, fired—or else they give you a DLO."

"DLO?"

"Disciplinary layoff. Which means you're out without pay for however long they say. Like maybe it'll be a three-day DLO or a week DLO."

Eddie explained it further: "Like this foreman comes up to me and says, 'Pick up that piece of paper.' Only he says it a little nastier, with a few references to my race, creed, and length of hair. So I says, 'That's not my job.' He says, 'I'm giving you a direct order to pick up that piece of paper.' Finally he takes me up to the office. My committeeman comes over and tells me I could of lost my job because you can't refuse a direct order. You do it, and then you put in a grievance—ha!"

"Calling your committeeman," says Duane. "That's just like the Army too. If your CO [commanding officer] is harassing you, you can file a complaint with the IG [Inspector General]. Only thing is you gotta go up to your CO and say, 'Sir, request permission to see the Inspector General to tell him my commanding officer is a shit.' Same thing here. Before you can get your committeeman, you got to tell the foreman exactly what your grievance is in detail. So meantime he's working out ways to tell the story different."

Here Stan took out an actual DLO form from his wallet. "Last week someone up the line put a stink bomb in a car. I do rear cushions, and the foreman says, 'You get in that car.' We said, 'If you can put your head in that car we'll do the job.' So the foreman says, 'I'm giving you a direct order.' So I hold my breath and do it. My job is every other car so I let the next one pass. He gets on me, and I say, 'It

---

[2]Since many workers were afraid of losing their jobs, I have changed names, juggled positions on the line, and given facsimiles for identifying details.

ain't my car. Please, I done your dirty work and the other one wasn't mine.' But he keeps at me, and I wind up with a week off. Now, I got a hot committeeman who really stuck up for me. So you know what? They sent *him* home too. Gave the committeeman a DLO!"

"See, just like the Army," Duane repeats. "No, its worse 'cause you're welded to the line. You just about need a pass to piss."

"That ain't no joke," says Eddie. "You raise your little hand if you want to go wee-wee. Then wait maybe half an hour till they find a relief man. And they write it down every time too. 'Cause you're supposed to do it on your own time, not theirs. Try it too often, and you'll get a week off."

"I'd rather work in a gas station," said Stan wistfully. "That way you pump gas, then you patch a tire, then you go to the bathroom. You do what needs doing."

"Why don't you work in a gas station?" I asked.

"You know what they pay in a gas station? I got a kid. Besides, I couldn't even get a job in a gas station. Before I got in here I was so hard up I wound up selling vacuum cleaners— $297 door to door. In a month I earned exactly $10 selling one vacuum cleaner to a laid-off steel worker for which I'll never forgive myself."

"No worse than making cars," Eddie said. "Cars are your real trap, not vacuum cleaners. You need the car to keep the job and you need the job to keep the car. And don't think they don't know it. They give you just enough work to keep up the payments. They got it planned exactly, so you can't quit."

"He's a little paranoid," Duane said.

"Look it," says the paranoid reasonably. "They give you 50, 55 hours' work for a couple of weeks. So your typical boob buys a color TV. Then they cut you back to 30 hours. There's not a married man who doesn't have bills. And the company keeps it like that so there's no way out. You're stuck for life."

I asked about future plans.

Eddie was getting out as soon as he saved enough money to travel. He thought he might work for three more months. He'd said three

months when he started, and it was nine months already, but "things came up."

Duane figured he'd stay till after his wife had the baby. That way he could use the hospital plan. After that? "Maybe we'll go live on the land. I don't know. I wish someone would hand me a discharge."

Stan was a reasonable man—or a boob, as Eddie might have it. He knew he was going to stay. "If I'm gonna do some dumb job the rest of my life, I might as well do one that pays."

Though none of them could afford to quit, they were all eager for a strike. They'd manage somehow. For Stan it was a good investment in his future job. The others just liked the idea of giving GM a kick in the ass from the inside.

The Blue-Collar Commune

Later in the week I stayed at an auto-workers' commune. Like so many other young people, they were trying to make a one-generational family—a homestead. Life centered, as of old, around the hearth, which was a waterpipe bubbling through bourbon. The family Bibles were the Books of the Dead —both Tibetan and Egyptian. Throughout the evening, 6 to 12 people drifted through the old house waiting for Indian Nut (out working night shift at Lordstown) and his wife Jane (out baby-sitting).

Jane returned at midnight to prepare dinner for her husband. By 2:00 A.M. she complained: "They can keep them two, three, four hours over." Overtime is mandatory for auto workers but it's not as popular at Lordstown as it is among older workers at other plants.

At 2:30 A.M. the Nut burst in, wild-haired, wild-eyed, and sweet-smiled. He had a mild, maniacal look because his glasses were speckled with welding spatter.

"New foreman, a real Gee-Mad-man. Sent a guy home for farting in a car. And another one home for yodeling."

"Yodeling?" I asked.

"Yeah, you know." (And he yodeled.)

(It's common in auto plants for men to break the monotony with noise, like the banging of tin cans in jail. Someone will drop something, his partner will yell "Whaa," and then "Whaa" gets transmitted all along the line.)

"I bet there's no shop rule against farting," the Nut conjectured. "You know those porkers have been getting their 101 off the line again, and not that many of them need repairs. It's the hillbillies. Those cats have no stamina. The union calls them to a meeting, says, 'Now don't you sabotage, but don't you run. Don't do more than you can do.' And everybody cheers. But in a few days it's back to where it was. Hillbillies working so fast they ain't got time to scratch their balls. Meantime these porkers is making money even faster than they're making cars."

I ask who he means by the hillbillies. "Hillbillies is the general Ohio term for assholes, except if you happen to be a hillbilly. Then you say Polack. Fact is everybody is a hillbilly out here except me and two other guys. And they must work day shift 'cause I never see them.

"Sabotage?" says the Nut. "Just a way of letting off steam. You can't keep up with the car so you scratch it on the way past. I once saw a hillbilly drop an ignition key down the gas tank. Last week I watched a guy light a glove and lock it in the trunk. We all waited to see how far down the line they'd discover it. . . . If you miss a car, they call that sabotage. They expect the 60-second minute. Even a machine has to sneeze. Look how they call us in weekends, hold us extra, send us home early, give us layoffs. You'd think we were machines the way they turn us on and off."

I apologized for getting Indian Nut so steamed up and keeping him awake late. "No," sighed Jane. "It always takes a couple of hours to calm him down. We never get to bed before four."

Later that day, about 1:00 P.M., Indian Nut cooked breakfast for all of us (about 10). One nice thing about a working-class commune: bacon and eggs and potatoes for breakfast—no granola.

It took about an hour and a half to do the day's errands—mostly dope shopping and car

repair. Then Indian Nut relaxed for an hour around the hearth.

As we talked some people listened to Firesign Theatre while others played Masterpiece or Monopoly. Everyone sucked at the pipe from time to time.

A college kid came by to borrow records. He was the editor of the defunct local underground paper called *Anonymity*. (It had lived up to its title before folding.)

"I've been trying to get Indian Nut to quit working there," he said.

"Why?" I asked.

"Don't you know? GM makes M-16s."

"Yeah, well, you live with your folks," said one of the Monopolists.

"You can always work some kind of rip-off," replied the ex-editor.

Everyone joined the ensuing philosophical inquiry about where it was moral to work and whom it was moral to rip off.

"Shit," sighed Indian Nut. "It's four-thirty. Someone help Jane with the dishes." Taking a last toke, the Nut split for the plant.

As I proceeded with my unscientific survey, I found that I couldn't predict a man's militancy from his hair length, age, or general freakiness. But you could always guess a man's attitudes by his comments on the car. When someone said, "I wouldn't even buy a Vega, not a '71 or a '72," then he would usually say, "General Motors—all they care about is money. Not the worker, not the car, just the goddamn money."[3]

A 19-year-old told me bitterly: "A black guy worked next to me putting sealer into the cracks. He used to get cut all the time on sharp edges of metal. One day his finger really got stuck and he was bleeding all over the car. So I stopped the line. [There's a button every so many feet.] Sure they rushed him to the hospital, but boy did they get down on me for stopping the line. That line runs no matter what the cost."

---

[3]Ironically, the Vega gets high marks from car buffs. In its May issue, for example, *Car and Driver* magazine reported that its readers had voted the Vega "Best Economy Sedan" (versus Datsun, Volkswagen, etc.) for the second year in a row. [Ed.]

The mildest man I met was driving a Vega. He was a long-haired, or at least shaggy-haired, 21-year-old. He thought the Vega was a "pretty little thing." When I asked about his job he said, "It's a very important job. After all, everybody's got to have a car." Yes, he had voted for the strike. "Myself, I'd rather work, but if they're gonna keep laying people off, might as well strike now and get it over with." Anyway, he figured the strike would give him time to practice: he was second guitarist in a band, and if his group could only "get it together," maybe he could quit GM. He had other hopes too. For instance: "The company lets you put in suggestions, and you get money if they use your suggestions." He was a cheerful, good-natured lad, and, as I say, he liked the Vega.

There's a good reason why attitudes toward the car correlate with attitudes toward the company. It's not just "hate them, hate their car." It's also hate your job and hate yourself when you think you're making a hunk of junk, or when you can't feel you've made anything at all. I was reminded of this by a worker's mother.

While her son and his friends talked shop —DLOs, strike, rock bands—I talked to her in the kitchen. Someone in the supermarket where she worked had said, those young kids are just lazy: "One thing, Tony is not lazy. He'll take your car apart and put it together any day. Ever since he's been in high school we haven't had to worry about car trouble. The slightest knock and he takes care of it. And he never will leave it half done. He even cleans up after himself.

"And I'm not lazy either. I love to cook. But supposing they gave me a job just cracking eggs with bowls moving past on a line. Pretty soon I'd get to a point where I'd wish the next egg was rotten just to spoil their whole cake."

At the Pink Elephant Bar I met a man who'd voted against the strike, one of the rare 3 percent. He was an older man who'd worked in other auto plants. "I seen it before. The international [union] is just giving them enough rope to hang themselves. They don't ever take on speed-up or safety. And they don't ever help with any strike *they* didn't call.

"Meany and his silk shirts! Reuther's daughter hobnobbed with Miss Ford, but at least he didn't wear silk shirts. . . . Woodcock?* Who cares what he wears.

"Like I was saying, they see a kicky young local so they go along. They authorize the strike. But it's just giving you enough rope to hang yourself.

"They see you got young inexperienced leadership—I'm not saying our leadership is young and inexperienced but what it is, is —young and inexperienced.

"So they let 'em go ahead. But they don't give 'em no help. They don't give 'em no funds. They don't even let the other locals come out with you. When it comes to humanizing working conditions you might as well be back before there was any unions.

"So the strike drags on, it's lost, or they 'settle' in Detroit. Everybody says, 'There, it didn't pay.' And the next time around the leadership gets unelected. See—they gave 'em enough rope to hang 'emselves."

Other GM plants are having labor troubles, but no coordinated union action has been authorized. It is difficult for an outsider to tell when the UAW International is giving wholehearted help. But with or without the international, workers will continue to agitate for better working conditions.

Local 1112 at Lordstown defined their demands as narrowly as possible. They asked GM to hire more men. They do not, they hasten to explain, want to limit the speed of the line. Gary Bryner, president of the local (an elder statesman at 29), said, "We recognize that it's management's prerogative to run the plant. But all we've got is our labor, so we want to see that our conditions of labor are okay."

Despite this humble goal, local 1112 is undertaking a fight that the international union has backed away from, even suppressed, in the past.

Every 3 years for the past 15, Walter

---

*President, UAW.

Reuther bargained with auto manufacturers for higher wages and better benefits—off the job. And every 3 years for the past 15, auto workers rejected Reuther's contracts, demanding, in addition, better conditions—on the job.

In 1955 more than 70 percent of GM workers went on strike when presented with a contract that failed to deal with speed-up or other local grievances. After the 1958 contract an even larger percentage wildcatted. In 1961 the post-contract strike closed all GM plants and many large Ford plants. Running from the rear to the front of the parade, Reuther declared the strike official. However, he failed to negotiate for the demands that caused the wildcat. In 1961 there was a rank-and-file campaign before negotiations began. Near all large plants, bumper stickers appeared on auto workers' cars, saying, HUMANIZE WORKING CONDITIONS.[4]

The underlying assumption in an auto plant is that no worker wants to work. The plant is arranged so that employees can be controlled, checked, and supervised at every point. The efficiency of an assembly line is not only in its speed but in the fact that the workers are easily replaced. This allows the employer to cope with high turnover. But it's a vicious cycle. The job is so unpleasantly subdivided that men are constantly quitting and absenteeism is common. Even an accident is a welcome diversion. Because of the high turnover, management further simplifies the job, and more men quit. But the company has learned to cope with high turnover. So they don't have to worry if men quit or go crazy before they're 40.

The UAW is not a particularly undemocratic union. Still, it is as hard for the majority of its members to influence their international as it is for the majority of Americans to end the war in Vietnam. The desire to reduce alienation is hard to express as a union demand, and it's hard to get union leaders to insist upon this demand. Harder still will be the actual struggle to take more control over production away from corporate management. It is a fight that questions the right to private ownership of the means of production.

---

[4]This information was given to me by Stan Weir, a former auto worker. His article "U.S.A.: The Labor Revolts" appears in *American Society Inc.* (Markham Publishing Co., Chicago, 1970).

Organizational Processes

There are many battles going on at the workplace. Some of these battles are between workers and other workers, some between supervisors and subordinates, and some between line and staff. But the most fundamental battle is between an abstraction called "the organization" and a reality called the worker. At lower levels of the organization, the worker is on only one side of the battle. As you move up the organizational ladder and accumulate increasing responsibility for acting as a management spokesperson, it becomes necessary to battle from both sides—against the organization on personal issues, and for the organization on other issues. The "prize" in this battle is the right of one combatant to organize the efforts of the other. Will the worker submit to the "rules," or will the organization adapt to the needs, preferences, and intentions of the worker?

In this section, we will consider the organizational "battle" from several perspectives. First, we will consider the history and current trends in organizational theory. Next, we will consider the role of the psychologist as referee in the battle. Finally, we will consider the implications of work for human development and well-being.

Since Max Weber introduced the notion of a bureaucracy, there has been a steady stream of organizational theories competing for canonization as the "right" theory. Some have emphasized the importance of order, planning, and regularity. Others have emphasized the emotional component of the members of the organization. Still others have concentrated on the nature of the work being accomplished in the organization. In this reading, Perrow takes a very strong position on the past and future of organizational theory. He identifies the "forces of light" and the "forces of darkness" and lays out a battle plan for the future.

■ READING 32 ■

The Short and Glorious History of Organizational Theory

Charles Perrow

From the beginning, the forces of light and the forces of darkness have polarized the field of organizational analysis, and the struggle has been protracted and inconclusive. The forces of darkness have been represented by the mechanical school of organizational theory—those who treat the organization as a machine. This school characterizes organizations in terms of such things as:

Centralized authority.

Clear lines of authority.

Specialization and expertise.

Marked division of labor.

Rules and regulations.

Clear separation of staff and line.

The forces of light, which by mid-20th century came to be characterized as the human relations school, emphasizes people rather than machines, accommodations rather than machine-like precision, and draws its inspiration

from biological systems rather than engineering systems. It has emphasized such things as:

Delegation of authority.

Employee autonomy.

Trust and openness.

Concerns with the "whole person."

Interpersonal dynamics.

THE RISE AND FALL OF SCIENTIFIC MANAGEMENT

The forces of darkness formulated their position first, starting in the early part of this century. They have been characterized as the scientific management or classical management school. This school started by parading simple-minded injunctions to plan ahead, keep records, write down policies, specialize, be decisive, and keep your span of control to about six people. These injunctions were needed as firms grew in size and complexity, since there were few models around beyond the railroad, the military, and the Catholic church to guide organizations. And their injunctions worked.

Executives began to delegate, reduce their span of control, keep records, and specialize. Planning ahead still is difficult, it seems, and the modern equivalent is Management by Objectives.

But many things intruded to make these simple-minded injunctions less relevant:

1. Labor became a more critical factor in the firm. As the technology increased in sophistication it took longer to train people, and more varied and specialized skills were needed. Thus, labor turnover cost more and recruitment became more selective. As a consequence, labor's power increased. Unions and strikes appeared. Management adjusted by beginning to speak of a cooperative system of capital, management, and labor. The machine model began to lose its relevancy.

2. The increasing complexity of markets, variability of products, increasing number of branch plants, and changes in technology all required more adaptive organization. The scientific management school was ill-equipped to deal with rapid change. It had presumed that once the proper structure was achieved the firm could run forever without much tampering. By the late 1930s, people began writing about adaptation and change in industry from an organizational point of view and had to abandon some of the principles of scientific management.

3. Political, social, and cultural changes meant new expectations regarding the proper way to treat people. The dark, satanic mills needed at the least a whitewashing. Child labor and the brutality of supervision in many enterprises became no longer permissible. Even managers could not be expected to accept the authoritarian patterns of leadership that prevailed in the small firm run by the founding father.

4. As mergers and growth proceeded apace and the firm could no longer be viewed as the shadow of one man (the founding entrepreneur), a search for methods of selecting good leadership became a preoccupation. A good, clear, mechanical structure would no longer suffice. Instead, firms had to search for the qualities of leadership that could fill the large

footsteps of the entrepreneur. They tacitly had to admit that something other than either "sound principles" or "dynamic leadership" was needed. The search for leadership traits implied that leaders were made, not just born, that the matter was complex, and that several skills were involved.

ENTER HUMAN RELATIONS

From the beginning, individual voices were raised against the implications of the scientific management school. "Bureaucracy" had always been a dirty word, and the job design efforts of Frederick Taylor were even the subject of a congressional investigation. But no effective counterforce developed until 1938, when a business executive with academic talents named Chester Barnard proposed the first new theory of organizations: Organizations are cooperative systems, not the products of mechanical engineering. He stressed natural groups within the organization, upward communication, authority from below rather than from above, and leaders who functioned as a cohesive force. With the spectre of labor unrest and the Great Depression upon him, Barnard's emphasis on the cooperative nature of organizations was well timed. The year following the publication of his *Functions of the Executive* (1938) saw the publication of F. J. Roethlisberger and William Dickson's *Management and the Worker*, reporting on the first large-scale empirical investigation of productivity and social relations. The research, most of it conducted in the Hawthorne plant of the Western Electric Company during a period in which the workforce was reduced, highlighted the role of informal groups, work restriction norms, the value of decent, humane leadership, and the role of psychological manipulation of employees through the counseling system. World War II intervened, but after the war the human relations movement, building on the insights of Barnard and the Hawthorne studies, came into its own.

The first step was a search for the traits of

good leadership. It went on furiously at university centers but at first failed to produce more than a list of Boy Scout maxims: A good leader was kind, courteous, loyal, courageous, etc. We suspected as much. However, the studies did turn up a distinction between "consideration," or employee-centered aspects of leadership, and job-centered, technical aspects labeled "initiating structure." Both were important, but the former received most of the attention and the latter went undeveloped. The former led directly to an examination of group processes, an investigation that has culminated in T-group programs and is moving forward still with encounter groups. Meanwhile, in England, the Tavistock Institute sensed the importance of the influence of the kind of task a group had to perform on the social relations within the group. The first important study, conducted among coal miners, showed that job simplification and specialization did not work under conditions of uncertainty and nonroutine tasks.

As this work flourished and spread, more adventurous theorists began to extend it beyond work groups to organizations as a whole. We now knew that there were a number of things that were bad for the morale and loyalty of groups—routine tasks, submission to authority, specialization of task, segregation of task sequence, ignorance of the goals of the firm, centralized decision making, and so on. If these were bad for groups, they were likely to be bad for groups of groups—i.e., for organizations. So people like Warren Bennis began talking about innovative, rapidly changing organizations that were made up of temporary leadership and role assignments, and democratic access to the goals of the firm. If rapidly changing technologies and unstable, turbulent environments were to characterize industry, then the structure of firms should be temporary and decentralized. The forces of light, of freedom, autonomy, change, humanity, creativity, and democracy were winning. Scientific management survived only in outdated text books. If the evangelizing of some of the human relations school theorists were excessive, and if Likert's System 4 or MacGregor's

Theory Y or Blake's 9×9 evaded us, at least there was a rationale for confusion, disorganization, scrambling, and stress: Systems should be temporary.

BUREAUCRACY'S COMEBACK

Meanwhile, in another part of the management forest, the mechanistic school was gathering its forces and preparing to outflank the forces of light. First came the numbers men —the linear programmers, the budget experts, and the financial analysts—with their PERT systems and cost-benefit analyses. From another world, unburdened by most of the scientific management ideology and untouched by the human relations school, they began to parcel things out and give some meaning to those truisms, "plan ahead" and "keep records." Armed with emerging systems concepts, they carried the "mechanistic" analogy to its fullest—and it was very productive. Their work still goes on, largely untroubled by organizational theory; the theory, it seems clear, will have to adjust to them, rather than the other way around.

Then the words of Max Weber, first translated from the German in the 1940s—he wrote around 1910, incredibly—began to find their way into social science thought. At first, with his celebration of the efficiency of bureaucracy, he was received with only reluctant respect, and even with hostility. All writers were against bureaucracy. But it turned out, surprisingly, that managers were not. When asked, they acknowledge that they preferred clear lines of communication, clear specifications of authority and responsibility, and clear knowledge of whom they were responsible to. They were as wont to say "there ought to be a rule about this," as to say "there are too many rules around here," as wont to say "next week we've got to get organized," as to say "there is too much red tape." Gradually, studies began to show that bureaucratic organizations could change faster than nonbureaucratic ones, and that morale could be higher where there was clear evidence of bureaucracy.

What was this thing, then? Weber had showed us, for example, that bureaucracy was the most effective way of ridding organizations of favoritism, arbitrary authority, discrimination, payola and kickbacks, and yes, even incompetence. His model stressed expertise, and the favorite or the boss's nephew or the guy who burned up resources to make his performance look good was *not* the one with expertise. Rules could be changed; they could be dropped in exceptional circumstances; job security promoted more innovation. The sins of bureaucracy began to look like the sins of failing to follow its principles.

ENTER POWER, CONFLICT, AND DECISIONS

But another discipline began to intrude upon the confident work and increasingly elaborate models of the human relations theorists (largely social psychologists) and the uneasy toying with bureaucracy of the "structionalists" (largely sociologists). Both tended to study economic organizations. A few, like Philip Selznick, were noting conflict and differences in goals (perhaps because he was studying a public agency, the Tennessee Valley Authority), but most ignored conflict or treated it as a pathological manifestation of breakdowns in communication or the ego trips of unreconstructed managers.

But in the world of political parties, pressure groups, and legislative bodies, conflict was not only rampant, but to be expected—it was even functional. This was the domain of the political scientists. They kept talking about power, making it a legitimate concern for analysis. There was an open acknowledgement of "manipulation." These were political scientists who were "behaviorally" inclined—studying and recording behavior rather than constitutions and formal systems of government—and they came to a much more complex view of organized activity. It spilled over into the area of economic organizations, with the help of some economists like R. A. Gordon and some sociologists who were studying conflicting goals of treatment and custody in prisons and mental hospitals.

The presence of legitimately conflicting goals and techniques of preserving and using power did not, of course, sit well with a cooperative systems view of organizations. But it also puzzled the bureaucratic school (and what was left of the old scientific management school), for the impressive Weberian principles were designed to settle questions of power through organizational design and to keep conflict out through reliance on rational-legal authority and systems of careers, expertise, and hierarchy. But power was being overtly contested and exercised in covert ways, and conflict was bursting out all over, and even being creative.

Gradually, in the second half of the 1950s and in the next decade, the political-science view infiltrated both schools. Conflict could be healthy, even in a cooperative system, said the human relationists; it was the mode of resolution that counted, rather than prevention. Power became reconceptualized as "influence," and the distribution was less important, said Arnold Tannenbaum, than the total amount. For the bureaucratic school—never a clearly defined group of people, and largely without any clear ideology—it was easier to just absorb the new data and theories as something else to be thrown into the pot. That is to say, they floundered, writing books that went from topic to topic, without a clear view of organizations, or better yet, producing "readers" and leaving students to sort it all out.

Buried in the political-science viewpoint was a sleeper that only gradually began to undermine the dominant views. This was the idea, largely found in the work of Herbert Simon and James March, that because man was so limited—in intelligence, reasoning powers, information at his disposal, time available, and means of ordering his preferences clearly—he generally seized on the first acceptable alternative when deciding, rather than looking for the best; that he rarely changed things unless they really got bad, and even then he continued to try what had worked before; that he limited his search for solutions to well-worn paths and traditional sources of information and established ideas; that he was wont to remain preoccupied with routine, thus preventing innovation. They called these characteristics "cognitive limits on rationality" and spoke of "satisficing" rather than maximizing or optimizing. It is now called the "decision-making" school, and is concerned with the basic question of how people make decisions.

This view had some rather unusual implications. It suggested that if managers were so limited, then they could be easily controlled. What was necessary was not to give direct orders (on the assumption that subordinates were idiots without expertise) or to leave them to their own devices (on the assumption that they were supermen who would somehow know what was best for the organization, how to coordinate with all the other supermen, how to anticipate market changes, etc.). It was necessary to control only the *premises* of their decisions. Left to themselves, with those premises set, they could be predicted to rely on precedent, keep things stable and smooth, and respond to signals that reinforce the behavior desired of them.

To control the premises of decision making, March and Simon outline a variety of devices, all of which are familiar to you, but some of which you may not have seen before in quite this light. For example, organizations develop vocabularies, and this means that certain kinds of information are highlighted, and others are screened out—just as Eskimos (and skiers) distinguish many varieties of snow, while Londoners see only one. This is a form of attention-directing. Another is the reward system. Change the bonus for salesmen and you can shift them from volume selling to steady-account selling, or to selling quality products or new products. If you want to channel good people into a different function (because, for example, sales should no longer be the critical function as the market changes, but engineering applications should), you may have to promote mediocre people in the unrewarded function in order to signal to the good people in the rewarded one that the game has changed. You cannot expect most people to make such

decisions on their own because of the cognitive limits on their rationality, nor will you succeed by giving direct orders, because you yourself probably do not know whom to order where. You presume that once the signals are clear and the new sets of alternatives are manifest, they have enough ability to make the decision but you have had to change the premises for their decisions about their career lines.

It would take too long to go through the dozen or so devices, covering a range of decision areas (March and Simon are not that clear or systematic about them, themselves, so I have summarized them in my own book), but I think the message is clear.

It was becoming clear to the human relations school, and to the bureaucratic school. The human relationists had begun to speak of changing stimuli rather than changing personality. They had begun to see that the rewards that can change behavior can well be prestige, money, comfort, etc., rather than trust, openness, self-insight, and so on. The alternative to supportive relations need not be punishment, since behavior can best be changed by rewarding approved behavior rather than by punishing disapproved behavior. They were finding that although leadership may be centralized, it can function best through indirect and unobtrusive means such as changing the premises on which decisions are made, thus giving the impression that the subordinate is actually making a decision when he has only been switched to a different set of alternatives. The implications of this work were also beginning to filter into the human relations school through an emphasis on behavioral psychology (the modern version of the much maligned stimulus-response school) that was supplanting personality theory (Freudian in its roots, and drawing heavily, in the human relations school, on Maslow).

For the bureaucratic school, this new line of thought reduced the weight placed upon the bony structure of bureaucracy by highlighting the muscle and flesh that make these bones move. A single chain of command, precise division of labor, and clear lines of communication are simply not enough in themselves.

Control can be achieved by using alternative communication channels, depending on the situation; by increasing or decreasing the static or "noise" in the system; by creating organizational myths and organizational vocabularies that allow only selective bits of information to enter the system; and through monitoring performance through indirect means rather than direct surveillance. Weber was all right for a starter, but organizations had changed vastly, and the leaders needed many more means of control and more subtle means of manipulation than they did at the turn of the century.

THE TECHNOLOGICAL QUALIFICATION

By now the forces of darkness and forces of light had moved respectively from midnight and noon to about 4 A.M. and 8 P.M. But any convergence or resolution would have to be on yet new terms, for soon after the political science tradition had begun to infiltrate the established schools, another blow struck both of the major positions. Working quite independently of the Tavistock Group, with its emphasis on sociotechnical systems, and before the work of Burns and Stalker on mechanistic and organic firms, Joan Woodward was trying to see whether the classical scientific principles of organization made any sense in her survey of 100 firms in South Essex. She tripped and stumbled over a piece of gold in the process. She picked up the gold, labeled it "technology," and made sense out of her otherwise hopeless data. Job-shop firms, mass-production firms, and continuous-process firms all had quite different structures because the type of tasks, or the "technology," was different. Somewhat later, researchers in America were coming to very similar conclusions based on studies of hospitals, juvenile correctional institutions, and industrial firms. Bureaucracy appeared to be the best form of organization for routine operations; temporary work groups, decentralization, and emphasis on interpersonal processes appeared to work best for nonroutine operations. A raft of studies ap-

peared and are still appearing, all trying to show how the nature of the task affects the structure of the organization.

This severely complicated things for the human relations school, since it suggested that openness and trust, while good things in themselves, did not have much impact, or perhaps were not even possible in some kinds of work situations. The prescriptions that were being handed out would have to be drastically qualified. What might work for nonroutine, high-status, interesting, and challenging jobs performed by highly educated people might not be relevant or even beneficial for the vast majority of jobs and people.

It also forced the upholders of the revised bureaucratic theory to qualify their recommendations, since research and development units should obviously be run differently from mass-production units, and the difference between both of these and highly programmed and highly sophisticated continuous-process firms was obscure in terms of bureaucratic theory. But the bureaucratic school perhaps came out on top, because the forces of evil—authority, structure, division of labor, etc.—no longer looked evil, even if they were not applicable to a minority of industrial units.

The emphasis on technology raised other questions, however. A can company might be quite routine, and a plastics division nonroutine, but there were both routine and nonroutine units within each. How should they be integrated if the prescription were followed that, say, production should be bureaucratized and R&D not? James Thompson began spelling out different forms of interdependence among units in organizations, and Paul Lawrence and Jay Lorsch looked closely at the nature of integrating mechanisms. Lawrence and Lorsch found that firms performed best when the differences between units were *maximized* (in contrast to both the human relations and the bureaucratic schools), as long as the integrating mechanisms stood half-way between the two —being neither strongly bureaucratic nor nonroutine. They also noted that attempts at participative management in routine situations were counterproductive, that the environments of some kinds of organizations were far from turbulent and customers did not want innovations and changes, that cost reduction, price and efficiency were trivial considerations in some firms, and so on. The technical insight was demolishing our comfortable truths right and left. They were also being questioned from another quarter.

ENTER GOALS, ENVIRONMENTS, AND SYSTEMS

The final seam was being mined by the sociologists while all this went on. This was the concern with organizational goals and the environment. Borrowing from the political scientists to some extent, but pushing ahead on their own, this "institutional school" came to see that goals were not fixed; conflicting goals could be pursued simultaneously, if there were enough slack resources, or sequentially (growth for the next four years, then cost-cutting and profit-taking for the next four); that goals were up for grabs in organizations, and units fought over them. Goals were, of course, not what they seemed to be, the important ones were quite unofficial; history played a big role; and assuming profit as the preeminent goal explained almost nothing about a firm's behavior.

They also did case studies that linked the organization to the web of influence of the environment; that showed how unique organizations were in many respects (so that, once again, there was no one best way to do things for all organizations); how organizations were embedded in their own history, making change difficult. Most striking of all, perhaps, the case studies revealed that the stated goals usually were not the real ones; the official leaders usually were not the real ones; the official leaders usually were not the powerful ones; claims of effectiveness and efficiency were deceptive or even untrue; the public interest was not being served; political influences were pervasive; favoritism, discrimination, and sheer corruption were commonplace. The accumula-

tion of these studies presented quite a pill for either the forces of light or darkness to swallow, since it was hard to see how training sessions or interpersonal skills were relevant to these problems, and it was also clear that the vaunted efficiency of bureaucracy was hardly in evidence. What could they make of this wad of case studies?

We are still sorting it out. In one sense, the Weberian model is upheld because organizations are not, *by nature,* cooperative systems; top managers must exercise a great deal of effort to control them. But if organizations are tools in the hands of leaders, they may be very recalcitrant ones. Like the broom in the story of the sorcerer's apprentice, they occasionally get out of hand. If conflicting goals, bargaining, and unofficial leadership exist, where is the structure of Weberian bones and Simonian muscle? To what extent are organizations tools, and to what extent are they products of the varied interests and group strivings of their members? Does it vary by organization, in terms of some typological alchemy we have not discovered? We don't know. But at any rate, the bureaucratic model suffers again; it simply has not reckoned on the role of the environment. There are enormous sources of variations that the neat, though by now quite complex, neo-Weberian model could not account for.

The human relations model has also been badly shaken by the findings of the institutional school, for it was wont to assume that goals were given and unproblematical, and that anything that promoted harmony and efficiency for an organization also was good for society. Human relationists assumed that the problems created by organizations were largely limited to the psychological consequences of poor interpersonal relations within them, rather than their impact on the environment. Could the organization really promote the psychological health of its members when by necessity it had to define psychological health in terms of the goals of the organization itself? The neo-Weberian model at least called manipulation "manipulation" and was skeptical of claims about autonomy and self-realization.

But on one thing all the varied schools of organizational analysis now seemed to be agreed: organizations are systems—indeed, they are open systems. As the growth of the field has forced ever more variables into our consciousness, flat claims of predictive power are beginning to decrease and research has become bewilderingly complex. Even consulting groups need more than one or two tools in their kitbag as the software multiplies.

The systems view is intuitively simple. Everything is related to everything else, though in uneven degrees of tension and reciprocity. Every unit, organization, department, or work group takes in resources, transforms them, and sends them out, and thus interacts with the larger system. The psychological, sociological, and cultural aspects of units interact. The systems view was explicit in the institutional work, since they tried to study whole organizations; it became explicit in the human relations school, because they were so concerned with the interactions of people. The political science and technology viewpoints also had to come to this realization, since they deal with parts affecting each other (sales affecting production; technology affecting structure).

But as intuitively simple as it is, the systems view has been difficult to put into practical use. We still find ourselves ignoring the tenets of the open-systems view, possibly because of the cognitive limits on our rationality. General systems theory itself had not lived up to its heady predictions; it remains rather nebulous. But at least there is a model for calling us to account and for stretching our minds, our research tools, and our troubled nostrums.

SOME CONCLUSIONS

Where does all this leave us? We might summarize the prescriptions and proscriptions for management very roughly as follows:

1. A great deal of the "variance" in a firm's behavior depends on the environment. We have become more realistic about the limited range of change that can be induced through internal efforts. The goals of organizations, including those of profit and efficiency, vary greatly among industries and vary systematically by industries. This suggests that the impact of better management by itself will be limited, since so much will depend on market forces, competition, legislation, nature of the workforce, available technologies and innovations, and so on. Another source of variation is, obviously, the history of the firm and its industry and its traditions.

2. A fair amount of variation in both firms and industries is due to the type of work done in the organization—the technology. We are now fairly confident in recommending that if work is predictable and routine, the necessary arrangement for getting the work done can be highly structured, and one can use a good deal of bureaucratic theory in accomplishing this. If it is not predictable, if it is nonroutine and there is a good deal of uncertainty as to how to do a job, then one had better utilize the theories that emphasize autonomy, temporary groups, multiple lines of authority and communications, and so on. We also know that this distinction is important when organizing different parts of an organization.

We are also getting a grasp on the question of what is the most critical function in different types of organizations. For some organizations it is production; for others, marketing; for still others, development. Furthermore, firms go through phases whereby the initial development of a market or a product or manufacturing process or accounting scheme may require a nonbureaucratic structure, but once it comes on stream, the structure should change to reflect the changed character of the work.

3. In keeping with this, management should be advised that the attempt to produce change in an organization through managerial grids, sensitivity training, and even job enrichment and job enlargement is likely to be fairly ineffective for all but a few organizations. The critical reviews of research in all these fields show that there is no scientific evidence to support the claims of the proponents of these various methods; that research has told us a great deal about social psychology, but little about how to apply the highly complex

findings to actual situations. The key word is *selectivity:* We have no broad-spectrum antibiotics for interpersonal relations. Of course, managers should be sensitive, decent, kind, courteous, and courageous, but we have known that for some time now, and beyond a minimal threshold level, the payoff is hard to measure. The various attempts to make work and interpersonal relations more humane and stimulating should be applauded, but we should not confuse this with solving problems of structure, or as the equivalent of decentralization or participatory democracy.

4. The burning cry in all organizations is for "good leadership," but we have learned that beyond a threshold level of adequacy it is extremely difficult to know what good leadership is. The hundreds of scientific studies of this phenomenon come to one general conclusion: Leadership is highly variable or "contingent" upon a large variety of important variables such as nature of task, size of the group, length of time the group has existed, type of personnel within the group and their relationships with each other, and amount of pressure the group is under. It does not seem likely that we'll be able to devise a way to select the best leader for a particular situation. Even if we could, that situation would probably change in a short time and thus would require a somewhat different type of leader.

Furthermore, we are beginning to realize that leadership involves more than smoothing the paths of human interaction. What has rarely been studied in this area is the wisdom or even the technical adequacy of a leader's decision. A leader does more than lead people; he also makes decisions about the allocation of resources, type of technology to be used, the nature of the market, and so on. This aspect of leadership remains very obscure, but it is obviously crucial.

5. If we cannot solve our problems through good human relations or through good leadership, what are we then left with? The literature suggests that changing the structures of organizations might be the most effective and certainly the quickest and cheapest method. However, we are now sophisticated enough to know that changing the formal structure by itself is not likely to produce the desired changes. In addition, one must be aware of a large range of subtle, unobtrusive, and even covert processes and change devices that exist. If inspection procedures are not working, we are now unlikely to rush in with sensitivity training, nor would we send down authoritative communications telling people to do a better job. We are more likely to find out where the authority really lies, whether the degree of specialization is adequate, what the rules and regulations are, and so on, but even this very likely will not be enough.

According to the neo-Weberian bureaucratic model, it has been influenced by work on decision-making and behavioral psychology, we should find out how to manipulate the reward structure, change the premises of the decision makers through finer controls on the information received and the expectations generated, search for interdepartmental conflicts that prevent better inspection procedures from being followed, and after manipulating these variables, sit back and wait for two or three months for them to take hold. This is complicated and hardly as dramatic as many of the solutions currently being peddled, but I think the weight of organizational theory is in its favor.

We have probably learned more, over several decades of research and theory, about the things that do *not* work (even though some of them obviously *should* have worked), than we have about things that do work. On balance, this is an important gain and should not discourage us. As you know, organizations are extremely complicated. To have as much knowledge as we do have in a fledgling discipline that has had to borrow from the diverse tools and concepts of psychology, sociology, economics, engineering, biology, history, and even anthropology is not really so bad.

REFERENCES

This paper is an adaptation of the discussion to be found in Charles Perrow, *Complex Organizations: A Critical Essay,* Glenview, Ill.; Scott,

Foresman, 1972. All the points made in this paper are discussed thoroughly in that volume.

The best overview and discussion of classical management theory and its changes over time is by Joseph Massie—"Management Theory" in the *Handbook of Organizations* edited by James March, Chicago, Ill.: Rand McNally, 1965, pp. 387–422.

The best discussion of the changing justifications for managerial rule and worker obedience as they are related to changes in technology, etc., can be found in Reinhard Bendix's *Work and Authority in Industry*, New York: John Wiley & Sons, 1956. See especially the chapter on the American experience.

Some of the leading lights of the classical view—F. W. Taylor, Col. Urwick, and Henry Fayol—are briefly discussed in *Writers on Organizations* by D. S. Pugh, D. J. Hickson, and C. R. Hinings, Penguin, 1971. This brief, readable, and useful book also contains selections from many other schools that I discuss, including Weber, Woodward, Cyert and March, Simon, the Hawthorne Investigations, and the Human Relations Movement as represented by Argyris, Herzberg, Likert, McGregor, and Blake and Mouton.

As good a place as any to start examining the human relations tradition is Rensis Likert, *The Human Organization*, New York: McGraw-Hill, 1967. See also his *New Patterns of Management*, McGraw-Hill, 1961.

The Buck Rogers school of organizational theory is best represented by Warren Bennis. See his *Changing Organizations*, McGraw-Hill, 1966, and his book with Philip Slater, *The Temporary Society*, New York: Harper & Row, 1968. Much of this work is linked into more general studies, e.g., Alvin Toffler's very popular paperback *Future Shock*, Random House, 1970, and Bantam Paperbacks, or Zbigniew Brzezinski's *Between Two Ages: America's Role in the Technitronic Era*, New York: Viking Press, 1970. One of the first intimations of the new type of environment and firm and still perhaps the most perceptive is to be found in the volume by Tom Burns and G. Stalker, *The Management of Innovation*, London: Tavistock,

1961, where they distinguished between "organic" and "mechanistic" systems. The introduction, which is not very long, is an excellent and very tight summary of the book.

The political science tradition came in through three important works. First, Herbert Simon's *Administrative Behavior*, New York: MacMillan, 1948, followed by the second half of James March and Herbert Simon's *Organizations*, New York: John Wiley & Sons, 1958, then Richard M. Cyert and James March's *A Behavioral Theory of the Firm*, Englewood Cliffs, N.J.: Prentice-Hall, 1963. All three of these books are fairly rough going, though chapters 1, 2, 3, and 6 of the last volume are fairly short and accessible. A quite interesting book in this tradition, though somewhat heavy-going, is Michael Crozier's *The Bureaucratic Phenomenon*, University of Chicago, and Tavistock Publications, 1964. This is a striking description of power in organizations, though there is a somewhat dubious attempt to link organization processes in France to the cultural traits of the French people.

The book by Joan Woodward, *Industrial Organisation: Theory and Practice*, London: Oxford University Press, 1965, is still very much worth reading. A fairly popular attempt to discuss the implications for this for management can be found in my own book *Organizational Analysis: A Sociological View*, Tavistock, 1970, chapters 2 and 3. The impact of technology on structure is still fairly controversial. A number of technical studies have found both support and nonsupport, largely because the concept is defined so differently, but there is general agreement that different structures and leadership techniques are needed for different situations. For studies that support and document this viewpoint see James Thompson, *Organizations in Action*, McGraw-Hill, 1967, and Paul Lawrence and Jay Lorsch, *Organizations and Environment*, Cambridge, Mass.: Harvard University Press, 1967.

The best single work on the relation between the organization and the environment and one of the most readable books in the field is Philip Selznick's short volume *Leadership in*

Administration, Evanston, Ill.: Row, Peterson, 1957. But the large number of these studies are scattered about. I have summarized several in my *Complex Organizations: A Critical Essay*.

Lastly, the most elaborate and persuasive argument for a systems view of organizations is found in the first 100 pages of the book by Daniel Katz and Robert Kahn, *The Social Psychology of Organizations*, Wiley, 1966. It is not easy reading, however.

At least on paper, America would seem to value and reward merit at both the individual and organizational levels. This is a general principle that most of us would accept as representative of the American culture. We see it each Olympic year; we see it in our childrearing practices; we see it at work. It pervades our response to the environment. As a result, when we see success in other cultures, our immediate reaction is to incorporate the instruments of that success into our culture.

For more than a decade, the Japanese have been competing successfully with their American counterparts in the production of cars, steel, and high-technology equipment. In addition, they have adopted very different management styles. It has occurred to more than one person that possibly these two facts are linked—perhaps the Japanese management style is responsible for their competitive success. As a result, a number of books have been written about ways of adapting the Japanese style of management to the typical American organization. In this reading Schein takes exception to the "me too" response of American organizations. He points out some of the other differences between American and Japanese organizations that might account for the success of the Japanese efforts in the international market.

Does Japanese Management Style Have a Message for American Managers?

Edgar H. Schein
Massachusetts Institute of Technology

One of the greatest strengths of U.S. society is our flexibility, our ability to learn. When we see a problem, we tinker with it until we have it solved, and we seem to be willing to try anything and everything. One of our greatest weaknesses, on the other hand, is our impatience and short-run orientation. This leads to fads, a preoccupation with instant solutions, a blind faith that if we put in enough effort and money anything is possible, and an inability or unwillingness to see the long-range conse-quences of some of the quick fixes which we try. Complicated solutions which require long-range planning, resolute implementa-tion, and patience in the face of short-run diffi-culties are harder for us to implement.[1]

The tension between flexibility and faddism can be seen clearly in the current preoccupa-tion with Japanese management. Two recent books, Ouchi's *Theory Z* and Pascale and Athos's *The Art of Japanese Management*, are currently on the *New York Times* best sellers list. Why this sudden interest and what are the implications for management theory? I would

Source: Reprinted from "Does Japanese Management Style Have a Message for American Managers?" by Edgar H. Schein, *Sloan Management Review*, Fall 1981, pp. 55–68, by permission of the publisher. Copyright © 1981 by the Sloan Management Review Association. All rights reserved.

[1]Slater, P. *The Pursuit of Loneliness.* Boston: The Beacon Press, 1970.

like to examine some of the theses of these two books and to put those theses into a historical perspective. From this perspective I will draw some tentative conclusions about cultural themes in the United States and the implications for U.S. management.

Some Historical Perspective: Indoctrination

In 1961, I published an article called "Management Development as a Process of Influence" which attempted to show that many of the socialization methods used by some of our largest corporations (such as IBM and General Electric) were essentially similar to processes of indoctrination which one could observe in many other settings.[2] Such socialization methods were under strong attack by W.H. Whyte (in *The Organization Man*) and others who saw in them a tendency to create "men in grey flannel suits" who would cease to think for themselves and just parrot the corporate line, thus reducing the innovative and creative capacity of the organization and the individuality of the employee.[3] Ironically, the companies which had built such indoctrination centers (such as IBM at Sands Point, N.Y. and General Electric at Crotonville, N.Y.) were very proud of the spirit and common way of thinking which they could induce in their employees and managers. Such spirit was viewed as one of the key sources of strength of these enterprises.

But the pendulum swung hard during the 1960s, and it became the fashion to move away from producing conformity toward stimulating self-actualization.[4] "Indoctrination" either moved underground, was relabeled, or was replaced by "development" programs which emphasized opportunities for the integration of individual goals with organizational goals. Models of development shifted from the engineering model of "molding or shaping people to fit the organization" to more agricultural models of permitting people to flourish according to their innate potential; the obligation of the organization was to provide sunshine, nutrients, water, and other environmental supports. (Little is said in this model about pruning, transplanting, and uprooting, by the way.) The IBM songbook was put away, and managers who used to be proud of their ability to motivate people by inspiring them through common rituals and activities were made to feel ashamed of using "manipulative" tactics.

In the 1970s we discovered the concept of "organizational culture" and have begun to rethink the issue once again.[5] Even if a company does not deliberately and consciously indoctrinate its new employees, its important beliefs, values, and ways of doing things will, in any case, powerfully socialize anyone who remains in the organization and wishes to move upward and inward in it.[6] Such socialization processes and their effects in producing either conformity or innovation have been described and analyzed, and the tactics which stimulate innovation have received special attention.[7]

Now, with the "discovery" that some Japanese companies are effective because of their ability to involve and motivate people, and the assertion that such involvement results from

---

[2]Schein, E. H. Management development as a process of influence, *Industrial Management Review* (now *Sloan Management Review*), May 1961, pp. 59–77; E. H. Schein, *Coercive Persuasion*, New York: Norton & Co., 1961.

[3]Whyte, W. H., Jr., *The Organization Man*, New York: Simon & Schuster, 1956.

[4]Argyris, C. *Integrating the Individual and the Organization*, New York: John Wiley & Sons, 1964; Maslow, A. H. *Motivation and Personality*, New York: Harper & Row, 1954; McGregor, D. M. *The Human Side of Enterprise*, New York: McGraw-Hill, 1960.

[5]Silverzweig, S. and Allen, R. F. Changing the corporate culture, *Sloan Management Review*, Spring 1976, 33–49; Pettigrew, A. M. On studying organizational cultures, *Administrative Science Quarterly*, 1979, 570–581; Schwartz, H. and Davis, S. M. Matching corporate culture and business strategy, *Organizational Dynamics*, Summer 1981, 30–48.

[6]Schein, E. H. The individual, the organization, and the career: a conceptual scheme, *Journal of Applied Behavioral Science*, 1971, 401–426; Schein, E. H. *Career Dynamics: Matching Individual and Organizational Needs*, Reading, MA: Addison-Wesley, 1978.

[7]Van Maanen, J. and Schein, E. H. Toward a theory of organizational socialization, in *Research in Organizational Behavior* (Vol. 1) B. Staw, ed. Greenwich, CT: JAI Press, 1979.

socialization tactics which induce a high degree of loyalty and conformity, we may be headed back toward the ideology of indoctrination which we so forcefully put aside a mere 20 years ago.

Human Relations and Participation

A similar pendulum swing can be identified with respect to two other human relations values: whether or not one should treat people wholistically and whether or not one should make decisions from the bottom up by participation and consensus mechanisms. Many Americans have grown up with a tradition of bureaucracy, of strong bosses, of hiring people as "hands" to provide certain activities in return for certain pay and benefits. But most students of industrial relations systems note that there has been a historical trend in such systems from a period of autocracy through a period of paternalism toward the present more consultative and participative models.[8] In the paternalistic phase American companies have treated employees very wholistically: building company towns; funding company sports activities; providing country clubs, counseling services, day care centers, medical facilities, uniforms, and so on. Indeed, one of Ralph Nader's most powerful films deals with the town of Kannapolis, N.C., where the Cannon Mills Co. not only provides lifetime employment but owns all of the housing, uses its own security force as the town police force, and provides all the services needed by the town. What alarmed Nader was the possibility that the citizens of this town were not developing any skills in self-government, which would leave them very vulnerable if the company should move or cease to be so totally paternalistic.

We may also recall that one of the major results of the now historic studies of the Hawthorne plant of the Western Electric Company was the recognition that employees were whole people who brought their personal problems with them to their place of work. In the 1930s the company launched a counseling program which involved company-employed counselors to help employees deal with any personal problems on a totally confidential basis.[9] Though it has been a tradition in our military services not to fraternize with the men (presumably because it might be difficult to be objective when individuals must be sent into dangerous situations), there is no such tradition in industry generally. Office parties, company picnics, and other forms of fraternization have been considered legitimate and desirable in many organizations and by many managers, though they are clearly not as institutionalized in the United States as they are in Latin America and Japan.

The human relations training programs for foremen which were rampant in the 1940s were clearly aimed at teaching managers to treat their employees as whole people, to consider their needs, to fight for them when necessary, and to build strong loyalty and team spirit. The leadership and sensitivity training which flourished in the 1960s was similarly aimed at truly understanding the needs and talents of subordinates, peers, and bosses, so that appropriate levels of participation could be used in solving increasingly complex problems in organizations.[10] The writings of McGregor on Theory Y showed the importance of trust and faith in people; the writings of Argyris showed the necessity of permitting people in organizations to function as adults instead of reducing them to dependent children.[11] Likert argued cogently for System 4, a more participative form of organization in which consensus management plays a big role;

[8]Harbison, F. and Myers, C. A. *Management in the Industrial World*, New York: McGraw-Hill, 1959.

[9]Dickson, W. J. and Roethlisberger, F. J. *Counseling in an Organization: A Sequel to the Hawthorne Researches*, Boston: Division of Research, Harvard Business School, 1966; Johnson, H. W. "The Hawthorne studies: The legend and the legacy," *Man and Work in Society*, E. L. Cass and F. G. Zimmer, eds. New York: Van Nostrand Reinhold, 1975.

[10]Schein, E. H. and Bennis, W. G. *Personal and Organizational Change through Group Methods*, New York: John Wiley & Sons, 1965.

[11]McGregor (1960); Argyris (1964).

and Maslow first introduced the idea of Theory Z, a self-actualizing organization.[12]

Many managers saw the point immediately, and either felt reinforcement for what they were already doing or began to retrain themselves and their organization toward some of the new values and technologies of participative decision making. But as a total ideology this approach clearly has not taken hold. Many organizations discovered:

That high morale did not necessarily correlate with high productivity;

That autocratic systems could outproduce democratic systems (at least in the short run);

That high productivity even when achieved by autocratic methods could build high morale;

That the costs in terms of time and effort which participation entailed were often not affordable in certain kinds of environments.

Human Relations Japanese Style

Now the pendulum appears to be swinging once again on the issue of paternalism, managing the whole worker, and creating worker involvement through participation. We are told that the Japanese are extremely paternalistic and wholistic in their approach to employees, that they tend to employ people for life, and that supervisors take care of the personal as well as the work needs of subordinates (sometimes even helping an employee find a wife). The Japanese use bottom-up consensual decision making and encourage high levels of trust across hierarchical and functional boundaries.

THEORY Z

Ouchi has for some time been arguing that the essential differences between American (Theory A) and Japanese (Theory J) manage-

ment systems lie in some key *structural* issues and *cultural* values which make it possible for certain kinds of management styles to flourish. Specifically, he points out that major Japanese companies:

Employ their key people for "life" (i.e., until forced retirement at age 55 to 60);

Rotate them through various functions;

Promote them very slowly and according to more of a seniority than merit system;

Place responsibility on groups rather than on individuals (a value of the Japanese culture).

These determinants make it possible for Japanese companies:

To treat their employees as total people;

To build the kind of trust that facilitates bottom-up consensual decision making; and

To control employees in a subtle, indirect manner.

In contrast, Ouchi points out, the bureaucratic model often associated with pure American management methods emphasizes:

Employment contracts which last only as long as the individual is contributing;

Specialization of function with rotation reserved only for people on a general manager track;

Little concern for the total person;

Rapid feedback and promotion;

Explicit formal control systems;

Individual responsibility (a strong cultural value in the United States);

Individual top-down decision making.

The crucial insight which Ouchi provides is to identify another model, which he calls Theory Z, which is found in many American companies, which fits into our culture, and which combines certain features of the A and J models. Such companies have:

Lifetime employment;

Slower rates of promotion;

---

[12]Likert, R. *The Human Organization,* New York: McGraw-Hill, 1967; Maslow, A. H. *The Farthest Reaches of Human Nature,* New York: The Viking Press, 1971.

Somewhat more implicit, less formal control systems;

More concern for the total person;

More cross-functional rotation and emphasis on becoming a generalist;

Some level of participation and consensual decision making;

A continued emphasis on individual responsibility as a core value.

Though he does not give much evidence in his book, Ouchi has shown in other papers that a U.S. company which approximates the Theory Z criteria generated higher morale, higher loyalty, and generally more healthy, positive feelings at all levels of the hierarchy than did a comparable Theory A company. What is missing, however, is convincing evidence that those companies which fit the Theory Z model are more *effective* than comparable companies which operate more on the Theory A bureaucratic model. Furthermore, Ouchi acknowledges that the Theory Z companies he has studied generate less professionalism, have a harder time integrating mavericks into their ranks because they generate strong conformity pressures (leading them to be sexist and racist), and may only be adaptive for certain kinds of technological or economic environments. In fact, the only way a Theory Z company can manage the instabilities which are inherent in running a successful business in a turbulent environment is to limit lifetime employment to a small cadre of key people and to keep a large percentage of the labor force in a temporary role which resembles more closely the bureaucratic A model. In order to survive, it may be necessary for Theory Z companies to subcontract much of their work or to rely on a set of satellite companies to absorb the instabilities. (The latter is the typical Japanese pattern.)

Implications of Theory Z

After describing how this notion of an industrial "clan" can facilitate certain kinds of long-range involvement on the part of employees, Ouchi argues strongly that U.S. companies should think seriously about becoming more like clans, and lays out a program of how to do it. Neither the argument that a company should be more like Z nor the proposed steps for how to get there are at all convincing, however. The theoretical sophistication which is displayed in the analysis of types of organizational control is followed by naive and superficial prescriptions about how one might think about a change program designed to help a company to become more like a clan (if, indeed, this is even possible). In effect, the manager is invited to be more open and trusting and to involve his or her people more. Little attention is given to the issue of why a given organization would be less trusting and participative in the first place, and to the problem of taking managerial values from a culture in which they fit very well to one in which the fit is not at all clear.

But Ouchi makes a strong sales pitch, and it is here that our tendency to embrace the quick fix may get us into trouble. If someone tells us that Theory Z is closer to the Japanese model, and that the Japanese are getting a lot of mileage out of their model, do we all get on the bandwagon and give our employees tenure, push decision making down the hierarchy, and slow down promotions? Do we turn everyone into a generalist, throw out formal control systems, and treat each person as a total human being? If we do, will our productivity shoot right back up so that we can regain our once dominant economic position? Sounds too simplistic, does it not? Unfortunately that is just what it is, because it takes into account neither the uniqueness of Japanese culture nor the uniqueness of U.S. culture, nor the technological and environmental conditions which ultimately will dictate whether an A, a Z, or some other form will be the most effective in a given situation. What the Ouchi book leaves out, unfortunately, are criteria which might help a manager to decide whether or not a Z, an A, or some other form is appropriate.

On the positive side, the analysis focuses on the importance of the human factor, and Ouchi's seven criterion categories are certainly an important grid for assessing the options for managing people. The identification of the clan mechanism as a way of organizing and controlling people brings us back to what many companies know intuitively—"we are one big family in this organization"—and legitimizes the kind of indoctrination which used to be more common. We can see more clearly that between autocracy and democracy there lies a full range of choices, and that a high degree of paternalism is not necessarily incompatible with bottom-up consensual, participative decision making. The manager can also see that the way people feel about an organization can be explicitly managed even if the relationship to long-range effectiveness is not completely clear. As Etzioni noted long ago, a person can be involved in an organization in a variety of ways, ranging from the "alienated prisoner" or calculative employee to the participating member who is fully and morally involved.[13] Two serious questions to consider are whether U.S. economic organizations can claim moral involvement (as some Japanese firms apparently do) and whether such levels of involvement are even desirable in our culture.

The Ouchi analysis closes with a useful reminder that what ties the Japanese company together is a *company philosophy*, some dominant values which serve as criteria for decisions. What permits bottom-up consensual decision making to occur is the wide sharing of a common philosophy which guarantees a similarity of outlook with respect to the basic goals of the organization. Ouchi provides some case examples and displays a method by which a company can determine its own philosophy.

INTEGRATING THE SEVEN S's

Pascale and Athos make their argument at a different level of analysis, though they also stress the importance of managing *people* as key resources and the importance of superordinate goals, sense of spirit, or company philosophy. Ouchi is more the social scientist, presenting a

theoretically grounded sociological argument for a structural approach to human resource management. Pascale and Athos are less theoretical and more didactic. They are the teachers/consultants, distilling some of the wisdom from the analysis of the Japanese experience, and they try to transmit that wisdom through a more down-to-earth writing style. The managerial reader will learn more from this book, while the social scientist will learn more from the Ouchi book.

As already indicated, Ouchi has seven basic criteria for distinguishing A from J. Pascale and Athos (with due apologies for the gimmicky quality of the scheme) draw on a formulation developed by the McKinsey Co. which includes the following seven basic variables:

1. Superordinate goals,
2. Strategy,
3. Structure,
4. Systems,
5. Staff (the concern for having the right sort of people to do the work),
6. Skills (training and developing people to do what is needed), and
7. Style (the manner in which management handles subordinates, peers, and superiors).

Within this structure, Pascale and Athos identify what they term the "soft S's" and the "hard S's," and explain that the superordinate goals are critical in tying everything together. They argue that Japanese companies are effective because of their attention to such integration and their concern for those variables which have to do with the human factor, the soft S's. These are the factors which American managers allegedly pay too little attention to: staff, skills, and, most importantly, style. The hard S's (which complete the Seven S model) are: strategy, structure, and systems.

Through a detailed comparison of the Matsushita Corp. and ITT under Geneen, the authors bring out the essential contrast between Japanese attention to the soft S's and Geneen's more "American" preoccupation with very tight controls, autocratic decision making, and concern for the bottom line. Yet the

---

[13]Etzioni, A. *Complex Organizations*, New York: Holt, Rinehart, and Winston, 1961.

Geneen story also illustrates that a system which is as internally consistent as ITT's was, can be very effective. Its weakness lay in its inability to survive without the personal genius of a Geneen to run it.

The Japanese Style

Following this dramatic contrast, Pascale and Athos analyze the Japanese management style and explain how a culture which values "face" and is collective in its orientation can breed managerial behavior which makes the most of ambiguity, indirection, subtle cues, trust, interdependence, uncertainty, implicit messages, and management of process (instead of attempting to develop complete openness, explicitness, and directness in order to minimize ambiguity and uncertainty). "Explicit communication is a cultural assumption; it is not a linguistic imperative," they remind us.[14]

The lesson for American managers here is diametrically opposite in the two books. Ouchi's proposal for how to get to Theory Z is to be more open; Pascale and Athos imply (from their positive case examples of U.S. managers who use indirection, implicit messages, and nondecision as strategies) that we might do well to learn more of the arts of how to be less open. Though we in the United States often imply that to worry about "face" is a weakness and that it is better to "put all the cards on the table," in fact, there is ample evidence that Americans no less than Japanese respond better to helpful face-saving hints than to sledgehammers. "When feedback is really clear and bad, it's usually too late."[15] "The inherent preferences of organizations are clarity, certainty, and perfection. The inherent nature of human relationships involves ambiguity, uncertainty, and imperfection. How one honors, balances, and integrates the needs of both is the real trick of management."[16]

The analysis of face-to-face communication, drawn from an article by Pascale called "Zen and the Art of Management," is full of valuable insights on the subtleties of how and why indirection, tact, and concern for face are not merely niceties but necessities in human relations. It is crucial to recognize, of course, the distinction between *task* relevant information (about which one should be as open as possible in a problem-solving situation) and *interpersonal* evaluative information (about which it may be impossible to be completely open without running the risk of permanently damaging relationships).[17] Sensitivity training in which people attempted to tell each other what they thought of each other only worked in so-called "stranger groups," where people did not know each other before and knew that they would not have to work or live with each other after the program.[18]

Interdependence

Pascale and Athos supplement their analysis of face-to-face relations with an excellent analysis of groups and the dilemmas of interdependence. Noting that the American tradition is one of independence and that the Japanese tradition (based on their limited space and the technology of rice farming) is one of interdependence, they show how groups and meetings can work in this context by members being more restrained, self-effacing, and trusting. As Ouchi points out, getting credit in the *long run*, instead of worrying (as Americans often do) about being recognized immediately for any and all accomplishments, is made possible by the knowledge of lifetime employment, i.e., if people have to work with each other for a long time, true contribution will ultimately be recognized. Both books indicate that such group relationships combined with lack of specialization of careers give the Japanese company the ability to integrate better across key functional interfaces, because everyone has

[14]Pascale, R. T. and Athos, A. G. *The Art of Japanese Management: Applications for American Executives*, New York: Simon & Schuster, 1981, p. 102.

[15]Ibid., p. 106.

[16]Ibid., p. 105.

[17]Schein, E. H. *Process Consultation*, Reading, MA: Addison-Wesley, 1969.

[18]See Schein and Bennis (1965).

more empathy and understanding for other functions.

Superior-Subordinate Relationships

Long-term relationships and a culture in which everyone knows his or her place in the status hierarchy lead to a different concept of superior-subordinate relationships in Japan. The boss is automatically more of a mentor, teaching through subtle cues rather than blunt feedback, exercising great patience while the subordinate learns how to interpret cues and to develop his or her own skills, and reinforcing the basic company philosophy as a conceptual source that helps subordinates to decide what to do in any given situation. This point is critical, because it highlights one of the most important functions of superordinate goals or organizational philosophy. If everyone understands what the organization is trying to do and what its values are for how to do things, then every employee who truly understands the philosophy can figure out what his or her course of action should be in an ambiguous situation. No directives or explicit control systems are needed because the controls are internalized.

Individualism and Authority

Pascale and Athos take the issues of power and authority into the cultural realm in a more subtle fashion than does Ouchi, who merely labels J companies as having collective responsibility and A and Z companies as having individual responsibility. But we must ask what individual or collective responsibility means in each culture. Can we assume that the American model of individual rights, independence, equal opportunity under the law, and related values and norms is in any sense the opposite of or even on the same dimension with the Japanese notion of group responsibility? Is the issue simply that the group would be sacrificed for the individual in the United States, while the individual would be sacrificed for the group in Japan?

A more appropriate formulation is to assume that in every culture and in every individual there is a core conflict about how self-seeking or self-effacing to be for the sake of one's group or organization. At the extremes where either nationalism or anarchy is involved, the conflict is easier to reduce, but in a pluralistic society (such as in the United States) it is a genuine dilemma. (This is exemplified in U.S. sports organizations which try to create a team while maximizing the individual talents of the players.) In a recent analysis of individualism, Waterman has indicated that in political and social science writings there have always been two versions of individualism: one which focuses on selfishness and takes advantage of the group and one which focuses on self-actualization in the interest of maximizing for both the individual and the group the talents latent in the members.[19] Those writers who argue for a humanistic solution to organizational problems are espousing the second definition which assumes that integration is possible.

In my experience the effective organization is neither individualistic nor collective; rather, it attempts to create norms and procedures which extol stardom and teamwork equally. The manager's job (just like the good coach's) is to find a way to weld the two forces together. The Japanese solution to this dilemma appears to be aided immensely by the fact that basic traditions and cultural values strongly favor hierarchy and the subordination of the individual to those above him or her. However, this solution has potentially negative consequences, because it reduces the creative talent available to the organization. One might suspect, however, that the effective organization in Japan finds ways of dealing with this dilemma, and that the highly talented individual is not as pressured to conform as the less talented individual.[20]

The Japanese company in the Ouchi model could be expected to be more innovative on

[19]Waterman, A. S. Individualism and interdependence, *American Psychologist*, 1981, 762–773.
[20]McLendon, J. *Rethinking Japanese groupism: individual strategies in a corporate context*, unpublished paper, Harvard University, 1980.

those tasks which require group solutions, while the American company could be expected to be more innovative on those tasks that require a high level of individual expertise and creativity. Company effectiveness would then depend on the nature of the tasks which face it, its ability to diagnose accurately what those tasks are, and its flexibility in transforming itself, what I have termed an "adaptive coping cycle."[21] Whatever its human virtues and in spite of its ability to integrate better, a Theory Z organization might have more trouble both in seeing changes in its environment and in making the necessary transformations to adapt to those changes. Because of its strong commitment to a given philosophy and the pressure for everyone to conform, it is more likely to produce rigid paradigms for dealing with problems.

Implications for U.S. Management

Both books call for a reexamination of U.S. paradigms of how to organize and how to manage. While one can only applaud this challenge and use the models which the books present to gain perspective for such reexamination, one must be concerned about the glibness of the lessons, recommendations, and advice given the meager data base on which they are based. Neither book makes much of an effort to decipher what may be happening in our own culture and society which would explain our tendency toward Theory A (if, indeed, it can be shown that such a tendency exists). Why do we have difficulty with some of the solutions which the Japanese apparently find natural and easy, and, most importantly, what are the strengths in the U.S. system which should be preserved and built upon?

For example, Ouchi is quick to point out the negative consequences of the American tendency to try to *quantify* everything. Most of us would agree that for managing the human system of the organization, quantification may be more of a trap than a help, but one might

also argue that our *desire* to quantify reflects some of the best traditions of western science and rationalism. The trick is to learn what to quantify and to know why quantification is helpful. In the design of quality control circles or in the setting of sales targets, it may be crucial to state a goal in quantifiable form in order to measure progress toward the goal. On the other hand, attempting to quantify managerial traits as part of a performance appraisal system may distort communication and reduce the effectiveness of the whole system, because people would begin to feel like "mere numbers." The effective manager in any cultural system would be the one who knows what to quantify.

Many of the formal control systems which have become associated with the concept of bureaucracy (and which are seen by Ouchi, Pascale, and Athos as dysfunctional relative to the more indirect controls associated with the Japanese style) imply that all organizations face similar control problems. One might suspect, however, that controlling the design and building of a large aerospace system might require more formal control mechanisms than the control of an R&D organization in a high-technology industry. Ouchi's comparison of formal bureaucratic with informal clan mechanisms misses the point that Galbraith made so effectively: as any organization evolves, it develops organizational structures which are needed *at that stage* to deal with its information processing and control problems. A geographically dispersed organization dealing with local variants of a given market has different problems than a high-technology company which has standard products that work more or less in any market. Galbraith's analysis reveals at least six or seven variants of control systems from simple rules to complex matrix structures.[22]

But the most important issue to examine before we race into new organizational paradigms is whether or not we even have the right explanation for Japanese success. Neither Ouchi nor Pascale and Athos present much evidence to justify the premise that the Japanese

---

[21]Schein, E. H. *Organizational Psychology*, 3d. ed. Englewood Cliffs, NJ: Prentice-Hall, 1980.

[22]Galbraith, J. *Designing Complex Organizations*, Reading, MA: Addison-Wesley, 1973.

organizations cited are successful because of the management system described. In addition, no evidence is shown that such organizations are, indeed, the most successful ones in Japan. For example, it may well be that both Japanese productivity and management style are the reflection of some other common historical, economic, and/or sociocultural factor(s) in Japan.[23] Neither book tells us enough about the following important issues:

The role of postwar reconstruction;

The opportunity to modernize the industrial base;

The close collaboration between industry and government;

The strong sense of nationalism which produces high levels of motivation in all workers;

That lifetime employment is possible for roughly one third of the employees in some Japanese organizations because of the system of *temporary* employment for the rest of the employees and the existence of satellite companies which absorb some of the economic fluctuations;

That all employees retire fairly early by U.S. standards (in their mid- to late 50s);

That many of the best companies are family dominated and their strong company philosophies may be a reflection of founder values which might be hard to maintain as these companies age;

That the cultural traditions of duty, obedience, and discipline strongly favor a paternalistic clan form of organization.

Neither book refers to the growing literature which compares managerial style and beliefs in different countries and which contradicts directly some of the books' assertions about U.S. and Japanese management

approaches.[24] For example, although both books extol the virtues of Japanese indirection, subtlety, and ability to live with uncertainty and ambiguity, Hofstede found in a sample of 40 countries that U.S. managers reported the highest levels of tolerance of ambiguity, while Japanese managers reported some of the lowest levels. On many dimensions U.S. and Japanese managers are surprisingly similar in their orientation which suggests that the real answer to organizational effectiveness may be to find those combinations of strategy, structure, and style which are either "culture free" or adaptable within a wide variety of cultures.

KNOWING WHAT IS CULTURAL

If we are to have a theory of organizations or management which is culture free or adaptable within any given culture, we must first know what culture is. This is surprisingly difficult because we are all embedded in our own culture. What can we learn from Japanese managers if we cannot decipher how their behavior is embedded in their culture? Can we attempt to adapt managerial methods developed in other cultures without understanding how they would fit into our own?

The first and perhaps the most important point is that we probably *cannot really understand another culture* at the level of its basic world view. The only one we can really understand is our own. Even understanding our own culture at this level requires intensive analysis and thought. One cannot suddenly become aware of something and understand it if one has taken it completely for granted. The true value of looking at other cultures is, therefore, to gain perspective for studying one's own culture. By seeing how others think about and do things, we become more aware of how we think about and do things, and that awareness is the first step in analyzing our own cultural assumptions and values. We can use analyses

[23]Fruin, W. M. "The Japanese company controversy," *Journal of Japanese Studies*, 1978, 267–300; Lawrence, B. S. *Historical perspective: Seeing through halos in social research*, unpublished paper, M.I.T., 1981.

[24]Hofstede, G. *Culture's Consequences: International Differences in Work-Related Values*, Beverly Hills, CA: Sage Publications, 1980; England, G. W. *The Manager and His Values*, Cambridge, MA: Ballinger, 1975.

FIGURE 1   The Levels of Culture

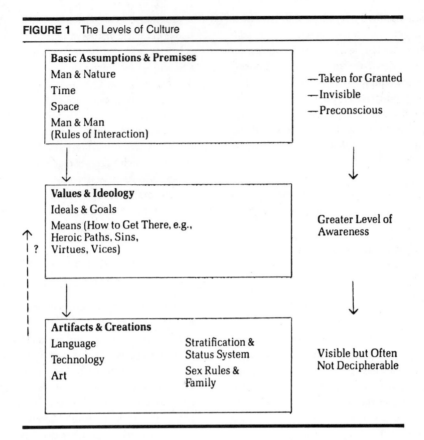

of Japanese management methods and their underlying cultural presumptions to learn about the hidden premises of U.S. managerial methods and our own cultural presumptions.

If we can grasp and become aware of our own premises and values, we can then examine analytically and empirically what the strengths and weaknesses of our own paradigm may be. This process of self-analysis is subtle and difficult. Not enough research has been done on managerial practices in our own culture; thus, the methods of analysis and tentative conclusions presented below should be treated as a rough first cut at analyzing our own cultural terrain.[25]

[25]Some excellent efforts in this direction can be found in: Newman, W. H. Cultural assumptions underlying U.S. management concepts, in *Management in an International Context*, J. L. Massie and Luytjes, eds. New York: Harper & Row, 1972; O'Toole, J. J. Corporate managerial cultures, in *Behavioral Problems in Organizations*, C. L. Cooper, ed. Englewood Cliffs, NJ: Prentice-Hall, 1979; England (1975).

Levels of Culture

In thinking about culture, one should distinguish surface manifestations from the essential underlying premises which tie together the elements of any given culture. As shown in Figure 1, there are at least three interconnected levels:

1. *Artifacts and creations* are the visible manifestations of a culture (which include its language, art, architecture, technology, and other material outputs) and its visible system of organizing interpersonal relationships, status levels, sex roles, age roles, etc. Though this level is highly visible, it is often not decipherable in the sense that the newcomer to the culture cannot figure out "what is really going on," what values or assumptions tie together the various visible manifestations.

2. *Values and ideology* are the rules, principles, norms, values, morals, and ethics which guide both the ends of a given society (group)

and the means by which to accomplish them. Values and ideological statements usually define *what* national goals, intergroup relationships, and interpersonal relationships are appropriate to strive for; they are taught to children and reinforced in adults. Generally the level of culture we first encounter is *how* to achieve the goals (i.e., the appropriate rules of conduct which govern relationships between nations, groups, and individuals within the society). This is also where differences are felt most strongly because of the penalties associated with behaving inappropriately. This level of culture, although partly conscious and partly unconscious, can be revealed if people reflect analytically about their own behavior.

3. *Basic assumptions and premises* are the underlying and typically unconscious assumptions about the nature of truth and reality, the nature of human nature, "man's" relationship to nature, "man's" relationship to "man," the nature of time, and the nature of space.[26] These assumptions create the cultural core or essence, provide the key to deciphering the values and artifacts, and create the patterning that characterizes cultural phenomena. It is also this level, however, which is hardest to examine, because it is taken for granted and, hence, outside of awareness.

If we analyze U.S. culture and managerial assumptions in terms of some of the categories around which basic assumptions are built, what perspective does this provide, and how does this help us to learn from Japanese managerial practices?

SOME KEY ASSUMPTIONS OF U.S. CULTURE

"Man's" Relationship to Nature: Proactive Optimism

It is a premise of most western societies (particularly of the United States) that nature can and should be conquered, that "man" is ultimately perfectible, and that anything is ultimately possible if we put enough effort into it. "Where there's a will there's a way," buttressed by "Every day we do difficult things; the impossible just takes a little longer," sets the tone for how we approach tasks. We feel constrained by the environment only if we do not have the knowledge or technology to control or alter it, and then we proactively seek whatever knowledge or technology is necessary to overcome the obstacle.

Such proactive optimism underlies the values surrounding equality of opportunity in that we take it for granted that anyone might be able to accomplish anything, if given the opportunity. In other words, man is ultimately perfectible, as the thousands of self-help books in airport book shops proclaim. The notion of accepting one's "fate" (limiting one's aspirations by one's social position or some other nontechnological constraint) is simply not part of the underlying ideology, however much empirical data might argue to the contrary.[27]

Given this core assumption, what kinds of organizational forms are possible in the United States? Can an industrial clan (a Theory Z organization) with its intrinsic conservative orientation survive in a cultural environment which emphasizes change, progress, innovation, and novelty? Or would this cultural orientation begin to erode the very core of such an organization—the stability which produces the comfort?

Similarly, can a culture which encourages people to find better ways to do things independently, to resist arbitrary authority if it interferes with pragmatic problem solving, and to value individual accomplishment produce an integrated system like the Pascale/Athos Seven S model? Perhaps the most notable characteristic of U.S. managerial practice is that we are never satisfied and are forever tinkering to find a better way. This will always undermine efforts toward integration. For many U.S. managers, integration equals stagnation;

[26]Kluckhohn, F. R. and Stodtbeck, F. L. *Variations in Value Orientations*, Evanston, IL: Row, Peterson, 1961.

[27]Evans, J. M. *America: The View from Europe*, Stanford, CA: The Portable Stanford, 1976.

I have observed repeatedly that as soon as a system becomes routine, managers begin to think about "reorganization." Perhaps we deeply mistrust stability and are culturally "pot stirrers."

"Man's" Relationship to "Man": Individualistic Egalitarianism

Every society or group must resolve the issue between individualism and collectivism. The underlying U.S. assumption appears to be that the individual always does and should do what is best for himself or herself, and is constrained only by respect for the law and the rights of others. The rule of law implies that there are no philosophical and moral principles which can ultimately determine when another's rights have been violated, and, therefore, the legislative and judicial process must decide this on a case-by-base basis through a confronting, problem-solving process judged by a jury of peers. Buried in these assumptions is a further assumption that the world can only be known through successive confrontations with natural phenomena and other people; that the nature of truth resides in empirical experience, not in some philosophical, moral, or religious system; and that the ultimate "philosophy," therefore, might as well be one of pragmatism. Ambition, maximizing one's opportunities, and fully utilizing one's capacities become the moral imperatives.

These assumptions, in turn, are related to the western rational scientific tradition which emphasizes experimentation; learning from experience; open debate of facts; and a commitment to truth, accuracy, measurement, and other aids to establish what is "real." The openness and pluralism which so many commentators on America emphasize are closely related to the assumption that truth can only be discovered through open confrontation and can come from anyone. The lowest level employee has as good a chance to solve a key problem as the president of the company, and one of the worst sins is *arbitrary* authority ("Do it because I am the boss, even if you think it is

wrong" or "If I'm the boss, that makes me right").

Yet teamwork is an important value in U.S. sports and organizational life. It is not clear to me how to reconcile the need for teamwork with the assumptions of individualism, and neither Ouchi nor Pascale and Athos offer much guidance on how consensual methods (such as those advocated) can be fitted to the notions of individual responsibility which U.S. managers take for granted. One of the greatest fears that U.S. managers have of groups is that responsibility and accountability will become diffused. We need to be able to identify who is accountable for what even when the realities of the task make shared responsibility more appropriate. According to Ouchi, and Pascale and Athos, the Japanese deliberately blur individual responsibility and adapt their decision making to such blurring. If that is so, their version of the consensus method may have little to teach us.

Participatory methods can work in the United States but they must be based on a different premise: the premise that teamwork and participation are *better* ways to *solve problems*, because knowledge, information, and skills are distributed among a number of people. We must, therefore, involve those people who have relevant information and skills. But the goal in terms of U.S. assumptions is better problem solving and more efficient performance, not teamwork, consensus, or involvement per se. Unless Japanese consensus methods are built on the same premise of effective problem solving, they are in many senses culturally irrelevant.

Similarly, the Japanese concern for the whole person may be based on premises and assumptions which simply do not fit our core assumptions of individualism and self-help. U.S. managers are scared of paternalism and excessive involvement with subordinates, because they see them as "invasions of privacy." If an individual is taken care of by an organization, he or she may lose the ability to fight for himself or herself. Our whole system is based on the assumptions that one must "be one's own best friend" and that the law is there to protect each and every one of us. Dependency, security orientation, and allowing others to solve our problems are viewed as signs of failure and lack of ambition, and are considered to be undeserving of sympathy. On the other hand, if it is necessary to take care of the whole family in an overseas transfer in order to enable the primary employee to function effectively, then we do it. Pragmatism, necessity, and efficiency override issues of what would be more humane, because of the underlying belief that we cannot philosophically agree on basic standards of what is "best" for everyone. What is best for people must be decided on the basis of negotiation and experience (ultimately expressed in laws, safety codes, and quality of work-life standards).

A culture based on such premises sounds harsh and cold, and the things we are told we should do to "humanize" organizations sound friendly and warm. But cultures are neither cold nor warm, because within any given culture both warmth and coldness have their own meaning. We may not like certain facets of our culture once we discover their underlying premises, and we may even set out to change our culture. However, we cannot produce such change simply by pointing to another culture and saying that some of the things they do *there* would be neat *here*. We have not yet begun to understand our own culture and the managerial paradigms which it has created. This paper is a beginning attempt to stimulate such self-understanding, and such understanding is a prerequisite for any "remedial" action.

If members of organizations are in a primitive battle (sometimes with themselves), then there is some value in identifying an impartial referee to clarify the rules of the battle and to keep the combatants from either destroying the arena in which the battle is taking place or destroying themselves. In this reading, Friedlander suggests that organizational development is the process for clarifying the rules of the battle and that the organizational consultant is the referee. He describes the techniques available and draws an important distinction between process consultation and other forms of consultation or intervention. For the organizational psychologist, how *things are done in an organization is often as important as* what *is done. Friedlander addresses the* how *part of organizational behavior.*

■ READING 34 ■

The Facilitation of Change in Organizations

Frank Friedlander

Professor of Organization Behavior, School of Management,
Case Western Reserve

Whereas much of psychology focuses on the individual as a coherent system (e.g., clinical and counseling psychology) or on the individual within a larger setting (e.g., social psychology, school psychology, industrial psychology), organizational development (OD) focuses on the organization itself. Organizational development draws on psychology as a basic discipline, particularly social psychology (group dynamics and small group theory), clinical and counseling psychology (diagnostic and counseling methods, personality theory), and industrial psychology (attitudes and motivation). It also draws on anthropology (the culture of the organization), sociology (organizations as social institutions), political science (the organization as politically governed by power and authority), organizational theory (organizational form and technology), and systems theory (the organization as an open system of interacting parts). Thus, OD treats the organization not only as a system composed of interacting parts but also as a system that interacts with its environment.

This article describes and critiques OD and explores its origins, its present condition and practice, and its future trends and issues.

THE EVOLUTION OF ORGANIZATIONAL DEVELOPMENT

Organizational development has emerged both from the demands of a changing environment and from knowledge provided by the evolution of the applied behavioral sciences (Friedlander & Brown, 1974). Rapid changes within organizational environments have demanded organizational processes and structures that are far more flexible and responsive

Source: *Professional Psychology, 11* (3), June 1980. Copyright 1980 by the American Psychological Association. Reprinted by permission of the publisher and author.

than traditional bureaucratic structures. Dramatic shifts have occurred in the social environment—in the lifestyles, needs, and values of the workforce; whereas increases in professionalization, educational level, and ease of mobility have decreased organizational loyalty and dependency. There have been efforts to challenge authority; there has been a gradual shift from organizational relevance to personal relevance; and there has been a trend toward preference for collaborative rather than hierarchical roles. Much of the alienation and disenchantment in our current society is attributed to the institution of work. Work is an arena in which considerable leverage can be exerted to improve the quality of life.

Concurrent with and in partial response to these changes in the environment, a number of developments have occurred in the behavioral science disciplines. These include the realization that a variety of social and psychological factors affect work performance (Mayo, 1933); the discovery that group decision making affects personal involvement, motivation, and commitment (Lewin, 1947); findings that participation increases ownership of change (Coch & French, 1948); and the use of groups as agents of change in organizations (Cartwright, 1951). In the late 1940s, T-groups and sensitivity training were used as an educational method that focused on group processes and group dynamics (Bradford, Gibb, & Benne, 1964). Recently, approaches to sociotechnical systems (Trist, Note 1) and work motivation (Herzberg, 1966) have incorporated the organizational tasks and social structures as important dimensions of organizational change.

During the past 10 years, OD has increasingly changed from a solely micro concern to a more integrated micro-macro perspective. Based on the assumption that the organization was merely a collection of individuals and small groups, OD was originally concerned with the individual and the small group. The next evolutionary step treated the organization as a closed system of people working within various social processes and structures on various technologies and influenced by the policies and culture of the organization. The organization is now conceived as an open system interacting with its external environment by receiving resources from it and exporting services or products to it. Each progression in this evolution has built on, rather than displaced, its antecedent phase. Thus, contemporary OD is concerned with the person, the organization's structures and technologies, and its environmental interchange.

Today OD is emerging as a field of interdisciplinary academic study and as a recognized profession. Increasing numbers of practitioners are employed by organizations. There is an accrediting agency for OD practitioners (the International Association for Applied Social Scientists) plus several professional organizations with OD divisions.

A description of some of the more important dimensions of OD follows from the discussion above: Organizational development is a profession and discipline (a) which is directed toward helping the organization explore and implement its needs for change through a long-range, systemwide effort, (b) in its personal-structural-technological-environmental processes, (c) in which a consultant (external or internal), utilizing behavioral science knowledge and skills, works with organizational members and helps them build into the organization a *capacity* for an increased awareness of present and desired conditions, for problem identification and problem solving, and for learning from experience. A further description of each of these elements forms the main body of this article.

EXPLORATION AND IMPLEMENTATION OF CHANGE

The need for OD frequently begins with a felt frustration by representative parts of the organization who are often upper level managers whose repeated efforts to resolve an issue have been unsuccessful. These issues may include an inability of the organization to plan adequately, to deal with organizational chaos, to meet performance standards, to implement a technical change, to coordinate component units, to work together collaboratively, and to manage internal conflicts. After the organization invites an OD consultant to visit and help the organization, the consultant contacts a variety of individuals and groups and works out a contract with the organization, specifying the expectations and roles of each party, the nature of the projected relationship, and the goals and general procedures of the project. Within the context of this entry phase, the consultant and client are building the open and trusting relationship so essential for the subsequent collaboration and confrontation between them. The consultant must listen to the underlying meaning and motives of the client and understand the systemic characteristics of the organization, not just the symptomatic problems presented.

During the entry and diagnosis phases, a gradual delineation of the "client" emerges. In the initial contact between client and consultant, the client is often the manager who requests the consultant to visit and help the organization. This format may change or expand during the early phases of the OD project to include key members of a manager's staff, a network of key managers, and so forth. If the OD effort is to involve unionized employees, it is important that acceptance for that part of the project be obtained from the union organization. Union cooperation is crucial to successful OD efforts involving unionized employees.

The second phase of an OD intervention is a diagnosis of the organization's issues as perceived and felt by its members. The consultant frequently works with a small group of organization members in designing and conducting interviews and questionnaires and in making observations. The data sources for the diagnosis include the client's straightforward presentation of its problems, the findings from the consultant's research, and the consultant's observations. The data from these form the basis of a joint diagnosis of the organization's issues and are fed back to a select group of key members, which often become the "client." Discussion of these issues follows, perhaps leading to a prioritization of those issues that are most salient and/or can be accomplished in a rela-

tively short period of time, in order to provide a successful experience. Action steps are planned around one or two key issues. During the feedback and discussions, the consultant may help group members become more aware of the group process by sharing observations, providing training in communication and in group functioning, or providing brief theory inputs. The diagnosis phase leads to and may include formulating plans for action. Planning includes the location or target within the organization for exploration and change, the people who will participate, time schedules, criteria for accomplishment, temporary protection this effort may require to get it launched, and the expected linkages between this action effort and others in the organization. Eventually, whatever action steps are taken by the organization are evaluated, and the new data are again fed back to the organization members.

Thus, an action research cycle is begun, which sequences through the stages of contracting, diagnosis, feedback, discussion, planning, action, and evaluation. With increasing experience of this cycle, gradually the OD function is "learned" and institutionalized within the organization.

THE PERSONAL–STRUCTURAL–TECHNOLOGICAL–ENVIRONMENTAL PROCESS

In this discussion an organization is seen as having four interacting phenomena. These are pictured in Figure 1. An organization is composed of *people* with different sets of values, styles, and skills; *technologies* with different characteristics; *processes and structures*, which reflect different kinds of relationships between people or between people and their work; and an *environment* with which the organization is continually interacting. First, OD focuses on exploration and change in the person: skills, knowledge, values, work style, management style, interpersonal style, personal growth and development. Second, OD is concerned with exploring and modifying the technology of the

FIGURE 1   Approaches to Organization Development (Friedlander & Brown, 1974)

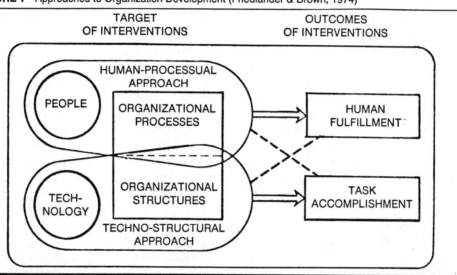

organization—the flow, pace, complexity, and arrangement of its technical procedures and resources—and with the application of its art, craft, and skill toward some productive end. Third, OD is concerned with relationships between people, their work roles, and the task—through such efforts as job design, procedures, and definitions. A fourth concern of OD is to analyze and deal with the various pressures from and opportunities in the organization's external environment—planning, environmental forecasting, and negotiating with relevant environmental components such as suppliers, consumers, regulators, and competitors.

Within this framework, processes and structures are the integrating mechanisms for applying human resources to technological methods for task accomplishment and for facilitating the utilization of technological methods for human fulfillment. The terms *process* and *structure* are used to differentiate two different but related aspects of the organization. Process describes the dynamic flow and developmental quality of relationships between people and their work as manifested in day-to-day interactions. Structure describes these relationships as ongoing sets of relatively durable roles and connections. Both process and structure are concerned with authority, communication,

decision making, and goal setting. Over time, structures can be changed by processes that are inconsistent with them, and processes are constrained or facilitated by organizational structures. Since process and structure are embedded in each other, it is almost impossible to create lasting change in one without modification of the other.

The target of exploration and change in OD is the total system of which its people, its processes and structures, its technologies, and its environments are interacting parts. Any attempt to change only one part of this system (e.g., individuals) must invariably affect other parts (e.g., structures and processes).

Unfortunately, many efforts labeled OD focus only on one of the following areas: efforts to revise technological processes (through technological, engineering, or operations design), efforts to change the organization's structure (through revisions in decision making, communications, or authority relationships), efforts to change individual human behavior (through training or assessment methods), or efforts to modify only the organization-environment interchange (through consumer or public relations efforts, diversification, merger, or lobbying). Common implicit assumptions are that changes in the task processes will automatically lead to changes in structure and individual behavior, or that changes in both task and process will conveniently follow structural change, or that behavioral changes in an individual will automatically lead to process and structural changes in the organization. Much individual counseling and training fails in organizational work because the organizational structures and processes are incongruent with the training or the organization will not change in ways that match the individual's new knowledge or growth. Sometimes the individual maintains changed behavior, the organization cannot tolerate the changes, and the individual quits (Sykes, 1962). Strong resistance is generally encountered when efforts are made to change only the organization's structure (Dalton, 1965) or only the technology of the organization (Trist & Bamforth, 1951). Finally, Lawrence and Lorsch (1969), using a model of congruence between the organization's internal structure and the degree and type of changes in its external environment, have shown the need to take the environment into account in OD work.

Many contemporary OD methods can be easily categorized into the person-process/structure-technology-environment framework. Most encompass at least two of these four areas. For example, interventions involving the individual person or group and organizational processes (human-process interventions) would include team building, intergroup problem solving, confrontation meetings, goal setting and planning, third-party facilitation, process consultation, data feedback, problem-solving meetings, and task force establishment. Note, however, that several of these might at a later time lead to structural or technological changes. Interventions in which the target is both the technology and the structure of the organization (technostructural interventions) include organization design, job enrichment, job enlargement, and sociotechnical analysis. An example of a process-environmental intervention would be open-systems planning, in which the organization increases its awareness and changes its processes to deal more effectively with changing aspects of the environment in which it exists.

In a recent review of the impact and effectiveness of OD, Friedlander and Brown (1974) noted that few OD efforts involve a simultaneous concern with the people, the technology, and the structure/process of the organization. Even fewer OD efforts include all three components as they relate to the organization's environment. Those that incorporate both the technology and the structure of the organization (technostructural) generally result in increased satisfaction, lower absenteeism, lower turnover, and quality increases. Sociotechnical systems approaches, in addition, consistently yielded increased performance and productivity. Most of those OD approaches that incorporate both the individual and the organizational processes have a positive effect on job attitudes, and sometimes on job behavior; but there is insufficient evidence that these approaches increase performance.

Further research reviews (Srivastva et al., 1976) have indicated that providing workers with autonomy, task variety, and feedback results in positive outcomes and that democratic and supportive supervisory styles improve job attitudes and performance. Factors of crucial importance in reaching these conditions appear to be worker engagement in the change process and support for change from the management and supervisory levels. An additional research review (Dunn & Swierczek, 1978) also found that the conditions for successful change efforts involved collaborative modes of intervention, participative change-agent orientation, and strategies emphasizing high levels of participation. In a recent comparative study (Pasmore & King, 1978), the differential impacts of sociotechnical system, job redesign, and survey feedback interventions were investigated on an array of attitudinal and performance measures in comparable units of an organization. The authors found that the attitudinal effects of the interventions were quite similar; however, only the sociotechnical system intervention resulted in major productivity improvements and cost savings.

Although little research has been done on interventions linking the organization to its environment, methods for the identification of such issues are being developed (Clark & Krone, 1972; Jayaram, 1978). Increasingly, a focus solely on internal organizational issues is likely to be inadequate. Pfeffer and Salencik (1978), for example, argue that most organizational dynamics are influenced by the organization's *external* environment rather than its internal happenings. Emery and Trist (1965) have noted that the external environment of most organizations is becoming increasingly unpredictable and unmanageable; that is, parts of that environment interact intensively with each other, regardless of the actions of any single individual or organization. Therefore, we cannot predict consistently the meaning of our own social actions or those of others. And as the complexity and pace of environmental change increase, the lead time for thoughtful individual or organizational responses is diminished. Parts of the environment that can be identified and influenced include elements of the social, political, cultural, technological, legal, marketing, supplier, and financial environment of the organization.

THE BEHAVIORAL SCIENCE CONSULTANT

The consultant (either external or internal), or change agent, in OD plays a far more collaborative role with the client system than in most other organizational improvement programs. The consultant helps the client become aware of present organizational conditions (what it is like to work and live in the organization) and of organizational forces that either create and maintain these conditions or impede change and improvement of these conditions. The consultant also helps the client expand its vision of alternative organizational futures. Comparison of these visions with the present condition creates energy for both planning and strategy on how to get from the present to the future.

At another level, the OD change agent's expertise is in *ways* to approach, diagnose, and solve organizational problems rather than to provide substantive answers to problems. The consultant is less likely to provide answers than to question the following: the methods used by a group or organization in discovering issues, the process that the group or organization employs in discovering and utilizing its resources, the relationships between people or units that hinder or facilitate problem solving and collaboration, the effect of autocratic or participatory methods on implementing technological change, the degree to which the design of a set of related jobs might cause functional or dysfunctional social interaction, and the effect of the social structure on the implementation of a new job design. In short, the consultant enables and facilitates the client's *process* of identifying issues, of considering and implementing solutions, and of evaluating the effectiveness of solutions after their implementation. The client and consultant must work collaboratively in an open and trusting relationship, each utilizing different but complementary areas of expertise. The responsibility for initiating and implementing organizational change rests ultimately with the client organization or manager, whereas the responsibility for consulting to facilitate this process rests with the consultant.

The meta-purpose of OD is to build into the organization an increased capacity for it to know *how* to set visions and revisions of its future, *how* to understand and accept its current condition, and *how* to move from the latter toward the former. The meta-purpose of OD includes building an organization's capacity to identify and find solutions to its own current and future problems. In one sense, this is a capacity of the organization to learn how to learn from its own experience; how to increase its sensitivity and awareness to its human resources, processes and structures, technology, and environment; and how to consider alternative courses of action and to evaluate the repercussion of these actions. Building such capacities into the organization implies changing the organization's cultural processes (i.e., making organization development a way of life) and teaching the organization the appropriate way to build relationships, diagnose issues, and take action. This capacity is learned, and it occurs only over an extended period of time.

Eventually the learning permeates the organization but is continually activated and reinforced through the internal OD consultant function. In the long run, durable OD implies building a learning organization.

TRENDS AND ISSUES

I have already discussed the trend from a sole reliance on micro approaches to a more integrated micro-macro perspective. This trend was in response to the limitations experienced by OD practitioners and researchers of a focus solely on the individual as a target of change. A gradual realization occurred that the work groups or teams to which individuals belong are an integral part of their work existence —that individuals cannot experience enduring change and development unless their work groups also experience change and development. Similarly, a realization occurred that durable change in the work group cannot occur without a corresponding change in the larger organizational unit to which it belongs. Recently, the OD field has recognized that lasting organizational change and development are also influenced by the organization's interactions with its environment and the mutual influences between change in the organization and change in the larger system of which it is a part. Such changes include those occurring in governmental laws and regulations, modifications in consumer and marketing patterns, shifts in the norms of the culture in which the organization operates, and innovations in the technological fields that affect it. The trend toward macro perspectives is a trend toward the holistic; it parallels, perhaps, the evolution from an early psychoanalytic orientation toward gestalt, community, and environmental psychologies; it reflects our evolutionary concern with the larger environment's impact on the system we study; and it also reflects our eventual intent to influence or even design that larger environment. It is hoped that this macro concern will inevitably return to enrich our understanding of the micro system initially studied.

Similarly, the trend in OD has sequenced from a psychological to a sociostructural to a sociotechnical perspective. Each perspective has built on the former base. Thus, a number of interventions and strategies focus not on individuals alone but on individuals embedded within specific structures and processes of the organization. And until recently, the organization as a human enterprise was differentiated (in the consultant's mind) from the organization as a technological enterprise. Now OD is incorporating technostructural perspectives and interventions that focus concurrently on the *way* work is done and the social structure in which it is done. The way a task is designed and achieved obviously has a high impact on the social structure in which it is done. Similarly, the social structure has clear repercussions on the way a task is performed and, thus, on the productivity of the unit.

A continuation of this trend would integrate all three perspectives, for example, *individuals* working in specific social *structures* in specific *task* methodologies. The effectiveness of OD will increase as its perspectives and strategies encompass a wider segment of the organizational realities with which it deals. In addition, this trend needs input not only from the cornerstone disciplines of psychology and social psychology but also from the disciplines of anthropology, sociology, political science, and systems theory.

As OD's role expands, the process must become longer-term, and working relationships with diverse agents of the organization must become more enduring. These diversities multiply the complexity of diagnosis and intervention as well as of theory and research.

OD has thrust itself into the political tension of both promoting the welfare of the organization and championing opportunities for individual self-actualization and control by employees of their own working lives. When these two outcomes are in conflict, tension and compromise are inevitable (Nord, 1978), either in the consultant or in the organization, or more likely in both. Organizational development's democratic and humanistic values proclaim that each individual has a right to a job that brings with it self-respect and a set of task requirements that are human and meaningful. On the other hand, OD professes (often implicitly) to its client systems an increased effectiveness of the organization as a whole—through some contribution to the organization's goals (e.g., better services, ideas, profits, etc.).

One of the ways this issue gets played out is in OD's role in influencing the organization to provide greater freedom for its workers—or greater constraint of its workers. Perhaps the proper role of OD is to help the organization confront the tension between freedom and constraint and redress the imbalance (Weisbord, 1977). For this redress, OD will draw on its theories of organization structure and, inevitably, on its value system, which underlies much of its theories.

A second way the personal growth versus organization welfare issue gets played out is by the choice of the political power system OD utilizes. Typically, OD entry, contracting, and recontracting are done through the formal power system: the upper part of the organizational hierarchy. Eventually, OD reports to upper management, just as does the remainder of the organization. If the OD practitioners do not nurture and receive continual support from this upper management level, they are likely to find themselves running furiously over a cliff into thin air. Yet many of the practitioner's activities may result in increased opportunity for worker respect, control, and actualization at lower levels. Philosophically, OD's power source is its humanistic and democratic values; politically, its power base is in the organizational hierarchy. Organizational development's appeal is in humanizing and democratizing the organizational goals and learning processes; politically, it is in maintaining and appealing to its current goals and power sources. The field has its statesmen and its politicians. The former espouse its values and its theory; the latter deal effectively with the pragmatics of the organizational system through innovative and constructive compromise. Organizational development must draw from and represent both. It must have the vision of the profession yet be grounded in the political realities of the organization it serves. And it is hoped that the head and feet are connected!

Another major OD issue (similar to issues faced in other practicing professions) is the separation of its theory, its research, and its practice. Each of these has emerged from a separate source; each conceives of the progress of OD as different and as dependent on the other's paying more attention to its own needs and issues. Practitioners of OD tend to find OD theory overly complex and academic and OD research too detailed, method bound, and irrelevant. Organizational development theorists claim OD practitioners are too interested in technique and method and OD researchers only study narrow slices of OD. Researchers perceive theorists as too expansive, complex, and nonempirical and practitioners as flying by the seat of their pants (overly intuitive). Practitioners would like researchers and theorists to understand and help their practice; theorists would like practitioners and researchers to appreciate and utilize their concepts and models; researchers would like practitioners to provide them with greater access to organizations in order to research OD on their own terms.

Because of poor interaction among these three areas of OD, advances in each are increasingly unrelated and irrelevant to the others. Each has become almost a separate "field" of OD. These are strange circumstances, given that each could be of great value to the others. They are, at root, completely interdependent. Indeed, OD as a field will advance to the extent that its research, its theory, and its practice are of mutual relevance and benefit to one another.

It has been argued that the strength of OD is its simultaneous footing in rationalism, pragmatism, and existentialism (Friedlander, 1976). The rationale brings to OD its emphasis on conceptualization, logic, and science; the pragmatic theme pushes OD to become useful, practical, applied; the existential theme within OD allows it to focus on experience, awareness, acceptance, choice, and commitment. The rational base is mostly, and perhaps stereotypically, centered in universities and publication systems where rational perspectives are encouraged, taught, and rewarded. The pragmatic base is endemic in most organizations (including universities!). It is concerned with organizational improvement and draws its knowledge through observation and analysis of organizational performance rather than relying on disciplinary knowledge. The existential theme in OD focuses primarily on the experience of the individual and on personal choices and commitments. The OD existentialist is less interested in diagnosis than in accepting the experiential flow of the individual; less interested in strategizing and planning for change than in offering clarification of individual choices; less interested in changing behavior than in allowing awareness and acceptance to occur; and less interested in evaluating change than in encouraging individuals' commitment to choice.

These three themes—to think, to do, and to be—quite obviously are all essential to the field of OD. Yet they conflict with each other in what each considers important. Organizational development must balance all of these if it is to grow and flourish.

Finally, OD, in its steadfast effort to facilitate *change*—a fresh, novel, different condition—has focused on the new, the beginning, the planning, and the implementation of tomorrow. It has thus avoided what is old, trustworthy, reliable, and comfortable—the organization and the people who live and work in it. Organizations, like individuals, resist giving up their ways of behaving and thinking, particularly if this calls for the death of a core part of their identity. The leap from the known to the unknown, from certainty to uncertainty, invites anxiety, defensiveness, and resistance. Tannenbaum (1976) sees change as a gradual shift from "holding on" to "letting go." Organizational development needs to focus on both of these parts of the change process—to understand and support both of these organizational needs. Organizational change implies not only a rebirth but also a mini-death. The organization's very identity lies in its individuals, technology, process, and structure as they currently exist. If the organization senses the consultant calling for radical surgery, it is likely to deny rather than accept its issues.

Historically, industrial and organizational psychology has depended very little on constructs such as personality. There has been little attention paid to traditional clinical approaches to adjustment. This has been true in spite of the fact that there is general agreement that work can do terrible things to the psychological well-being of workers. In this reading, Maccoby introduces the psychoanalytic tradition into the analysis of the effect of work on workers. His basic premise is that work can often produce abnormal patterns of human development, patterns that have their effects not only in work but also outside of work.

■ READING 35 ■

Work and Human Development

Michael Maccoby

At a time when many people limit the issue of employment to one of providing jobs for everyone, less attention is paid to *what* people are employed to do and *how* they do it. Work stimulates feelings and attitudes that can lead either in the direction of human development or of psychopathology. If a job contributes to an individual's development, it will strengthen our society; if it does not, both the individual and society will suffer.

How does work influence human development?

In his approach to psychoanalytic theory, Erich Fromm suggests that development, when described as a process strengthening capacities for reason and love, be contrasted to both psychopathology *and* normality.[1] This approach clarifies and provides a way for psychologists to evaluate work in terms of whether it stimulates human development, psychopathology (mental illness), or normality.

The very concept of mental illness has been challenged by writers who maintain that the concept is meaningless or misleading and that either so-called "normals" are sick (Laing, 1967) or that much so-called sickness is merely a label for bad behavior (Szasz, 1960). On the other side, the mental health profession tends to label all psychic suffering as treatable illness, to the point where psychotherapists sometimes seem out of touch with the experience of those who suffer.

For example, a psychiatric institute established a pilot project to treat factory workers. One of the project directors invited me to study intake interviews, as possibly useful for the study of social character. The interviews were of no use because the mental health workers explored neither the goals and strivings nor the actual conditions of the factory workers. Rather, they assumed psychopathology and illness from the presence of symptoms such as extreme anxiety or feelings of persecution by the foreman without even asking whether these symptoms were rational reactions to the working conditions or real persecutions by the foreman. The worker might be extremely neurotic, but the symptom might result from his efforts to adapt to, or struggle with, humanly

---

Source: *Professional Psychology, 11*(3), June 1980. Copyright 1980 by the American Psychological Association. Reprinted by permission of the publisher and author.

[1]On Fromm's approach to human development and psychopathology, see Fromm (1941, 1955, 1964).

destructive conditions. To find out which is the case, a psychologist must explore the relationships among work, character, modes of adaptations, and symptoms. If the work causes inner conflict, which may not even be conscious to the worker, this cannot be determined merely by describing symptoms, but must be explored; sometimes psychoanalytic methods are required.

Elsewhere I have cited (Maccoby, 1976) the case of a Mexican factory worker interviewed by Dr. Alejandro Cordova (Note 1). This automobile worker said that he was satisfied with his work, which consisted of mounting the suspension of the car (i.e., he tightened screws in the same way hundreds of times a day). Although he was a craftsman before becoming an auto worker, he even maintained that fractionating improved the work, and he offered no criticism of his job, at least consciously. Despite these opinions, there were other indications that he was far from happy with his work. He complained that he often felt nervous at the factory and tended to take it out on other workers. When he got home, he felt exhausted and was often in a bad humor, which was not the case when he worked in a small craft shop. He also reported that since he had begun working in the factory, he had suffered from constant headaches, frequent colds, and colitis. In contrast to his statement that he was satisfied with his work, these symptoms suggested a deep conflict between what he (consciously) thought—that the work was satisfying—and what he knew in his body and spirit—that the work was infuriating. This conflict appeared to be expressed in a repetitive dream, "I dream that at my work there is a man who is a stranger and we are arguing. I don't know who he is, and I don't remember what I am arguing with him about." This dream helped clarify why this worker did not connect his anger and symptoms to his experience at work. I suggest that it is a precise symbolization of alienation. Unconsciously, this worker was two people. One was the conscious self who was satisfied at work. The other was the unconscious "stranger" who had a different point of view. These two aspects of the self were constantly arguing with each other. What were they arguing about? The dreamer could not remember. What the evidence of the interview points to is that the unconscious stranger was telling the dreamer that he had to leave the workplace if he were to become whole and remain sane. That this knowledge remained repressed is understandable especially when we consider that the worker needed this job to support his family and could imagine no way of changing the production technology or organization to improve the quality of his work.

Is this automobile worker mentally ill? I would contend that he is not. He is extremely disturbed by the conditions of work, but there is no evidence of the deep-rooted psychopathology that should be part of the definition of mental or emotional illness. He is like the American automobile workers studied by Kornhauser (1965), who found that routine and repetitive jobs led to feelings of hostility and anxiety. These workers suffered from a reactive condition that could not be treated by a doctor except in terms of symptomatic relief through tranquilizers that merely exchanged one symptom for another, that is, insensitivity in the place of anxiety. In these cases, a "cure" would have required social change, not treatment.

But this does not mean that there is no such thing as psychopathology or mental-emotional illness. Workers themselves understand better the distinction between mental illness versus suffering due to dehumanizing conditions than do many health professionals. In a report from Bertram S. Brown (Note 2), then director of the National Institute of Mental Health, we discover that the two groups view reality differently. Brown asks why so few workers sought treatment, even when it was offered free of charge. The reason why, he maintains, is that workers and union officials are uneducated about the benefits of psychotherapy, but the evidence of a study he cites suggests that the mental health professionals are the ones who most need education. Samples of workers and providers of care were both asked whether they thought that mental health care was required in a number of situations. In some cases, a large majority of both groups agreed that an individual needed psychotherapy. Examples were the man who drinks too much or the one who often fights on the job. But in some cases, the two groups disagreed. For example, a large majority of the psychotherapists thought that a husband and wife who have "marital problems and seldom see each other because they both work and they work on different shifts" needed psychotherapy, whereas the workers thought they did not. I assume that the more intelligent psychotherapists would argue that if the couple did not have problems, they would arrange their lives in order to be together. But the workers know this may not be possible, and most workers are not fools who need a professional to tell them the obvious.

The biases of the mental health providers are expressed in their responses to the following situation: A woman works at a job every day and goes home to cook and clean at night and feels that no one appreciates what she does. How is one to respond to such a situation?

A majority of the psychotherapists thought she needed treatment. We are not told why. Is it so she will adapt to her role and not complain? Or should she get angry and leave the situation in which she is unappreciated? The fact that an overwhelming percentage of workers thought that she did not require treatment is interpreted by Brown as a lack of sympathy. But is it? More likely, the workers considered that the family of this woman needed a talking-to and that it was not a problem that could be solved by treating the woman as a patient.

When I have made this point with psychotherapists, they have defended themselves by maintaining that they would help the woman to confront her family and to demand more respect. However, unless the psychotherapist understood the husband, such a process might lead to a conflict that the woman would not choose to initiate. Even if the therapist were able to start a dialogue in the family, it would not be a case of curing a patient but of encouraging her and others to consider alternatives.

Workers are sensitive about being labeled mentally ill. Those surveyed did not reject the concept of mental illness. Rather, they distinguished clearly between probable symptoms of illness needing treatment (alcoholism, aggressiveness) and problems caused by situational factors. They are aware that to earn a living they may have to accept stress. The question is, at what point does this stress become so great that it causes mental illness?

SYMPTOM VERSUS CAUSE

Although workers may be able to distinguish mental illness from symptoms of stress, the mental health professional will be confused as long as the *cause* of the symptom is not questioned. To avoid confusion, the psychoanalytically oriented investigator should withhold diagnosis until the roots of symptoms in an individual's character structure have been explored.[2] This does not require a lengthy psychoanalysis or study of the individual's early childhood experiences. The method may be an interview or open-ended questionnaire (Fromm & Maccoby, 1970). The essential question for the psychoanalyst should be whether any symptom—destructive behavior, fear, inability to act, and so forth—is a rational reaction to a threatening situation or whether it would persist even if the situation from an objective point of view were benign. If the symptom appears irrational, the psychoanalyst should expect to discover unconscious strivings, motives, and passions that, when brought to light, account for the individual's thoughts, feelings, and behavior. However, psychoanalytic theory has paid little attention to work, and psychoanalysts have little experience with factory or clerical workers. To make use of psychoanalysis in better understanding the relation between work and mental illness, we must examine critically Freud's theory of psychopathology.

---

[2]Erich Fromm has clearly presented a model of forces leading to psychopathology and health in *The Heart of Man* (1964). In what follows, I have essentially followed this model but changed some of the names Fromm uses to describe pathological forces.

When the psychoanalyst speaks of psychopathology, he or she refers not merely to symptoms but also to unconscious and irrational strivings, wishes, or fears such as hatred, cannibalistic impulses, lust to kill, incestuous desires, or the wish to return to the womb. Freud's genius was to develop a technique to bring these hidden emotions to consciousness through talking and taking seriously communications such as dreams, slips of the tongue, and inadvertent expressions. However, it is one thing to confront the unconscious in the consulting room and another to understand theoretically the causes of irrational passions. Freud constantly revised his theory of psychopathology, although he never wavered in his view that infantile sexuality and destructiveness were to be found in all serious neuroses.

An unresolved question is whether irrational strivings are part of human nature or whether they are caused by negative circumstances. Freud's view is complex. On the one hand, he recognized that severe frustration or oppression of children would increase the incidence of neurosis, particularly in those individuals with a constitutional (genetic) vulnerability. On the other hand, Freud (1927/1975) believed that certain "instinctual wishes" are born afresh with every child and "among these instinctual wishes are those of incest, cannibalism, and lust for killing" (p. 10).

From Freud's point of view, neurosis may be caused either by too much frustration in childhood of instinctual wishes for pleasure or by too little socialization of inborn destructiveness, because of the child's failure to resolve the Oedipal struggle (rivalry with the father) and develop a superego (a punishing conscience that turns destructiveness inward).

One can accept Freud's basic clinical discoveries about unconscious irrational strivings and the strategy of psychoanalysis (including the role of resistance and transference), which are confirmed time and again by the practicing psychoanalyst, and at the same time reject his unproven theories about the nature of man. As Fromm (1973) argues, Freud himself, while holding to his view that destructiveness was

instinctual, constantly revised his metapsychology and failed to resolve important contradictions between his earlier libidinal theory and later more vitalistic theory.

Without ignoring the importance of genetic factors in vulnerability to experiences, evidence from anthropology and developmental psychology supports Fromm's view that destructive urges are not innate but are the result of unfavorable early childhood experiences, such as oppression or smothering, that provoke hatred or set the stage for sadomasochistic attitudes. Clinical evidence further indicates that incestuous strivings often are provoked by incestuous parents, that narcissism results from lack of love and ambitious parents, and so on.

In revising Freud's theory of psychopathology (emotional illness), Fromm (1964, 1973) proposes that emotional illness implies some combination of regressive incestuous strivings, narcissism, and hatred of life that is unconscious and in conflict with healthier attitudes. Alcoholism, destructive behavior, paranoia, and other symptoms of mental illness are fed by these emotional attitudes that are deeply embedded in character. Character syndrome of dynamic traits or emotional attitudes is a key concept in understanding the meaning of a symptom and its resistance to change.

Fromm integrates psychoanalytic findings with the humanistic, philosophical, and religious traditions that have defined human development as the process of overcoming childishness, egocentrism, and resentment. Fromm conceives of normality in relationship to both illness and human development in terms of three character vectors: independence versus passive dependency (symbiosis); love and concern for others versus egocentrism and narcissism; and reverence for life, joyful spontaneity (biophilia) versus deadening control, hatred of life (necrophilia). The positive role of human development represents conscious, spontaneous, and humanly responsible activity, whereas the negative pole of psychopathology represents unconscious, regressive infantile strivings—a primitive illusion of total security that resists all reason.

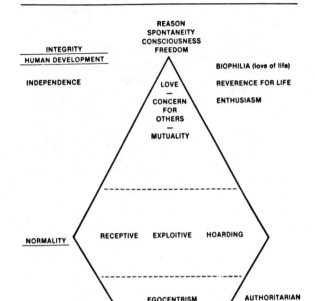

FIGURE 1 Human Development versus Psychopathology (adapted from Erich Fromm, 1964)

These irrational strivings are expressed in complex beliefs and actions described by both Fromm and Harry Stack Sullivan (1956), who show how the deeply regressive and distrustful individual manipulates the environment to prove irrational beliefs (e.g., the paranoid creates enemies). Without skillful treatment, such a person remains locked within a system that blocks the chance for healthy development (see lower part of diagram, Figure 1). Theories of psychopathology also influence treatment techniques. Some psychotherapists believe that by exclusively exploring infantile experiences they will uncover and correct the causes of neurosis. Although this is a misunderstanding of Freud's technique, his instinctual theory lends itself to this approach in contrast to Fromm's, which focuses attention on the individual's *present practice of life as well as origins in childhood.* A process of cure depends not only on making the irrational conscious, but on improving work, on the family, and in general, on a practice of life that supports the internal (and external) struggle for health.[3]

On the negative side, but less extremely regressive, are the orientations of dependency, egocentrism, and authoritarianism that approach the range of "normal character." As Fromm points out (1964), there is a wider variety of character types within the normal range than at either the regressive or progressive extremes.

---

[3]This is not to contradict evidence that some mental illness may be totally or partially caused by a physiological imbalance and can be cured by medication (e.g., manic-depressive illness and lithium treatment).

NORMALITY AND SOCIAL CHARACTER

Normality, as it is defined in any particular society, describes the "social character" types shared by a class or group that are adaptive to particular social and environmental conditions. For example, in rural villages throughout the world, the "normal" people tend to be cautious, self-protective, methodical, thrifty, and self-reliant, with the character orientation Fromm has called "productive-hoarding" (Fromm & Maccoby, 1970). Such individuals express traditional values of self-reliance, respect, and personal integrity. These character traits and values are adaptive to the life of a small farmer who must depend on himself and his family against the uncertainties of the weather, natural disasters, changing markets, and tricky middlemen. Only those with such inner-directed emotional attitudes survive and prosper; these same attitudes are taught by parents to children from early infancy and become the message of religion and folk culture.

Within the normal range there are, of course, extensive variations of temperament and talents. Subtypes can also be distinguished in terms of character. For example, some craftsmen are more receptive and life affirming, whereas others tend to be more dutiful and unbending. These differences may stem from the constitutional endowment of the individual and/or from variations in family subculture.

The quality of the social character and of normality in terms of its developmental level depends, in large measure, on how it fits with the social conditions, particularly modes of work that determine survival and security.

For Freud (1927), work is inevitably oppressive to the masses because it blocks the expression of instinctual drives. Only the elite are able to sublimate their instinctual drives in their work and thus gain pleasure from it. For Fromm (1955), in contrast, work is a way of relating to the world. He writes,

> But work is not only an inescapable necessity for man. Work is also his liberator from nature, his creator as a social and independent being. *In the process of work, that is, the molding and changing of value outside of himself, man molds, and changes himself* . . . he develops his powers of cooperation, of reason, his sense of beauty. (pp. 177–178)

Modes of work can either stimulate life-affirming attitudes or depress them through frustration and oppression. Work is thus necessary for human development, but this depends not only on the nature of work but its relation to social character. According to Fromm's theory, if a social character adaptive to one environment is thrust into another, a situation of stress can stimulate negative traits. The farmer-craftsman forced to work in a factory experiences frustration of his characteristic self-reliance and sense of respect. Behaviorally he adapts, but like the Mexican auto worker described above, he unconsciously rebels and suffers the symptoms of his conflict. Or he may consciously rebel if he can join a union. In other cases, the frustrating social conditions stimulate the negative side of the social character, for example, obstinacy in place of self-reliance. At a certain point, the individual can no longer adapt and may be driven toward psychopathology.

The often-used concept of "stress" becomes mechanical, unless it is understood in terms of experience: frustration of creative strivings, heartbreak, hardening, despair. Some individuals near the borderline between normality and pathology may be pushed over the edge by "stressful" work that blocks their creative impulses (Caplan, Note 3). They may respond by fear and anger and then regressive escape, narcissistic isolation, or deep hatred of life. To measure the limits of stress, one must understand individual and social character. Cordova (Note 1) describes how stress results when engineers install new safety measures in coal mines without considering the miners' attitudes. From their dreams, Cordova finds that miners repress their feelings of fear and powerlessness, but they gain confidence from their keen sensing of changes underground that might threaten safety. When the engineers substituted metal beams for wood underground, the miners became anxious. They had learned to detect slight changes in the creaking of wood, but the "safer" metal provided no clues and thus diminished the feeling of having some control over the environment.

A normal social character is vulnerable to stress that might affect other social characters differently. Erik Erikson (1963) describes how the Sioux Indians became depressed and hostile when they were deprived of the right to be hunters and warriors. The Sioux could not develop the social character of farmers. Their traditional daring and discipline learned in childhood became meaningless without the chance to hunt or fight; the result was apathy and impotent anger.

In studying the relationship between character and work, like Fromm (1947), I have asked not only how individuals adapt to their work (and at what cost) but how they potentially might work to develop the most creative or productive aspects of their character, given that character sets boundaries and directions for change (Maccoby, 1976). My colleagues and I have studied different types of workers and managers not only in factories but also in business and government offices.

Based on interviews with individuals about their values and goals, emotional attitudes and conflicts are explored and social character types are determined inductively. This method is in contrast to typing workers only in terms of their attitudes toward a particular job, as though that expressed a character orientation to work.

For example, Jacob and Jacob (1976) distinguish two personality types among auto workers: those who work for "self-expression" and are satisfied by greater challenge, autonomy, and responsibility versus those who work for pay and promotion and are more concerned with material rewards and physical conditions of work. In light of our findings in an auto parts factory (Duckles, 1977; Maccoby, Note 4), this dichotomy is misleading. It describes two modes of adaptation to factory work, but not necessarily different character types. Many workers who do not find self-expression in factory work do so outside the plant in arts and crafts, gardening, housework, or farming. In some cases, their most meaningful work is not what they are paid to do. These workers may not want more challenge or responsibility at the paid job, but they do respond favorably to respect and the chance to have a say in how work is organized. Projects to improve work can make the factory less oppressive and encourage increased concern for others. However, human development would be stimulated more in an environment where individuals could be paid to develop their creative interests.

HUMAN DEVELOPMENT

Just as we can evaluate work organizations according to whether they push people toward psychopathology, so can we assess whether they stimulate human development. Human development or character development is a process leading to an integrity of character that is at the opposite pole of psychopathology. Psychopathology implies a regressive attempt to rediscover the infant's sense of total protectiveness by controlling the world with a sense of omnipotence, resulting in becoming more unconscious, helpless, and despairing. Integrity of character describes the process of individuation and mutuality that unfolds the human potential for reason, independence, courage, love, spontaneity, and confidence.

All the great religions and humanistic traditions agree that the process of human development is one of liberation from greed and egocentrism, with the goal being development of one's capacity for love and knowledge. The most developed people are typically those who have struggled with impulses that enslave them. This development can itself heighten the conflict between individual and society as a person becomes more aware of social pressures that limit human development.

Ultimately, human development depends on individual decision making, discipline, and everyday practice. It requires caring for others and commitment to goals and projects beyond oneself. The organization of work cannot determine this development, but it can either stimulate or limit it. Furthermore, in our society both education and family are responsive to what pays off at work. Therefore, the workplace plays a particularly important role in determining human development.

What are the conditions that will stimulate human development in the workplace? To some extent, that depends on both the character and life goals of workers. Different people may respond differently to the same conditions because of character. Herrick's (Note 5) research shows that the most humanly developed workers—those who have a sense of independence, mutuality, and love of life—suffer and protest under dehumanizing conditions; whereas more hardened, self-protective, and less hopeful workers are more satisfied with these conditions. These latter conditions parallel the reactions of managers to their work (Maccoby, 1976). Successful managers are competitive and detached. Those who experience the most painful conflict are those who care most about people.

Almost everyone can be stimulated to examine work in terms of its effects on him or her, especially if social circumstances encourage hope of improving conditions. At the Harman International factories in Bolivar, Tennessee, and Coatbridge, Scotland, management and union (United Auto Workers, and General and Municipal Workers Union) have sponsored projects to improve work, based on interrelated principles of human development (Harvard Project, Note 6). These principles can be summarized as security (of employment, health, and safety), equity (fairness of rewards in relation to contribution), participation, and individuation. Security and equity are basic protection against exploitation, and these principles encourage the individual to contribute ideas for improving work. The principles of participation and individuation are the basis of democratic practices, respect for different viewpoints, and creative needs.

The Harvard Project on Technology, Work, and Character was invited by management and union to help establish these programs (Maccoby, Note 4). Part of this role has been to initiate discussion about the relationship between work and human development. At Bolivar we began by interviewing individuals about their work and stimulating them to analyze and evaluate it in terms of the principles. A next step was to open up the study and raise it to the level of public discussion. Together management and union committees began to analyze work and were encouraged to experiment with alternatives that were evaluated according to the principles (Duckles, Duckles, & Maccoby, 1977).[4] As individuals discovered that they could influence change, many were stimulated to think of new possibilities and to take more account of other people with different goals. A result of this exercise in making work more satisfying was increased cooperation and productivity.

The Harvard Project is now developing a similar program in the federal government, including managers and office and production workers. A central element is the exploration of social character and its implications in creating an effective and humanly developing organization.

All persons have the potential for human development, but the path will be different for each person, according to his or her individual experiences. Since human development depends so much on social relationships, each society must be organized to stimulate this development. Human needs for physical survival and sanity must be met in such a way as to protect the individual's sense of security and dignity. Otherwise, fear, distrust, and resentment inevitably increase psychopathology. Ideally, society will also be organized to provide a meaningful and productive role for individuals, depending on age and ability, and will encourage the fullest possible development of individual talents.

Although this ideal and these principles are totally consistent with the official values of our society, they have not generally been applied to work organization in America. A hundred years ago, it might have been argued that a

---

[4]This involves the kind of active learning, essential to developing independent and critical thought, described by Piaget (1973).

large percentage of the workforce was self-employed and no one was stuck in an organization. This is no longer the case. Today, many Americans have given up hope that work will be fulfilling. They seek their main satisfactions at home and in leisure activities. However, to be creative at leisure while feeling dehumanized at work requires superhuman detachment. For most Americans, work is central to self-definition and personality development, both directly and indirectly. Although people will accept stressful employment out of necessity, work that does not stimulate human development will weaken a democratic society.

Work and Task Design

In an earlier section, we considered the broad issue of job design. In those readings, we considered big concepts such as job enrichment, and we looked at how one might go about consciously changing the entire psychosocial profile of a job. There is another perspective that one might take in considering the effects of job changes on work behavior. One might consider the effect of changing individual tasks. There is little doubt that there is a connection between changing jobs and changing tasks, but there is also a unique perspective to be gained from examining readings about task change.

Individual work tasks are assumed to be embedded in a larger system of tasks called a job. One way of thinking of this system is as a man-machine system. In this broader conception, various equipment and various operators are linked in a communication-action network. Changing the nature of that communication network can often have dramatic effects on the efficiency of the system. In this reading, Voevodsky presents an example of how a modification in an information exchange process saved a cab company a great deal of time and money.

■ READING 36 ■

Evaluation of a Deceleration Warning Light for Reducing Rear-End Automobile Collisions

John Voevodsky
Portola Valley, California

The possibility of designing automotive equipment to prevent automobile collisions has been greatly overshadowed by attempts to design automotive equipment to protect occupants during a crash (Bowen, 1972). Prevention of a significant number of rear-end collisions may be possible by the use of a light system warning other drivers that the car ahead is decelerating. The theoretical basis for the design of such a deceleration warning light system was published earlier (Voevodsky, 1967). The present study is an evaluation of the collision prevention effectiveness of a deceleration warning light under normal driving conditions.

METHOD

The deceleration warning light system designed for this study was an amber warning

light, center mounted on the rear of a vehicle at the same height as existing stop lights, which communicated a component of deceleration initiated by the driver of that vehicle to the driver of a following vehicle. A device for measuring deceleration, essentially an inertial pendulum, hence independent of any mechanical adjustments of the car such as brake pedal position, was rigidly attached to the vehicle. The warning light, activated by use of the brake pedal, was pulsed in a controlled fashion at a rate that varied exponentially with the component of deceleration. A 50 percent increase in frequency of the light pulses from 1.0 pulse per second to 7.6 pulses per second for each .1 gravity force increase in deceleration from 0 to .5 gravity provides the exponential relationship.

Subjects

A commercial taxicab company, to be referred to as the Cab Company, participated in

Source: *Journal of Applied Psychology*, 59(3), 1974, pp. 270–273. Copyright 1974 by the American Psychological Association. Reprinted by permission of the publisher and author.

the experiment at no cost to itself other than time out of service for equipping the cabs and operating them so equipped.[1] The Cab Company was asked to make their San Francisco fleet of 503 cabs available for two reasons: (a) The San Francisco fleet travels almost two million miles per month, thereby enabling a testing of the equipment over significant mileage in a relatively short time period. (b) The Cab Company's complete records of cab accidents were available for the five years prior to 1972, thus providing a statistical base from which to evaluate the test data.

Procedure

On March 1, 1972, 343 taxis began operation with deceleration warning lights. The remaining 160 taxis were to be traded in on new vehicles and therefore were not equipped, but served as a concurrent control group. The new vehicles were equipped when delivered to the Cab Company. Later, between June 1 and August 28, 1972, the deceleration warning lights were removed from previously equipped cabs in order to equalize the mileage driven by the equipped and nonequipped cabs. This approximately equal monthly mileage was continued through the end of the experiment, February 1, 1973. The changes in the proportions of cabs equipped or unequipped were corrected by expressing all collision rates as collisions per million miles driven.

The dispatcher assigned taxi drivers to equipped or unequipped taxis at his discretion, disregarding any preferences expressed by the drivers.

No massive education program on the operation and function of the deceleration warning light system was undertaken prior to the experiment or during the experiment. Limited news coverage at the start of the test provided the only source of public information.

RESULTS

At the end of the reporting period, January 31, 1973, the vehicles equipped with the deceleration warning lights had traveled a total of 12.3 million miles with a rear-end collision rate of 3.51 collisions per million miles (Figure 1).[2] This is a 60.6 percent reduction in the rear-end collision rate from the concurrent control group, which had 8.91 collisions per million miles over a total of 7.2 million miles. The rate for the concurrent control group is almost identical to the 1971 rate of 8.89 over 21.5 million miles, and is near the mean rate of 7.9 for the five years prior to January 1, 1972, computed over 125 million miles from the Cab Company records.

The 10 months for which comparative data are available can be taken as 10 independent experiments. The month of April 1972 was excluded from the analysis as there were no control data for this month. When the rear-end collisions are treated as collisions per million miles within each month, a paired t test of the differences for equipped and nonequipped cabs is significant ($t = 4.06$, $df = 8$, $p = .006$).[3]

The rate of personal injury to taxicab drivers struck in the rear by other vehicles for the equipped vehicles was .65 per million miles, or a 61.1 percent reduction from the 1.67 rate of the concurrent control group (see Table 1). The costs of repairs to the cab vehicles struck in the rear by other vehicles declined from $1,041 per million miles for the concurrent control group to $398 per million miles for the deceleration warning light vehicles. This is a reduction of 61.8 percent. Damage figures for the vehicles that collided with taxis are not known. Because the Cab Company is not at

[1] Acknowledgment is made of the cooperation of the Yellow Cab Company of San Francisco for their participation and for making their accident records available.

[2] The months appear at different points above the abscissa for equipped and nonequipped cabs because in the earlier months the total mileage driven by the equipped cabs was greater than that of the nonequipped cabs.

[3] The division of accident rates into units of months is somewhat arbitrary, but to produce a statistical test at all it was necessary to use the data available from the Cab Company. Mileage data are reported monthly, rather than by miles to accident, which would permit the use of Poisson statistics.

FIGURE 1 Rear-End Collisions of Cabs Equipped and Not Equipped with Deceleration Warning Light

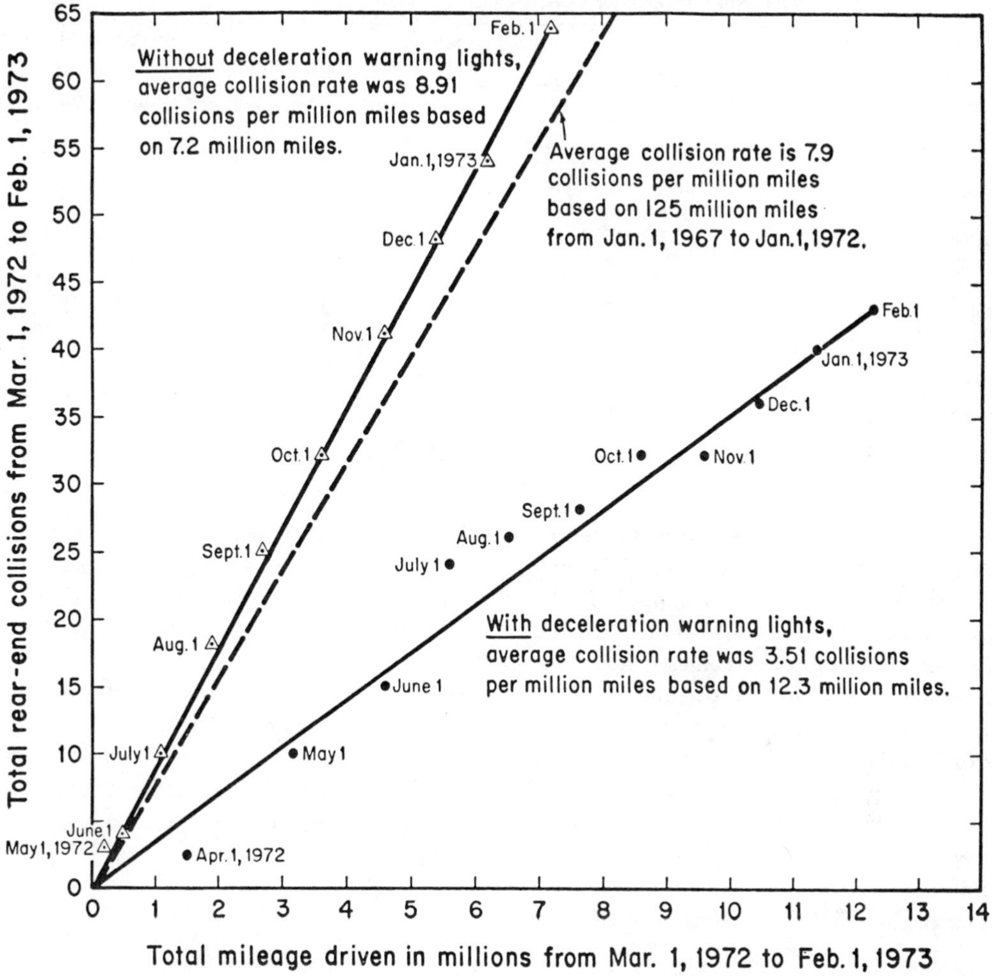

Without deceleration warning lights, average collision rate was 8.91 collisions per million miles based on 7.2 million miles.
Average collision rate is 7.9 collisions per million miles based on 125 million miles from Jan. 1, 1967 to Jan. 1, 1972.
With deceleration warning lights, average collision rate was 3.51 collisions per million miles based on 12.3 million miles.
Feb. 1
Jan. 1, 1973
Dec. 1
Nov. 1
Oct. 1
Sept. 1
Aug. 1
July 1
June 1
May 1, 1972
May 1
Apr. 1, 1972
Total rear-end collisions from Mar. 1, 1972 to Feb. 1, 1973
Total mileage driven in millions from Mar. 1, 1972 to Feb. 1, 1973

fault these amounts are not included in their records.

DISCUSSION

A common criticism of social experiments that involve innovative arrangements is that the operators are sensitive to the new arrangements and behave differently because of the so-called Hawthorne effect (Roethlisberger & Dickson, 1939). This criticism does not apply because the collisions are due to the drivers of the cars that follow the taxis and not to the taxi drivers. That the taxi driver has not become more cautious because of driving a taxi equipped with a safety device is attested by the lack of change in the collisions in which the taxicab driver ran into the rear-end of a car in front of him. The drivers of equipped taxis produced 7.1 such collisions per million miles, and those not equipped produced 8.1 such collisions per million miles. When this difference is tested statistically by the same procedure previously described, the difference is not significant ($t = .65$, $df = 8$, $p = .52$).

The results of this 11-month, 19.5-million mile test of a deceleration warning light system in natural driving conditions indicate that a significant reduction in rear-end collisions

TABLE 1   Rear-End Collisions, Drivers Injured, and Cab Damage Is a Function of Miles Driven, for Cabs Equipped and Not Equipped with Deceleration Warning Lights

Month/Year	Mileage		Rear-End Collisions		Drivers Injured		Cab Damage (Dollars)	
	With	Without	With	Without	With	Without	With	Without
March 1972	1,515,793	197,903	2	3	0	1	200	1,275
April 1972	1,661,455	0	8	0	2	0	252	0
May 1972	1,439,438	245,316	5	1	1	0	394	0
June 1972	987,941	711,234	9	6	1	1	3,090	227
July 1972	959,977	757,510	2	8	0	0	8	1,408
August 1972	1,085,868	826,081	2	7	0	0	88	425
September 1972	921,800	855,596	4	7	0	1	0	765
October 1972	1,038,207	1,002,130	0	9	0	2	0	2,124
November 1972	876,549	844,301	4	7	3	1	270	189
December 1972	875,895	835,591	4	6	0	4	507	853
January 1973	899,105	908,877	3	10	1	2	67	211
Totals	12,262,028	7,184,539	43	64	3	12	4,876	7,477
Per million miles			3.51	8.91	.65	1.67	398	1,041

and injury can be achieved. During the experiment, the deceleration warning light prevented rear-end collisions to equipped vehicles by 5.4 collisions per million miles, reduced the number of cab drivers injured from such collisions by 1.02 injured per million miles, and reduced the cost of repairs to cab vehicles struck in the rear by $643 per million miles. These figures do not include taxi passenger injuries and the personal injuries and property damage prevented for the vehicles which ran into the rear of the cabs. With the U.S. public driving approximately 1,115,000 million miles each year (National Safety Council, 1971) the potential reduction in personal injury and property damage from rear-end collisions for American society is enormous. The same report from the National Safety Council indicates that rear-end collisions account for 2,000 deaths per year. If 60 percent of these are avoidable, the savings of 1,200 lives per year would be a human benefit.

Hence, this quantitative experiment also illustrates the kind of "on the street" field evaluation possible with the cooperation of public and private agencies.[4]

[4]The California Highway Patrol granted the permit to place the deceleration warning lights on the cabs for the experiment. This investigation could not have been possible without their approval

There are few who would assert that the introduction of a computer, robot, or other instrument of automation would not change a production process. While most workers would probably grudgingly admit to the probability of increased efficiency and reliability, there would also be protestations that work "wouldn't be the same" with the new equipment. In this reading, Buchanan and Boddy document how the work of a cookie maker changed when a computer took over the production process. When you are reading this article, decide which job you would rather have—cookie maker or the baker?

■ READING 37 ■

Advanced Technology and the Quality of Working Life: The Effects of Computerized Controls on Biscuit-Making Operators

David A. Buchanan and David Boddy

Department of Management Studies, University of Glasgow

Developments in microelectronics have rapidly expanded the range of applications of computing devices in manufacturing. There has been much speculation about the impact of this new technology on the experience of work, but there are few accounts of its effects in practice.

Barron and Curnow (1979) argue that microelectronics will extend automation in manufacturing simply by replacing mechanical and electromechanical control devices in piecemeal fashion, and that this will not materially affect the roles of operators. They claim that for the worker, "such an approach could be attractive,

since it is likely to provide him with tools and instruments which enhance his skills and make the job more interesting" (Barron & Curnow, 1979, p. 35). They also claim that human intervention in manufacturing is not likely to be eliminated by electronics as "it is not expected that it will be possible, even in the longer term, to achieve systems with the degree of adaptability provided by the human" (Barron & Curnow, 1979, p. 35).

This optimism about the impact of technical progress is shared by numerous commentators (Mann & Hoffman, '960; Marek, 1962; Woodward, 1965; Hunter et al., 1970; Taylor, 1971*a, b;* Williamson, 1973; Davis & Taylor, 1975, 1976; Davis, 1976, 1977; Vine & Price, 1977; Singleton, 1974, 1979;

Source: *Journal of Occupational Psychology*, 56, 1983, pp. 109–119. (Printed in Great Britain).

Bainbridge, 1978; Paternotte, 1978; Landeweerd, 1979; Umbers, 1979). These researchers have been mainly concerned with computerized continuous production, and portray the process control operator as a skilled and knowledgeable information processor and decision maker with responsibility, discretion, and good working conditions.

Other commentators have presented an alternative perspective on the effects of technical advance (Braverman, 1974; Nichols & Beynon, 1977; Gallie, 1978; Clegg & Dunkerley, 1980; Boddy & Buchanan, 1981; Buchanan & Boddy, 1982). These researchers have emphasized the importance of management objectives as determinants of the organization and experience of work, and argue that managers use technical change to improve management control over work flow and workers.

The objective of this paper is therefore to provide tentative answers to the following questions:

1. How did computer controls affect the job characteristics and attitudes to work of biscuit-making operators?
2. To what extent was the organization of work that accompanied these technical changes due to: (*a*) the capabilities of the technology, (*b*) management objectives?

The computer controls had affected several operating and managerial jobs in the biscuit-making factory studied. This paper focuses on the effects on two operating jobs, the doughman and the ovensman, which were affected in significant and contrasting ways.

RESEARCH METHODOLOGY

Research Design

This was a one-shot case study, to investigate the effects of two applications of computerized equipment in biscuit making, one for mixing dough, and the other for weighing packed biscuits. The dough-mixing computer

was introduced in 1971, and was being replaced by smaller and more powerful computing equipment in 1981. The packet-weighing device was introduced in 1979. The data were collected between January and June 1981.

This design was used because the more recent changes concerned contemporary developments in microelectronics and little empirical research had been carried out into their potential effects. The overall aim of the study was to generate fresh insights for further research, and rich rather than rigorous data were thus considered to be important at this stage.

The main limitations of this design are that no information was collected before the changes were introduced, and the generalizability of the findings may be weak as the organization studied was unique in several respects. The company's employment policy was welfare orientated, and it was common to find managers and operators who had worked in the factory for over 20 years. Several respondents were therefore familiar with both old and new technologies.

Research methods

1. Various company documents were examined, mainly internal memoranda and reports concerning the functions and advantages of current and future computer systems. These documents helped to explain the reasoning behind the use of the technology, and what was expected of it.
2. Semi-structured interviews were conducted with:
    (*a*)   the eight production managers (see Figure 1) concerned with the section of biscuit production studied—this provided information about the operation of the technology and further insights into management expectations and the reasoning behind its use;
    (*b*)   three training officers, one management development adviser, and the technical services manager

FIGURE 1 Partial Organization Chart, Biscuit Production

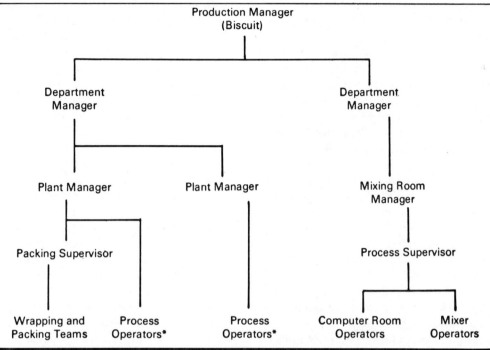

*Machine operators and ovensmen.

—this provided information about the effects of technical change on other related functions within the company;

(c) seven operators of the line studied, including: one computer room operator, two doughmen or mixer operators, one machine-man, one ovensman, and two wrapping machine operators. They were asked how their jobs had changed with the introduction of new computing technologies, and about their attitudes to these changes.

These interviews lasted around 45 minutes each, and the production managers were interviewed several times during the fieldwork.

3. Observation of the biscuit-making process, and in particular of the computerized controls—further informal discussion with managers and operators on the functions of the equipment and their reactions to it took place during this phase of the fieldwork.

4. A report of the findings was fed back to managers and operators for their comments; this procedure confirmed the accuracy of the findings, and some factual errors were corrected.

MAKING BISCUITS

The company had been making biscuits in Glasgow since 1925. In 1981, the factory employed around 2,000 people, and was a subsidiary of one of the largest biscuit manufacturers in Britain. The factory had 15 production lines. This study concerned line number 4, which made one of the company's most popular and profitable products. Computer-controlled mixing was introduced to all lines in 1971. Line 4 was the first, since 1979, to use computerized packet weighing and updated mixing control computers. Figure 1 is a partial organization chart showing positions concerned with line 4.

Line 4 was run by: a computer room operator (mostly female; also ran other lines), a doughman or mixer operator (mostly male), a machine operator (male), an ovensman (male), and a packing team of 10, with one supervisor (female). The ovensmen were paid more than the mixer and machine operators.

Biscuits were made in four stages: mixing, cutting, baking, and wrapping. The flour was first pumped into storage silos from tankers. The recipe for each product was stored on punched paper tape which was fed into a computer by the computer room operators. The computer controls fed flour, water, and sugar to the mixing machines in accordance with the recipe. The computer room had a wall display or "mimic board" showing the current state of the process on each line. The recipe tape for each product normally remained constant for long periods. When a recipe change was required, operators used programming skills to create a new recipe tape.

At the time of this study, the computer system installed in 1971 was being replaced with "recipe desks." These were located in the computer room, and allowed adjustments to be made to the recipes faster, using small thumbwheels on the desk panels. They did not require paper tapes.

At the start of each shift, the doughman checked with the computer room operators that the correct recipe tape was loaded, and made sure that enough "sundries" (ingredients added in small quantities) were available. The doughman then pressed a "call button" to start the mixing cycle. When the main ingredients had been delivered to the mixing machine, a light told the doughman to start the mixer. The sundries were added by him manually during the mixing process; automating this had proved extremely difficult.

The computer controlled the mix recipe, time, speed, temperature, and timing of interruptions. Mixing normally involved three stages: dissolving (the sugar), creaming (mixing in the fat), and doughing (mixing everything). Each mix took about 20 minutes with up to three interruptions for the sundries to be added. While a mix was taking place, the hoppers above the mixer were refilled and the cycle was ready to begin again.

A sample of dough from each mix went through an "oven test." If the doughman decided that the mix was good, it was emptied into a dough hopper and was then rolled to the right thickness by passing it through rollers adjusted by the machine operator. The flat dough sheet then passed through a cutter which stamped out biscuits of the appropriate shape.

The process was continuous from the cutting machine to the packing benches. The biscuits were baked as they travelled by conveyor, in about four minutes, through the 90-metres long oven. The ovensman checked the thickness, or "bulk," of each batch of biscuits by measuring the length of a set number of biscuits in a graduated tray or gauge. If the bulk was wrong, the ovensman could change the temperatures in the various zones of the oven to correct it. The colour and moisture content of the biscuits could also be adjusted in this way. Incorrect moisture content reduced the shelf life of the biscuits and made them liable to "check" or break.

When they left the oven, the biscuits went onto a cooling conveyor and were then fed to an automatic wrapping machine. Before going to despatch, each packet passed over a computerized "checkweigher" and was rejected if it was light. Packets had to be as close to their stated weight as possible, to comply with consumer protection legislation, and to avoid giving customers "free" biscuits. The amount of excess biscuit wrapped was called "turn of scale." This term derives from the time when packets were weighed manually on a scale whose pointer was deflected (turned) from the vertical by underweight or overweight packets. The main function of the computerized checkweigher was therefore to reduce turn of scale. The wrapping machine operator got a digital display of the weight of each packet. If the weight was consistently wrong, she could make small adjustments to the number of biscuits being put into each packet. Information on packet weights also appeared on a video display screen in the ovensman's work area. The weights were shown as a graph and in numbers and the display was updated every two minutes. The computer also printed regular production analyses for management on another terminal.

THE DECISION TO USE COMPUTER CONTROLS

Investment in computing technology reflected the thinking of the company chairman. In the words of one production manager, he was an "evangelist for investment," particularly for improvements in production technology that cut costs and improved product quality. This policy influenced management thinking and behaviour throughout the company.

Managers were free to introduce technical changes to improve productivity in their sections. The company had a special internal group that monitored and developed process control technologies. This group also circulated details of new developments relevant to the company; "mail order microchips," as one manager commented.

The long-term management objective was to automate production fully. This objective was based on the assumption that management control over production, and productivity, would be improved by reducing human intervention in the process and controlling production by computer. A company report explained this policy by identifying three "key concepts":

Firstly that the adoption of further automatic monitoring and control equipment will result in higher productivity and less waste through lower manning levels and greater product consistency.

Secondly that computer systems can offer significant benefits in the display and communication of relevant process information to production staff, and also carry out pertinent statistical analyses on such information. The latter part being a prerequisite for a complete understanding of process relationships and the development of new control loops.

Thirdly that with an automatic system, it is desirable to have the facility for remote operator monitoring and control. There are obvious advantages to be obtained with the facility to, at one central point, monitor and adjust the set points of a number of different processes spread out across the factory floor.

The immediate objective, however, was to improve production control by introducing systems that gave managers and operators more information more quickly to control the process more effectively.

These developments had met teething problems. The electronic checkweigher was installed in 1979, but was not considered to be working properly until 1980. There were problems in linking it to the wrapping machine. The computer at the mixing end was reliable and downtime was caused mainly by mechanical failures in control actuators, and not in the computer.

These technical changes had increased the capacity of the plant by making output more continuous and had made the product quality more consistent. Turn of scale on line 4 was reduced from an average 3.5 percent in 1977 to 1.8 percent in 1981.

COMPUTING TECHNOLOGY AND THE DOUGHMAN

Before 1971, the job of mixing dough was done by time-served master bakers. They were each responsible for a team of workers who brought flour manually from the storage area. They also supervised the mixing of the ingredients in "spindle mixers," which were open vats like large domestic foodmixers. When they could see and hear the mix, the doughmen could tell by the feel of the dough, and by the sound that it made, if it was too dry or too wet, and could add small amounts of required ingredients to compensate. They were therefore skilled craftsmen in charge of other workers and had considerable status in the plant.

When the mixing control computer was introduced, the job became repetitive, with a cycle time of around 20 minutes a mix, no longer involved the supervision of others, and was classed as semi-skilled. The doughman's tasks now were:

(a) to start the machine (by pressing a button).

(b) to add the sundries when the computer stopped the mix.

(c) to pass a sample of the finished mix to the ovensman.

(d) to empty the finished mix into the dough hopper for the machineman.

The mixing vessel was enclosed and the operator could neither see nor hear the mix, and had to leave it only to collect the sundries, which were weighed in advance for him. When the equipment failed, skilled electronic technicians were required to track down the cause and repair it. One manager stated, "The mixer operators do not understand the equipment and have no expertise in fault finding."

Doughmen sometimes forgot to add sundries, such as salt. This was only discovered at the end of the mix or at the oven test. The computer controls, however, had reduced the number of bad mixes by removing some of the main sources of (human) error.

The skilled and varied craft of the doughman was thus replaced by the computer controls, and management preferred the job title "mixer operator". The comments of several managers illustrated how this job had changed:

> There was more variation in the things he did. Now they seem to lose all interest. There are three or four operators who've been here longer than the computer, and I can see they've really switched off. I've seen it happen to new people coming in as well. It destroys the human contact.
>
> The job has got much more boring and routine. It's changed the atmosphere of the work entirely. They used to have much more to do, but it has done away with much of the manhandling. There's no outlet on the job now and people are desperate to get away from the job.
>
> If automatic control goes too far, operators may lose interest in the work. When the plant is running smoothly, operators start talking and

stop checking. Operators may lose concentration on the job.

> It's made it a very boring job. We try to make it a bit more interesting with rotation and training courses about biscuit making. But some operators are very happy with the job and don't want any complications. We found that one of the reasons they forgot to add sundries was that they were talking to "visitors" from other parts of the factory. So now we keep people out of their area, unless they're there for a reason.
>
> The main requirement is to get a continuous supply of dough of a consistent quality. Management don't want the human element. The computer was put in to make less manual work and more accurate weighing and checking.
>
> It affects our ability to get foremen and managers from the operators. They don't want to get out of the rut. It's the repetitiveness of the thing which makes it so boring—he doesn't need to move.
>
> One problem with the whole mixer set-up seems to be that the new generation of operators don't appreciate as fully as before the consequences of what they do. It's all so automatic they have difficulty visualizing the effects of, say, half a minute extra mixing time on later stages in production.

Talking about their work and how it had changed, the two doughmen made the following comments:

> Our job is to give a constant supply of dough at the right consistency. It's a responsible job. You're at the top of the line and all the others are waiting.
>
> It's very repetitious. The computer controls it. We just press the button. If something goes wrong, it's more difficult to fix it.
>
> We used to have much more humour. You had your own group of manual workers working with you doing the manhandling and this gave a lot more fun. It's much more routine now. The recipe desk makes it much easier, but if it breaks down we have to do it by hand.
>
> It also takes the responsibility off us. They can't blame the doughmen. If we had to weigh it ourselves it would be our fault if anything went wrong. The old system used to take about twice as long to do a mix as the new one.
>
> It's much less interesting, more routine, very little scope for human error now. Initially, it's more skilled, till you get to know the set-up,

then there's a fair amount of boredom. Except when something goes wrong.

COMPUTING TECHNOLOGY AND THE OVENSMAN

The ovensman was responsible for baking biscuits that had the correct bulk, weight, moisture content, colour, shape, and taste. This was complex, because action to correct a deviation on one of these biscuit features could affect the others. The training time was 12 to 16 weeks.

Two of the most important features were biscuit bulk and weight. The ovensman checked these manually at least once during the baking of every mix. This allowed him to adjust the baking process to ensure consistency, and tell the wrapping machine operators about any potential difficulties. Every mix could have different properties. Some flours absorbed more moisture than others; some doughs were soft and others were tough.

At the end of every baking line, after the biscuits had been wrapped, there used to be an electromechanical checkweigher. The biscuit packets travelled on a conveyor over this machine which contained a weigh cell that weighed each individual packet and compared this weight with a (manually) preset standard weight. Light packets were pushed off the conveyor, and those at or above the set weight passed on to despatch. This machine could not record packet weights. A manual, random sample, check was made every half hour, to find out precisely how over- or underweight the packets were. The computer-controlled checkweigher was installed on line 4 in 1979 to replace the electromechanical system. The new checkweigher gave the ovensman information on the performance of the line, at a speed and in a format that enabled him to make rapid adjustments to the oven controls and to reduce turn of scale. If the packet weights were high, and the wrapping machine operator could not compensate, the ovensman could tell the machine operator to adjust the rollers, or he could increase the oven temperature to in-

crease bulk and reduce the number of biscuits per packet.

The information from the electronic checkweigher showed that something was wrong, but did not indicate what was causing the problem, or what action to take to correct it. The ovensman and machine operator had to take into account the properties of the flour being used. When the turn of scale wandered, the ovensman and machine operator decided what to do to correct it. It was vital they took this decision together, otherwise they may have overcompensated by taking independent action simultaneously to correct the same fault. The ovensman's opinion carried more weight.

The ovensman felt that the new system had reduced the pressure on him; management kept out of the way when there were no problems. The new system was used to settle disputes about the responsibility for inaccurate packet weights. The ovensman also felt that the new package had increased the interest and challenge in the job because it gave him a goal that he could influence, related to turn of scale and the number of packets of biscuits that left the factory. This was reflected in the bonus payment, and he felt that he had the satisfaction of knowing that he was cutting waste and costs. He commented that "Management want a straight graph on the video showing minimum turn of scale. We are working to finer tolerances now." One supervisor explained the changes to the job thus:

There is now no need for a constant physical check. The new package highlights problems making it easier to make corrections quicker. The operators are continually on top of the job, and the feedback from the package makes operators more aware of passing problems down the line.

The pressures on operators have been reduced. The turn of scale package acts as a double check for the ovensman; it's an assistant, a second opinion. More people can now see what is happening, are aware of the state of production and level of performance. The checkweigher provides an instant reminder of the need to take corrective action. As that check acts as a check on the ovensman's own check, it probably means that the ovensman takes more care over his own checking.

If things start to go wrong, we can regain the situation faster. Before, when packets were way over or under weight, everything had to be trayed off, which wasted time. This also meant more breakages. The new package gives more information faster, whereas before those "unforgiving minutes" were lost.

Another effect of this spread of information is that nobody can hide their mistakes because everyone has a clearer idea of where the problem lies when things go wrong.

CONCLUSIONS

Computer Controls and Job Characteristics

Tavistock Institute researchers (Emery, 1963; Hill, 1971) have suggested that the following job characteristics are significant determinants of the quality of working life. At the individual level, work should provide variety, meaning, control over operations, feedback of results, preparation and auxiliary tasks, and use of skills and knowledge. At the group level, the organization of work should provide job rotation for interdependent or stressful tasks, interdependent groupings to enhance meaning, feedback and control, communication channels, and promotion opportunities.

At the individual level, the introduction of computerized mixing affected the job of the doughman adversely on all of the significant characteristics. It replaced the doughman's craft skills, but did not overcome the need for human intervention at that stage of the process. It created what may be described as a *distanced* role with the following eight features:

1. Operators had a poor understanding of the production process and equipment.
2. Operators could not visualize the consequences of personal action or inaction.
3. Operators could not trace sources or diagnose causes of process and equipment faults.
4. There was no mechanical or manual backup system.
5. Specialist maintenance was required.
6. Operators became bored, apathetic, and careless.
7. Operators rejected responsibility for breakdown.
8. Operators developed no knowledge or skills through the work experience that made them promotable, and management lost a source of supervisory recruitment.

These features may be typical of jobs in "nearly automated" systems, where traditional skills are replaced, and where the work experience equips the operator with neither the capabilities nor the motivation to carry out residual but key functions effectively.

In contrast, the introduction of computerized packet weighing affected the job of the ovensman beneficially on the significant characteristics at the individual level, except for preparation and auxiliary tasks, which were not affected. The new system *complemented* his skill and knowledge, and created a role in which the operator:

(a) retained discretion to monitor and control the process.

(b) got rapid feedback on performance.

(c) had good understanding of the relationships between process stages.

(d) was able to control the process more effectively.

(e) had a visible goal that could be influenced.

(f) felt that the job had more interest and challenge.

The concept of complementarity was introduced by Jordan (1963). Singleton (1974, 1979) has also argued for this perspective in the design of human-machine systems.

At the group level, the jobs of the doughman and the ovensman were not affected by recent technical changes. Promotion opportunities for doughmen were reduced when the first mixing control computer was introduced in

1971 and a separate group of computer operators was formed. Job rotation took place within the mixing operator and ovensman groups to cover for meal breaks and absenteeism, but there was no rotation of jobs between mixing operators and ovensmen. The interdependencies between the several operators on each line could have led to the establishment of line teams, with rotation along the line, but management had not considered this.

Developments in technology are essentially developments in the way in which work operations are controlled (Bright, 1958; Braverman, 1974; Bessant et al., 1980). The extent to which machinery can replace human intervention, therefore, depends on the nature of the control task. Awkward and variable raw materials, sensitive equipment, and a product with tight quality constraints inhibit automation and guarantee a key role for human operators in maintaining system reliability.

The optimistic predictions of Barron and Curnow (1979), and others, are thus substantiated by the ovensman's example. The popular assumption that as machines do more people do less may not be generally accurate. The piecemeal introduction of electronic devices may give operators tools that complement skills, create information-processing, problem-solving and decision-making jobs, and enhance the quality of working life. But the pessimism of Braverman (1974) and others is reinforced by the doughman's example, which demonstrates that improvements in work experience are not guaranteed by technical advance.

Management Objectives and Work Organization

The organization and experience of work of the biscuit line operators in this case appear to have been determined by three sets of factors.

First, the information-handling and control capabilities, and limitations, of the equipment—these replaced the need for some operating skills, but complemented the use of other skills. But these capabilities and limitations do not uniquely constrain the organiza-

tion of work. They enable a range of different organizational arrangements to be established (Child, 1972; Buchanan, 1979).

Second, management objectives. These were concerned mainly with improving information about production performance, and extending computer control over the process to reduce operator intervention. Would the jobs of the doughman and ovensman be different if management had not pursued these control objectives? Management in this case may have used:

> (a) a different equipment design, to allow the doughman to see and hear the mixing process;
>
> (b) another layout, to give the doughman the recipe desk and responsibility for adjusting ingredient quantities;
>
> (c) autonomous work groups, each responsible for one production line.

These suggestions are speculative, but indicate some of the choices that appear to have been closed by management's preoccupation with production information and control. The management desire to remove control from operators frustrates the development of forms of work organization that enhance the quality of working life. By interfering with complementary relationships between operators and production equipment, these management objectives may also frustrate the pursuit of improvements in productivity.

Third, the physical and organizational structures created by past decisions and technical changes. The new recipe desk system to control the mixing process could have been located with and operated by the mixer operators. But the factory layout and organizational grouping established when the first computer was installed in 1971 made it difficult for management to consider not giving the new system to the computer room operators in 1981. The pay differentials among line operators may also have inhibited autonomous group working.

Management in this case got the extra production information and control required. One consequence was to make the work of the line operators, and in particular the ovensman, much more visible. Any errors in performance appeared within minutes on a computer terminal and also appeared automatically in computer analyses of production. The ovensman's information about and understanding of the process also increased. Computing technology thus alters patterns of access to information in organizations, and this may be a key issue for further research.

The organization of work that accompanies technical change is thus strongly influenced by management beliefs about machine and human capabilities and reliability. If Barron and Curnow are correct, management expectations of contemporary computing technologies may be unrealistic. The ability of electronic controls to design people out of manufacturing is limited. New technology creates new opportunities for the organization of work. It may therefore be necessary to examine traditional assumptions in the face of technical change, and to identify and evaluate systematically the organizational options.

If given a few minutes, most of us would be able to predict what would happen if a robot were introduced into our workplace. We would have some preconceptions of the speed and accuracy of the robot compared to a human operator. We would also have some preconceptions about whether we would benefit individually or not. In this reading, the authors show how preconceptions are often wrong and make suggestions of how to prepare for the introduction of new technology into the workplace.

■ READING 38 ■

The Human Side of Robotics: How Workers React to a Robot

Linda Argote, Paul S. Goodman, and David Schkade
Carnegie-Mellon University

Robots are being used in increasing numbers in offices and factories throughout the world. However, little is known about how robots affect either individual workers or the structure, functioning, and effectiveness of organizations. This article focuses on workers' reactions to the introduction of a robot in a factory. We examine how workers react to the robot itself, as well as how the firm's strategy for introducing the robot affects these reactions. This knowledge should enable managers to make better decisions about the use of robots in their organizations.

In general, robots can be thought of as machines that can sense, think, and act in repeatable cycles. However, given the current state of robotic technology, the sensing and learning functions are not well developed. Thus, we will view robots as (electromechanical) devices with multiple task capability and programmability. The current functions of most robots in U.S. factories are to transfer material and to do certain processes, such as welding.

Currently, industrial robots are in limited use; it is estimated that from 3,500 to 5,000 robots were used in the United States in 1980.[1] There are, however, many reasons that an increasing number of robots will be used in this country, including high labor costs, the current emphasis on productivity, and technological improvements in capabilities and costs of robots.[2]

As the use of robots increases, there is growing interest in the social impact of robotics. How will the use of robots affect employment levels?[3] Which jobs can be performed by

[1]Robots join the labor force, *Business Week*, June 9, 1980.

Salpukas, A. Manufacturing using robots, *New York Times*, October 23, 1980.

[2]Engelberger, J. *Robotics in Practice*. New York: AMACOM, 1980.

[3]Ayres, R.U. The future of robotics: A meta review (prepared for The UNESCO/11 ASA Symposium on Scientific Forecasting and Human Needs: Methods, Trends, and Messages, Tbilisi, USSR, December 1981).

robots?[4] What types of educational and training programs are needed for workers whose jobs are affected by robots?[5]

This study differs from other work on the social impact of robotics by examining how individual workers react to the introduction of a robot at their factory. Our focus is on understanding workers' psychological reactions (e.g., their attitudes and motivations) to the robot and to the manner in which the robot was introduced. The more positive workers' reactions to robots are, the more likely organizations will experience positive economic consequences, such as increased productivity through the use of robots.

While this study appears to be one of the first to examine the effects on individual workers of introducing a robot in a factory, there is literature on the impact of technological change on individuals and organizations. Several themes emerge from that literature which should help our understanding of the effects of robots in the workplace. One theme emphasizes the need to take into account the compatibility between an organization's technology, its structure, and its members.[6] Failure to consider these factors often results in unintended negative consequences, including increased absenteeism, higher accident rates, and decreased productivity.

Another theme from studies of technological change is that changes in technology often lead to changes in the job activities of individual workers. Whyte found that automation increased the extent to which jobs were mentally demanding.[7] Elizur and Mann and Hoffman reported that workers in automated organizations felt a greater sense of control and respon-

sibility than their counterparts in less automated organizations.[8] Workers in automated organizations often experienced a greater sense of pressure than workers in less automated organizations.[9]

Technological change also affects social interaction patterns at work. Whyte found that increased automation decreased the opportunities workers had to interact with their co-workers.[10] Williams and Williams noted that new technologies often created new demands on support personnel and required more coordination activities between support and production personnel.[11]

Another theme from the organizational change literature is that worker involvement in the design of change affects worker acceptance of and commitment to the change.[12] In their classic study, Coch and French found that worker participation in the design of change was associated with higher productivity, lower turnover, and fewer acts of aggression against the company.[13] Similarly, Griener and Crockett both stressed that a change attempt was more likely to be successful if everyone affected by the change was involved in its design and implementation.[14]

While this review is not exhaustive, it indicates that workers can resist technological change, that the opportunity to participate in

---

[4]Ayres, R.U. and Miller, S.M. Preparing for the growth of industrial robots, (unpublished paper), Carnegie-Mellon University, 1981.

[5]Technology assessment: The impact of robotics, Technical Report EC/2405801-FR-1, Eikonix Corporation, 1979.

[6]Emery, F.E. and Trist, E.L. Socio-technical systems, in *Organizational Systems: General Systems Approaches to Complex Organizations*, F. Baker, ed. Homewood, IL: Richard D. Irwin, 1973.

[7]Whyte, W.F. *Men at Work*. Homewood, IL: Richard D. Irwin, 1961.

---

[8]Elizur, D. *Adapting to Innovation*, Jerusalem: Jerusalem Academic Press, 1970.

Mann, F.C. and Hoffman, L.R. *Automation and the Worker*, New York: Holt, 1960.

[9]Mumford, E. and Banks, D. *The Computer and the Clerk*, London: Routledge and Kegan Paul, 1967.

[10]Whyte, 1961.

[11]Williams, L.K. and Williams, C.B. The impact of numerically controlled equipment on factory organization, *California Management Review*, Winter 1964, pp. 25–34.

[12]Beer, M. *Organization Change and Development*. Santa Monica, CA: Goodyear, 1980.

[13]Coch, L. and French, J.R.P. Overcoming resistance to change, *Human Relations*, August 1948, pp. 512–532.

[14] Griener, L.E. Patterns of organization change, *Harvard Business Review*, May–June 1967, pp. 119–128;

Crockett, W. Introducing change to a government agency, in *Failures in Organization Development and Change*, P. H. Mirvis and D. N. Berg, eds. New York: John Wiley & Sons, 1977.

a change may reduce resistance, and that technological change can affect social interaction patterns on the job. A decrease in the opportunity to interact with others is generally associated with increases in worker alienation, stress, and absenteeism. This review also suggests that new technologies can change work activities. If the change decreases variety, autonomy, and challenge in jobs, or if it introduces activities that are incompatible with the workers' abilities and preferences, workers' attitudes will probably become more negative and their motivational levels are likely to fall.

While robots may be viewed as another advance in automation, we believe that workers may view robots as qualitatively different from other forms of automation. Workers have been exposed to robots with glorified capabilities on television and in the movies. In addition, a robot often directly takes the place of a worker. We think these factors combine to make the introduction of a robot a very salient and possibly threatening event for workers.

RESEARCH SITE AND METHODOLOGY

To understand how workers react to the introduction of a robot, data were collected at a manufacturing plant that was installing its first robot. The plant, which had been in operation for approximately 10 years, was involved in the forging and machining of various metal alloys. The workforce, which numbered about 1,000, was nonunion, predominantly blue collar, and fairly stable. The average length of service for employees in the department where the robot was introduced was eight years. Relationships between labor and management appeared to be good; no walkouts or other examples of industrial strife had occurred at the plant in recent years.

The company had used a fairly comprehensive set of strategies to introduce the robot into the plant, including an open house to demonstrate the operation of the robot, talks by the plant manager, discussions with first-line supervisors, and notices posted in the cafeteria. The company had informed employees about a year in advance that a robot was going to be introduced at the plant.

The robot was introduced in a department that handled the milling and grinding of bar stock; this involved approximately 10 different operations. The department had 40 employees who worked in three shifts. Each person operated one or more of the milling and grinding machines, which were arranged in a horseshoe-like configuration.

The work flow in the department was primarily sequential. Workers moved products from one operation to another by hand. There was some flexibility in the order in which products went through the various operations. Although the majority of the products went through most of the operations, not every product went through every operation. There were some buffer inventories between operations.

The robot, which was placed at the beginning of the work flow in the department, loaded and unloaded two milling machines. One person operated the robot on each shift.

We interviewed production workers on each shift in the department before and after the robot was put on-line. These production workers were our primary sample. Interviews were conducted during two separate visits to the plant in 1981, about two and a half months before and two and a half months after the introduction of the robot. We interviewed the same individuals during both our first and second visits, however, some workers were not available during the second visit because of such factors as vacations and illness. During the first visit, 37 employees were interviewed; during the second visit, 25 were interviewed. Our sample at Time 2 appears to have been representative of our population at Time 1 with respect to such characteristics as tenure, job grades, and shifts.[15]

---

[15]Our Time 2 sample was drawn without replacement from the population of employees we interviewed at Time 1. Therefore, we used the hypergeometric distribution to construct a likelihood ratio test to investigate whether our Time 2 sample was representative of our Time 1 population on characteristics such as tenure, job grades, and shifts. The χ^2 values computed from the likelihood ratio

In addition to interviews with members of our primary sample, approximately 30 supplemental interviews were conducted with first- and second-line supervisors and managers; production workers in an adjacent department; individuals from engineering, maintenance, and personnel relations; and other plant staff. Each interview lasted about 30 minutes and contained both structured response and open-ended questions concerning the robot and the circumstances surrounding its introduction. We also observed the workforce during the introduction of the robot and administered a satisfaction questionnaire to production workers.

RESULTS

We will first discuss the results of our study in terms of the effect the robot had on workers' beliefs, activities, and interactions. We will then examine how the organization was affected by the introduction of the robot.

WORKERS' BELIEFS

Beliefs about the Robot. We were curious about how workers in our sample think about robots, so we asked the respondents an open-ended question: How would you describe a robot to a friend? Table 1 lists the phrases used to describe a robot. The major concepts seem to be: mechanical man, preprogrammed machine, something that loads machines, something that increases productivity, or something that reduces manual work. This list of descriptions falls into three categories: general descriptions (mechanical man), functions (loads machines), and consequences (reduces manual work). The general types of categories used by workers to describe robots show no significant changes between Time 1 and Time

TABLE 1   Workers' Descriptions of Robots

	Percent of Total Mentions	
	Time 1	Time 2
Mechanical Man	15%	9%
Hydraulic Arm	2	9
Computer	6	0
Preprogrammed Machine	15	16
TV Image	10	7
Moves Material	4	9
Loads Machine	12	14
Better Productivity	15	5
Reduces Manual Work	15	23
Works Continuously	6	8
	100%	100%

2.[16] However, we found a significant increase in the number of concepts mentioned by each individual over time, which is consistent with the idea that more experience should lead to a more differentiated view of robots.[17]

As a follow-up to the first question, we asked workers how they learned about robots. The movie *Star Wars* and television shows depicting humanlike robots were frequently mentioned. These humanlike robots in the media probably contributed to the tendency of workers to anthropomorphize the robot: workers on each shift named the robot and endowed it with human qualities. This tendency was evident both in the interviews and in observations of people in the workplace.

Beliefs about the Effects of Robots. Table 2 presents workers' beliefs about robots in general at Time 2. Seven questions or statements were read to the workers, who re-

statistic were not large enough to reject at more than moderate levels of significance ($p < .25$) the hypothesis that our Time 2 sample was a random sample drawn without replacement from the population of employees we interviewed at Time 1. Results of these analyses are available on request from the authors.

[16]To test whether the frequency of mentions in various categories changed from Time 1 to Time 2, we pooled the frequency of mentions in each category at Time 1 and Time 2 to arrive at the frequency of mentions in the population. Using the hypergeometric distribution, we then tested whether the distribution of mentions at Times 1 and 2 were random samples drawn without replacement from our population. There was no evidence for rejecting the hypothesis that our Time 1 distribution was a random sample from the population, $\chi^2(2) = 1.04$, $p < .75$, or for rejecting the hypothesis that our Time 2 distribution was a random sample from the population, $\chi^2(2) = 0.82$, $p < .75$.

[17]The significance level is $t(24) = 1.89$, $p < .10$.

TABLE 2 Workers' Beliefs about Robots in General at Time 2

	Percent of Workers Agreeing/Strongly Agreeing*
Robots will:	
Make U.S. more competitive	87%
Be capable of doing my job	29
Be capable of doing clerical jobs	8
Be capable of doing management jobs	17
Displace workers	50
Create less desirable jobs	21
Require more job retaining	87

*Questions were asked in this order.

sponded by strongly agreeing, agreeing, slightly agreeing, slightly disagreeing, disagreeing, or strongly disagreeing. The results indicate that workers in our sample had positive attitudes toward robots. The workers felt that robots will help the United States remain competitive. There is some indication that workers believed that robots will displace other workers but not themselves, and will be limited to certain types of jobs. Workers perceived that the use of robots will require additional education and skill training for workers.

Table 3 focuses on workers' perceptions of the effects of the robot in their department, rather than on their general beliefs about robots. The respondents were presented with an outcome and asked at Time 1 whether the robot would increase, decrease, or have no effect on that outcome. Respondents were asked at Time 2 whether the robot had actually increased, decreased, or had no effect on the outcome. For example, let us consider one outcome: the chances for an accident. Table 3 indicates that 11 percent of our respondents at Time 1 thought the robot would increase the chances of an accident; this had increased to 29 percent at Time 2. At Time 1, 41 percent thought the robot would decrease the chances of an accident; 21 percent of our Time 2 respondents thought the robot had decreased the chances of an accident.

The results of the probit analyses which tested whether there were significant changes in respondents' answers from Time 1 to Time 2 are also presented in Table 3.[18] For example, the results of the probit analysis on the chances of an accident outcome reveal that the coefficient of the time variable for accidents was $- 0.687$. Thus, respondents were more likely at Time 2 than at Time 1 to say that the introduction of the robot increases the chances of an accident.

Table 3 indicates that a majority of the workers at Time 2 felt that robots increased productivity, but did not have much effect on the quality of output or the number of people who work in the department. The results of the probit analyses indicate that workers were significantly more likely at Time 2 than at Time 1 to say that the robot increased the chances of an accident, increased costs, and lowered the quality of the output. In short, Table 3 suggests that workers in the department where the robot was introduced became less optimistic over time about the effects of the robot.

We also asked respondents about the effect of the robot on jobs of individual workers. A majority of the workers at Time 2 believed that the robot had decreased the number of boring jobs and had reduced fatigue on the job. A majority of the workers also reported

[18]The N-Chotomous probit model requires independence of the error terms. This requirement might be violated if, for example, observations for the same individual at different points in time were correlated. In using the probit model, we have assumed that this dependence, if it exists, is weak.

TABLE 3 Perceptions of the Effect of a Robot in a Production Department

	Percent of Respondents Who Said Robot Had Effect on:[a]									
	Productivity		Accidents		Costs		Quality		Number of People Employed	
Effect	Time 1	Time 2	Time 1	Time 2	Time 1	Time 2	Time 1	Time 2	Time 1	Time 2
Increase	81%	67%	11%	29%	10%	33%	51%	17%	6	0
No effect	8	12	32	46	7	4	30	54	44	83
Decrease	3	12	41	21	55	42	3	21	44	17
Coefficient of Time Variable in Probit Model[b]	0.607		-0.687^d		-0.760^c		1.167^e		-0.533	

[a]The percent of respondents who said "Don't know" is not included in this table; hence, percentages for some outcomes will total less than 100%.
[b]A positive coefficient indicates that respondents were more likely at Time 2 than at Time 1 to move in the direction of saying the particular outcome decreased: a negative coefficient indicates that respondents were more likely at Time 2 than at Time 1 to move in the direction of saying the outcome increased.
[c]Statistically significant at 90 percent level.
[d]Statistically significant at 95 percent level.
[e]Statistically significant at 99 percent level.

that robots required workers to learn greater skills, which is consistent with the information in Table 2.

We also asked these questions of production workers in a department adjacent to the one in which the robot was introduced in order to understand how perceptions of workers in other departments were affected by the introduction of the robot. Workers in this adjacent department had access to some of the same sources of information about the robot (e.g., the demonstration, the plant manager's talk, and the notices) as did workers in the department with the robot. Workers in the adjacent department were also able to watch the robot operate. The pattern of results obtained from workers in the adjacent department was similar to that described for our primary sample.[19] There was some evidence that workers in the adjacent department were more optimistic about the effects of the robot at Time 2 than were their counterparts in the department with the robot. For example, workers in both departments

were more likely at Time 2 than at Time 1 to say that the chances for an accident increased and that costs increased; however, workers in the adjacent unit thought that the chances for an accident and costs increased to a smaller extent than did workers in the department with the robot.

Beliefs about Introducing Change. In order to understand how workers learned about the robot, we asked the employees at Time 1 whether they learned about the robot from a particular source and about the extent to which the source increased their understanding of the robot. As Table 4 indicates, the most frequently mentioned source of information about robots was the weekly workplace meeting between supervisors and workers. However, these meetings increased workers' understanding of robots only to a small extent. Written communication and the demonstration at the open house were the most effective sources of information about the robot. However, less than half of our respondents attended the open house, and only 16 percent reported that they received a written communication. Thus, the various communication sources do not seem to have been very helpful in increasing workers' understanding of the robot.

In addition, we asked workers how much influence or involvement they *actually had* on

[19]The probit analyses on the outcomes discussed above were run separately for each department with time (Time 1 versus Time 2) as the predictor of the outcomes. The probit analyses were also performed on the data from both departments combined, with both time and department (department with the robot, adjacent department) as predictors of the outcomes. A similar pattern of results was obtained from the different analyses.

TABLE 4 Effectiveness of Communication about the Robot at Time 1

Communication Source	Percent of Workers Who Reported They Received Communication	Average Extent Communication Increased Workers' Understanding*
Written communication	16%	2.6
Workplace meetings	89	4
Communication from supervisor	46	4.1
Movies or audiovisual presentations	13	3
Demonstrations	42	2.7
Informal sources, including the grapevine	37	4

*Questions were asked in this order. The response alternatives were: (1) to a very great extent, (2) to a great extent, (3) to a fair extent, (4) to a little extent, (5) not at all.

decisions about: (*a*) whether the robot would be introduced in their department, (*b*) where it would be placed, and (*c*) who would run it. We also asked them how much influence they *should* have had. The workers reported that they had no influence on any of these decisions. They said they should have had a little influence on decisions about whether the robot would be introduced and who should run it. However, workers did not think they should be involved in decisions about where the robot was placed.

Activities

Our analysis thus far has focused on workers' beliefs; we will now address the question of how the robot introduction affected workers' activities. For this analysis our sample is composed of the individual on each shift who operated the robot. Special interview schedules were developed to measure the activities, work cycle, and interaction patterns of the operators' jobs before and after the robot was introduced.

When the robot was introduced, a manufacturing cell (i.e., a set of interdependent machines operated by a worker) was created. The robot provided material handling functions for two milling machines. An operator was then responsible for the two milling machines and the robot. The introduction of the robot removed the materials handling activity from

the operator's job and added a new activity — robot operator.

Before the robot's introduction, approximately 12 different products were passed through both milling machines to begin the work flow sequence for this production department. The work cycle for each machine included set-up activities and then relatively short milling times (one to two minutes) during a product run. Work was done to fine tolerances, and it was possible for the operator to determine, through some measurement procedures, whether the parts were milled correctly. The major quality control activity, however, was at the end of all the machine operations.

After the change, the number of products remained the same. The two milling machines were still located at the beginning of the work cycle where the bar stock went through the first two milling operations. The other machine operations were unchanged, and quality control activities were still at the end of all the machine operations.

The major change in activities in the new manufacturing cell came in the material handling activities. In the old system, the operator would pick up the stock, place it on machine one, clamp it in, start the machine, and then the milling machine would perform its work. The operator would then stop the machine, unclamp the stock, place it on the second machine, and the cycle would repeat. Each new stock would follow this cycle. When we asked the operators about the differences between their jobs before and after the robot introduction, they said:

> Now it's mainly watching . . . walking around the machines to be sure everything is running.

> We do more activities. Now you have to set up all three machines.

> There are also more functions . . . you need to program the robot.

The operators also reported that they were doing more activities and that the total work cycle had increased. They attributed the increased work cycle to more setups and delays in getting the new robot operational.

The change in activities was related to a change in skill requirements. The operators said:

> The job now requires more skills. . . . You have to learn how to program the robot and run it. . . . With more skills, of course, comes more responsibility.

> Operating the robot requires more skills . . . the job is more sophisticated.

If we combine the ideas in these quotations with those in the preceding ones, it is clear that the new skills are in observing and detecting problems in the interface between the three machines and in programming and operating the robot.

What are some of the consequences for the worker of these changes in activities? The literature on the relationship between job activities and individual characteristics indicates that improving the fit between the new job activities and the personal characteristics of the worker can lead to more positive attitudes and higher motivation. Conversely, introducing activities that are incompatible with a worker's abilities and preferences is likely to generate stress, negative attitudes, and lower motivation. Because we are examining the introduction of a single robot and are dealing with only three operators, it is difficult to identify statistically significant changes in our study. However, some trends are evident. The operators in

our study experienced more stress or pressure. Two of the operators said:

> There is more stress now. . . . We have more responsibility. . . . They want the robot to run and we have to keep it going. . . . That's hard because it is still relatively new.

> It's nerve racking . . . there are lots of details . . . it's an expensive piece of equipment.

This stress stems partly from the new tasks and responsibilities of the operators and partly from operating a new costly piece of equipment. There was also a more subtle source of stress when workers compared themselves to the robot. There was much speculation during our first visit to the plant about whether an operator who was particularly quick would be able to beat the robot. By our second visit, workers seemed resigned to the fact that the robot would always be able to outproduce a human worker. The reason was simple: robots do not take breaks or go to lunch! Although objectively the operators controlled the robot and the two milling machines, they subjectively felt that there was competition between them and the machine. Operators reported that the robot could load and unload the two milling machines faster than they could when they operated the machines manually.

One of the operators in our sample said that although he found observing and monitoring more boring than manual activities, he was currently satisfied with his job because it still included many manual set-up activities. He commented, however, that without these set-up activities, the current job would be more boring than his previous job. We suspect that this incompatibility between activities required by the job and preferences of the worker was another source of potential stress.

We do not want to create a picture of unhappy operators. All these individuals voluntarily accepted the job of operating the manufacturing cell, and all received considerable recognition because of the "newness" of the robot. All operators acknowledged that the use of the robot eliminated the prior heavy and fatiguing work, and they reported approximately the same degree of satisfaction with most aspects of their job before and after the robot was introduced.

At the same time, however, workers experienced more stress than they had in their prior job. It would be premature at this point to speculate about whether this increased stress was good or bad for the individual or for the organization. Studies have shown that increased stress is associated with increased turnover and absenteeism, and that stress can lead to either increments or decrements in performance.[20]

Since the introduction of the robot could affect support personnel as well as operators, we interviewed people in engineering, maintenance, quality control, and scheduling. Engineering and maintenance were responsible for getting the machine up and running. Changes in the functioning of the machine could affect quality control and scheduling. Several themes emerged from our discussions with support personnel. First, some felt that the use of the robot had changed their job activities. Since the robot represented a new generation of technology, new knowledge and new job activities were necessary. Second, there were some feelings of frustration since not all support personnel were involved in planning for the robot and yet their job activities were affected by the robot. Third, there were positive feelings created by the recognition the workers received and by their personal pride in the successful operation of the robot.

Interactions

The formal and informal interactions that develop around job activities are important in the workplace. The introduction of a robot can change these interaction patterns, which in turn may have psychological and behavioral

consequences. For example, if the new technology breaks up existing social interactions and isolates the worker, we would expect increases in feelings of alienation and more resistance to the new technology.

The operators reported at Time 2 that they had less opportunity to talk with people on the job than they had before the robot was introduced. Two of the operators said:

> I haven't been able to talk as much. . . . I'm too involved with the robot. . . . You really have to concentrate.

> I don't have time to talk with anyone . . . I don't want them breaking my concentration. . . . I'm isolated now.

The decreased opportunity to interact with others seemed to come mainly from the increased mental demands of the job. Because workers had to concentrate more, they did not have time to talk with their co-workers.

The introduction of the robot did not change the work flow in the department. All the workers, including the robot operator, were located in the same area and participated in the same part of the work flow. Thus, while our operators reported less opportunity to interact with others in the department, the set of people they interacted with in the department remained roughly the same. This might have provided built-in support mechanisms to buffer the workers from some of the effects of the change.

The major changes in interactions occurred between support personnel from the engineering and maintenance departments and the operators of the manufacturing cell. There was more frequent contact between engineering and maintenance personnel and the operators. Perhaps because the robot was new and represented the first major installation in the plant, support personnel as well as the operators were highly motivated to get the robot up and running, and they cooperated with each other. If many robots were being placed on-line and the support personnel had great demands on their time, then we might find more conflict between support personnel and the operators.

[20]Porter, L.W. and Steers, R.M. Organizational, work, and personal factors in employee turnover and absenteeism, *Psychological Bulletin*, 1973, pp. 151–176; Scott, W.E. Activation theory and task design, *Organizational Behavior and Human Performance*, 1977, pp. 111–128.

Organizational Unit

Our discussion thus far has focused exclusively on the effects of the robot on the individual. The introduction of this new technology also affected the department, requiring a reevaluation and reclassification of the operator's job. Some of the operator's job activities were eliminated and others were added. Given the net change, should the job retain the same grade or be upgraded? Although management upgraded the job, the workers felt that the new grade and associated pay for the operator's job were still too low.

We also examined whether the introduction of the robot affected other department policies, procedures, or formal coordination mechanisms. There was no evidence of any effect other than the changes in the pay system.

CONCLUSION

The purpose of this article is to focus attention on the consequences for the worker of introducing robots into the factory. Workers in our sample held positive beliefs about robots in general. When we asked them about the effect of the robot on their department, they initially reported that the robot would increase productivity, reduce costs, increase quality, make the job easier and less boring, and increase skill requirements. As workers acquired more experience with the robot, their beliefs about robots became more complex and somewhat more pessimistic (greater chances for accidents, cost increases, quality decreases).

We think this study has several major strengths. To our knowledge, it is the first systematic evaluation of the effect on workers of introducing a robot. The study used a variety of methods, including interviews, questionnaires, and observations. We collected data before and after the change to get some base line to study the effects of the robot introduction over time. In addition, we used a broad sample perspective to identify both individuals directly affected by the change and individuals indirectly affected (e.g., support personnel).

The study, of course, has certain limitations. Data were collected from only one organization. There was only one robot installation, and it was the first robot installation. The change also took place in a nonunion organization, and there were positive relations between labor and management. While interview data on the effects of the robot on such various outcomes as productivity were collected, company records data on these outcomes were not collected. Future research is needed involving multiple organizations and including records or archival data and interview data collected over several points in time (e.g., before, shortly after, and a year or so after the robot introduction).

What can we learn from this study that will help in new installations of robotics in factories? Despite the small sample size and the difficulty of systematically testing certain relationships, a number of findings have emerged from this study. These findings *combined with* findings from other studies of increased automation suggest some recommendations for managers introducing new technologies.

1. Before introducing the robot, important questions need to be resolved. For example, workers are likely to be most concerned about job security and pay. Failure to resolve such questions before introducing the robot is likely to reduce the effectiveness of the introduction.

2. It is critical to analyze the organization before introducing change. What effects will the technological change have on the activities, interactions, and beliefs of workers? Managers must anticipate potential problems that the change may bring—both obvious problems (such as job loss) and subtle ones (e.g., new job activities).

3. Management must develop a strategy for worker involvement in introducing the new technology. There is a wide variety of possible strategies. In our study management provided virtually no opportunities for worker involvement in the robot introduction. The workers wanted some level of involvement in certain decisions but not in others. Some involvement is likely to increase understanding about the robot and may perhaps lead to greater commitment to the change process.

4. Certain communication techniques seem more effective than others in introducing robots. Demonstrations that illustrate the operations of a robot seem to be a powerful technique.

5. Some feedback mechanism to monitor communication effectiveness in introducing this technology is necessary. Our study showed a discrepancy between what management was trying to communicate to workers and what the workers actually received.

6. It is vital that first-line supervisors be given information about the robot and support from upper management in dealing with workers' reactions to the robot. In times of change workers are likely to go to their supervisors more frequently for information and advice. The attitudes and behaviors of supervisors are likely to have a big effect on the success of the robot introduction.

7. The robot will create new job activities. It is very important to do a careful analysis of the new job and to maximize the fit between job characteristics and the personal characteristics of the worker. The literature indicates that if there is a poor fit between a job and a particular worker, this may have a dysfunctional effect on both the individual and the organization. The question is not just whether the worker can do the new activities, but whether the worker *can do* and *prefers* these activities. If there is a poor fit between the job and the worker, management must consider alternatives in job redesign or in the selection procedures.

8. If the change in activities is from "doing" to "observing," workers may experience more boredom on the job. If this occurs, some mechanism to alleviate boredom, such as job rotation, may be helpful. Job rotation would increase task variety and build up a backlog of skills for future expansion of robotics.

9. It is important to train backup operators for the robot. In our study only one person per shift was initially trained to operate the robot. This led to disruptions in the work process when one of the operators was absent. Training backup operators would provide the organization with more flexibility and individual workers with more job variety.

10. The introduction of robots can affect the nature of social interaction patterns at work. Prior research shows that attempts to change these patterns can generate resistance to change. If analysis indicates that the change will break up existing social relationships, alternative strategies should be developed. For example, involving the worker in this part of the change may generate new work arrangements that will facilitate acceptance of the change.

11. A successful introduction of robots requires the cooperation of support personnel. Our study showed that not all support personnel were involved in planning for the introduction of the robot, and this created some stress. Involvement of support personnel and operators early in the change process should facilitate the introduction process.

SECTION TWELVE

Stress

Industrial and organizational psychology is now in the enviable position of having more theory than data in the area of stress. This is in stark contrast to the old days of dust bowl empiricism when theory was thought to be cancer causing. At present, we have at least three viable approaches to understanding stress at work. The first might be called the constitutional or trait approach and it is embodied in the work of those making distinctions between Type A and Type B behavior patterns. The second approach is the environmental approach. From this perspective, there are things "out there" that have similar effects on all people. Those "things" might be environmental stressors such as noise, pressure for production, or inappropriate organizational structure. A third approach is the cognitive one. From the cognitive perspective, stress develops when individuals perceive themselves to be unable to meet an environmental demand. In this section, we will consider a few of these approaches as well as an attempt to demonstrate how stress might be reduced.

Following the pioneering work of Selye, many researchers have been pursuing the link between environmental demands, typical reactions to those demands, and the results or consequences of those reactions. In the simplest possible terms, it is proposed that when certain types of individuals are faced with environmental demands, they react in a way that increases their vulnerability to cardiovascular and gastrointestinal disease and malfunction. They get ulcers, have strokes, and generally degenerate. In this reading, we consider various types of reactions to stress and their possible consequences. In particular, Glass and his colleagues warn of the consequences of Type A behavior patterns.

■ READING 39 ■

Stress, Type A Behavior, and Coronary Disease

David C. Glass, Richard Contrada, and Barry Snow

Epidemiologists trace the beginnings of the heart disease problem in the United States at least to the turn of the century. Since then, mortality rates due to cardiovascular disease have increased dramatically. Between 1940 and 1950, for example, the rate for white males, ages 35 to 64, increased by 23 percent (Borhani, 1966). Although recent data from 1968 to 1972 suggest a decline in coronary mortality in American men, the disease still remains the major cause of death in the United States. A large percent of the cases is classified as "premature" deaths, since they occur during the middle years, ages 35 to 50.

CORONARY HEART DISEASE

Coronary heart disease (CHD) refers to a set of clinical disorders that results from damage to the coronary arteries supplying the heart;

this damage is called atherosclerosis or coronary artery disease. There are several major forms of clinical CHD. In angina pectoris, the individual experiences paroxysmal attacks of chest pain, which are the result of failure of the coronary arteries to deliver an adequate supply of blood to the heart. Although angina can be painful, it may persist for years in stable form without significant damage to heart tissue. However, angina pectoris is a serious disease. Affected persons have been known to die suddenly, or they may develop an acute myocardial infarction (MI).

MI, commonly termed *heart attack*, represents necrosis or death of a part of the heart due to a prolonged state of inadequate blood supply. The pathophysiological processes underlying this event remain unclear. Many cases of MI are associated with the presence of thrombosis (clot formation) in one or more of the coronary arteries. However, whether coronary thrombosis plays a precipitating or a secondary role in MI has been debated in recent years. In addition, several studies indicate that the presence of coronary thrombosis is a rare event in

Source: *Weekly Psychology Update* (Vol. I, No. 1), 1980. Princeton, N.J.: Biomedia Incorporated.

cases of sudden death due to cardiac arrhythmias. This has led some investigators to argue that MI and **sudden cardiac death** are two forms of myocardial necrosis with distinct pathophysiological mechanisms (Eliot, 1979). Other forms of clinical coronary heart disease include congestive heart failure and disturbances in the electrical activity of the heart.

FACTORS ENHANCING RISK FOR CHD

Data collected in various epidemiological studies suggest that the following factors are associated with increased risk of CHD: (*a*) aging, (*b*) sex (being male), (*c*) elevated levels of serum cholesterol and related low-density lipoproteins, (*d*) hypertension, (*e*) heavy cigarette smoking, (*f*) diabetes mellitus, (*g*) parental history of heart disease, (*h*) obesity, (*i*) physical inactivity, and (*j*) specific anomolies on the electrocardiogram (Kennel, McGee, & Gordon, 1976).

Although identification of these risk factors represents a significant advance in understanding CHD, some investigators question the predictive importance of such variables as dietary fats and physical inactivity in precipitating a later coronary event (Friedman, 1969). Moreover, the precise mechanisms whereby still other risk factors (e.g., elevated blood pressure) lead to CHD remain unclear. Even if these mechanisms were precisely understood, a search for additional causes of CHD would be indicated, since even the best combination of risk factors fails to identify most new cases of the disease. Accordingly, researchers are now considering the role of social and psychological factors in the etiology and pathogenesis of coronary disease (Jenkins, 1971, 1976, 1978).

Clinicians have long pointed out the hard-driving, competitive, time-urgent, and aggressive qualities of coronary patients (Osler, 1892). Nevertheless, when the growing pandemic of CHD in the 1930s and 1940s gave rise to a series of prospective studies of CHD risk factors, psychosocial factors were largely ignored in favor of biomedical variables. The role of psychological variables in the disease process was neglected for a variety of reasons. Unlike physical variables, which can usually be defined and measured with a good deal of precision, psychological factors frequently elude efforts at conceptualization and quantification. Indeed, reviews of the literature published as late as 1968 concluded that most personality traits could not distinguish between healthy and disease groups with any degree of reliability (Mordkoff & Parsons, 1968). Faced with the limited success of the trait approach, Friedman and Rosenman developed an interactionist perspective to the study of psychosocial risk factors (Rosenman & Friedman, 1974; Friedman & Rosenman, 1974). In their opinion, the increased rate of heart disease in modern times is associated with the stresses and challenges of an increasingly industrialized society. These pressures give rise to a complex set of behaviors, which Friedman and Rosenman define as the Type A coronary-prone behavior pattern.

TYPE A BEHAVIOR PATTERN

Type A behavior may be defined as "an action-emotion complex that can be observed in any person who is aggressively involved in a chronic, incessant struggle to achieve more and more in less and less time, and, if required, to do so against the opposing efforts of other things or persons" (Friedman & Rosenman, 1974). A series of laboratory studies by Glass and associates has provided empirical documentation for the competitive, achievement-striving, time-urgent, and hostile components of Type A behavior pattern (Glass, 1977). For example, Type A individuals strive harder to succeed than Type B, as is reflected in their attempts to solve a greater number of arithmetic problems irrespective of the presence or absence of a deadline. Another study showed that compared to Type B individuals, Type A individuals work at a level closer to the limits of their endurance on a treadmill test, while simultaneously admitting to less fatigue. Still other studies indicated that Type A individuals perceive time as passing more slowly than it actually does and experience greater difficulty with tasks that require delayed responses. As for the hostility component, two experiments showed that in contrast to Type B, Type A individuals deliver higher levels of electric shock to a confederate who has previously harassed them.

It is generally agreed that the Type A concept does not refer to the stressful conditions that elicit these behaviors, to the responses themselves, or to some hypothetical personality trait that produces them. Pattern A refers to a set of overt behaviors that occur in susceptible individuals given appropriately eliciting conditions. This interactionist approach—focusing on the interplay between the situation and the individual—is reflected in the traditional techniques used to assess the Type A behavior pattern.

MEASUREMENT OF PATTERN A

There are two major methods for assessing Type A behavior. The first, the **structured interview**, was developed by Rosenman and Friedman (Rosenman, 1978). In this method, the subject is asked a series of questions dealing with the intensity and quality of his competitive drive, time urgency, and hostility. Although the content of the subject's answers is considered important in making a behavior pattern diagnosis, the trained interviewer gives more attention to the manner and tone of the subject's responses. The questions are asked in a brisk manner, with emphasis on key words and phrases. The interviewer will occasionally challenge the subject by interrupting a response in midsentence. Type A individuals typically become impatient at these interruptions and try to override the interviewer. Frequent use of explosive vocal intonations, as well as rapid and accelerated speech, intermittent (and perhaps impatient) sighing, and rhythmic motor responses are also apparent in the Type A individual. Assessments based on the interview are typically made on a four-point scale, where A1 and A2 represent, respectively, the fully developed and the incom-

pletely developed Type A pattern. B represents the relative absence of Type A characteristics, and X represents an intermediate mixture of both behavior patterns. Assessments of recorded interviews by two independent raters reveal agreement rates ranging from 75 to 90 percent in various studies. Moreover, 80 percent of the interviewed subjects in one study showed the same classification over periods of 12 to 20 months (Rosenman, 1978).

Jenkins et al. have developed an alternative to the structured interview known as the **Jenkins Activity Survey for Health Prediction** (JAS) (Jenkins, Zyzanski, & Rosenman, 1979). This self-administered questionnaire requires that the subject respond to a group of items that reflect the content of the interview. A typical question is: "How would your wife (or closest friend) rate you?" The reply, "Definitely hard driving and competitive," is a Pattern A response, and "Definitely relaxed and easygoing" is a Pattern B response. Another question is: "Do you ever set deadlines or quotas for yourself at work or at home?" Where "Yes, once a week or more often" is a Pattern A response, "No" or "Yes, but only occasionally" are Pattern B responses. Although the self-administered JAS questionnaire has the advantage of providing an objective score on the A-B continuum, this score agrees only moderately with A-B classification based on the interview (i.e., 73 percent). It should be noted, however, that the agreement rate goes up to 90 percent if only the extremes of the A-B distribution (± 1 standard deviation) are considered. The JAS has a test-retest reliability, which ranges from .60 to .70 across one- to four-year intervals (Jenkins, Zyzanski, & Rosenman, 1979).

ASSOCIATION OF PATTERN A WITH CHD

The strongest available evidence for an association between Type A behavior and CHD comes from a prospective, double-blind study known as the Western Collaborative Group Study (Rosenman, Friedman, Straus, et al., 1964). A sample of approximately 3,000 men, ages 39 to 59, was identified and independently examined for behavior patterns and medical and demographic factors. Rosenman et al. reported that about 1,500 men were judged at intake to be Type A. An eight-and-one-half-year follow-up study showed that more than twice the rate of CHD occurred in these men compared to those who had originally been judged as Type B (Rosenman, Brand, Jenkins, et al., 1975). Further analysis of these data revealed that the traditional risk factors (e.g., elevated serum cholesterol and smoking cigarettes) could not account for the differential rate of CHD among Type A and B cases. This finding suggests that Pattern A does not exert its major pathogenic influence through the other risk factors for CHD.

Still other research, using coronary arteriography, has documented a greater degree of coronary occlusion among Type A compared to Type B patients (Blumenthal, Williams, Kong, et al., 1978). It would appear, then, that Pattern A behavior is related to clinical manifestations of coronary heart disease, as well as to the underlying atherosclerotic disease process.

PATTERN A AS A PSYCHOLOGICAL CONSTRUCT

A large proportion of the population is typically classified as Type A, but there is a relatively low incidence of CHD among Type A individuals (albeit significantly greater than in the Type B population). Therefore, the causal mechanisms underlying CHD may not be distributed evenly throughout the Type A group. It is possible that some facets of Pattern A behavior have little or no association with CHD, since they appear in all A individuals rather than in only those who show increased risk. This line of thought underscores the importance of understanding the psychological mechanisms that produce and sustain Type A behavior.

There are at least three approaches to identifying such mechanisms. Consider the work of Glass and associates, who suggest that Type A behavior is elicited in susceptible individuals by uncontrollable, stressful situations (Glass, 1977). Psychological stress may be defined as the internal state of the individual when he is faced with threats of psychic and/or physical harm (Lazarus, 1966). An uncontrollable stressor would be a condition that an individual believes he cannot influence or alter. A controllable stressor, by contrast, implies a perception on the part of the individual that he can escape or avoid the event. Pattern A behavior is conceptualized by Glass as a characteristic style of coping with environmental stressors that threaten the individual's sense of control. Compared with the Type B group, Type A individuals are expected to strive harder initially to assert and maintain control over uncontrollable events (hyperreactivity). However, continued exposure to uncontrollable stress must end in failure and frustration. Type A individuals are believed to react to this eventuality by giving up efforts at control more quickly and intensely than their Type B counterparts (hyporeactivity). Experimental studies have provided some support to these hypothesized Type A reactions.

Another approach to identifying the psychological mechanisms underlying Pattern A behavior is found in the work of Scherwitz et al. (Scherwitz, Berton, & Leyenthal, 1978). They suggest that the descriptors of Type A behavior (achievement striving, competition, time urgency, and hostility) require an involvement in the self and usually a comparison with a standard. In the case of achievement, for example, the self is where it wants to be, whereas in competition the self is compared with another. Scherwitz et al. argue that the construct of self-involvement is thus useful in explaining why Type A behaviors arise. Experimental data suggest that self-involvement is, indeed, correlated with cardiovascular variables that might be routes to CHD.

Still a third approach to conceptualization is found in an article by Matthews et al., which showed that only two factors in the Pattern A complex, competitive drive (including hostility) and impatience, were associated with the subsequent occurrence of CHD (Matthews,

Glass, Rosenman, & Bortner, 1977). Dembroski et al. have developed a component scoring system for the structured interview based on these findings (Dembroski, MacDougall, Shields, et al., 1978). The same components that were the best predictors of CHD were also the best predictors of experimentally induced cardiovascular elevations.

PHYSIOLOGICAL MECHANISMS

Researchers have been concerned with the physiological mechanisms that might mediate the association between Pattern A and CHD. The suggested mechanisms include elevated cardiovascular activity (e.g., blood pressure), acceleration of the rate of damage to the coronary arteries over time, facilitation of platelet aggregation leading to thrombus (clot) formation, induction of myocardial lesions, and initiation of cardiac arrhythmias. In some quarters, it is believed that these effects are influenced by enhanced activity of the sympathetic nervous system and consequent discharge of catecholamines such as epinephrine and norepinephrine (Eliot, 1979). Indeed, research has shown greater urinary norepinephrine excretion during the work day and plasma norepinephrine responses to competition and stress among Type A compared with Type B men (Rosenman & Friedman, 1974). More recent research indicates greater elevations in plasma epinephrine among Type A than among Type B individuals when both types were exposed to a hostile competitor (Glass, Krakoff, Contrada, et al., in press). Increases in systolic blood pressure and heart rate accompanied the epinephrine changes. Such cardiovascular activity has been reported by other investigators to be characteristic of the Type A group (Dembroski, MacDougall, Shields, et al., 1978).

Glass has proposed the following integration of these physiological results with his conception of Type A behavior as a style for coping with uncontrollable stressors (Glass, 1977). Evidence exists showing that stress influences the rise and fall of catecholamines and related cardiovascular activity. More specifically, active coping with a stressor may heighten these responses, whereas a decline in efforts to master a stressful event has been linked to a decline in catecholamine activity. Moreover, some investigators have suggested that the rise and fall of catecholamines and associated shifts between sympathetic and parasympathetic activity may be the mechanisms underlying sudden cardiac death (Glass, 1977; Engel, 1970).

One should recall that the Type A group initially exhibits enhanced efforts to master uncontrollable stressors followed by greater signs of giving up after prolonged exposure to such stimulation. Glass's argument is that this alternation of active coping and giving up, accompanied by the potentially damaging physiological processes outlined above, is experienced more frequently and intensely by Type A than by Type B individuals. To the extent that coronary disease is influenced by a cycle of hyperreactivity and hyporeactivity, the greater likelihood of the disease occurring in Type A individuals might be explained in terms of the cumulative effects of the excessive rise and fall in catecholamines released by the repeated interplay of Pattern A and uncontrollable stress. Research is currently being conducted to test this line of thought (Glass, Krakoff, Contrada, et al., in press).

INTERVENTION

A long-range goal for Pattern A research is to generate programs of intervention that will reduce coronary heart disease. Efforts in this area have so far accomplished little more than suggesting approaches which warrant further investigation.

Three interrelated considerations must be made in the design of intervention studies, the first being the choice of a target of intervention. Likely candidates include social and environmental factors that promote and sustain Type A behavior, psychological processes that interact with environmental factors in eliciting potentially pathogenic behaviors, and Type A behavior itself.

A second consideration that is related to the first is the nature of the treatment process. Social and environmental targets call for intervention at an organizational level. One possibility is to alter the conditions that seem to produce uncontrollable stressful experiences. For example, work efficiency and time management might be improved so that the number of hassles and deadlines occurring in an individual's day-to-day work environment is reduced.

Psychotherapeutic approaches may prove effective in altering psychological processes that give rise to Pattern A behavior. For example, modification of the way in which Type A individuals perceive and appraise uncontrollable events might be accomplished through the use of rational approaches to treatment (Roskies, Spevack, Surkis, et al., 1978). Programs of behavior modification might also be used with the aim of reinforcing Type B behavior while reducing the incidence and intensity of Type A behavior (Friedman & Rosenman, 1974). Relevant physiological processes have been the target of some behavior modification programs, in which subjects were trained to recognize and control their somatic reactions in stressful situations (Roskies, Spevack, Surkis, et al., 1978). Pharmacological methods have also received attention in efforts to alter Type A behavior, including the use of agents called beta blockers (e.g., propranolol), which inhibit the production of catecholamines.

A third consideration in designing an intervention program is the choice of criterion measures. Since a reduction in CHD is perhaps the most important criterion, considerable research on the pathophysiological processes associated with Type A behavior is the first order of business. In this connection, it should be noted again that most Type A individuals do not develop coronary heart disease. It becomes necessary, therefore, to identify the components of Pattern A that lead to physiological processes that may be routes to CHD. Once these components are identified, intervention programs could focus their attention exclusively on the CHD-relevant aspects of Type A behavior. Indeed, many facets of the behavior pattern may be socially desirable and adaptive for individuals in this society.

CONCLUSION

It seems clear that the past decade or two has provided systematic documentation for the observations of clinical cardiologists concerning coronary-prone behavior (Dembroski, Weiss, Shields, et al., 1978). It is apparent, however, that additional research remains to be done. Complexities abound at each level of analysis, including the psychological variables that account for Type A behavior, the situations that elicit the behavior, and the physiological processes whereby Pattern A leads to CHD. One must also consider the enormity of the task of integrating these factors with the traditional biomedical risk factors. Although an attempt has been made to provide an overview of the knowledge that now exists, the current state of affairs may be more aptly compared with the fitting of one small piece into a large puzzle. It is hoped that the shadings and minute detail on this small puzzle piece will lead to the eventual completion of the picture.

Most of us have had an opportunity to say "I wouldn't have the pressure of that job for all the money in the world." Some examples that come to mind are a taxicab dispatcher, an air traffic controller, an exchange clerk in a department store on the day after Christmas, and possibly a hockey goalie. Karasek has considered various job titles from two perspectives: (a) the extent to which there is substantial demand made of the people who occupy the job, and (b) the extent to which there are constraints or limits placed on the capacity of those people to respond to the job demands. As a result, he presents a template for describing the type of job that is most likely to produce stress. It might be interesting for you to consider your "job" as a student and analyze its stress potential in terms of Karasek's dimensions.

■ READING 40 ■

Job Demands, Job Decision Latitude, and Mental Strain: Implications for Job Redesign

Robert A. Karasek, Jr.
Columbia University

Well-known organizational case studies have indirectly referred to the important interactive effects of job demands and job decision latitude. Whyte's restaurant workers (1948) experienced the severest strain symptoms when they faced heavy customer demands which they were not able to control; Gouldner (1954) notes that personal and organizational tensions increase when close supervision is applied to miners under heavy work loads; and Crozier (1964) and Drabek and Hass (1969) discuss organizational strain which arises among groups of workers simultaneously facing heavy work loads and rigid rule structures or limited decision alternatives. Unfortunately, these case studies and their consistent findings have had little influence on survey analyses of mental

strain among large groups of working individuals.

Instead, two survey research traditions have emerged to deal with the psychosocial effects of work environments. One tradition focuses on job decision latitude (decision authority or skill level), the other treats "stressors" on the job. Most of the vast literature on job satisfaction and mental strain focuses primarily on job decision latitude (for example, Kornhauser, 1965; even Hackman & Lawler, see p. 290), while the "life stress" tradition of epidemiological studies of mental health (for example, Holmes & Rahe, 1967; Dohrenwend & Dohrenwend, 1974) focuses on the illnesses induced by environmental stressors or job stressors alone (for example, Sundbom, 1971; Caplan et al., 1976; Theorell, 1976). Unfortunately, job decision latitude research rarely includes systematic discussion of job demands

Source: *Administrative Science Quarterly*, 24, June 1979.

and the job demand literature rarely includes systematic discussion of decision latitude (Karasek, 1978a).

I suspect that many contradictory findings in the literature can be traced to incomplete models derived from these mutually exclusive research traditions. I suggest that a correct analysis must distinguish between two important elements of the work environment at the individual level: (*a*) the job demands placed on the worker and (*b*) the discretion permitted the worker in deciding how to meet these demands.

Both of these characteristics of the work environment must be analyzed to avoid misinterpretation and/or inconsistencies. A typical paradox which arises from omitting one of them is alluded to by Quinn et al. (1971, p. 411): They found that both executives and assembly-line workers could have stressful jobs, but could not explain differences in their job satisfaction. It is probable that the obvious differences in the omitted variable of decision latitude for executives and workers account for the differences observed in their strain symptoms and satisfaction:

> A major paradox of the study was that workers in higher status occupations were more satisfied than others with their jobs, were more mentally healthy, but at the same time experienced greater emotional tension concerning the events occurring on their jobs. Conversely, workers totally free of labor standards problems were not always among the most satisfied, since many of their jobs lacked the quality of self-developing challenge that appeared to be a major determinant of high job satisfaction.

Failure to distinguish between job stressors and job decision latitude is also reflected in the tendency to describe all structurally determined job characteristics as "job demands," regardless of their drastically different effects on psychological functioning. While the environmental determinacy of all of these characteristics supports the uniform terminology of demands, the lack of homogeneity of effects can lead to substantial misinterpretation, as in the case where decision authority is referred to

as a "demand" (Blood & Hulin, 1967, p. 268). The implication is that job strain increases with all such "demands," but as we will see this is definitely not the case. Failure to distinguish between work load stressors and job decision latitude (skill level and decision authority) and their different effects could account for Ritti's inconsistent finding that "time pressure demands" are associated with strain symptoms, while "intellectual demands" are not. Kahn (1979) finds a similar difference in effects for "qualitative versus quantitative job demands." Another version of this interpretive ambiguity occurs for a few conventional measures of job content, such as "responsibility," which mix aspects of both job demands and job decision latitude (Turner & Lawrence, 1965, p. 53).

A related problem is that the empirical association between job conditions and mental strain or dissatisfaction disappears in some well-known research findings, leading some authors (Hulin & Blood, 1968) to conclude that cultural values or individual differences overwhelm the effects of job condition on the individual. Two types of analytical errors could account for the lack of relationships. First, studies which fail to distinguish between demands and discretion and add the measures together would find relationships with strain symptoms cancelled out if, as we propose, the opportunity to use skill and make decisions *reduces* the undesirable effects of job demands. Second, failure to account for the possible nonlinear, nonadditive associations with mental strain that could occur from the interaction of two independent variables would produce different relationships for different subgroups, or insignificant relationships when findings are examined for linear trends (Turner & Lawrence, 1965; Hulin & Blood, 1968; Caplan et al., 1975; Andrews & Withey, 1976). A conclusive analysis thus requires examining broad representative data which include all types of working situations.

Another type of difficulty occurs with current definitions of "overload" (or "underload") as a source of strain (McGrath, 1970; Harrison, 1978). Overload is usually defined as occurring when the environmental situation poses demands which exceed the individual's capabilities for meeting them. While this formulation correctly identifies the mediating role played by personal capabilities, it introduces the individual level of analysis prematurely. Attention should first be directed to other types of environmental variables which can moderate job stressors, such as decision latitude, and then to the moderating effects of individual capabilities or perceptions. Mixing both the environmental and the individual characteristics into a single measure, such as "overload," not only shifts attention away from environmental moderators but makes it difficult to derive unambiguous implications for either work environment or personnel policy.

THE JOB STRAIN MODEL

The model postulates that psychological strain results not from a single aspect of the work environment, but from the joint effects of the demands of a work situation and the range of decision-making freedom (discretion) available to the worker facing those demands. These two aspects of the job situation represent, respectively, the instigators of action (work load demands, conflicts, or other stressors which place the individual in a motivated or energized state of "stress") and the constraints on the alternative resulting actions. The individual's job decision latitude is the constraint which modulates the release or transformation of "stress" (potential energy) into the energy of action. Thus, this is a stress-management model of strain which is environmentally based. If no action can be taken (Zeigarnik, 1927), or if the individual must forego other desires because of low decision latitude (Henry & Cassell, 1969, p. 179), the unreleased energy may manifest itself internally as mental strain.

A note on definitions is in order. Hereafter we will not use the term *stress* (referring to an internal state of the individual) because our research does not measure it directly. Instead, three related terms should be defined: The first

term is an independent variable that measures stress sources (stressors), such as work load demands, present in the work environment. These are called "job demands." The second measures decision latitude and is called "job control" or "discretion." The third is a derived composite measure that is called "job strain." Job strain occurs when job demands are high and job decision latitude is low (see Figure 1). I predict that this composite independent measure, job strain, is related to the dependent variable, symptoms of mental strain.

In practical terms, the task-level dimensions of the model may be relevant to important issues at the organizational level: output level and authority structure. Job demands (especially work load demands) probably express the overall output level of the firm, and job decision latitude is probably closely related to the firm's authority structure and technology, although further research would be required to establish the nature of those linkages. Thus, an important potential implication of the model is that the mental strain consequences of high organizational output levels may be contingent on the flexibility and equity of the organizational decision structure.

Figure 1 summarizes the types of jobs that might result from different combinations of job demands and job decision latitude. The labeled diagonals actually represent two interactions: situations where job demands and job decision latitude *diverge* ("A"), and situations where they are *matched* ("B"). The first situation, when demands are relatively greater than decision latitude, is of primary importance in predicting mental strain. Although the exact mathematical form of the interaction can probably not be distinguished clearly with the present data, the present theory best fits the pattern of a "relative excess" interaction (Southwood, 1978): Strain equals the excess of demands over decision latitude.

The model contains two predictions. First, following Diagonal A, strain increases as job demands increase (Friedman, Rosenman, & Carroll, 1958; Quinn et al., 1971), relative to decreasing job decision latitude (Frankenhaeuser & Rissler, 1970; Glass & Singer,

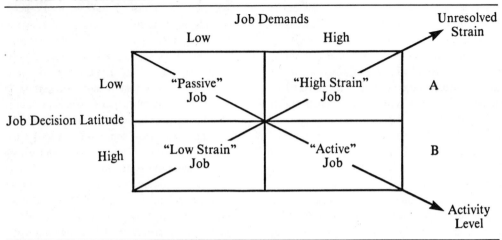

FIGURE 1   Job Strain Model

1972; Beehr, 1976; Frankenhaeuser & Gardell, 1976; Langer & Rodin, 1976). Second, incremental additions to competency are predicted to occur when the challenges of the situation are matched by the individual's skill or control in dealing with a challenge. When job demands and job decision latitude are simultaneously high (Csikszentmihalyi, 1975), we define the job as "active" and hypothesize that it leads to development of new behavior patterns both on and off the job (Diagonal B toward lower right). The model predicts that

jobs at the opposite extreme (defined as "passive job") induce a decline in overall activity and a reduction in general problem-solving activity (Suomi & Harlow, 1972; see also the "learned helplessness" literature: Maier & Seligman, 1976).

The utility of the overall model is based on the separation of job demands and job decision latitude. Ideally, these two aspects of the job should be highly correlated: "Authority is commensurate with responsibility." In fact, there is considerable empirical evidence that

TABLE 1   Factor Analysis of Job Content Dimensions, U.S. Quality of Employment Survey, 1972 (Employed males, ages 20–65; $N = 950$)

Varimax Factor Loadings	Factor I Job Decision Latitude	Factor II Job Demands
High skill level	(.59)	.21
Learn new things	(.55)	.27
Nonrepetitious	.27	.01
Creative	(.71)	.07
Allows freedom	(.42)	.19
Make one's decisions	(.77)	.01
Participate in decisions	(.73)	.08
Have say on the job	(.74)	.03
Work fast	.05	(.44)
Work very hard	.20	(.55)
Lots of work	.23	(.40)
Not enough time	.32	(.46)
Excessive work	.04	(.51)
No time to finish	.07	(.58)
Conflicting demands	.13	.35

Note: Loadings greater than .40 in parentheses.

the correlation is low, which implies that there are substantial groups of workers with discrepant demands and decision latitude. A varimax factor analysis of an approximately equal number of job demand and job decision latitude measures from the U.S. Quality of Employment Survey Data 1972 (Table 1) confirms empirically the dichotomy of job demands and job decision latitude. Composite indicators additively constructed from responses to the questions in Table 1 are correlated at .11, and Swedish data show similarly low correlations ($r = .25$ in the data base used here; $r = .02$ to .14 in a large Swedish white-collar union data base, Karasek, 1978b).

THE DATA

The data used to test the stress-management model come from recent national surveys in the United States and Sweden. The Swedish survey (Johansson, 1971a) is a random sample of the full adult population (approximately 1: 1,000) aged 15 to 75, with a response rate of 92 percent for 1968 and a response rate of 85 percent for 1968 and 1974. The U.S. survey, the University of Michigan Quality of Employment Survey for 1972, is based on a national stratified sample of housing units with a response rate of 76 percent. The Swedish data contain both expert and self-reported evaluations for some job content characteristics and are also longitudinal: The same workers were interviewed in 1968 and in 1974. The U.S. data are not longitudinal but are richer in detailed job descriptions. Both data sets represent attempts to sample randomly the full national working population. This analysis is based on male workers only; other research has indicated that the relationship between work and mental status for women is often complicated by the additional demand of housework (Karasek, 1976). The analysis of the Swedish data only includes employed workers (82 percent of the male work force). I also limit the analysis to job content at the level of the individual and do not address the undeniably important effects of work group and organizational level processes, except as they affect individual jobs.

JOB DECISION LATITUDE: INDIVIDUAL CONTROL AT THE WORKPLACE

Job decision latitude is defined as the working individual's potential control over his tasks and his conduct during the working day. Two measures, "decision authority" and "intellectual discretion," were selected for this study because of their similarity to other measures in the literature ("discretion and qualification scale," Gardell, 1971; "intellectual discretion," Kohn & Schooler, 1973) and their importance in job and organizational design strategies. These measures are also similar to the two central components of the Hackman and Oldham (1975) and Turner-and-Lawrence-derived (1965) Motivating Potential Score: autonomy in task organization decisions and variety in skill use (these appear to account for the bulk of the variance on the M.P.S. score: scale-item correlations .80 and .62, respectively.)

In analyses of surveys with large samples, "decision authority" and "intellectual discretion" are correlated ($r = .48$ in the U.S. data; see also high correlations between similar measures in Hackman and Lawler, 1971, p. 282; and Jenkins et al., 1975, p. 175). Thus, highly skilled work that allows little decision authority appears to be a relatively rare combination in practice (although Frankenhaeuser & Gardell, 1976, describe such a job for lumber graders). Therefore, in analyzing the U.S. data, we additively combined four measures of decision authority and four measures of intellectual discretion into an aggregate scale (Cronbach, $\alpha = .82$, see Appendix A). In future research it would be desirable to distinguish between the effects of several different aspects of decision latitude (i.e., with respect to skill, task organization, time pacing, organizational policy influence, control over potential uncertainties, decision resources). However, our aggregate decision latitude scale appears to

TABLE 2 Test of the Job Strain Model with Symptoms of Exhaustion and Depression

U.S. Quality of Employment Survey, 1972, Male Workers, Aged 20-65 (N = 911)[a]

Swedish Level of Living Survey, 1968 Employed Males, Aged 18-66 (N = 1,896)[b]

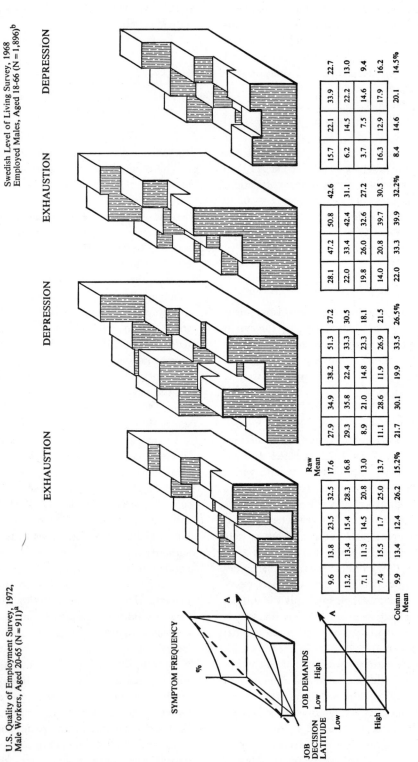

TABLE 2 *(concluded)*

	β coefficient	β coefficient	β coefficient	β coefficient
A. Regression estimates[c]				
1. Decision latitude	- .065***	- .150***	- .135***	- .117***
2. Demands	.150***	.118***	.159***	.143***
Regression estimates[c] (with interaction term)				
1. Decision latitude	- .004	- .109***	- .110***	- .009
2. Demands	.077*	.075*	.140***	.060**
3. Abs. diff. interaction term[e]	.111**	.066	.031	.137***
	S.R.R.	S.R.R.	S.R.R.	S.R.R.
B. Regression estimates (logit-0, 1 symp.)[d]				
1. Decision latitude	- 1.14	- 1.41**	- 1.30***	- 1.29*
2. Demands	1.57***	1.20*	1.46***	1.45***
C. Analysis of variance (log-linear-0, 1 symp.)				
1. Decision latitude		***	***	***
2. Demands	***	*	***	***
3. Interaction				

*p ≤ .05
**p ≤ .01
***p ≤ .001

[a] U.S. cell sizes, row by row: 73,58,34,40,76,67,52,46,56,80,55,48,27,71,60,68
[b] Swedish cell sizes, row by row: 89,163,65,287,449,144,81,146,144,43,101,184
[c] Using the full symptom scale without dichotomization
[d] Standardized Risk Ratio. This is the change in the odds of having the symptom for each standard deviation of the independent variable. This value can be determined by logistic regression, in which the dependent variable is the "logit" of the probability of the predicted event (log (p/ (1-p)), and the independent variables are in the form used in conventional linear regression (Morris and Rolph, 1978).
[e] See Appendix B for interaction term formulation.

TABLE 3 Test of the Job Strain Model with Reports of Dissatisfaction, Pill Consumption, and Sick Days

U.S. Quality of Employment Survey,
Employed Males, Aged 20-65 (N=911)[a]

Swedish Level of Living Survey,
Employed Males, Aged 18-66 (N=1,896)[b]

JOB DISSATISFACTION

				Raw Mean
40.9	26.3	42.9	55.3	39.8
21.6	19.7	12.5	27.3	20.3
9.4	11.3	23.5	23.9	16.2
18.5	10.9	14.3	13.8	13.7
Column Mean 24.1	16.5	21.6	27.5	22.0

LIFE DISSATISFACTION

19.7	10.5	14.3	29.3	18.1
6.4	5.9	9.4	15.2	8.6
1.8	2.4	1.8	6.3	2.9
7.1	4.3	3.3	1.5	2.5
9.4	5.4	6.4	11.3	8.0%

PILL CONSUMPTION
(Tranquilizers and Sleeping Pills)

4.5	9.8	13.9	9.2
4.9	5.2	13.9	6.5
1.2	3.4	7.6	4.6
2.3	6.9	8.7	7.3
4.0	6.0	10.4	6.7%

SICK DAYS
(5 or more days per year)

38.2	40.2	46.2	40.9
30.7	39.4	47.9	37.9
34.6	31.5	24.3	29.4
14.0	20.8	17.8	18.2
31.2	36.1	31.0	33.4%

SYMPTOM FREQUENCY

UNRESOLVED STRAIN A

ACTIVE-PASSIVE B

JOB DEMANDS

JOB DECISION LATITUDE — Low / High

closely approximate a "core" of generally correlated measurements of this type. This scale is
divided at approximately the quartile points
for use in Tables 2 and 3.

The Swedish intellectual discretion indicator was constructed from a measure of the skill
level required for the worker's job and his evaluation of the work as repetitious (lacking in
variety). We reason that repetitious work,
even if it once required skill, loses its capacity
for intellectual challenge after constant rehearsal. Indeed, the vast majority (79 percent)
of repetitious job responses were from workers
specifying that no formal training beyond elementary education was required for their job
(see also Gardell, 1971; Kohn and Schooler,
1973). Thus a repetitive, low-skill level job is
the lowest step on the intellectual discretion
measure. The other steps are, respectively: elementary skill level job (not repetitive); job requiring at least one year additional training;
job requiring at least three years additional
training.

It is certainly possible that a worker's personality affects his perception of decision latitude. Fortunately, the Swedish data provide
both self- and expert assessments of "intellectual discretion" to assess the magnitude of this
difference. Occupational evaluators at the
Swedish Central Statistical Bureau use a six-
level rating scheme to measure the "education
demanded, assigned, or expected of a particular occupation" (Carlsson et al., 1974, p. 387).
The Swedish self-reported intellectual discretion measure correlates highly with these expert ratings ($r = .69$ (1968); $r = .64$ (1974),
which corroborates other findings (Kohn &
Schooler, 1973, $r = .78$; Hackman & Lawler,
1971, $r = .87$ [average for autonomy and vari-
ety]; Gardell, 1971) and suggests that self-as-
sessments are a reasonably accurate measure of
job decision latitude.

JOB DEMANDS

The goal in constructing the scale of job demands is to measure the psychological stressors
involved in accomplishing the work load,
stressors related to unexpected tasks, and

stressors of job-related personal conflict. There
is no attempt in this article to measure the impact of physical job stressors, which may affect
the individual by other mechanisms than those
discussed here (and possibly lead to further
physiological strain, particularly for blue-
collar workers, Sundbom, 1971). Stressors
such as fear of unemployment or occupational
career problems might also contribute to these
measures, but Buck (1972) finds that the demands related to accomplishing the task are
the most commonly cited source of job pressure when a wide variety of potential sources
are reviewed.

There is much less research assessing the
congruence of self- and objective ratings for
job demands than there is for job decision latitude. A self-report of a "demanding" job on
the indicator probably will also express an element of subjective perception of stress (Lazarus, 1966). However, this subjective aspect
could lead to underestimating the job content
and mental strain associations: The social desirability of certain responses would probably
reduce reports of depression.

Questions about job demands in the U.S.
data clearly measure the pressure of output on
the job: "Does your job require you to work
very fast, hard, or to accomplish large amounts
of work? Are you short of time?" (see Appendix A). Seven items forming an acceptable
scale (Cronbach's $\alpha = .64$) were added together to construct a final index of psychological job demands. One confirmation of the construct validity of the scale is that it can be used
to discriminate occupations one would normally consider to be psychologically demanding using the U.S. Quality of Employment
Survey and the 1970 Census Occupational
Codes (Karasek, 1978a, p. 11). This scale is
divided at approximately the quartile points
for use in Tables 2 and 3.

The Swedish psychological job demands
indicator is a Guttman scale of responses to
questions about whether the job is hectic and
psychologically demanding (coefficient of re-
producibility = .94, coefficient of scalabil-
ity = .78; Karasek, 1976). Although task
pressures are probably the primary source of

the job demands measured here, the indicator is broad in coverage and cannot distinguish specific job demands. The content validity of the indicator is confirmed by the fact that it correlates with known job stressors such as piece rate work, lack of rest breaks, and anticipation of job loss. The indicator does not correlate highly with stressors from other spheres of life such as family problems or small-child care.

MENTAL STRAIN INDICATORS

The Swedish survey contains questions inspired by the American Health Survey of mental and physical well being. A set of indicators was drawn from both the U.S. and Swedish surveys roughly measuring mental strain symptoms. These items are similar to questions in the Gurin, Veroff, and Feld (1960) Mental Status Index and the Langner (1962) 22-item scale. Several findings have confirmed the usefulness of self-reports of mental health impairment (for a discussion of this literature, see Langner and Michael, 1963; Schwartz, Meyers, and Astrachan, 1973; Seiler, 1973). The scales were originally constructed to screen mental patients; however, Seiler (1973) concludes that the scales are best interpreted as measures of psychological strain.

The complete group of mental and physical illness symptoms available in both the U.S. and Swedish data is factor analyzed to avoid the possibility (suggested by Seiler, 1973) that our indicators also identify physical or psychosomatic ailments. We isolated two factors corresponding to two aspects of mental strain: exhaustion and depression. The exhaustion indicator is based on responses of tiredness in the morning and complete exhaustion in the evening. The depression indicator is constructed from responses of nervousness, anxiety, sleeping problems, worry, and depression (see Appendix A).

FINDINGS

Table 2 presents the findings from the test of the job strain model in two formats. In the upper portion, the percentage of workers with "severe" levels of depression or exhaustion is displayed as the vertical axis of a three-dimensional diagram. Psychological job demands and job decision latitude are the other two axes, as presented in Figure 1. In these diagrams, the dependent variable has been dichotomized (0,1). The percentages shown represent the probability that the worker with each specific combination of job demands and job decision latitude has experienced relatively severe exhaustion or depression ("often" have such a problem in the U.S. data).

Inspecting Table 2, we find that the symptom variations conform to the predictions of the job strain model for both countries. First, it is primarily workers with jobs simultaneously low in job decision latitude and high in job demands who report exhaustion after work, trouble awakening in the morning, depression, nervousness, anxiety, and insomnia or disturbed sleep. Second, the relation between job content and mental strain is similar for both Swedish and U.S. workers, using self-reported data.

Regression-based summary estimates of the job content and mental strain association are presented in Table 2, part B. The strength of the regression associations is presented in terms of "standardized risk ratios," a statistic commonly used in epidemiological studies of illness where the dependent variables are dichotomous (Rosenman et al., 1976; Morris & Rolph, 1978). The intuitive meaning of the ratio is the change in the odds of having the illness for each standard deviation change in the independent variable (a Standardized Risk Ratio of 1.42 implies a top-to-bottom decile difference in illness risk of 4:1). Translating the odds back into symptom percentages, depression in the United States ranged from 43 to 17 percent, decile-to-decile, while in Sweden it ranged from 30 to 11 percent. In the United States, exhaustion varied from 34 to 11 percent from the top to bottom deciles; in Sweden, it varied from 49 to 20 percent. Although the meaning of the symptom levels differs somewhat in the two national questionnaires, the general range of variation, and its association with job demands and job decision latitude, is remarkably similar when the two national samples are compared.

The three-dimensional diagrams based on the dichotomized dependent variables give an easily interpretable picture of the relationship between job content and mental strain, including interactions. It is also desirable to assess the interaction effects by statistical procedures, but this is difficult to do. The model proposes a specific mathematical form for the relationship, a "relative excess" interaction (Southwood, 1978), where job strain increases with the relative excess of demands over decision latitude. (This formulation is analogous to other theories of relative deprivation and conflict.) While this formulation clearly qualifies as a joint relationship or interaction according to Southwood's definition (1978, p. 1155), in many cases it is impossible to distinguish it empirically from a linear, additive relationship. A regression analysis to compare different mathematical interaction forms can be performed, but this really presumes a more precise theory and data than we have. Our theory is not yet sufficiently precise to warrant excluding related mathematical forms—such as a model based on the absolute value of difference. (Underestimation of interaction significance is also a problem; see Althauser, 1971.) On the other hand, the alternative statistical procedure used to test for the significance of interactions, analysis of variance, is too insensitive; it fails to give credit for deviations from linearity which display a particular pattern based on an ordinal level of the dependent variable.

In spite of these shortcomings, results of two such tests are presented in Table 2, parts A and C. The first test is a regression analysis with the interaction term added to the regression along with decision latitude and demands; the second is an analysis of variance adapted for a (0, 1) dependent variable (Bishop, Fienberg, & Holland, 1975). The interaction term for the regression analysis is an "absolute difference model," with a constant term chosen to give greater emphasis to problems of too many job demands and less emphasis to the problem of too much decision latitude (see Appendix B).

Table 2 shows that there is only moderate evidence for an interaction effect, understood as a departure from a linear, additive model. However, both the demands and the decision latitude regression terms are significant and of the appropriate sign to confirm an interactive "relative excess" model, which is the simplest statement of our theory. In addition, there is evidence of a nonlinear interaction for depression among Swedish workers (clearer evidence of interaction is available in Table 3).

Judgments about job characteristics by both workers and experts are possible only with the Swedish data base. The findings based on the objective ratings of job discretion are approximately the same as those based on the workers' own reports (Karasek, 1978a; see also Gardell, 1971). Thus, objective data suggest that the findings are not artifacts of the "perception" of control (Geer, Davison, & Gatchel, 1970) or due to self-reporting "bias." The hypothesis that the findings represented only biased reports by "strain-filled" workers about their jobs is also contradicted by the similarity of the findings for two countries (similarly industrialized), in spite of potential differences due to language and culture.

ALTERNATIVE STRAIN INDICATORS: ABSENTEEISM, PILL CONSUMPTION, AND JOB DISSATISFACTION

If the job strain model has general validity, it should predict a broad range of mental strain findings. The test below uses several alternative dependent variables. I examined the more "subjective" job satisfaction indicators, which have been shown to depend primarily on intrinsic job qualities (Kalleberg, 1977). Here the model clearly reveals interactive effects which may have clouded earlier linear, or unidimensional, analyses. A second set of alternative dependent variables offers more "objective" evidence that the work environment takes its toll on job-related behavior; the job strain model predicts both pill consumption and sick-day absences.

Swedish survey measures of behavior patterns allow us to test for "objective" evidence

of job strain. Table 3 displays data on tranquil-
izer and sleeping pill consumption in 1968,
and on the number of sick days taken in the
previous year. Findings for both the expert's
rating and the self-reported measure of job decision latitude reveal that jobs with low decision latitude and high demand are as strongly
associated with pill consumption and sick days
as they are with reports of mental strain.

The long tradition of equivocal findings
with variously defined job satisfaction indicators has given job satisfaction research an
equally equivocal reputation. Although the
ambiguity inherent in the job satisfaction indicators is difficult to avoid, the analysis in
Table 3 is based on two often-utilized scales:
one 10-item scale measuring job-related depression ("feel blue when thinking of job,"
I.S.R. scale, see Appendix A) and another 5-
item scale measuring attachment to the job
("Would you recommend it to a friend? Are
you planning to change jobs?" Kalleberg,
1977). The three-dimensional diagrams are
again utilized to show the joint effects of job
decision latitude and job demands on a combined indicator of severe dissatisfaction (dissatisfaction on at least two measures on either
scale).

It is evident from the diagrams in Table 3
that the overall relationships are quite complex
and the interaction terms in the regression
equation are highly significant (p always $\leq$
.001). Nevertheless, the results are consistent
with the job strain model. The job dissatisfaction indicator displays a strong increase (workers in the top job strain decile have six times
the dissatisfaction of workers in the bottom job
strain decile) in the same manner as the indicators of Table 2. A small secondary peak at *low*
job strain is also observable for the dissatisfaction indicator. A small percentage of jobs may
be too comfortable. While not directly predicted by our model, this finding of an unbal-
anced U-shaped relationship is consistent with
Selye's (1956) paradigm of stress adaptation:
Neither too much nor too little strain is good
for the organism. We would add that too
much strain is clearly worse than too little
(Naatanen, 1973).

The other obvious feature of the dissatisfaction distributions is the secondary peak for
"passive" jobs. This phenomenon is consistent
with the second prediction activity level
change, made by the model. Although the
mental strain symptoms showed no marked relation to "passive" work, the model proposed a
separate mechanism to govern the development of "active" and "passive" behavior patterns on the job. I hypothesize that "passive"
job content is also associated with job dissatisfaction. This conclusion is bolstered by the
strongly significant ($F \leq 7.9$) coefficient for an
interaction term which combines both job
strain and activity level effects (see Appendix
B). Although a full discussion of this mechanism is beyond the scope of this article, recent
research has bolstered the finding that behavior patterns in general are affected by the "active" or "passive" quality of the job (Karasek,
1976; Elden, 1977; Karasek, 1979; see also
Langer & Rodin, 1976). Thus, "active" or "passive" job content could quite plausibly be a
component of job-related feelings of satisfaction.

DISCUSSION

It was suggested that two major paradoxes
in job strain research might result from failure
to consider the joint interactive effects of job
demands and job decision latitude. First, misinterpretation of the true source of job strain
could occur when the contribution of either
job decision latitude or job demands is overlooked, or when these job characteristics,
which operate differently, are mixed indiscriminately. Second, "disappearance" could occur when the counteracting effects of job demands and job decision latitude cancel each
other out. "Disappearance" could also result
when generally applicable nonlinear or interactive findings vanish in small subpopulations
when the relationships are summarized line-
arly. This problem is especially important in
job satisfaction studies in light of the complex
relationships found in Table 3.

Ritti (1971) found a "paradox" in a test of

job demand indicators: an increase in one measure of job demands, time pressure, was associated with diminished satisfaction (misutilization); while an increase in another measure, intellectual demands, was associated with increased satisfaction. A further surprise was that the greatest satisfaction was associated with heavy time demands plus heavy intellectual demands.

The first finding is consistent with our model if, as we suggest, intellectual responsibility is treated as a measure of decision latitude and time pressure as a measure of job demands related to work load. Ritti's second finding is also consistent with the activity level mechanism of our model and our finding in Table 3: The highest satisfaction occurs with "active jobs," where both the challenge of high job demands and the opportunity for significant use of judgment and discretion are available.

Turner and Lawrence's (1965) findings illustrate a possible paradox of disappearance. Although some of their findings display a positive or a curvilinear relationship between job satisfaction and job decision latitude (measured as "responsibility," but recall its problems, p. 286) they conclude that no clear relationship exists. The findings presented in this article show that nonlinearities per se do not prevent a conclusion in support of a plausible model. Another Turner-and-Lawrence finding —a positive association between job decision latitude and job satisfaction existed only in rural areas— is contradicted by my tests controlling for urban or rural location with national population samples (Karasek, 1978a; Table 6). I find that the associations are at least as strong in urban areas. Turner and Lawrence's findings were based on 11 plants; the urban factories possibly represented an unusual subpopulation with restricted variance (located on the inflection point in the job strain curve).

Blood and Hulin (1967) and Hulin (1971, p. 166) fail to discriminate between job demands and job decision latitude. They contend that an absence of an increase in job satisfaction as job "level" (job decision latitude) increases is evidence of alienation from middle class values. However, their interpretation of alienation from the work ethic (Hulin & Blood, 1968, p. 49) and, in part, their criteria for identifying alienated workers, are based on increased satisfaction when job *demands* are reduced (Blood & Hulin, 1967, p. 268). Our model shows that for the vast majority of workers, lower work load demands are associated with increased satisfaction. The "work ethic" has always had its limitations. The failure to distinguish between job demands and job decision latitude, and failure to consider their counteracting results, may be responsible for the "paradox of disappearance" in the Hulin and Blood findings.

Hulin and Blood also find that rural workers display a strong job content/job satisfaction association, while urban blue-collar workers do not (corroborating Turner and Lawrence's results). Hulin and Blood further infer that the cause of this discrepancy is "urban alienation from middle class values," although they do not measure feelings of alienation directly. Recent studies controlling for attitudes and alienation (Shepard, 1970; White & Ruh, 1973) have found that these controls do not diminish content-job satisfaction findings. This finding, plus our finding that the association is as strong in urban areas as in rural areas, suggests that the Hulin and Blood conclusion is really the product of a special subpopulation and an inappropriate generalization of their findings. Hulin and Blood's policy implication that "job enrichment" strategies should not be recommended for low status, blue-collar urban workers is also not supported by secondary controls in our analysis (Karasek, 1978a; Table 6). Indeed, I conclude that this group is the one most affected by problems of strain and related feelings of dissatisfaction, and should be the focus of job redesign programs.

The last example of a contradiction that can be resolved refers to overall life satisfaction. Table 3 shows that life dissatisfaction is as strongly related to job characteristics as job dissatisfaction is. The relationship, predictable by the job strain model, is obviously nonlinear and has the characteristic interactions between job demand and job decision latitude variables ($p \leq .001$). This may explain the Andrews and Withey's "paradox of disappearance" (using a linear model and no interaction)—"job concerns show only a modest relationship . . . to satisfaction with life-as-a-whole" (1976, p. 129). The Andrews-and-Withey life-satisfaction measure is very similar to the one used here, and their analysis is based on a representative survey of the U.S. population ($N = 1,927$).

CONCLUSIONS

The job strain model predicts significant variations in mental strain. This prediction was borne out by nationally representative data for two industrialized countries, for a variety of mental strain symptoms, for a range of job content definitions, and for both expert and self-reported data.

An important implication of the job decision associations is that most working individuals in countries with advanced economies, such as the United States and Sweden, find that the "requirement" of using intellectual skill or making decisions represents an opportunity to exercise judgment. This enhances the individual's feelings of efficacy and ability to cope with the environment; it is not a source of stress. Table 2 demonstrates that the opportunity for a worker to use his skills and to make decisions about his work activity is associated with reduced symptoms at every level of job demands. We do not find, therefore, support for the belief that individuals "overburdened" with decisions face the most strain (Janis & Mann, 1977) in an industrialized economy. Literature lamenting the stressful burden of executive decision making misses the mark (for a fuller discussion of this literature, see Zaleznik, Kets de Vries, & Howard, 1977). Constraints on decision making, not decision making per se, are the major problem, and this problem affects not only executives but workers in low status jobs with little freedom for decision. Indeed, if we search the U.S. data for the most common occupation codes with high levels of job demands and low levels of job decision latitude, we find assembly workers, garment stitchers, freight-and-material handlers, nurse's aides and orderlies, and telephone operators. The working individual with few opportunities to make job decisions in the face of output pressure is most subject to job strain (Kerckhoff & Back, 1968).

Furthermore, both the satisfaction measures and the depression indicators show some covariation with the "activity level" of the job. That is, more "active" jobs are associated with satisfaction and reduced depression, even though they are more demanding. "Passive" jobs (with low demands as well as low decision latitude) are dissatisfying. Thus, our findings should not be interpreted as showing that the adverse effects of low job decision latitude are limited to workers with highly demanding jobs or even that such jobs should be changed by decreasing job demands (although this would appear at least to alleviate symptoms of mental strain). Related research findings suggest that employees with low decision latitude and low job demands face the different problem of passivity and apathy (for further discussion, see Karasek, 1976; Langer & Rodin, 1976; Elden, 1977; Karasek, 1979).

Possibly the most important implication of this study is that it may be possible to improve job-related mental health without sacrificing productivity. It would appear that job strain can be ameliorated by increasing decision latitude, independently of changes in work load demands. If, as would be expected, work load is related to organizational output levels, these levels could be kept constant if mental health "externalities" were improved. Changes in the administrative structure would have to be made which improve the worker's ability to make significant decisions about his task structure, increase his influence on organizational decisions, and allow him discretion over the use of his existing and potential skills.

These job design suggestions contradict major principles of job design as proposed by Frederick Taylor. For a promised increase in economic compensation (by no means always realized), the worker allowed management to assume tight control of job-related decisions. While it was claimed that increased output would come from elimination of "wasted effort and unnecessary decisions" the overall workload probably increased in many cases. Not only have Taylor's policies probably led to mental strain that was overlooked when these theories were advocated, but in some circumstances demoralization associated with these jobs may even cancel the presumed productivity benefits. Policy decisions to centralize decision-making and job design expertise are often assumed to lead to the technological progress and production reliability that are needed for economic efficiency. However, unless these important economic linkages are reexamined in light of the effects of psychosocial mechanisms, many potentially more humane and productive forms of work organizations may continue to be overlooked.

The findings of a secondary peak in the job content and dissatisfaction associations could also have policy significance. There is evidence that at high levels of job decision latitude, symptoms level out or even begin to increase with increasing decision latitude. This leads to the conclusion that job redesign strategies attempting to reduce strain in already comfortable jobs may reach a point of "diminishing returns" and in fact create problems. Elimination of unnecessary constraints on decision making for managerial jobs may be a desirable strategy to reduce job strain in specific instances, but a broad increase in decision responsibility for this group may only increase their strain. However, for the lowest status jobs the reduction of strain associated with increases in decision latitude is substantial. While the problem of job strain affects employees at all levels in the organization, the solution must certainly focus attention on the most oppressive jobs.

Given the fact that stress can be harmful to workers, both physically and psychologically, it is natural to consider ways of reducing stress. There are two basic approaches taken. The first is to reduce stress by providing individuals with various coping mechanisms. The second is to redesign the work environment to reduce or eliminate the source of the stress. In this reading, the coping approach is illustrated—but a surprising conclusion is drawn by those responsible for the stress-reduction program.

■ READING 41 ■

Managing Organizational Stress: A Field Experiment

Daniel C. Ganster and Bronston T. Mayes, *Department of Management, University of Nebraska–Lincoln*
Wesley E. Sime, *Stress Physiology Laboratory, University of Nebraska–Lincoln*
Gerald D. Tharp, *School of Life Sciences, University of Nebraska–Lincoln*

The growing body of literature concerning organizational stress, although still inconclusive, strongly suggests at least two conclusions. First, stress at work is a critical factor in the determination of employee health and well-being and also has important implications for organizational effectiveness. Occupational and workplace characteristics have been found to be directly related to mental ill health (e.g., Kasl, 1973; Kornhauser, 1965) and coronary heart disease (see, for example, Cooper & Marshall, 1976). The combined effects of such personal outcomes also represent serious costs to employing organizations. In 1963 cardiovascular diseases were estimated to account for 12 percent of lost working time in the United States, amounting to a total economic loss of $4 billion that year (Felton & Cole, 1963). In the United Kingdom, Aldridge (1970) has indicated that 22.8 million work days were lost

Source: *Journal of Applied Psychology*, 67(5), 1982, pp. 533–542. Copyright 1982 by the American Psychological Association. Reprinted by permission of the publisher and author.

in 1968 alone from mental disorders, nervousness, and migraine headaches.

Second, there is a critical need for research that rigorously evaluates the many potential strategies for managing organizational stress. It is the contention of Newman and Beehr (1979) that theirs is the only "comprehensive and critical review of both personal and organizational strategies for handling job stress" (p. 2). Based on our review of the literature, theirs is a contention with which we concur. The Newman and Beehr (1979) review addressed a wide range of stress management strategies, ranging from such techniques as meditation, diet, and exercise to organizational interventions in task design. For virtually all of these strategies, evaluations employed only subjective assessments of effectiveness made in settings lacking experimental controls. Newman and Beehr (1979) concluded:

> Perhaps the most glaring impression we received from the review was the lack of evaluative research in this domain. Most of the strategies re-

viewed were based on professional opinions and "related" research. Very few have been evaluated directly with any sort of scientific rigor. (p. 35)

The research reported in the present article is an attempt to begin to fill this void.

THE CHOICE OF A STRESS MANAGEMENT STRATEGY

We considered several criteria in choosing a stress management strategy. First, the potential strategy needed to be feasible given organizational and researcher resources. This criterion precluded the use of intervention programs that involve the extensive redesigning of organizational characteristics such as work-group composition, schedules, reporting relationships, and tasks. This is not to deny the potential utility of such interventions in removing stressors from the work environment. In fact, it might well be argued that changing jobs and organizations so that employees face fewer strain-inducing stimuli represents the most potent approach to dealing with stress.

Second, we sought a strategy that had a strong a priori probability of success. To assess this probability, we sought an intervention that was based on a solid theoretical and empirical foundation and at least had some evidence attesting to its usefulness in nonorganizational settings. Finally, we wanted to test a stress management strategy that had enough generality to be applicable in a wide range of different organizational settings, as opposed to one designed for a specific organizational situation (e.g., police work; see Sarason, Johnson, Berberich, & Siegel, 1979). The strategy chosen for the present study was judged consistent with these criteria.

The training program that was evaluated is based on the work of Ellis (1962) and on Meichenbaum's (1973, 1975) work in cognitive behavior modification, supplemented with progressive relaxation training. Although cognitive training programs have not been tested rigorously in organizational settings, a number of investigators have reported encouraging findings in the treatment of test anxiety

(Meichenbaum, 1972; Sarason, 1972; Wine, 1970). One case where such a program was tested in an organizational environment was reported by Sarason et al. (1979), who evaluated a program composed of cognitive and progressive relaxation training applied to police academy trainees. Although an experimental and control group design was used, the study was nevertheless beset with methodological flaws. Of major concern was the selection of criterion variables used to evaluate the program. Sarason et al. (1979) used one-item observer ratings of trainees' performance in simulated police activities. Experimental subjects were rated as better performers than controls on two of five such simulations. Furthermore, Sarason et al. reported that they were not certain that the performance raters were blind with regard to the subjects' group membership. In sum, the study did not produce convincing evidence that the training actually altered subjects' strain responses to job stressors.

Given the solid theoretical and empirical bases of cognitive and relaxation training and the lack of rigorous evaluations in organizational settings, it was deemed useful to attempt a test of such a program.

Specifically, it was hypothesized that treatment subjects would exhibit lower levels of (*a*) epinephrine, (*b*) norepinephrine, (*c*) anxiety, (*d*) depression, and (*e*) somatic complaints than no-treatment control subjects.

METHOD

Subjects

The study population consisted of all members of a public agency employing approximately 230 individuals. The agency is charged with delivering social services and benefits to clients in the community. Tasks involve determining eligibility for benefits, counseling, and the handling of emergency cases. Employees were polled previously by management and indicated a strong desire for assistance in managing stress in their jobs. Workers typically cited heavy work loads, inadequate resources, and the frequency of crisis situations as sources of stress on the job. The researchers recruited participants by conducting an informational seminar on stress which all employees were invited to attend. The seminar was conducted at the workplace during working hours and consisted of a presentation of information about job stress and its potential effect on people's health and well-being. The last half of the seminar (about 30 minutes) was devoted to explaining the proposed study and offering the training (free of charge) to the participants. Potential participants were told what they would be required to do if they volunteered for the training (e.g., fill out questionnaires, provide urine specimens, etc.), and that their involvement would last about six months. From the employee population, 79 individuals volunteered to participate. These 79 subjects were then given further briefing as to the study procedures. In order to randomly assign subjects to treatments, it was explained to subjects that demand for the treatment exceeded supply (see Cook & Campbell, 1976) and that the training would proceed at two times, one program starting two weeks from then, and another after three months. In order to ensure equity, subjects were instructed that a lottery would be used to determine who received the training first. The subjects accepted this condition as fair and reasonable, and all agreed to continue their participation.

The subjects were predominantly female (92 percent), averaged 39 years of age, had a mean education of 14.5 years, and had been employed in the agency an average of about four years. The organizational level of the participants ranged from secretary to director of the agency, and represented all the functions of the organization.

Design

The design of the study consisted of a true experiment (Cook & Campbell, 1976) with a treatment and control group and pre- and postmeasures on all criterion variables. In addition, the true experiment was supplemented with two quasi-experimental designs, one of which provided a replication of the treatment whereas the other constituted a four-month follow-up on the first treatment group. The study design is presented schematically in Table 1.

Criterion Variables

The dependent variables were chosen in order to represent three classes of strain responses: psychological, physiological, and somatic complaints.

Psychological strains. The psychological strain variables consisted of paper-and-pencil measures of anxiety, depression, and irritation. Anxiety was measured with the 20-item scale of Spielberger, Gorsuch, and Lushene (1970). Each item is accompanied by a four-point response format ranging from 1 (almost never) to 4 (almost always). Sample items are "I worry too much about things that really don't matter," and "I get in a state of tension or turmoil as I think over my recent concerns and interests." Reliability for the present sample was estimated at .92 (coefficient alpha).

TABLE 1   Study Design

Group	n	Assignment to Groups	Measurement Episode (October)	Eight-week Treatment Program	Measurement Episode (December)	Eight-week Treatment Program	Measurement Episode (April)
Treatment	40	Random	T_1	X	T_2		T_3
Control	39	Random	T_1		T_2	X	T_3

Note: T = time; X = exposure to treatment. All dependent variables were measured during each measurement episode.

A six-item measure developed by Cobb (Note 1) was used to measure depression. Like the anxiety scale, these items were followed by four-point response scales (sample items: "I feel sad"; "I feel depressed"). Reliability for the present sample was estimated at .81. Irritation was also measured with a three-item scale developed by Cobb (Note 1). This measure had the same response format as the anxiety and depression scales, and an estimated reliability of .80 (coefficient alpha).

Somatic Complaints. A 17-item scale assessing the frequency of a variety of somatic complaints was included in the questionnaire packet containing the anxiety, depression, and irritation scales. The items asked subjects to report the frequency, at work, of such complaints as migraine headaches, dizziness, nausea, sweating palms, and flushing of the face. Each item had a five-point response format ranging from 1 (never) to 5 (very often). The 17 items were averaged to yield a total score for somatic complaints. Despite the diversity of complaints sampled, the measure yielded a reliability estimate of .88.

Subjects completed the measures on the same day of the week at each of the three measurement waves of the study. Questionnaire administrations were conducted on site during working hours in groups containing experimental and control group subjects.

Physiological Strains. To provide measures of physiological strain at work, levels of the catecholamines—epinephrine and norepinephrine—were assessed from urine samples provided by subjects. The rationale for using the urinary catecholamines as indexes of strain is based upon the fact that they are crucial in the activation of the sympathetic nervous system during exposure to stressors. When a person is placed in a stressful situation, the body responds by engaging its "fight or flight" mechanism, which includes increased release of norepinephrine from the sympathetic nerve endings and epinephrine from the adrenal gland. These amine compounds elevate blood pressure, heart rate, and blood flow, and mobilize glucose and the fatty acids so as to pro-

vide increased energy for resistance to stress. Frankenhaeuser (1977) has been one of the major proponents for the use of the catecholamines in stress research.

Urine samples were collected from subjects at each of the three measurement waves of the study, under as controlled conditions as possible in a field setting. At each measurement wave, all urine samples were collected on the same day of the week for all subjects. Subjects were instructed to eat a normal breakfast on the day of urine collection, and to refrain from cigarette and caffeine consumption, if possible. All subjects arrived at work at approximately 8:00 A.M. and collected their urine throughout the morning hours at work until approximately 11:00 A.M. when samples were collected by the researchers. This procedure was followed for two reasons. First, we desired to have physiological indicants of subjects' strain response to a morning's exposure to their job. Second, in order to achieve a reliable determination of catecholamine excretion, one needs at least 90 minutes to get a specimen. Upon collection, 10 ml of each urine sample were acidified with 1 ml of 1 percent hydrochloric acid and frozen until assaying could be completed by the fourth author in his laboratory. Samples were assayed using the Bio-Rad Catecholamine by Column Test, a fluorometric technique that allows for differential analysis of epinephrine and norepinephrine. Levels are reported as micrograms/100 ml urine.

Treatment Program

The treatment consisted of a standardized group training program, and was conducted by a clinical psychologist who has had extensive experience in individual and group stress management programs. The present program consisted of eight two-hour group sessions, conducted for eight consecutive weeks during working hours in a training room provided by the organization.

The first four sessions involved teaching participants to recognize their own stress-inducing cognitions aroused when they encounter environmental stimuli. This cognitive restructuring procedure is based upon the rational-emotive therapy model of Ellis (1962) and is also similar to programs described by Meichenbaum (1973, 1975). It proceeds from several assumptions. First, it is assumed that organizational members encounter psychosocial stimuli in the workplace that behave as stressors. These stressors, in turn, may evoke a variety of psychological, physiological, and behavioral manifestations of strain. A second assumption is that the link between stressors and strains is mediated by cognitive processes ultimately under the control of the person. Lazarus (1968), for example, has argued that the degree to which a particular situation elicits an emotional response is largely a function of the person's cognitive appraisal of the situation. Sarason (1975) has also asserted that individuals under strain display a variety of self-defeating cognitions. Finally, it is assumed that such negative cognitive appraisals can be extinguished and supplanted by ones more adaptive to the person's functioning. In sum, participants were taught that much of their experienced strain (anxiety, tension, etc.) is caused by their cognitions ("self-talks"). This part of the treatment program, then, consisted of lectures and interactive discussions designed to help participants (a) recognize events at work and what cognitions they elicit; (b) become aware of the effects of such cognitions on their physiological and emotional responses; (c) systematically evaluate the objective consequences of events at work; and (d) replace self-defeating cognitions that unnecessarily arouse strain (e.g., "I'm an incompetent worker who cannot handle the workload") with more adaptive appraisals (e.g., "I handle this workload as well as anyone else," or "the workload is too high and I should approach my supervisor").

The last four sessions of the treatment were devoted primarily to muscle relaxation, using techniques adapted from Jacobson's (1938) program. Attention was focused on most of the major muscle groups, including hand and forearm flexors/extensors, upper arm flexors/extensors, foot and ankle flexors/extensors, abdominal group, paravertebral back extensors, pectoralis, rhomboids, neck flexors/extensors,

and facial muscles. During the initial sessions, biofeedback (using the galvanic skin response) was used to demonstrate the effects of stressful thoughts on physiology. Similar biofeedback techniques were used to demonstrate the calming effects of muscular relaxation on emotional and physiological responses. In addition, some session time was used to explain and demonstrate the impact of hyper- and hypoventilation, with instruction and practice in abdominal breathing.

In sum, the progressive relaxation and biofeedback training was used to reinforce and supplement the cognitive restructuring so that the whole program was an integrated approach to coping with stress.

RESULTS

Analysis of Experimental Design

The analyses of the data were conducted in several steps because of the mixed experimental and quasi-experimental properties of the design. The replication phase of the study is not a true experimental design because the second treatment group subjects served as their own controls. It is not appropriate to compare the two groups at Time 3 (T_3) because, for one, treatment and history effects are confounded at this point. For this reason, a multivariate analysis of variance with repeated measures is not an appropriate analytical method. However, the design at T_2 is a true experiment. Since multiple dependent variables were employed that were correlated to some extent, a multivariate analysis was deemed appropriate.

The first analysis consisted of a two-group discriminant analysis of T_1 data to provide a check on the efficacy of the randomization procedures. A stepwise inclusion criterion was used to maximize discrimination. The analysis indicated no significant discrimination between the groups; thus the randomization was judged to be adequate.

A second discriminant analysis was computed for T_2 data to provide a multivariate assessment of the treatment effects. In this case a significant discriminant function emerged (Wilks's lambda $= .91$, $p < .05$). The criterion variables with the highest discriminant function coefficients were epinephrine (.98) and irritation (.55). The centroid for the control group was .25, whereas the centroid for the treatment group was $-.38$, indicating that the treatment subjects displayed significantly lower levels of epinephrine and irritation.

Given the significant multivariate findings, a series of six univariate regressions were computed to further explore the data. Each dependent variable was used as the criterion in a multiple regression and was regressed on its T_1 value and group membership (coded as a dummy variable). These regressions constitute analyses of covariance (Cohen & Cohen, 1975) and provide greater precision in estimating experimental effects to the extent that T_1 and T_2 measures are correlated.

In two of the regressions, the group dummy variable contributed a significant increment to squared multiple correlation. In the case of epinephrine, group differences accounted for 7 percent of the variance. Epinephrine at T_1 was not a significant covariate. The other significant regression involved depression, where group differences accounted for 5 percent of the variance. Surprisingly, group membership did not account for a statistically significant amount of the variance in irritation. Hence, the findings of the regression analyses are somewhat at odds with those from the discriminant analysis regarding depression and irritation. Two factors could account for this apparent discrepancy. First, the discriminant analysis takes into account the correlations among the criterion variables. At T_2, depression and irritation are correlated .51; thus there is some redundancy in their discriminatory power. A second factor that may contribute to this discrepancy is that the variables differentially benefit from the covariance analyses. Depression at T_1 accounts for 53 percent of the variance of depression at T_2; thus a sizable portion of the variance is removed from the error term for the test of group differences. Irritation at T_1, however, accounts for only 27 percent of T_2 irritation variance, so irritation does not benefit as much from the covariance analysis. In both cases, however, the covariance

TABLE 2 Criterion Means and Standard Deviations by Group and Time

Variable	Time 1		Time 2		Time 3	
	Treatment ($n = 40$)	Control ($n = 39$)	Treatment ($n = 36$)	Control ($n = 34$)	Treatment ($n = 30$)	Control ($n = 31$)
Epinephrine						
M	1.53	1.52	.30	.51	.80	1.06
SD	1.57	1.49	.38	.53	.76	.83
Norepinephrine						
M	5.68	7.37	3.41	4.58	2.38	1.82
SD	5.41	6.52	3.43	5.72	3.31	3.13
Anxiety						
M	2.31	2.23	2.12(1.77)	2.21(1.86)	2.11	2.09
SD	.53	.38	.52	.34	.48	.51
Depression						
M	2.26	2.07	2.05(1.58)	2.16(1.80)	2.05	1.93
SD	.57	.39	.58	.40	.54	.44
Irritation						
M	2.12	2.06	1.97(.99)	2.20(1.12)	1.97	1.97
SD	.55	.44	.41	.45	.47	.52
Somatic complaints						
M	2.00	1.91	1.88(1.60)	1.94(1.16)	1.87	1.92
SD	.63	.58	.55	.61	.49	.57

Note: Covariance adjusted means at Time 2 are shown in parentheses. These are repeated only for those variables whose Time 1 values were significant ($p < .05$) covariates.

adjusted means are lower for the treatment group. Raw means for all variables are listed in Table 2, which also includes covariance adjusted means at T_2. Whether the treatment should be considered as having significant effects on either irritation or depression, or both, is left to the discretion of the reader. Our bias is to treat the discriminant analysis as an alpha protection measure, and to make interpretations of treatment effects from the covariance analyses. In either case, however, the treatment demonstrated a significant effect on epinephrine excretion.

Analysis of Four-Month Follow-Up

Whereas the results of the experimental design indicate that the treatment produced significant effects for at least epinephrine, T_3 data provide some indication of how long-lasting these effects are. As noted above, comparisons between groups at T_3 are uninterpretable. Thus comparisons were made between T_3, T_2, and T_1 for the original experimental group subjects. However, even these comparisons do not yield unambiguous conclusions because time effects are confounded with history effects. An inspection of the criterion means for both groups across different times (Table 2) indicates a very probable period effect for the catecholamines. There appears to be a rather dramatic drop in both epinephrine and norepinephrine from T_1 to T_2 for treatment and control subjects. This effect is not very alarming, however, since catecholamine levels are typically found to vary significantly across seasons

(Selye, 1976). Caplan, Cobb, French, Harrison, and Pinneau (1976) have also reported similar period effects for thyroid hormones. Although the existence of a period effect for catecholamines does not preclude the interpretation of the treatment effects for the true experimental design, it does render the follow-up analyses somewhat ambiguous. Nevertheless, correlated t tests were computed comparing T_3 with T_1 and T_2, and are listed in Table 3. Inspection of Table 3 reveals significant differences between T_1 and T_3 for epinephrine, norepinephrine, anxiety, and depression (column 1), and a significant increase in epinephrine between T_2 and T_3 (column 2). These results suggest that the treatment effect on epinephrine began to fade between T_2 and T_3, but did not regress to pretest levels. Similarly, there are no differences in levels of norepinephrine, anxiety, and depression between T_2 and T_3, but T_3 levels of these variables are significantly lower than at the pretest. Overall, these findings are consistent with the conclusion that the treatment effects do not regress to pretest levels after four months. Of course, one cannot be completely confident in this conclusion because of the confounding of history (seasonal) and time effects in this phase of the study.

DISCUSSION

This article reports the evaluation of a stress management training program in an organizational setting. Before discussing the findings,

TABLE 3 Within-Group Contrasts across Times (T)

Variable	Follow-Up Comparisons on Treatment Group		Replication Comparisons on Control Group	
	T_1–T_3	T_2–T_3	T_1–T_3	T_2–T_3
Epinephrine	2.13*	−4.92†	1.74	−3.60†
Norepinephrine	2.75*	1.94	3.15	3.46†
Anxiety	3.45†	.75	2.58*	2.02
Depression	2.52*	−.14	2.11*	3.61†
Irritation	1.36	0	.95	2.30*
Somatic complaints	1.71	.12	−.09	.22

Note: Within-group contrasts are correlated t ratios. * $p < .05$. † $p < .01$.

several features of the study design should be noted.

Internal Validity

First, the treatment itself was tested with a true experimental design. Consequently all the typical threats to internal validity were controlled. However, a few internal validity threats are worthy of discussion. Cook and Campbell (1976) noted that "resentful demoralization of respondents receiving less desirable treatments" (p. 229) may lead to spurious differences between groups. In the present study, all subjects volunteered for, and presumably desired, the stress management training. However, half of them were denied the treatment until a later time. If resentful demoralization produced a spurious treatment effect, these control subjects should have exhibited significant increases in strain responses. There is no evidence at T_2 that this was the case. In addition, the randomization procedures were carefully explained to all subjects in advance, and they appeared genuinely accepting of these conditions. Furthermore, one would expect a differential experimental mortality rate for control subjects under conditions of resentful demoralization. Again, this was not found to be the case. Another general threat to internal validity that might produce spurious treatment effects is the operation of demand characteristics (Fromkin & Streufert, 1976). For instance, there is every reason to expect that the general hypothesis of the experiment was completely transparent to all the participants. Although we do not feel that the "good subject" effect is very likely in the present case, one cannot, for certain, rule out such an effect on the questionnaire criterion variables. However, the strongest treatment effect was found for the epinephrine measure, and it seems highly implausible that subjects altered their rate of urinary catecholamine excretion in order to confirm the hypothesis.

On the other hand, Cook and Campbell (1976) described three validity threats that can have the effect of equalizing treatment and control groups. In the present study, the most probable of these is that the treatment was diffused to or imitated by the control subjects. Although treatment subjects were asked not to talk about the training to their co-workers, some of whom were control subjects, it is safe to assume that some of them probably did. However, it is highly unlikely, given the nature of the training, that such discussion would actually constitute diffusion of the treatment. In any event, the treatment did produce some significant effects.

External and Construct Validity

Whereas internal validity might be regarded as the sine qua non of experimental research, in the present case the issues of construct and external validity are particularly salient because of the applied nature of the research. Each of these issues is discussed in turn.

Cook and Campbell (1976) described both "construct validity of the cause" and "construct validity of the effect" (pp. 238–241). Taking the latter first, the effect construct is employee strain and was operationalized with multiple methods (catecholamines, anxiety, depression, irritation, and somatic complaints). Aside from the apparent face validity of the psychological and health measures as indicants of strain, they have been empirically linked to a variety of organizational stressors in a diverse national sample (Caplan et al., 1975). Evidence for the validity of the catecholamines as indicants of strain comes from experimental research in both laboratory and field settings. The extensive laboratory work of Frankenhaeuser clearly demonstrated that epinephrine and norepinephrine excretion can be manipulated with a variety of psychosocial and task stressors (see, for example, Frankenhaeuser, 1977). In addition, Timio and Gentili (1976) found the same types of effects in a field experiment where workers were randomly assigned to piece work and salary pay systems in a fully balanced repeated measures design. Finally, the catecholamines take on added practical significance in light of Selye's (1976) conclusion that "it is now generally accepted that a stress-induced excess of corticoids or catecholamines does play a role in the development of many diseases" (p. 725). In short, we feel that the criteria used in the present study represent meaningful and valid dimensions of employee strain. An external validity issue concerns the nature of the study population. There is no way to determine if the responses of this particular nonrandom and mostly female sample are typical of those that might be exhibited by employees in other organizational contexts. Although we know of no strong a priori reason why they should be considered atypical, more replications with different trainers are needed before we can become confident in the utility of such stress management programs.

CONCLUSION

In light of the above discussion, it appears that a stress management training program involving cognitive restructuring and progressive relaxation can produce a statistically significant reduction in employee strain at work. In addition, the replication and follow-up phases of the study, although yielding data of a weaker inferential nature, suggest that the treatment effects are not completely spurious or ephemeral in nature.

In spite of the somewhat favorable findings of the present evaluation experiment, however, we are reluctant to advocate the enthusiastic adoption of such stress management interventions for several reasons. First of all, there is a plethora of commercially available seminars and training programs for stress management offered by consulting firms. Many of these interventions consist of discussions or lectures lasting from as little as two or three hours to two days. The program described in this study consisted of 16 hours of exposure distributed over 8 weeks. Whereas the treatment effects for epinephrine excretion, and perhaps depression and irritation, are statistically significant, the effect sizes are not dramatic. Our hunch is that this amount of training is close to the minumum required to produce reliable changes in employee strain. In addition, the present trainer was a clinical psychologist with much experience in cognitive therapy techniques who was assisted by an exercise and stress physiologist for the relaxation training. The efficacy of such a program when implemented by less specialized management consultants is unknown.

Finally, we would argue that there are ethical and empirical reasons for *not* choosing to implement such a stress management intervention. The present program is one that attempts to alter the reactions of employees to presumed noxious and stressful organizational, task, and role characteristics. In this sense it represents an inoculation approach, and does not, in fact, remove objective stressors from the employee's organizational environment. Training employees to better tolerate poorly designed organizations would seem to be a less desirable strategy than one that attempts to make the organization inherently less stressful. In this regard we tend to concur with the opinions recently espoused by Shore (1980; Note 2). Empirically, the field experiment of Timio and Gentili (1976) demonstrates that just the manipulation of pay systems (piecework versus salary) for assembly line workers produces much larger effects on catecholamines than are reported in the present article. This could be considered as further justification for giving the highest priority to making organizational changes in order to deal with employee stress.

In conclusion, the greatest value of stress management programs like that evaluated in the present study may well be as supplements to organizational change programs. After all, some stressors may be imposed by the external environment and may not be under the control of management. Tax accountants will be exposed to deadline pressures every April no matter how their employing organization is designed (Friedman, Rosenman, & Carrol, 1958). Perhaps this is the proper perspective to maintain when considering the implementation of such stress management programs.

SECTION THIRTEEN

Work Schedules

In a discussion of environmental sources of stress, it is common to discuss temperature, noise, and work pace. Another potent variable for consideration is work schedule. When you report to work and leave work can have a substantial effect on all other aspects of your life. The most dramatic example of this effect is seen in shiftwork, either fixed or rotating. Consider the worker on the 3-to-11 shift. She goes to work at 2:30 P.M. before the kids are home from school. She comes home at 11:30 P.M. after the kids (and friends and neighbors and maybe even spouse) are asleep. She is keyed up after a day of work and she is no more ready to get into bed than her day shift counterpart would be at 3:30 P.M. As a result, she stays up and does things around the house, watches some TV, and so forth. Finally, at 6:00 A.M., she is tired and goes to bed. The kids get up at 6:30 and are off to school before she arises. When she gets up her spouse is gone, her friends are at work, and the neighbors are busy with their housework.

The example above is of a fixed shift pattern. Consider, now, the more extensive consequences of moving from afternoon, to night, to day shift every three days or every week. In this section we will consider some of the consequences of shiftwork as well as a more positive intervention that reduces some of the stressful aspects of work schedule.

There is little doubt that shiftwork can be debilitating. In fixed shift operations, particular attention is paid to the night shift. It is assumed that the night shift requires the greatest adaptation in personal scheduling and various biological and psychological rhythms. Some research, however, has indicated that night shiftwork might not be as debilitating as originally thought. In this paper, Frese and Okonek describe some of the effects of long-term night shiftwork as well as some subtle issues in the measurement of these effects that tend to obscure the effects of this work schedule.

■ READING 42 ■

Reasons to Leave Shiftwork and Psychological and Psychosomatic Complaints of Former Shiftworkers

Michael Frese, *University of Pennsylvania*
Klaus Okonek, *Bundesgesundheitsamt, Berlin, Federal Republic of Germany*

In the literature on the relation between health and night- and shiftwork, one often finds the paradoxical result that shiftworkers show fewer health complaints than do non-shiftworkers. It is known from longitudinal studies that shiftworkers are a select group (e.g., Angersbach et al., 1980; Meers, Maasen, & Verhaegen, 1978). Therefore, many studies have investigated the health of those who have once worked in shifts but are now working during the daytime (Aanonson, 1964; Angersbach et al., 1980; Koller, Kundi, & Cervinka, 1978; Taylor & Pocock, 1972). The assumption is that these former shiftworkers have left shiftwork because they were not able to adapt to shiftwork. Therefore, one would expect that this group would show the highest degree of ill health. This appears to

be true in most of the studies (Aanonson, 1959; Koller et al., 1978; Angersbach et al., 1980), but there are important exceptions (e.g., Taylor & Pocock, 1972).

There is, of course, more than one reason to leave shiftwork, for example, personal ones (like changing jobs or location), occupational ones (like better chances of advancement), social ones (e.g., better chances to participate in social events), and, finally, health ones. If one lumps all these groups together on the assumption that they all left shiftwork because of health reasons, one may underestimate the health problems of the group that truly stopped working shifts because of health reasons. Because health problems are the target of this article, we will differentiate between workers who left shiftwork for health reasons versus those who left for other reasons.

Besides this methodological reason for differentiating between these groups, there is a substantive reason as well. The reason why former shiftworkers have been included in

Source: *Journal of Applied Psychology*, 69(3), 1984, pp. 509–514. Copyright 1984 by the American Psychological Association. Reprinted by permission of the publisher and author.

cross-sectional studies on night- and shiftwork has been to rule out plausible alternative causal hypotheses for the above-mentioned paradoxical results in this field (the selection problem). Therefore, differentiating between those who left shiftwork for health reasons and those who had other reasons for leaving shiftwork helps us to decide among possible causal hypotheses even in cross-sectional studies. This article examines three conceptualizations on the relationship between night- and shiftwork and ill health. They are as follows: (a) shiftwork has a direct negative effect on health; (b) the shiftworkers' ill health is a result of constitutional weakness; and (c) a combination of these viewpoints into a vulnerability-stress model.

METHOD

Sample

The sample of former shiftworkers was part of a larger study on the effects of shiftwork. A scientific study group for the chemical labor unions in the Federal Republic of Germany arranged for the distribution of questionnaires in 24 factories that were selected from 69 companies whose local labor union chapters had expressed a willingness to participate in the study. They are representative of the areas in which the labor union "Industriegewerkschaft Chemie, Papier, Keramik" operates. A random sample was not feasible because only labor union members could have been included, and it would have been impossible to specifically approach former shiftworkers. Therefore, shop stewards distributed consent forms to qualified native German blue- and white-collar workers. Their instruction was to make a special effort to approach former shiftworkers and workers who do not belong to the labor union. Workers who returned the consent forms received the questionnaire which they were asked to return anonymously to the local labor union in a closed envelope. Each factory was allotted a certain number of consent forms so that 15 percent of all the shiftworkers and 5 percent of the nonshiftworkers were sampled. The minimum number of consent forms distributed to each factory was 100. This led to an oversampling in the smaller factories.

Of those who received the questionnaire, an average of 61.5 percent returned it (total $N = 5,448$, former shiftworkers $N = 764$). The return rate was the same for shiftworkers and for nonshiftworkers. The return rate ranged from 27 percent to 100 percent across the different factories. As is true of other research in the applied area, it is difficult to estimate the "real" refusal rate, because workers could refuse to sign the consent form. Thus, we could only ascertain the rate of people who did not return a completed questionnaire after they had signed the consent form. In order to keep cultural, social, and workplace influences equal, the following steps were taken to homogenize the sample for this report: White-collar employees and women were excluded. Furthermore, only former shiftworkers were included who had previously worked nights. This reduced the sample of former shiftworkers to 261. Slight additional reductions of the sample size arise in the analyses because of missing data.

Three groups of former shiftworkers were determined by the answer to the question whether they had left shiftwork for health reasons. Those who said that this was *very true* or *predominantly true* are considered members of the "former shiftworkers due to health reasons" (abbreviated HR; $N = 122$); those who answered *not at all true* or *a little true* are members of the "former shiftworkers for other reasons" (OR; $N = 36$); and those who checked the middle category (*is partly true*) are called "middle group" (MR; $N = 43$).

Instruments

All of the scales have been tested in pilot studies (Projekt Schichtarbeit, 1980). The items typically have a five-point answer scale and an equidistant item format (taken from Rohrmann, 1978) was used to insure interval scaling.

The following scales were used: (a) Environmental stress (10 items, developed by Semmer, 1982, e.g., "How much are you stressed by noise on your workplace?"), Cronbach's Alpha = 84; (b) psychological stress (Semmer, 1982, six items, e.g., "How often are you under time pressure in your work?"), Alpha = .80; (c) psychosomatic complaints, nine items, e.g., "Do you have headaches?"), Alpha = .84; this is a short form of the "Freiburger Beschwerdeliste" by Fahrenberg (1975)

(slightly adapted by Mohr, 1984); it is similar to English scales of somatic complaints like the one used by Caplan, Cobb, French, Harrison, & Pinneau, 1975; (d) irritation/strain (Mohr, 1984, four items, e.g., "Are you rather nervous when you come home tired from work?"), Alpha = .88; (e) a summation index on health complaints of the last two years (10 items,

TABLE 1 Differences between the Three Groups of Former Shiftworkers

Variable	Mean or Percentage			F or x^2
	HR	MR	OR	
1. Demographic variables				
Age (years)	45.2	39.2	40.6	$F(2,252) = 9.63§$
Unemployment (yes)	1%	7%	7%	$x(2, N = 253) = 6.14‡$
Membership in labor union				$x^2(4, N = 257) = .70$
Function in labor union	35%	32%	38%	
Member without function	57%	57%	55%	
Not member	8%	11%	7%	
Return rate				$x^2(2, N = \quad) = .11$
Low	55%	52%	55%	
High	45%	48%	45%	
How long shiftwork (years)	10.43	6.42	6.31	$F(2,252) = 11.20§$
How long ago stopped shiftwork (years)	9.85	8.68	10.54	$F(2,251) = .80$
2. Skills				
How much skill necessary in present job*	3.52	3.72	3.83	$F(2,254) = 3.59‡$
Length of on the job training (Median; present job)	4.27	6.75	5.85	$x^2(16, N = 257) = 24.2$
Formal skills				$x^2(2, N = 258) = 8.83‡$
Semiskilled	56%	35%	39%	
Skilled	44%	65%	61%	
3. Ill Health				
Psychosomatic complaints*	2.68	2.42	2.03	$F(2,249) = 15.46§$
Irritation/strain*	2.92	2.85	2.06	$F(2,249) = 13.11§$
Health complaints of last two years†	3.30	3.14	2.51	$F(2,255) = 6.38$
4. Stress at present workplace				
Environment*	2.65	2.70	2.66	$F(2,237) = .07$
Psychological*	3.45	3.48	3.51	$F(2,254) = .26$
5. Reasons for leaving shiftwork				
More time for family*	3.01	3.83	2.63	$F(2,243) = 7.61§$
Better leisure time possibilities*	3.04	3.77	2.90	$F(2,244) = 4.04§$
Could not adjust to the constant changes in shifts*	3.43	3.74	2.26	$F(2,245) = 24.36§$
Wanted to work in my occupation*	1.55	2.74	1.88	$F(2,241) = 5.8§$
Better chances to advance*	1.61	2.08	2.19	$F(2,241) = 5.92§$
More interesting work*	2.83	3.31	3.41	$F(2,244) = 1.70$
Better possibilities to further education*	2.13	2.56	2.37	$F(2,243) = 1.64$
Reasons related to company policy*	1.85	2.47	2.52	$F(2,245) = 5.0§$
Physician counselled change (yes)	75%	21%	4%	$x(2, N = 253) = 116.4§$
Would go back to shiftwork				$x(4, N = 253) = 10.67‡$
In any case	5%	2%	6%	
Only if I had no other choice	29%	48%	49%	
In no case	66%	50%	45%	

Note: HR = former shiftworkers due to health reasons; MR = middle group; OR = former shfitworkers for other reasons.
*Five-step scale.
†Summation index, lowest = 1, highest = 9.
‡$p<.05$. §$p<.01$.

e.g., "I had an illness in the stomach or bowels within the last two years"; Mohr, 1984). All of the other variables relating to reasons for entering and leaving shiftwork, improvements after leaving shiftwork, skills, and type of shiftwork system are single items (see Table 1).

RESULTS AND DISCUSSION

Health Differences

The means and one-way analyses of variance (ANOVAS) of health complaints are given in Table 1. On all three indicators of ill health —psychosomatic complaints, irritation/ strain, and health complaints of the last 2 years —the group HR shows the highest values. This is similar to the results reported by Aanonson (1964). The results suggest that studies that do not differentiate between different groups of former shiftworkers along the variable "leaving for health reasons" tend to underestimate the true situation of the relevant group of former shiftworkers: the ones who really left because of health reasons.

Other Differences

Although the three groups do not differ in regard to the reasons for going into shiftwork, their reasons for leaving shiftwork are clearly different (as displayed in Table 1). The MR and the OR group gave mainly positive reasons that attracted them to day work (like better chances to advance), whereas the HR workers left shiftwork because of medical and adjustment reasons and because they were counselled to do so. The HR group is also less well skilled than the other two groups. It is interesting that the HR workers were less often unemployed than the other two groups. In addition, the HR group spent about 10 years in shiftwork, whereas the other two groups worked only an average of six years in shifts. However, there are no significant differences in the time span since they had left shiftwork. Thus, it appears that the OR and MR groups are more highly skilled, have positive reasons to leave shiftwork, and leave it much earlier than is true for HR. Furthermore they seem to risk unemployment more readily.

The Vulnerability-Stress Model

With regard to conceptualizations of the relationship between night- and shiftwork and ill health, the results given so far could be interpreted as being consistent with the hypothesis that shiftworkers become sicker the longer they work in shifts. However, the correlations between years of shiftwork and current ill health are essentially zero for all former shiftworkers and for each of the three subgroups. Furthermore, there are no significant correlations between the question "How long ago did you stop working shifts" and ill health. A reasonable interpretation is that HR workers have worked nights and shifts up to their biological/psychological breaking point (vulnerability-stress model). Some break down earlier, some later. Once this breaking point is reached there are strong signs of ill health, which persist even after shiftwork is abandoned. Why do the shiftworkers stay up to this point? The most important reason given by nearly all the workers for going into shiftwork is the financial one, although the three groups do not differ significantly for the respective item. Apparently, financial incentives lead one to persist in shiftwork as long as one does not have adequate alternatives. Because of their higher skills, special circumstances (e.g., changes in the company), and greater willingness to risk unemployment, the OR workers conceive of and have more alternatives to shiftwork and therefore change to day work earlier, in contrast to the HR members, who stay in shiftwork until the physician warns them to leave. Thus, the OR workers do not typically approach their breaking point. It is obvious from the data in Table 1 that this reasoning is more clearly substantiated for the two extreme groups than for the MR group, which has high skills and unemployment on the one hand and relatively high ill health on the other.

The conceptualization that ill health is only

due to constitutional weakness does not seem to be a viable alternative. Shiftworkers in at least the larger West German corporations are usually medically screened before becoming employed. Thus, the more healthy workers are already selected. Nevertheless, shiftworkers show signs of ill health similar to the HR group (Frese, 1983). Furthermore, the constitutional weakness model cannot readily explain the higher skill and unemployment level in OR and the long time the HR group has worked in shifts (up to 29 years). Therefore, the vulnerability-stress model accounts better for the data.

Problems of Interpretation

Two possible objections still have to be dealt with that relate to sampling problems and to questionnaire research on ill health. One would argue that having shop stewards distribute questionnaires or consent forms leads to sampling problems. Two kinds of difficulties might arise: Workers who want to influence the public or the labor union could be more motivated to participate and would

therefore be overrepresented in the sample, or shop stewards' selection of subjects could lead to biased results. It is not completely possible to rule out these potential problems. It seems likely that they should lead to differences between active labor union participants, passive members, or nonmembers. One would assume that active members paint a bleaker picture of the situation of shiftworkers in accordance with the labor union policy in order to convince the public that their situation needs special attention. Furthermore, the return rate of a certain factory could be affected by the way shop stewards have approached potential participants of this study.

It is possible to study the effect of these variables in this study. Additionally it seems useful to control for stress in the present job and for age. Therefore a three-way analysis of covariance was run with the following variables (the sums of squares were adjusted for all other effects because of unequal Ns in the cells): groups of former shiftworkers, membership in the labor union, and return rate (with two levels of return rate, higher than 70 percent and lower than 70 percent). Age and environmental

FIGURE 1   Interaction of Union Membership and Groups of Former Shiftworkers

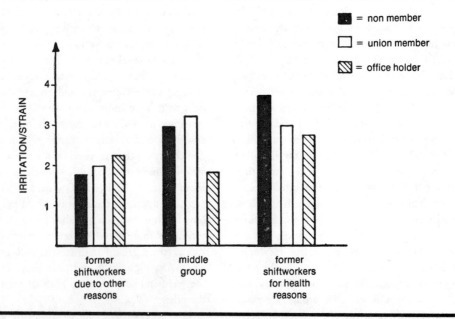

and psychological stress were employed as control variables. The variables denoting membership in the labor union and return rate do not show any significant main effects. There are significant main effects of the variable denoting groups of former shiftworkers on irritation/strain, $F(2, 209) = 9.09$, $p < .01$, and psychosomatic complaints, $F(2, 209) = 6.66$, $p < .01$. Thus the results of the one-way ANOVAS shown in Table 1 are reproduced for two of the health measures, irritation/strain and psychosomatic complaints, but not for the variable health complaints of last two years. Additionally, there are some unexpected significant interaction effects of the variables denoting groups of former shiftworkers and membership in the labor union on irritation/strain, $F(4, 209) = 3.18$, $p < .05$, and on psychosomatic complaints, $F(4, 209) = 2.41$, $p = .05$. However, in no case do the results lend support to the interpretation that persons active in the labor union show a higher level of ill health or that HR workers who are active in the labor union show higher ill health (compare the example displayed in Figure 1). In all, the potentially confounding effects do not seem to account for the differences in irritation/strain and psychosomatic complaints between the different groups of former shiftworkers.

The second objection is that questionnaires measure health complaints but do not adequately measure existing physiological and psychological disturbance: the HR group consists primarily of "lamenting" persons, who report more ill health or reconstruct the reasons for their leaving shiftwork in this light. It is not possible to extensively deal with this argument here, but this interpretation would also suggest that there are differences between the groups on reported stress in the present job. This is not the case (cf. Table 1). Furthermore, the strong correlations of the reported physician's advice to leave shiftwork with the indexes of ill health bolster this interpretation because it is unlikely that the physician was completely dependent on "lamenting" for his or her advice. The point biserial correlations (rs) are .39 ($N = 247$, $p < .001$) with psychosomatic complaints, .33 ($N = 247$, $p < .001$) with irritation strain, and .29 ($N = 253$, $p < .001$) with health complaints of the last two years. Finally, Meltzer and Hochstim (1970) have shown that there is a larger number of false negatives than false positives in questionnaire answers, that is, more people will underestimate their ill health than will overestimate it in comparison to medical ratings.

In summary, it is profitable to differentiate between different groups of former shiftworkers so that the true situation of the relevant group of former shiftworkers — the ones who left because of health reasons — is not underestimated. The recommendation is, therefore, to routinely differentiate between these groups in future research. Furthermore, the differences between the three groups of former shiftworkers are compatible with the hypothesis that the HR group is less skilled and takes fewer risks of unemployment and therefore stays longer in jobs with night- and shiftwork. Thus, they may come to the breaking point, where the physician has to advise them to leave shiftwork.

Although fixed shifts can have negative effects on workers, rotating shifts seem to be even more problematic. The dilemma is that certain manufacturing, process, and service functions are 24-hour operations. If that is the case, the problem changes from one of eliminating afternoon and night shifts completely to one of identifying the least harmful method for introducing and maintaining shiftwork schedules. In this paper, Wolinsky describes a successful intervention in the mining industry that seemed to reduce the harmful effects of rotating shifts.

■ READING 43 ■

Beat the Clock
Efforts to Limit Damage from Night- , Shiftwork are Slowed by Economy

Joan Wolinsky

The war between the forces of light and darkness, a fantasy limited to storybooks and movies for most of us, is all too real for millions of Americans who report to work when the rest of us turn in for the night, or whose work schedule changes frequently. And their health is often a casualty of that battle.

Recent studies have shown that workers on the night and rotating shifts have a higher incidence of stomach and sleep disorders, cardiovascular disease, marital discord, and poorer work performance. Often they feel socially isolated from friends and family, are irritable, and are plagued by fatigue.

That gloomy picture is of concern to a number of psychologists and other scientists, who are combining their knowledge of performance, sleep, and biological clocks to evaluate and perhaps alleviate the psychological and physiological effects of a rotating or night shift.

Researchers at The Center for the Design of Industrial Schedules in Boston, for example, have applied chronobiological interventions at a Utah potash mine, claiming that production and worker satisfaction climbed significantly. It was the first time knowledge of biological clocks was put to use in an industrial setting, said the researchers.

Meanwhile, a sleep center at the Illinois Institute of Technology (IIT) has recently completed a comprehensive survey to measure the impact of varying work schedules on the health and performance of shiftworkers.

As a result of the study's findings, psychologist Donald I. Tepas, director of the project, concludes that workers on the night shift suffer from chronic sleep deprivation primarily because they are lured by the demands of our day-oriented society. In response, he has devised some behavioral interventions to improve the sleep of workers on the graveyard or rotating turn.

The issue of shiftwork has become important to more workers with the recent explosion in round-the-clock computer operations.

Source: *Monitor, 13,* 1982, pp. 28–29.

Night and rotating employment have grown to the point where they affect not only the blue-collar or service industry worker but also the white-collar employee, sleep experts say.

Yet with the flagging economy and an administration that favors the deregulation of the rules governing the workplace, scientists and union officials indicate that, for the time being most interventions to help the shiftworker will remain on paper.

Much of what is known today about the hazards or benefits of shiftwork is culled from relatively recent discoveries in Europe and Japan. In the last decade, for example, scientists have discovered that many physiological functions in humans, such as body temperature, urinary output, and blood pressure, are regulated by an internal biological clock, or circadian rhythm.

Until recently, most psychologists interested in work-sleep schedules have focused their attention on performance research, according to noted sleep researcher and psychologist Wilse Webb of the University of Florida. However, the study of work-sleep schedules has matured to the point where it must take into account work on biological rhythms, sleep, and performance, he added.

DIGGING FOR DATA

A team of scientists from the Center for the Design of Industrial Schedules, including psychologist John Coleman from Stanford University, conducted an experiment at the Utah potash mine to learn if the application of chronobiological principles to a work setting could improve worker productivity, health, and job satisfaction.

At the experiment site, the Great Salt Lake Minerals & Chemical Corp., the researchers divided 85 rotating shiftworkers into two groups whose schedule each week jumped from night to evening to daytime duty. In both groups, workers reversed the direction of their shifts, while the second group also extended its schedule from a week to 21 days. These groups were compared with a control group of 68 nonrotating day and evening shiftworkers with comparable jobs.

The reversed schedule is more compatible with the body's internal clock, explained Charles A. Czeisler, the center's director, which actually operates on a 25-hour cycle. Although humans reset their clocks to the earth's 24-hour light-dark cycle without too much trouble, they cannot adjust well to any further compression of the day, which occurred when the subjects adhered to the original schedule sequence.

Lengthening the cycle of the shift in the second group gave workers more time to adapt to the new sleep-wake cycle, Czeisler said, a process which usually takes as long as a week. Complaints among these workers that the schedule changed too rapidly dropped significantly after this longer schedule was imposed, the study reported.

Several months after the introduction of these interventions, the researchers reported ". . . a substantial increase on the schedule satisfaction index, improvements in the health index, and a reduction in personnel turnover. At the same time, the rate of potash harvesting . . . increased and the increases in productivity were maintained in the harvest season which followed the completion of our study period." Those on the 21-day schedule led the two other groups in all these categories.

But those on a permanent night turn may also lack a regulated cycle since many workers revert to a daytime schedule on days off, most sleep specialists agree. Such irregular cycles can result in a sleep timing disorder in which the worker has difficulty falling asleep and waking up at the prescribed times. Although no one knows the long-term effects of this permanent "jet lag," haphazard sleep-wake cycles have been blamed for producing digestive disorders, fatigue, and poor performance resulting in serious safety hazards, Czeisler noted.

Some psychologists, however, believe that social and personal factors play a role at least equally important to the circadian cycle in the sleep habits of shiftworkers. While most of the research on sleep and the circadian cycle is confined to the artificial environment of the lab, it "must balance a whole set of values," observed Michael Colligan, a psychologist specializing

in shiftwork at the National Institute for Occupational Safety and Health (NIOSH). "Physical health, personal situation and needs, domestic relationships, and stage of life, all
combine to produce different emotional and
physical concerns," he added.

PERSONAL PREFERENCES

The NIOSH-funded work-sleep study at IIT
is one of the first to address the social and personal factors influencing the shiftworker's
sleep, said Tepas. With the assistance of labor
unions, who recruited workers of day, evening, night, and rotating shifts in St. Louis
and Chicago, researchers were able to gather
data as the subjects went about their normal
routines.

The study consisted of a general survey, a
lab study of a subsample of workers, and field
interviews about community, home, and leisure life. In the lab study, workers slept in the
lab on four consecutive nights during the work
week, reporting there at the end of the day.
Brain waves were recorded while the workers
slept.

Data from the lab studies of St. Louis workers indicated that night shift workers sleep less
than their day shift counterparts and scored
worse on a task measuring performance.

Tepas said the abbreviated sleep of night
shift employees cannot be solely attributed to
the fact that chronobiologically they were attempting to sleep at the wrong time of day.
Rather, he said, "we live in a day-oriented
world, and . . . people want to do things with
other people. The fact they're not getting
enough sleep is simply a function of the fact
they decide how much sleep they're going to
get."

A recent follow-up of some of the respondents shows no indication they have adapted to
their topsy-turvy work schedule, Tepas said,
such as learning to hit the sack as soon as they
get off duty.

"It's fair to say that night shift cuts down on
your sleep and changes your whole social life
around. People go through all types of gym-
nastics to make it acceptable," he said, adding

that the stresses of such a schedule could explain why the divorce rate of night shift workers is "almost double that of day workers."

However, the project's research staff has
developed a number of behavioral strategies
to minimize chronic sleep deprivation, said
Tepas. Some are simple, such as limiting shift
work to short sleepers or encouraging workers
to eliminate napping, which reduces the main
sleep period.

Other interventions are more intricate. For
example, maintaining a constant sequence of
sleep, work, and time off would allow the
worker to adopt a permanent sleep-work cycle.
This particular sequence also enables the night
worker to avoid sleeping during the morning
hours, the worst time of day chronobiologically to sleep.

But this intervention is much more difficult
to apply, Tepas admitted, since workers on a
night shift would be sleeping during the evening hours when other family members are en-
joying their leisure time. "Thus, what makes
good chronobiological sense to some may make
little sense to the worker who values off-the-
job social contacts other than fellow shiftworkers."

LITTLE INTEREST

Tepas said his "damn simple interventions"
have little chance of being recognized by industry or workers given the present ill health
of the economy. Employers mistakenly believe
that these strategies will cost money, he said,
while employees are more concerned with just
holding onto their jobs.

John Zalusky, an economic researcher with
the AFL-CIO, said that the issue of shiftwork
schedules isn't as important as it was five years
earlier because of the failing economy, although he believes "most workers hate the
night shift and would like to see it abol-
ished." He added, however, that union members would like to adopt the European shiftwork schedule of only two to three days on the
night shift.

Zalusky's main concern is that job layoffs

will mean that older workers, who are less able to tolerate a night shift, will once again be drawing the graveyard turn as their seniority causes them to replace younger workers.

Airline pilots, many of whom constantly experience jet lag, recently received a setback when the federal government proposed loosening the rules limiting flight time and duty time hours. The rule changes, as yet to be enacted, would mean that pilots could be on duty for as much as 78 hours in one week, according to the Air Line Pilots Association. The current rule allows a maximum of 30 hours flight time in any seven consecutive days.

"Airlines are the least responsive to the dark side of the clock," Webb commented about the corporate world's general apathetic stance on shiftwork. "Most decisions (about shiftwork schedules) are based on a linear 24-hour system, as if persons were robots.

"Unnaturally we have created a 24-hour world, and shiftwork is a symptom of our inability to recognize our own biology. We are ripping off the cocoon of night."

Flexitime is a concept that has achieved some popularity, at least in the press, in the last decade. Flexitime is a scheduling system that allows the worker some flexibility in the time that he reports to and leaves work. Many organizations and managers have been resisting flexitime schedules, fearing that there will be a radical alteration of work patterns, making it more difficult to complete the assigned work of the unit. They are afraid that no one will show up until 10:00 in the morning, or that everyone will leave at 3:00 in the afternoon. In this reading, we are presented with the results of a field study that examined the actual effect of a flexitime schedule on reporting and leaving times of workers. The results are surprising. It turns out that there is only a modest alteration of work schedules even when workers are given great latitude in start and stop times.

■ READING 44 ■

Arrival and Departure Patterns of Public Sector Employees before and after Implementation of Flexitime

Simcha Ronen

Graduate School of Business Administration, New York University

Alternative work schedules are gaining acceptance as interventions which can address individual needs and organizational effectiveness (Cohen & Gadon, 1978; Nolen, 1979; Ronen, 1981; Ronen & Primps, 1980, 1981). One such innovation is flexible working hours, or flexitime. The main objective of flexitime is to create an alternative to the traditional, fixed working schedule by granting employees the freedom to choose their arrival and departure times within a range (designated as "flexband") set by the employer. Certain hours during the day when all employees must be present is also specified by the employer (designated as "coretime").

By defining a broad range of appropriate membership behavior, the organization allows the individual employee to choose the behavior-attendance pattern which is most appropriate to him/her. This allows an adjustment of work patterns to the individual's own bioclock, and an improved fit between work and nonwork life domains. Such areas as family commitments, educational endeavors, and recreational activities may be better coordinated, and traveling patterns, scheduling, and the duration of commuting time adjusted in order to reduce travel cost, time, and stress (Ronen, 1981). Tardiness, under flexitime, is virtually eliminated, since an employee's workday begins when he/she arrives at work; the only way in which an employee can be late is if he/she arrives at work during the coretime instead of during the flexband.

Despite the advantages associated with flexible working hours, many supervisors have expressed anxiety about the degree of variation in

Source: *Personnel Psychology, 34,* 1981.

433

an employee's arrival and departure times during the flexbands—especially during the implementation stages. First-line supervisors, in particular, express concerns over the need for additional coordination and communication in order to insure that all job responsibilities are covered during the flexbands. In an attempt to limit potential problems, managers often recommend a strict rather than a permissive flexitime system, and may curtail some of the advantages of the system as a result. Data on employee arrival behavior may demonstrate these concerns to be largely unfounded.

The purpose of this paper is to examine the effect of a flexible working hours schedule on the arrival and departure times of employees. The issues addressed are the following:

What is the magnitude of the change?

How constant is the change over time?

To what extent do employees exhibit a characteristic pattern of arrival/departure?

What is the effect of flexitime on tardiness?

METHOD

Data were collected from 200 randomly selected full-time employees in four government agencies in Israel, employing close to 700 employees. One hundred sixty-two employees fulfilled the research requirements. The information was obtained six months prior to and six months after the implementation of the flexitime program. Four months of readings were obtained for both the pre- and post-cases. Arrival and departure times were gathered from individual time-clock records. There were 60 percent males and 40 percent females in the sample, but no significant differences based on sex were found in any of the variables.

The flexitime system allowed a three-hour flexband in the morning and a four-hour flexband in the afternoon. The coretime was 10:00 A.M. to 2:00 P.M. Carry-over of debit or credit hours was allowed within the accounting period of one month, and banking of up to 10 hours of debit or credit hours was allowed from one accounting period to the next. Pre-implementation arrival and departure times were 7:30 A.M. and 3:30 P.M. respectively.

RESULTS AND DISCUSSION

To determine how flexitime affects the employees' arrival and departure times, data available for 160 workers are compared before and after the implementation of flexitime, and presented in Table 1. Under pre-flexitime conditions, 65 percent of the employees arrived at work by 7:30, 85 percent were present by 8:00 and 95 percent by 8:30. Thus, 35 percent were typically tardy. Under flexitime conditions 46 percent were present by 7:30, 69 percent by 8:00, and 85 percent by 8:30, although the flexband ended at 10:00 A.M. Under pre-flexitime conditions 91 percent of the employees departed by 4:00 while under flexitime 61 percent departed by that time. Despite the variations in percentiles, average arrival and departure times after flexitime implementation show a relatively small change when compared with the pre-flexitime period: 8 and 22 minutes respectively. These results indicate that while workers have the flexibility to suit their own needs, the majority of them still tend to arrive and depart at times not very different from their pre-flexitime schedule. This finding is similar to data gathered from four U.S. government agencies located in four different states (Ronen, 1981). It indicates that when American public sector employees use the flexibility allowed them to tailor arrival times to suit their own needs, they do not vary their arrival markedly nor do they behave in an inconsistent manner. They do however, tend to arrive somewhat earlier than under fixed hours. Over 85 percent of these employees were at work by 8:30 A.M., whereas the official starting time prior to implementation of flexitime was the typical 9:00 A.M.

Magnitude and Consistency of the Change

In order to ascertain whether under flexitime *individual patterns* for arrival and departure times emerged, the workers were grouped

TABLE 1 Distributions of Arrivals and Departures—Cumulative Percentage

	Present on the Job at:	Pre-Flexitime	Under Flexitime
Arrivals	06:30	0%	2%
	07:00	0%	11%
	07:30	65%	46%
	08:00	85%	69%
	08:30	95%	85%
	09:00	100%	92%
	10:00	100%	99%
	10:30	100%	100%
	Average	07:36 A.M.	07:44 A.M.
Departures	14.00	100%	100%
	14:30	98%	90%
	15:00	81%	73%
	15:30	40%	57%
	16:00	9%	39%
	16:30	4%	23%
	17:00	3%	16%
	18:00	0%	10%
	Average	03:17 P.M.	03:39 P.M.

Note: Results represent percent of arrivals and departures, not percent of employees.

according to their arrival and departure behavior. An employee is said to exhibit a characteristic pattern, or belong to a *typology*, if over half of either his/her arrival or departure times occur within a specified range of one hour or less. An employee belonging to a typology exhibits less variability in his/her arrival (or departure) times than a worker who does not belong to a typology. The typologies were calculated based on 75 arrivals per worker over four months, and 60 departures per worker during the same period (Fridays were excluded).

The data presented in Table 2 describe the relationship between the employees' arrival and departure typologies. The employees were grouped into three categories—those displaying an arrival pattern, a departure pattern, and those displaying no pattern at all. The data indicate that 83 percent of the workers display a characteristic arrival pattern and 68 percent display a characteristic departure pattern. Sixty percent of the workers belong to both an arrival and departure typology. Twenty-three percent belong to an arrival typology but exhibit no departure pattern, and 8

TABLE 2 Comparison of Arrival and Departure Typologies after Implementation of Flexitime

		No Arrival Typology	Have Arrival Typology		Total
Departure	Arrival		Early	Late	
No Departure Typology		9	21	2	32
	Early	3	41 [60]	3	47
Have Departure Typology				[60]	
	Late	5	4	12	21
Total		17	66	17	100

percent exhibit a departure typology but not an arrival typology. Of this sample, only 9 percent display no characteristic pattern for either arrival or departure. The data also indicate that for 69 percent of the employees with an arrival typology, the arrival times center around the pre-flexitime mode (7:15–8:14 A.M.); for 73 percent of workers with a departure typology, departure coincided with the pre-flexitime mode (2:45–3:45 P.M.).

The implication of this finding is that under flexitime conditions the majority of workers establish a fairly consistent pattern of arrival and departure behavior, and to a large extent, a pattern that is similar to the pre-flexitime behavior.

Tardiness

The data based on approximately 12,000 workdays indicate that an effect of a flexible working hours program is a drastic reduction in employee tardiness. This results in increased hours available for productive activities for the organization, and an average saving of over four hours per worker per month. The number of late arrivals decreased from an average of 6 to 0.67 per worker per month. The tardiness in these organizations prior to flexitime implementation was excessive but the implemented system virtually eliminated the problem. The average monthly rate per employee of coretime tardiness after flexitime implementation was 1 percent. Time lost as a result of coretime tardiness was deducted from the monthly salary.

CONCLUSION

This study indicates that with the implementation of a flexible working hours program, employees tailor their schedule to suit their personal needs and that these needs dictate the characteristics of arrival and departure patterns. Their behavior is not markedly different, however, from the pre-implementation schedule, and tends to remain relatively stable. Although discretion is available daily, it is clear that commuting schedules, carpools, family schedules and other similar considerations may influence the amount of personal discretion the employee actually utilizes.

The implication of these findings is that even under flexitime conditions, which allow daily variations of arrivals and departures, management is able to forecast the scheduling of the organization's activities with a relative degree of certainty. These patterns emerged within the context of a scheduling system allowing a maximum amount of flexibility. Under a more conservative flexitime schedule, with no banking and narrower flexbands as is typical of most schedules offered by organizations in the United States, one might predict even higher levels of stability in arrival and departure patterns from employees. On the other hand, even under the most lenient of systems, patterns do emerge which allow the undisrupted functioning of the organization. Employees, while exercising the freedom to schedule their workday for themselves, do not behave in a random, haphazard fashion. The ability to estimate with a relative degree of certainty the workforce's arrival/departure patterns should allay managers' concerns about flexitime's interference with the work flow of the organization, and the efficient use of human resources.

The Field of Industrial and Organizational Psychology

Industrial and organizational psychology, like most other disciplines, sets up certain boundaries. These boundaries help to distinguish industrial and organizational psychology from other interest areas within psychology and from other nonpsychological behavioral sciences. Having drawn those boundaries, it is tempting to extend the meaning of those boundaries and see them as a protection from having to consider the principles of these other disciplines. This is a mistake. The boundaries are there as an aid in describing to others what our primary interests are. In this section, we will consider two readings that address this issue of what is and what is not a legitimate knowledge base for research and application in industrial and organizational psychology.

One of the things conspicuously absent from much of the industrial and organizational literature is the topic of conflict. Serious consideration of broad social and political systems and their effects on industrial behavior represents another substantial gap. The history of the labor movement illustrates the fact that these two realities—the dynamics of conflict and the reality of sociopolitical systems—are inextricably bound together. It is interesting to note that some of the most intense criticisms of the classic Hawthorne studies come from the failure to consider the effects of the emergence of trade unionism and the effects of the Great Depression (and the memory of that event) on the responses of the subjects of the various Hawthorne experiments.

Nord argues that we continue to ignore the forces of disharmony and the sociopolitical realities of the workplace. As a result, he asserts, we will be condemned to repeat mistakes of the past. Industrial and organizational psychology will continue to fail to make the contribution to the human condition that it could were we to be more expansive in our view of work.

■ READING 45 ■

Continuity and Change in Industrial/Organizational Psychology: Learning from Previous Mistakes

Walter R. Nord
Washington University, St. Louis, Missouri

Efforts by industrial organization (I/O) psychologists to predict their own future and the future nature of work in organizations have not been very successful. This article attempts to look at the future by taking the inaccuracy of previous predictions as problematic; it assumes that analysis of the inaccuracy of these predictions is more informative than the predictions themselves. Although predictions such as the inevitable death of bureaucracy, the satisfac-

tion of lower level needs, self-actualization at work, and increased participation in management by lower level participants may ultimately come true, for most people life along these dimensions has barely improved; on the contrary, in the context of the current recession, things for many people have gotten considerably worse.

In this article I speculate about the reasons for the failures and assert that by understanding these failures, we will better understand I/O psychology and more accurately predict its future.

Undoubtedly, many reasons account for the

Source: *Professional Psychology, 13*(6), December 1982, pp. 942–952. Copyright 1982 by the American Psychological Association. Reprinted by permission of the publisher and author.

failure of previous forecasts, including the following latent characteristics in the field of I/O psychology itself: (*a*) I/O psychology proceeds in an ahistorical fashion; (*b*) I/O psychologists tend to focus their analysis on current changes and consequently give too little attention to underlying continuity and sources of stability; (*c*) despite recognition that organizations are open systems, I/O psychologists systematically understate the consequences for internal organizational functioning of the political/economic processes in the larger social system. Before detailing these three characteristics, I want to emphasize that I see them as pathologies in I/O psychology, in general, and their consequences on predictions as symptoms of the pathology. However, these symptoms are manifested more in discussions of the future than in the routine day-to-day work of I/O psychologists.

AHISTORICAL NATURE OF I/O PSYCHOLOGY

Herbert Gutman (1977) observed: "However carefully the present is studied and however refined the techniques of analysis, the present is not fully comprehended if the past is ignored or distorted" (p. 259). Gutman's observation deserves serious consideration by anyone attempting to comprehend the future (as well as the past and present) of I/O psychology.

In our field, important aspects of history are typically ignored and/or misunderstood. Our ahistorical proclivities have contributed to important distortions in our view of the evolution of organizational forms and the influence of historical processes on the development of I/O psychology.

Often we appear to assume that the evolution of organizational forms occurs through a rational process in which certain technological and market conditions are taken as given, and the structures that survive do so because of their efficiency. Chandler (1977) has shown that these considerations have been very important historically, and I am *not* arguing with that premise. What I will argue is that the scenario is more complex; the evolution of organi-

zational forms, especially those aspects related to the management of people, is also heavily influenced by social, economic, moral, ideological, and political processes. To understand organizations of the past, present, and future, we must understand how these elements have become embedded in and continue to influence modern organizational forms.

Consider, for example, the period in U.S. history between 1880–1920—a critical era of great social turmoil, which influenced the development of American work organizations and their environments (see Chandler, 1977; Nelson, 1975; Weinstein, 1968) and witnessed the beginnings of modern management theory and applied social science.

The essence of these fields—their assumptions, structures, problems, and omissions—was shaped by the struggles of this critical period in their development. Although our I/O psychology field took root in this era, we have given little attention to the social context of these formative years. In fact, whereas historians focus on the years between 1880 to 1914 or 1920, writers in our field (e.g. Greiner, 1979; Tausky, 1970) typically make some passing reference to the formal organizations of the ancients or of biblical times and then begin their serious analysis in the early 1900s with F. W. Taylor. This approach omits detailed treatment of the context in which Taylor's work developed and flourished. In fact, historians who have extensively examined this period differ from I/O psychologists in their picture of the evolution of organizations. In particular, the doctrine of efficiency and the development of social and political institutions, which contributed to the development and viability of modern corporations, were much less the result of technical considerations and more a response to historical conditions than I/O psychologists assumed.

Several historians (e.g., Hays, 1957; Nelson, 1975; Weinstein, 1968; Wiebe, 1967) have argued that at the beginning of the 20th century, Americans were searching for social order. As Wiebe (1967) wrote, "America in the late 19th century was a society without a core" (p. 12). As far as businessmen were concerned, the disorder was expressed in terms of the "labor problem"; the violent strikes of the 1890s, labor turnover, the breakdown of discipline in the factory, and problems of motivating workers loomed as serious threats to both efficiency and managerial legitimacy. Modern management theory appears to have been shaped by this concern over disorder. It was in this context that the role of science in solving social conflicts and the doctrine of efficiency became dominant.

Moreover, as Hays (1957) has shown, during this period some assumptions that have played such an important role in modern applied social science took shape. He observed that important social philosophers and early figures in the history of social science of the time had the same major concerns as did ministers and moralists, namely, fears about modern industrialism threatening the creative individual and fears about socialism. These people placed supreme value on the individual and "abhorred the notion that society was composed basically of groups which struggled to gain power and influence; they were horrified at the evidence of class conflict in American life." They directed their efforts to reforming individuals by education and government action so as to "regenerate the individual mind and moral conscience" (Hays, 1957, p. 75). American social scientists and management theorists attempted to cope with social unrest by focusing on the individual instead of on the collectivity and by defining problems in a manner that reflected their understanding of the elitists' rather than the lower classes' outlook. Recent critiques, such as by Bramel and Friend (1981), suggest that these trends have continued well past the pre-1920 era.

The acceptance of Taylorism and the origin of modern organizational forms, including wage and incentive schemes, welfare programs, complex systems of job grades, and a clear promotion hierarchy (Stone, 1974), modern personnel practices (Watson, 1977), and other characteristics of modern organization are seen by many historians as a partial response to the search for order and the need of businessmen to exercise greater control and power over the factory laborer. In an effective summary of these conclusions, Nelson (1975) states,

> Through a process that bore striking resemblances to the steps by which managers increased their control over production, the employer extended his control over the factory. The manager perceived a problem (whether it was an inadequate supply of skilled workers, labor unrest, or a growing gap between the management and the worker), adopted various ad hoc solutions, finally employed specialists to deal with the problem, and slowly increased the specialists' responsibility at the expense of the foremen. The apprentice supervisors and welfare workers (they were occasionally the same) in turn standardized and systematized their functions as their authority increased. The process seldom occurred exactly in this way, of course, and welfare secretaries still occupied precarious positions in the factory of 1915. But the seed had been planted which, under wartime conditions, would grow into the personnel management movement of the postwar period. (pp. 120–121)

As with Taylor's work, middle-class professionals became major beneficiaries of these developments. Not only did the personnel administration profession get its start but, as Watson (1977) noted, so did the demand for social scientists who came to provide the continuous flow of new knowledge used by personnel people to enhance their power and legitimacy as professionals.

In sum, although technological conditions and the drive for economic efficiency played a major role in these developments (Chandler, 1977), so did the social context and conflicts of the times. By studying the two approaches together rather than separately, we can better understand the formative years of our field. Although the effects of these early developments on modern practice need to be traced, the predominant view is that in its formative years, the applied social science of organizations existed in a context in which an orderly and conservative solution to the "labor problem" was a major concern. The features of organizations and of the substance of I/O psychology and management theory that we often treat as natural, inevitable outcomes were, at least in part, attempts of individuals and groups to cope with a particular set of concerns, from a particular set of interests, at a particular point in time. The future of I/O psychology, as well as its present, must be understood in this context.

CONTINUITY AND STABILITY

A second aspect of I/O psychology that has contributed to errors in forecasts of the future stems, in part, from the ahistorical stance described herein. With little awareness of major historical trends, events that are minor, recurring "blips" are often mistakenly seen as substantial changes. Just as a severely truncated axis on a line graph can make a relatively constant trend appear to be a radical change, so too can we overlook the historical foundations of organizations and our society and fail to see the pattern of continuity.

Daniel Yankelovich (1981) observed:

> In any culture there will usually be more continuity than change. . . . In American life, continuity and far-reaching change do coexist with each other. So variegated is American culture that an observer who wishes to highlight its continuity can easily do so; and conversely, an observer who wishes to document the changing nature of American life can also have his way. The subtle question of judgment is always: Have the important things remained the same, or have *they* changed? (p. xvii)

Yankelovich's attention to both sources of error is important. My focus here is on the elements of continuity. I do not mean to imply that important changes have not and will not continue to occur; but I do suggest that many important things have remained pretty much the same. By putting what appear to be major changes in the context of continuity, they will appear far less sweeping. Several aspects of continuity can serve to illustrate this position.

First, the so-called norms of rationality and the corollary importance attached to quantification continue to play important roles in influencing the weighting of criteria in decisions. Rationality is not a politically neutral process (McNeil, 1978). For example, it is useful to certain elites for legitimating their own control. Moreover, Gross (1968) noted that easily quantified variables are often given undue weight in decisions. Variables such as job satisfaction and individual growth, to name just two, often are difficult to quantify and hence may be "underweighted" in decisions. This state of affairs is apt not only to continue but to accelerate. Consequently, organizations will continue to give less attention to outcomes such as human growth, job satisfaction, and the impact of work on the total individual, all of which are advocated by many I/O psychologists.

A second source of continuity is embedded in organizations themselves. As leading theorists, such as Lindblom (1959), Cyert and March (1963), Thompson (1967), and Mintzberg (1979), have noted, organizations often change incrementally. Major changes in the design of work and structure of organizations—if they occur at all—take place gradually. Nelson's (1975) analysis of the development of factories and managerial practices around the turn of the century illustrates the probable course of events. Nelson concluded that changes in technical and human aspects of management came slowly, locally, and in a piecemeal fashion. A major barrier to more rapid change was the paradigm that businessmen held of the factory: They saw the factory as merely a place to house machinery. Major changes in concerns with accidents and safety required legislation. Major revisions in management practices, including the introduction of Taylorism and the use of modern technical methods, often were successful only when a new factory was opened. Finally, debates were often vigorous over the need for businessmen to provide things we now take as givens, for example, drinking fountains, lockers, toilets, and lavatories.

All this suggests that the nature of organizations, the work environment, and work itself are not apt to change rapidly. Chandler (1977), Thompson (1967), and others have been persuasive in showing that organizations appear to be driven to reduce uncertainty. Current practices are imbedded in a network of paradigms, institutions, and technologies that constrain change. Moreover, as Hackman (1978) observed, past practices help to define those things we know how to do and those things we do not know how to do in managing people and organizations. We do the former and retreat from the latter.

Continuity can also be predicted because of the nature of the relationship between I/O psychology and organizations. For whatever reasons, as Nord (1977) noted, I/O psychologists have historically taken their dependent variables directly from the problems managers confront. Similarly, as I will suggest in the next section, the independent variables considered seem limited by the acceptance of certain aspects of the political economic system. In this article, I will not seek to explain these relationships; I will merely assert their empirical existence. In the absence of major changes in the training, socialization, source of resources and research cites, and numerous other factors that might account for this empirical relationship, the definition of dependent variables and the approaches we propose to deal with these issues will most likely continue to be quite conservative despite our tendency to label them as radical.

In sum, I see continuity as a major feature of I/O psychology's past, present, and future. As will be clear later on when I speculate about future trends, I do not envision a static situation. However, I predict that many of the changes that will occur can be better anticipated and understood when a strong prevailing wind of continuity is assumed.

I/O PSYCHOLOGY AND THE POLITICAL ECONOMIC CONTEXT

I have argued in more depth elsewhere (Nord, in press) that organizational psychologists have failed to specify the relationship between the effectiveness of individual organizations and social welfare. For the most part, we have relied heavily on the assumptions of economists that social welfare is maximized when each unit in the system pursues its own self-interest efficiently; the free market system ensures this relationship. Although there is considerable merit to the market system, it has serious deficiencies as well (see Lindblom, 1977; Scitovsky, 1976). In this article, I will not examine the pros and cons of the market system but will focus only on some consequences for I/O psychology when I/O psychologists implicitly accept this particular political-economic logic.

I must stress that I am not saying that the free market logic is necessarily an inappropriate foundation for I/O psychology. My major point is that failure to recognize the implications of this foundation has caused problems including an inadequate recognition of the political roles played by formal organizations and an inadequate view of conflict.

The impact of organizations on the lives of individuals and society as a whole goes far beyond technical and economic roles played by organizations. Organizations influence the socialization and training of young people who are preparing for adult life; they also influence the lives of adults through their day-to-day work and through changes they must make in order to respond to the requirements of the organization. These processes are not new. With the advent of larger, more bureaucratic systems, the organization of work and other economic activity have always influenced the noneconomic aspects of individual lives. What seems to have changed over the last century or so is the role played by large formal organizations in determining allocation of life chances (Dahrendorf, 1979), criteria for social decisions (McNeil, 1978), and governmental policy (Lindblom, 1977). Through both conscious and unconscious activity and through both formal and informal influence, many decisions and actions of large organizations are quite properly viewed as political. As Karpik (1978), Lindblom (1977), and Pfeffer (1978) have argued, creation of their environments is a major activity that makes for successful organizations. The trends for organizations and organization networks to become larger, more international in scope, and more powerful in comparison with other social institutions seem to make it increasingly difficult for I/O psychologists to ignore the political roles that organizations play; yet I/O psychologists continue to overlook the political dimensions of their efforts as they serve these organizations. The maintenance of the arbitrary distinction between economic and political activity—although always misleading—is a more serious error than before.

The absence of an explicit treatment of the political-economic context has distorted I/O psychologists' perceptions of organizations in a second way. The model of the organization assumed in classical economics is the firm. An important characteristic of the concept of the firm is the assumption of goal congruity among the actors. Although both modern economics and modern organization theory have gone well beyond this view, their initial formulation, based on the assumption of a harmony of interests among participants, has had lasting consequences. This assumption is embedded, to varying degrees, in many of the dominant approaches to management, including scientific management, human relations, and human resources. Moreover, the model of the firm assumes that various sets of actors voluntarily choose their courses of action based on rational calculation. Harmony of interests and rational calculations are mutually supportive because agreed upon goals—especially when they are readily quantifiable in a measure such as profit—make rational calculation feasible. Rational calculation, in turn, is a procedure that leads people to believe that decisions—even ones they may not personally like—are not disputable. Means become the subject of debate; ends or values are ignored. Within this framework, I/O psychologists are freed from the need to deal with certain value issues and conflicting interests. Their legitimacy is assured; and whether they work on selection, training, firing, decision making, and so forth, they are helping the system become more rational.

There is, of course, a quite different view of organizations. This view assumes conflict among many of the goals of various participants, and hence, rational calculation is an imperfect means to allocate resources. Since harmony of interests does not exist or exists only on such general goals as survival, social order is a constant problem for management. Under these assumptions, it is reasonable to expect that dominant coalitions in organizations would seek means to control participants who have competing interests and vice versa. For the most part, the dominant coalitions have more resources to employ I/O psychologists than do other participants.

Management works to solve the problem of order under two general sets of constraints. First, the means available to create social order inside the organization are constrained by social norms and laws that exist outside the organization. Given the laws, norms, and goals of the dominant coalitions in organizations in American society, the particular means of control apt to be most useful would be consistent with or draw on individualism, economic efficiency, productivity, and the work ethic, as opposed to collectivism, enjoyment at work, or minimization of work. American I/O psychology is rife with prescriptions resting on the former set of values. A second set of constraints on the means to assure social control in the workplace stems from the relative power positions of the various interest groups. Skill levels, demand in the product and labor markets, laws governing employer/employee relationships, and import and immigration policies are some of the elements in this struggle.

Undoubtedly, both the rational/harmony perspective and the conflict perspective account for past trends and the present state of affairs at the workplace. Since the former is so well known and widely accepted, I will focus on the latter. A great deal of evidence supports this conflict view; space permits brief reference to only a few of the most important sources.

First, Rodgers (1978) has argued convincingly that, historically, efforts to preserve the work ethic have been driven by a fundamental tension in our society between the ideology of freedom and democracy and the coercive nature of work. Although Rodgers' analysis stops with 1920, his description of incentive systems, industrial democracy movements, efforts to increase cooperation and preserve meaningful work (all of which were developed prior to that time) reveals that many of the proposals made since 1950 to "humanize the workplace" are new only in detail, not basic substance. Moreover, the rapid rise, the popularity, and the "premature" death of these earlier efforts make them appear discomfortingly similar to events in recent I/O psychology. Although much has changed since 1920, the hypothesis that I/O psychologists are responding to and constrained by many of the same forces as those that influenced the moralists, educators, and social philosophers, discussed by Rodgers, appears to be a worthy one. The nature of the problems, the proposed solutions, and the ultimate fate of those solutions are all compatible with the political-economic conflict scenario.

A second body of work has been summarized by Clegg and Dunkerley (1980). These writers argued that the structure of organizations and the control processes organizations employ are determined by long-standing institutions (e.g., private property) as well as by short-run factors (e.g., points in economic cycles and the demand for particular types of workers): For example, when work is routine and "deskilled," the workers can be controlled through technology, tight job specifications, and the threat of being replaced. For these jobs, especially at low points in the economic cycle, traditional, coercive types of control are effective. In other words, for a large segment of the workforce, the lower portion of economic cycles substitutes for other means of securing cooperation or compliance. It is clear that a major lacuna in previous predictions about the quality of work life and I/O psychology, in general, has been macroeconomics. On the other hand, many jobs require more highly skilled individuals who are difficult to replace. These individuals are apt to be controlled more by hegemonic sources. Hegemonic control is exercised through institutions, tastes, customs, social and moral relations, religion, and political principles. Intellectuals play an important role in hegemonic control by helping to produce hegemonic ideas and rationalizations of the current social relationships. Many critics have charged I/O psychology as performing this function.

Previous predictions of the future of work, as well as recent ones (Miles & Rosenberg, 1982) that suggest that technical efficiency will lead inevitably to a rather radical restructuring of the nature of work and of organizations, seem to assume the rational perspective and to ignore the conflict viewpoint. These predictions overlook the historical patterns portrayed by Marglin (1974), Clawson (1980), Braverman (1974), Edwards (1979), and numerous others who show that control and predictability are often more important than technical efficiency in the design of work and organizations. They give little attention to the role of economic cycles and conflicting interests. They give little attention to the role of economic cycles and conflicting interests. They give little attention to how the particular issues that I/O psychologists take as problematic and the solutions they propose are shaped by existing issues and institutions. In short, their inattention to fundamental elements of political economy threatens their predictions.

THE FUTURE

So far I have attempted to make three closely related arguments. First, when we look at the history of work and organizations, we see that modern organization forms and the principles of management theory did not evolve solely on the basis of their technical efficiency. They were heavily influenced by social disorder of the particular period in which they arose. Second, I have suggested that the failure to recognize sources of continuity has led I/O psychologists to overestimate the degree of change that will take place. Third, the particular model of the political-economic system that appears to underlie I/O psychology is a limited one. One of the latent consequences of this limited perspective has been a tendency for I/O psychologists to overstate the roles of rationality and harmony in organizations and to understate the role of conflict. Consequently, I/O psychologists often mislead themselves and others through their use of their metaphors of science, choice, rationality, and concepts derived from the work ethic. Paradoxically, these metaphors make our work extremely useful as raw material for hegemonic control—quite the reverse of what our humanistically oriented language suggests that we are doing.

My view of the future is derived from these thoughts. Although there will be change, the substance of the change will be constrained by the continuity of political economic processes of the postcapitalistic era. Change will occur, but it will occur *within* fundamental constraints. For example, a major problem for organizations—as in the past—will be control. However, given changes in the work force, the nature of that control may be modified. One role I/O psychology will play is in the development of methods, tools, and concepts that are useful in maintaining such control in a manner consistent with the prevailing social norms, ideologies, and economic conditions. Since I believe that *both* the rational point of view and the conflict perspective continue to have merit, the actual consequences of I/O psychology will be mixed. As the rational view implies, I/O psychology will help organizations function better technically. In addition, as the conflict perspective suggests, I/O psychology will also function to legitimate and perpetuate the current social order. There will, of course, be changes with respect to the techniques used to perform these functions, but the basic patterns will be consistent with business as usual.

Within these basic patterns, there will be pressures for change. Before concluding, I will speculate as to the nature and direction of some of these pressures.

First, the impact of economic organizations on other arenas in society will grow. As a result of this trend, there will be a great pressure to recognize the fallacy of the long-standing assumption that economic and political activity can be treated separately. Consequently, I/O psychologists will be challenged to more

fully consider their political-economic assumptions and the interests that their work serves.[1] Although these pressures may increase, their impact is difficult to predict. As in the past, these challenges are easily ignored in the operations of our day-to-day routines.

Second, the recent emphasis on productivity—although it too is not new in our history—could lead to a greater awareness that "bottom line" financial data are far less adequate guides for managing various functions in organizations than is often assumed. On-line measures of quality, waste, efficiency, and, perhaps, even information about the value of human resources may be more in demand and —because of the growth of micro and personal computers—more readily available. Psychologists may be able to help in solving the measurement problems in collecting this type of information. This information should be extremely useful as a data source for research by I/O psychologists. Moreover, the information provided by these sophisticated monitoring systems ought to stimulate more interest in various incentive systems that attempt to tie rewards to performance. Although there may be some ways in which these developments increase individual autonomy (e.g., people can work more at home on their own terminal), the major gains in discretion will occur mainly because the new systems permit even greater control over central functions.

Third, as the nature of the workforce changes, so will the relative emphasis given to different forms of control. It is tempting to predict that the growth in the service sector and the relative decline in blue-collar jobs will increase the latitude employees require and hence increase the emphasis on autonomy and/or hegemonic control. On the other hand, service jobs can be routinized and closely monitored; consider McDonald's hamburgers and

---

[1]Saying that it will be increasingly difficult to avoid the recognition of these issues is not a prediction that such recognition will occur. Given the theme of continuity developed in the previous section, the inattention to these issues may well continue. In this light, an interesting process to observe may be the mechanisms that have functioned and will continue to function to buffer mainstream I/O psychology from this recognition.

airline reservation personnel. As Hackman (1978) argued, we know how to fit people to jobs better than we know how to fit jobs to people. Short-run events resulting from new technology should not be mistaken for long-run trends. Whereas the innovation process may require flexibility, long-run effective operation is apt to require routinization and control in many operations.

In addition to changes in the type of work, much has been written on changes in the attitudes and expectations of members of the workforce. For example, Yankelovich (1981) has described a growing tendency of members of American society to exercise greater personal choice against institutional encroachments. Cooper, Morgan, Foley, & Kaplan (1979) have reported an overall decline in job satisfaction due to a decrease in satisfaction with "esteem"-related items—fairness, responsiveness to employees, respect shown to employees. They found that the satisfaction of managers on these variables has declined dramatically and is now similar to that of clerical and hourly employees. Thus it appears that organizations may be pressured to respond more fully to employee desires for respect and discretion than in the past. Again, whereas a rational paradigm suggests the need for more humanized management, the conflict perspective suggests the probability of an increased demand for hegemonic controls that certain segments of I/O psychology have provided in the past. The degree to which I/O psychology contributes to greater humanization or merely to more effective hegemonic control deserves continuing attention. Neither outcome can be assumed. Moreover, the time frame used in this evaluation must be made explicit. In the short run, what seem to be mere palliatives may contribute to changes in norms, values, and paradigms we hold about organizations and may also be the raw materials for fundamental changes in the realities of organizations.

Fourth, several forces appear to be inducing I/O psychologists to take differences among organizational participants more seriously. At least some of this pressure is coming from the academic portion of our field. The work of

Weick (1979) and others has put new emphasis on the subjective side of organizations. Writers, such as Pfeffer (1978), have shown the need to treat organizations as political systems. Frost, Mitchell, and Nord (1982) have demonstrated the importance of adopting different perspectives on the experience of life in organizations. Often I/O psychologists have failed to take major differences among groups of workers as problematic. There is growing recognition that such differences are important and are based, to some degree, on differences in location in the organization hierarchy and in social/economic status and demographic variables (e.g., sex). Exactly what impact this recognition will have on I/O psychology is difficult to know. However, it could center attention on the value issues pointed to by writers such as Van de Ven and Astley (1981).

Fifth, what changes and what remains constant in the workplace will be heavily influenced by general economic conditions as well as by events in particular labor and product markets. Industrial/organizational psychologists, who have seen the workplace as becoming increasingly humane, seem to have taken their cues from parts of the economy that are growing and have assumed rather continuous economic growth. Quite different assumptions must be incorporated if we are to deal with the decline of large numbers of industries and with recurrence of economic cycles.

Sixth, the basic pattern of trying to reconcile routine work and rigid control in the workplace with our liberal economic and democratic values will continue. The short-term results will be the continuous outpouring of the type of fads that have characterized our field. These fads will serve various functions. To some degree their major impact will be merely to make the careers of their originators and promoters as well as their users in organizations whose own internal legitimacy depends in part on being up to date with recent advances. On the other hand, these fads may have a very positive impact in certain locations—particularly in new plants. In the long run, however, the results of these fads might be quite different. People may get tired of them and begin to look in other directions to solve their rational problems and preserve their legitimacy. However, gradually over time, in conjunction with other forces, the various notions promoted by I/O psychologists may influence the paradigms that members of society hold about the nature of work and organizations. Perhaps, just as toilets and drinking fountains are now relatively noncontroversial additions to humanizing the workplace, so in the future, aspects of social organization may become more responsive to human dignity.

Perhaps then the real problem with I/O psychology—whether it is written from an optimistic view by people such as Miles and Rosenberg (1982), who look at a few organizations and see the widespread quest for their human resource model as inevitable, or from what I consider to be a more realistic view that sees far less substantive change on central issues—is that both the optimists and I have adopted too short a time horizon in developing our views. The nature of organizations and the major features of society will change, more or less together, over time. The optimists may do a serious disservice by making the changes seem to come too easily and too quickly. People such as myself may do a serious disservice by failing to see how the local successes of the optimists may be part of a piecemeal change process that is both a consequence of and a contributor to social progress over time.

To the degree that these assertions are valid, the future of I/O psychology will be most promising if we become more conscious of our place in history and in the political economy and more aware of how the future is shaped by continuity with the past. It is hoped that this article has contributed to that perspective.

As you look back over the sections of this reading book, you get a certain feeling of disaggregation. There are neat little piles of studies on selection and job analysis and training and motivation and work design. While that may be convenient for both student and teacher alike, it does not do justice to the phenomenon of work. Workers do not think of leadership patterns at one particular time and work design on a different occasion. Similarly, although we tend to ignore variables of temperament in selection research, there can be little doubt that emotional factors will play a role in ultimate success on a job. In fact, as we progressed through the book, we have been increasingly assaulted with the fact that work, in its entirety, has substantial effects on many aspects of a worker's life.

In this final reading, Stagner argues for a refocusing of the efforts of industrial and organizational psychologists around the theme of humanism and its manifestation in work design. He suggests that industrial and organizational psychology begin to deal with the emotions of workers as a way of understanding the intricate and powerful relationships between work and workers.

■ READING 46 ■

Past and Future of Industrial/Organizational Psychology

Ross Stagner
Professor Emeritus, Department of Psychology, Wayne State University

Some of us are fond of the aphorism that "psychology has a short past but a long history." In this vein, we could argue that industrial psychology goes all the way back to the Biblical instance of Gideon selecting prospective soldiers by a simple performance test. More realistically, the history of industrial psychology begins with the argument between Wilhelm Wundt and J. McKeen Cattell on the importance of universal laws of the mind versus individual differences in the functioning of these laws. Moore (1962) chose this incident as symbolizing the genesis of industrial psychology; he wrote:

Source: *Professional Psychology*, *13*(6), December 1982, pp. 892–902. Copyright 1982 by the American Psychological Association. Reprinted by permission of the publisher and author.

There was a breaking away from orthodox Wundtian psychology confined to the laws common to all men, and an increasing interest in individual differences. This had begun with Galton in England, and had been brought to this country by Cattell; but there had been comparatively little consideration of industrial problems until Münsterberg published his *Psychology and Industrial Efficiency* in 1913. (pp. 1–2)

Münsterberg laid the foundation for studies of selection and training, but Scott (1911) had already published his *Influencing Men in Business* in which he expanded on some generalizations about motivation of salesmen and of employees in general. Thus both the cognitive and the dynamic aspects of industrial psychology were recognized almost 100 years ago. Although industry and science have changed, it is surprising to re-read these classics and discover that the major problems of today were already matters of concern at that time.

The historical background of organizational psychology is more diffuse. In a sense it goes back to Max Weber (who, surprisingly, wrote a paper on the psychophysics of industrial work) and the study of bureaucracy. Taylor (1911) wrote of group influences on work behavior, but mostly in a pejorative manner, bewailing "systematic soldiering" (p. 17) and other means of restricting output. Taylor's hostility to unions represented a kind of attention (but not scientific research) to social influences. Other early industrial psychologists differed with Taylor; Muscio (1920), for example, wrote that "The most valuable possession of the worker is the union, and the power that he possesses by means of it for collective bargaining" (p. 253). Somewhat later we have the Hawthorne studies, particularly the Bank Wiring Room data, that show the potent influences of the group on worker behavior (Roethlisberger & Dickson, 1939).

Leavitt (1962) covers some of the early history of organizational psychology and notes a useful distinction between "human relations" and organizational behavior. Regrettably, he endorsed a charge that many I/O psychologists reject, namely, that "classical industrial psychology had been, ideologically at least, an ally of Taylorism and scientific management" (p. 25). It is of course true that the work of Münsterberg, Viteles, Tiffin, Guion, and others is, on the whole, not antithetical to Taylor, but the word *ally* seems farfetched. As Ferguson (1962) demonstrated, early relations between organized labor and industrial psychology were good; the charge of critics that psychologists were "servants of power" came much later.

CHANGES IN CONTEXT AND PHILOSOPHY OF I/O PSYCHOLOGY

Changes in Context

Modern industry presents problems quite different from those faced by Scott and Münsterberg. Most factory jobs then involved heavy labor and direct manipulation of machines. Thus Münsterberg's pioneer work on selection of streetcar motormen could focus on visual and auditory perception, reaction time, and distance judgment and produce convincing results regarding the benefits of testing applicants for these psychological functions. Today we face a high-technology environment in which more and more jobs involve watching dials, making decisions, closing valves, pressing buttons. The relevant functions are nearly all cognitive in nature. Along with this, the selection procedures used by personnel psychologists have changed.

The legal context has also changed. Münsterberg did not have to cope with problems of test bias, although he did note that one employer refused to hire Swedes as machinists and another thought Swedes were the best for that job. Today personnel psychologists must exercise considerable skill in trying to predict job performance without discriminating against racial or sexual groups. Discrimination on the basis of age has also been forbidden, and this will further complicate matters.

The educational level of the population is also changing. Seventy years ago it was unheard-of for a college student to apply for a manual labor job. Today many applicants have attended or even graduated from college. This change is significant because a major complaint on job satisfaction surveys is "My abilities are underutilized." It is to be hoped that job redesign and higher technology will make this complaint obsolete.

Finally, we note that the American economy is shifting from an economy based on producing goods to one based on private and public services. The impact of this trend on I/O psychology is not clear. Some studies in which attitudes and behaviors of workers in private enterprise are compared with those in public agencies suggest that the problems of selection, training, motivation, unionization, and so forth are parallel in the two settings.

Change in Philosophy

Finally, one observes a change within the discipline of psychology. At the turn of the century, most industrial psychologists ignored the problem of perception. Observers assumed that they knew the "real facts" regarding the industrial situation. Today most I/O psychologists are more sophisticated; they realize that they must consider conditions as perceived by managers, employees, and union officials and that none of these may be identical to the "facts," as seen by the psychologist. Paradoxically, this change in philosophy has led to greater realism in dealing with problems in job design, organizational development, and industrial relations.

THE FUTURE OF INDUSTRIAL PSYCHOLOGY

Industrial/organizational psychology has changed and is changing. This process will continue into the 21st century, perhaps at a less rapid pace. Given the societal changes already visible, we can predict at least some of the probable modifications in our discipline.

Selection is obviously an area in which changes will be required. High-technology jobs will require more emphasis on cognitive functions. Tests of manual dexterity will still be used, especially for fine coordination. Personality variables will become more salient; stress tolerance and ability to cope with emergencies (cf. Three-Mile Island) will be explored. Assessment centers will expand even further. As the cost of equipment handled by an employee goes up, the expense of careful selection is less of an obstacle to management.

These changes must be accomplished without violating Equal Employment Opportunity Commission (EEOC) requirements. Although we have no reason to assume important minority group differences either in cognitive functioning or in stress tolerance, the introduction of age discrimination poses a problem. Considerable evidence indicates that older persons are more cautious, slower to make decisions, and slower to react in a choice situation. This may represent a danger in an automatic-process chemical or nuclear industry.

Viteles (1934) studied the problem of aging workers and warned against the stereotype that older employees are inefficient. He found that many workers of advanced years learned new tasks as rapidly as their younger cohorts. He suggested that the apparent decline was a function of environment, not of changes in the central nervous system. Developmental psychologists are now confirming his speculation. Blieszner, Willis, and Baltes (1981) demonstrated that older subjects could increase their scores markedly on tests of inductive reasoning if they were given daily practice and feedback on similar problems for a period of two weeks. Since this is one of the so-called "fluid" intelligence functions, alleged to be uninfluenced by practice, the finding is important. Viteles has been supported, and concern about aging is now shifting to the detrimental influences imposed by the environment, especially the work environment.

If selection criteria are to become more complex and the bases for rejection of an applicant more subtle, more industrial psychologists will find themselves in counseling roles. In a society full of litigation over alleged wrongs by industry, skill in reducing the rejectee's anger and hostility will become important.

It is also likely that private testing-counseling services and state agencies will also proliferate. Cognitive testing of older applicants may lead to erroneous results because of anxiety, unfamiliarity with testing procedures, lack of practice, and so forth. The independent psychologist can do a better job of reducing insecurity and anxiety than a factory personnel staffer.

Psychologists devising selection procedures will pay more attention to "face validity" because rejectees will be less likely to challenge the procedure. For an information-processing job, a test using word-processing equipment will be challenged less often than one using pencil-and-paper tests.

The Study of Individual Differences

Industrial psychology began as an assertion of the principle that although all persons are human, they are not interchangeable. Differences in sensory acuity, speed of response, memory, and so on were demonstrated and shown to be important. Regrettably, experimental psychologists continued to focus on mean differences among groups. "Individual diversities were hidden in averages or even discarded as erroneous," wrote Young (1924, p. 44). But industrial psychologists have lapsed into the same error, and so we read research reports that "younger workers were significantly more efficient than older workers," a type of statement that supports personnel managers in a stereotyped rejection of elderly applicants. An individual-differences report might have concluded that "20 percent of older workers equaled or exceeded the median of the younger group." Phrasing results in this fashion reminds the unsophisticated reader of statistics that many older applicants may be superior to the average younger job seekers.

Industrial psychologists have developed some very sophisticated statistical techniques, and it is no surprise that graduate training programs in our field have come to emphasize the quantitative side of instruction, perhaps to the exclusion of human psychology. In a recent report, the American Psychological Association (APA), Education and Training Committee of Division 14 (I/O Psychology) ranked training in quantitative methods very high in its priorities for graduate education (APA, Note 1). To the extent that such emphasis develops an enthusiasm for canonical analysis, nonorthogonal analysis of variance, and other esoteric procedures, it may prove a detriment to I/O psychology. And to the extent that such training repels graduate students who are relatively sensitive to the perceptions of managers or of employees, it may be detrimental to American industry.

The Study of Workplace Behavior

Viteles (1934) quoted the Gilbreths (without citation) as asserting that "more output can be achieved by applying oneself steadily for short periods, and then resting, than by applying oneself less steadily and having no rest periods" (p. 297). This phenomenon has almost disappeared from industrial psychology, but workers regularly rediscover it for themselves. Reporters studying the troubled Lordstown GM plant were puzzled that the workers complained of the speed of the line, yet "doubling up" was often observed. This consisted of one worker covering two positions, working furiously for 15 or 30 minutes while his partner loafed, and then exchanging roles. It seems likely that an ingenious psychologist or even an ingenious manager could start from this observation and devise ways of operating an assembly line that would evoke less resentment than present practices.

Job redesign, of course, is needed far more extensively than just modifying assembly lines (Hackman & Oldham, 1976). Taylor (1911) was of course an early advocate of job redesign but in a way that most modern psychologists would reject: "The work of every workman is fully planned out by the management. . . . This task specifies not only what is to be done but how it is to be done and the exact time allowed for doing it" (p. 39). In fact, the urgent need for redesign of factory jobs derives precisely from this Taylorizing of tasks. All decision making by the worker and all free choices of movement, of tools, and of location of materials were eliminated. It is hardly surprising that dissatisfied workers say, "My abilities are underutilized" and that researchers find desire for autonomy to account for much of the dissatisfaction encountered.

It is clear that job redesign is too important to leave to managers or even to industrial psychologists. Unless workers have a voice in the changing pattern of work, they will be frustrated and rebellious.

Performance Appraisal

Evaluating the success of the worker is not often mentioned in the classical literature of industrial psychology. Münsterberg (1913) evaluated the success of his selection devices by accident rates, because accidents had been a major cost item for the street railway company involved. Today it is generally recognized that evaluation of employee performance is essential, but astonishingly little has been done to improve practices. Most firms use ratings by supervisors, but ample research shows that these ratings are unsatisfactory. Lifson (1953) showed that experts in time and motion study could not even agree with each other in the evaluation of filmed job performances. Cleveland and Landy (1981) reported that performance ratings by supervisors were of low reliability and thus lacked validity. Cleveland and Landy did succeed in training supervisors to make ratings that were reliable; but as is shown in the ingenious studies of Borman (1978), the increase in reliability is not necessarily accompanied by an increase in validity.

An improvement in appraisal, which would also eliminate stereotypes and halo effects, would be to evaluate products while ignorant of the identity of the employee. This is not feasible on some factory jobs, but with increased computerization, many products can be evaluated without identifying the worker. Ratings thus could be of performance exclusive of friendship, ethnic stereotypes, and other irrelevant factors.

Kleiman and Durham (1981) remind us that this is not a trivial problem. The EEOC constraints on hiring are also being applied to promotions, advanced training assignments, early retirement recommendations, and so on. Employers are going to demand that I/O psychologists provide appraisal methods that will stand close scrutiny.

In addition to job performance, there are other outcomes of employment, some of which are just now receiving attention. As far back as 1913, Münsterberg was emphasizing that the satisfaction of the worker was an important consideration for the psychologist, and Viteles (1934) stressed reduction of the physiological cost (fatigue) to the worker as well as awareness of the importance of job satisfaction (p. 293). Even Taylor (1911) included side comments regarding satisfactions, although he treated this mainly as satisfaction with pay. Most of us probably assume that the questionnaire study of satisfaction began with Hoppock (1935), but Münsterberg (1913, p. 238) mentioned a

questionnaire study of workers that had been done in Germany in 1912. Regrettably, he did not record any summary of the findings.

Although job satisfaction might seem to be a gestalt, all-or-nothing kind of phenomenon, greatest progress in recent decades has resulted from the shift to facet studies. It has become clear that satisfaction with pay may vary widely in relation to satisfaction with the work itself, with supervision, or with opportunities for decision making. Herzberg, Mausner, Peterson, and Capwell (1957) proposed a rather broad categorization of factors as intrinsic and extrinsic satisfiers. Although the Taylor-Skinner emphasis on pay or other concrete incentives is widely accepted by industrial executives, union leaders, and some I/O psychologists, evidence is accumulating that this view has unfortunate consequences. Hackman and Oldham (1976) relate higher effort and more efficient performance to intrinsic satisfiers, that is, the work itself; and Deci (1975) has found evidence that extrinsic incentives weaken or destroy intrinsic motivation.

Beyond job satisfaction, psychologists are becoming concerned with industrial impacts on mental health. The work of Kornhauser (1965) first brought into sharp focus the damaging effects of Taylorized (fragmented, mechanically repetitive) jobs. Employees on such assignments reported more worries, more depressions, more irritations, and other symptoms of mental ill health than employees doing the same kind of work but on a flexible schedule. In addition to this kind of problem, the phenomenon of "burnout" has recently attracted attention (Jones, 1981). Nurses, physicians, and others responsible for patient care come under repeated emotional strain until they decide to leave; or they may develop a callous attitude, indifferent to the needs of the client or patient. As we move toward a "service economy," such phenomena must necessarily receive more attention from I/O psychologists.

Repetitive, machine-paced jobs may also have detrimental consequences for cognitive functions. Broadbent (1978) reported that workers on such assignments experience more episodes of absent-mindedness, forgetfulness, disorientation, and so forth than fellow workers on more flexible jobs. Since these symptoms are commonly associated with advancing age, it may be that future research will relate Taylorized jobs to premature aging. Along the same line, Martin, Ackerman, Udris, and Oergerli (1980) studied Swiss watchmaking employees on repetitive, boring jobs and found a possible adverse effect on verbal ability. They correlated tenure on such a job with score on a verbal test; the result was a highly significant $-.55$. Age, interestingly, did not correlate significantly with the verbal test. Industrial/organizational psychologists need to design longitudinal research that will point to significant independent variables influencing the development of job dissatisfaction, mental ill health, and decline in cognitive functioning. In the meantime, job redesign to reduce the frequency of machine-paced, fragmented jobs would seem to be a needed public health measure.

Aside from toxic chemicals and the like, jobs may also be hazardous to one's physical health. Caplan, Cobb, French, Harrison, and Pinneau (1975) showed that workers on repetitive jobs had more dispensary visits and more complaints of health problems than similar workers on more flexible jobs. A Soviet study of this problem (Samilova, 1971) reported that women on machine-paced tasks suffered more cardiovascular, neurological, and arthritic illnesses than women in the same establishments but on self-paced operations.

One of Studs Terkel's interviewees made the judicious observation that "When the arm starts movin', the brain stops" (Terkel, 1972). On a more sophisticated level, O'Hanlon (1981) speculates about the inhibitory effect of repetitive stimulation on cortical centers. This would seem to be compatible with the data of Broadbent (1978) and of Martin et al. (1980). The connection with symptoms of physical and mental ill health may be found to depend on activation of autonomic nervous system reflexes by the frustration of tendencies toward spontaneous movements; on a rigidly defined job, little variation in movement is permissible.

Developmental psychologists are finding evidence to support a view of aging as environmentally imposed deterioration of function. The studies cited above suggest that if the environment is a rigidly constraining job demanding rapid repetition of a precisely defined set of movements, mental processes show symptoms of aging at an accelerated rate. Seventy years ago Münsterberg (1913) expressed the hope that industrial psychology could aid in the elimination of "mental dissatisfaction in the work, mental depression and discouragement" (p. 309). The hope is still with us as an agenda item for the future.

Motivation

Motivation seems not to have been a problem for early industrial psychologists. Taylor (1911) advocated a highly simplified view: "all the worker wants is money." Scott (1911), on the other hand, was offering a more complex approach including egoistic and altruistic motives. Over the succeeding 70 years, psychologists alternated between "single motive" and "multimotive" conceptualizations. Sigmund Freud, C. L. Hull, and Carl Rogers can be cited as single-motive theorists. B. F. Skinner writes in the same vein but avoids commiting himself to a theory of motivation. In the multimotive group, we may cite Maslow (1954), Alderfer (1972), Vroom (1964), and others. (Vroom is doubtful, since he does not discuss the origins of valences, his term for incentives.) The Hawthorne studies were generally interpreted as supporting a multimotive view; for example, in the Bank Wiring Room, the employees clearly subordinated their own income to protect the earnings of slower coworkers.

The hierarchical theories (Maslow, Alderfer) are particularly useful to industrial psychologists because they offer a conceptual handle on a difficult problem. Studies of job satisfaction show that when one source of discontent is removed by management, another pops up to take its place. Thus, when workers are poorly paid, money is the major demand; but when pay levels are perceived as adequate, demands for autonomy, responsibility, decision making, and so forth begin to appear. If pay, as argued by Locke (1982), is the only demand of any importance, the introduction of these self-enhancement goals would be hard to understand.

Most of the recent work on job redesign, organizational development, quality of work life, and so forth has assumed that a hierarchical theory of motivation is correct. Since these theories treat pay as a symbol of physiological needs such as hunger and thirst, they do not discard financial motivation but simply treat it as one of several human needs to be satisfied by work.

It should be noted that the capitalist-Marxist view of man as being motivated solely by economic considerations may be responsible for some of the difficulties of American industry in the 1980s. Management has in the past bribed workers to tolerate aversive work assignments; to quote Taylor (1911), "workmen will not submit to this rigid standardization . . . unless they receive extra pay for doing it" (p. 83). Thus, in the 1960s, instead of cooperative efforts with unions to redesign jobs and make work more satisfying, management merely raised pay and benefits. An unintended consequence of this may have been pricing certain commodities (e.g., automobiles) out of the market, both in the United States and throughout the world. It seems clear that in the next decade, I/O psychologists must work on the development of jobs that are more satisfying in themselves. This is not to be a device for cutting wages but to put an end to the practice of paying higher wages to maintain rigid managerial control of job structure.

Another aspect of the motivational problem in industry is related to another Taylor principle, namely, immediate gratification. Taylor emphasized that workers must be able to see a relationship between their increased expenditure of energy and their increased income. Further, the time lapse must be very short. Hence, piecework and individual incentives became standard industrial procedures. This is clearly compatible with the views of Skinner

on immediate reinforcement, and some of his disciples are developing applications to industry. The philosophy has also been adapted to compensation of executives, for example, where increases in short-run profits, as by mergers, lead to immediate bonuses. This approach to executive compensation has crowded out policies of long-term maximization of market share and productivity through research, plant modernization, and so forth. Industrial/organizational psychologists need to remind their clients of Freud's dichotomy of pleasure principle and reality principle. Infantile personalities demand immediate gratification and short-run maximization; mature personalities can tolerate delay in order to optimize long-term gratifications. Life based on the pleasure principle is not good for children, for corporations, or for the American economy.

Psychoanalytic theory has had little impact on American I/O psychologists. McMurry (1944) made an effort to examine a variety of industrial problems in a psychoanalytic frame of reference, with variable outcomes. Occasionally he made an excellent point, for example, regarding unconscious motives: "all workers are to some degree ambivalent (unconsciously hostile . . .) toward their employers . . . the son whose father mistreated him may be spurred to open revolt by an equally brutal foreman" (p. 3). Thus he warned managers not to make job changes in an authoritarian manner—advice needed as much today as in 1944, and perhaps more so in 1994. However, his book has not been widely cited by his colleagues.

SATISFACTION AND ENERGY MOBILIZATION

The ultimate dilemma posed to I/O psychology by motivation theory is this: *A satisfied motive does not energize behavior.* Thus, if money is the sole incentive, workers arrive at an acceptable income level and then behave in ways obnoxious to employers; they take off work on Mondays and/or Fridays, quit on slight provocation, pay little attention to the job, and so on. A similar outcome could be predicted if any other extrinsic incentive is used repetitively. Job redesign to make the work intrinsically interesting is the only hopeful prospect. Intrinsic motives are relatively nonsatiating; if today's job was interesting, tomorrow's work may also be.

Intrinsic motives are not easily manipulated to increase actual production. Kurt Lewin (1951) pointed out that the level of productive effort may be conceptualized as an equilibrium of vectors. One can raise the level by adding an external incentive, but this runs the risk of increasing the tension level in the system. It is more effective to remove negative vectors (in this case, group disapproval of higher output) so that any intrinsic motives may have freedom to influence behavior. It is this motivational model that seems to offer most encouragement to quality-of-work-life efforts.

It is relevant to observe that although managers have exactly the same motives as workers, the tasks facing managers are intrinsically more complex, less fractionated, free of machine pacing, and more challenging and interesting. The manager who copes successfully with a problem gets more of a "feeling of achievement" than a worker assembling a carburetor. Thus, it is not solely a difference in income that accounts for the higher satisfaction reported by managers.

I/O PSYCHOLOGY
AND UNIONS

Labor unions constitute, for many I/O psychologists, a kind of Freudian complex—repressed material that influences behavior without entering conscious awareness. The word *union* will be found rarely if at all in the index to a textbook or monograph in this field, although investigators occasionally admit to having begun a project that was blocked by union opposition. It seems surprising that so little research has been done, even if only to find out how to avoid such frustrating interventions.

In the 1980s there seems to have been a resurgence of concern by psychologists with unions (cf. Gordon & Nurick, 1981). In addition to such impartial research, regrettably, there has been an increase in efforts at identifying prounion employees so that they can be removed from the work force in roundabout ways.

As noted earlier in this article, the founding fathers of I/O psychology took a more favorable attitude. Ferguson (1962) went to some pains to document Scott's refusal to cooperate in a union-busting plan in Chicago. He also observed that the president of the American Federation of Labor served on the board of the Personnel Research Federation, an early venture in applied psychology.

The economy of the 1980s is not favorable to unions; in fact, many formerly strong unions have been impelled to grant concessions on wages and benefits, which would have been inconceivable only a few years back. However, unions will probably come back in great strength by 1990. In part, this prediction is based on the predilection of executives for instant gratification. One notes, for example, that only a few days after winning union votes for wage freezes and benefit reductions, General Motors announced a plan for increased bonuses for top executives, as did International Harvester, McLouth Steel, and other firms. This completely egocentric view of the economy will necessarily pump strength back into the unions.

Jobs provide satisfaction for a variety of motives, as outlined earlier. The same is true for union membership. A worker may join a union to win increased wages but stay for friendship, loyalty to leaders, felt power in opposition to management. A bright, ambitious young worker may seek satisfaction for ego motives in union office.

Industrial/organizational psychologists, however, will not find the unions to be rich sources of fees for consulting. The typical union does not have the resources required. Contacting a union for a research study, on the other hand, may lead to mutual confidence and to involvement, perhaps at lower compensation than for management, in decisions about organizational development in the union.

It is perhaps inevitable that I/O psychologists would be accused of being promanagement. Even Münsterberg (1913) unconsciously indicated that the problems of his profession were defined by managers; he asked how far "the study of attention, or of perception, or of memory, and so on, can be useful *for the purposes of the business man*" (p. 22; italics added). This does not seem to be an adequate excuse for ruling unions out of the field of I/O psychology; in fact, some very interesting problems of leader-follower relations, loyalty to a group, bargaining processes, and alienation can probably be investigated more adequately in the union-management context than in any other setting.

I/O PSYCHOLOGY AND THE UNITARY ORGANISM

In a way, I/O psychology today suffers from Taylorism, task fragmentation, and loss of a unified perspective. Just as the worker is arbitrarily assigned to a task that includes no awareness of how it fits into the product ultimately envisioned, so students of psychology are likely to perceive the industrial/organizational field as a set of specific specialties having no ineluctable interconnections. That is, selection may become a specialized function having no connection with job satisfaction, stress, or mental health problems. Psychologists working in organizational development often show no sensitivity to the anxieties and insecurities of the managers affected by the changes initiated. If a production line is changed to a set of small teams producing subassemblies, selection procedures, training programs, performance appraisal procedures, and so on will have to be reconsidered.

Workers are human beings who also experience anxiety, fear, hostility, and similar emotions. Psychologists need to be aware of these emotions and to be sensitive to the impact of their interventions. They also need to keep in mind the concept of individual differences,

including rigidity, fear of change, and preference for the old ways. Workers, Taylor commented, resist arbitrary changes in their tasks, methods, and work environment. The I/O practitioner needs to be a competent general psychologist sensitive to the total personality of the individual who is having work-connected problems. This points to a recommendation that graduate training in this field should revert to more emphasis on general psychology, with perhaps some postponement of specialized skill training to the postdoctoral level.

Future I/O psychologists will live in a complex world. They will need some sophistication in economic theory and in sociological concepts. If they are working in areas affected by EEOC (as are most industrial people), they may even need a smattering of labor law. Within the broad territory now called "psychology," they will need greater understanding of developments in such fields as information processing (from whence will come most of the advances in selection tests), social psychology (for new developments in attitude measurement, attitude change, attribution research, small group behavior), and developmental psychology (e.g., for the most sophisticated research on aging). Advances in these fields must be assimilated to current I/O practices—or, perhaps more precisely, in Piagetian terms, I/O conceptualizations must be accommodated to the developments of other psychological specialties. If such changes in psychologists' thought patterns occur, we may hear fewer bitter protests from our colleagues about the intransigent opposition of union leaders, entrenched bureaucrats, or crotchety chief executives when the consultant tries to restructure a task or an organization. Varela (1971) has prepared an analysis of how knowledge from social psychology can be utilized to resolve industrial problems. Nord (1980) recommended that I/O psychology devise an organizational psychology for redesigning I/O psychology. Although his analysis relies on systems concepts, as opposed to Varela's individual psychology, the outcomes are similar. For example, Nord recommends an improved search process for psychology that would extend beyond our traditional fences to include relevant concepts from economics, sociology, and systems theory. He returns to the individual level in urging that psychologists recognize that the environment has changed and that they must abandon some traditional beliefs (Kurt Lewin called this "unfreezing") to adapt to these changes. In the foregoing pages, I have identified a few frozen concepts that appear to need thawing.

Industrial/organizational psychology has its quantitative side and its humanist side. The humanist side involves sensitivity to the perceptions and emotions of workers, executives, and others involved in a given industrial situation. The quantitative side involves logical analysis and devotion to statistical techniques (which are not always relevant to the real-life situation). Nord (1980) suggested that we require our graduate students to design "neat" researches, regrettably often on trivial points. It would be undesirable to let either of these aspects of our discipline wither, but we may need to bring the humanist side into clearer focus. "Humanizing industrial organizations" has become a popular slogan (cf. Meltzer & Wickert, 1976); but the human element easily gets lost in a thicket of methodology. Further, there seems to be minimal agreement on what constitutes "humanizing." Tentatively, I would like to suggest that "humanizing" occurs when we treat a person in an industrial setting as a total personality, complete with emotions and perceptions, not simply as a set of test scores, an aggregate of skills, or a role receiver. Only in this way can we restore the humanist side of industrial psychology.

REFERENCES

SECTION ONE

Alluisi, E. A. Methodology in the use of synthetic tasks to assess complex performance. *Human Factors*, 1967, *9*, 375–384.

Annett, J., and Duncan, K. D. Task analysis and training design. *Occupational Psychology*, 1967, *41*, 211–221.

Archer, W. B. Computation of group job descriptions from occupational survey data. USAF, Personnel Research Laboratory, PRL–TR–66–12, 1966.

Archer, W. B. and Fruchter, D. A. The construction, review, and administration of Air Force job inventories. USAF, Personnel Research Laboratory, Technical Documentary Report No. 63–21, 1963.

Armstrong, J. S., and Soelberg, P. On the interpretation of factor analysis. *Psychological Bulletin*, 1967, *70*, 361–364.

Arvey, R. D. and Mossholder, K. V. A proposed methodology for determining similarities and differences among jobs. *Personnel Psychology*, 1977, *30*, 363–73.

Arvey, R. D., Passino, E. M., and Lounsbury, J. W. Job analysis results as influenced by sex of incumbent and sex of analyst. *Journal of Applied Psychology*, 1977, *62*, 411–16.

Baehr, M. E. A factorial framework for job descriptions for higher-level personnel. Industrial Relations Center, The University of Chicago, 1967.

Balma, M. J. The concept of synthetic validity. *Personnel Psychology*, 1959, *12*, 395–396.

Bloom, B. S. (Ed.). *Taxonomy of Educational Objectives. Handbook I: Cognitive Domain.* New York: McKay, 1956.

Boese, R. R. and Cunningham, J. W. Systematically derived dimensions of human work. Center for Occupational Education, North Carolina State University, 1975.

Brumback, G. B., Romashko, T., Hahn, C. P., and Fleishman, E. A. Model procedures for job analysis, test development and validation. City of New York, Department of Personnel, July 1974.

Brumback, G. B. and Vincent, J. W. Factor analysis of work-performed data for a sample of administrative, professional, and scientific positions. *Personnel Psychology*, 1970, *23*, 101–07.

Carr, M. J. The Samoa method of determining technical, organizational, and communicational dimensions of task clusters. USN, Naval Personnel Research Activity, Technical Bulletin STB 68–5, 1967.

Center for Vocational Education, The Ohio State University. Directory of task inventories (Volumes 1, 2, and 3).

Chambers, A. N. Development of a taxonomy of human performance: A heuristic model for the development of classification systems. *JSAS Catalog of Selected Documents in Psychology*, 1973, *3*, 24–25. (Ms. No. 320) (Also available as AIR Tech. Rep. 726–4. Washington, D.C.: American Institutes for Research, October 1969.)

Christal, R. E. Stability of consolidated job descriptions based on task inventory survey information. USAF, Personnel Research Division, Air Force Systems Command, AFHRL–TR–71–48, 1971.

Christal, R. E. New directions in the Air Force occupational research program. USAF, Personnel Research Division, AFHRL, 1972.

Christal, R. E. The United States Air Force occupational research project. USAF, Air Force Systems Command, Brooks Air Force Base, Texas, January 1974.

Christal, R. E., and Madden, F. M. Air Force research on job evaluation procedures. Lackland Air Force Base, Tex.: Personnel Laboratory, Aeronautical Systems Division, Air Force Systems Command, ASD–TN–61–46, June 1961.

Christal, R. E., Madden, F. M., and Harding, F. D. Reliability of job evaluation ratings as a function of number of raters and length of job descriptions. Lackland Air Force Base, Tex.: Personnel Laboratory, Wright Air Development Division, Air Research and Development Command, WADD–TN–60–257, October 1960.

Cragun, J. R. and McCormick, E. J. Job inventory information: task and scale reliabilities and scale interrelationships. USAF, Personnel Research Laboratory, PRL–TR–67–15, 1967.

Cunningham, J. W. An S-O-R approach to the study of job commonalities relevant to occupational education. Center for Occupational Education, North Carolina State University, 1968.

Cunningham, J. W. The job-cluster concept and its curricular implications. Center for Occupational Education, Center Monograph No. 4, North Carolina State University, 1969.

Cunningham, J. W., and McCormick, E. J. Factor analyses of "worker-oriented" job variables. Occupational Research Center, Purdue University, June 1964. (Prepared for Office of Naval Research under contract Nonr–1100 [19], Report No. 4.)

Cunningham, J. W., Tuttle, T. C., Floyd, J. R., and Bates, J. A. The development of the Occupation Analysis Inventory: an "ergometric" approach to an educational problem. Center for Occupational Education, Center Research Monograph No. 6, North Carolina State University, 1971.

Farina, A. J., Jr. Development of a taxonomy of human performance: A review of descriptive schemes for human task behavior. JSAS *Catalog of Selected Documents in Psychology*, 1973, 3, 23. (Ms. No. 318) (Also available as AIR Tech. Rep. 726–7. Washington, D. C.: American Institutes for Research, February 1971.)

Farina, A. J., Jr., and Wheaton, G. R. Development of a taxonomy of human performance: The task characteristics approach to performance prediction. JSAS *Catalog of Selected Documents on Psychology*, 1973, 3, 26–27. (Ms. No. 323) (Also available as AIR Tech. Rep. 726–7. Washington, D.C.: American Institutes for Research, February 1971.)

Farrell, W. T. Hierarchical clustering: A bibliography. Evaluation of the Marine Corps task analysis program. California State University, Los Angeles, July 1975.

Farrell, W. T., Stone, C. H., and Yoder, D. Guidelines for research planning and design in task analysis, Technical Report No. 4, Evaluation of the Marine Corps Task Analysis Program. California State University, Los Angeles, September 1975.

Fine, S. A. Functional job analysis as a method of indirect validation: A study in synthetic validity. Unpublished doctoral dissertation, George Washington University, 1962.

Fine, S. A. Functional job analysis. *Personnel Administration and Industrial Relations*, 1955, 2, 1–16.

Fine, S. A. Functional Job Analysis Scales: A Desk Aid. W. E. Upjohn Institute for Employment Research, Kalamazoo, Mich., April 1973.

Fine, S. A., and Heinz, C. A. The estimates of worker trait requirements for 4,000 jobs. *Personnel and Guidance Journal*, 1957, 36, 168–174.

Fitts, P. M. Factors in complex skill training. In R. Glaser (Ed.) *Training Research and Education*. Pittsburgh, Pa.: University of Pittsburgh Press, 1962.

Fleishman, E. A. Factor structure in relation to task difficulty in psychomotor performance. *Educational and Psychological Measurement*, 1957, 17, 522–532.

Fleishman, E. A. Abilities at different stages of practice in rotary pursuit performance. *Journal of Experimental Psychology*, 1960, 60, 162–171.

Fleishman, E. A. The description and prediction of perceptual-motor skill learning. In R. Glaser (Ed.), *Training Research and Education*. Pittsburgh, Pa.: University of Pittsburgh Press, 1962.

Fleishman, E. A. *The Structure and Measurement of Physical Fitness.* Englewood Cliffs, N.J.: Prentice-Hall, 1964.

Fleishman, E. A. The prediction of total task performance from prior practice on task components. *Human Factors*, 1965, 7, 18–27.

Fleishman, E. A. Development of a behavior taxonomy for describing human tasks: A correlational-experimental approach. *Journal of Applied Psychology*, 1967, *51*, 1–10.

Fleishman, E. A. Individual differences and motor learning. In R. M. Gagné (Ed.), *Learning and Individual Differences.* Columbus, Ohio: Charles E. Merrill, 1967. *(a)*

Fleishman, E. A. Performance assessment based on an empirically derived task taxonomy. *Human Factors*, 1967, 9, 349–366. *(b)*

Fleishman, E. A. On the relation between abilities, learning, and human performance. *American Psychologist*, 1972, *27*, 1017–1032.

Fleishman, E. A., and Ellison, G. D. Prediction of transfer and other learning phenomena from ability and personality measures. *Journal of Educational Psychology*, 1969, 60, 300–314.

Fleishman, E. A., and Hempel, W. E., Jr. Changes in factor structure of a complex psychomotor test as a function of practice. *Psychometrika*, 1954, *18*, 239–252.

Fleishman, E. A., and Hempel, W. E., Jr. The relation between abilities and improvement with practice in a visual discrimination reaction task. *Journal of Experimental Psychology*, 1955, 49, 301–312.

Fleishman, E. A., Kinkade, R. G., and Chambers, A. N. Development of a taxonomy of human performance: A review of the first year's progress. American Institutes for Research, Technical Progress Report No. 1. November 1968.

Fleishman, E. A. and Parker, J. F. Factors in the retention and relearning of perceptual-motor skill. *Journal of Experimental Psychology*, 1962, 64, 215–226.

Fleishman, E. A., Teichner, W. H., and Stephenson, R. W. Development of a taxonomy of human performance: A review of the second year's progress. American Institutes for Research, Technical Progress Report No. 2, January 1970.

Fleishman, E. A., and Stephenson, R. W. Development of a taxonomy of human performance: A review of the third year's progress. American Institutes for Research, Technical Progress Report No. 3. September 1970.

Fugill, J. W. K. Task difficulty and task aptitude benchmark scales for the mechanical and electronics career fields. USAF, Air Force Systems Command, Brooks Air Force Base, Texas, April 1972.

Gagné, R. M. Human functions in systems. In R. M. Gagné (Ed.), *Psychological Principles in System Development.* New York: Holt, Rinehart & Winston, 1962.

Gagné, R. M. *Conditions of Learning.* New York: Holt, Rinehart & Winston, 1964.

Gagné, R. M., and Bolles, R. C. A review of factors in learning efficiency. In E. Galanter (Ed.), *Automatic Teaching: The State of the Art.* New York: John Wiley & Sons, 1963.

Galbraith, J. K. The economics of the American housewife. *Atlantic*, August 1973, pp. 78–83.

Galloway, S. and Archuleta, A. Sex and salary: Equal pay for comparable work. *American Libraries*, 1978, 9, 281–285.

Gilbert, A. C. F. Dimensions of certain army officer positions derived by factor analysis. U.S. Army Research Institute for the Behavioral and Social Sciences, December 1975.

Gordon, G. G., and McCormick, E. J. The identification, measurement and factor analyses of "worker-oriented" job variables. Occupational Research Center, Purdue University, July 1963. (Prepared for Office of Naval Research under contract Nonr–1100 (19), Report No. 3.)

Gragg, D. B. Identification of logistics officer job type groups. USAF, AFHRL–70–39, 1970.

Gragg, D. B. An occupational survey of an airman career ladder: supply warehousing-inspection. USAF, Personnel Research Laboratory, Technical Report No. 62–19, 1962.

Gregory, Robert G., and Duncan, Ronald C. The relevance of segmented labor market theories: the Australian experience of the achievement of equal pay for women. *Journal of Post Keynesian Economics*, 1981, *3*, 403–428.

Guilford, J. P. *Nature of Human Intelligence*. New York: McGraw-Hill, 1967.

Guion, R. M. Synthetic validity in a small company: A demonstration. *Personnel Psychology*, 1965, *18*, 49–63.

Hackman, J. R. Tasks and task performance in research on stress. In J. E. McGrath (Ed.), *Social and Psychological Factors in Stress*. New York: Holt, Rinehart & Winston, 1970.

Hemphill, J. K. Describing managerial work. The Conference on the Executive Study. Educational Testing Service, 1961.

Hemphill, J. K. Job descriptions for executives. *Harvard Business Review*, 1959, *37*, 53–67.

Jaspen, N. A factor study of work characteristics. *Journal of Applied Psychology*, 1949, *33*, 449–459.

Jeanneret, P. R. Personal communication, 1978.

Jeanneret, P. R. Equitable job evaluation and classification with the Position Analysis Questionnaire. *Compensation Review*, First Quarter, 1980, pp. 32–42. AMACOM, American Management Associations.

Jeanneret, P. R. A study of the job dimensions of "worker-oriented" job variables and of their attribute profiles. Unpublished doctoral dissertation, Purdue University, 1969.

Jeanneret, P. R., and McCormick, E. J. The job dimensions of "worker-oriented" job variables and of their attribute profiles as based on data from the Position Analysis Questionnaire. Occupational Research Center, Purdue University, June 1969. (Prepared for Office of Naval Research under contract Nonr–1100 (28), Report No. 2.)

Kleiger, W. A., and Mosel, J. N. The effect of opportunity to observe and rater status on the reliability of performance ratings. *Personnel Psychology*, 1953, *6*, 57–63.

Lawshe, C. H. Employee selection. *Personnel Psychology*, 1952, *5*, 31–34.

Lecznar, W. B. Three methods for estimating difficulty of job tasks. USAF, AFHRL–TR–71–30, July 1971.

Levine, J. M., Kramer, G. G., and Levine, E. N. Effects of alcohol on human performance: An integration of research findings based on an abilities classification. *Journal of Applied Psychology*, 1975, *60*, 285–293.

Levine, J. M., Romashko, T., and Fleishman, E. A. Development of a taxonomy of human performance: evaluation of an abilities classification system for integrating and generalizing research findings. American Institutes for Research, Technical Report No. 12, 1971.

Levine, J. M., Romashko, T., and Fleishman, E. A. Evaluation of an abilities classification system for integrating and generalizing human performance research findings: An application to vigilance tasks. *Journal of Applied Psychology*, 1973, *58*, 149–157.

Lewis, L. Job analysis in the United States Training and Employment Service. Proceedings of Division of Military Psychology Symposium: Collecting, Analyzing, and Reporting Information, Describing Jobs and Occupations. 75th Annual Convention of the American Psychological Association. Personnel Research Division, Air Force Human Resources Laboratory, Lackland Air Force Base, Tex.: September 1969.

McCormick, E. J. The development of processes for indirect or synthetic validity: III. Application of job analysis to indirect validity. A symposium. *Personnel Psychology*, 1959, *12*, 402–413.

McCormick, E. J. *Job Analysis: Methods and Applications*. New York: AMACOM, American Management Associations, 1979.

McCormick, E. J., Cunningham, J. W., and Gordon, G. G. Job dimensions based on factorial analyses of worker-oriented job variables. *Personnel Psychology*, 1967, *20*, 417–430.

McCormick, E. J., Cunningham, J. W., and Thornton, G. C. The prediction of job requirements by a structured job analysis procedure. *Personnel Psychology*, 1967, *20*, 431–440.

McCormick, E. J., Finn, R. H., and Scheips, C. D. Patterns of job requirements. *Journal of Applied Psychology*, 1957, *41*, 358–364.

McCormick, E. J., and Ilgen, D. R. *Industrial Psychology* (8th ed.). Englewood Cliffs, N.J.: Prentice-Hall, 1980.

McCormick, E. J., Jeanneret, P. R., and Mecham, R. C. The development and background of the Position Analysis Questionnaire (PAQ). Occupational Research Center, Purdue University, 1969. (Prepared for Office of Naval Research under contract Nonr–1100 [28], Report No. 5.) AD–691 737. (a)

McCormick, E. J., Jeanneret, P. R., and Mecham, R. C. A study of job characteristics and job dimensions as based on the Position Analysis Questionnaire (PAQ). *Journal of Applied Psychology*, 1972, *56*, 347–68.

Mayo, C. C. A method for determining job types for low aptitude airmen. USAF, AFHRL–TR–69–35, 1969.

Mead, D. F., and Christal, R. E. Development of a constant standard weight equation for evaluating job difficulty. USAF, AFHRL–TR–70–44, 1970.

Mead, D. F. Development of an equation for evaluating job difficulty. USAF, AFHRL–TR–70–42, 1970.

Mecham, R. C. Ratings of attribute requirements of job elements in a structured job analysis format. Unpublished master's thesis, Purdue University, 1968.

Mecham, R. C. The synthetic prediction of personnel test requirements and job evaluation points using the Position Analysis Questionnaire. Unpublished doctoral dissertation, Purdue University, 1970.

Mecham, R. C., and McCormick, E. J. The rated attribute requirements of job elements in the Position Analysis Questionnaire. Occupational Research Center, Purdue University, January 1969. (Prepared for Office of Naval Research under contract Nonr–1100 [28], Report No. 1). AD–682 490. (a)

Mecham, R. C., and McCormick, E. J. The use of data based on the Position Analysis Questionnaire in developing synthetically-derived attribute requirements of jobs. Occupational Research Center, Purdue University, June 1969. (Prepared for Office of Naval Research under contract Nonr–1100 [28], Report No. 4.) (c)

Mecham, R. C., and McCormick, E. J. The use in job evaluation of job elements and job dimensions based on the Position Analysis Questionnaire. Psychology Department, Purdue University, Report No. 3, 1969. (b)

Melching, H. W., and Boucher, S. D. Procedures for constructing and using Task Inventories. Center for Vocational and Technical Education, The Ohio State University, Research Development Series No. 91, 1973.

Melton, A. W. The taxonomy of human learning: Overview. In A. Melton (Ed.), *Categories of Human Learning*. New York: Academic Press, 1964.

Melton, A. W., and Brigg, G. Engineering psychology. In P. R. Farnsworth and Q. McNemar (Eds.), *Annual Review of Psychology* (Vol. 11). Palo Alto, Calif.: Annual Reviews, 1960.

Miles, M. C. Studies in job evaluation: a. Validity of a check list for evaluating office jobs. *Journal of Applied Psychology*, 1952, *36*, 97–101.

Miller, Ann R., Treiman, Donald J., Cain, Pamela S., and Roos, Patricia A. (Eds.), *Work, Jobs, and Occupations: A Critical Review of The Dictionary of Occupational Titles*. Report of the Committee on Occupational Classification and Analysis to the U.S. Department of Labor. Washington, D.C.: National Academy Press, 1980.

Miller, R. B. Analysis and specification of behavior in training. In R. Glaser (Ed.), *Training Research and Education*. Pittsburgh, Pa.: University of Pittsburgh Press, 1962.

Miller, R. B. *Task Taxonomy: Science or Technology?* Poughkeepsie, N.Y.: IBM, 1966.

Morsh, J. E. Analyzing work behavior. A paper presented at the American Psychological Association, 1963.

Morsh, J. E. Evolution of a job inventory and tryout of task rating factors. USAF, Personnel Research Laboratory, Technical Report No. 65–22, 1965.

Morsh, J. E. Identification of job types in the personnel career field. USAF, Personnel Research Laboratory, Technical Report No. 65–9, 1965.

Morsh, J. E. Job analysis in the United States Air Force. *Personnel Psychology*, 1964, *17*, 7–17.

Morsh, J. E. Job types identified with an inventory constructed by Telectronics engineers. USAF, Personnel Research Laboratory, Technical Report No. 66–6, 1966.

Morsh, J. E., and Archer, W. B. Procedural guide for conducting occupational surveys in the United States Air Force. USAF, Personnel Research Laboratory, Technical Report 67–11, 1967.

Morsh, J. E., and Christal, R. E. Impact of the computer on job analysis in the United States Air Force. USAF, Personnel Research Laboratory, Technical Report 66-19, 1966.

Nunnally, J. C. *Psychometric Theory*. New York: McGraw-Hill, 1967.

Pass, J. J., and Cunningham, J. W. A systematic procedure for estimating the attribute requirements of occupations. Report No. 11 of the Ergometric Research and Development Series. Center for Occupational Education, North Carolina State University, 1975.

Perlman, Nancy D., and Ennis, Bruce J. *Preliminary Memorandum on Pay Equity: Archieving Equal Pay for Work of Comparable Value*. Albany: State University of New York, Center for Women in Government, 1980.

Primoff, E. S. The J-coefficient approach to jobs and tests. *Personnel Administration*, 1957, *20*, 30–40.

Primoff, E. S. The development of processes for indirect or synthetic validity: IV. Empirical validations of the J-coefficient. A symposium. *Personnel Psychology*, 1959, *12*, 413–418.

Remick, Helen. Strategies for creating sound, bias free job evaluation plans. In *Job Evaluation and EEO: The Emerging Issues*. New York: Industrial Relations Counselors, Inc., 1978.

Remick, Helen. Beyond equal pay for equal work: comparable worth in the State of Washington. In Ronnie Steinberg Ratner (Ed.), *Equal Employment Policy for Women: Strategies for Implementation in the United States, Canada, and Western Europe*. Philadelphia: Temple University Press, 1980, 405–448.

Riccobono, J. A., and Cunningham, J. W. Work dimensions derived through systematic job analysis: a study of the Occupation Analysis Inventory. Center for Occupational Education, Center Research Monograph No. 8, North Carolina State University, 1971.

Riccobono, J. A., and Cunningham, J. W. Work dimensions derived through systematic job analysis: a replicated study of the Occupation Analysis Inventory. Center for Occupational Education, Center Research Monograph No. 9, North Carolina State University, 1971.

Riccobono, J. A., Cunningham, J. W., and Boese, R. R. Clusters of occupations based on systematically derived work dimensions: an exploratory study. Report No. 10 of the Ergometric Research and Development Series. Center for Occupational Education, North Carolina State University, 1974.

Silverman, J. A computer technique for clustering tasks. USN, Naval Personnel Research Activity, Technical Bulletin STB 66–23, 1966.

Silverman, J. New techniques in task analysis. USN, Naval Personnel Research Activity, Research Memorandum No. SRM 68–12, 1967.

Smith, P. C., and Kendall, L. M. Retranslation of expectations: An approach to the construction of unambiguous anchors for rating scales. *Journal of Applied Psychology*, 1963, *47*, 149–155.

Sprecher, T. B. Dimensions of engineers' job performance. Educational Testing Service, Research Bulletin, 1965.

Stone, C. H. Evaluation of the Marine Corps Task Analysis Program, Technical Report No. 16. California State University, Los Angeles, June 1976.

Taylor, L. R., and Colbert, G. A. Empirically derived job families as a foundation for the study of validity generalization: Study II. The construction of job families based on company-specific PAQ job dimensions. *Personnel Psychology*, 1978, *31*, 341–55.

Teichner, W. H., and Whitehead, J. Development of a taxonomy of human performance: Evaluation of a task classification system for generalizing research findings from a data base. American Institutes for Research, Technical Report No. 8, April 1971.

Theologus, G. C. Development of a taxonomy of human performance: A review of biological taxonomy and classification. JSAS *Catalog of Selected Documents in Psychology*, 1973, *3*, 23–24. (Ms. No. 319) (Also available as AIR Tech. Rep. 726–3. Washington, D.C.: American Institutes for Research, December 1969.

Theologus, G. C., and Fleishman, E. A. Development of a taxonomy of human performance: Validation study of ability scales for classifying human tasks. JSAS *Catalog of Selected Documents in Psychology*, 1973, *3*, 29. (Ms. No. 326) (Also available as AIR Tech. Rep. 726–10. Washington, D.C.: American Institutes for Research, April 1971.)

Theologus, G. C., Romashko, T., and Fleishman, E. A. Development of a taxonomy of human performance. American Institutes for Research, Technical Report No. 5, January 1970.

Theologus, G. C., Wheaton, G. R., and Fleishman, E. A. Effects of intermittent, moderate intensity noise stress on human performance. *Journal of Applied Psychology*, 1974, *59*, 539–547.

Tornow, W. W., and Pinto, P. R. The development of a managerial job taxonomy: A system for describing, classifying, and evaluating executive positions. *Journal of Applied Psychology*, 1976, *61*, 410–18.

Trattner, N. H., Fine, S. A., and Kubis, J. F. A comparison of worker requirement ratings made by reading job descriptions and by direct observation. *Personnel Psychology*, 1955, *8*, 183–194.

Treiman, Donald. *Job Evaluation: An Analytic Review*. Interim Report to the Equal Employment Opportunity Commission. Committee on Occupational Classification and Analysis, National Research Council. Washington, D.C.: National Academy of Sciences, 1979.

Tucker, L. R. A method of synthesis of factor analysis studies. Personnel Research Section Report No. 984. Washington, D.C.: Department of the Army, 1951.

Tuttle, T. C. and Cunningham, J. W. Affective correlates of systematically derived work dimensions: Validation of the Occupation Analysis Inventory. Ergometric research and development series, Report No. 7. Center research monograph No. 10. Center for Occupational Education, North Carolina State University, 1972.

U.S. Department of Commerce, Bureau of the Census. *1970 Census of Population*. Washington, D.C.: U.S. Government Printing Office, 1970.

U.S. Department of Health, Education, and Welfare. Major tasks and knowledge clusters involved in performance of electronic technicians' work. U.S. Government Printing Office, 1966.

United States Employment Service. *Dictionary of occupational titles: Vol. I. Definitions of titles. Vol. II. Occupational classification.* (3d ed.) Washington, D.C.: U.S. Government Printing Office, 1965.

Viteles, M. S. Job specifications and diagnostic tests of job competency designed for the auditing division of a street railway company. *Psychological Clinic*, 1922, *14*, 83–105.

Viteles, M. S. *Industrial Psychology*. New York: Norton, 1932.

Walker, K. Household work time: Implication for family decisions. *Journal of Home Economics*. 1973, *65*(7), 7–15.

Wheaton, G. R. Development of a taxonomy of human performance: A review of classificatory systems relating to tasks and performance. JSAS *Catalog of Selected Documents in Psychology*, 1973, *3*,

22–23. (Ms. No. 317) (Also available as AIR Tech. Rep. 726–1. Washington, D.C.: American Institutes for Research, December 1968.)

Winer, B. J. *Statistical Principles in Experimental Design.* New York: McGraw-Hill, 1962.

Wood, P. J. A taxonomy of instrumental conditioning. *American Psychologist,* 1974, *29,* 584–597.

SECTION TWO

Adams, L. P. *The Public Employment Service in Transition, 1933–1968: Evolution of a Placement Service into a Manpower Agency.* Cornell Studies in Industrial and Labor Relations No. 16. Ithaca, N.Y.: New York State School of Industrial and Labor Relations, Cornell University, 1969.

Adkins, D. C. Selecting public employees. *Public Personnel Review,* 1956, *17,* 260–261.

Albright, L. E., Glennon, J. R., and Smith, W. J. *The Uses of Psychological Tests in Industry.* Cleveland, Oh.: Allen, 1963.

American Psychological Association, American Educational Research Association, and National Council on Measurement in Education. *Standards for Educational and Psychological Tests.* Washington, D.C.: American Psychological Association, 1974.

American Psychological Association, Division of Industrial and Organizational Psychology. *Principles for the Validation and Use of Personnel Selection Procedures* (2d ed.). Berkeley, Calif.: Author, 1980. (Copies may be ordered from Lewis E. Albright, Kaiser Aluminum & Chemical Corporation, 300 Lakeside Drive—Room KB 2140, Oakland, Calif. 94643.)

American School of Correspondence. *Employment Management and Safety Engineering: A Practical Reading Course,* 7 vols. Chicago: American School of Correspondence, 1919.

Amrin, M. The 1965 congressional inquiry into testing. *American Psychologist,* 1965, *20,* 869.

APA pushing "truth in testing" alternative—More study. *APA Monitor,* October 1979, p. 9.

Aronson, A. H. *Biography of an Ideal: A History of the Federal Civil Service.* Washington, D.C.: U.S. Government Printing Office, 1973.

Baritz, L. *Servants of Power: A History of the Use of Social Science in American Industry.* Middletown, Conn.: Wesleyan University Press, 1960.

Bartlett, C. J., Bobko, P., Mosier, S. B., and Hannan, R. Testing for fairness with a moderated multiple regression strategy: An alternative to differential analysis. *Personnel Psychology,* 1978, *31,* 233–241.

Benge, E. J. *The Use of Tests in Employment and Promotion.* Studies in Personnel Policy No. 14. New York: National Industrial Conference Board, 1939.

Berle, A. A., and Means, G. C. *The Modern Corporation and Private Property.* Chicago: Commerce Clearinghouse, 1932.

Berliner, D. C. Tempus Educare. In P. Peterson and H. Walberg (Eds.), *Research in Teaching: Concepts, Findings and Implications.* Berkeley, Calif.: McCutchan, 1979.

Bingham, W. V. Psychology applied. *Scientific Monthly,* 1923a, 16.

Bingham, W. V. Cooperative business research. *Annals of the American Academy of Political Science,* 1923b, 110.

Bingham, W. V. *Aptitudes and Aptitude Testing.* New York: Harper & Row, 1937.

Bingham, W. V. Report of the committee on classification of military personnel advisory to the Adjutant General's office. *Science,* 1941, *93,* 572–574.

Bingham, W. V. In E. G. Boring, H. S. Langfield, H. Warner, and R. M. Yerkes, (Eds.) *A History of Psychology in Autobiography.* New York: Russell and Russell, 1952.

Blackford, K. M. H., and Newcomb, A. *The Job, the Man, the Boss.* New York: Doubleday, Page and Co., 1919.

Blake, D. H., Frederick, W. C., and Myers, M. S. *Social Auditing: Evaluating the Impact of Corporate Programs*. New York: Praeger Publishers, 1976.

Boehm, V. R. Differential prediction: A methodological artifact? *Journal of Applied Psychology*, 1977, *62*, 146–154.

Bolanovich, D. J. Interest tests reduce factory turnover. *Personnel Psychology*, 1948, *1*, 81–92.

Boring, E. G. *A History of Experimental Psychology*, 2d ed. New York: Appleton-Century-Crofts, 1942.

Boring, E. G., Langfeld, H. S., Warner, H., and Yerkes, R. M. (Eds) *A History of Psychology in Autobiography*. New York: Russell and Russell, 1952.

Borrow, H. C. The growth and present status of occupational testing. *Journal of Consulting Psychology*, 1944, *8*, 70–73.

Bray, D. W., Campbell, R. J., and Grant, D. L. *Formative Years in Business*. New York: John Wiley & Sons, 1974.

Bray, D. W., and Grant, D. L. The assessment center in the measurement of potential for business management. *Psychological Monographs*, 1966, *80*, Whole number.

Brewer, J. M. *History of Vocational Guidance: Origins and Early Development*. New York: Harper & Row, 1942.

Brogden, H. E. When testing pays off. *Personnel Psychology*, 1949, *2*, 171–183.

Brogden, H. E., and Taylor, E. K. A theory and classification of criterion bias. *Educational & Psychological Measurement*, 1950, *20*, 159–186.

Bureau of National Affairs. *Supervisory Selection Procedures*. Personnel Policies Forum No. 48. Washington, D.C.: Bureau of National Affairs, 1958.

Bureau of National Affairs. *Employee Selection Procedures*. Personnel Policies Forum No. 70. Washington, D.C.: Bureau of National Affairs, 1963.

Burnham, J. *The Managerial Revolution: What is Happening in the World*. New York: John Day Co., Inc., 1941.

Business Week. Sharper tools for talent hunt, March 27, 1965, 70–74.

Callender, J. C., and Osburn, H. G. Development and test of a new model of validity generalization. *Journal of Applied Psychology*, 1980, *65*, 543–558.

Camfield, T. M. Psychologists at War: The History of American Psychology and the First World War. Ph.D. dissertation, University of Texas at Austin, 1969.

Campbell, J. T., Crooks, L. A., Mahoney, M. H., and Rock, D. A. *An Investigation of Sources of Bias in the Prediction of Job Performance: A six year study* (Final Project Report No. PR-73-37). Princeton, N.J.: Educational Testing Service, 1973.

Carp, A. Testimony before the Senate Subcommittee on Constitutional Rights of the Committee on the Judiciary, June 7–10. *American Psychologist*, 1965, *20*, 917.

Cattell, J. M. The psychological corporation. *Annals of the American Academy of Political Science*, 1923, *110*, 165–171.

Chapman, J. C. *Trade Tests: The Scientific Measurement of Trade Proficiency*. New York: H. Holt and Co., 1921.

Chapman, J. C. Tests for trade proficiency. *Annals of the American Academy of Political Science*, 110, 1923.

Cherry-Burrell. Square peg 'problem employees' find square holes with aptitude tests. *Sales Management*, 1941, *48*, 19–20.

Cleary, T. A., and Hilton, T. I. Test bias: Prediction of grades of Negro and white students in integrated colleges. *Journal of Educational Measurement*, 1968, *5*, 115–124.

Cole, N. S. Bias in testing. *American Psychologist*, 1981, *36*, 1067–1077.

Committee on Standards for Providers of Psychological Services, American Psychological Association.

Standards for Providers of Industrial and Organizational Psychological Services. Washington, D.C.: Author, 1979.

Cronbach, L. J., and Gleser, G. *Psychological Tests and Personnel Decisions.* Urbana: University of Illinois Press, 1957.

Cronbach, L. J., Yalow, E., and Schaeffer, G. A mathematical structure for analyzing fairness in selection. *Personnel Psychology*, 1980, *33*, 693–704.

Cuts raise new social-science query: Does anyone appreciate social science? *The Wall Street Journal*, March 27, 1981, p. 54.

Davis, H. V. *Frank Parsons: Prophet, Innovator, Counselor.* Carbondale, Ill.: University of Southern Illinois Press, 1969.

Dorsch, F. *Geschichte und Probleme der angewandten Psychologie.* Stuttgart: Verlag Franz Huber, 1963.

Dunlap, K. Fact and fable in character analysis. *Annals of the American Academy of Political Science*, 1923, *110*, 74–80.

Eilbirt, H. The development of personnel management in the United States. *Business History Review*, 1959, *33*, 345–64.

Emmet, B., and Jeuck, J. E. *Catalogues and Counters: A History of Sears, Roebuck and Company.* Chicago: University of Chicago Press, 1950.

Equal Employment Opportunity Commission, Civil Service Commission, Department of Labor, and Department of Justice. Adoption by four agencies of Uniform Guidelines on Employee Selection Procedures. *Federal Register*, 1978, *43*, 38290–38315.

Equal Employment Opportunity Commission, Office of Personnel Management, Department of Justice, Department of Labor, and Department of the Treasury. Adoption of questions and answers to clarify and provide a common interpretation of the "Uniform guidelines on employee selection procedures." *Federal Register*, 1979, *44*, 11996–12009.

Ethical Standards of Psychologists. Washington, D.C.: American Psychological Association, 1977.

Ewing, D. W. *Freedom Inside the Organization: Bringing Civil Liberties to the Workplace.* New York: Dutton, 1977.

Federal Board for Vocational Education. *The Turnover of Labor.* Employment Management Series No. 46. Washington, D.C.: U.S. Government Printing Office, 1919.

Feiss, R. A. Personal relationships as a basis of scientific management. *Bulletin of the Society to Promote the Science of Management*, 1915, 1.

Filer, H. A., and O'Rourke, L. J. Progress in civil service tests. *Journal of Personnel Research*, 1923, *1*, 484–493.

Flanagan, J. C., ed. *The Aviation Psychology Program in the Army Air Forces.* Army Air Forces Aviation Psychology Research Reports No. 1. Washington, D.C.: U.S. Government Printing Office, 1948.

Flinn, A. D. Development of the Personnel Research Federation. *Journal of Personnel Psychology*, 1922, *1*, 7–13.

Fuess, C. M. *The College Board: Its First Fifty Years.* New York: Columbia University, 1950.

Gael, S., and Grant, D. L. Employment test validation for minority and nonminority telephone company service representatives. *Journal of Applied Psychology*, 1972, *56*, 135–139.

Gael, S., Grant, D. L., and Ritchie, R. J. Employment test validation for minority and nonminority clerks with work sample criteria. *Journal of Applied Psychology*, 1975, *60*, 520–426. (a)

Gael, S., Grant, D. L., and Ritchie, R. J. Employment test validation for minority and nonminority telephone operators. *Journal of Applied Psychology*, 1975, *60*, 411–419. (b)

Gaudet, F. J. *Labor Turnover: Calculation and Cost,* American Management Association Research Study 39. New York: American Management Association, 1960.

Ghiselli, E. E. *The Validity of Occupational Aptitude Tests.* New York: John Wiley & Sons, 1966.

Glass, G. V. Primary, secondary, and meta-analysis of research. *Educational Researcher*, 1976, *5*, 3–8.

Grant, D. L., and Bray, D. W. Validation of employment tests for telephone company installation and repair occupations. *Journal of Applied Psychology*, 1970, *54*, 7–14.

Gross, M. L. *The Brain Watchers*. New York: Random House, 1962.

Guion, R. M. *Personnel Testing*. New York: McGraw-Hill, 1965.

Habbe, S. Introduction in *Experience with Psychological Tests*. Studies in Personnel Policy No. 92. New York: National Industrial Conference Board, 1948.

Haber, S. *Efficiency and Uplift: Scientific Management in the Progressive Era*. Chicago: University of Chicago Press, 1960.

Hale, M., Jr. *Human Science and Social Order: Hugo Münsterberg and the Origins of Applied Psychology*. Philadelphia: Temple University Press, 1980.

Haney, W. Validity, vaudeville, and values: A short history of social concerns over standardized testing. *American Psychologist*, 1981, *36*, 1021–1034.

Hathaway, S. R. MMPI: Professional use by professional people. *American Psychologist*, 1964, *19*, 204–210.

Hinrichs, J. R. Comparison of "real life" assessments of management potential with situational exercises, paper-and-pencil ability tests, and personality inventories. *Journal of Applied Psychology*, 1969, *53*, 425.

Hinrichs, J. R. An eight-year follow-up of a management assessment center. *Journal of Applied Psychology*, 1978, *63*, 596.

Hohenstein, W. V. National Influence and Control over State and Local Personnel Practices in the United States. Ph.D. dissertation, University of Minnesota, 1956.

Hollingworth, H. L. Specialized vocational tests and methods. *School and Society* 1, 1915.

Hollingworth, H. L. *Vocational Psychology: Its Problems and Methods*. New York: D. Appleton and Co., 1916.

Huck, J. R. Assessment centers: A review of the external and internal validities. *Personnel Psychology*, 1973, *26*, 191–212.

Humphreys, L. G. Statistical definitions of test validity for minority groups. *Journal of Applied Psychology*, 1973, *58*, 1–4.

Hunter, J. E. *Validity generalization for 12,000 jobs: An application of synthetic validity and validity generalization to the General Aptitude Test Battery (GATB)*. Washington, D.C.: U.S. Employment Service, U.S. Department of Labor, 1980.

Hunter, J. E., and Schmidt, F. L. A critical analysis of the statistical and ethical implications of five definitions of test fairness. *Psychological Bulletin*, 1976, *83*, 1053–1071.

Hunter, J. E., and Schmidt, F. L. Differential and single group validity of employment tests by race: A critical analysis of three recent studies. *Journal of Applied Psychology*, 1978, *63*, 1–11.

Hunter, J. E., and Schmidt, F. L. Fitting people to jobs: Implications of personnel selection for national productivity. In E. A. Fleishman (Ed.), *Human Performance and Productivity*. Hillsdale, N.J.: Erlbaum, 1984.

Hunter, J. E., Schmidt, F. L., and Hunter, R. Differential validity of employment tests by race: A comprehensive review and analysis. *Psychological Bulletin*, 1979, *86*, 721–735.

Hunter, J. E.., Schmidt, F. L., and Rauschenberger, J. M. Fairness of psychological tests: Implications of four definitions for selection utility and minority hiring. *Journal of Applied Psychology*, 1977, *62*, 245–260.

Hunter, W. S. Psychology in the war. *American Psychologist*, 1946, *1*, 479–492.

Irwin, R. R. Lockheed's full testing program. *Personnel Journal*, 1942, *21*, 103–106.

Jensen, A. R. *Bias in Mental Testing.* New York: Free Press, 1980.

Justices uphold utility's stand on job testing. *The Wall Street Journal,* March 6, 1979, p. 4.

Katzell, R. A., and Dyer, F. J. Differential validity revived. *Journal of Applied Psychology,* 1977, *62,* 137–145.

Kavruk, S. Thirty-three years of test research: A short history of test development in the U.S. Civil Service Commission. *American Psychologist,* 1956, *11,* 329–333.

Kevles, D. M. Testing the Army's intelligence: Psychologists and the military in World War I. *Journal of American History,* 1968, *55,* 565–581.

Kinslinger, H. J. Application of projective techniques in personnel psychology since 1940. *Psychological Bulletin,* 1966, *66,* 134–149.

Klaw, S. The management psychologists have landed. *Fortune,* 1950, *81,* 107.

Kornhauser, A. W., and Kingsbury, F. W. *Psychological Tests in Business.* Chicago: University of Chicago Press, 1924.

Lawshe, C. H., and Balma, M. J. *Principles of Personnel Testing,* 2d ed. New York: McGraw-Hill, 1946.

Ledvinka, J. The statistical definition of fairness in the federal selection guidelines and its implications for minority employment. *Personnel Psychology,* 1979, *32,* 551–562.

Lee, R. D., Jr. *Public Personnel Systems.* Baltimore, Md.: University Park Press, 1979.

Lent, R. H., Aurbach, H. A., and Levin, L. S. Predictors, criteria, and significant results. *Personnel Psychology,* 1971, *24,* 519–533. (a)

Lent, R. H., Aurbach, H. A., and Levin, L. S. Research and design and validity assessment. *Personnel Psychology,* 1971, *24,* 247–274. (b)

Lerner, B. *Washington* v. *Davis:* Quantity, quality, and equality in employment testing. In P. Kurland (Ed.), *The 1976 Supreme Court Review.* Chicago: University of Chicago Press, 1977.

Lerner, B. Employment discrimination: Adverse impact, validity, and equality. In P. Kurland & G. Casper (Eds.), *The 1979 Supreme Court Review.* Chicago: University of Chicago Press, 1979.

Lilienthal, R. A., and Pearlman, K. *The Validity of Federal Selection Tests for Aid/Technicians in the Health, Science, and Engineering Fields.* Washington, D.C.: U.S. Office of Personnel Management, Personnel Research and Development Center, in press.

Link, H. C. *Employment Psychology: The Application of Scientific Methods to the Selection, Training and Grading of Employees.* New York: Macmillan, 1919.

Link, H. C. Psychological tests in industry. *Annals of the American Academy of Political Science,* 1923, *110.*

Linn, R. L. Single-group validity, differential validity, and differential predictions. *Journal of Applied Psychology,* 1978, *63,* 507–514.

Lopez, F. M. *The Making of a Manager: Guidelines to His Selection and Promotion.* New York: American Management Association, 1970.

Mack, M. J., Schmidt, F. L., and Hunter, J. E. Estimating the productivity costs in dollars of minimum selection test cutoff scores. Washington, D.C.: U.S. Office of Personnel Management, Personnel Research and Development Center, in press.

Macy, J. W. Psychological Testing. *American Psychologist,* 1965a, *20,* 883–884.

Macy, J. W. Testimony before the Senate Subcommittee on Constitutional Rights of the Committee on the Judiciary, June 7–10. *American Psychologist,* 1965b, *20,* 931–932.

Mann, A. *Yankee Reformers in the Urban Age.* Cambridge, Mass.: Harvard University Press, 1954.

Mayo, E. *The Social Problems of an Industrial Civilization.* Boston: Graduate School of Business Administration, Harvard University, 1945.

McCormick, E. J., and Tiffin, J. *Industrial Psychology.* London: George Allen and Unwin, 1975.

Mirvis, P. H., and Seashore, S. E. Being ethical in organizational research. *American Psychologist,* 1979, *34,* 766–780.

Moore, B. V. Personnel selection of graduate engineers: The differentiation of apprentice engineers for training as salesmen, designers, and executives of production. *Psychological Monographs*, 1921, *20*, 1–84.

Moses, J. L., and Byham, W. C. (Eds.). *Applying the Assessment Center Method*. New York: Pergamon Press, 1977.

Münsterberg, H. *American Problems from the Point of View of a Psychologist*. New York: Moffat, Yard and Co., 1910.

Münsterberg, H. *Psychology and Industrial Efficiency*. New York: Houghton Mifflin, 1913.

Napoli, D. S. The Architects of Adjustment: The Practice and Professionalization of American Psychology, chapter 5. Ph.D. dissertation, University of California at Davis, 1975.

National Industrial Conference Board. *What Employers Are Doing for Employees: A Survey of Voluntary Activities for Improvement of Working Conditions in American Business Concerns*. New York: National Industrial Conference Board, 1936.

National Industrial Conference Board. *The Use of Tests in Employment and Promotion*. Studies in Personnel Policy No. 14. New York: National Industrial Conference Board, 1939.

National Industrial Conference Board. *Experience with Employment Tests*. Studies in Personnel Policy No. 32. New York: National Industrial Conference Board, 1941.

National Industrial Conference Board. *Personnel Activities in American Business*. Studies in Personnel Policy No. 86. New York: National Industrial Conference Board, 1947.

National Industrial Conference Board. *Experience with Employment Tests*. Studies in Personnel Policy No. 92. New York: National Industrial Conference Board, 1948.

National Industrial Conference Board. *Personnel Practices in Factory and Office*. Studies in Personnel Policy No. 145. New York: National Industrial Conference Board, 1964a.

National Industrial Conference Board. *Personnel Practices in Factory and Office: Manufacturing*. Studies in Personnel Policy No. 194. New York: National Industrial Conference Board, 1964b.

National Industrial Conference Board. *Office Personnel Practices: Nonmanufacturing*. Studies in Personnel Policy No. 197. New York: National Industrial Conference Board, 1964c.

Nelson, D. M. *Managers and Workers: Origins of the New Factory System in the United States, 1880–1920*. Madison, Wis.: University of Wisconsin Press, 1975.

Noble, D. A. *America by Design: Science, Technology, and the Rise of Corporate Capitalism*. New York: Alfred A. Knopf, 1977.

Novick, M. R. Federal guidelines and professional standards. *American Psychologist*, 1981, *36*, 1035–1046.

O'Connor, E. J., Wexley, K. N., and Alexander, R. A. Single group validity: Fact or fallacy? *Journal of Applied Psychology*, 1975, *60*, 352–355.

Parsons, F. *Our Country's Needs: Or the Development of a Scientific Industrialism*. Boston: Arena Publishing Co., 1894.

Parsons, F. The vocation bureau. *Arena* 40, 1908.

Partington, J. E., and Bryant, T. R. The personnel consultant and psychological testing at armed forces induction stations. *American Psychologist*, 1946, *1*, 111.

Paterson, D. G., and Ludgate, K. E. Blond and brunette traits: A quantitative study. *Personnel Research*, 1922, *1*, 122–27.

Pearlman, K., Schmidt, F. L., and Hunter, J. E. Validity generalization results for tests used to predict training success and job proficiency in clerical occupations. *Journal of Applied Psychology*, 1980, *65*, 373–406.

Petersen, D. J. The impact of *Duke Power* on testing. *Personnel*, 1974, *51*, 30–37.

Roethlisberger, F. J., and Dickson, W. J. *Management and the Worker: An Account of a Research Program Conducted by the Western Electric Company, Hawthorne Works, Chicago*. Cambridge, Mass.: Harvard University Press, 1939.

Samelson, F. World War I intelligence testing and the development of psychology. *Journal of the History of the Behavioral Sciences*, 1977, *13*, 274–282.

Schmidt, F. L., Berner, J. G., and Hunter, J. E. Racial differences in validity of employment tests: Reality or illusion? *Journal of Applied Psychology*, 1973, *53*, 5–9.

Schmidt, F. L., Gast-Rosenberg, I., and Hunter, J. E. Validity generalization results for computer programmers. *Journal of Applied Psychology*, 1980, *65*, 643–661.

Schmidt, F. L., and Hunter, J. E. Development of a general solution to the problem of validity generalization. *Journal of Applied Psychology*, 1977, *62*, 529–540.

Schmidt, F. L., and Hunter, J. E. Moderator research and the law of small numbers. *Personnel Psychology*, 1978, *31*, 215–231.

Schmidt, F. L., and Hunter, J. E. Racial and ethnic bias in psychological tests: Divergent implications of two definitions of test bias. *American Psychologist*, 1974, *29*, 1–8.

Schmidt, F. L., Hunter, J. E., and Caplan, J. R. Validity generalization results for two jobs in the petroleum industry. *Journal of Applied Psychology*, 1981, *66*, 261–273.

Schmidt, F. L., Hunter, J. E., McKenzie, R., and Muldrow, T. The impact of valid selection procedures on workforce productivity. *Journal of Applied Psychology*, 1979, *64*, 609–626.

Schmidt, F. L., Hunter, J. E., and Pearlman, K. Task differences and validity of aptitude tests in selection: A red herring. *Journal of Applied Psychology*, 1981, *66*, 166–185.

Schmidt, F. L., Hunter, J. E., Pearlman, K., and Shane, G. S. Further tests of the Schmidt–Hunter Bayesian validity generalization procedure. *Personnel Psychology*, 1979, *32*, 250–281.

Schmidt, F. L., Hunter, J. E., and Urry, V. M. Statistical power in criterion-related validity studies. *Journal of Applied Psychology*, 1976, *61*, 473–485.

Schmidt, F. L., Pearlman, K., and Hunter, J. E. The validity and fairness of employment and educational tests for Hispanic Americans: A review and analysis. *Personnel Psychology* 1980, *33*, 705–724.

Scott, W. D. Review of Hugo Münsterberg. *Psychology and Industrial Efficiency. Psychological Bulletin, 10*, 1913.

Scott, W. D. The scientific selection of salesmen. *Advertising and Selling*, 1915, *24*(October): 5–6, 94–96. (November):*11*, 55. (December):*11*, 69–70.

Scott, W. D., Clothier, R. C., and Spriegel, W. R. *Personnel Management: Principles, Practices, and a Point of View*, 6th ed. New York: McGraw-Hill, 1961.

Sewell, W. H., Hauser, R. M., and Featherman, D. L. (Eds.) *Schooling and Achievement in American Society*. New York: Academic Press, 1976.

Shafritz, J. M. *Public Personnel Management: The Heritage of Civil Service Reform*. New York: Praeger Publishers, 1975.

Shriver, S. Suggestions to the American Psychological Association. *American Psychologist*, 1965, *20*, 876–877.

Siegel, J. B. The use of psychological testing in industry. *Pittsburgh Business Review*, 1968, *38*, 1–3.

Spencer, L. M. What's the score now with psychological tests. *American Business*, 1959, *29*, 7–10.

Standards for Providers of Psychological Services. Washington, D.C.: American Psychological Association, 1977.

Stead, W. H., Shartle, C. L., and Otis, J. L. *Occupational Counseling Techniques*. U.S.E.S. study. New York: American Book Company, 1940.

Stead, W. H., and Masincup, W. E. *The Occupational Research Program of the United States Employment Service*. Chicago: Public Administration Service, 1942.

Stessin, L. How private are personnel files? *New York Times*, April 9, 1978, pp. 1F; 14F.

Tenopyr, M. L. The realities of employment testing. *American Psychologist*, 1981, *36*, 1120–1127.

Terman, L. The status of applied psychology in the United States. *Journal of Applied Psychology*, 1919, *5*, 1–4.

Thorndike, E. L. Educational diagnosis. *Science*, 1913, n.s., 37.

Thorndike, R. L. *Personnel Selection: Test and Measurement Techniques.* New York: John Wiley & Sons, 1949.

U.S. Adjutant General's Office. *The Personnel System of the United States Army.* Vol. 1: *History of the Personnel System.* Committee on Classification of Personnel in the Army. Washington, D.C.: U.S. Government Printing Office, 1919.

U.S. Adjutant General's Office. Personnel Research in the Army. Personnel Research Section, War Department. *Personnel Journal,* 1943, *21,* 352.

U.S. Bureau of Labor Statistics. *Proceedings of the Employment Managers' Conference,* Philadelphia, Pa. Bulletin no. 227. Washington, D.C.: U.S. Department of Labor, 1917.

U.S. Bureau of Labor Statistics. Hiring and separation methods in American factories. *Monthly Labor Review,* 1932, *35,* 1008.

U.S. Civil Service Commission. *Twenty-Seventh Annual Report of the United States Civil Service Commission for the Fiscal Year Ending June 30, 1910.* Washington, D.C.: U.S. Government Printing Office, 1911.

U.S. Civil Service Commission. *Twenty-Eighth Annual Report of the United States, Civil Service Commission for the Fiscal Year Ending June 30, 1911.* Washington, D.C.: U.S. Government Printing Office, 1912.

U.S. Civil Service Commission. *Fortieth Annual Report of the United States Civil Service Commission for the Fiscal Year Ending June 30, 1923.* Washington, D.C.: U.S. Government Printing Office, 1924.

U.S. Congress. *History of Civil Service Merit Systems of the United States and Selected Foreign Countries.* Subcommittee on Manpower and Civil Service. Committee on Post Office and Civil Service, U.S. House of Representatives. 94th Congress, 2d session. Washington, D.C.: U.S. Government Printing Office, 1976.

U.S. Department of Labor. *Dictionary of Occupational Titles* (4th ed.). Washington, D.C.: U.S. Government Printing Office, 1977.

U.S. Office of Strategic Services. *Assessment of Men: Selection of Personnel for the Office of Strategic Services.* New York: Rinehart and Co., 1948.

Van Riper, P. *History of the United States Civil Service.* Evanston, Ill: Row, Peterson and Co., 1958.

Viteles, M. The mental status of the Negro. *Annals of the American Academy of Political Science,* 1928, *140,* 166–177.

Viteles, M. *Industrial Psychology.* New York: W. W. Norton and Co., 1932.

Wadsworth, G. W., Jr. Humm-Wadsworth Temperament Scale. In *Experience with Employment Tests.* Studies in Personnel Policy No. 32. New York: National Industrial Conference Board, 1941.

Westin, A. F. A new move toward employee rights. *New York Times,* April 23, 1978, p. 18F.

Whyte, W. H., Jr. The fallacies of "personality" testing. *Fortune,* 1954, *50,* 118–119.

Wiebe, R. *The Search for Order, 1877–1920.* New York: Hill and Wang, 1967.

Wiley, D. E. Another hour, another day: Quality of schooling a potent path for policy. *Studies of Educational Process* No. 3, University of Chicago, July 1973.

Wolins, L. Responsibility for raw data. *American Psychologist,* 1962, *17,* 657–658.

Woodward Governor Company. How and why Woodward Governor Co. uses aptitude tests for employees. *Sales Management,* 1941, *48,* 66–67.

Worthy, J. C. "Planned executive development: The experience of Sears, Roebuck and Co." *Personnel Series 137.* New York: American Management Association, 1951.

Yerkes, R. M., ed. *Psychological Examining in the United States Army.* Memoirs of the National Academy of Sciences 15. Washington, D. C.: U.S. Government Printing Office, 1921.

Yerkes, R. M. Psychological work of the National Research Council. *Annals of the American Academy of Political Science,* 1923, *110,* 172–78.

Yoakum, C. S., and Yerkes, R. M., eds. *Army Mental Tests.* New York: Henry Holt and Co., 1920.

Young, K. The history of mental testing. *Pedagogical Seminary*, 1923, *31*, 1–47.

SECTION THREE

Abrams, S. Polygraph validity and reliability: A review. *Journal of Forensic Sciences*, 1973, *18*, 313–326.

Alderfer, C. P., and Brown, L. D. Designing an "empathic questionnaire" for organizational research. *Journal of Applied Psychology*, 1972, *56*, 456–460.

Ash, P. Validation of an instrument to predict the likelihood of employee theft. *Proceedings of the 78th Annual Convention of the American Psychological Association*, 1970, 579–580.

Ash, P. Screening employment applicants for attitudes toward theft. *Journal of Applied Psychology*, 1971, *55*, 161–164.

Ash, P. Attitudes of work applicants toward theft. *Proceedings of the XVIIth International Congress of Applied Psychology*, 1972, 985–988.

Ash, P. Predicting dishonesty with the Reid Report. *Polygraph*, 1975, *5*, 139–153.

Ash, P. The assessment of honesty in employment. *South African Journal of Psychology*, 1976, *6*, 68–79.

Barland, G. H. *Detection of deception in criminal suspects: A field validation study.* Unpublished doctoral dissertation, University of Utah, 1975.

Barland, G. H. and Raskin, D. C. Detection of deception. In W. F. Proskasy & D. C. Raskin (Eds.), *Electrodermal activity in psychological research.* New York: Academic Press, 1973.

Barland, G. H. and Raskin, D. C. An evaluation of field techniques in detection of deception. *Psychophysiology*, 1975, *12*, 321–330.

Barrett, G. V., Phillips, J. S., and Alexander, R. A. Concurrent and predictive validity designs: A critical reanalysis. *Journal of Applied Psychology*, 1981, 66, 1–6.

Belt, J. A. and Holden, P. B. Polygraph usage among major U.S. corporations. *Personnel Journal*, 1978, *57*, 80–86.

Bemis, S. E. Occupational validity of the general aptitude test battery. *Journal of Applied Psychology*, 1968, *52*, 240–249.

Bersh, P. V. A validation study of polygraph examiner judgments. *Journal of Applied Psychology*, 1969, *53*, 399–403.

Boehm, V. R. Are we validating more but publishing less? (The impact of governmental regulation on published validation research—an explanatory investigation). *Personnel Psychology*, 1982, *35*, 175–187.

Bray, D. W., Campbell, R. J., and Grant, D. L. *Formative Years in Business.* New York: John Wiley & Sons, 1974.

Business buys the lie detector. *Business Week*, February 6, 1978, pp. 100–101, 104.

Callender, J. C., and Osburn, H. G. Development and test of a new model for generalization of validity. *Journal of Applied Psychology*, 1980, *65*, 543–558.

Causey v. *Ford Motor Company.* 10 Employment Practices Decisions 10321.

Chaiken, S., and Eagly, A. H. Communication modality as a determinant of message comprehensibility. *Journal of Personality and Social Psychology*, 1976, *34*, 605–614.

Circle K Corporation v. *EEOC.* 50 Federal Reporter 1052–54.

Corporate Lie Detector comes under fire. *Business Week*, January 13, 1973, pp. 88–89.

Dean, R. A. Reality shock, organizational commitment, and behavior: A realistic job preview experiment. *Dissertation Abstracts International*, 1981, *42*, 12A, 5226. (University Microfilms No. 82-12, 381).

Dunnette, M. D., Arvey, R. D., and Banas, P. A. Who do they leave? *Personnel*, 1973, *50*, 25–39.

Flanagan, J. C. The critical incident technique. *Psychological Bulletin*, 1954, *51*, 327–358.

Ghiselli, E. E. The validity of aptitude tests in personnel selection. *Personnel Psychology*, 1973, *26*, 461–477.

Ghiselli, E. E. The validity of a personnel interview. *Personnel Psychology*, 1966, *19*, 389–395.

Glass, G. V., McGaw, B., and Smith, M. L. *Meta-analysis in Social Research*. Beverly Hills, Calif.: Sage, 1981.

Guion, R. M. *Personnel Testing*. New York: McGraw-Hill, 1965.

Guion, R. M., and Gottier, R. F. Validity of personality measures in personnel selection. *Personnel Psychology*, 1965, *18*, 135–164.

Hackman, J. R., and Oldham, G. R. *Work Redesign*. Reading, Mass.: Addison-Wesley, 1980.

Hays, W. L. *Statistics for Psychologists*. New York: Holt, Rinehart & Winston, 1963.

Hester v. *Southern Railway*. 5 Fair Employment Practices 121.

Hoiberg, A., and Berry, N. H. Expectations and perceptions of Navy life. *Organizational Behavior and Human Performance*, 1978, *21*, 130–145.

Horvath, F. The effect of selected variables on interpretation of polygraph records. *Journal of Applied Psychology*, 1977, *62*, 127–136.

Horvath, F. An experimental comparison of the psychological stress evaluator and the galvanic skin response in detection of deception. *Journal of Applied Psychology*, 1978, *63*, 338–344.

Horvath, F. S. and Reid, J. E. Reliability of polygraph examiner diagnosis of truth and deception. *Journal of Criminal Law, Criminology and Police Science*, 1971, *62*, 276–281.

Hunter, J. E., Schmidt, F. L., and Jackson, G. B. *Meta-analysis: Cumulating Research Findings across Studies*. Beverly Hills, Calif.: Sage, 1982.

Ilgen, D. R., and Feldman, J. M. Performance appraisal: A process focus. *Research in Organizational Behavior*, 1983, *5*, 141–197.

Johnson, L. C. and Corah, N. L. Racial differences in skin resistance. *Science*, 1963, *139*, 766–767.

Keeler, L. A method for detecting deception. *American Journal of Police Science*, 1930, *1*(1), 38.

Kugelmass, S. and Lieblich, I. Relation between ethnic origin and GSR reactivity in psychophysiological detection. *Journal of Applied Psychology*, 1968, *52*, 54–59.

Lancaster, H. Failing system: Job tests are dropped by many companies due to antibias drive. *The Wall Street Journal*, September 3, 1975, p. 1.

Landy, F. J., and Farr, J. L. Performance rating. *Psychological Bulletin*, 1980, *87*, 72–107.

Larson, J. A. Modification of the Marston deception test. *Journal of Criminal Law and Criminology*, 1921, *12*, 390.

Latham, G. P., Fay, C., and Saari, L. M. The development of behavioral observation scales for appraising the performance of foremen. *Personnel Psychology*, 1979, *32*, 299–311.

Latham, G. P., and Wexley, K. N. Behavioral observation scales for performance appraisal purposes. *Personnel Psychology*, 1977, *30*, 255–268.

Latham, G. P., Wexley, K. N., and Pursell, E. D. Training managers to minimize rating errors in the observation of behavior. *Journal of Applied Psychology*, 1975, *60*, 550–555.

Latham, G. P., and Yukl, G. A review of research on the application of goal setting in organizations. *Academy of Management Journal*, 1975, *18*, 824–845.

Lazarus, R. S., Tomita, M., Opton, E. O., Jr., and Kodama, M. A cross-cultural study of stress-reaction patterns in Japan. *Journal of Personality and Social Psychology*, 1966, *4*, 622–633.

Lee, R., Miller, K. J., and Graham, W. K. Corrections for restriction of range and attenuation in criterion-related validation studies. *Journal of Applied Psychology*, 1982, *67*, 637–639.

Lent, R. H., Aurbach, H. D., and Levin, L. S. Predictors, criteria, and significant results. *Personnel Psychology*, 1971, *24*, 519–533.

Levine, J., and Butler, J. Lecture versus group discussion in changing behavior. *Journal of Applied Psychology*, 1952, *36*, 29–33.

Lieblich, I., Ben-Shakhar, G., Kugelmass, S., and Cohen, Y. Decision theory approach to the problem of polygraph interrogation. *Journal of Applied Psychology*, 1978, *63*, 489–498.

Linn, R. L. Pearson selection formulas: Implications for studies of predictive bias and estimates of educational effects in selected samples. *Journal of Educational Measurement*, 1983, *20*, 1–16.

Linn, R. L., Harnisch, D. L., and Dunbar, S. B. Corrections for range restriction: An empirical investigation of conditions resulting in conservative corrections. *Journal of Applied Psychology*, 1981, *66*, 655–663.

Locke, E. A. Toward a theory of task motivation and incentives. *Organizational Behavior and Human Performance*, 1968, *3*, 157–189.

Lombroso, C. *Crime: Its Causes and Remedies*. (trans. by Horton, H. P.). Boston: Little, Brown, 1912.

Lykken, D. T. Psychology and the lie detection industry. *American Psychologist*, 1974, *29*, 725–739.

Lykken, D. T. Uses and abuses of the polygraph. In H. L. Pick (Ed.) *Psychology: From Research to Practice*. New York: Plenum Press, 1978.(a).

Lykken, D. T. Where science fears to tread. (Review of *Truth and deception: The polygraph ("lie detector") technique* (2d ed.) by J. E. Reid & F. E. Inbau). *Contemporary Psychology*, 1978, *23*, 81–82.(b).

Lykken, D. T. The detection of deception. *Psychological Bulletin*, 1979, *86*, 47–53.

Maas, J. B. Patterned expectation interview: Reliability studies on a new technique. *Journal of Applied Psychology*, 1965, *49*, 431–433.

Mayfield, E. C. The selection interview—re-evaluation of published research. *Personnel Psychology*, 1964, *17*, 239–260.

McGuire, W. J. Inducing resistance to persuasion. In L. Berkowitz (Ed.) *Advances in experimental social psychology* (Vol. 1, pp. 191–229). New York: Academic Press, 1964.

Mobley, W. H., Griffeth, R. W., Hand, H. H., and Meglino, B. M. Review and conceptual analysis of the employee turnover process. *Psychological Bulletin*, 1979, *86*, 493–522.

Orne, M. T., Thackray, R. I., and Paskewitz, D. A. On the detection of deception: A model for the study of the physiological effects of psychological stimuli. In N. Greenfield, & R. Steinbach, (Eds.) *Handbook of Psychophysiology*. New York: Holt, 1972, pp. 743–785.

Pearlman, K., Schmidt, F. L., and Hunter, J. E. Validity generalization results for tests used to predict job proficiency and training success in clerical occupations. *Journal of Applied Psychology*, 1980, *65*, 373–406.

Podlesny, J. A., and Raskin, D. C. Physiological measures and the detection of deception. *Psychological Bulletin*, 1977, *84*, 782–799.

Popovich, P., and Wanous, J. P. The realistic job preview as a persuasive communication. *Academy of Management Review*, 1982, *7*, 570–578.

Porter, L. W., Steers, R. M., Mowday, R. T., and Boulian, P. V. Organizational commitment, job satisfaction, and turnover among psychiatric technicians. *Journal of Applied Psychology*, 1974, *59*, 603–609.

Premack, S., and Wanous, J. P. *A meta-analysis of realistic job preview experiments*. Unpublished manuscript. Columbus, Ohio: Ohio State University, College of Administrative Science, 1983.

Pursell, E. D., Dossett, D. L., and Latham, G. P. Obtaining valid predictors by minimizing rating errors in the criterion. *Personnel Psychology*, 1980, *33*, 91–96.

Raskin, D. C. and Podlesny, J. A. Truth and deception: a reply to Lykken. *Psychological Bulletin*, 1979, *86*, 54–59.

Reid, J. E. and Inbau, F. E. *Truth and Deception: The Polygraph ("Lie Detector") Technique* (2d ed.). Baltimore, Md.: Williams and Wilkins, 1977.

Reilly, R. R., Brown, B., Blood, M. R., and Malatesta, C. Z. The effects of realistic previews: A study and discussion of the literature. *Personnel Psychology*, 1981, *34*, 823–834.

Reilly, R. R., and Chao, G. T. Validity and fairness of some alternative employee selection procedures. *Personnel Psychology*, 1982, *35*, 1–62.

Rice, B. The new truth machines. *Psychology Today*, June 1978, pp. 61–78.

Rosenbaum, R. W. Predictability of employee theft using weighted application blanks. *Journal of Applied Psychology*, 1976, *61*, 94–98.

Rosenthal, R. *Experimenter Effects in Behavioral Research*. New York: Appleton-Century-Crofts, 1966.

Salton v. *Western Electric*. 7 Employment Practices Decisions 9327.

Schmidt, F. L., Gast-Rosenberg, I., and Hunter, J. E. Validity generalization results for computer programmers. *Journal of Applied Psychology*, 1980, *65*, 643–661.

Schmidt, F. L., and Hunter, J. E. Development of a general solution to the problem of validity generalization. *Journal of Applied Psychology*, 1977, *62*, 529–540.

Schmidt, F. L., Hunter, J. E., and Caplan, J. Validity generalization results for two job groups in the petroleum industry. *Journal of Applied Psychology*, 1981, *66*, 261–273.

Schmidt, F. L., Hunter, J. E., Pearlman, K., and Shane, G. S. Further tests of the Schmidt-Hunter Bayesian validity generalization procedure. *Personnel Psychology*, 1979, *32*, 257–281.

Schmitt, N., and Schneider, B. Current issues in personnel selection. In K. M. Rowland and J. Ferris (Eds.), *Research in Personnel and Human Resources Management, 1*. Greenwich, Conn.: JAI Press, 1983.

Skolnick, J. H. Scientific theory and scientific evidence: An analysis of lie detection. *Yale Law Journal*, April 1961, *70*, 694–728.

Smith, P. C., Kendall, L. M., and Hulin, C. L. *The Measurement of Satisfaction in Work and Retirement*. Chicago: Rand McNally, 1969.

Smith, P. C., and Kendall, L. M. Retranslation of expectations: An approach to the construction of unambiguous anchors for rating scales. *Journal of Applied Psychology*, 1963, *47*, 149–155.

Thorndike, R. L. *Personnel Selection*. New York: John Wiley & Sons, 1949.

Ulrich, L., and Trumbo, D. The selection interview since 1949. *Psychological Bulletin*, 1965, *63*, 100–116.

U. S. House of Representatives. The use of polygraphs and similar devices by federal agencies. (House Report No. 94–795 of the Committee on Government Operations.) January 1976.

U. S. Senate. Privacy, polygraphs, and employment. (93d Congress, 2d Session, prepared by the staff of the Subcommittee on Constitutional Rights of the Committee on the Judiciary.) November 1974.

Wanous, J. P. Organizational entry: From naive expectations to realistic beliefs. *Journal of Applied Psychology*, 1976, *61*, 22–29.

Wanous, J. P. Realistic job previews: Can a procedure to reduce turnover also influence the relationship between abilities and performance? *Personnel Psychology*, 1978, *31*, 249–258.

Wanous, J. P. *Organizational entry: Recruitment, selection, and socialization of newcomers*. Reading, Mass.: Addison-Wesley, 1980.

Wagner, R. The employment interview: A critical review. *Personnel Psychology*, 1949, *2*, 17–46.

Wernimont, P. F., and Campbell, J. Signs, samples, and criteria. *Journal of Applied Psychology*, 1968, *52*, 372–376.

Wexley, K. N., and Klimoski, R. Performance appraisal: An update. In K. M. Rowland and G. D. Ferris (Eds.), *Research in Personnel and Human Resources Management, 2*. Greenwich, Conn.: JAI Press, 1984.

Wexley, K. N., Sanders, R. D., and Yukl, G. A. Training interviewers in employment interviews. *Journal of Applied Psychology*, 1973, *57*, 233–236.

SECTION FOUR

Albemarle Paper Co. v. *Moody*. 422 U.S. 405 (1975).

American Psychological Association, Division of Industrial-Organizational Psychology. *Principles for the validation and use of personnel selection procedures* (2d ed.) Berkeley, Calif.: author, 1980.

Arvey, R. D. *Fairness in Selecting Employees.* Reading, Mass.: Addison-Wesley, 1979.

Balzer, W. K. *Biased attention to and encoding of behaviors during performance appraisal: The effects of initial impression and centrality of the appraisal task.* Unpublished dissertation. Department of Psychology, New York University, 1983.

Banks, C. G. *A laboratory study of the decision-making processes underlying performance appraisal.* Unpublished dissertation. Department of Psychology, University of Minnesota, 1979.

Banks, C. G. *Cue Selection and Evaluation.* Unpublished manuscript, 1982.

Banks, C. G., and Roberson, L. Performance appraisers as test developers. *Academy of Management Review*, 1985, *10*, 128–142.

Barnes-Farrell, J.L. and Coutkure, K. *Effects of appraisal salience on immediate and memory-based judgments.* Paper presented at the 91st Annual American Psychological Association Meeting, Anaheim, Calif., 1983.

Barrett, R. S. Influence of supervisor's requirements on ratings. *Personnel Psychology*, 1966, *19*, 375–387. *(a)*

Barrett, R. S. *Performance Rating.* Chicago: Science Research Associates, 1966. *(b)*

Bass, B. M. Further evidence on the dynamic nature of criteria. *Personnel Psychology*, 1962, *15*, 93–97.

Bass, B. M., and Barrett, G. V. *People, Work and Organizations (2d ed.).* Boston: Allyn & Bacon, 1981.

Bernardin, H. J. Implications of the Uniform Selection Guidelines for performance appraisals of police officers. *Proceedings of the national workshop on the selection of law enforcement officers*, 1979, 97–102.

Bernardin, H. J. *Rater training strategies: An integrative model.* Paper presented at the 89th Annual American Psychological Association Meeting, Los Angeles, Calif., 1981.

Bernardin H. J., and Beatty, R. W. *Performance Appraisal: Assessing Human Behavior of Work.* Boston: Kent, 1983.

Bernardin, H. J., and Buckley, M. R. A consideration of strategies in rater training. *Academy of Management Review*, 1981, *2*, 205–212.

Bernardin, H. J., and Pence, E. C. Effects of rater training: Creating new response sets and decreasing accuracy. *Journal of Applied Psychology*, 1980, *65*, 60–66.

Bernardin, H. J. and Smith P. C. A clarification of some issues regarding the development and use of behaviorally-anchored rating scales (BARS). *Journal of Applied Psychology*, 1981, *66*, 458–463.

Bernardin, H. J. and Walter, C. S. The effects of rater training and diary keeping on psychometric error in ratings. *Journal of Applied Psychology*, 1977, *62*, 64–69.

Blood, M. R. Spin-offs from behavioral expectation scale procedures. *Journal of Applied Psychology*, 1974, *59*, 513–515.

Blum, M. L., and Naylor, J. C. *Industrial Psychology.* New York: Harper & Row, 1968.

Boice R. Observational skills. *Psychological Bulletin*, 1983, *93*, 3–29.

Bolton v. *Murray Envelope Corp.* 493 F.2d 191 (5th Cir., 1974).

Borman, W. C. The rating of individuals in organizations: An alternate approach. *Organizational Behavior and Human Performance*, 1974, *12*, 105–124.

Borman, W. C. Consistency of rating accuracy and rating error in the judgment of human performance. *Organizational Behavior and Human Performance*, 1977, *20*, 238–252.

Brito v. *Zia Co.* 478 F.2d 1200 (10th Cir. 1973). Cascio, W. F. *Applied Psychology in Personnel Management.* Reston, Va.: Reston, 1978.

Bruner, J. S., and Tagiuri, R. The perception of people. In G. Lindzey (Ed.), *Handbook of Social Psychology* (Vol. 2). Cambridge, Mass.: Addison-Wesley, 1954.

Campbell, J. P., Dunnette, M. D., Lawler, E. E., III, and Weick, K. E. *Managerial Behavior, Performance, and Effectiveness.* New York: McGraw-Hill, 1970.

Campbell, J. P. Psychometric theory. In M. D. Dunnette, (Ed.), *Handbook of Industrial and Organizational Psychology.* Chicago: Rand-McNally, 1976.

Carroll, S. J., and Schneier, C. E. *Performance Appraisal and Review Systems.* Glenview, Ill.: Scott, Foresman, 1982.

Cascio, W. F., and Valenzi, E. R. Relations among criteria of police performance. *Journal of Applied Psychology,* 1978, *63,* 22–28.

Cleverly v. *Western Electric Co.* 594 F.2d 638 (8th Cir. 1979).

Cooper W. Ubiquitous halo. *Psychological Bulletin,* 1981a, *90,* 218–244.

Cooper W. Conceptual similarity as a source of halo in job performance ratings. *Journal of Applied Psychology,* 1981b, *66,* 302–307.

Cronbach, L. J. Processes affecting scores on "understanding of others" and "assumed similarity." *Psychological Bulletin,* 1955, *52,* 177–193.

DeCotiis, T. A. An analysis of the external validity and applied relevance of three rating formats. *Organizational Behavior and Human Performance,* 1977, *19,* 247–266.

DeNisi, A., Meglino, B., and Cafferty, T. P. A cognitive view of the performance appraisal process: A model and research propositions. *Organizational Behavior and Human Performance,* 1984, *33,* 360–396.

DeVries, D., Morrison, A., Shullman, S., and Gerlach, M. *Performance Appraisal on the Line.* New York: Wiley-Interscience, 1981.

Dipboye, R. L. Some neglected variables in research on discrimination in appraisals. *Academy of Management Review,* 1985, *10,* 116–127.

Donaldson v. *Pillsbury Co.* 554 F.2d 825 (8th Cir. 1977).

Dunnette, M. D. A note on the criterion. *Journal of Applied Psychology,* 1963, *47,* 251–254.

Dunnette, M. D. *Personnel Selection and Placement.* Belmont, Calif.: Wadsworth, 1966.

E.E.O.C. v. *Radiator Specialty Co.* 610 F.2d 178 (4th Cir. 1979).

Feldman, J. M. Beyond attribution theory: Cognitive processes in performance appraisal. *Journal of Applied Psychology,* 1981, *66,* 127–148.

Feldman, J. M. *Practice, practicality, and prospects of training for performance appraisal.* Paper presented at the 91st Annual American Psychological Association Meeting. Anaheim, Calif., 1983.

Feldman, J. M. Instrumentation and training implications for performance appraisal: A perceptual-cognitive viewpoint. In K. M. Rowland, and J. Ferris (Eds.), *Research in Personnel and Human Resources Management, 1.* Greenwich, Conn.: JAI Press, 1983.

Flanagan, J. C. The critical incident technique. *Psychological Bulletin,* 1954, *51,* 327–358.

Friedman, B. A. and Cornelius, E. T. III. Effect of rater participation in scale construction on the psychometric characteristics of two rating scale formats. *Journal of Applied Psychology,* 1976, *61,* 210–216.

Ghiselli, E. E. and Haire, M. The validation of selection tests in light of the dynamic character of criteria. *Personnel Psychology,* 1960, *13,* 225–231.

Gilmore v. *Kansas City Terminal Railway Co.* 509 F2d 48 (8th Cir. 1975).

Gordon, M. E. The effect of the correctness of the behavior observed on the accuracy of ratings. *Organizational Behavior and Human Performance,* 1970, *5,* 366–377.

Guion, R. M. Criterion measurement and personnel judgments. *Personnel Psychology,* 1961, *14,* 141–149.

Guion, R. M. *Personnel Testing.* New York: McGraw-Hill, 1965.

Hausman, H. J. and Strupp, H. H. Non-technical factors in superiors' ratings of job performance. *Personnel Psychology,* 1955, *8,* 201–217.

Hays, W. H. *Statistics.* New York: Holt, Rinehart & Winston, 1981.

Horstman, D. A. New judicial standards for adverse impact: Their meaning for personnel practices. *Public Personnel Management*, 1978, 7, 347–353.

Jacobs, R., Kafry, D., and Zedeck, S. Expectations of behaviorally anchored rating scales. *Personnel Psychology*, 1980, 33, 595–640.

James v. Stockholm Valves & Fittings Co. 559 F.2d 310 (5th Cir. 1977).

James, L. R. Criterion models and construct validity for criteria. *Psychological Bulletin*, 1973, 80, 75–83.

Jenkins, G. D., and Taber, T. A Monte Carlo study of factors affecting three indices of composite scale reliability. *Journal of Applied Psychology*, 1977, 62, 392–398.

Kane, J. S., and Lawler, E. E., III. Methods of peer assessment. *Psychological Bulletin*, 1978, 85, 555–586.

Kelly, G. A. *The Psychology of Personal Constructs*. New York: Norton, 1955.

Kleiman, L. and Faley, R. Assessing content validity: Standards set by the court. *Personnel Psychology*, 1978, 31, 701–713.

Koltuv, B. Some characteristics of intrajudge trait intercorrelations. *Psychological Monographs*, 1962, 76 (33, Whole No. 552).

Landy, F. J., Barnes, J., and Murphy, K. Correlates of perceived fairness and accuracy in performance appraisal. *Journal of Applied Psychology*, 1978, 63, 751–754.

Landy, F. J., and Farr, J. L. Police performance appraisal. JSAS *Catalog of Selected Documents in Psychology*, 1976, 6, 83. (Ms. No. 1315).

Landy, F. J., Farr, J. L., Saal, F. G., and Freytag, W. R. Behaviorally anchored scales for rating the performance of police officers. *Journal of Applied Psychology*, 1976, 61, 752–758.

Landy, F. J., and Farr J. Performance rating. *Psychological Bulletin*, 1980, 87, 172–177.

Landy, F. J., and Trumbo, D. A. *The Psychology of Work Behavior* (Rev. ed.). Homewood, Ill.: Dorsey Press, 1980.

Landy, F. J., and Vance, R. J. *Statistical Control of Halo*. Unpublished manuscript, 1978. (Available from Frank J. Landy, Department of Psychology, Pennsylvania State University, University Park, Penn. 16802.)

Latham, G. P., and Locke, F. A. Goal setting: A motivational technique that works. *Organizational Dynamics*, 1979, 8, 68–80.

Lawler, E. E., III. The multitrait-multirater approach to measuring managerial job performance. *Journal of Applied Psychology*, 1967, 51, 369–381.

Lopez, F. M. *Evaluating Employee Performance*. Chicago: Public Personnel Association, 1968.

Lord, R. G. Accuracy in development measurement: An alternative definition based on raters' cognitive schema and signal detection theory. *Journal of Applied Psychology*, 1985, 70, 66–71.

Lord, R. G. (in press). An information processing approach to social perception, leadership perception, and behavioral measurement in organizational settings. In B. Staw and L.L. Cummings (Eds.), *Research in Organizational Behavior*. Greenwich, Conn.: JAI Press.

Marquez v. Omaha District Sales Office, Ford Division of Ford Motor Co. 440 F2d 1157 (8th Cir. 1971).

McDonnell Douglas Corp. v. Green. 411 US. 792 (1973).

Meyer v. Missouri State Highway Commission. 567 F.2d 804 (8th Cir. 1977).

Miner, J. B. Management appraisal: A review of procedures and practices. In H. L. Tosi, R. J. House, and M. D. Dunnette (Eds.) *Managerial Motivation and Compensation*. East Lansing, Mich.: Michigan State University, Graduate School of Business Administration, 1972.

Mohrman, A. and Lawler, E. E. Motivation and performance behavior. In F. Landy, S. Zedeck, and J. Cleveland (Eds.). *Performance Measurement and Theory*. Hillside, N.J.: Lawrence Erlbaum, 1983.

Mullins, C. J. and Force, R. C. Rater accuracy as a generalized ability. *Journal of Applied Psychology*, 1962, 46, 191–193.

Murphy, K. R. and Balzer, W. *Systematic distortions in memory-based ratings: Consequences for rating accuracy.* Paper presented at the 91st Annual American Psychological Association Meeting, Anaheim, Calif., 1983.

Murphy, K. R., Balz, W., Kellam, K., and Armstrong, J. Effects of the purpose of rating on accuracy in observing teaching behavior and evaluating teaching performance. *Journal of Educational Psychology*, 1984, 76, 45–54.

Murphy, K. R., Balzer, W., Lockhart, M., and Eisenman, E. Effects of previous performance on evaluation of present performance. *Journal of Applied Psychology*, 1985, 70, 72–84.

Murphy, K. R., Garcia, M., Kerkar, S., Martin, C., and Balzer, W. Relationship between observational accuracy and accuracy in evaluating performance. *Journal of Applied Psychology*, 1982, 67, 320–325.

Murphy, K. R., Martin, C., and Garcia, M. Do behavioral observation scales measure observation? *Journal of Applied Psychology*, 1982, 67, 562–567.

Myers, J. H. Removing halo from job evaluation factor structure. *Journal of Applied Psychology*, 1965, 49, 217–221.

Norman, W. T., and Goldberg, L. R. Rater, ratees, and randomness in personality structure. *Journal of Personality and Social Psychology*, 1966, 4, 681–691.

Passini, F. T., and Norman, W. T. Ratee relevance in peer nominations. *Journal of Applied Psychology*, 1969, 53, 185–187.

Patterson v. *American Tobacco Co.* 535 F.2d 275 (4th Cir. 1976). Also 586 f.2d 300 (4th Cir. 1978).

Prien, E. P. Dynamic character of criteria: Organizational change. *Journal of Applied Psychology*, 1966, 50, 501–504.

Ritti, R. R. Control of "halo" in factor analysis of a supervisory behavior inventory. *Personnel Psychology*, 1964, 17, 305–318.

Robinson v. *Union Carbide Corp.* 538 F.2d 652 (5th Cir. 1976).

Rowe v. *General Motors Corp.* 457 F.2d 348 (5th Cir. 1972).

Schmidt, F. L., and Kaplan, L. B. Composite versus multiple criteria: A review and resolution of the controversy. *Personnel Psychology*, 1971, 24, 419–434.

Schneider, D. J. Implicit personality theory. *Psychological Bulletin*, 1973, 79, 294–309.

Schneier, D. B. The impact of EEO legislation on performance appraisals. *Personnel*, 1978, *July-August*, 24–34.

Schwab, D. P., Heneman, H. G., III, and DeCotiis, T. Behaviorally anchored rating scales: A review of the literature. *Personnel Psychology*, 1975, 28, 549–562.

Sledge v. *J. P. Stevens & Co.* 585 F.2d 625 (4th Cir. 1978).

Smith, P. C. Behaviors, results, and organizational effectiveness: The problem of criteria. In M. D. Dunnette (Ed.), *Handbook of Industrial and Organizational Psychology.* Chicago: Rand McNally, 1976.

Spool, M. D. Training programs for observers of behavior: A review. *Personnel Psychology*, 1978, 31, 853–888.

Tajfel, H., and Wilkes, A. L. Salience of attributes and commitment to extreme judgments in perception of people. *British Journal of Social and Clinical Psychology*, 1963, 2, 40–49.

Thornton, G. C. and Zorich, S. Training to improve observer accuracy. *Journal of Applied Psychology*, 1980, 65, 351–354.

U.S.A. v. *City of Chicago.* 573 F.2d 416 (7th Cir. 1978).

Wade v. *Mississippi Cooperative Extension Service.* 528 F.2d 508 (5th Cir. 1976).

Watkins v. *Scott Paper Co.* 503 F.2d 159 (5th Cir, 1976).

Weahkee v. *Perry.* 587F.2d 1256 (D.C. Div. 1978).

Wherry, R. J. *The Control of Bias in Rating: A Theory of Rating* (Personnel Research Board Rep. 922). Washington, D.C.: Department of the Army, Personnel Research Section, February 1952.

Whitla, D. K., and Tirrell, J. E. The validity of ratings of several levels of supervisors. *Personnel Psychology*, 1953, *6*, 461–466.

Zedeck, S., and Baker, H. T. Nursing performance as measured by behavioral expectation scales: A multitrait-multirater analysis. *Organizational Behavior and Human Performance*, 1972, *7*, 457–466.

Zedeck, S., Jacobs, R., and Kafry, D. Behavioral expectations: Development of parallel forms and analysis of scale assumptions. *Journal of Applied Psychology*, 1976, *61*, 112–115.

SECTION FIVE

Adam, E. E., Jr. Behavior modification in quality control. *Academy of Management Journal*, 1975, *18*, 662–679.

Anderson, C. R. *OSHA and Accident Control through Training.* New York: Industrial Press, 1975.

Bandura, A. *Social Learning Theory.* Englewood Cliffs, N.J.: Prentice-Hall, 1977.

Box, G. E. P., and Jenkins, G. M. *Time-Series Analysis: Forecasting and Control.* San Francisco: Holden Day, 1970.

Burnaska, R. F. The effects of behavioral modeling training upon managers' behaviors and employees' perceptions. *Personnel Psychology*, 1976, *29*, 329–335.

Byham, W. C., Adams, D., and Kiggins, A. Transfer of modeling training to the job. *Personnel Psychology*, 1976, *29*, 345–349.

Campbell, D. T., and Stanley, J. C. *Experimental and Quasi-Experimental Designs for Research.* Chicago: Rand McNally, 1966.

Campbell, J. P., Dunnette, M. D., Lawler, E. E., III, and Weick, K. E., Jr. *Managerial Behavior, Performance, and Effectiveness.* New York: McGraw-Hill, 1970.

Catano, V. M. Improvement in workers' performance through feedback of information of system performance. *Perceptual and Motor Skills*, 1976, *42*, 487–490.

Cooper, M. L., Thomson, C. L., and Baer, D. M. The experimental modification of teacher attending behavior. *Journal of Applied Behavior Analysis*, 1970, *3*, 153–157.

Erez, M. Feedback: A necessary condition for goal-setting performance relationship. *Journal of Applied Psychology*, 1977, *62*, 624–627.

Glass, G. V., Wilson, V. L., and Gottman, J. M. *Design and Analysis of Time Series Experiments.* Boulder: Colorado Associated University Press, 1975.

Goldstein, A. P., and Sorcher, M. *Changing Supervisory Behavior.* New York: Pergamon Press, 1974.

Gray, J. L. The myths of the myths about behavior mod in organizations: A reply to Locke's criticisms of behavior modification. *Academy of Management Review*, 1979, *4*, 121–129.

Guthrie, E. R. *The Psychology of Learning.* New York: Harper, 1935.

Hegarty, W. H. Using subordinate ratings to elicit behavioral changes in supervisors. *Journal of Applied Psychology*, 1974, *6*, 764–766.

Hull, C. L. The conflicting psychologies of learning—A way out. *Psychological Review*, 1936, *42*, 491–516.

Jones, R. R., Vaught, R. S., and Weinrott, M. Time-Series Analysis in Operant Research. *Journal of Applied Behavior Analysis*, 1977, *10*, 151–166.

Katzell, R. A., Bienstock, P., and Faerstein, P. H. *A Guide to Worker Productivity Experiments in the United States, 1971–1975.* New York: New York University Press, 1977.

Kim, J. S., and Hamner, W. C. Effect of performance feedback and goal setting on productivity and satisfaction in an organizational setting. *Journal of Applied Psychology*, 1976, *61*, 48–57.

Komaki, J., Barwick, K. D., and Scott, L. R. A behavioral approach to occupational safety: Pinpointing and reinforcing safe performance in a food manufacturing plant. *Journal of Applied Psychology*, 1978, *63*, 434–445.

Kraut, A. I. Developing managerial skills via modelling techniques: Some positive research findings—A symposium. *Personnel Psychology*, 1976, *29*, 325–369.

Laner, S., and Sell, R. G. An experiment on the effect of specially designed safety posters. *Occupational Psychology*, 1960, *34*, 153–169.

Latham, G. P., and Dossett, D. L. Designing incentive plans for unionized employees: A comparison of continuous and variable ratio reinforcement schedules. *Personnel Psychology*, 1978, *31*, 47–61.

Latham, G. P., Fay, C., and Saari, L. M. The development of behavioral observation scales for appraising the performance of foremen. *Personnel Psychology*, 1979, *32*, 299–311.

Latham, G. P., and Wexley, K. N. Behavioral observation scales for performance appraisal purposes. *Personnel Psychology*, 1977, *30*, 255–268.

Latham, G. P., Wexley, K. N., and Pursell, E. D. Training managers to minimize rating errors in the observation of behavior. *Journal of Applied Psychology*, 1975, *60*, 550–555.

Latham, G. P., and Yukl, G. A. A review of research on the application of goal setting in organizations. *Academy of Management Journal*, 1975, *18*, 824–845.

Leamon, T. B. An investigation into the effects of knowledge of results on operator performance. *Ergonomics*, 1974, *17*, 639–650.

Leslie, J., Jr., and Adams, S. K. Programmed safety through programmed learning. *Human Factors*, 1973, *15*, 223–236.

Locke, E. A. Toward a theory of task motivation and incentives. *Organizational Behavior and Human Performance*, 1968, *3*, 157–189.

Locke, E. A. The myths of behavior mod in organizations. *Academy of Management Review*, 1977, *2*, 543–553.

Locke, E. A. The myths of the myths about behavior mod in organizations. *Academy of Management Review*, 1979, *4*, 131–135.

Locke, E. A. Latham versus Komaki: A tale of two paradigms. *Journal of Applied Psychology*, 1980, *65*, 16–23.

Mager, R. F. *Preparing Instructional Objectives*. Palo Alto, Calif.: Fearon, 1962.

Milutinovich, J. S., and Phatak, A. V. Carrying the safety training load—tips for all managers. *Industrial Engineering*, 1978, *10*, 24–32.

Moses, J. L., and Byham, W. C. *Applying the Assessment Center Method*. New York: Pergamon Press, 1977.

Moses, J. L., and Ritchie, R. J. Supervisory relationships training: A behavioral evaluation of a behavior modelling program. *Personnel Psychology*, 1976, *29*, 337–343.

Nadler, D. A., Mirvis, P. H., and Cammann, C. The ongoing feedback system: Experimenting with a new managerial tool. *Organizational Dynamics*, 1976, *4*, 63–80.

National Safety Council. *Work injury and illness rates*. Chicago: Author, 1978.

O'Connor, R. D. Relative efficacy of modeling, shaping, and the combined procedures for modification of social withdrawal. *Journal of Abnormal Psychology*, 1972, *79*, 327–334.

Operator training, OSHA's hidden failure: How you can correct it. *Modern Materials Handling*, October 1975, 45–60.

Panyan, M., Boozer, H., and Morris, N. Feedback to attendants as a reinforcer for applying operant techniques. *Journal of Applied Behavior Analysis*, 1970, *3*, 1–4.

Performance audit, feedback, and positive reinforcement. *Training and Development Journal*, November 1972, *26*, 8–13.

Quilitch, H. R. A comparison of three staff-management procedures. *Journal of Applied Behavior Analysis*, 1975, *8*, 59–66.

Skinner, B. F. *The Behavior of Organisms: An Experimental Approach*. New York: Appleton-Century, 1938.

Smith, P. E. Management modeling training to improve morale and customer satisfaction. *Personnel Psychology*, 1976, *29*, 351–359.

Steers, R. M., and Porter, L. W. The role of task-goal attributes in employee performance. *Psychological Bulletin*, 1974, *81*, 434–452.

Stogdill, R. *Handbook of Leadership*. New York: Free Press, 1974.

Sulzer-Azaroff, B. Behavioral ecology and accident prevention. *Journal of Organizational Behavior Management*, 1978, *2*, 11–44.

Tolman, E. C. *Purposive Behavior in Animals and Men*. New York: Appleton-Century, 1932.

Yukl, G. A., and Latham, G. P. Consequences of reinforcement schedules and incentive magnitudes for employee performance: Problems encountered in an industrial setting. *Journal of Applied Psychology*, 1975, *60*, 294–298.

Yukl, G. A., Latham, G. P., and Pursell, E. D. The effectiveness of performance incentives under continuous and variable ratio schedules of reinforcement. *Personnel Psychology*, 1976, *29*, 221–231.

SECTION SIX

Adam, E. E., Jr. An analysis of changes in performance quality with operant conditioning procedures. *Journal of Applied Psychology*, 1972, *56*, 480–486.

Adam, E. E., Jr., and Scott, W. E., Jr. The application of behavioral conditioning procedures to the problems of quality control. *Academy of Management Journal*, 1971, *14*, 175–193.

Adam, E. E. Behavior modification in quality control. *Academy of Management Journal*, 1975, *18*, 662–679.

Adams, J. S. Toward an understanding of inequity. *Journal of Abnormal and Social Psychology*, 1963, *67*, 422–436. (a)

Adams, J. S. Wage inequities, productivity, and work quality. *Industrial Relations*, 1963, *3*, 9–16. (b)

Adams, J. S. Inequity in Social Exchange. In L. Berkowitz (Ed.), *Advances in Experimental Social Psychology* (Vol. 2). New York: Academic Press, 1965.

Adams, J. S. Effects of overpayment: Two comments on Lawler's paper. *Journal of Personality and Social Psychology*, 1968, *10*, 315–316.

Adams, J. S., and Freedman, S. Equity theory revisited: Comments and annotated bibliography. In L. Berkowitz and E. Walster (Ed.), *Advances in Experimental Social Psychology* (Vol. 9). New York: Academic Press, 1976.

Adams, J. S., and Jacobsen, P. Effects of wage inequities on work quality. *Journal of Abnormal and Social Psychology*, 1964, *69*, 19–25.

Adams, J. S., and Rosenbaum, W. B. The relationship of worker productivity to cognitive dissonance about wage inequities. *Journal of Applied Psychology*, 1962, *46*, 161–164.

Andrasik, F. Organizational behavior modification in business settings: A methodological and content review. *Journal of Organizational Behavior Management*, 1979, *2*, 85–102.

Andrews, F. M., and Farris, G. F. Time pressure and performance of scientists and engineers: A five-year panel study. *Organizational Behavior and Human Performance*, 1972, *8*, 185–200.

Andrews, G. W. Wage inequity and job performance. *Journal of Applied Psychology*, 1967, *51*, 39–45.

Annett, J. *Feedback and Human Behaviour*. Baltimore, Md.: Penguin Books, 1969.

At Emery Air Freight: Positive reinforcement boosts performance. *Organizational Dynamics*, 1973, *1*(3), 41–50.

Bandura, A. *Social Learning Theory*. Englewood Cliffs, N.J.: Prentice-Hall, 1977.

Bandura, A., and Simon, K. M. The role of proximal intentions in self-regulation of refractory behavior. *Cognitive Therapy and Research*, 1977, *1*, 177–193.

Barker, R. G. Explorations in ecological psychology. *American Psychologist*, 1965, *20*, 1–14.

Bassett, G. A. A study of the effects of task goal and schedule choice on work performance. *Organizational Behavior and Human Performance*, 1979, *24*, 202–227.

Bavelas, J. B. Systems analysis of dyadic interaction: Prediction from individual parameters. *Behavioral Science*, 1978, *23*, 177–186.

Bavelas, J. B., and Lee, E. S. Effects of goal level on performance: A trade-off of quantity and quality. *Canadian Journal of Psychology*, 1978, *32*(4), 219–240.

Becker, L. J. Joint effect of feedback and goal setting on performance: A field study of residential energy conservation. *Journal of Applied Psychology*, 1978, *63*, 428–433.

Berger, C. J., Cummings, L. C., and Heneman, H. G., III. Expectancy theory and operant conditioning predictions of performance under variable ratio and continuous schedules of reinforcement. *Organizational Behavior and Human Performance*, 1975, *14*, 227–243.

Berkowitz, L., and Walster, E. Equity theory: Toward a general theory of social interaction. In L. Berkowitz and E. Walster (Eds.), *Advances in Experimental Social Psychology* (Vol. 9). New York: Academic Press, 1976.

Blau, P. M. *Exchange and Power in Social Life*. New York: John Wiley & Sons, 1967.

Blumenfeld, W. S., and Leidy, T. R. Effectiveness of goal setting as a management device: Research note. *Psychological Reports*, 1969, *24*, 752.

Bobb, H. W., and Kopp, D. G. Applications of behavior modification in organizations: A review and critique. *Academy of Management Review*, 1978, *3*, 281–292.

Bragg, J. E., and Andrews, I. R. Participative decision making: An experimental study in a hospital. *Journal of Applied Behavioral Science*, 1973, *2*, 727–735.

Brass, D. J., and Oldham, G. R. Validating an in-basket test using an alternative set of leadership scoring dimensions. *Journal of Applied Psychology*, 1976, *61*, 652–657.

Burke, R. J., and Wilcox, D. S. Characteristics of effective employee performance review and development interviews. *Personnel Psychology*, 1969, *22*, 291–305.

Campbell, D. J., and Ilgen, D. R. Additive effects of task difficulty and goal setting on subsequent task performance. *Journal of Applied Psychology*, 1976, *61*, 319–324.

Campbell, D. T., and Stanley, J. C. *Experimental and Quasi-Experimental Designs for Research*. Chicago: Rand McNally, 1963.

Campbell, J. P., and Pritchard, R. D. Motivation theory in industrial and organizational psychology. In M. Dunnette (Ed.), *Handbook of Industrial and Organizational Psychology*. Chicago: Rand McNally, 1976.

Carrell, M. R., and Dittrich, J. E. Equity theory: The recent literature, methodological considerations, and new directions. *Academy of Management Review*, 1978, *3*, 202–210.

Carroll, S. J., Jr., and Tosi, H. L. Goal characteristics and personality factors in a management-by-objectives program. *Administrative Science Quarterly*, 1970, *15*, 295–305.

Christensen-Szalanski, J. J. A further examination of the selection of problem-solving strategies: The effects of deadlines and analytic aptitudes. *Organizational Behavior and Human Performance*, 1980, *25*, 107–122.

Christie, R., and Geis, F. L. (Eds.). *Studies in Machiavellianism*. New York: Academic Press, 1970.

Chung, K. H., and Vickery, W. D. Relative effectiveness and joint effects of three selected reinforcements in a repetitive task situation. *Organizational Behavior and Human Performance*, 1976, *16*, 114–142.

Cohen, J. Multiple regression as a general data-analytic system. *Psychological Bulletin*, 1968, *70*, 426–443.

Connolly, T. Some conceptual and methodological issues in expectancy models of work performance motivation. *Academy of Management Review*, 1976, *1*(4), 37–47.

Cook, T. D., and Campbell, D. The design and conduct of quasi-experimental and true experiments in field settings. In M. D. Dunnette (Ed.), *Handbook of Industrial and Organizational Psychology*. Chicago: Rand McNally, 1976.

Cummings, L. L., Schwab, D. P., and Rosen, M. Performance and knowledge of results as determinants of goal setting. *Journal of Applied Psychology*, 1971, *55*, 526–530.

Dachler, H. P., and Mobley, W. H. Construct validation of an instrumentality–expectancy–task-goal model of work motivation: Some theoretical boundary conditions. *Journal of Applied Psychology*, 1973, *58*, 397–418. (Monograph)

Davis, T. R. V., and Luthans, F. Leadership re-examined: A behavioral approach. *Academy of Management Review*, 1979, *4*, 237–248.

Deci, E. L., and Porac, J. Cognitive evaluation theory and the study of human motivation. In M. R. Lepper and D. Greene (Eds.), *The Hidden Costs of Reward*. Hillsdale, N.J.: Erlbaum, 1978.

Dossett, D. L., Latham, G. P., and Mitchell, T. R. The effects of assigned versus participatively set goals, KR, and individual differences when goal difficulty is held constant. *Journal of Applied Psychology*, 1979, *64*, 291–298.

Dyer, L. D., and Parker, D. F. Classifying outcomes in work motivation research: An examination of the intrinsic–extrinsic dichotomy. *Journal of Applied Psychology,* 1975, *60*, 455–458.

Dyer, L. D., and Weyrauch, W. MBO and motivation: An empirical study. *Academy of Management Proceedings*, 1975, pp. 134–136.

Erez, M. Feedback: A necessary condition for the goal setting–performance relationship. *Journal of Applied Psychology*, 1977, *62*, 624–627.

Feyerabend, P. K. How to be a good empiricist—A plea for tolerance in matters epistemological. In D. Baurin (Ed.), *Philosophy of Science: The Delaware Seminar* (No. 2). New York: John Wiley & Sons, 1963.

Fishbein, M., and Ajzen, I. *Belief, Attitude, Intention, and Behavior: An Introduction to Theory and Research.* Reading, Mass: Addison-Wesley, 1975.

Forward, J., and Zander, A. Choice of unattainable group goals and effects on performance. *Organizational Behavior and Human Performance*, 1971, *6*, 184–199.

Frank, J. D. Recent studies of the level of aspiration. *Psychological Bulletin*, 1941, *38*, 218–226.

French, J. R. P., Kay, E., and Meyer, H. H. Participation and the appraisal system. *Human Relations*, 1966, *19*, 3–20.

Friedman, M., and Rosenman, R. H. *Type A Behavior and Your Heart.* New York: Knopf, 1974.

Frost, P. J., and Mahoney, T. A. Goal setting and the task process: I. An interactive influence on individual performance. *Organizational Behavior and Human Performance*, 1976, *17*, 328–350.

Garland, H. The effects of piece-rate underpayment and overpayment on job performance: A test of equity theory with a new induction procedure. *Journal of Applied Social Psychology*, 1973, *3*, 325–334.

Georgopoulos, B. S., Mahoney, G. M., and Jones, N. W. A path-goal approach to productivity. *Journal of Applied Psychology*, 1957, *41*, 345–353.

Goodman, P. S., and Friedman, A. An examination of Adams' theory of inequity. *Administrative Science Quarterly*, 1971, *16*, 271–288.

Gough, H. G., and Heilbrun, A. B. *The Adjective Checklist Manual.* Palo Alto, Calif.: Consulting Psychologists Press, 1965.

Graen, G. Instrumentality theory of work motivation: Some experimental results and suggested modifications. *Journal of Applied Psychology Monograph*, 1969, *53*(1, Pt. 2).

Greller, M. M. Evaluation of feedback sources as a function of role and organizational level. *Journal of Applied Psychology*, 1980, *65*, 24–27.

Haan, M., Smith, M. B., and Block, J. Moral reasoning of young adults: Political-social behavior, family background, and personality correlates. *Journal of Personality and Social Psychology*, 1968, *10*, 183–201.

Hackman, J. R., and Lawler, E. E. Employee reactions to job characteristics. *Journal of Applied Psychology*, 1971, *55*, 259–286. (Monograph)

Hackman, J. R., and Porter, L. W. Expectancy theory predictions of work effectiveness. *Organizational Behavior and Human Performance*, 1968, *3*, 417–426.

Hall, D. T., and Foster, L. W. A psychological success cycle and goal setting: Goals, performance, and attitudes. *Academy of Management Journal*, 1977, *20*, 282–290.

Hall, D. T., and Hall, F. S. The relationship between goals, performance, success, self-image, and involvement under different organizational climates. *Journal of Vocational Behavior*, 1976, *9*, 267–278.

Hall, D. T., and Lawler, E. E. Job pressures and research performance. *American Scientist*, 1971, *59*(1), 64–73.

Hamner, W. C., and Hamner, E. P. Behavior modification on the bottom line. *Organizational Dynamics*, 1976, *4*, 2–21.

Hamner, W. C., and Harnett, D. L. Goal-setting, performance and satisfaction in an interdependent task. *Organizational Behavior and Human Performance*, 1974, *12*, 217–230.

Hannan, R. L. *The effects of participation in goal setting on goal acceptance and performance: A laboratory experiment*. Unpublished doctoral dissertation, University of Maryland, 1975.

Heneman, H. G., III and Schwab, D. P. Evaluation of research on expectancy theory predictions of employee performance. *Psychological Bulletin*, 1972, *78*, 1–9.

Hermann, J. A., de Montes, A. I., Dominguez, B., Montes, F., and Hopkins, B. L. Effects of bonuses for punctuality on the tardiness of industrial workers. *Journal of Applied Behavior Analysis*, 1973, *6*, 563–570.

Hermans, H. J. M. A questionnaire measure of achievement motivation. *Journal of Applied Psychology*, 1970, *54*, 353–363.

Heyns, R., and Lippitt, R. Systematic observation techniques. In G. Lindzey (Ed.), *The Handbook of Social Psychology* (Vol. 1). Reading, Mass.: Addison-Wesley, 1954.

Hilgard, E. R. Success in relation to level of aspiration. In C. L. Stacey and M. F. DeMartino (Eds.), *Understanding Human Motivation*. Cleveland, Ohio: Howard Allen, 1958.

Hinkley, D. On quick choice of power transformation. *Applied Statistician*, 1977, *26*, 67–69.

Hinrichs, J. R. *Practical Management for Productivity*. New York: Van Nostrand Reinhold, 1978.

Hogan, R. Moral conduct and moral character: A psychological perspective. *Psychological Bulletin*, 1973, *79*, 217–232.

Homans, G. C. *Social Behavior: Its Elementary Forms*. New York: Harcourt Brace Jovanovich, 1961.

House, R. J., Shapiro, H. J., and Wahba, M. A. Expectancy theory as a predictor of work behavior and attitude: A re-evaluation of empirical evidence. *Decision Sciences*, 1974, *5*, 481–506.

Ilgen, D. R., Fisher, C. D., and Taylor, M. S. Consequences of individual feedback on behavior in organizations. *Journal of Applied Psychology*, 1979, *64*, 349–371.

Ivancevich, J. M. Changes in performance in a management by objectives program. *Administrative Science Quarterly*, 1974, *19*, 563–574.

Ivancevich, J. M. Effects of goal setting on performance and job satisfaction. *Journal of Applied Psychology*, 1976, *61*, 605–612.

Ivancevich, J. M. Different goal setting treatments and their effects on performance and job satisfaction. *Academy of Management Journal*, 1977, *20*, 406–419.

Ivancevich, J. M., and McMahon, J. T. Black-white differences in a goal-setting program. *Organizational Behavior and Human Performance*, 1977, *20*, 287–300. (a)

Ivancevich, J. M., and McMahon, J. T. Education as a moderator of goal setting effectiveness. *Journal of Vocational Behavior*, 1977, *11*, 83–94. (b)

Ivancevich, J. M., and McMahon, J. T. A study of task-goal attributes, higher order need strength, and performance. *Academy of Management Journal*, 1977, *20*, 552–563. (c)

Jablonsky, S. F., and DeVries, D. L. Operant conditioning principles extrapolated to the theory of management. *Organizational Behavior and Human Performance*, 1972, *7*, 340–358.

Jacques, E. *Equitable Payment*. New York: John Wiley & Sons, 1961.

Kahneman, D. *Attention and Effort*. Englewood Cliffs, N.J.: Prentice-Hall, 1973.

Kaplan, R., and Rothkopf, E. Z. Instructional objectives as directions to learners: Effect of passage length and amount of objective-relevant content. *Journal of Educational Psychology*, 1974, *66*, 448–456.

Kazdin, A. E. Methodological and assessment considerations in evaluating reinforcement programs in applied settings. *Journal of Applied Behavior Analysis*, 1973, *6*, 517–531.

Kempen, R. W., and Hall, R. V. Reduction of industrial absenteeism: Results of a behavioral approach. *Journal of Organizational Behavior Management*, 1977, *1*, 1–21.

Kerlinger, F. N. *Foundations of Behavioral Research*. New York: Holt, Rinehart & Winston, 1973.

Kim, J. S., and Hamner, W. C. Effect of performance feedback and goal setting on productivity and satisfaction in an organizational setting. *Journal of Applied Psychology*, 1976, *61*, 48–57.

Kish, L. Confidence intervals for clustered samples. *American Sociological Review*, 1957, *22*, 154–165.

Koch, J. L., and Rhodes, S. R. Problems with reactive instruments of field research. *Journal of Applied Behavioral Science*, 1979, *15*, 485–506.

Kohlberg, L. The development of children's orientations toward a moral order. *Vita Humana*, 1963, *6*, 11–33.

Kohlberg, L. The child as a moral philosopher. *Psychology Today*, 1968, *2*(4), 24–30.

Kohlberg, L. The cognitive-developmental approach to socialization. In D. A. Goslin (Ed.), *Handbook of Socialization Theory and Research*. Chicago: Rand McNally, 1969.

Kolb, D. A., and Boyatzis, R. E. Goal-setting and self-directed behavior change. *Human Relations*, 1970, *23*, 439–457.

Komaki, J. Alternative evaluation strategies in work settings: Reversal and multiple-baseline designs. *Journal of Organizational Behavior Management*, 1977, *1*, 53–77.

Komaki, J., Barwick, K. D., and Scott, L. R. A behavioral approach to occupational safety: Pinpointing and reinforcing safe performance in a food manufacturing plant. *Journal of Applied Psychology*, 1978, *64*, 434–445.

Komaki, J., Waddell, W. M., and Pearce, M. G. The applied behavior analysis approach and individual employees: Improving performance in two small businesses. *Organizational Behavior and Human Performance*, 1977, *19*, 337–352.

Kopelman, R. E., and Thompson, P. H. Boundary conditions for expectancy theory predictions of work motivation and job performance. *Academy of Management Journal*, 1976, *19*, 237–258.

Korman, A. K. Toward a hypothesis of work behavior. *Journal of Applied Psychology*, 1970, *54*, 31–41.

Kunin, T. The construction of a new type of attitude measure. *Personnel Psychology*, 1955, *8*, 65–78.

LaPorte, R. E., and Nath, R. Role of performance goals in prose learning. *Journal of Educational Psychology*, 1976, *68*, 260–264.

Latham, G. P., and Baldes, J. J. The "practical significance" of Locke's theory of goal setting. *Journal of Applied Psychology*, 1975, *60*, 122–124.

Latham, G. P., and Dossett, D. L. Designing incentive plans for unionized employees: A comparison of continuous and variable ratio reinforcement schedules. *Personnel Psychology*, 1978, *31*, 47–61.

Latham, G. P., and Kinne, S. B., III. Improving job performance through training in goal setting. *Journal of Applied Psychology*, 1974, *59*, 187–191.

Latham, G. P., and Locke, E. A. Increasing productivity with decreasing time limits: A field replication of Parkinson's law. *Journal of Applied Psychology*, 1975, *60*, 524–526.

Latham, G. P., and Locke, E. A. Goal-setting: A motivational technique that works. *Organizational Dynamics*, 1979, *8*(2), 68–80.

Latham, G. P., Mitchell, T. R., and Dossett, D. L. Importance of participative goal setting and anticipated rewards on goal difficulty and job performance. *Journal of Applied Psychology*, 1978, *63*, 163–171.

Latham, G. P., and Saari, L. M. The effects of holding goal difficulty constant on assigned and participatively set goals. *Academy of Management Journal*, 1979, *22*, 163–168. (a)

Latham, G. P., and Saari, L. M. Importance of supportive relationships in goal setting. *Journal of Applied Psychology*, 1979, *64*, 151–156. (b)

Latham, G. P., and Yukl, G. A. Assigned versus participative goal setting with educated and uneducated woods workers. *Journal of Applied Psychology*, 1975, *60*, 299–302. (a)

Latham, G. P., and Yukl, G. A. A review of research on the application of goal setting in organizations. *Academy of Management Journal*, 1975, *18*, 824–845. (b)

Latham, G. P., and Yukl, G. A. Effects of assigned and participative goal setting on performance and job satisfaction. *Journal of Applied Psychology*, 1976, *61*, 166–171.

Lawler, E. E., III. Ability as a moderator of the relationship between job attitudes and job performance. *Personnel Psychology*, 1966, *19*, 153–164.

Lawler, E. E. Equity theory as a predictor of productivity and work quality. *Psychological Bulletin*, 1968, *70*, 596–610. (a)

Lawler, E. E. Effects of hourly overpayment on productivity and work quality. *Journal of Personality and Social Psychology*, 1968, *10*, 306–313. (b)

Lawler, E. E. *Pay and Organizational Effectiveness: A Psychological View.* New York: McGraw-Hill, 1971.

Lawler, E. E., Koplin, C. A., Young, T. E., and Fadem, J. A. Inequity reduction over time in an induced overpayment situation. *Organizational Behavior and Human Performance*, 1968, *3*, 253–268.

Lawler, E. E., and O'Gara, P. W. The effects of inequity produced by underpayment on work output, work quality, and attitudes toward the work. *Journal of Applied Psychology*, 1967, *51*, 503–510.

Lawler, E. E., III, and Suttle, J. L. Expectancy theory and job behavior. *Organizational Behavior and Human Performance*, 1973, *9*, 482–503.

Lewin, K. Psychology of success and failure. In C. L. Stacey and M. F. DeMartino (Eds.), *Understanding Human Motivation*. Cleveland, Ohio: Howard Allen, 1958.

Lieberman, D. A. Behaviorism and the mind: A (limited) call for a return to introspection. *American Psychologist*, 1979, *34*, 319–333.

Lied, T. R., and Pritchard, R. D. Relationships between personality variables and components of the expectancy–valence model. *Journal of Applied Psychology*, 1976, *61*, 463–467.

Locke, E. A. Motivational effects of knowledge of results: Knowledge or goal setting? *Journal of Applied Psychology*, 1967, *51*, 324–329.

Locke, E. A. Toward a theory of task motivation and incentives. *Organizational Behavior and Human Performance*, 1968, *3*, 157–189.

Locke, E. A. Purpose without consciousness: A contradiction. *Psychological Reports*, 1969, *25*, 991–1009.

Locke, E. A. Critical analysis of the concept of causality in behavioristic psychology. *Psychological Reports*, 1972, *31*, 175–197.

Locke, E. A. Personnel attitudes and motivation. *Annual Review of Psychology*, 1975, *26*, 457–480.

Locke, E. A. The myths of behavior mod in organizations. *Academy of Management Review*, 1977, *2*, 543–553.

Locke, E. A. The ubiquity of the technique of goal setting in theories of and approaches to employee motivation. *Academy of Management Review*, 1978, *3*, 594–601.

Locke, E. A. Latham versus Komaki: A tale of two paradigms. *Journal of Applied Psychology*, 1980, *65*, 16–23.

Locke, E. A., and Bryan, J. F. Cognitive aspects of psychomotor performance: The effects of performance goals on level of performance. *Journal of Applied Psychology*, 1966, *50*, 286–291.

Locke, E. A., and Bryan, J. F. Performance goals as determinants of level of performance and boredom. *Journal of Applied Psychology*, 1967, *51*, 120–130.

Locke, E. A., and Bryan, J. F. Goal-setting as a determinant of the effect of knowledge of score on performance. *American Journal of Psychology*, 1968, *81*, 398–406.

Locke, E. A., and Bryan, J. F. The directing function of goals in task performance. *Organizational Behavior and Human Performance*, 1969, *4*, 35–42. (a)

Locke, E. A., and Bryan, J. F. Knowledge of score and goal level as determinants of work rate. *Journal of Applied Psychology*, 1969, *53*, 59–65. (b)

Locke, E. A., Bryan, J. F., and Kendall, L. M. Goals and intentions as mediators of the effects of monetary incentives on behavior. *Journal of Applied Psychology*, 1968, *52*, 104–121.

Locke, E. A., Cartledge, N., and Knerr, C. S. Studies of the relationship between satisfaction, goal setting, and performance. *Organizational Behavior and Human Performance*, 1970, *5*, 135–158.

Locke, E. A., Cartledge, N., and Koeppel, J. Motivational effects of knowledge of results: A goal-setting phenomenon? *Psychological Bulletin*, 1968, *70*, 474–485.

Locke, E. A., Feren, D. B., McCaleb, V. M., Shaw, K. N., and Denny, A. T. The relative effectiveness of four methods of motivating employee performance. In K. Duncan, M. Gruneberg, and D. Wallis (Eds.), *Changes in Working Life*. New York: John Wiley & Sons, 1980.

Locke, E. A., Mento, A. J., and Katcher, B. L. The interaction of ability and motivation in performance: An exploration of the meaning of moderators. *Personnel Psychology*, 1978, *31*, 269–280.

Locke, E. A., and Schweiger, D. M. Participation in decision-making: One more look. In B. M. Staw (Ed.), *Research in Organizational Behavior* (Vol. 1). Greenwich, Conn.: JAI Press, 1979.

London, M., and Oldham, G. R. Effects of varying goal types and incentive systems on performance and satisfaction. *Academy of Management Journal*, 1976, *19*, 537–546.

Lopes, L. L. Individual strategies in goal-setting. *Organizational Behavior and Human Performance*, 1976, *15*, 268–277.

Luthans, F., and Bond, K. M. The use of reversal designs in organizational behavior research. In R. L. Taylor, M. J. O'Connell, R. A. Zawacki, and D. D. Warrick (Eds.), *Proceedings of the Annual Meeting of the Academy of Management*, 1977, 86–90.

Luthans, F., and Kreitner, R. *Organizational Behavior Modification*. Glenview, Ill.: Scott, Foresman, 1975.

Luthans, F., and White, D. D. Behavior modification: Application to manpower management. *Personnel Administration*, 1971, *34*, 41–47.

Masters, J. C., Furman, W., and Barden, R. C. Effects of achievement standards, tangible rewards, and self-dispensed achievement evaluations on children's task mastery. *Child Development*, 1977, *48*, 217–224.

Matsui, T., and Terai, T. A cross-cultural study of the validity of the expectancy theory of work motivation. *Journal of Applied Psychology*, 1975, *50*, 263–265.

Mawhinney, R. C. Operant terms and concepts in the description of individual work behavior: Some problems of interpretation, application, and evaluation. *Journal of Applied Psychology*, 1975, *60*, 704–712.

McCall, M. W., Morrison, A. M., and Hannan, R. L. *Studies of Managerial Work: Results and Methods*. Greensboro, N.C.: Center for Creative Leadership, 1978.

McClelland, D. C. *Power: The Inner Experience*. New York: Irvington, 1975.

McClelland, D. C., and Winter, D. G. *Motivating Economic Achievement*. New York: Free Press, 1971.

Meichenbaum, D. *Cognitive-Behavior Modification*. New York: Plenum Press, 1977.

McGhee, W., and Tullar, W. L. A note on evaluating behavior modification and behavior modeling as industrial training techniques. *Personnel Psychology*, 1978, *31*, 477–484.

Mento, A. J., Cartledge, N. D., and Locke, E. A. Maryland versus Michigan versus Minnesota: Another look at the relationship of expectancy and goal difficulty to task performance. *Organizational Behavior and Human Performance*, 1980, *25*, 419–440.

Migliore, R. H. *MBO: Blue collar to top executive*. Washington, D.C.: Bureau of National Affairs, 1977.

Milgram, S. Behavioral study of obedience. *Journal of Abnormal and Social Psychology*, 1963, *67*, 371–378.

Miller, G. A., Galanter, E., and Pribram, K. H. *Plans and the Structure of Behavior*. New York: Holt, 1960.

Miller, H. E., Katerberg, R., and Hulin, C. L. Evaluation of the Mobley, Horner, and Hollingsworth model of employee turnover. *Journal of Applied Psychology*, 1979, *64*, 509–517.

Miller, L. K. Methodological and assessment considerations in applied settings: Reviewers' comments. *Journal of Applied Behavior Analysis*, 1973, *6*, 532–539.

Mintzberg, H. *The Nature of Managerial Work*. New York: Harper & Row, 1973.

Mitchell, S. Interobserver agreement, reliability, and generalizability of data collected in observational studies. *Psychological Bulletin*, 1979, *86*, 376–390.

Mitchell, T. R. Expectancy models of job satisfaction, occupational preference and effort: A theoretical, methodological, and empirical appraisal. *Psychological Bulletin*, 1974, *81*, 1053–1077.

Mitchell, T. R., and Albright, D. W. Expectancy theory predictions of the satisfaction, effort, performance, and retention of naval aviation officers. *Organizational Behavior and Human Performance*, 1972, *8*, 1–20.

Mitchell, T. R., and Biglan, A. Instrumentality theories: Current uses in psychology. *Psychological Bulletin*, 1971, *76*, 432–454.

Mobley, W. H., Horner, S. O., and Hollingsworth, A. T. An evaluation of precursors of hospital employee turnover. *Journal of Applied Psychology*, 1978, *63*, 408–414.

Mobley, W. H., Hand, H. H., Baker, R. L., and Meglino, B. M. Conceptual and empirical analysis of military recruit training attrition. *Journal of Applied Psychology*, 1979, *64*, 10–18.

Mossholder, K. W. Effects of externally mediated goal setting on intrinsic motivation: A laboratory experiment. *Journal of Applied Psychology*, 1980, *65*, 202–210.

Motowidlo, S. J. *A laboratory study of the effects of situational characteristics and individual differences on task success and motivation to perform a numerical task*. Unpublished doctoral dissertation, University of Minnesota, 1976.

Motowidlo, S., Loehr, V., and Dunnette, M. D. A laboratory study of the effects of goal specificity on the relationship between probability of success and performance. *Journal of Applied Psychology*, 1978, *63*, 172–179.

Mowday, R. T. Equity theory predictions of behavior in organizations. In R. M. Steers and L. W. Porter (Eds.), *Motivation and Work Behavior*. New York: McGraw-Hill, 1979.

Nemeroff, W. F., and Cosentino, J. Utilizing feedback and goal setting to increase performance appraisal interviewer skills of managers. *Academy of Management Journal*, 1979, *22*, 566–576.

Ness, R. G., and Patton, R. W. The effect of beliefs on maximum weight-lifting performance. *Cognitive Therapy and Research*, 1979, *3*, 205–211.

Nisbett, R. E., and Wilson, T. D. Telling more than we can know: Verbal reports on mental processes. *Psychological Review*, 1977, *84*, 231–259.

Nord, W. R. Beyond the teaching machine: The neglected area of operant conditioning in the theory and practice of management. *Organizational Behavior and Human Performance*, 1969, *4*, 375–401.

Nord, W. R. Improving attendance through rewards. *Personnel Administration*, 1970, *33*, 37–41.

Nunnally, J. C. *Psychometric Theory*. New York: McGraw-Hill, 1967.

Odiorne, G. S. MBO: A backward glance. *Business Horizons*, October 1978, pp. 14–24.

Oldham, G. R. The impact of supervisory characteristics on goal acceptance. *Academy of Management Journal*, 1975, *18*, 461–475.

Oldham, G. R. The motivational strategies used by supervisors: Relationships to effectiveness indicators. *Organizational Behavior and Human Performance*, 1976, *15*, 66–86.

Oliver, R. L. Expectancy theory predictions of salesmen's performance. *Journal of Marketing Research*, 1974, *11*, 243–252.

Opshal, R., and Dunnette, M. D. The role of financial compensation in industrial motivation. *Psychological Bulletin*, 1966, *66*, 94–118.

Organ, D. W. Intentional versus arousal effects of goal-setting. *Organizational Behavior and Human Performance*, 1977, *18*, 378–389.

Orpen, C. Effects of bonuses for attendance on absenteeism of industrial workers. *Journal of Organizational Behavior Management*, 1978, *1*, 118–124.

Ottemann, R., and Luthans, F. An experimental analysis of the effectiveness of an organizational behavior modification program in industry. In A. G. Bedeian, A. A. Armenakis, W. H. Holley, Jr., and H. S. Feild, Jr. (Eds.), *Proceedings of the Annual Meeting of the Academy of Management*, 1975, 140–142.

Ouchi, W. G. *Theory Z*. Reading, Mass.: Addison-Wesley, 1981.

Patchen, M. *The Choice of Wage Comparisons*. Englewood Cliffs, N.J.: Prentice-Hall, 1961.

Pedalino, E., and Gamboa, V. U. Behavior modification and absenteeism: Intervention in one industrial setting. *Journal of Applied Psychology*, 1974, *59*, 694–698.

Peters, T. J. and Waterman, R. H. *In Search of Excellence*. New York: Harper & Row, 1982.

Piaget, J. *The Moral Judgment of the Child*. Glencoe Ill.: Free Press, 1948.

Porter, L. W., and Lawler, E. E. *Managerial Attitudes and Performance*. Homewood, Ill.: Dorsey Press, 1968.

Pritchard, R. D. Equity theory: A review and critique. *Organizational Behavior and Human Performance*, 1969, *4*, 176–211.

Pritchard, R. D., and Curtis, M. I. The influence of goal setting and financial incentives on task performance. *Organizational Behavior and Human Performance*, 1973, *10*, 175–183.

Pritchard, R. D., and Sanders, M. S. The influence of valence, instrumentality, and expectancy on effort and performance. *Journal of Applied Psychology*, 1973, *57*, 55–60.

Rand, A. *Introduction to Objectivist Epistemology*. New York: The Objectivist, 1967.

Reynolds, R. E., Standiford, S. N., and Anderson, R. C. Distribution of reading time when questions are asked about a restricted category of text information. *Journal of Educational Psychology*, 1979, *71*, 183–190.

Ronan, W. W., Latham, G. P., and Kinne, S. B., III. Effects of goal setting and supervision on worker behavior in an industrial situation. *Journal of Applied Psychology*, 1973, *58*, 302–307.

Rosen, N. *Leadership, Change and Work Group Dynamics: An Experiment*. Staples Press, 1969.

Rosswork, S. G. Goal setting: The effects on an academic task with varying magnitudes of incentive. *Journal of Educational Psychology*, 1977, *69*, 710–715.

Rothkopf, E. Z., and Billington, M. J. A two-factor model of the effect of goal-descriptive directions on learning from text. *Journal of Educational Psychology*, 1975, *67*, 692–704.

Rothkopf, E. Z., and Billington, M. J. Goal-guided learning from text: Inferring a descriptive processing model from inspection times and eye movements. *Journal of Educational Psychology*, 1979, *71*, 310–327.

Rothkopf, E. Z., and Kaplan, R. Exploration of the effect of density and specificity of instructional objectives on learning from text. *Journal of Educational Psychology*, 1972, *63*, 295–302.

Ryan, T. A. *Intentional Behavior: An Approach to Human Motivation.* New York: Ronald Press, 1970.

Sales, S. M. Some effects of role overload and role underload. *Organizational Behavior and Human Performance*, 1970, *5*, 592–608.

Sayles, L. R. *Behavior of Industrial Work Groups: Prediction and Control.* New York: John Wiley & Sons, 1958.

Schmidt, F. L. Implications of a measurement problem for expectancy theory research. *Organizational Behavior and Human Performance*, 1973, *10*, 243–251.

Schneier, C. E. Behavior modification in management: A review and critique. *Academy of Management Journal*, 1974, *17*, 528–548.

Schrauger, J. S., and Rosenberg, S. F. Self-esteem and the effects of success and failure feedback on performance. *Journal of Personality*, 1970, *38*, 404–417.

Schriesheim, C. A., and Kerr, S. Theories and measures of leadership: A critical appraisal of current and future directions. In J. G. Hunt and L. L. Larson (Eds.), *Leadership: The Cutting Edge.* Carbondale: Southern Illinois University Press, 1977.

Schriesheim, C. A., Kinicki, A. J., and Schriesheim, J. F. The effect of leniency on leader behavior descriptions. *Organizational Behavior and Human Performance*, 1979, *23*, 1–29.

Schwab, D. P., and Dyer, L. D. The motivational impact of a compensation system on employee performance. *Organizational Behavior and Human Performance*, 1973, *9*, 215–225.

Searfoss, D. G., and Monczka, R. M. Perceived participation in the budget process and motivation to achieve the budget. *Academy of Management Journal*, 1973, *16*, 541–554.

Sheridan, J. E., Slocum, J. W., Jr., and Richards, M. D. Expectancy theory as a lead indicator of job behavior. *Decision Sciences*, 1974, *5*, 507–522.

Singh, J. P. *Some personality moderators of the effects of repeated success and failure on task-related variables.* Unpublished doctoral dissertation, University of Akron, 1972.

Snyder, C. A. Application of organizational behavior modification in the public sector: Case studies in a hospital environment (Doctoral dissertation, University of Nebraska, 1978). *Dissertation Abstracts International*, 1978, *39*, 5036A.

Staw, B. M. Motivation in organisations: towards synthesis and redirection. In B. M. Staw, and G. R. Salancik, (Eds.) *New Directions in Organisational Behaviour.* Chicago: St. Clair Press, 1977.

Steers, R. M. Task-goal attributes, n achievement, and supervisory performance. *Organizational Behavior and Human Performance*, 1975, *13*, 392–403.

Steers, R. M., and Porter, L. W. The role of task-goal attributes in employee performance. *Psychological Bulletin*, 1974, *81*, 434–452.

Stephens, T. A., and Burroughs, W. A. An application of operant conditioning to absenteeism in a hospital setting. *Journal of Applied Psychology*, 1978, *63*, 518–521.

Strang, H. R., Lawrence, E. C., and Fowler, P. C. Effects of assigned goal level and knowledge of results on arithmetic computation: A laboratory study. *Journal of Applied Psychology*, 1978, *63*, 446–450.

Taylor, F. W. *The Principles of Scientific Management.* New York: Norton, 1967. (Originally published, 1911.)

Terborg, J. R. The motivational components of goal setting. *Journal of Applied Psychology*, 1976, *61*, 613–621.

Terborg, J. R., and Miller, H. E. Motivation, behavior, and performance: A closer examination of goal setting and monetary incentives. *Journal of Applied Psychology*, 1978, *63*, 29–39.

Turney, J. R. Activity outcome expectancies and intrinsic activity values as predictors of several motivation indexes for technical-professionals. *Organizational Behavior and Human Performance*, 1974, *11*, 65–82.

Umstot, D. D., Bell, C. H., Jr., and Mitchell, T. R. Effects of job enrichment and task goals on satisfaction and productivity: Implications for job design. *Journal of Applied Psychology*, 1976, *61*, 379–394.

Vroom, V. H. *Work and Motivation.* New York: John Wiley & Sons, 1964.

Wahba, M. A., and House, R. J. Expectancy theory in work and motivation: Some logical and methodological issues. *Human Relations*, 1974, *27*, 121–147.

Walster, E., Berscheid, E., & Walster, G. W. New directions in equity research. *Journal of Personality and Social Psychology*, 1973, *27*, 151–176.

Wanous, J. P., Keon, T. L., and Latack, J. C. Expectancy theory and occupational/organisational choices: a review and test. *Organisational Behaviour and Human Performance*, 1983, *32*.

Weick, K. E. Systematic observational methods. In G. Lindzey and E. Aronson (Eds.), *The Handbook of Social Psychology* (Vol. 2). Reading, Mass.: Addison-Wesley, 1968.

Weiner, B. *Achievement Motivation and Attribution Theory.* New York: General Learning Press, 1974. Also Hewstone, M. (Ed.), *Attribution Theory.* London: Blackwell.

Weiner, Y. The effects of task-and-ego-oriented performance on two kinds of over-compensation inequity. *Organizational Behavior and Human Performance*, 1970, *5*, 191–208.

Wexley, K. N., and Nemeroff, W. F. Effectiveness of positive reinforcement and goal setting as methods of management development. *Journal of Applied Psychology*, 1975, *60*, 446–450.

White, F. M., and Locke, E. A. Perceived determinants of high and low productivity in three occupational groups: A critical incident study. *Journal of Management Studies*, in press.

White, S. E., Mitchell, T. R., and Bell, C. H., Jr. Goal setting, evaluation apprehension, and social cues as determinants of job performance and job satisfaction in a simulated organization. *Journal of Applied Psychology*, 1977, *62*, 665–673.

Willems, E., and Raush, H. *Naturalistic Viewpoints in Psychological Research.* New York: Holt, Rinehart & Winston, 1969.

Wilsted, W. D., and Hand, H. H. Determinants of aspiration levels in a simulated goal setting environment of the firm. *Academy of Management Journal*, 1974, *17*, 172–177.

Wine, J. Test anxiety and direction of attention. *Psychological Bulletin*, 1971, *76*, 92–104.

Yates, J. F., and Kulick, R. M. Effort control and judgments. *Organizational Behavior and Human Performance*, 1977, *20*, 54–65.

Yukl, G. A., and Latham, G. P. Consequences of reinforcement schedules and incentive magnitudes for employee performance: Problems encountered in an industrial setting. *Journal of Applied Psychology*, 1975, *60*, 294–298.

Yukl, G. A., and Latham, G. P. Interrelationships among employee participation, individual differences, goal difficulty, goal acceptance, goal instrumentality, and performance. *Personnel Psychology*, 1978, *31*, 305–323.

Yukl, G. A., Latham, G. P., and Pursell, E. D. The effectiveness of performance incentives under continuous and variable ratio schedules of reinforcement. *Personnel Psychology*, 1976, *29*, 221–231.

Yukl, G. A., Wexley, K. N., and Seymore, J. D. Effectiveness of pay incentives under variable ratio and continuous reinforcement schedules. *Journal of Applied Psychology*, 1972, *56*, 19–23.

Zander, A. *Motives and Goals in Groups.* New York: Academic Press, 1971.

Zander, A., Forward, J., and Albert, R. Adaptation of board members to repeated failure or success by their organization. *Organizational Behavior and Human Performance*, 1969, *4*, 56–76.

Zedeck, S. Problems with the use of "moderator" variables. *Psychological Bulletin*, 1971, *76*, 295–310.

SECTION SEVEN

Bales, R., and Strodtbeck, F. Phases in group problem solving. *Journal of Abnormal and Social Psychology*, 1951, *46*, 485–495.

Bass, B., and Valenzi, E. Contingent aspects of effective management styles. In J. G. Hunt and L. L. Larson (Ed.), *Contingency Approaches to Leadership*. Carbondale: Southern Illinois University Press, 1974.

Blake, R., and Mouton, J. *The Managerial Grid*. Houston: Gulf, 1964.

Bock, R. D. Programming univariate and multivariate analysis of variance. *Technometrics*, 1963, *5*, 95–117.

Bordua, D., and Reiss, A. Command, control, and charisma: Reflections on police bureaucracy. *American Journal of Sociology*, 1966, *72*, 68–76.

Borgatta, E., and Bales, R. Task and accumulation of experience as factors in the interaction of small groups. *Sociometry*, 1953, *16*, 239–252.

Campbell, J., Dunnette, E., Lawler, E., and Weick, K. *Managerial Behavior, Performance and Effectiveness*. New York: McGraw-Hill, 1970.

Cashman, J., and Graen, G. The nature of leadership in the vertical dyad: The team building process. *Organizational Behavior and Human Performance*, in press.

Cronbach, L. J., and Furby, L. L. How we should measure "change"—or should we? *Psychological Bulletin*, 1970, *74*, 68–80.

Dansereau, F., Cashman, J., and Graen, G. Instrumentality theory and equity theory as complementary approaches in predicting the relationship of leadership and turnover among managers. *Organizational Behavior and Human Performance*, 1973, *10*, 184–200.

Dansereau, F., Graen, G., and Haga, W. J. A vertical dyad linkage approach to leadership in formal organizations. *Organizational Behavior and Human Performance*, 1975, *13*, 46–78.

DeCharms, R. *Personal Causation*. New York: Academic Press, 1968.

Deci, E. Intrinsic motivation, extrinsic reinforcement, and inequity. *Journal of Personality and Social Psychology*, 1972, *22*, 113–120.

Deci, E. *Instrinsic Motivation*. New York: Plenum, 1975.

Dubin, R. Theory building in applied areas. In M. Dunnette (Ed.), *Handbook of Industrial and Organizational Psychology*. Chicago: Rand McNally, 1976.

Fiedler, F. E. A contingency model of leadership effectiveness. In L. Berkowitz (Ed.), *Advances in Experimental Social Psychology*. New York: Academic Press, 1964.

Fiedler, F. E. *A Theory of Leadership Effectiveness*. New York: McGraw-Hill, 1967.

Fiedler, F. E., and Chemers, M. M. *Leadership and Effective Management*. Glenview, Ill.: Scott, Foresman, 1974.

Filley, A. C., House, R. J., and Kerr, S. *Managerial Process and Organizational Behavior* (2d ed.). Glenview, Ill.: Scott, Foresman, 1976.

Graen, G. Role making processes within complex organizations. In M. D. Dunnette (Ed.), *Handbook of Industrial and Organizational Psychology*. Chicago: Rand McNally, 1976.

Graen, G., and Cashman, J. A role making model of leadership in formal organizations: A developmental approach. In J. G. Hunt and L. L. Larson (Eds.), *Leadership Frontiers*. Kent, Ohio: Kent State University Press, 1975.

Graen, G., Dansereau, F., Jr., and Minami, T. Dysfunctional leadership styles. *Organizational Behavior and Human Performance*, 1972, *7*, 216–236.

Graham, W. K., and Oleno, T. Perceptions of leader behavior and motivations of leaders. *Journal of Industrial Psychology*, 1970, *5*, 63–70.

Green, S. G., and Mitchell, T. R. Attributional processes of leaders in leader-member interactions. *Organizational Behavior and Human Performance*, 1979, *23*, 429–458.

Greller, M., and Herold, D. Sources of feedback: A preliminary investigation. *Organizational Behavior and Human Performance*, 1975, *13*, 244–256.

Hackman, R., and Oldham, G. Motivation through the design of work: Test of a theory. *Organizational Behavior and Human Performance*, 1976, *16*, 250–279.

Hall, A. T., and Hall, F. S. The relationship between goals, performance, success self-image, and involvement under different organizational climates. *Journal of Vocational Behavior*, 1976, *9*, 267–278.

Hall, D., and Lawler, E. Unused potential in R&D labs. *Research Management*, 1969, *12*, 339–354.

Hammer, T. H., and Dachler, H. P. A test of some assumptions underlying the path goal model of supervision: Some suggested conceptual modifications. *Organizational Behavior and Human Performance*, 1975, *14*, 60–75.

Hays, W. L. *Statistics for Psychologists*. New York: Holt, Rinehart & Winston, 1963.

Heise, D. R. Separating reliability and stability in test-retest correlation. *American Sociological Review*, 1969, *34*, 93–101.

Heller, F. A. *Managerial Decision Making*. Assen, The Netherlands: Royal VanGorcum Ltd., 1971.

Heller, F. A., and Yukl, G. Participation, managerial decision-making, and situational variables. *Organizational Behavior and Human Performance*, 1969, *4*, 227–234.

House, R. J. A path-goal theory of leader effectiveness. *Administrative Science Quarterly*, 1971, *16*, 321–338.

House, R. J., and Dessler, G. The path-goal theory of leadership: Some post hoc and a priori tests. In J. G. Hunt and L. L. Larson (Eds.), *Contingency Approaches to Leadership*. Carbondale: Southern Illinois University Press, 1974.

House, R. J., Filley, A. C., and Kerr, S. Relation of leader consideration and initiating structure to R&D subordinates' satisfaction. *Administrative Science Quarterly*, 1971, *16*, 19–30.

House, R. J., and Mitchell, T. R. Path-goal theory of leadership. *Journal of Contemporary Business*, 1974, *3*, 81–97.

House, R. J., and Rizzo, J. R. Toward the measurement of organizational practices: Scale development and validation. *Journal of Applied Psychology*, 1972, *56*, 288–296.

Hunt, J. G., and Osborn, R. N. An adaptive-reactive theory of leadership: The role of macro variables in leadership research. In J. G. Hunt and L. L. Larson (Eds.), *Leadership Frontiers*. Carbondale: Southern Illinois University Press, 1975.

Huse, E. F. *Organization Development and Change*. St. Paul: West, 1975.

Jaccard, J., King, G. W., and Bomazal, R. Attitudes and behavior: An analysis of specifity of attitudinal predictors. *Human Relations*, 1977, *30*, 817–824.

Jones, E., and Nisbett, R. The actor and the observer: Divergent perceptions of the causes of behavior. In E. Jones, D. Kanouse, H. Kelley, R. Nisbett, S. Valins, and B. Weiner (Eds.), *Attribution: Perceiving the Causes of Behavior*. Morristown, N.J.: General Learning Press, 1972. pp. 79–94.

Kaplan, Abraham. *The Conduct of Inquiry*. San Francisco: Chandler, 1964.

Kelley, H. H. Attribution in social interaction. In E. Jones, D. Kanouse, H. Kelley, R. Nisbett, S. Valins, and B. Weiner (Eds.), *Attribution: Perceiving the Causes of Behavior*. Morristown, N.J.: General Learning Press, 1972. pp. 1–26.

Kerr, S., Schriesheim, C., Murphy, C. J., and Stogdill, R. M. Toward a contingency theory of leadership based upon the consideration and initiating structure literature. *Organizational Behavior and Human Performance*, 1974, *12*, 62–82.

Korman, A. Toward a hypothesis of work behavior. *Journal of Applied Psychology*, 1970, *54*, 31–41.

Lord, F. M. Problems in the measurement of growth. *Educational and Psychological Measurement*, 1956, *16*, 421–457.

Lott, A., and Lott, B. Group cohesiveness as interpersonal attraction: A review of relationships with antecedent and consequent variables. *Psychological Bulletin*, 1965, *64*, 259–302.

Manning, F. W. H., and DuBois, P. H. Correlation methods in research on human learning. *Perceptual and Motor Skills*, 1962, *25*, 287–321.

McNamara, J. Uncertainties in police work: The relevance of police recruits' backgrounds and training. In D. Bordua (Ed.), *The Police: Six Sociological Essays*. New York: Wiley, 1967.

Miner, J. The uncertain future of the leadership concept: An overview. In J. G. Hunt and L. L. Larson (Eds.), *Leadership Frontiers*. Carbondale: Southern Illinois University Press, 1975.

Mitchell, T. R. Organizational behavior. *Annual Review of Psychology*, 1979, *30*, 243–281.

Mitchell, T. R., and Green, S. G. *Leader responses to poor performance: An attributional analysis*. Paper presented at the National Meetings of the American Psychological Association, Toronto, Canada, September 1978.

Mitchell, T. R., Green, S. G., and Wood, R. E. An Attributional Model of Leadership and the Poor Performing Subordinate: Development and Validation. In B. M. Staw and L. L. Cummings (Eds.) *Research in Organizational Behavior*, Vol 3. Greenwich, Conn.: JAI Press, 1977.

Oldham, G. Job characteristics and internal motivation: The moderating effect of interpersonal and individual variables. *Human Relations,* 1976, *29*, 559–570.

Ouchi, W. The relationship between organizational structure and organizational control. *Administrative Science Quarterly*, 1977, *22*, 95–113.

Parker, J. W., Taylor, E. K., Barrett, R. S., and Martins, L. Rating scale content, III: Relationship between supervisory and self-ratings. *Personnel Psychology*, 1959, *12*, 49–63.

Porter, L., Steers, R., Mowday, R., and Boulian, P. Organizational commitment, job satisfaction, and turnover among psychiatric technicians. *Journal of Applied Psychology*, 1974, *59*, 603–609.

Rizzo, J. R., House, R. J., and Lirtzman, S. I. Role conflict and ambiguity in complex organizations. *Administrative Science Quarterly*, 1970, *15*, 150–163.

Rosen, B., and Jerdee, T. H. Factors influencing disciplinary judgments. *Journal of Applied Psychology*, 1974, *3*, 327–331.

Schuler, R., Aldag, R., and Brief, A. Role conflict and ambiguity: A scale analysis. *Organizational Behavior and Human Performance*, 1977, *20*, 111–128.

Stogdill, R. *Individual Behavior and Group Achievement*. New York: Oxford University Press, 1959.

Tannenbaum, R., and Schmidt, W. How to choose a leadership pattern. *Harvard Business Review*, 1958, *36*, 95–101.

Templer, A. J. Self-perceived and others-perceived leadership style using the LBDQ. *Personnel Psychology*, 1973, *26*, 359–367.

Thornton, C. C. The relationship between supervisory and self-appraisals of executive performance. *Personnel Psychology*, 1968, *21*, 441–455.

Tucker, M. F., Cline, V. B., and Schmitt, J. R. Prediction of creativity and other performance measures from biographical information among pharmaceutical scientists. *Journal of Applied Psychology*, 1967, *51*, 131–138.

Van de Ven, A., Delbecq, A., and Koenig, R. Determinants of coordination modes within organizations. *American Sociological Review*, 1976, *41*, 322–338.

Vroom, V., and Yetton, P. *Leadership and Decision Making*. Pittsburgh: University of Pittsburgh Press, 1973.

Weiner, B., Frieze, I., Kukla, A., Reed, L., Rest, S., and Rosenbaum, R. Perceiving the causes of success and failure. In E. Jones, D. Kanouse, H. Kelley, R. Nisbett, S. Valins, and B. Weiner (Eds.), *Attribution: Perceiving the Causes of Behavior*. Morristown, N.J.: General Learning Press, 1972.

Wherry, R. Test selection and suppressor variables. *Psychometrika*, 1946, *11*, 239–247.

Wilson, O., and McLaren, R. *Police Administration* (3d ed.). New York: McGraw-Hill, 1972.

Winer, B. J. *Statistical Principles in Experimental Design*. New York: McGraw-Hill, 1962.

Woodward, J. Technology, material control, and organizational behavior. In A. Negandhi (Ed.), *Modern Organization Theory*. Kent: Kent State University, 1973.

Zander, A. Group aspirations. In D. Cartwright and A. Zander (Eds.), *Group Dynamics: Research and Theory* (3d ed.). New York: Harper & Row, 1968.

Zedeck, S. Problems with the use of "moderator" variables. *Psychological Bulletin*, 1971, 76, 295–310.

SECTION EIGHT

Andrisani, P., and Nestel, G. Internal-external control as a contributor to and outcome of work experience. *Journal of Applied Psychology*, 1976, 61, 156–165.

Australian Bureau of Statistics. *A Census of Population and Housing*. Canberra: Australian Government Printing Service, 1971.

Bacon, A. W. Leisure and the alienated worker: A critical reassessment of three radical theories of work and leisure. *Journal of Leisure Research*, 1975, 7, 179–190.

Banks, M. H. and Jackson, P. R. Unemployment and risk of minor psychiatric disorder in young people: Cross-sectional and longitudinal evidence. *Psychological Medicine*, 1982, 789–798.

Bishop, D. W. Stability of the factor structure of leisure behavior: Analyses of four communities. *Journal of Leisure Research*, 1970, 2, 160–170.

Bishop, D., Jeanrenaud, C., and Lawson, K. Comparison of time diary and recall questionnaire for surveying leisure activities. *Journal of Leisure Research*, 1975, 7, 73–80.

Brewin, C. R. Work-role transitions and stress in managers: Illustrations from the clinic. *Personnel Review*, 1980, 9, 27–30.

Brown, G. W. and Harris, T. *Social Origins of Depression: A Study of Psychiatric Disorder in Women*. London: Tavistock, 1978.

Cheek, N. H., Jr. Toward a sociology of not work. *Pacific Sociological Review*, 1971, 14, 245–258.

Cherlin, A., and Bourque, L. B. Dimensionality and reliability of the Rotter I-E scale. *Sociometry*, 1974, 37, 565–582.

Cooley, W. W., and Lohnes, P. R. *Multivariate Data Analysis*. New York: Wiley, 1971.

Craik, K. H., and McKechnie, G. E. Personality and the environment. *Environment and Behavior*, 1977, 9, 155–168.

Driver, B. L., and Knopf, R. C. Personality, outdoor recreation and expected consequences. *Environment and Behavior*, 1977, 9, 169–193.

Dubin, R. Industrial workers' worlds: A study in the central life interests of industrial workers. *Social Problems*, 1956, 4, 3–13.

Dubin, R., and Champoux, J. E. Central life interests and job satisfaction. *Organizational Behavior and Human Performance*, 1977, 18, 366–377.

Dubin, R., Champoux, J. E., and Porter, L. W. Central life interests and organizational commitment of blue collar and clerical workers. *Administrative Science Quarterly*, 1975, 20, 411–421.

Duffy, P. J., Shiflett, S., and Downey, R. G. Locus of control: Dimensionality and predictability using Likert scales. *Journal of Applied Psychology*, 1977, 62, 214–219.

Dunnette, M. D. Introduction. In M. D. Dunnette (Ed.), *Work and Non-Work in the Year 2001*. Monterey, Calif.: Brooks/Cole, 1973.

Emery, F. *Futures We Are In*. The Hague, The Netherlands: Nijhoff, 1977.

Emery, F., and Phillips, C. *Living at Work*. Canberra: Australian Government Printing Service, 1976.

Firth, J. Experiencing uncertainty: A case from the clinic. *Personnel Review*, 12(2), 11–15.

Freud, S. *Civilization and its Discontents*. London: Hogarth Press, 1930.

Fryer, D. and Payne, R. L. (1984). Proactive behavior in unemployment: findings and implications. *Leisure Studies 3,* 273–95.

Gardell, B. Reactions at work and their influence on nonwork activities: An analysis of a sociopolitical problem in affluent societies. *Human Relations*, 1976, *29*, 885–904.

Gilmor, T. M. Locus of control as a mediator of adaptive behavior in children and adolescents. *Canadian Psychological Review*, 1978, *19*, 1–26.

Gorz, A. Work and consumption. In P. Anderson and R. Blackburn (Eds.) *Towards Socialism*. London: Fontana, 1965.

Hepworth, S. J. Moderating factors of the psychological impact of unemployment. *Journal of Occupational Psychology*, 1980, *53*, 139–145.

Jackson, P. R. and Warr, P. B. (1984). Unemployment and psychological ill-health: the moderating role of duration and age. *Psychological Medicine 14*, 605–14.

Jackson, P. R., Stafford, E. M., Banks, M. H., and Warr, P. B. (1983). Unemployment and psychological distress in young people: The moderating role of employment commitment. *Journal of Applied Psychology 68*, 525–35.

Jahoda, M. Notes on work. In R. M. Loewenstein, L. M. Newman, M. Schnur, and A. J. Solnit (eds.), *Psychoanalysis: A General Psychology*. New York: International Universities Press, 1966.

Jahoda, M. (1981). Work, employment and unemployment. *American Psychologist*, 1981, *36*, 184–191.

Kabanoff, B. Work and nonwork: A review of models, methods, and findings. *Psychological Bulletin*, 1980, *88*, 60–77.

Kando, T., and Summers, W. The impact of work on leisure. *Pacific Sociological Review*, 1971, *14*, 310–327.

Kelly, J. R. Work and leisure: A simplified paradigm. *Journal of Leisure Research*, 1972, *4*, 50–62.

Kelly, J. R. Situational and social factors in leisure decisions. *Pacific Sociological Review*, 1978, *21*, 313–330.

Kish, L. *Survey Sampling*. New York: Wiley, 1965.

Klecka, W. R. Discriminant analysis. In N. H. Nie, C. Hadlai Hull, J. G. Jenkins, K. Steinbrenner, & D. H. Bent (Eds.), *SPSS: Statistical Package for the Social Sciences* (2nd ed.). New York: McGraw-Hill, 1975.

Kornhauser, A. W. *Mental Health of the Industrial Worker*. New York: Wiley, 1965.

Lefcourt, H. *Locus of Control*. New York: Wiley, 1976.

London, M., Crandall, R., and Fitzgibbons, D. The psychological structure of leisure: Activities, needs, people. *Journal of Leisure Research*, 1977, *9*, 252–263.

London, M., Crandall, R., and Seals, G. W. The contribution of job and leisure satisfaction to the quality of life. *Journal of Applied Psychology*, 1977, *62*, 328–334.

Mansfield, R., and Evans, M. G. Work and non-work in two occupational groups. *Industrial Relations*, 1975, *6*, 48–54.

Meissner, M. The long arm of the job: A study of work and leisure. *Industrial Relations*, 1971, *10*, 239–260.

Meyersohn, R. Leisure. In A. Campbell and P. Converse (Eds.), *The Human Meaning of Social Change*. New York: Oxford University Press, 1972.

Mills, C. W. *White Collar*. Oxford University Press, 1951.

Neulinger, J. *The Psychology of Leisure*. Springfield, Ill.: Charles C Thomas, 1974.

O'Brien, G. E. The measurement of cooperation. *Organizational Behavior and Human Performance*, 1968, *3*, 427–439.

O'Brien, G. E. The centrality of skill-utilization for job design. In K. Duncan, M. Gruenwald, and D. Wallis (Eds.), *Changes in Working Life*. New York: Wiley, 1980.

O'Brien, G. E. Leisure attributes and retirement satisfaction. *Journal of Applied Psychology*, in press.

O'Brien, G. E., Biglan, A., and Penna, J. Measurement of the distribution of potential influence and participation in groups and organizations. *Journal of Applied Psychology*, 1972, *56*, 11–18.

O'Brien, G. E., and Dowling, P. The effects of congruency between perceived and actual job attributes upon job satisfaction. *Journal of Occupational Psychology*, 1980, *53*, 121–130.

Oeser, O. A., and O'Brien, G. E. A mathematical model for structural role theory, III. The analysis of group tasks. *Human Relations*, 1967, *20*, 83–97.

Orpen, C. Work and nonwork satisfaction: A causal-correlational analysis. *Journal of Applied Psychology*, 1978, *63*, 530–532.

Parker, S. R. *The Future of Work and Leisure*. London: MacGibbon & Kee, 1971.

Parker, S. *The Sociology of Leisure*. London: Allen & Unwin, 1976.

Parry, G. The mental health of employed and unemployed mothers: Beyond the global comparison. MRC/SSRC SAPU Memo 576, 1983.

Payne, R. L., Warr, P. B., and Hartley, J. (1984). Social class and psychological health during unemployment. *Sociology of Health and Illness*, 6, 152–174.

Phares, E. J. *Locus of Control in Personality*. Morristown, N.J.: General Learning Press, 1976.

Porter, L. W., Lawler, E. E., and Hackman, J. R. *Behavior in Organizations*. New York: McGraw-Hill, 1975.

Rapaport, R., and Rapaport, R. N. Four themes in the sociology of leisure. *British Journal of Sociology*, 1974, *25*, 215–229.

Rotter, J. B. Generalized expectancies for internal versus external control of reinforcement. *Psychological Monographs*, 1966, *80* (1, Whole No. 609).

Rousseau, D. M. Relationship of work to nonwork. *Journal of Applied Psychology*, 1978, *63*, 513–517.

Seashore, S. E. Defining and measuring the quality of working life. In L. E. Davis and A. B. Cherns (Eds.), *The Quality of Working Life*. (Vol. 1): *Problems, Prospects and State of the Art*. Glencoe, N.Y.: Free-Press, 1975.

Seeman, M. The urban alienations: Some dubious theses from Marx to Marcuse. *Journal of Personality and Social Psychology*, 1971, *19*, 135–143.

Shapiro, D. A., Parry, G. and Brewin, C. R. Stress, coping and psychotherapy: Foundations of a clinical approach. In C. Mackay and T. Cox (Eds.), *Response to Stress: Occupational Aspects*. London: International Publishing Corporation, 1979.

Spink, P. Some comments on the quality of working life. *Journal of Occupational Psychology*, 1975, *48*, 179–184.

Stafford, E. M., Jackson, P. R. and Banks, M. H. Employment, work involvement and mental health in less qualified young people. *Journal of Occupational Psychology*, 1980, *53*, 291–304.

Tatsuoka, M. M. *Multivariate Analysis*. New York: John Wiley & Sons, 1971.

Wall, T. D. and Clegg, C. W. A longitudinal field study of group work design. *Journal of Occupational Behaviour*, 1981, *2*, 31–49.

Warr, P. B. A study of psychological well-being. *British Journal of Psychology*, 1978, *69*, 111–121.

Warr, P. B. A national study of non-financial employment commitment. *Journal of Occupational Psychology*, 1982, *55*, 297–312.

Warr, P. B. Job loss, unemployment and psychological well-being. In E. van de Vliert and V. Allen (Eds.), *Role Transitions*. New York: Plenum, 1983, (a.)

Warr, P. B. Work and unemployment. In P. J. D. Drenth, H. Thierry, P. J. Willems, and C. J. de Wolff (Eds.), *Handbook of Work and Organization Psychology*. London: John Wiley & Sons, 1983, (b.)

Warr, P. B. and Jackson, P. R. (1983). Self-esteem and unemployment among young workers. *Le Travail Humain*, 46, 355–66.

Warr, P. B. and Lovatt, D. J. Retraining and other factors associated with job finding after redundancy. *Journal of Occupational Psychology*, 1977, *50*, 67–84.

Warr, P. B. and Parry, G. Paid employment and women's psychological well-being. *Psychological Bulletin*, 1982, *91*, 498–516. (a)

Warr, P. B. and Parry, G. Depressed mood in working-class mothers with and without paid employment. *Social Psychiatry*, 1982, *17*, 161–165. (b)

Warr, P. B. and Payne, R. L. Experiences of strain and pleasure among British adults. *Social Science and Medicine*, 1982, *16*, 1691–1697.

Warr, P. B. and Payne, R. L. Social class and reported changes in behavior after job loss. *Journal of Applied Social Psychology*, *13*, 206–22.

Warr, P. B., Cook, J. D., and Wall, T. D. Scales for the measurement of some work attitudes and aspects of psychological well-being. *Journal of Occupational Psychology*, 1979, *52*, 129–148.

Warr, P. B., Jackson, P. R., and Banks, M. H. Duration of unemployment and psychological well-being in young men and women. *Current Psychological Research*, 1982, *2*, 207–214.

Wilensky, H. Work, careers and social integration. *International Social Science Journal*, 1960, *12*, 543–560.

Zuzanek, J. Society of leisure or the harried leisure class? Leisure trends in industrial societies. *Journal of Leisure Research*, 1974, *6*, 293–304.

SECTION NINE

Cherns, A. The principles of sociotechnical design. *Human Relations*, 1976, *29*, 783–792.

Cummings, T. G. Self-regulating work groups: A socio-technical synthesis. *Academy of Management Review*, 1978, *3*, 625–634.

Cummings, T. G., and Srivastva, S. *Management of Work: A Socio-Technical Systems Approach.* Kent, Ohio: Kent State University Press, 1977.

Davis, L. E. Developments in job design. In P. B. Warr (Ed.), *Personal Goals and Work Design.* London: Wiley, 1975.

Davis, L. E., and Trist, E. L. Improving the quality of work life: Sociotechnical case studies. In J. O'Toole (Ed.), *Work and the Quality of Life.* Cambridge: Massachusetts Institute of Technology Press, 1974.

Emery, F. E. and Trist, E. L. Socio-technical systems. In F. E. Emery (Ed.) *Systems Thinking.* London: Penguin Books, 1969.

Fein, M. Job enrichment: A reevaluation. *Sloan Management Review*, Winter 1974, pp. 69–88.

Ford, R. N. *Motivation through the Work Itself.* New York: American Management Associations, 1969.

Gulowsen, J. A measure of work group autonomy. In L. E. Davis and J. C. Taylor (Eds.), *Design of Jobs.* Middlesex, England: Penguin Books, 1972.

Hackman, J. R. The design of self-managing work groups. In B. King, S. Streufert, and F. E. Fiedler (Eds.), *Managerial Control and Organizational Democracy.* Washington, D.C.: V. H. Winston, 1978.

Hackman, J. R., and Lawler, E. E. Employee reactions to job characteristics. *Journal of Applied Psychology*, 1971, *55*, 259–285. (Monograph)

Hackman, J. R., and Oldham, G. R. Development of the job diagnostic survey. *Journal of Applied Psychology*, 1975, *60*, 159–170.

Hackman, J. R., and Oldham, G. R. Motivation through the design of work: Test of a theory. *Organizational Behavior and Human Performance*, 1976, *16*, 250–279.

Hackman, J. R., and Oldham, G. R. *Work Redesign.* Reading, Mass.: Addison-Wesley, 1980.

Hackman, J. R., Oldham, G., Janson, R., and Purdy, K. A new strategy for job enrichment. *California Management Review*, Summer 1975, pp. 57–71.

Herzberg, F. One more time: How do you motivate employees? *Harvard Business Review*, January–February 1968, pp. 53–62.

Herzberg, F. The wise old Turk. *Harvard Business Review*, September–October 1974, pp. 70–80.

Herzberg, F. *The Managerial Choice*. Homewood, Ill.: Dow Jones-Irwin, 1976.

Herzberg, F., Mausner, B., and Snyderman, B. *The Motivation to Work*. New York: Wiley, 1959.

House, R. J., and Wigdor, L. Herzberg's dual-favor theory of job satisfaction and motivation: A review of the evidence and a criticism. *Personnel Psychology*, 1967, *20*, 369–389.

Katzell, R. Work attitudes, motivation, and performance. *Professional Psychology*, 1980, *11*, 409–420.

Katzell, R. A., Bienstock, P., and Faerstein, P. H. *A Guide to Worker Productivity Experiments in the United States 1971–1975*. New York: New York University Press, 1977.

Katzell, R. A. and Yankelovich, D. *Work, Productivity and Job Satisfaction*. New York: The Psychological Corporation, 1975.

King, N. A clarification and evaluation of the two-factor theory of job satisfaction. *Psychological Bulletin*, 1970, 74, 18–31.

Kornhauser, A. *Mental Health of the Industrial Worker*. New York: Wiley, 1965.

Lawler, E. E., III, Nadler, D. A., and Cammann, C. *Observing and Measuring Organizational Change: A Guide to Field Practice*. New York: Wiley-Interscience, 1980.

Macy, B. A., and Mirvis, P. H. Measuring the quality of work and organizational effectiveness in behavioral-economic terms. *Administrative Science Quarterly*, 1976, *21*, 212–226.

Oldham, G. R., and Hackman, J. R. Work design in organizational context. In B. M. Staw and L. L. Cummings (Eds.), *Research in Organizational Behavior* (Vol. 2). Greenwich, Conn.: JAI Press, 1980.

Paul, W. J., Jr., Robertson, K. B., and Herzberg, F. Job enrichment pays off. *Harvard Business Review*, March–April 1969, pp. 61–78.

Pierce, J. L., and Dunham, R. B. Task design: A literature review. *Academy of Management Review*, 1976, *1*, 83–97.

Salancik, G. R., and Pfeffer, J. An examination of need satisfaction models of job attitudes. *Administrative Sciences Quarterly*, 1977, *22*, 427–456.

Schwab, D. P., and Cummings, L. L. A theoretical analysis of the impact of task scope of employee performance. *Academy of Management Review*, 1976, *1*, 23–25.

Scott, W. E. Activation theory and task design. *Organizational Behavior and Human Performance*, 1966, *1*, 3–30.

Sirota, D., and Wolfson, A. D. Job enrichment: Surmounting the obstacles. *Personnel*, July–August 1972, pp. 8–19.

Strauss, G. Job satisfaction, motivation, and job redesign. In G. Strauss, R. E. Miles, C. C. Snow, and A. S. Tannenbaum (Eds.), *Organizational Behavior: Research and Issues*. Madison, Wis.: Industrial Relations Research Association, 1974.

Trist, E. L., Higgin, G. W., Murray, H., and Pollock, A. B. *Organizational Choice*. London: Tavistock, 1963.

Turner, A. N., and Lawrence, P. R. *Industrial Jobs and the Worker*. Boston: Harvard Graduate School of Business Administration, 1965.

Van de Ven, A. H., and Ferry, D. L. *Measuring and Assessing Organizations*. New York: Wiley-Interscience, 1980.

Van der Zwaan, A. H. The sociotechnical systems approach: A critical evaluation. *International Journal of Production Research*, 1975, *13*, 149–163.

Vernon, H. M. *On the Extent and Effects of Variety in Repetitive Work* (Industrial Fatigue Research Board Report No. 26). London: H. M. Stationery Office, 1924.

Walker, C. R., and Guest, R. H. *The Man on the Assembly Line.* Cambridge, Mass.: Harvard University Press, 1952.

Walton, R. E. How to counter alienation in the plant. *Harvard Business Review*, November–December 1972, pp. 70–81.

Walton, R. E. The diffusion of new work structures: Explaining why success didn't take. *Organizational Dynamics*, Winter 1975, pp. 3–22.

Walton, R. E. Work innovations at Topeka: After six years. *Journal of Applied Behavioral Science*, 1977, *13*, 422–433.

Walton, R. Quality of work life activities: A research agenda. *Professional Psychology*, 1980, *11*, 484–493.

Walton, R. E., and Schlesinger, L. S. Do supervisors thrive in participative work systems? *Organizational Dynamics*, Winter 1979, pp. 24–38.

Whitsett, D. A., and Winslow, E. K. An analysis of studies critical of the motivator-hygiene theory. *Personnel Psychology*, 1967, *20*, 391–415.

SECTION TEN

Bradford, L. P., Gibb, J. R., and Benne, K. D. *T-group Theory and Laboratory Method.* New York: John Wiley & Sons, 1964.

Cartwright, D. Achieving change in people: Some applications of group dynamics theory. *Human Relations*, 1951, *4*, 381–392.

Clark, J. V., and Krone, C. G. Towards an overall view of organizational development in the early seventies. In J. M. Thomas and W. G. Bennis (Eds.), *Management of Change and Conflict.* New York: Viking Press, 1972.

Coch, L., and French, J. R. P. Overcoming resistance to change. *Human Relations*, 1948, *1*, 512–532.

Dalton, M. Managing the managers. *Human Organization*, 1965, *14*, 4–10.

Duckles, M. M., Duckles, R., and Maccoby, M. The process of change at Bolivar. *Journal of Applied Behavioral Sciences*, 1977, *13*(3), 387–400.

Duckles, R. *Work, workers and democratic change.* Doctoral dissertation, Wright Institute Graduate School, 1977.

Dunn, W. N., and Swierczek, F. W. Planned organizational change: Toward grounded theory. *Journal of Applied Behavioral Science*, 1978, *13*, 135–158.

Emery, F. E., and Trist, E. L. The causal texture of organizational environments. *Human Relations*, 1965, *18*, 21–32.

Erikson, E. *Childhood and Society.* New York: Norton, 1963.

Freud, S. *The Future of an Illusion* (1927). Standard Edition (Vol. 21). London: Hogarth Press, 1975.

Friedlander, F. OD reaches adolescence. *Journal of Applied Behavioral Science*, 1976, *12*, 7–12.

Friedlander, F., and Brown, L. D. Organization development. *Annual Review of Psychology*, 1974, *25*, 313–341.

Fromm, E. *Escape from Freedom.* New York: Holt, Rinehart & Winston, 1941.

Fromm, E. *Man for Himself.* New York: Holt, Rinehart & Winston, 1947.

Fromm, E. *The Sane Society.* New York: Holt, Rinehart & Winston, 1955.

Fromm, E. *The Heart of Man.* New York: Harper & Row, 1964.

Fromm, E. *The Anatomy of Human Destructiveness.* New York: Holt, Rinehart & Winston 1973.

Fromm, E., and Maccoby, M. *Social Character in a Mexican Village*. Englewood Cliffs, N.J.: Prentice-Hall, 1970.

Herzberg, F. *Work and the Nature of Man*. Cleveland, Ohio: World, 1966.

Jacob, P., and Jacob, B. Life on the automated line. *The Wharton Magazine*, Fall 1976, *1*(1), 56–60.

Jayaram, F. K. Open systems planning. In W. A. Pasmore and J. J. Sherwood (Eds.), *Sociotechnical Systems*. La Jolla, Calif.: University Associates, 1978.

Kornhauser, A. *Mental Health of the Industrial Worker*. New York: John Wiley & Sons, 1965.

Laing, R. D. *The Politics of Experience*. New York: Pantheon Books, 1967.

Lawrence, P. R., and Lorsch, J. W. *Developing Organizations: Diagnosis and Action*. Reading, Mass.: Addison-Wesley, 1969.

Lewin, K. Group decision and social change. In T. Newcomb and E. Hartley (Eds.), *Readings in Social Psychology*. New York: Holt, 1947.

Maccoby, M. *The Gamesman, the New Corporate Leaders*. New York: Simon & Schuster, 1976.

Mayo, E. *The Human Problems of an Industrial Civilization*. New York: Macmillan, 1933.

Nord, W. R. Dreams of humanization and the realities of power. *The Academy of Management Review*, 1978, *3*, 674–678.

Pasmore, W. A., and King, D. C. Understanding organizational change: A comparative study of multifaceted interventions. *Journal of Applied Behavioral Science*, 1978, *14*, 455–468.

Pfeffer, J., and Salencik, G. *The External Control of Organizations*. New York: Harper & Row, 1978.

Piaget, J. *To Understand is to Invent: The Future of Education*. New York: Grossman, 1973.

Srivastva, S., Salipante, P. F., Cummings, T. G., Notz, W. W., Bigelow, J. D., and Waters, J. A. *Job Satisfaction and Productivity*. Kent, Ohio: Kent State University Press, 1976.

Sullivan, H. S. *Clinical Studies in Psychiatry*. New York: Norton, 1956.

Sykes, A. J. M. The effects of a supervisory training course in changing supervisor's perceptions and expectations of the role of management. *Human Relations*, 1962, *15*, 227–243.

Szasz, T. S. The myth of mental illness. *American Psychologist*, 1960, *15*, 113–118.

Tannenbaum, R. Some matters of life and death. *OD Practitioner*, 1976, *8*, 1–7.

Trist, E., and Bamforth, K. W. Some social and psychological consequences of the Longwall method of coal getting. *Human Relations* 1951, *4*, 3–38.

Weisbord, M. R. How do you know it works if you don't know what it is? *OD Practitioner*, 1977, *9*, 1–8.

SECTION ELEVEN

Bainbridge, L. The process controller. In W. T. S. Singleton (Ed.), *The Study of Real Skills*, Volume 1. *The Analysis of Practical Skills*. Lancaster: MTP Press, 1978, pp. 236–263.

Barron, I. and Curnow, R. *The Future with Microelectronics*. London: Frances Pinter, 1979.

Bessant, J., Braun, E., and Moseley, R. Microelectronics in manufacturing industry: The rate of diffusion. In T. Forester (Ed.), *The Microelectronics Revolution*. Oxford: Basil Blackwell, 1980, pp. 198–218.

Boddy, D. and Buchanan, D. A. Information technology and the experience of work. Paper presented to the EEC Conference on the Information Society, Dublin, Ireland, 18–20 November 1981.

Bowen, W. Auto safety needs a new roadmap. *Fortune*, April 1972, *85*, 98–101; 142–145.

Braverman, H. *Labour and Monopoly Capital: The Degradation of Work in the Twentieth Century*. New York: Monthly Review Press, 1974.

Bright, J. *Automation and Management*. Boston, MA: Division of Research, Harvard Business School, 1958.

Buchanan, D. A. *The Development of Job Design Theories and Techniques*. Aldershot, Hants: Saxon House, 1979.

Buchanan, D. A. and Boddy, D. Advanced technology and the quality of working life: The effects of word processing on video typists. *Journal of Occupational Psychology*, 1982, 55, 1–11.

Child, J. Organization structure, environment and performance: The role of strategic choice. *Sociology*, 1972, 6, 1–22.

Clegg, S. and Dunkerley, D. *Organization: Class and Control*. London: Routledge & Kegan Paul, 1980.

Davis, L. E. Developments in job design. In P. Warr (Ed.), *Personal Goals and Work Design*. New York: Wiley, 1976, pp. 67–80.

Davis, L. E. Evolving alternative organizational designs: Their sociotechnical bases. *Human Relations*, 1977, 30, 261–273.

Davis, L. E. and Taylor, J. C. Technology effects on job, work, and organizational structure: A contingency view. In L. E. Davis and A. B. Cherns (Eds.), *The Quality of Working Life: Problems, Prospects and the State of the Art*. New York: The Free Press, 1975, pp. 220–241.

Davis, L. E. and Taylor, J. C. Technology, organization and job structure. In R. Dubin (Ed.), *Handbook of Work, Organization and Society*. Chicago: Rand McNally, 1976, pp. 379–419.

Emery, F. E. Some hypotheses about the ways in which tasks may be more effectively put together to make jobs (Tavistock Institute of Human Relations), 1963. Reprinted in P. Hill (1971), *Towards a New Philosophy of Management*. Aldershot, Hants: Gower Press.

Gallie, D. *In Search of the New Working Class: Automation and Social Integration Within the Capitalist Enterprise*. Cambridge: Cambridge University Press, 1978.

Hill, P. *Towards a New Philosophy of Management*. Aldershot, Hants: Gower Press, 1971.

Hunter, L. C., Reid, G. L., and Boddy, D. *Labour Problems of Technological Change*. London: George Allen & Unwin, 1970.

Jordan, N. Allocation of functions between man and machines in automated systems. *Journal of Applied Psychology*, 1963, 47, 161–165.

Landeweerd, J. A. Internal representation of a process, fault diagnosis and fault correction. *Ergonomics*, 1979, 22, 1343–1351.

Mann, F. C. and Hoffman, L. R. *Automation and the Worker: A Study of Social Change in Power Plants*. New York: Henry Holt, 1960.

Marek, J. Effects of automation in an actual control work situation. Tavistock Institute of Human Relations Document no. 669, 1962.

National Safety Council. *Accident Facts*. Chicago: Author, 1971.

Nichols, T. and Beynon, H. *Living with Capitalism: Class Relations and the Modern Factory*. London: Routledge & Kegan Paul, 1977.

Paternotte, P. H. The control performance of operators controlling a continuous distillation process. *Ergonomics*, 1978, 21, 671–679.

Roethlisberger, F. J., and Dickson, W. J. *Management and the Worker*. Cambridge, Mass.: Harvard University Press, 1939.

Singleton, W. T. *Man-Machine Systems*. London: Penguin, 1974.

Singleton, W. T. *The Study of Real Skills*. Volume 2: *Compliance and Excellence*, Lancaster: MTP Press, 1979.

Taylor, J. C. *Technology and Planned Organizational Change*. Ann Arbor, MI: Institute for Social Research, University of Michigan, 1971. (a)

Taylor, J. C. Some effects of technology in organizational change. *Human Relations* 1971, 24, 105–123. (b)

Umbers, I. G. A study of the control skills of gas grid control engineers. *Ergonomics*, 1979, 22, 557–571.

Vine, D. R. and Price, F. C. Automated hot strip mill operation: A human factors study. *Iron and Steel International*, 1977, *50*, 95–101.

Voevodsky, J. Inferences from visual perception and reaction time to requisites for a collision-preventing cyberlite stop lamp. *Proceedings of the National Academy of Sciences of the United States of America*, 1967, *57*, 688–695.

Williamson, D. T. N. The anachronistic factory. *Personnel Review*, 1973, *2*, 26–38.

Woodward, J. *Industrial Organization: Theory and Practice*. London: Oxford University Press, 1965.

SECTION TWELVE

Aldridge, J. F. L. Emotional illness and the working environment. *Ergonomics*, 1970, *13*, 613–621.

Althauser, Robert P. Multicollinearity and nonadditive regression models. In H. Blalock (Ed.), *Causal Models in the Social Sciences*. Chicago: Aldine, 1971, 453–472.

Andrews, Frank M., and Withey, Stephen B. *Social Indicators of Well-being: The Development and Measurement of Perceptual Indicators*. New York: Plenum, 1976.

Beehr, Terry, Perceived situational moderators of the relationship between subjective role ambiguity and role strain. *Journal of Applied Psychology*, 1976, *61*, 35–40.

Bishop, Yvonne M. M., Fienberg, Stephen E., and Holland, Paul W. *Discrete Multivariate Analysis, Theory and Practice*. Cambridge, M.I.T., 1975.

Blau, P. M. and Duncan, O. D. *The American Occupational Structure*. New York: Wiley, 1967.

Blood, Milton R., and Hulin, Charles L. Alienation, environmental characteristics, and worker's responses. *Journal of Applied Psychology*, 1967, *51*, 284.

Blumenthal, J. A., Williams, R., Kong, Y., et al., Type A behavior and angiographically documented coronary disease. *Circulation*, 1978, *58*, 634–639.

Borhani, N. O., Magnitude of the problem of cardiovascular-renal disease. In A. M. Lilienfeld and A. J. Gifford (Eds.), *Chronic Diseases and Public Health*. Baltimore: Johns Hopkins University Press, 1966.

Breer, Paul E., and Locke, Edwin A., *Task Experience as a Source of Attitudes*. Homewood, IL: Dorsey, 1965.

Buck, Vernon, E. *Working Under Pressure*. New York: Crane, Russak, 1972.

Caplan, R. D., Cobb, S., French, J. R. P., Harrison, R. V., and Pinneau, S. R. *Job Demands and Worker Health* (HEW Publication No. NIOSH). Washington, D.C.: U.S. Government Printing Office, 1976.

Caplan, R. D., Cobb, S., French, J. R. P., Van Harrison, R., and Dineau S. R., Jr. *Job Demands and Worker Health: Main Effects and Occupational Differences*. Washington, D.C.: U.S. Department of Health, Education and Welfare (U.S.G.P.O. Stock No. 1733-00083), 1976.

Carlsson, Güsta, Eriksson, Robert, Lofwall, Christina, and Warneryd, Bo. *Socio-ekonomiska grupperingar" Statistisk Tidskrift*, 1974, *75*, 381–400.

Cohen, J., and Cohen, P. *Applied Multiple Regression/Correlation Analysis for the Behavioral Sciences*. Hillsdale, N.J.: Erlbaum, 1975.

Cook, T. D., and Campbell, D. T. The design and conduct of quasi-experiments and true experiments in field settings. In M. D. Dunnette (Ed.), *Handbook of Industrial and Organizational Psychology*. Chicago: Rand McNally, 1976.

Cooper, C. L., and Marshall, J. Occupational sources of stress: A review of the literature relating to coronary heart disease and mental ill health. *Journal of Occupational Psychology*, 1976, *49*, 11–28.

Cronbach, Lee J., and Furby, Lita, How should we measure change—Or should we? *Psychological Bulletin*, 1970, *74*, 68–80.

Crozier, Michael. *The Bureaucratic Phenomenon*. Chicago: University Press, 1964.

Csikszentmihalyi, Mihaly. *Beyond Boredom and Anxiety*. San Francisco: Jossey-Bass, 1975.

Dembroski, T. M., MacDougall, J. M., Shields, J. L., et al., Components of the Type A coronary prone behavior pattern and cardiovascular responses to psychomotor performance challenge. *Journal of Behavioral Medicine*, 1978, *40*, 593–609.

Dembroski, T. M., Weiss, S. M., Shields, J. L., et al., *Coronary Prone Behavior*. New York: Springer-Verlag, 1978.

Dohrenwend, Barbara S., and Dohrenwend, Bruce P. *Stressful Life Events: Their Nature and Effects*. New York: Wiley, 1972.

Drabek, Thomas E., and Hass, J. Eugene. Laboratory simulation of organizational stress. *American Sociological Review*, 1969, *39*, 222–236.

Elden, J. Maxwell, Political Efficacy at Work: More Autonomous Forms of Workplace Organization Link to a More Participatory Politics. Seminar on social change and organizational development, Inter-university Center, Dubrovnik, 1977.

Eliot, R. S., *Stress and the Major Cardiovascular Disorders*. New York: Futura, 1979.

Ellis, A. *Reason and Emotion in Psychotherapy*. New York: Lyle Stuart, 1962.

Engel, G. L. Sudden death and the "medical model" in psychiatry. *Canadian Psychiatric Association Journal*, 1970, *15*, 527–538.

Felton, J. S., and Cole, R. The high cost of heart disease. *Circulation*, 1963, *27*, 957–962.

Frankenhaeuser, M. Job demands, health, and well-being. *Journal of Psychosomatic Research*, 1977, *21*, 313–321.

Frankenhaeuser, Marianne, and Gardell, Bertil, Underload and overload in working life: Outline of a multidisciplinary approach. *Journal of Human Stress*, 1976, *2*, 35–46.

Frankenhaeuser, Marianne, and Rissler, Anita. Effects of punishment on catecholamine release and efficiency of performance. *Psychopharmacologia*, 1970, *17*, 378–390.

French, John R. P., and Caplan, Robert D. Psychosocial factors in coronary heart disease. *Industrial Medicine*, 1970, *39*, 31–44.

Friedman, M., *Pathogenesis of Coronary Artery Disease*. New York: McGraw-Hill, 1969.

Friedman, M., and Rosenman, R. H., *Type A Behavior and Your Heart*. New York: Knopf, 1974.

Friedman, Meyer, Rosenman, Ray H., and Carroll, Vernice. Changes in serum cholesterol and blood clotting time in men subjected to cyclic variation of occupational stress. *Circulation*, 1970, *17*, 852–861.

Fromkin, H. L., and Streufert, S. Laboratory experimentation. In M. D. Dunnette (Ed.), *Handbook of Industrial and Organizational Psychology*. Chicago: Rand McNally, 1976.

Gardell, Bertil. *Produktionsteknik och arbetsgladje*. Stockholm: Personaladministrativa Rader, 1971.

Gardell, Bertil. Reactions at work and their influence on nonwork activities. *Human Relations*, 1976, *29*, 885–904.

Gaer, James H., Davison, Gerald C., and Gatchel, Robert I. Reduction of stress in humans through nonvertical perceived controls of aversive stimulation. *Journal of Personality and Social Psychology*, 1970, *16*, 731–738.

Glass, D. C., *Behavior Patterns, Stress and Coronary Disease*. Hillsdale, N.J.: Lawrence Erlbaum, 1977.

Glass, D. C., Krakoff, L. R., Contrada, R., et al., Effect of harassment and competition upon cardiovascular and plasma catecholamine responses in Type A and Type B individuals. *Psychophysiology*, in press.

Grass, David C., and Singer, Jerome E. *Urban Stress: Experiments on Noise and Social Stressors*. New York: Academic Press, 1972.

Gouldner, Alvin W., *Patterns of Industrial Bureaucracy*. New York: Free Press, 1954.

Gurin, Gerald, Veroff, Joseph J., and Feld, Shiela. *Americans View Their Mental Health*. New York: Basic Books, 1960.

Hackman, J. Richard, and Lawler, Edward E. Employee reactions to job characteristics. *Journal of Applied Psychology Monograph*. 1971, 55, 259–286.

Hackman, Richard, J., and Oldham, Greg R., Development of the Job Diagnostic Survey. *Journal of Applied Psychology*, 1975, 60, 159–170.

Harrison, R. V. Person-environment fit and job stress. In Cary L. Cooper and Roy Payne (Eds.), *Stress at Work*. New York: Wiley, 1978, 175–209.

Henry, J., and Cassel, J. Psychological factors in essential hypertension, recent epidemiological and animal experimental evidence. *American Journal of Epidemiology*, 1969, 90, 171–200.

Holmes, Thomas H., and Rahe, Richard H. The social readjustment rating scale. *Journal of Psychosomatic Research*, 1967, 11, 213–218.

Hulin, Charles L. Individual differences and job enrichment—The case against general treatments. In J. Maher (Ed.). *New Perspectives in Job Enrichment*. New York: Van Nostrand, 1971.

Hulin, Charles L., and Blood, Milton R., Job enlargement, individual differences and worker responses. *Psychological Bulletin*, 1968, 69, 41–55.

Jacobson, E. *Progressive Relaxation*. Chicago: University of Chicago Press, 1938.

Janis, Irving, and Mann, Lawrence. *Decision Making: A Psychological Analysis of Conflict Choice, and Commitment*. New York: Free Press, 1977.

Jenkins, C. D., Psychologic and social precursors of coronary disease. *New England Journal of Medicine*, 1971, 284, 244–255.

Jenkins, C. D., Recent evidence supporting psychologic and social risk factors for coronary disease. *New England Journal of Medicine*, 1976, 294, 987–994.

Jenkins, C. D., Behavioral risk factors in coronary heart disease. *Annual Review of Medicine*, 1978, 29, 543–562.

Jenkins, C. D., Zyzanski, S. J., and Rosenman, R. H., *Manual for the Jenkins Activity Survey*. New York: Psychological Corp., 1979.

Jenkins, G. Douglas, Nadler, David A., Lawler, Edward E., and Cammon, Cortlandt. Standardized observations: An approach to measuring the nature of jobs. *Journal of Applied Psychology*, 1975, 60, 171–181.

Johansson, Sten. *Om Levnadsnivaundersokningen*. Laginkomstutredningen. Stockholm: Allmänna Forlaget, 1971a.

Johansson, Sten. *Den Vuxna Befolkningens Haisotillstand*. Laginkomstutredningen Stockholm: Allmänna Forlaget, 1971b.

Kahn, Robert, Work and health. Some psychological effects of advanced technology. 1979. In B. Gardell and G. Johansson (Eds.), *Man and Working Life*. London: Wiley. (in press)

Kalleberg, Arne Work values and job rewards: A theory of job satisfaction. *American Sociological Review*, 1977, 42, 124–143.

Karasek, Robert A., *The impact of the work environment on life outside the job*. Doctoral dissertation. Massachusetts Institute of Technology, 1976. Distributed by Institute for Social Research, Stockholm University.

Karasek, Robert A., A stress-management model of job strain. Working paper, Swedish Institute for Social Research, Stockholm University, 1978a.

Karasek, Robert A., Managing job stress through redesign of work processes. Paper presented at the American Public Health Association Meeting, Los Angeles, 1978b.

Karasek, Robert A., Job socialization and job strain, the implications of two related mechanisms for job design. 1979. In B. Gardell and G. Johannson (Eds.), *Man and Working Life*. London: Wiley (in press).

Kasl, S. V. Mental health and the work environment. *Journal of Occupational Medicine*, 1973, 15, 509–518.

Kennel, W. B., McGee, D., and Gordon, T. A general cardiovascular risk profile: The Framingham study. *American Journal of Cardiology*, 1976, 38, 46–51.

Kerckhoff, Alan C., and Back, Kurt W. *The June Bug*. New York: Appleton-Century-Crofts, 1968.

Kohn, Melvin L., and Schooler, Carmi, Occupational experience and psychological functioning, an assessment of reciprocal effects. *American Sociological Review*, 1973, *38*, 97–118.

Kornhauser, Arthur, *The Mental Health of the Industrial Worker*. New York: Wiley, 1965.

Langer, Ellen J., and Rodin, Judith, The effects of choice and enhanced personal responsibility for the aged: A field experiment in an institutional setting. *Journal of Personality and Social Psychology*, 1976, *34*, 191–198.

Langner, Thomas S. A twenty-two item screening score of psychiatric symptoms indicating impairment. *Journal of Health and Human Behavior*, 1962, *3*, 269–276.

Langner, Thomas S., and Michael, Stanley T. *Life Stress and Mental Health*. New York: Free Press, 1963.

Lazarus, R. S., *Psychological Stress and the Coping Process*. New York: McGraw-Hill, 1966.

Lazarus, R. S. Emotions and adaptation: Conceptual and empirical relations. In W. J. Arnold (Ed.) *Nebraska Symposium on Motivation* (Vol. 16). Lincoln: University of Nebraska Press, 1968.

Lazarus, Richard S. *Psychological Stress and the Coping Press*. New York: McGraw-Hill, 1966.

Maier, Steven F., and Seligman, Martin E. P., Learned helplessness—Theory and evidence. *Journal of Experimental Psychology-General*, 1976, *105*, 4–46.

Matthews, K. A., Glass, D. C., Roenman, R. H., and Bortner, R. W., Competitive drive, Pattern A and coronary heart disease: A further analysis of some data from the Western collaborative group study. *Journal of Chronic Disease*, 1977, *30*, 489–498.

McGrath, Joseph Edward, A conceptual formulation for research of stress. In Joseph Edward McGrath (Ed.), *Social and Psychological Factors in Stress*. New York: Holt, Rinehart & Winston, 1970.

Meichenbaum, D. H. Cognitive modification of test anxious college students. *Journal of Consulting and Clinical Psychology*, 1972, *39*, 370–378.

Meichenbaum, D. H. Cognitive factors in behavior modification: Modifying what clients say to themselves. In C. M. Franks and G. T. Wilson (Eds.), *Annual Review of Behavior Therapy and Practice*. New York: Brunner/Mazel, 1973.

Meichenbaum, D. H. A self-instructional approach to stress management: A proposal for stress inoculation training. In C. D. Spielberger and J. G. Sarason (Eds.), *Stress and Anxiety* (Vol. 1). New York: Halsted Press, 1975.

Mordkoff, A., and Parsons, O., The coronary personality: A critique. *International Journal of Psychiatry*, 1968, *5*, 413–426.

Morris, Carl, and Rolph, John *Introduction to Data Analysis and Statistical Inference*. Santa Monica: Rand, 1978.

Naatanen, Risto. The inverted-U relationship between activation and performance: A critical review. In S. Kornblum (Ed.), *Activation and Performance*. New York: Academic Press, 1973, 155–174.

Newman, J. E., and Beehr, T. A. Personal and organizational strategies for handling job stress: A review of research and opinion. *Personnel Psychology*, 1979, *32*, 1–43.

Osler, W., *Lectures on Angina Pectoris and Allied States*. New York: Appleton-Century-Crofts, 1982.

Palmore, E. B. Predicting longevity, a follow-up controlling for age. *Gerontologist*, 1969, *9*, 247–250.

Quinn, R. P., Seashore, S. W., Kahn, R., Magione, T., Campell, D., Stines, R., and McCullough, M. Survey of Working Conditions. Final Report on Univariate and Bivariate Tables. Washington: U.S. Department of Labor, Employment Standards Administration. (U.S.G.P.O. Document No. 2916-0001), 1971.

Quinn, Robert P., Magione, Thomas W., and Seashore, Stanley E. 1972–73, Quality of Employment Survey (codebook). Ann Arbor: University of Michigan, Institute for Social Research, 1975.

Ritti, Richard Job enrichment and skill utilization in engineering organizations. In J. Maher (Ed.) *New Perspective in Job Enrichment.* New York: Van Nostrand, 1971, 131–156.

Rosenman, R. H., The interview method of assessment of the coronary prone behavior pattern. In T. M. Dembroski, S. M. Weiss, J. L. Shields, S. G. Haynes, and M. Feinleib (Eds.), *Coronary Prone Behavior.* New York: Springer-Verlag, 1978.

Rosenman, R. H., Brand, R. J., Jenkins, C. D., et al., Coronary heart disease in the Western collaborative group study; Final follow-up experience of 8½ years. *Journal of the American Medical Association,* 1975, *233,* 872–877.

Rosenman, Ray H., Brand, Richard J., Sholtz, Robert I., and Friedman, Meyer, Multivariate prediction of coronary heart disease during 8.5 year follow-up in the Western collaborative group study. *American Journal of Cardiology,* 1976, *37,* 903–910.

Rosenman, R. H., and Friedman, M., Neurogenic factors in pathogenesis of coronary heart disease. *Med Clin North Amer,* 1974, *58,* 269–279.

Rosenman, R. H., Friedman, J., Straus, R., et al., A predictive study of coronary heart disease: The Western collaborative group study. *Journal of the American Medical Association,* 1964, *189,* 15–22.

Roskies, E., Spevack, M., Surkis, A., et al., Changing the coronary prone (Type A) behavior pattern in a nonclinical population. *Journal of Behavioral Medicine,* 1978, *1,* 201–216.

Sales, Stephen M., and House, J. Job dissatisfaction as a possible risk factor in coronary heart disease. *Journal of Chronic Diseases,* 1974, *23* 861–873.

Sarason, I. G. Experimental approaches to test anxiety: Attention and the uses of information. In C. D. Spielberger (Ed.), *Anxiety: Current Trends in Theory and Research* (Vol. 2). New York: Academic Press, 1972.

Sarason, I. G. Anxiety and self-preoccupation. In I. G. Sarason and C. D. Spielberger (Eds.), *Stress and anxiety* (Vol. 2). New York: Halsted Press, 1975.

Sarason, I. G., Johnson, J. H., Berberich, J. P., and Siegel, J. M. Helping police officers to cope with stress: A cognitive-behavioral approach. *American Journal of Community Psychology,* 1979, 7, 593–603.

Scherwitz, L., Berton, K., and Leventhal, H. Type A behavior, self involvement and cardiovascular response. *Psychosomatic Medicine,* 1978, *40,* 593–609.

Schwartz, Carol C., Myers, Jerome K., and Astrachan, Boris M. Comparing three measures of mental status: A note on the validity of estimate of psychological disorder in the community. *Journal of Health and Social Behavior,* 1973, *14,* 265–273.

Seiler, L. H. The 22-item scale used in field studies of mental illness: A question of method, a question of substance, and a question of theory. *Journal of Health and Social Behavior,* 1973, *14,* 252–264.

Selye, Hans *The Stress of Life.* New York: McGraw-Hill, 1956.

Selye, H. *Stress in Health and Disease.* Boston: Butterworths, 1976.

Shephard, Jon M. Functional specialization, alienation and job satisfaction. *Industrial and Labor Relations Review,* 1970, *23,* 207–219.

Shore, R. "Servants of power." *APA Monitor,* November 1979, p. 2.

Southwood, Kenneth E., Substantive theory and statistical interaction: Five models. *American Journal of Sociology,* 1978, *83,* 1154–1203.

Spielberger, C. D., Gorsuch, R. L., and Lushene, R. E. *Manual for the State-Trait Anxiety Inventory.* Palo Alto, Calif.: Consulting Psychologist Press, 1970.

Sundbom, Lars, *De Forvarvsarbetandes Arbetsplats Forhalianden.* Láginkomstutredningen. Stockholm: Allmänna Forlaget, 1971.

Suomi, S., and Harlow, H., Depressive behavior in young monkeys subjected to vertical chamber confinement. *Journal of Comparative and Physiological Psychology,* 1972, *80,* 11–18.

Swedish Institute for Social Research Questionnaire: 1968 Survey of Levels of Living in Sweden (English translation) Stockholm University, 1975.

Theorell, Tores, Selected illnesses and somatic factors in relation to two psychological stress indices: A prospective study on middle-aged construction building workers. *Journal of Psychosomatic Research*, 1976, *20*, 7–20.

Timio, M., and Gentili, S. Adrenosympathetic overactivity under conditions of work stress. *British Journal of Preventive Social Medicine*, 1976, *30*, 262–265.

Tuma, Nancy Brandon. Rewards, resources, and the rate of mobility: A non-stationary multivariate stocastic model. *American Sociological Review*, 1976, *41*, 338–360.

Turner, Arthur N., and Lawrence, Paul R. *Industrial Jobs and the Worker*. Boston: Harvard, 1965.

White, J. Kenneth, and Ruh, Robert A. Effects of personal values on the relationship between participation and job attitudes. *Administrative Science Quarterly*, 1973, *18*, 506–514.

Wine, J. *Investigations of an Attentional Interpretation of Text Anxiety*. Unpublished doctoral dissertation, University of Waterloo, Waterloo, Ontario, Canada, 1970.

Whyte, William F. *Human Relations in the Restaurant Industry*. New York: McGraw-Hill, 1948.

Zaleznik, A., de Vries, M. Kets, and Howard, J. Stress reactions in organizations: Syndromes, causes, and consequences. *Behavioral Science*, 1977, *22*, 151–162.

Zaleznik, A., Ondrack, J., and Silver, A. Social class, occupation, and mental health. In A. McLean (ed.), *Mental Health and Work Organization*. New York: Rand McNally, 1970, 117–139.

Zeigarnik, Bluma *Das Behalten erledigter und unerledigter Handlungen*. *Psychologische Forschung*, 1927, *9*, 1–85.

SECTION THIRTEEN

Aanonson, A. *Shiftwork and Health*. Kopenhagen: Universitet forlaget, 1964.

Angersbach, D., Knauth, P., Loskant, H., Karvonen, M. J., Undeutsch, K., and Rutenfranz, J. A retrospective cohort study comparing complaints and diseases in day and shift workers. *International Archives of Occupational Environment and Health*, 1980, *5*, 127–140.

Daplan, R. D., Cobb, S., French, J. R. P., Jr., Harrison, R. V., and Pinneau, S. R., Jr. *Job Demands and Worker Health*. Washington, DC: National Institute for Occupational Safety and Health, U.S. Department of Health, Education and Safety, 1975.

Cohen, A. R. and Gardon, H. *Alternative Schedules: Integrating Individual and Organizational Needs*. Reading, Mass.: Addison-Wesley, 1978.

Fahrenberg, J. Die Freiburger Beschwerdeliste FBL. (The Freiburg complaint list FBL). *Zeitschrift fuer Klinische Psychologie*, 1975, *4*, 79–100.

Frese, M. *Night and shiftwork, stress at work, and psychological and psychosomatic complaints: A comparison between shiftworkers, nonshiftworkers and former shiftworkers and between different shiftwork schedules*. Unpublished manuscript, 1983, available from the author.

Koller, M., Kundi, M., and Cervinka, R. Field studies of shiftwork at an Austrian oil refinery (1): Health and psychosocial wellbeing of workers who drop out of shiftwork. *Ergonomics*, 1978, *21*, 835–47.

Meers, A., Maasen, A., and Verhaegen, P. Subjective health after six months and after four years of shiftwork. *Ergonomics*, 1978, *21*, 857–860.

Meltzer, J. W., and Hochstim, J. R. Reliability and validity of survey data on physical health. *Public Health Report*, 1970, *85*, 1075–1086.

Mohr, G. *Die Erfassung des Psychischen Befindens bei Arbeitern*. (Measuring psychological well-being in blue collar workers). Unpublished manuscript, Freie Universitaet, Department of Psychology, Berlin, 1984.

Nolen, S. *New Patterns of Work*. New York: Work in America Institute, 1979.

Projekt Schichtarbeit. *Entwicklung und Erprobung von Vermittlungskonzeptionen zur Umsetzung von arbeitswissenschaftlichen und arbeitsorganisatorischen Erkenntnissen im Bereich Schichtarbeit.* (Development and test of a conceptualization of teaching knowledge regarding work sciences and work organization on shiftwork). Zwischenbericht No. 2, 1980.

Rohrmann, B. Empirische Studien zur Entwicklung von Antwortskalen fuer die sozialwissenschaftlicke Forschung. (Empirical studies for the development of answering scales for social science research). *Zeitschriftfuer Sozialpsychologie,* 1978, 9, 222–245.

Ronen, S. *Flexible Working Hours: An Innovation in the Quality of Working Life.* New York: McGraw-Hill, 1981.

Ronen, S. and Primps, S. B. The impact of flexitime on performance and attitude in 25 public agencies. *Public Personnel Management,* 1980, 9, 201–207.

Ronen, S. and Primps, S. B. The compressed work week as organizational change: Behavioral and attitudinal outcomes. *Academy of Management Review,* 1981, 6, 61–74.

Semmer, N. Stress at work, stress in private life, and psychological well-being. In W. Bachmann, I. Udris, and J. Daniel (Eds.), *Mental Load and Stress in Activity: European Approaches.* Berlin: Deutscher Verlag der Wissenschatten, and Amsterdam: North Holland, 1982.

Taylor, P. J., and Pocock, S. J. Mortality of shift and day workers, 1956–68. *British Journal of Industrial Medicine,* 1972, 29, 201–207.

SECTION FOURTEEN

Alderfer, C. P. *Existence, Relatedness, and Growth.* London: Collier-Macmillan, 1972.

Blieszner, R., Willis, S. L., and Baltes, P. B. Training research in aging on the fluid ability of inductive reasoning. *Journal of Applied Developmental Psychology,* 1981, 2, 247–265.

Borman, W. C. Exploring upper limits of reliability and validity in job performance ratings. *Journal of Applied Psychology,* 1978, 63, 135–144.

Bramel, D., and Friend, R. Hawthorne: The myth of the docile worker and class bias in psychology. *American Psychologist,* 1981, 36, 867–878.

Braverman, H. *Labor and Monopoly Capital.* New York: Monthly Review Press, 1974.

Broadbent, D. E. Chronic effects from the physical nature of work. In B. Gardell (Ed.), *Man and Working Life.* New York: John Wiley & Sons, 1978.

Caplan, R. D., Cobb, S., French, J. R. P., Jr., Harrison, R. V., and Pinneau, S. R., Jr., *Job Demands and Worker Health* (National Institute of Occupational Health and Safety 75-160). Washington, D.C.: U.S. Government Printing Office, 1975.

Chandler, A. D. *The Visible Hand: The Managerial Revolution in American Business.* Cambridge, Mass.: Harvard University Press, 1977.

Clawson, D. *Bureaucracy and the Labor Process: The Transformation of U.S. Industry, 1860–1920.* New York: Monthly Review Press, 1980.

Clegg, S., and Dunkerley, D. *Organization, Class and Control.* London: Routledge & Kegan Paul, 1980.

Cleveland, J. N., and Landy, F. J. Influence of rater and ratee age on two performance judgments. *Personnel Psychology,* 1981, 34, 19–30.

Cooper, M. R., Morgan, B. S., Foley, P. M., and Kaplan, L. B. Changing employee values: Deepening discontent? *Harvard Business Review,* 1979, 57, 117–125.

Cyert, R. M., and March, J. G. *A Behavioral Theory of the Firm.* Englewood Cliffs, N.J.: Prentice-Hall, 1963.

Dahrendorf, R. *Life Chances.* Chicago: University of Chicago Press, 1979.

Deci, E. L. *Intrinsic Motivation.* New York: Plenum Press, 1975.

Edwards, R. *Contested Terrain: The Transformation of the Workplace in the Twentieth Century*. New York: Basic Books, 1979.

Ferguson, L. W. *The Heritage of Industrial Psychology*. Hartford, Conn.: Finlay Press, 1962.

Frost, P. J., Mitchell, V. F., and Nord, W. R. (Eds.). *Organization Reality: Reports from the Firing Line* (2d ed.). Glenview, Ill.: Scott, Foresman, 1982.

Gordon, M. E., and Nurick, A. J. Psychological approaches to the study of unions and union-management relations. *Psychological Bulletin*, 1981, 90, 293–306.

Greiner, L. E. A recent history of organizational behavior. In S. Kerr (Ed.), *Organizational Behavior*. Columbus, Ohio: Grid, 1979.

Gross, B. M. *Organizations and Their Managing*. New York: Free Press, 1968.

Gutman, H. G. *Work, Culture and Society in Industrializing America*. New York: Vintage, 1977.

Hackman, J. R. The design of work in the 1980's. *Organizational Dynamics*, 1978, 7, 3–17.

Hackman, R. J., and Oldham, G. R. Motivation through the design of work: Test of a theory. *Organizational Behavior and Human Performance*, 1976, 16, 250–279.

Hays, S. P. *The Response to Industrialism 1885–1914*. Chicago: University of Chicago Press, 1957.

Herzberg, F., Mausner, B., Peterson, R. O., and Capwell, D. F. *Job Attitudes: Review of Research and Opinion*. Pittsburgh, Pa.: Psychological Service of Pittsburgh, 1957.

Hoppock, R. *Job Satisfaction*. New York: Harper, 1935.

Jones, J. W. (Ed.). *The Burnout Syndrome*. Park Ridge, Ill.: London House Press, 1981.

Karpik, L. Organizations, institutions, and history. In L. Karpik (Ed.), *Organizations and Environment*. Beverly Hills, Calif.: Sage, 1978.

Kleiman, L. S., and Durham, R. L. Performance appraisal, promotion, and the courts. *Personnel Psychology*, 1981, 34, 103–121.

Kornhauser, A. *Mental Health of the Industrial Worker*. New York: John Wiley & Sons, 1965.

Leavitt, H. J. Toward organizational psychology. In B. V. H. Gilmer (Ed.), *Walter Van Dyke Bingham*. Pittsburgh, Pa.: Carnegie Institute of Technology, 1962.

Lewin, K. *Field Theory in Social Science*. New York: Harper, 1951.

Lifson, K. A. Errors in time-study judgments of industrial work pace. *Psychological Monographs*, 1953, 67, (Whole No. 355).

Lindblom, C. E. The science of "muddling through." *Public Administration Review*, 1959, 19, 78–88.

Lindblom, C. E. *Politics and Markets*. New York: Basic Books, 1977.

Locke, E. A. The ideas of Frederick W. Taylor: An evaluation. *Academy of Management Review*, 1982, 7, 14–24.

Marglin, S. A. What do bosses do? The origins and functions of hierarchy in capitalist production. *Review of Radical Politics Economics*, 1974, 6, 60–112.

Martin, E., Ackerman, U., Udris, I., and Oergerli, K. *Monotonie in der Industrie*. Bern: Hans Huber Verlag, 1980.

Maslow, A. H. *Motivation and Personality*. New York: Harper, 1954.

McMurry, R. N. *Handling Personality Adjustment in Industry*. New York: Harper, 1944.

McNeil, K. Understanding organizational power: Building on the Weberian legacy. *Administrative Science Quarterly*, 1978, 23, 65–90.

Meltzer, H., and Wickert, F. R. *Humanizing Organizational Behavior*. Springfield, Ill.: Charles C Thomas, 1976.

Miles, R. E., and Rosenberg, H. R. The human resources approach to management: Second-generation issues. *Organizational Dynamics*, 1982, 10, 26–41.

Mintzberg, H. *The Structuring of Organizations*. Englewood Cliffs, N.J.: Prentice-Hall, 1979.

Moore, B. V. Some beginnings of industrial psychology. In B. V. H. Gilmer (Ed.) *Walter Van Dyke Bingham*. Pittsburgh, Pa.: Carnegie Institute of Technology, 1962.

Münsterberg, H. *Psychology and Industrial Efficiency*. Boston: Houghton Mifflin, 1913.

Muscio, B. *Lectures on Industrial Psychology*. London: G. Rutledge, 1920.

Nelson, D. *Managers and Workers: Origins of the New Factory System in the United States 1880–1920*. Madison: University of Wisconsin Press, 1975.

Nord, W. R. Job satisfaction reconsidered. *American Psychologist*, 1977, *32*, 1026–1035.

Nord, W. R. A political-economic perspective on organizational effectiveness. In K. Cameron and D. A. Whetten (Eds.), *Organizational Effectiveness: A Comparison of Multiple Models*. New York: Academic Press, in press.

Nord, W. R. Toward an organizational psychology for organizational psychology. *Professional Psychology*, 1980, *11*, 531–542.

O'Hanlon, J. F. Boredom: Practical consequences and a theory. *Acta Psychologica*, 1981, *49*, 53–82.

Pfeffer, J. *Organizational Design*. Arlington Heights, Ill.: AHM, 1978.

Rodgers, D. T. *The Work Ethic in Industrial America 1850–1920*. Chicago: University of Chicago Press, 1978.

Roethlisberger, F. J., and Dickson, W. J. *Management and the Worker*. Cambridge, Mass.: Harvard University Press, 1939.

Samilova, A. J. [Morbidity with temporary loss of working capacity of female workers engaged in monotonous work.] *Sovetskaya Zdravookhranenie*, 1971, *30*, 41–46. (Abstracted in O'Hanlon, 1981.)

Scitovsky, T. *The Joyless Economy*. New York: Oxford University Press, 1976.

Scott, W. D. *Influencing Men in Business*. New York: Ronald Press, 1911.

Stone, K. The origins of job structures in the steel industry. *Review of Radical Political Economics*, 1974, *6*, 113–173.

Tausky, C. *Work Organizations: Major Theoretical Perspectives*. Itasca, Ill.: Peacock, 1970.

Taylor, F. W. *Principles of Scientific Management*. New York: Harper, 1911.

Terkel, S. *Working*. New York: Pantheon Books, 1972.

Thompson, J. O. *Organizations in Action*. New York: McGraw-Hill, 1967.

Van de Ven, A. H., and Astley, W. G. A commentary on organizational behavior in the 1980's. *Decision Sciences*, 1981, *12*, 388–398.

Varela, J. A. *Psychological Solutions to Social Problems*. New York: Academic Press, 1971.

Viteles, M. S. *The Science of Work*. New York: Norton, 1934.

Vroom, V. H. *Work and Motivation*. New York: Wiley, 1964.

Watson, T. J. *The Personnel Managers: A Study in the Sociology of Work and Employment*. London: Routledge & Kegan Paul, 1977.

Weick, K. E. Cognitive processes in organizations. In B. M. Staw (Ed.), *Research in Organizational Behavior* (Vol. 1). Greenwich, Conn.: JAI Press, 1979.

Weinstein, J. *The Corporate Ideal in the Liberal State: 1900–1918*. Boston: Beacon Press, 1968.

Wiebe, R. H. *Search for Order, 1877–1920*. New York: Hill & Wang, 1967.

Yankelovich, D. *New Rules: Seaching for Self-Fulfillment in a World Turned Upside Down*. New York: Random House, 1981.

Young, K. The history of mental testing. *Pedagogical Seminary*, 1924, *31*, 32–44.

ABOUT THE EDITOR

Frank Landy has been a professor of psychology at Penn State University since he received his Ph.D. from Bowling Green State University in 1969. As a Fulbright Fellow in 1975 and 1979, he examined studies on the work environment and job enrichment in Sweden. Recently, his interests have shifted to Central and Eastern Europe. In the spring of 1986, he was a National Academy of Sciences exchange Fellow with the Romanian Academy of Sciences. He has also conducted research in Hungary, Czechoslovakia and Yugoslavia.

Professor Landy is an active consultant and frequently appears as an expert witness in Equal Employment Opportunity court cases. He also serves as editor of *Human Performance*, and is an associate editor of the *Journal of Applied Psychology*. He has published articles on job satisfaction, work motivation, performance evaluation, and testing. In addition, he has written texts on introductory psychology, industrial and organizational psychology, and performance evaluation.

A NOTE ON THE TYPE

The text of this book was set in 10/12 Garamond via computer-driven cathode ray tube. Claude Garamond (1480–1561), the respected French type designer and letter cutter, produced this beautiful typeface for François I at the king's urging. Garamond is a fine example of the Old Style typeface, characterized by oblique stress and relatively little contrast between thicks and thins. Full of movement and charm, this elegant face influenced type design down to the end of the eighteenth century.

Composed by Eastern Graphics, Binghamton, New York.

Printed and bound by Kingsport Press, Inc., Kingsport, Tennessee.